RUSSIA
St. Petersburg
Moscow
FINLAND
ESTONIA
LATVIA
LITHUANIA
BELARUS
UKRAINE
MOLDOVA
ROMANIA
BULGARIA
GEORGIA
AZERBAIJAN
ARMENIA
KAZAKHSTAN
UZBEKISTAN
TURKMENISTAN
KYRGYZSTAN
TAJIKISTAN
MONGOLIA
Beijing (Peking)
Shenyang
NORTH KOREA
Tianjin
Seoul
SOUTH KOREA
JAPAN
Tokyo
Osaka
CHINA
Wuhan
Shanghai
Chongqing
Hong Kong
TAIWAN
Asia
PACIFIC
OCEAN
Tropic of Cancer
Equator
Tropic of Capricorn
Antarctic Circle
Greenwich
TURKEY
GREECE
CYPRUS
SYRIA
LEBANON
IRAQ
IRAN
Tehran
ISRAEL
JORDAN
Baghdad
KUWAIT
Cairo
EGYPT
LIBYA
BAHRAIN
QATAR
SAUDI ARABIA
OMAN
YEMEN
Lahore
PAKISTAN
Delhi
NEPAL
BHUTAN
BANGLADESH
Karachi
Ahmadabad
Kolkata (Calcutta)
Dacca
BURMA (Myanmar)
Mumbai (Bombay)
Hyderabad
INDIA
Chennai (Madras)
Bangalore
SRI LANKA
MALDIVES
Bangkok
LAOS
THAILAND
CAMBODIA
VIETNAM
Ho Chi Minh City
Manila
PHILIPPINES
NORTHERN MARIANAS
Guam (U.S.A.)
PALAU
FEDERATED STATES OF MICRONESIA
BRUNEI
MALAYSIA
SINGAPORE
Borneo
Sumatra
INDONESIA
Jakarta
EAST TIMOR
New Guinea
PAPUA NEW GUINEA
Christmas Island (Australia)
Cocos Islands (Australia)
INDIAN
OCEAN
Oceania
AUSTRALIA
Sydney
New Caledonia (Fr.)
NEW ZEALAND
Prince Edward Islands (South Africa)
Crozet Is. (Fr.)
Kerguelen Is. (Fr.)
OUTHERN OCEAN
ica
CHAD
SUDAN
ERITREA
DJIBOUTI
ETHIOPIA
SOMALI REP
KENYA
UGANDA
RWANDA
BURUNDI
CENTRAL AFRICAN REP
CONGO (Dem. Rep. of the)
TANZANIA
SEYCHELLES
COMOROS
ANGOLA
ZAMBIA
MALAWI
MOZAMBIQUE
MADAGASCAR
MAURITIUS
Réunion (Fr.)
NAMIBIA
BOTSWANA
ZIMBABWE
SWAZILAND
LESOTHO
SOUTH AFRICA
COPYRIGHT PHILIP'S

T0079598

OXFORD

POCKET WORLD ATLAS

SIXTH EDITION

Copyright © 2008 Philip's
Reprinted 2018

Philip's, a division of Octopus Publishing Group Limited
50 Victoria Embankment, London EC4Y 0DZ
www.octopusbooks.co.uk
An Hachette Livre UK Company
www.hachettelivre.co.uk

Cartography by Philip's

CITY PLANS
Page 29, Dublin: The town plan of Dublin is based on Ordnance Survey Ireland by permission of the Government Permit Number 8408. © Ordnance Survey Ireland and Government of Ireland.

Ordnance Survey®

Page 31, London: This product includes mapping data licensed from Ordnance Survey® with the permission of the Controller of Her Majesty's Stationery Office. © Crown copyright 2008. All rights reserved. Licence number 100011710.

Vector data: Courtesy of Gräfe and Unser Verlag GmbH, München, Germany (city-center maps of Bangkok, Cape Town, Mexico City, Singapore, Sydney, and Tokyo).

Published in North America by Oxford University Press, Inc., 198 Madison Avenue, New York, NY 10016

www.oup.com/us/atlas

OXFORD UNIVERSITY PRESS

Oxford is a registered trademark of Oxford University Press

All rights reserved. No part of this publication may be reproduced, stored in a retrieval system, or transmitted in any form or by any means, electronic, electrical, chemical, mechanical, optical, photocopying, recording, or otherwise, without the prior permission of the Publisher.

Library of Congress Cataloging-in-Publication Data available

ISBN 978-0-19-537453-7

Printing (last digit): 9 8 7 6 5 4

Printed in Malaysia

CONTENTS

WORLD STATISTICS

4–7 Countries
8–9 Cities
10–11 Time zones
12–13 Flight paths
14–15 Distance table
16–19 World climate

CITY PLANS

20 City plans – legend
21 Amsterdam
22 Athens
23 Bangkok
24 Barcelona
25 Berlin
26 Brussels
27 Cape Town
28 Chicago
29 Dublin
30 Hong Kong
31 London
32 Madrid
33 Mexico City
34 Moscow
35 Mumbai
36 New York
37 Paris
38 Prague
39 Rio de Janeiro
40 Rome
41 San Francisco
42 Singapore
43 Sydney
44 Tokyo
45 Toronto
46 Vienna

GAZETTEER OF NATIONS

47 Gazetteer of Nations – contents
48–72 Country-by-country profiles

NOTE:
For reasons of safety or politics, there may be times when it is not advisable, or desirable, to visit one or more of the countries described in the Gazetteer of Nations section. If in doubt, please check with the US Department of State (www.state.gov/travel).

WORLD MAPS

1 World Maps – general reference
2–3 The Land Hemisphere 1:133.3M
4–5 The Water Hemisphere 1:133.3M

EUROPE

6–7 Europe 1:26.7M
8–9 Scandinavia and the Baltic Lands 1:13.3M
10–11 British Isles 1:6.7M
12–13 France 1:6.7M
14–15 Germany and Benelux 1:6.7M
16–17 Central Europe 1:6.7M
18–19 Spain and Portugal 1:6.7M
20–21 Italy and the Adriatic 1:6.7M
22–23 Greece and the Balkans 1:6.7M
24–25 Eastern Europe 1:13.3M

ASIA

26–27 Asia 1:67M
28–29 Western Russia and Central Asia 1:26.7M
30–31 Eastern Siberia 1:26.7M
32–33 Japan 1:8.5M
34–35 China 1:26.7M
36–37 Philippines and Eastern Indonesia 1:16.7M
38–39 Southeast Asia 1:16.7M
40–41 Eastern India, Bangladesh and Burma 1:13.3M
42–43 Western India, Pakistan and Sri Lanka 1:13.3M
44–45 Persian Gulf, Iran and Afghanistan 1:13.3M
46–47 The Middle East and Turkey 1:13.3M
48–49 Arabia and the Horn of Africa 1:20M

AFRICA

50–51 Africa 1:56M
52–53 Northwest Africa 1:20M
54–55 Northeast Africa 1:20M
56–57 Central Africa 1:20M
58–59 Southern Africa 1:20M

AUSTRALASIA

60–61 Australia 1:26.7M
62–63 Southeast Australia 1:10.7M
64–65 New Zealand 1:8M
Central and Southwest Pacific

NORTH AMERICA

66–67 North America 1:46.7M
68–69 Western Canada and Alaska 1:20M
70–71 Eastern Canada 1:20M
72–73 Northwest USA 1:8M
74–75 North-central USA 1:8M
76–77 Northeast USA 1:8M
78–79 Southwest USA 1:8M
80–81 Southern USA 1:8M
82–83 Southeast USA 1:8M
84–85 Mexico 1:20M
86–87 Caribbean and Central America 1:20M

SOUTH AMERICA

88–89 South America 1:46.7M
90–91 South America – Northwest 1:21.3M
92–93 South America – Northeast 1:21.3M
94–95 South America – South 1:21.3M

POLAR REGIONS

96 Antarctica 1:46.7M

INDEX

97–160 Index to World Maps

Country/Territory	Area (1,000 sq km)	Area (1,000 sq mi)	Population (1,000s)	Density (persons per sq km)	Capital City	Annual Income US$
Afghanistan	652	252	31,890	49	Kabul	800
Albania	28.7	11.1	3,601	125	Tirana	5,500
Algeria	2,382	920	33,333	14	Algiers	8,100
American Samoa (US)	0.20	0.08	58	290	Pago Pago	5,800
Andorra	0.47	0.18	72	153	Andorra La Vella	38,800
Angola	1,247	481	12,264	10	Luanda	6,500
Anguilla (UK)	0.10	0.04	14	134	The Valley	8,800
Antigua & Barbuda	0.44	0.17	69	157	St John's	10,900
Argentina	2,780	1,074	40,302	15	Buenos Aires	13,000
Armenia	29.8	11.5	2,972	100	Yerevan	5,700
Aruba (Netherlands)	0.19	0.07	100	518	Oranjestad	21,800
Australia	7,741	2,989	20,434	3	Canberra	37,500
Austria	83.9	32.4	8,200	98	Vienna	39,000
Azerbaijan	86.6	33.4	8,120	94	Baku	9,000
Azores (Portugal)	2.2	0.86	236	107	Ponta Delgada	15,000
Bahamas	13.9	5.4	306	22	Nassau	22,700
Bahrain	0.69	0.27	709	1,066	Manama	34,700
Bangladesh	144	55.6	150,448	1,045	Dhaka	1,400
Barbados	0.43	0.17	281	652	Bridgetown	19,700
Belarus	208	80.2	9,725	47	Minsk	10,200
Belgium	30.5	11.8	10,392	340	Brussels	36,500
Belize	23.0	8.9	294	13	Belmopan	7,800
Benin	113	43.5	8,078	72	Porto-Novo	1,500
Bermuda (UK)	0.05	0.02	66	1,196	Hamilton	69,900
Bhutan	47.0	18.1	2,328	50	Thimphu	1,400
Bolivia	1,099	424	9,119	8	La Paz/Sucre	4,400
Bosnia-Herzegovina	51.2	19.8	4,552	89	Sarajevo	6,600
Botswana	582	225	1,816	3	Gaborone	14,700
Brazil	8,514	3,287	190,011	22	Brasília	9,700
Brunei	5.8	2.2	372	65	Bandar Seri Begawan	25,600
Bulgaria	111	42.8	7,323	66	Sofia	11,800
Burkina Faso	274	106	14,326	52	Ouagadougou	1,200
Burma (= Myanmar)	677	261	47,374	70	Rangoon/Naypyidaw	1,900
Burundi	27.8	10.7	8,391	301	Bujumbura	800
Cambodia	181	69.9	13,996	77	Phnom Penh	1,800
Cameroon	475	184	18,060	38	Yaoundé	2,300
Canada	9,971	3,850	33,390	3	Ottawa	38,200
Canary Is. (Spain)	7.2	2.8	1,682	234	Las Palmas/Santa Cruz	19,900
Cape Verde Is.	4.0	1.6	424	105	Praia	7,000
Cayman Is. (UK)	0.26	0.10	47	178	George Town	43,800
Central African Republic	623	241	4,369	7	Bangui	700
Chad	1,284	496	9,886	8	Ndjamena	1,600
Chile	757	292	16,285	22	Santiago	14,400
China	9,597	3,705	1,321,852	138	Beijing	5,300
Colombia	1,139	440	44,380	39	Bogotá	7,200
Comoros	2.2	0.86	711	328	Moroni	600
Congo	342	132	3,801	11	Brazzaville	3,700
Congo (Dem. Rep. of the)	2,345	905	65,752	28	Kinshasa	300
Cook Is. (NZ)	0.24	0.09	22	91	Avarua	9,100
Costa Rica	51.1	19.7	4,134	79	San José	13,500
Croatia	56.5	21.8	4,493	80	Zagreb	15,500
Cuba	111	42.8	11,394	103	Havana	4,500
Cyprus	9.3	3.6	788	85	Nicosia	24,600
Czech Republic	78.9	30.5	10,229	130	Prague	24,400
Denmark	43.1	16.6	5,468	127	Copenhagen	37,400

Listed above are the principal countries and territories of the world. If a territory is not completely independent, then the country it is associated with is named. The area figures give the total area of land, inland water, and ice. The population figures are 2007 estimates. The annual income is the Gross Domestic Product per capita in US dollars. [Gross Domestic Product per capita has been measured

Country/Territory	Area (1,000 sq km)	Area (1,000 sq mi)	Population (1,000s)	Density (persons per sq km)	Capital City	Annual Income US$
Djibouti	23.2	9.0	496	22	Djibouti	1,000
Dominica	0.75	0.29	72	96	Roseau	3,800
Dominican Republic	48.5	18.7	9,366	192	Santo Domingo	9,200
East Timor	14.9	5.7	1,085	72	Dili	800
Ecuador	284	109	13,756	49	Quito	7,100
Egypt	1,001	387	80,335	80	Cairo	5,400
El Salvador	21.0	8.1	6,948	330	San Salvador	5,200
Equatorial Guinea	28.1	10.8	551	20	Malabo	4,100
Eritrea	118	45.4	4,907	40	Asmara	1,000
Estonia	45.1	17.4	1,316	29	Tallinn	21,800
Ethiopia	1,104	426	76,512	68	Addis Ababa	700
Faroe Is. (Denmark)	1.4	0.54	48	34	Tórshavn	31,000
Fiji	18.3	7.1	919	50	Suva	4,100
Finland	338	131	5,238	16	Helsinki	35,500
France	552	213	60,876	111	Paris	33,800
French Guiana (France)	90.0	34.7	196	1	Cayenne	8,300
French Polynesia (France)	4.0	1.5	279	67	Papeete	17,500
Gabon	268	103	1,455	5	Libreville	13,800
Gambia, The	11.3	4.4	1,688	149	Banjul	800
Gaza Strip	0.36	0.14	1,482	4,118	–	1,100
Georgia	69.7	26.9	4,646	67	Tbilisi	4,200
Germany	357	138	82,401	231	Berlin	34,400
Ghana	239	92.1	22,931	96	Accra	1,400
Gibraltar (UK)	0.006	0.002	28	4,303	Gibraltar Town	38,200
Greece	132	50.9	10,706	81	Athens	30,500
Greenland (Denmark)	2,176	840	56	0.03	Nuuk (Godthåb)	20,000
Grenada	0.34	0.13	90	262	St George's	3,900
Guadeloupe (France)	1.7	0.66	449	264	Basse-Terre	7,900
Guam (US)	0.55	0.21	173	316	Agana	15,000
Guatemala	109	42.0	12,728	117	Guatemala City	5,400
Guinea	246	94.9	9,948	40	Conakry	1,000
Guinea-Bissau	36.1	13.9	1,473	41	Bissau	600
Guyana	215	83.0	769	4	Georgetown	5,300
Haiti	27.8	10.7	8,706	314	Port-au-Prince	1,900
Honduras	112	43.3	7,484	67	Tegucigalpa	3,300
Hong Kong (China)	1.1	0.42	6,980	6,392	–	42,000
Hungary	93.0	35.9	9,956	107	Budapest	19,500
Iceland	103	39.8	302	3	Reykjavik	39,400
India	3,287	1,269	1,129,866	344	New Delhi	2,700
Indonesia	1,905	735	234,694	122	Jakarta	3,400
Iran	1,648	636	65,398	40	Tehran	12,300
Iraq	438	169	27,500	63	Baghdad	3,600
Ireland	70.3	27.1	4,109	58	Dublin	45,600
Israel	20.6	8.0	6,427	309	Jerusalem	28,800
Italy	301	116	58,148	193	Rome	31,000
Ivory Coast (= Côte d'Ivoire)	322	125	18,013	56	Yamoussoukro	1,800
Jamaica	11.0	4.2	2,780	253	Kingston	4,800
Japan	378	146	127,433	337	Tokyo	33,800
Jordan	89.3	34.5	6,053	66	Amman	4,700
Kazakhstan	2,725	1,052	15,285	6	Astana	11,100
Kenya	580	224	36,914	63	Nairobi	1,600
Kiribati	0.73	0.28	108	133	Tarawa	1,800
Korea, North	121	46.5	23,302	193	Pyŏngyang	1,900
Korea, South	99.3	38.3	49,045	498	Seoul	24,600
Kosovo	10.9	4.2	2,127	195	Priština	1,800

using the purchasing power parity method. This enables comparisons to be made between countries through their purchasing power (in US dollars), showing real price levels of goods and services rather than using currency exchange rates.] The figures are the latest available, usually 2007 estimates. *OPT = Occupied Palestinian Territory; N/A = Not available.

Country/Territory	Area (1,000 sq km)	Area (1,000 sq mi)	Population (1,000s)	Density (persons per sq km)	Capital City	Annual Income US$
Kuwait	17.8	6.9	2,506	141	Kuwait City	55,300
Kyrgyzstan	200	77.2	5,284	27	Bishkek	2,000
Laos	237	91.4	6,522	28	Vientiane	1,900
Latvia	64.6	24.9	2,260	35	Riga	17,700
Lebanon	10.4	4.0	3,926	377	Beirut	10,400
Lesotho	30.4	11.7	2,125	70	Maseru	1,500
Liberia	111	43.0	3,196	29	Monrovia	500
Libya	1,760	679	6,037	3	Tripoli	13,100
Liechtenstein	0.16	0.06	34	214	Vaduz	25,000
Lithuania	65.2	25.2	3,575	55	Vilnius	16,700
Luxembourg	2.6	1.0	480	186	Luxembourg	80,800
Macau (China)	0.02	0.007	457	18,280	–	24,300
Macedonia (FYROM)	25.7	9.9	2,056	81	Skopje	8,400
Madagascar	587	227	19,449	33	Antananarivo	1,000
Madeira (Portugal)	0.78	0.30	241	309	Funchal	22,700
Malawi	118	45.7	13,603	115	Lilongwe	800
Malaysia	330	127	24,821	75	Kuala Lumpur/Putrajaya	14,400
Maldives	0.30	0.12	369	1,230	Malé	3,900
Mali	1,240	479	11,995	10	Bamako	1,200
Malta	0.32	0.12	402	1,272	Valletta	23,200
Marshall Is.	0.18	0.07	62	342	Majuro	2,900
Martinique (France)	1.1	0.43	433	394	Fort-de-France	14,400
Mauritania	1,026	396	3,270	3	Nouakchott	1,800
Mauritius	2.0	0.79	1,251	613	Port Louis	11,900
Mexico	1,958	756	108,701	55	Mexico City	12,500
Micronesia, Fed. States of	0.70	0.27	108	154	Palikir	2,300
Moldova	33.9	13.1	4,320	128	Chişinău	2,200
Monaco	0.001	0.0004	33	33,000	Monaco	30,000
Mongolia	1,567	605	2,952	2	Ulan Bator	2,900
Montenegro	14.0	5.4	685	49	Podgorica	3,800
Montserrat (UK)	0.10	0.04	10	94	Plymouth	3,400
Morocco	447	172	33,757	76	Rabat	3,800
Mozambique	802	309	20,906	26	Maputo	900
Namibia	824	318	2,055	2	Windhoek	5,200
Nauru	0.02	0.008	14	644	Yaren District	5,000
Nepal	147	56.8	28,902	205	Katmandu	1,100
Netherlands	41.5	16.0	16,571	399	Amsterdam/The Hague	38,600
Netherlands Antilles (Neths)	0.80	0.31	224	233	Willemstad	16,000
New Caledonia (France)	18.6	7.2	222	12	Nouméa	15,000
New Zealand	271	104	4,116	15	Wellington	27,300
Nicaragua	130	50.2	5,675	44	Managua	3,200
Niger	1,267	489	12,895	10	Niamey	700
Nigeria	924	357	135,031	146	Abuja	2,200
Northern Mariana Is. (US)	0.46	0.18	85	177	Saipan	12,500
Norway	324	125	4,628	14	Oslo	55,600
Oman	310	119	3,205	15	Muscat	19,100
Pakistan	796	307	164,742	205	Islamabad	2,600
Palau	0.46	0.18	21	46	Melekeok	7,600
Panama	75.5	29.2	3,242	41	Panamá	9,000
Papua New Guinea	463	179	5,796	13	Port Moresby	2,900
Paraguay	407	157	6,669	16	Asunción	4,000
Peru	1,285	496	28,675	22	Lima	7,600
Philippines	300	116	91,077	304	Manila	3,300
Poland	323	125	38,518	123	Warsaw	16,200
Portugal	88.8	34.3	10,643	115	Lisbon	21,800
Puerto Rico (US)	8.9	3.4	3,944	433	San Juan	19,600
Qatar	11.0	4.2	907	79	Doha	29,400
Réunion (France)	2.5	0.97	777	311	St-Denis	6,200

Country/Territory	Area (1,000 sq km)	Area (1,000 sq mi)	Population (1,000s)	Density (persons per sq km)	Capital City	Annual Income US$
Romania	238	92.0	22,276	94	Bucharest	11,100
Russia	17,075	6,593	141,378	8	Moscow	14,600
Rwanda	26.3	10.2	9,908	376	Kigali	1,000
St Kitts & Nevis	0.26	0.10	39	151	Basseterre	8,200
St Lucia	0.54	0.21	171	277	Castries	4,800
St Vincent & Grenadines	0.39	0.15	118	304	Kingstown	3,600
Samoa	2.8	1.1	214	73	Apia	2,100
San Marino	0.06	0.02	30	485	San Marino	34,100
São Tomé & Príncipe	0.96	0.37	200	199	São Tomé	1,200
Saudi Arabia	2,150	830	27,601	14	Riyadh	20,700
Senegal	197	76.0	12,522	64	Dakar	1,700
Serbia	77.5	29.9	8,024	104	Belgrade	7,700
Seychelles	0.46	0.18	82	180	Victoria	18,400
Sierra Leone	71.7	27.7	6,155	86	Freetown	800
Singapore	0.68	0.26	4,553	6,570	Singapore City	48,900
Slovak Republic	49.0	18.9	5,448	112	Bratislava	19,800
Slovenia	20.3	7.8	2,009	99	Ljubljana	27,300
Solomon Is.	28.9	11.2	567	20	Honiara	600
Somalia	638	246	9,119	14	Mogadishu	600
South Africa	1,221	471	43,998	36	Cape Town/Pretoria	10,600
Spain	498	192	40,448	80	Madrid	33,700
Sri Lanka	65.6	25.3	20,926	319	Colombo	4,100
Sudan	2,506	967	39,379	16	Khartoum	2,500
Suriname	163	63.0	471	3	Paramaribo	7,800
Swaziland	17.4	6.7	1,133	65	Mbabane	4,800
Sweden	450	174	9,031	20	Stockholm	36,900
Switzerland	41.3	15.9	7,555	183	Bern	39,800
Syria	185	71.5	19,315	104	Damascus	4,500
Taiwan	36.0	13.9	22,859	635	Taipei	29,800
Tajikistan	143	55.3	7,077	49	Dushanbe	1,600
Tanzania	945	365	39,384	42	Dodoma	1,100
Thailand	513	198	65,068	127	Bangkok	8,000
Togo	56.8	21.9	5,702	100	Lomé	900
Tonga	0.65	0.25	117	156	Nuku'alofa	2,200
Trinidad & Tobago	5.1	2.0	1,057	206	Port of Spain	21,700
Tunisia	164	63.2	10,276	63	Tunis	7,500
Turkey	775	299	71,159	91	Ankara	7,500
Turkmenistan	488	188	5,097	10	Ashkhabad	9,200
Turks & Caicos Is. (UK)	0.43	0.17	22	51	Cockburn Town	11,500
Tuvalu	0.03	0.01	12	461	Fongafale	1,600
Uganda	241	93.1	30,263	128	Kampala	1,100
Ukraine	604	233	46,300	77	Kiev	6,900
United Arab Emirates	83.6	32.3	4,444	53	Abu Dhabi	55,200
United Kingdom	242	93.4	60,776	248	London	35,300
United States of America	9,629	3,718	301,140	31	Washington, DC	46,000
Uruguay	175	67.6	3,461	20	Montevideo	10,700
Uzbekistan	447	173	27,780	62	Tashkent	2,200
Vanuatu	12.2	4.7	212	17	Port-Vila	2,900
Venezuela	912	352	26,024	29	Caracas	12,800
Vietnam	332	128	85,262	259	Hanoi	2,600
Virgin Is. (UK)	0.15	0.06	24	154	Road Town	38,500
Virgin Is. (US)	0.35	0.13	108	308	Charlotte Amalie	14,500
Wallis & Futuna Is. (France)	0.20	0.08	16	60	Mata-Utu	3,800
West Bank (OPT)*	5.9	2.3	2,536	433	–	1,100
Western Sahara	266	103	383	1	El Aaiún	N/A
Yemen	528	204	22,231	42	Sana'	2,400
Zambia	753	291	11,477	15	Lusaka	1,400
Zimbabwe	391	151	12,311	32	Harare	500

	Population (1,000s)
Afghanistan	
Kabul	3,288
Algeria	
Algiers	3,260
Angola	
Luanda	2,839
Argentina	
Buenos Aires	13,349
Córdoba	1,592
Rosario	1,312
Mendoza	1,072
Armenia	
Yerevan	1,103
Australia	
Sydney	4,388
Melbourne	3,663
Brisbane	1,769
Perth	1,484
Adelaide	1,137
Austria	
Vienna	2,260
Azerbaijan	
Baku	1,856
Bangladesh	
Dhaka	12,560
Chittagong	4,171
Khulna	1,497
Rajshahi	1,035
Belarus	
Minsk	1,778
Belgium	
Brussels	1,012
Bolivia	
La Paz	1,533
Santa Cruz	1,352
Brazil	
São Paulo	18,333
Rio de Janeiro	11,469
Belo Horizonte	5,304
Pôrto Alegre	3,795
Recife	3,527
Brasília	3,341
Salvador	3,331
Fortaleza	3,261
Curitiba	2,871
Campinas	2,640
Belém	2,097
Goiânia	1,878
Manaus	1,673
Santos	1,634
Vitória	1,602
Maceió	1,137
Natal	1,049
Bulgaria	
Sofia	1,093
Burma (= Myanmar)	
Rangoon	4,107
Cambodia	
Phnom Penh	1,364
Cameroon	
Douala	1,980
Yaoundé	1,727
Canada	
Toronto	5,312
Montréal	3,640
Vancouver	2,188
Ottawa	1,156
Calgary	1,058
Edmonton	1,015
Chile	
Santiago	5,683

	Population (1,000s)
China	
Shanghai	14,503
Beijing	10,717
Guangzhou	8,425
Shenzhen	7,233
Wuhan	7,093
Hong Kong	7,041
Tianjin	7,040
Chongqing	6,363
Shenyang	4,720
Dongguan	4,320
Chengdu	4,065
Xi'an	3,926
Harbin	3,695
Nanjing	3,621
Guiyang	3,447
Dalian	3,073
Changchun	3,046
Zibo	2,982
Kunming	2,837
Hangzhou	2,831
Qingdao	2,817
Taiyuan	2,794
Jinan	2,743
Zhengzhou	2,590
Fuzhou	2,453
Changsha	2,451
Lanzhou	2,411
Xiamen	2,371
Shijiazhuang	2,275
Jinxi	2,268
Jilin	2,255
Wenzhou	2,212
Nanchang	2,188
Zaozhuang	2,096
Nanchong	2,046
Nanning	2,040
Linyi	2,035
Ürümqi	2,025
Yantai	1,991
Wanxian	1,963
Xuzhou	1,960
Baotou	1,920
Hefei	1,916
Suzhou	1,849
Nanyang	1,830
Tangshan	1,825
Ningbo	1,810
Datong	1,763
Yancheng	1,678
Tianmen	1,676
Shangqui	1,650
Lu'an	1,647
Wuxi	1,646
Luoyang	1,644
Hohhot	1,644
Anshan	1,611
Qiqihar	1,607
Tai'an	1,598
Daqing	1,594
Xinghua	1,587
Pingxiang	1,562
Handan	1,535
Xiantao	1,528
Zhanjiang	1,514
Weifang	1,498
Shantou	1,495
Fushun	1,456
Xianyang	1,450
Luzhou	1,447
Neijiang	1,441

	Population (1,000s)
Changde	1,429
Huainan	1,420
Liuzhou	1,409
Suining, Sichuan	1,401
Quanzhou	1,377
Xintai	1,334
Mianyang	1,322
Heze	1,318
Yiyang	1,318
Yueyang	1,286
Suqian	1,258
Changzhou	1,249
Huaian	1,243
Chifeng	1,238
Jingmen	1,228
Yuzhou	1,226
Zaoyang	1,210
Huzhou	1,203
Tianshui	1,199
Yongzhou	1,182
Mudanjiang	1,171
Liupanshui	1,149
Leshan	1,143
Jining, Shandong	1,143
Xiaoshan	1,130
Yixing	1,129
Zigong	1,087
Xianyang	1,072
Fuyu	1,068
Yulin	1,060
Baoding	1,042
Xinyi, Jiangsu	1,022
Zhuzhou	1,016
Jixi	1,012
Linqing	1,009
Jiamusi	1,006
Xiangfan	1,006
Zhangjiakou	1,001
Colombia	
Bogotá	7,594
Medellín	3,236
Cali	2,583
Barranquilla	1,918
Bucaramanga	1,069
Cartagena	1,002
Congo	
Brazzaville	1,173
Congo (Dem. Rep.)	
Kinshasa	6,049
Kolwezi	1,207
Lubumbashi	1,179
Costa Rica	
San José	1,217
Croatia	
Zagreb	1,067
Cuba	
Havana	2,192
Czech Republic	
Prague	1,171
Denmark	
Copenhagen	1,091
Dominican Republic	
Santo Domingo	2,563
Ecuador	
Guayaquil	2,387
Quito	1,514
Egypt	
Cairo	11,146
Alexandria	3,760

	Population (1,000s)
El Salvador	
San Salvador	1,517
Ethiopia	
Addis Ababa	2,899
Finland	
Helsinki	1,091
France	
Paris	9,820
Lyons	1,403
Marseilles	1,382
Lille	1,029
Georgia	
Tbilisi	1,406
Germany	
Berlin	3,387
Hamburg	1,705
Munich	1,195
Ghana	
Accra	1,981
Kumasi	1,517
Greece	
Athens	3,238
Guatemala	
Guatemala City	3,242
Guinea	
Conakry	1,465
Haiti	
Port-au-Prince	2,129
Honduras	
Tegucigalpa	1,061
Hungary	
Budapest	1,693
India	
Mumbai	18,336
Delhi	15,334
Kolkata	14,299
Chennai	6,915
Bangalore	6,532
Hyderabad	6,145
Ahmedabad	5,171
Pune	4,485
Surat	3,671
Kanpur	3,040
Jaipur	2,796
Lucknow	2,589
Nagpur	2,359
Patna	2,066
Indore	1,941
Vadodara	1,686
Bhopal	1,656
Coimbatore	1,628
Ludhiana	1,583
Agra	1,526
Visakhapatnam	1,468
Cochin	1,461
Nashik	1,408
Meerut	1,340
Faridabad	1,330
Varanasi	1,300
Ghaziabad	1,277
Asansol	1,272
Jamshedpur	1,246
Madurai	1,245
Jabalpur	1,234
Rajkot	1,205
Dhanbad	1,195
Amritsar	1,162
Allahabad	1,153
Vijayawada	1,093
Srinagar	1,093
Aurangabad	1,065

	Population (1,000s)
Bhilainagar-Durg	1,051
Solapur	1,012
Indonesia	
Jakarta	13,215
Bandung	4,126
Surabaya	2,992
Medan	2,287
Palembang	1,733
Ujung Pandang	1,284
Iran	
Tehran	7,352
Mashhad	2,147
Esfahan	1,547
Tabriz	1,396
Karaj	1,235
Shiraz	1,230
Qom	1,045
Iraq	
Baghdad	5,910
Mosul	1,236
Basra	1,187
Ireland	
Dublin	1,037
Israel	
Tel Aviv-Yafo	3,025
Italy	
Rome	3,348
Milan	2,953
Naples	2,245
Turin	1,660
Ivory Coast (= Côte d'Ivoire)	
Abidjan	3,516
Japan	
Tokyo	12,064
Yokohama	6,427
Osaka	2,599
Nagoya	2,172
Sapporo	1,922
Kobe	1,493
Kyoto	1,468
Fukuoka	1,341
Kawasaki	1,250
Hiroshima	1,126
Kitakyushu	1,011
Sendai	1,008
Jordan	
Amman	1,292
Kazakhstan	
Almaty	1,156
Kenya	
Nairobi	2,818
Korea, North	
Pyŏngyang	3,351
N'ampo	1,102
Korea, South	
Seoul	9,888
Busan	3,830
Incheon	2,884
Daegu	2,675
Daejeon	1,522
Gwangju	1,379
Seongnam	1,353
Ulsan	1,340
Lebanon	
Beirut	2,070
Libya	
Tripoli	2,098

	Population (1,000s)
Benghazi	1,114
Madagascar	
Antananarivo	1,808
Malaysia	
Kuala Lumpur	1,405
Mali	
Bamako	1,379
Mexico	
Mexico City	19,013
Guadalajara	3,905
Monterrey	3,517
Toluca	1,987
Puebla	1,880
Tijuana	1,570
Ciudad Juárez	1,469
León	1,438
Torreón	1,057
Morocco	
Casablanca	3,743
Rabat	1,859
Fès	1,032
Mozambique	
Maputo	1,316
Nepal	
Katmandu	1,176
Netherlands	
Amsterdam	1,157
Rotterdam	1,112
New Zealand	
Auckland	1,152
Nicaragua	
Managua	1,165
Nigeria	
Lagos	11,135
Kano	2,884
Ibadan	2,375
Kaduna	1,329
Benin City	1,022
Pakistan	
Karachi	11,819
Lahore	6,373
Faisalabad	2,533
Rawalpindi	1,794
Gujranwala	1,466
Multan	1,459
Hyderabad	1,392
Peshawar	1,255
Panama	
Panamá	1,216
Paraguay	
Asunción	1,858
Peru	
Lima	8,180
Philippines	
Manila	10,677
Davao	1,326
Poland	
Warsaw	1,680
Portugal	
Lisbon	2,761
Porto	1,309
Puerto Rico	
San Juan	2,604
Romania	
Bucharest	1,934
Russia	
Moscow	10,672
Saint Petersburg	5,315

	Population (1,000s)
Novosibirsk	1,425
Nizhniy Novgorod	1,288
Yekaterinburg	1,281
Samara	1,140
Omsk	1,132
Kazan	1,108
Rostov	1,081
Chelyabinsk	1,067
Ufa	1,035
Volgograd	1,016
Perm	1,014
Saudi Arabia	
Riyadh	5,514
Jedda	3,807
Mecca	1,529
Medina	1,044
Senegal	
Dakar	2,313
Serbia	
Belgrade	1,116
Sierra Leone	
Freetown	1,007
Singapore	
Singapore City	4,372
Somalia	
Mogadishu	1,320
South Africa	
Johannesburg	3,254
Cape Town	3,083
Durban	2,631
Pretoria	1,271
Vereeniging	1,027
Port Elizabeth	1,006
Spain	
Madrid	5,608
Barcelona	4,795
Sudan	
Khartoum	4,518
Sweden	
Stockholm	1,729
Syria	
Aleppo	2,505
Damascus	2,317
Taiwan	
Taipei	2,606
Kaohsiung	1,515
T'aichung	1,033
Tanzania	
Dar es Salaam	2,683
Thailand	
Bangkok	6,604
Togo	
Lomé	1,337
Tunisia	
Tunis	2,063
Turkey	
Istanbul	9,712
Ankara	3,573
Izmir	2,487
Bursa	1,414
Adana	1,245
Uganda	
Kampala	1,345
Ukraine	
Kiev	2,621
Kharkov	1,521
Dnepropetrovsk	1,122
Donetsk	1,065

	Population (1,000s)
Odessa	1,027
United Arab Emirates	
Dubai	1,330
United Kingdom	
London	8,505
Birmingham	2,280
Manchester	2,228
Liverpool	1,519
Glasgow	1,159
United States of America	
New York	18,718
Los Angeles	12,298
Chicago	8,814
Miami	5,434
Philadelphia	5,392
Dallas–Fort Worth	4,655
Boston	4,361
Houston	4,320
Atlanta	4,304
Washington	4,238
Detroit	4,034
Phoenix–Mesa	3,416
San Francisco	3,385
Seattle	2,989
San Diego	2,852
Minneapolis–St Paul	2,556
Tampa–St Petersburg	2,252
Denver	2,239
Baltimore	2,205
St Louis	2,159
Cleveland	1,855
Portland	1,810
Pittsburgh	1,806
Las Vegas	1,720
San Bernardino	1,690
San Jose	1,631
Cincinnati	1,599
Sacramento	1,555
Norfolk–Virginia Beach	1,460
Kansas City	1,437
San Antonio	1,436
Indianapolis	1,387
Milwaukee	1,316
Orlando	1,306
Providence	1,248
Columbus	1,236
Austin	1,107
Memphis	1,053
New Orleans	1,010
Uruguay	
Montevideo	1,353
Uzbekistan	
Tashkent	2,181
Venezuela	
Caracas	3,276
Valencia	2,330
Maracaibo	2,182
Maracay	1,138
Vietnam	
Ho Chi Minh City	5,065
Hanoi	4,164
Haiphong	1,873
Yemen	
Sana'	1,801
Zambia	
Lusaka	1,450
Zimbabwe	
Harare	1,527

Listed above are the principal cities with more than 1,00,000 inhabitants. The figures are taken from the most recent census or estimate available (usually 2007), and as far as possible are for the metropolitan area or urban agglomeration.

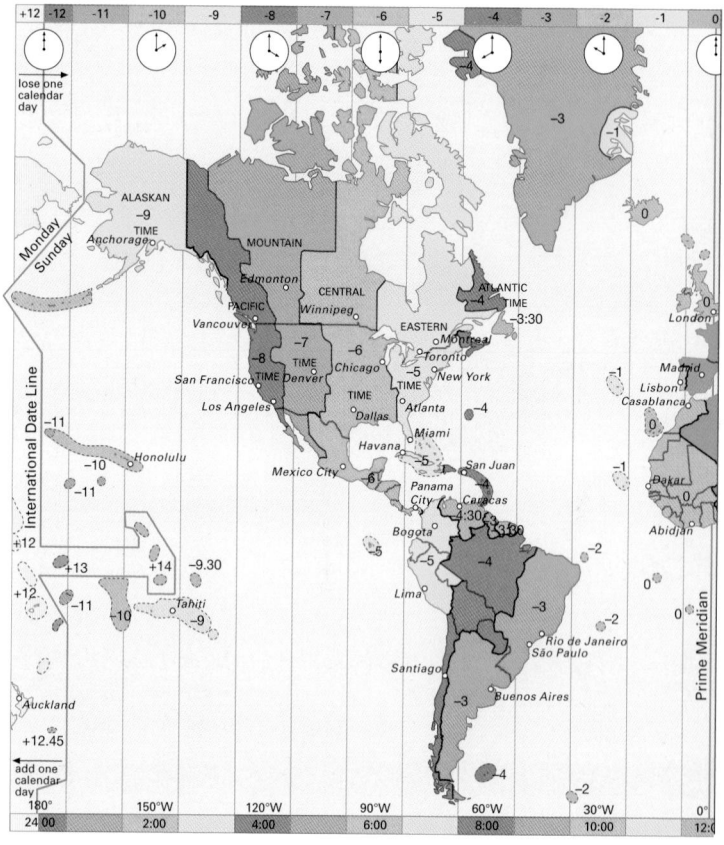

The world is divided into 24 time zones, each centered on meridians at 15° intervals, which is the longitudinal distance the Sun travels every hour. The Prime Meridian running through Greenwich in London, England, passes through the middle of the first time zone. Zones to the east of Greenwich are ahead of Universal Time (UT) by one hour for every 15° of longitude, while zones to the west are behind UT by one hour.

When it is 12 noon at the Greenwich meridian, 180° east it is midnight of the same day, while at 180° west the day is only just beginning. To overcome this, the International Date Line was established in 1883 – an imaginary line which approximately follows the 180th meridian. Therefore, if one traveled eastward from Japan (140° East) toward Samoa (170° West), one would pass from Sunday night straight into Sunday morning.

TIME DIFFERENCES FROM EASTERN STANDARD TIME

BEIJING	+13	LONDON	+5
CAIRO	+7	LOS ANGELES	–3
CHICAGO	–1	MOSCOW	+8
DALLAS	–1	MEXICO CITY	–1
DELHI	+10.5	SANTIAGO	+1
DENVER	–2	SYDNEY	+15
HONOLULU	–5	TOKYO	+14
KUWAIT	+8	VANCOUVER	–3

KEY TO TIME ZONES MAP

10 — Hours behind or ahead of UT or Coordinated Universal Time

Zones using UT (GMT)

Zones behind UT (GMT)

International boundaries

Actual solar time, when time at Greenwich is 12:00 (noon)

Zones ahead of UT (GMT)

Half-hour zones

Time zone boundaries

International Date Line

Note: Certain time zones are affected by the incidence of daylight saving time in countries where it is adopted.

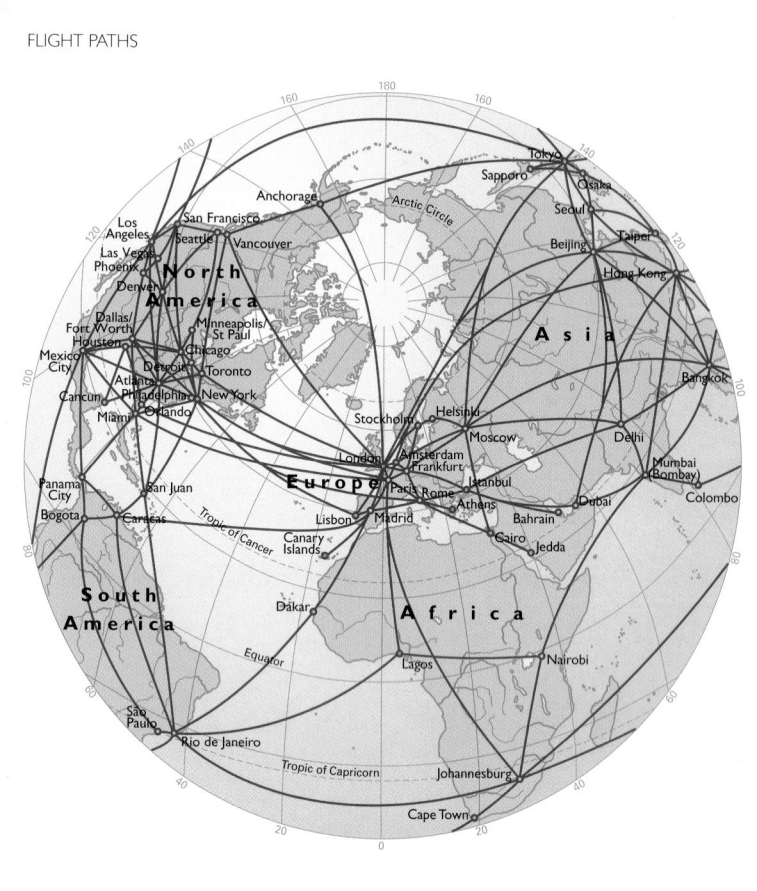

WORLD'S BUSIEST AIRPORTS

TOTAL NUMBER OF PASSENGERS IN MILLIONS (2006)

ATLANTA HARTSFIELD INTL. (ATL)	84.8
CHICAGO O'HARE INTL. (ORD)	77.0
LONDON HEATHROW (LHR)	67.5
TOKYO HANEDA (HND)	65.8
LOS ANGELES INTL. (LAX)	61.0
DALLAS/FORT WORTH INTL. (DFW)	60.2
PARIS CHARLES DE GAULLE (CDG)	56.8
FRANKFURT INTL. (FRA)	52.8
BEIJING CAPITAL INTL (PEK)	48.7

The flight paths shown on the maps above usually follow the shortest, most direct route from A to B, known as the ***great-circle route***. A great circle is any circle that divides the globe into equal halves. Aircraft do not always fly along great-circle routes, however. Lack of search and rescue and emergency landing provisions, together with limits on fuel consumption and minimum flying altitudes, mean that commercial aircraft do not usually fly across Antarctica.

FLIGHT TIMES FROM NEW YORK	
FRANKFURT	8hrs 35mins
JOHANNESBURG	17hrs 45mins
MEXICO CITY	5hrs 45mins
PARIS	8hrs 15mins
ROME	9hrs 35mins
SANTIAGO	12hrs 55mins
SINGAPORE	23hrs 10mins
TOKYO	14hrs 35mins
VANCOUVER	7hrs 25mins

FLIGHT TIMES FROM LONDON	
ATHENS	4hrs 05mins
AUCKLAND	24hrs 20mins
BANGKOK	14hrs 30mins
BUENOS AIRES	14hrs 20mins
HONG KONG	14hrs 10mins
LOS ANGELES	12hrs 00mins
MOSCOW	3hrs 50mins
MUMBAI (BOMBAY)	11hrs 15mins
NEW YORK	6hrs 50mins

Kms	Beijing	Buenos Aires	Cairo	Caracas	Chicago	Hong Kong	Honolulu	Johannesburg	Kolkata	Lagos	London	Los Angeles
Beijing		11972	4688	8947	6588	1220	5070	7276	2031	7119	5057	6251
Buenos Aires	19268		7341	3167	5599	11481	7558	5025	10268	4919	6917	6122
Cairo	7544	11814		6340	6127	5064	8838	3894	3541	2432	2180	7580
Caracas	14399	5096	10203		2502	10166	6009	6847	9609	4810	4664	3612
Chicago	10603	9011	3206	4027		7783	4247	8689	7978	5973	3949	1742
Hong Kong	1963	18478	8150	16360	12526		5543	6669	1653	7360	5980	7232
Honolulu	8160	12164	14223	9670	6836	8921		11934	7048	10133	7228	2558
Johannesburg	11710	8088	6267	11019	13984	10732	19206		5256	2799	5637	10362
Kolkata	3269	16524	5699	15464	12839	2659	11343	8459		5727	4946	8152
Lagos	11457	7916	3915	7741	9612	11845	16308	4505	9216		3118	7713
London	8138	11131	3508	7507	6356	9623	11632	9071	7961	5017		5442
Los Angeles	10060	9852	12200	5812	2804	11639	4117	16676	13120	12414	8758	
Mexico City	12460	7389	12372	3586	2726	14122	6085	14585	15280	11071	8936	2493
Moscow	5794	13477	2902	9938	8000	7144	11323	9161	5534	6254	2498	9769
Mumbai	4757	14925	4355	14522	12953	4317	12914	6974	1664	7612	7190	14000
Nairobi	9216	10402	3536	11544	12883	8776	17282	2927	6179	3807	6819	15544
New York	10988	8526	9020	3430	1145	12950	7980	12841	12747	8477	5572	3936
Paris	8217	11051	3210	7625	6650	9630	11968	8732	7858	4714	342	9085
Rio de Janeiro	17338	1953	9896	4546	8547	17704	13342	7113	15073	6035	9299	10155
Rome	8126	11151	2133	8363	7739	9284	12916	7743	7219	4039	1431	10188
Singapore	4478	15879	8267	18359	15078	2599	10816	8660	2897	11145	10852	14123
Sydney	8949	11800	14418	15343	14875	7374	8168	11040	9138	15519	16992	12073
Tokyo	2099	18362	9571	14164	10137	2874	6202	13547	5141	13480	9562	8811
Wellington	10782	9981	16524	13122	13451	9427	7513	11761	11354	16050	18814	10814

The table above shows air distances in miles and kilometers between 30 major cities.

	Mexico City	Moscow	Mumbai	Nairobi	New York	Paris	Rio de Janeiro	Rome	Singapore	Sydney	Tokyo	Wellington
Beijing	7742	3600	2956	5727	6828	5106	10773	5049	2783	5561	1304	6700
Buenos Aires	4591	8374	9275	6463	5298	6867	1214	6929	9867	7332	11410	6202
Cairo	7687	1803	2706	2197	5605	1994	6149	1325	5137	8959	5947	10268
Caracas	2228	6175	9024	7173	2131	4738	2825	5196	11407	9534	8801	8154
Chicago	1694	4971	8048	8005	711	4132	5311	4809	9369	9243	6299	8358
Hong Kong	8775	4439	2683	5453	8047	5984	11001	5769	1615	4582	1786	5857
Honolulu	3781	7036	8024	10739	4958	7437	8290	8026	6721	5075	3854	4669
Johannesburg	9063	5692	4334	1818	7979	5426	4420	4811	5381	6860	8418	7308
Kolkata	9494	3438	1034	3839	7921	4883	9366	4486	1800	5678	3195	7055
Lagos	6879	3886	4730	2366	5268	2929	3750	2510	6925	9643	8376	9973
London	5552	1552	4467	4237	3463	212	5778	889	6743	10558	5942	11691
Los Angeles	1549	6070	8700	9659	2446	5645	6310	6331	8776	7502	5475	6719
Mexico City		6664	9728	9207	2090	5717	4780	6365	10321	8058	7024	6897
Moscow			3126	3942	4666	1545	7184	1477	5237	9008	4651	10283
Mumbai				2816	7793	4356	8332	3837	2432	6313	4189	7686
Nairobi					7358	4029	5548	3350	4635	7552	6996	8490
New York	10724					3626	4832	4280	9531	9935	6741	8951
Paris	15656	5031					5708	687	6671	10539	6038	11798
Rio de Janeiro	14818	6344	4532					5725	9763	8389	11551	7367
Rome	3264	7510	12541	11842					6229	10143	6127	11523
Singapore	9200	2486	7010	6485	5836					3915	3306	5298
Sydney	7693	11562	13409	8928	7777	9187					4861	1383
Tokyo	10243	2376	6175	5391	6888	1105	9214					5762
Wellington	16610	8428	3914	7460	15339	10737	15712	10025				
Miles	12969	14497	10160	12153	15989	16962	13501	16324	6300			
	11304	7485	6742	11260	10849	9718	18589	9861	5321	7823		
	11100	16549	12370	13664	14405	18987	11855	18545	8526	2226	9273	

Known as "great-circle" distances, these measure the shortest routes between the cities.

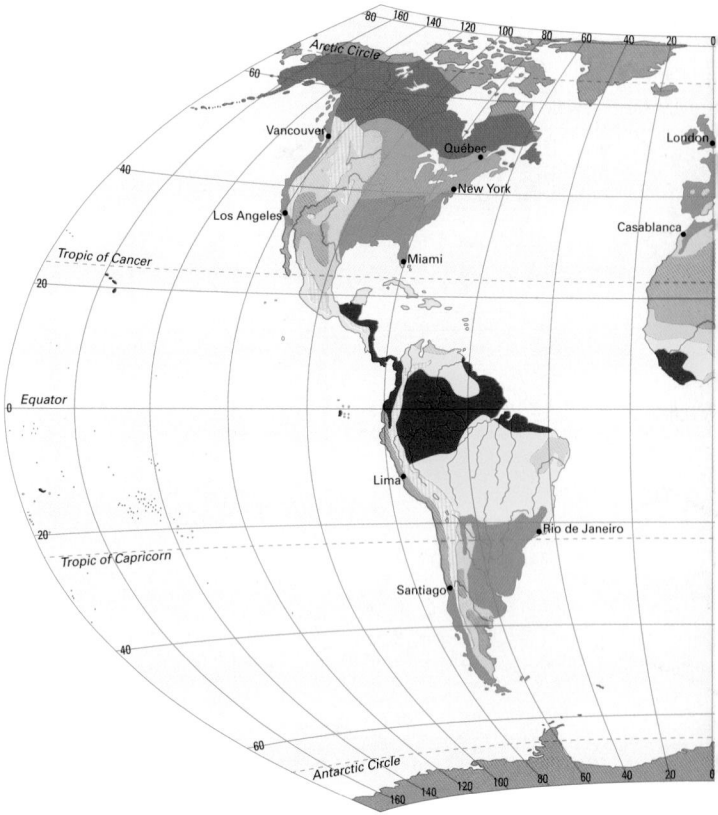

Climate is weather in the long term: the seasonal pattern of temperature and precipitation averaged over a period of time. Temperature roughly follows latitude, and is warmest near the equator and coldest near the poles. The interplay of various factors, however, namely the differential heating of land and sea, the influence of landmasses and mountain ranges on winds and ocean currents, and the effect of vegetation, all combine to add complexity. Thus New York and Naples share almost the same latitude, but their resulting climates are quite different. Most scientists are now in agreement that the world's climate is changing, due partly to atmospheric pollution. By the year 2050, average world temperatures are predicted to rise by approximately 3°F to make the climate hotter than it has been at any time during the last 120,000 years. Climate graphs for 24 cities are given on pages 18 and 19.

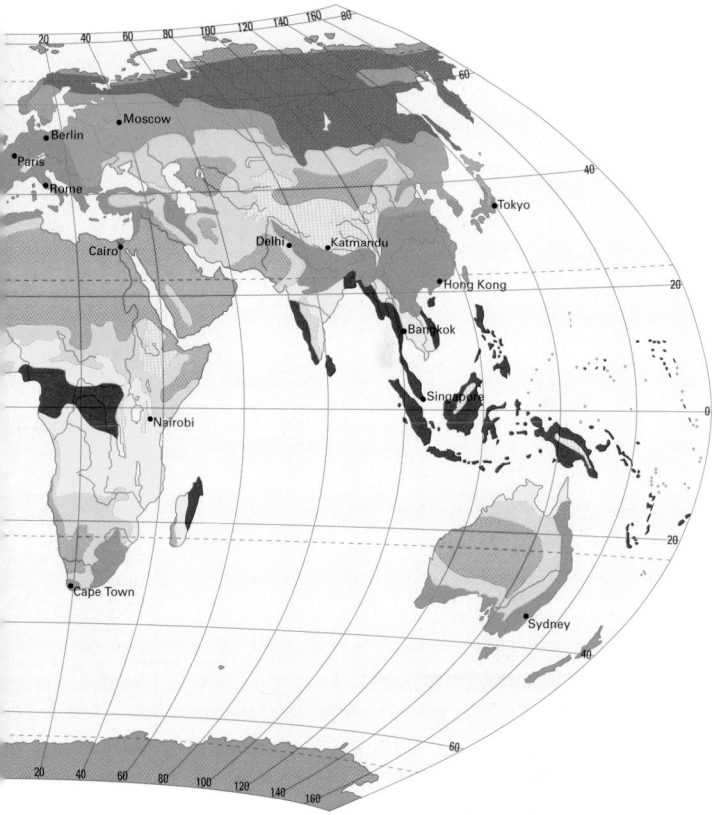

SEASONAL WEATHER EXTREMES

- **Caribbean**
  Hurricanes – August to October
- **Northern Latitudes**
  Blizzards – November to March
- **Southern Asia**
  Cyclones and typhoons – June to November
- **Southern Asia**
  Monsoon rains – July to October

CLIMATIC REGIONS

- Tropical climate (hot and wet)
- Desert climate (hot and very dry)
- Savanna climate (hot with dry season)
- Steppe climate (Warm and dry)
- Mild climate (Warm and wet)
- Continental climate (cold with wet winter)
- Subarctic climate (very cold winter)
- Polar climate (very cold and dry)
- Mountainous climate (altitude affects climate)

Lima • Climate graphs on pages 18 and 19

Note: Climate comprises a description of the condition of the atmosphere over a considerable area for a long time (at least 30 years).

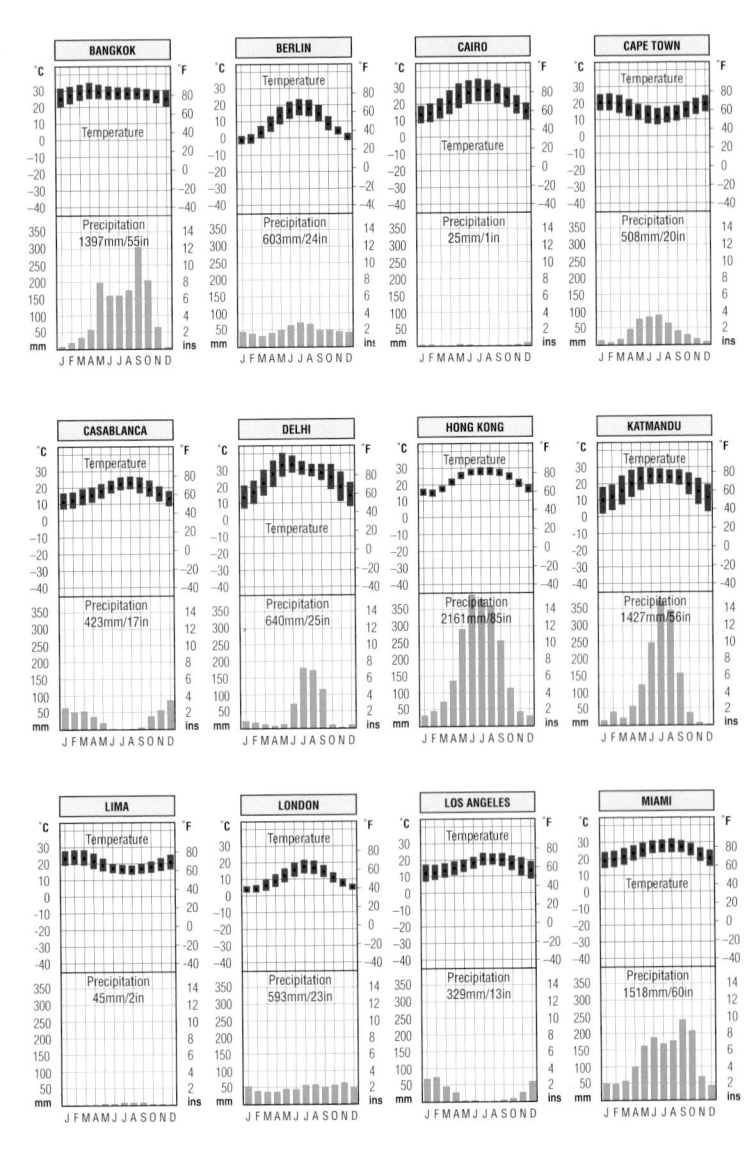
BANGKOK
Temperature
Precipitation
1397mm/55in
BERLIN
Temperature
Precipitation
603mm/24in
CAIRO
Temperature
Precipitation
25mm/1in
CAPE TOWN
Temperature
Precipitation
508mm/20in
CASABLANCA
Temperature
Precipitation
423mm/17in
DELHI
Temperature
Precipitation
640mm/25in
HONG KONG
Temperature
Precipitation
2161mm/85in
KATMANDU
Temperature
Precipitation
1427mm/56in
LIMA
Temperature
Precipitation
45mm/2in
LONDON
Temperature
Precipitation
593mm/23in
LOS ANGELES
Temperature
Precipitation
329mm/13in
MIAMI
Temperature
Precipitation
1518mm/60in
°C
°F
mm
ins
J F M A M J J A S O N D

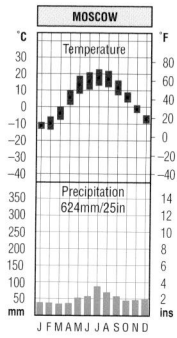
MOSCOW
°C
°F
Temperature
Precipitation
624mm/25in
mm
ins
J F M A M J J A S O N D

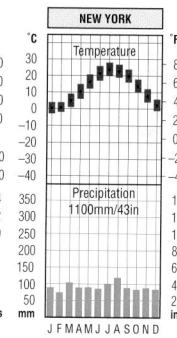
NEW YORK
°C
°F
Temperature
Precipitation
1100mm/43in
mm
ins
J F M A M J J A S O N D

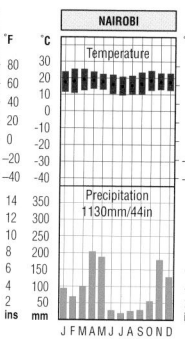
NAIROBI
°C
°F
Temperature
Precipitation
1130mm/44in
mm
ins
J F M A M J J A S O N D

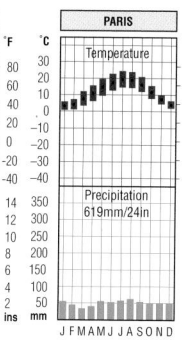
PARIS
°C
°F
Temperature
Precipitation
619mm/24in
mm
ins
J F M A M J J A S O N D

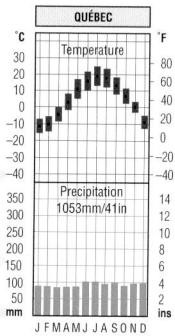
QUÉBEC
°C
°F
Temperature
Precipitation
1053mm/41in
mm
ins
J F M A M J J A S O N D

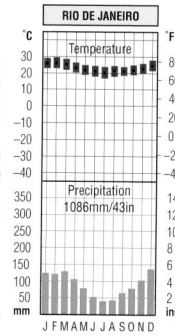
RIO DE JANEIRO
°C
°F
Temperature
Precipitation
1086mm/43in
mm
ins
J F M A M J J A S O N D

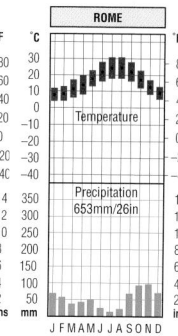
ROME
°C
°F
Temperature
Precipitation
653mm/26in
mm
ins
J F M A M J J A S O N D

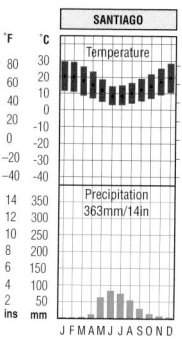
SANTIAGO
°C
°F
Temperature
Precipitation
363mm/14in
mm
ins
J F M A M J J A S O N D

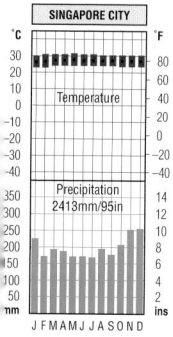
SINGAPORE CITY
°C
°F
Temperature
Precipitation
2413mm/95in
mm
ins
J F M A M J J A S O N D

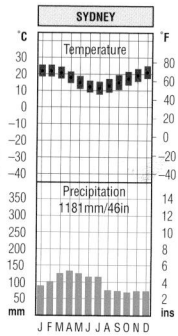
SYDNEY
°C
°F
Temperature
Precipitation
1181mm/46in
mm
ins
J F M A M J J A S O N D

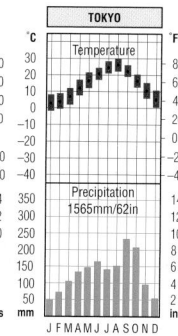
TOKYO
°C
°F
Temperature
Precipitation
1565mm/62in
mm
ins
J F M A M J J A S O N D

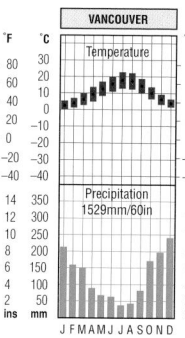
VANCOUVER
°C
°F
Temperature
Precipitation
1529mm/60in
mm
ins
J F M A M J J A S O N D

CITY PLANS

21 Amsterdam
22 Athens
23 Bangkok
24 Barcelona
25 Berlin
26 Brussels
27 Cape Town
28 Chicago
29 Dublin
30 Hong Kong
31 London
32 Madrid
33 Mexico City
34 Moscow
35 Mumbai
36 New York
37 Paris
38 Prague
39 Rio de Janeiro
40 Rome
41 San Francisco
42 Singapore
43 Sydney
44 Tokyo
45 Toronto
46 Vienna

LEGEND TO CITY PLANS

	Motorway		Abbey/cathedral
	Through route		Church of interest
	Secondary road		Hospital
	Other road		Mosque
	Limited access / pedestrian road		Shrine
	Railroad		Synagogue
	Tramway/monorail		Temple
	Elevated rail lines		Tourist information center
	Rail/bus station		Public building
S U M S	Underground/Metro station	*Museum*	Place of interest

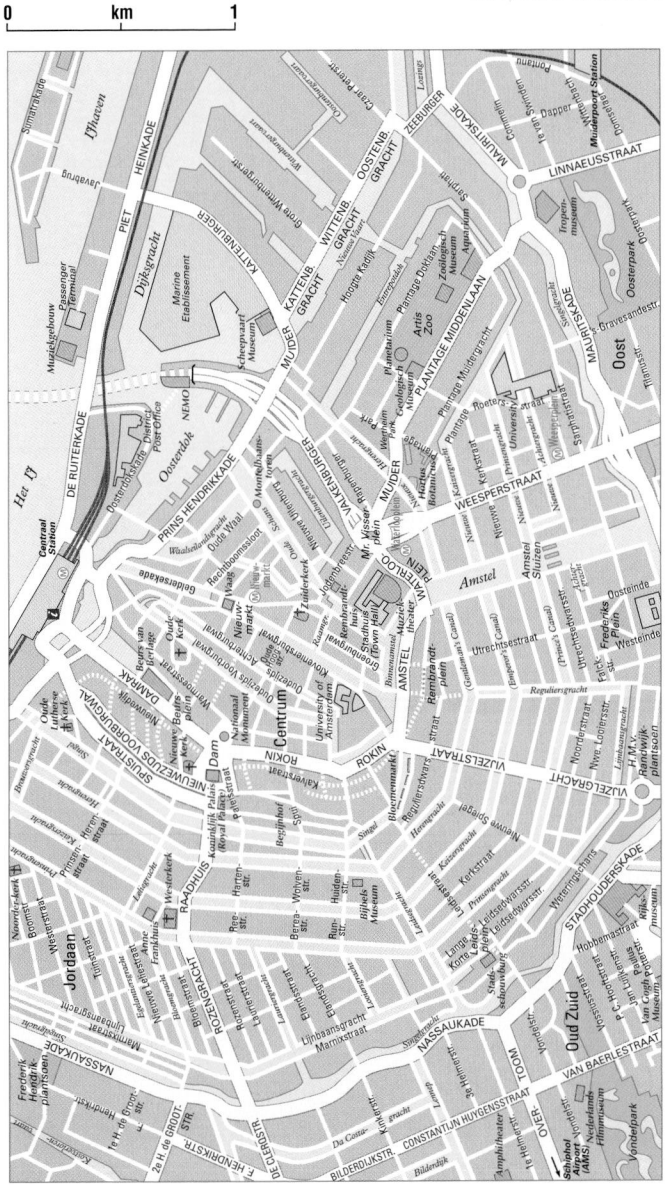
0
km
1
IJhaven
Muziekgebouw
Passenger Terminal
Marine Etablissement
Schepenhaven Museum
Het IJ
Central Station
DE RUITERKADE
PIET HEINKADE
KATTENBURGER
Oosterdok
NEMO
District Post Office
Oosterdokskade
PRINS HENDRIKKADE
Waterlooplein
Muziek theater
Rembrandt plein
Amstel
Amstel Sluizen
Frederiks plein

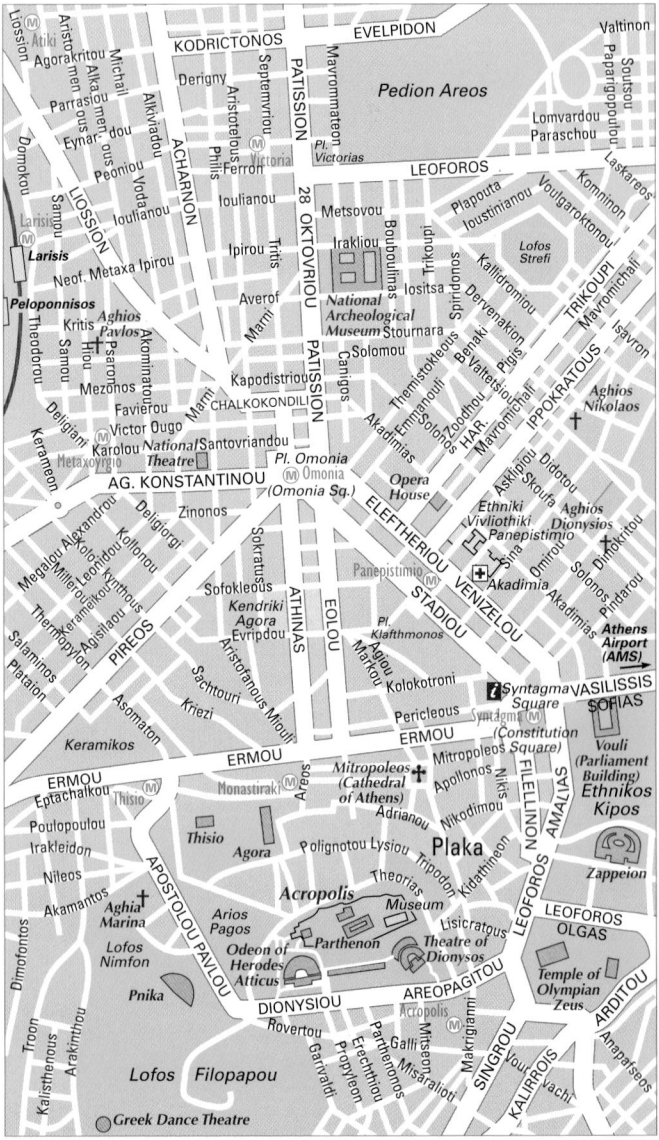

COPYRIGHT PHILIP'S

0 km 2

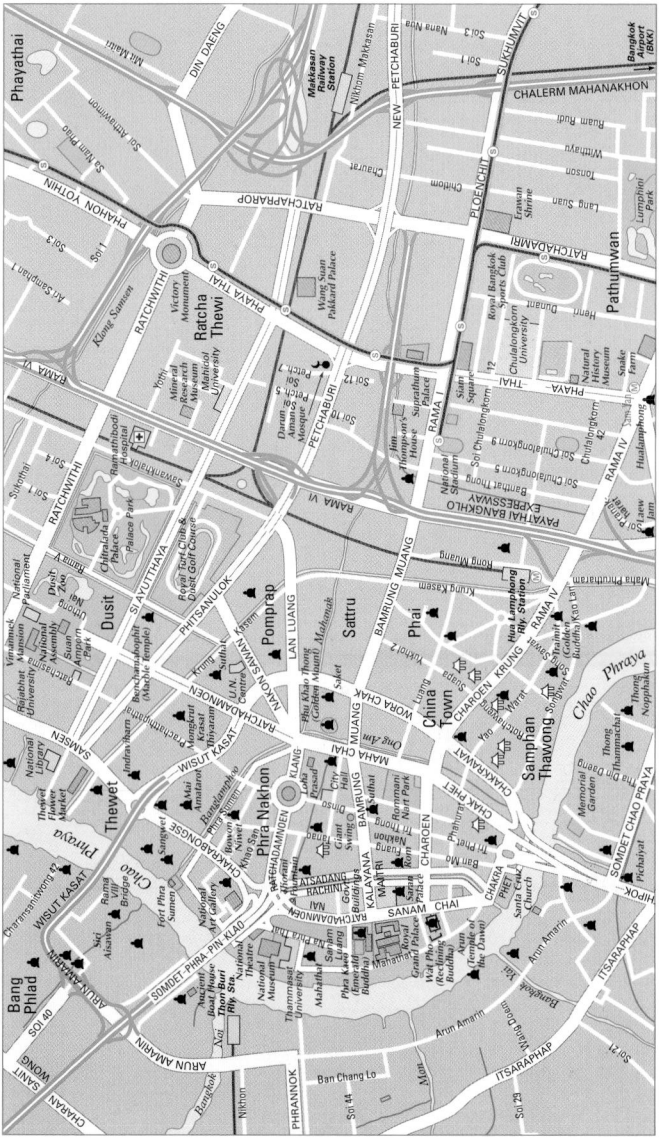
Phayathai
Ratcha Thewi
Pathumwan
Dusit
Pomprap
Sattru Phai
China Town
Samphan Thawong
Thewet
Phra Nakhon
Bang Phlad
Bangkok Airport (BKK)
Lumphini Park
Chao Phraya
Klong Ong Ang
Klong Mahanak
Klong Bangkok Noi
Klong Bangkok Yai
Klong Phadung Krung Kasem
Klong Ong Ang
Klong Bang Luang
Klong Bang Sue

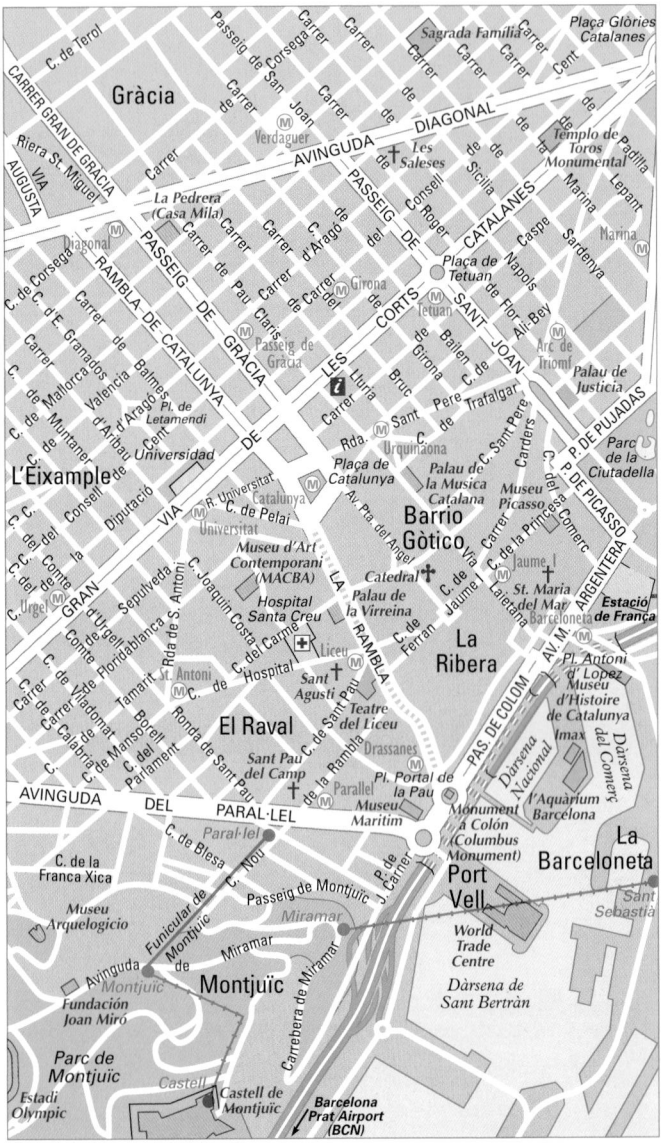

COPYRIGHT PHILIP'S

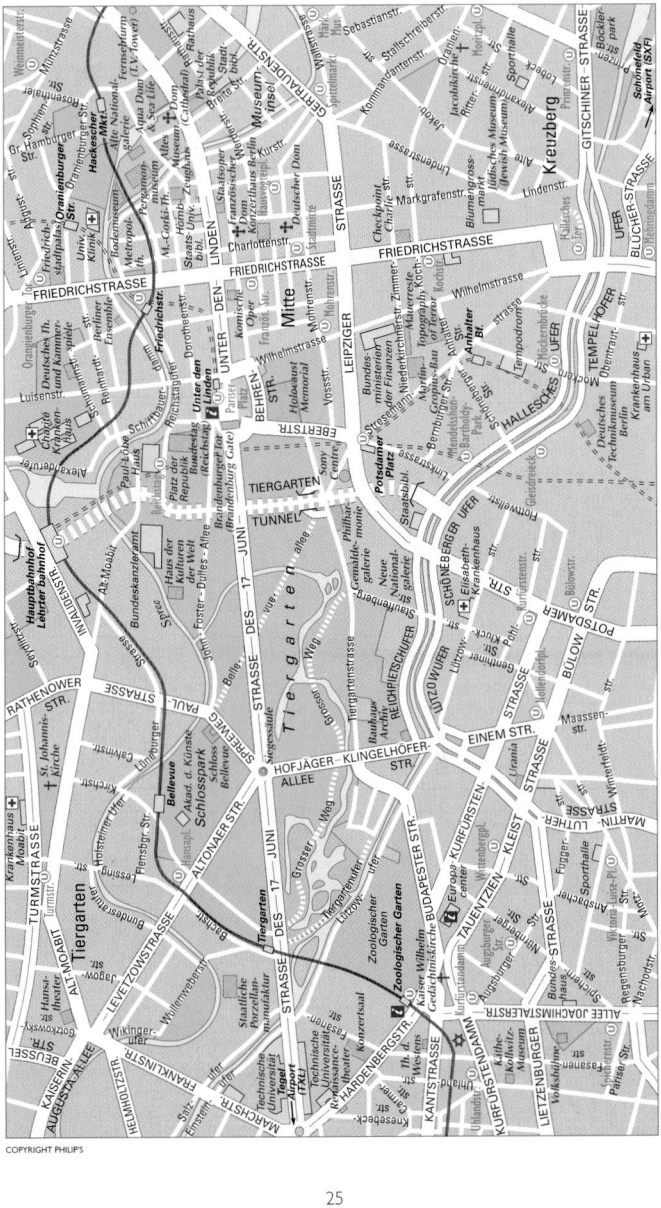
0 km 1
Tiergarten
Mitte
Kreuzberg
Schloss Bellevue
Bundeskanzleramt
Reichstag
Brandenburger Tor
Potsdamer Platz
Philharmonie
Neue Nationalgalerie
Zoologischer Garten
Kaiser Wilhelm Gedächtniskirche
Europa-Center
Hauptbahnhof
Lehrter bahnhof
Airport (TXL)
Airport (SXF)
Friedrichstr.
Unter den Linden
Potsdamer Platz
Leipziger Str.
Tiergarten
Bellevue
Zoologischer Garten
Friedrichstr.

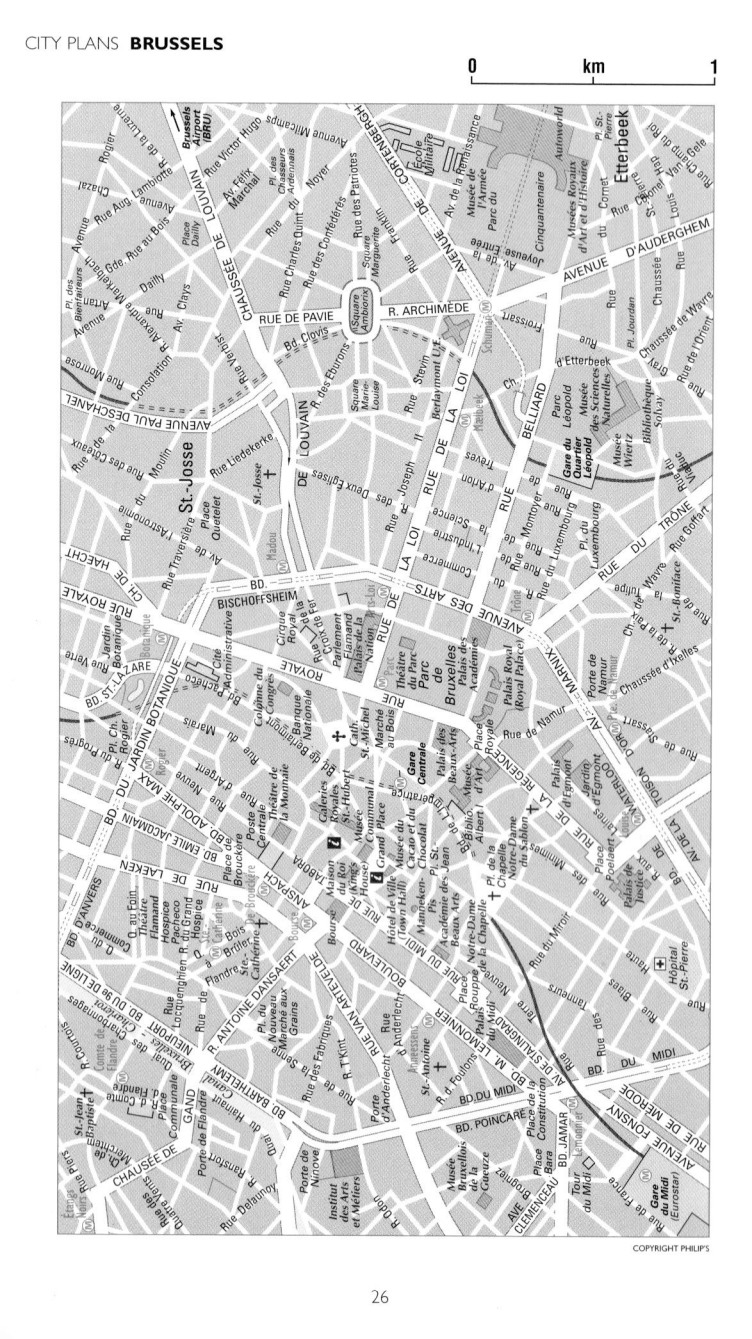
0
km
1
Brussels Airport (BRU)
Av. Victor Hugo
Av. Felix Marchal
Pl. des Chasseurs Ardennais
Av. de la Renaissance
Musée de l'Armée Parc du Cinquantenaire
Autoworld
Musées Royaux d'Art et d'Histoire
Pl. St. Pierre
Etterbeek
Rue du Comet
Rue Chemin de fer
Rue Gelé
Av. de la Joyeuse Entrée
Ecole Militaire
AVENUE D'AUDERGHEM
AVENUE DE CORTENBERGH
Rue des Patriotes
Rue des Confédérés
Rue Charles Quint
Rue du Noyer
Square Marguerite
Square Ambiorix
R. ARCHIMÈDE
RUE DE PAVIE
Bd. Clovis
R. des Eburons
Square Marie-Louise
Rue Stevin
Berlaymont U.E.
Rue de la Loi
Rue Joseph II
Rue d'Arlon
Rue Trèves
Rue Belliard
Parc Léopold
Musée des Sciences Naturelles
Gare du Quartier Leopold
Musée Wiertz
Bibliothèque Solvay
Chaussée de Wavre
Rue de l'Orient
Pl. Jourdan
Rue Froissart
Rue d'Etterbeek
Rue Montoyer
Rue du Luxembourg
Pl. du Luxembourg
Rue Gossart
RUE DU TRÔNE
Rue de la Loi
Rue de la Science
Rue de l'Industrie
Rue de la Loi
Rue de la Loi
Rue de la Loi

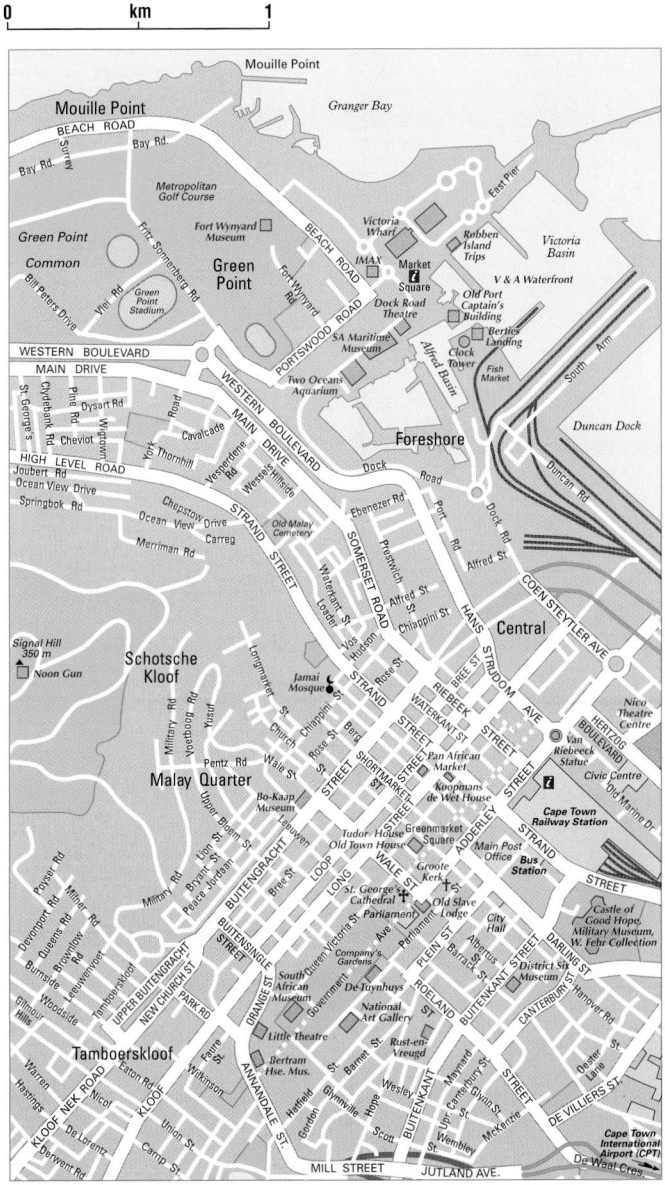

COPYRIGHT PHILIP'S

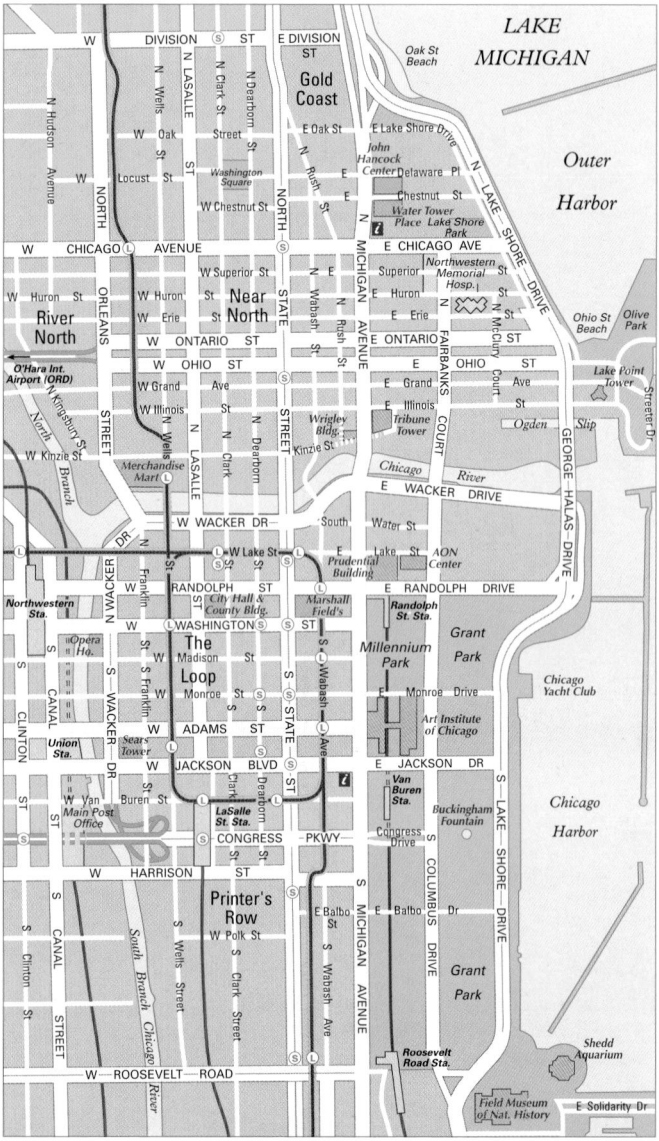

Elevated rail lines

COPYRIGHT PHILIP'S

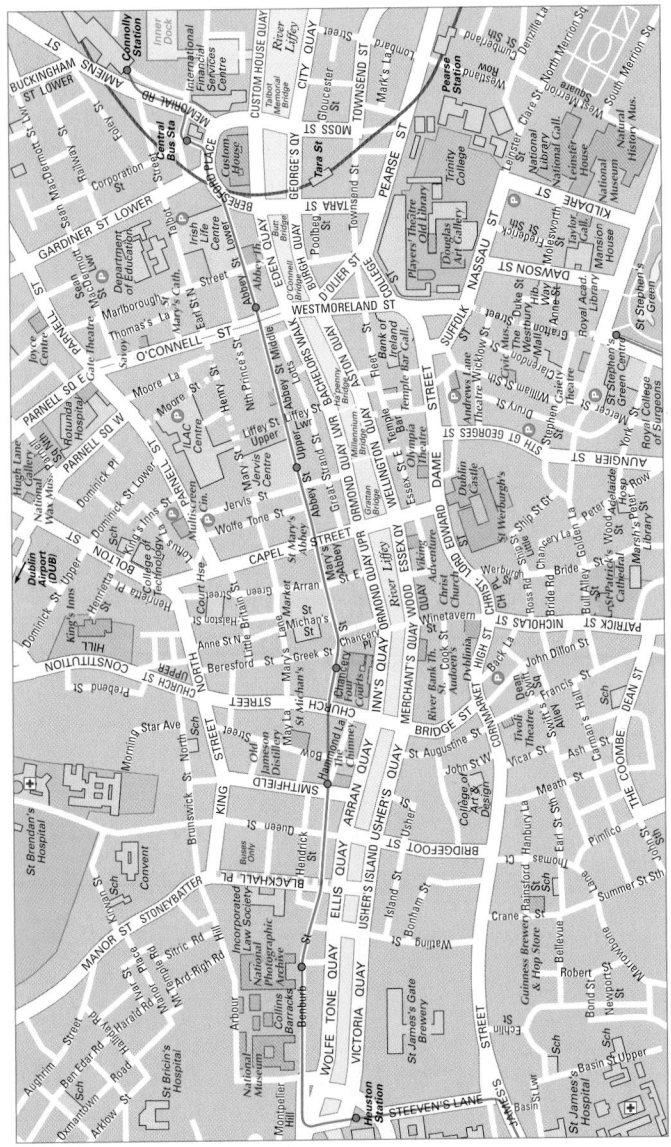
0
km
0.5
Connolly Station
Inner Dock
International Financial Services Centre
Custom House
River Liffey
Talbot Memorial Bridge
Pearse Station
Tara St
Central Bus Sta
Custom House Quay
Westland Row
Merrion Sq
Clare St
Merrion Sq
Leinster House
National Museum
National Library
National Gall.
Trinity College
Old Library
Dublin Bus
Pearse St
Townsend St
Lombard St
Mark's La
Moss St
Townsend St
Tara St
Pearse St
Pearse Station
Buckingham St Lower
Amiens St
Corporation
Foley St
Railway
Gardiner St Lower
Beresford Place
Eden Quay
Abbey St Middle
Abbey St Lower
Burgh Quay
Butt Bridge
Eden Quay
Aston Quay
Westmoreland St
Dublin Bus
Dublin Bus
Dublin Bus

The width of Victoria Harbour has been compressed so that the land area is better represented.

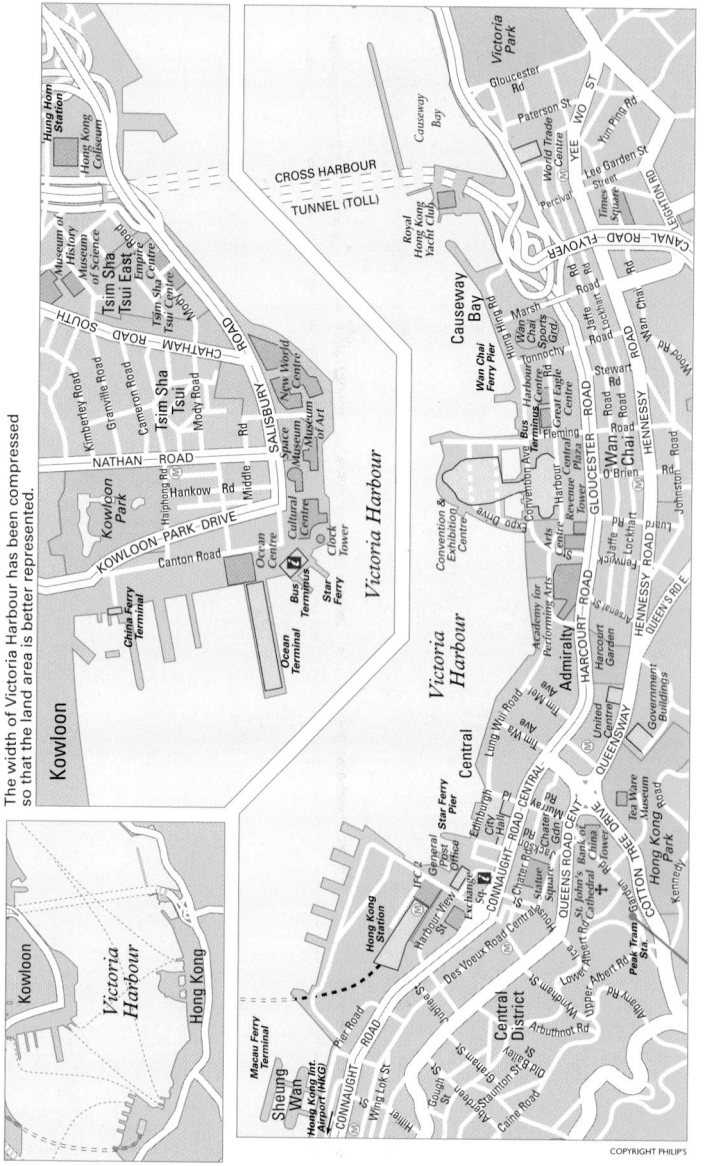

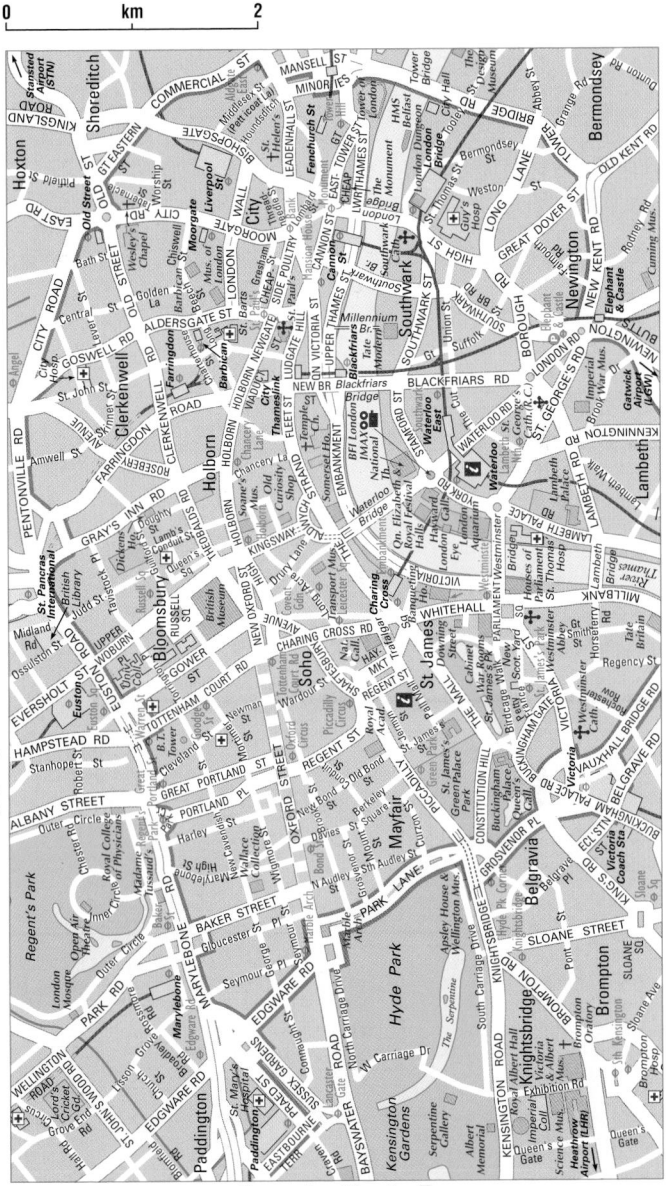
0
km
2
Hoxton
Shoreditch
Bermondsey
Clerkenwell
Holborn
City
Southwark
Newington
Bloomsbury
Soho
St James
Lambeth
Regent's Park
Mayfair
Belgravia
Hyde Park
Knightsbridge
Brompton
Paddington
Kensington Gardens
Stanstead Airport (MSA)
Gatwick Airport (GW)
Heathrow Airport (HR)
Tower Bridge
Millennium Bridge
Waterloo Bridge
Blackfriars Bridge
Westminster Bridge
Lambeth Bridge
Vauxhall Bridge
Victoria Coach Sta.
Victoria
Euston
Liverpool St
Fenchurch St
Cannon St
Blackfriars
Waterloo East
Waterloo
Charing Cross
Marylebone
Paddington
Victoria
Knightsbridge
Kensington Gardens
Hyde Park
Regent's Park
Tate Modern
Tate Britain
Tate Britain
Tate Britain

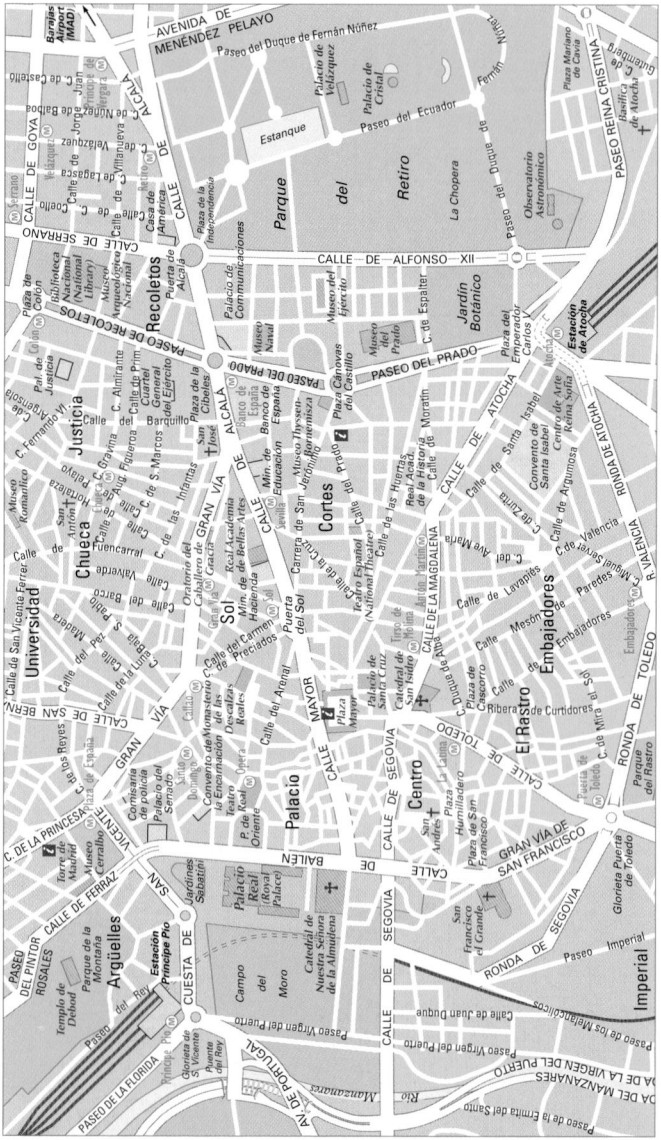
0
km
1
Barajas Airport (MAD)
AVENIDA DE MENÉNDEZ PELAYO
Paseo del Duque de Fernán Núñez
Estanque
Parque del Retiro
Palacio de Velázquez
Palacio de Cristal
Paseo del Ecuador
La Chopera
Observatorio Astronómico
Plaza Mariano de Cavia
Basílica de Atocha
PASEO REINA CRISTINA
CALLE DE ALFONSO XII
Palacio de Comunicaciones
Museo del Ejército
Jardín Botánico
Plaza del Emperador Carlos V
Estación de Atocha
PASEO DEL PRADO
Museo del Prado
Museo Naval
Plaza Canovas del Castillo
Banco de España
Mín. de Educación y Ciencia
Real Academia de Bellas Artes
Real Acad. de la Historia
Convento de Santa Isabel
Centro de Arte Reina Sofía
RONDA DE ATOCHA
CALLE DE ATOCHA
Recoletos
Biblioteca Nacional (National Library)
Museo Arqueológico Nacional
Plaza de Colón
Pal. de Justicia
Justicia
Chueca
Universidad
Sol
Cortes
Palacio
Centro
Embajadores
El Rastro
Argüelles
Imperial
Campo del Moro
Palacio Real (Royal Palace)
Catedral de Nuestra Señora de la Almudena
Jardines Sabatini
Estación Príncipe Pío
Templo de Debod
Parque de la Montaña
Torre de Madrid
Museo Cerralbo
Comisaría de policía
Palacio del Senado
Convento de Monjas de la Encarnación
Teatro Español (National Theatre)
Teatro Real
Palacio de Santa Cruz
Catedral de San Isidro
Plaza Mayor
Puerta del Sol
Plaza de Cascorro
Plaza de San Francisco
Iglesia de San Francisco el Grande
Glorieta Puerta de Toledo
Parque del Rastro
Glorieta de San Vicente del Ferrer
Glorieta de San Vicente
Glorieta de Carlos V
Glorieta de Carlos V

0 km 1

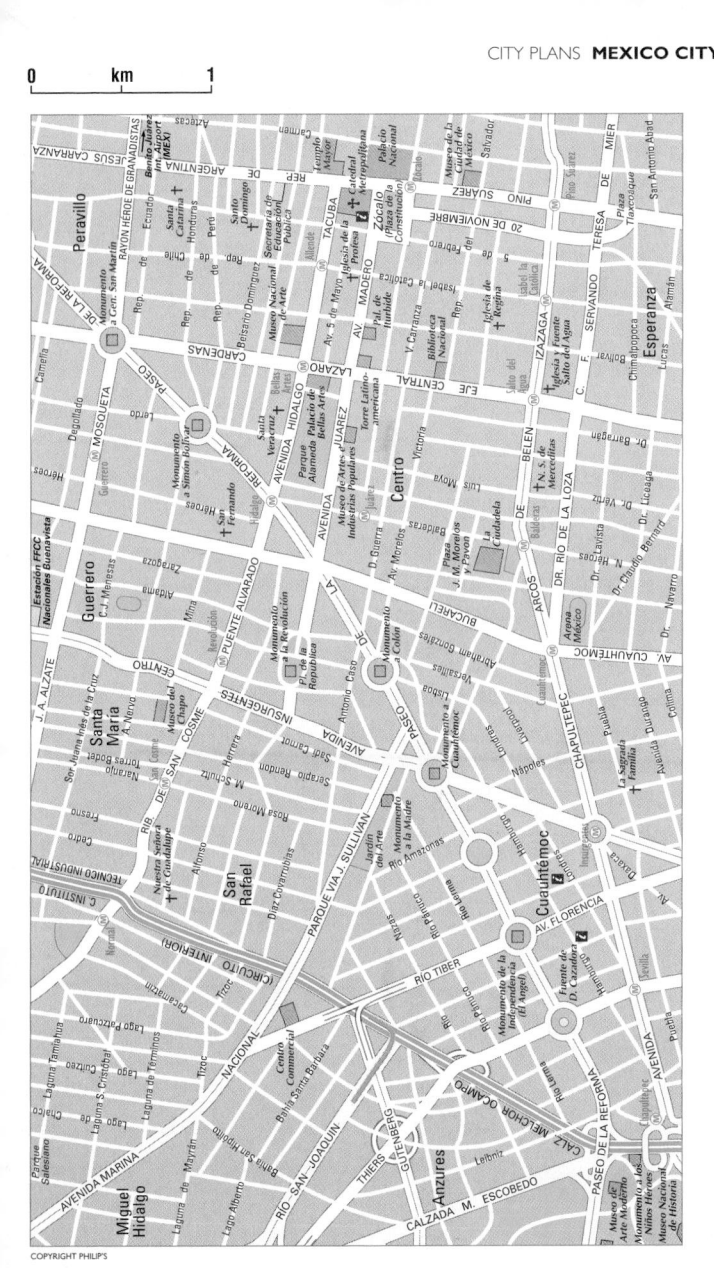
Peravillo
Guerrero
Santa María
San Rafael
Centro
Cuauhtémoc
Anzures
Miguel Hidalgo
Esperanza
Estación FFCC Nacionales Buenavista
Monumento a Cuauhtémoc
Monumento a la Revolución
Monumento a Colón
Monumento a la Independencia (El Ángel)
Monumento a Simón Bolívar
Monumento a Cuauhtémoc
Monumento a los Niños Héroes
Museo Nacional de Historia
Museo de Arte Moderno
Museo de Arte Indígena Popular
Museo Nacional de Arte
Museo de la Ciudad de México
Palacio Nacional
Catedral Metropolitana
Zócalo (Plaza de la Constitución)
Iglesia de Regina
Iglesia y Fuente Salto del Agua
Iglesia de San Fernando
Iglesia de Santa Veracruz
Iglesia de Santo Domingo
Templo Mayor
Torre Latinoamericana
Parque Alameda
Palacio de Bellas Artes
Bellas Artes
Secretaría de Hacienda y Crédito Público
Secretaría de Educación Pública
Biblioteca Nacional
Jardín Luis Arte
Jardín Morelos
Jardín Santa Veracruz
Jardín Santa María
Jardín Santa Catarina
Jardín Santa Ana
Jardín Santa Bárbara
Jardín Santa Cruz
Jardín Santa Fe
Jardín Santa Rosa
Jardín Santa Teresa
Jardín Santa Zita
Jardín Santa Zyta
Jardín Santa Zyta
Jardín Santa Zyta

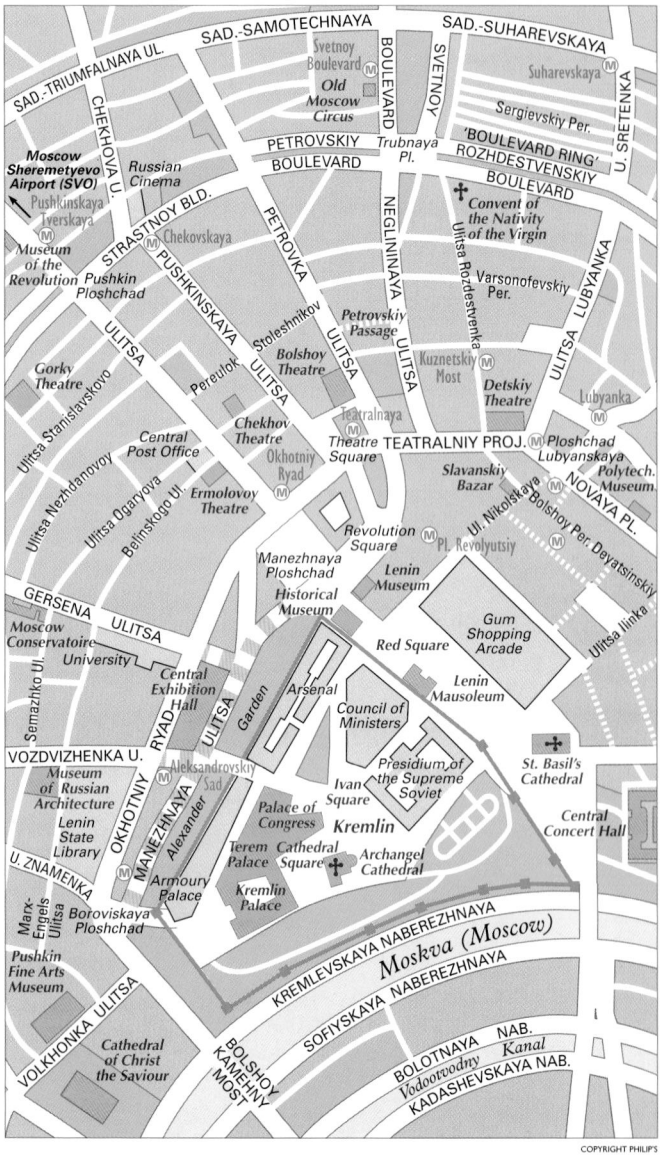

COPYRIGHT PHILIP'S

0 km 2

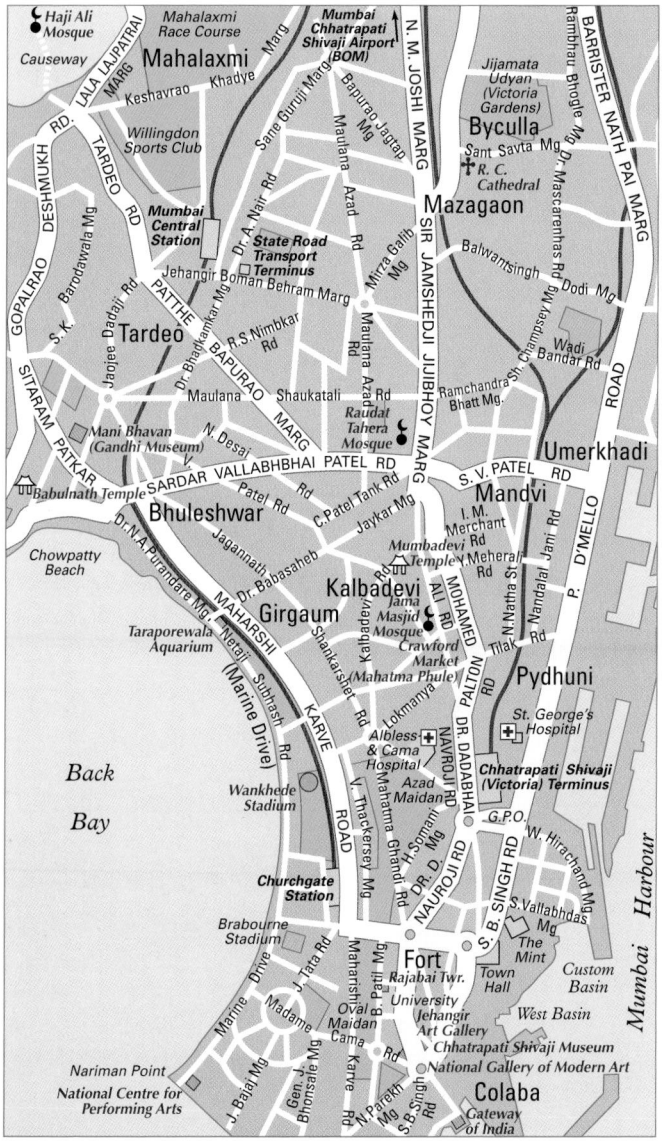

COPYRIGHT PHILIP'S

0 km 2

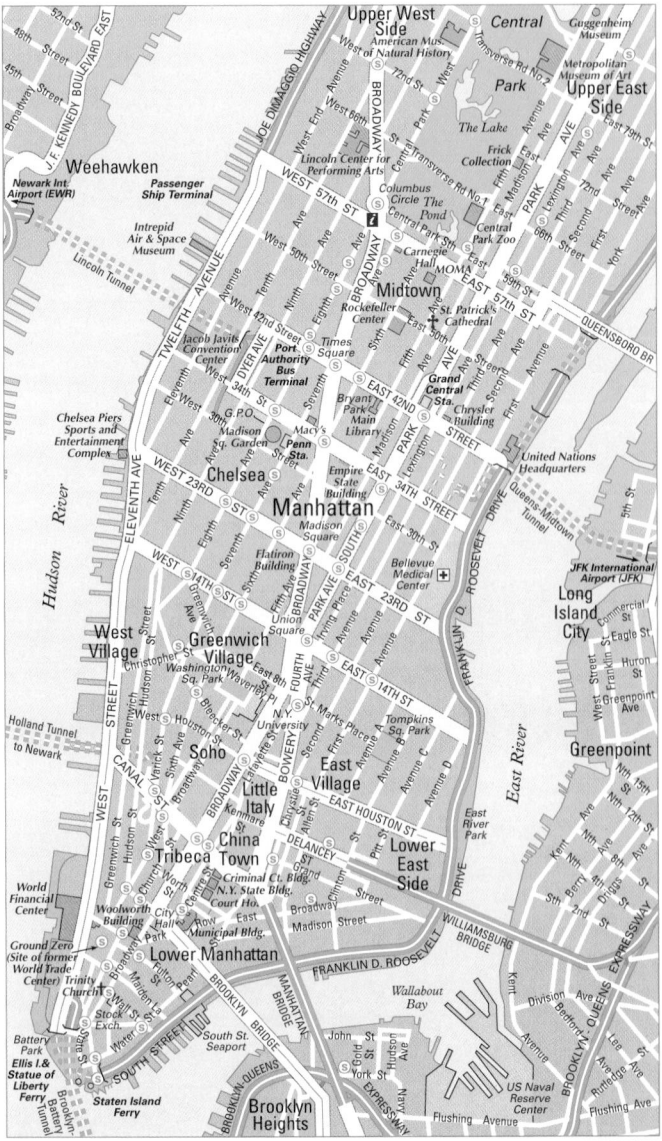
Upper West Side
Central Park
Upper East Side
Weehawken
Midtown
Chelsea
Manhattan
West Village
Greenwich Village
Soho
East Village
Little Italy
China Town
Tribeca
Lower East Side
Lower Manhattan
Brooklyn Heights
Long Island City
Greenpoint
Hudson River
East River
Newark Int. Airport (EWR)
Passenger Ship Terminal
Intrepid Air & Space Museum
Lincoln Tunnel
Holland Tunnel to Newark
Chelsea Piers Sports and Entertainment Complex
Port Authority Bus Terminal
Penn Sta.
Grand Central Sta.
Empire State Building
Madison Square
Flatiron Building
Union Square
Bellevue Medical Center
United Nations Headquarters
JFK International Airport (JFK)
Lincoln Center for Performing Arts
Columbus Circle
The Pond
Central Park Zoo
Carnegie Hall
MOMA
Rockefeller Center
St. Patrick's Cathedral
Times Square
Bryant Park
Main Library
Chrysler Building
Madison Sq. Garden
Macy's
Jacob Javits Convention Center
American Mus. of Natural History
Guggenheim Museum
Metropolitan Museum of Art
The Lake
Frick Collection
Tompkins Sq. Park
N.Y. University
Criminal Ct. Bldg.
N.Y. State Bldg.
Court Hse.
City Hall
Municipal Bldg.
Woolworth Building
World Financial Center
Ground Zero (Site of former World Trade Center)
Trinity Church
Battery Park
Ellis I. & Statue of Liberty Ferry
Staten Island Ferry
Stock Exch.
South St. Seaport
Wallabout Bay
US Naval Reserve Center
East River Park
Broadway
Fifth Ave
Madison Ave
Park Ave
Lexington Ave
Third Ave
Second Ave
First Ave
Avenue A
Avenue B
Avenue C
Avenue D
West End Ave
Central Park West
Columbus Ave
Eighth Ave
Ninth Ave
Tenth Ave
Eleventh Ave
Twelfth Ave
West Side Hwy
Hudson St
Greenwich St
Canal St
Varick St
Lafayette St
Bowery
Broadway
Bleecker St
Houston St
East Houston St
Delancey St
Grand St
Canal St
Fulton St
Wall St
Liberty St
Water St
Pearl St
Broad St
Battery Place
Greenwich St
Washington St
Christopher St
Bleecker St
Waverly Pl
Washington Sq. Park
Fourth Ave
Park Ave South
Irving Place
Lexington Ave
Madison Ave
Fifth Ave
Sixth Ave
Seventh Ave
Eighth Ave
Ninth Ave
Tenth Ave
Eleventh Ave
West 23rd St
West 14th St
East 14th St
East 23rd St
East 30th St
West 34th St
West 42nd St
West 50th St
West 57th St
East 57th St
West 72nd St
Central Park South
Central Park North
Transverse Rd No. 1
Transverse Rd No. 2
Transverse Rd No. 3
Transverse Rd No. 4
Lexington Ave
Third Ave
Second Ave
First Ave
York Ave
East River Drive
Franklin D. Roosevelt Drive
Queensboro Br.
Queens-Midtown Tunnel
Williamsburg Bridge
Brooklyn Bridge
Manhattan Bridge
Brooklyn-Queens Expressway
Flushing Ave
Kent Ave
Bedford Ave
Lee Ave
Rutledge Ave
Division Ave
Grand St
Gold St
John St
Hudson Ave
Navy St
Clinton St
Fulton St
Fulton St
Flushing Ave
Lafayette Ave
Clinton Ave
Bedford Ave
Brooklyn Ave
Fulton St
Liberty Ave
Grand Central Pkwy
Long Island Expy
Roosevelt Ave

0 km 1

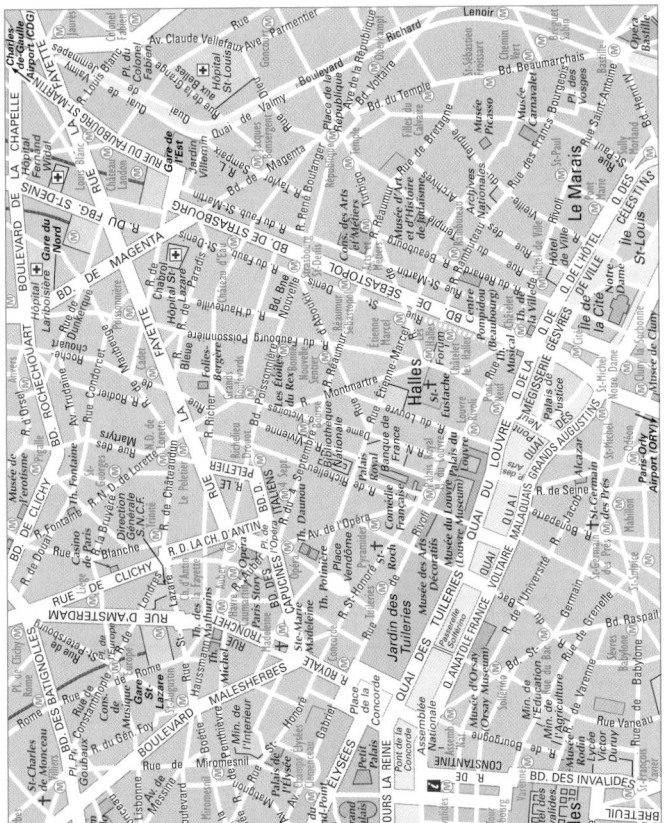
Monceau
Champ de Mars
Invalides
Le Marais
Halles
Jardin des Tuileries
Place de la Concorde
Place de la Bastille
Place de la République
Place de l'Etoile
Place de Clichy
Place de Rome
Place de Magenta
Place de Vienne
Place Fernand Wybot
Place Fernand Widal
Place Fernand Léger

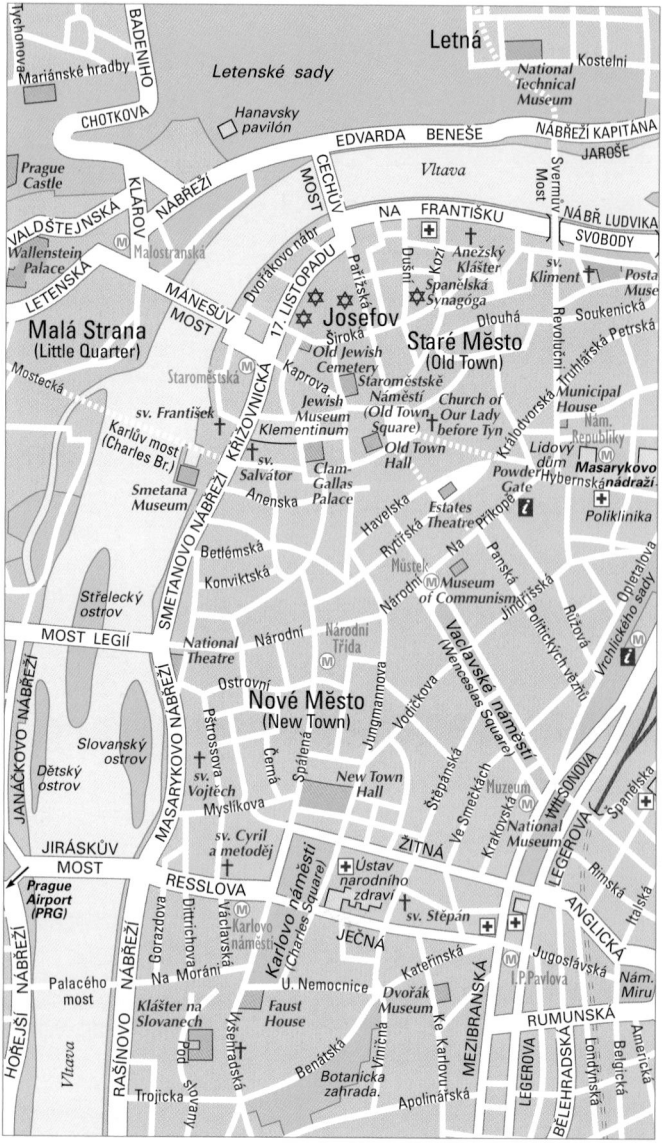

COPYRIGHT PHILIPS

0 km 0.5

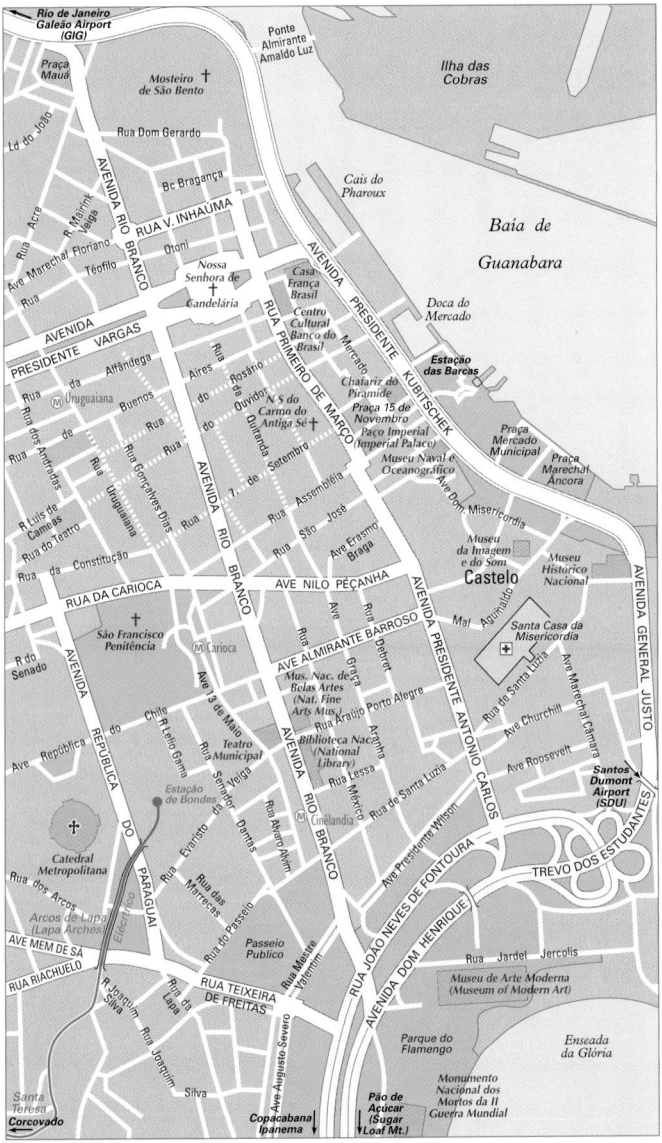

COPYRIGHT PHILIP'S

0 km 1

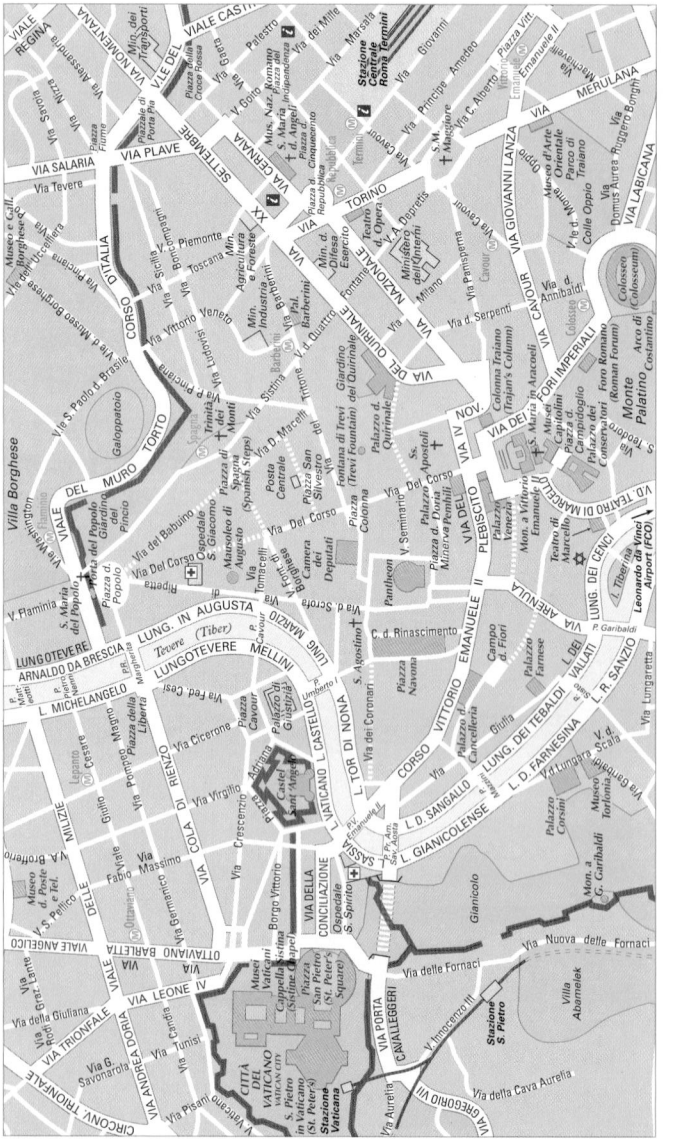
VIALE REGINA
Min. dei Trasporti
Piazzale di Porta Pia
Piazza della Croce Rossa
Palestro
Via Goito
Via Nizza
Via Savoia
Piazza Fiume
Via Palermo
Via Sicilia
Via Piemonte
Via Toscana
Via Lucania
Via Vittorio Veneto
Via Sistina
Via Boncompagni
Via Piemonte
Via Tevere
Via Flaminia
Via Pinciana
Via d. Museo Borghese
Museo e Gall. Borghese
Villa Borghese
Via S. Paolo d. Brasile
Galoppatoio
VIALE DEL MURO TORTO
Via Gianicolo
Via Aurelia
Via Del Babuino
Via Del Corso
Ospedale S. Giacomo
Piazza d. Popolo
Piazza del Popolo
Porta del Popolo
Giardino del Pincio
Mausoleo di Augusto
Piazza di Spagna (Spanish Steps)
Trinità dei Monti
Via D. Manelli
Via Tomacelli
Via Ripetta
Via Ripetta
Via Flaminia
Via Del Corso
Via Del Corso
Via Cavour
Via Cicerone
Via Fed. Cesi
Via Pompeo Magno
Via Virgilio
Via Crescenzio
Via Cola di Rienzo
Via Germanico
Via Fabio
Via Giulio
Via Massimo
Via Ottaviano
Via Cola di Rienzo
Via Cola di Rienzo
Via Tunisi
Via Pisani
Via Tunisi
Via Pisani
Via Savoiardi
Via Cola di Rienzo
Via Ottaviano
Via Germanico
Via Fabio
Via Giulio
Via Cola di Rienzo
Via Cola di Rienzo
Via Cola di Rienzo
Via Crescenzio
Via Virgilio
Via Pompeo Magno
Via Fed. Cesi
Via Cicerone
Via Cola di Rienzo
Via Cola di Rienzo
Via Cola di Rienzo

0 km 0.5

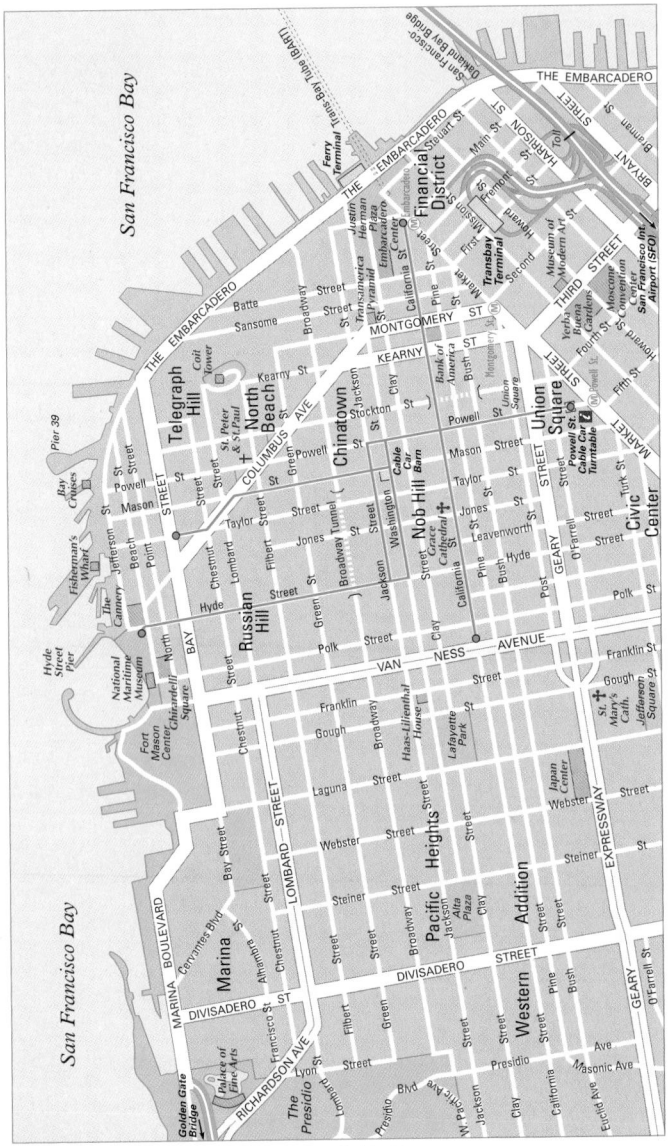
San Francisco Bay
San Francisco Bay
Pier 39
Bay Cruises
Fisherman's Wharf
The Cannery
Hyde Street Pier
National Maritime Museum
Fort Mason Center
Ghirardelli Square
Golden Gate Bridge
Palace of Fine Arts
The Presidio
Marina
Pacific Heights
Western Addition
Russian Hill
Telegraph Hill
Coit Tower
North Beach
St. Peter & St. Paul
Chinatown
Nob Hill
Cable Car Barn
Grace Cathedral
Financial District
Transbay Terminal
Transamerica Pyramid
Embarcadero Center
Ferry Terminal
Bank of America
Union Square
Union Square
Powell St. Cable Car Turntable
Civic Center
Haas-Lilienthal House
Lafayette Park
Alta Plaza
Japan Center
St. Mary's Cath.
Jefferson Square Sq
Museum of Modern Art
Yerba Buena Gardens
Moscone Convention Center
San Francisco Int. Airport (SFO)
Trans Bay Tube (BART)
San Francisco-Oakland Bay Bridge
THE EMBARCADERO
MONTGOMERY ST
KEARNY
COLUMBUS AVE
MARKET STREET
VAN NESS AVENUE
GEARY
EXPRESSWAY
DIVISADERO STREET
LOMBARD STREET
MARINA BOULEVARD
RICHARDSON AVE
BRYANT
HARRISON
HOWARD
MISSION
THIRD STREET
FIRST
FREMONT
MAIN
SANSOME
BATTERY
STEUART
MASON
TAYLOR
JONES
LEAVENWORTH
HYDE
POLK
FRANKLIN
GOUGH
WEBSTER
STEINER
LAGUNA
GOLDEN GATE
FRANKLIN
FIFTH
FOURTH
TURK
EUCLID
MASONIC
PRESIDIO
LYON
PRESIDIO BLVD
CAYWINES BLVD
BAY STREET
CHESTNUT
LOMBARD
GREEN
FILBERT
JACKSON
PACIFIC
CLAY
CALIFORNIA
PINE
BUSH
POST
O'FARRELL
JEFFERSON
BEACH
POINT
MASON
TAYLOR
JONES
HYDE
LEAVENWORTH
POLK
VAN NESS
FRANKLIN
GOUGH
WEBSTER
STEINER
LAGUNA
GOLDEN GATE

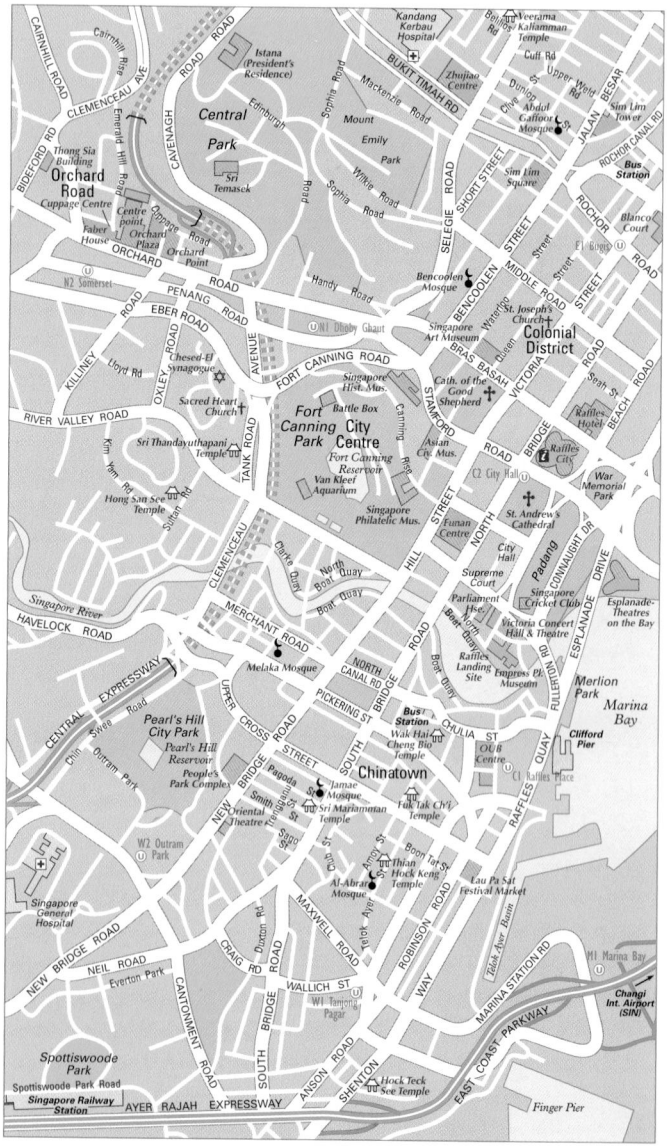

COPYRIGHT PHILIP'S

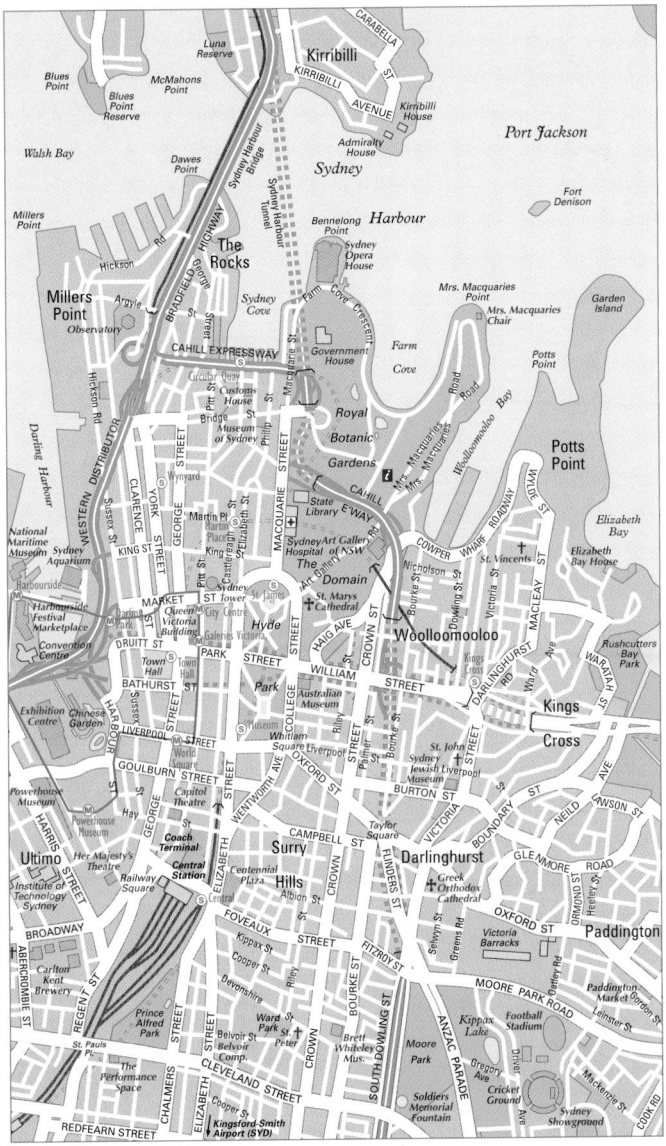

COPYRIGHT PHILIP'S

Monorail

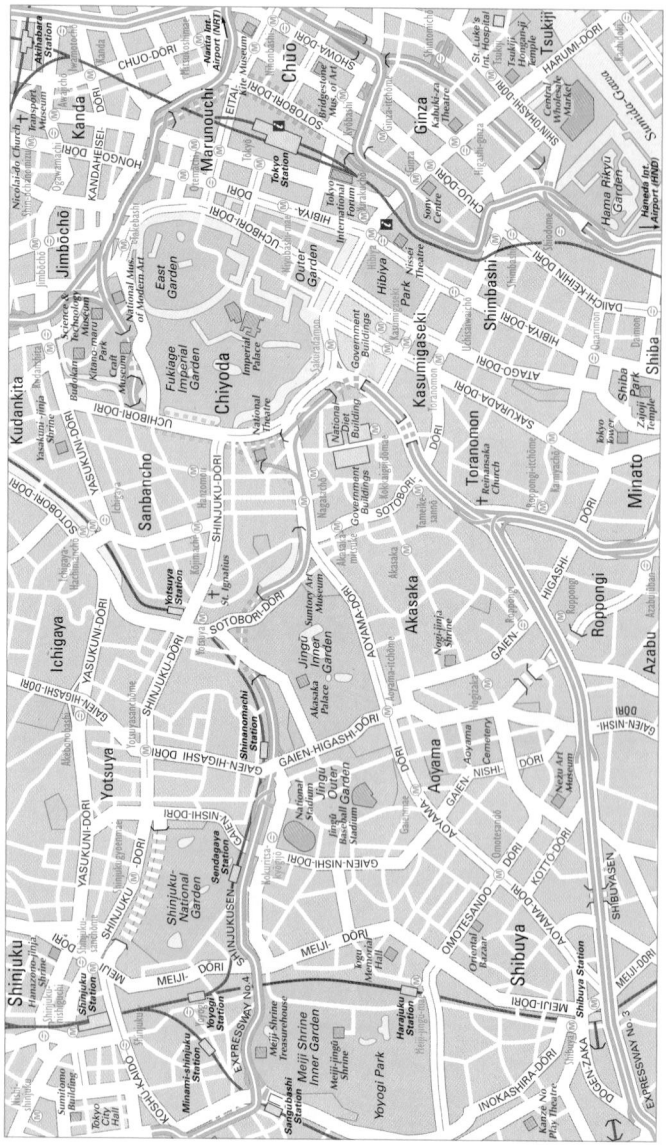
0
km
2
Shinjuku
Shinjuku Station
Hanazono Jinja Shrine
Tokyo City Hall
Sumitomo Building
Shinjuku National Garden
Sendagaya Station
Meiji-Shrine Treasure House
Meiji Shrine Inner Garden
Meiji-jingū Shrine
Yoyogi Station
Yoyogi Park
Harajuku Station
Shibuya
Shibuya Station
Oriental Bazaar
Kanze No Nō Theatre
Aoyama
Aoyama Cemetery
Nezu Art Museum
Jingū Outer Garden
Jingū Baseball Stadium
Jingū Inner Garden
Akasaka Palace
Akasaka
Suntory Art Museum
Nogi-jinja Shrine
Roppongi
Azabu
Yotsuya
Yotsuya Station
Shinanomachi Station
St. Ignatius
Ichigaya
Sanbancho
Kudankita
Kitano-mura Park Craft Museum
Yasukuni-jinja Shrine
Chiyoda
Fukiage Imperial Garden
Imperial Palace
National Theatre
National Diet Building
Government Buildings
Kasumigaseki
Toranomon
Benkyosaka Church
Minato
Zōjō-ji Temple
Tokyo Tower
Shiba
Shiba Park
Shimbashi
Nissay Theatre
Hibiya
Hibiya Park
Ginza
Kabuki-za Theatre
Sony Center
Tsukiji
Tsukiji Hongan-ji Temple
St. Luke's Int. Hospital
Hama Rikyū Garden
Tokyo Int. Forum
Tokyo Station
Marunouchi
Chūō
Bridgestone Mus. of Art
Kanda
Jimbocho
Nicolai-do Church
Akihabara Station
Kanda Station
Ochanomizu Station
Ochanomizu
Yasukuni Shrine
Kudan-shita
Jimbocho Station
Kanda Station
Tokyo Station
Yurakucho Station
Yurakucho
Hibiya Station
Kasumigaseki Station
Kamiyacho Station
Kamiyacho
Roppongi Station
Tokyo Station
Tokyo
Tokyo National Museum
National Museum of Modern Art
Kitanomaru Park
Kitanomaru Park Craft Museum
Yasukuni-jinja Shrine
Kudan-shita
Jimbocho Station
Kanda Station
Ochanomizu Station
Ochanomizu
Akihabara Station
Akihabara
Nicolai-do Church

0 km 1

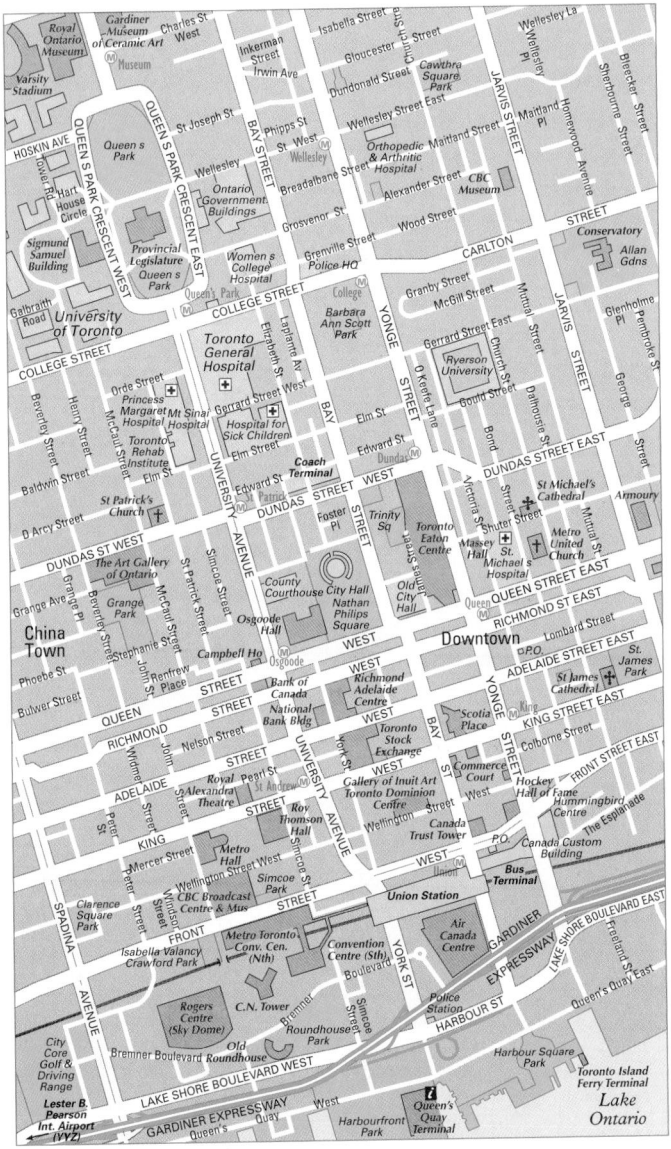

COPYRIGHT PHILIP'S

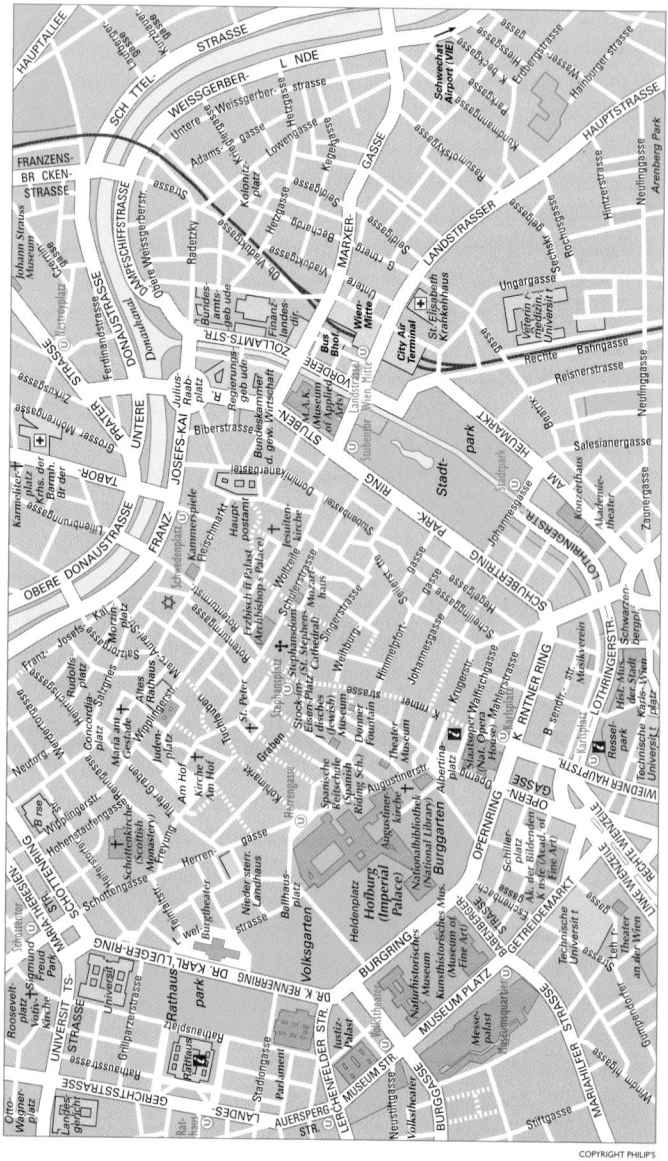

COPYRIGHT PHILIPS

GAZETTEER OF NATIONS

48 Afghanistan
Albania
Algeria
American Samoa
Andorra
Angola

49 Anguilla
Antigua & Barbuda
Argentina
Armenia
Aruba
Australia

50 Austria
Azerbaijan
Azores
Bahamas
Bahrain
Bangladesh

51 Barbados
Belarus
Belgium
Belize
Benin
Bermuda

52 Bolivia
Bosnia-Herzegovina
Botswana
Brazil
Bulgaria
Burma

53 Cambodia
Canada
Canary Is.
Cape Verde
Cayman Is.
Chad

54 Chile
China
Colombia
Comoros
Costa Rica
Croatia

55 Cuba
Cyprus
Czech Rep.
Denmark
Dominica
Dominican Rep.

56 Ecuador
Egypt
El Salvador
Estonia
Ethiopia
Fiji Is.

57 Finland
France
French Polynesia
Gambia, The
Georgia
Germany

58 Gibraltar
Greece
Grenada
Guadeloupe
Hong Kong
Hungary

59 Iceland
India
Indonesia
Iran
Ireland
Israel

60 Italy
Jamaica
Japan
Jordan
Kenya
Korea, South

61 Kuwait
Latvia
Lebanon
Libya
Liechtenstein
Lithuania

62 Luxembourg
Madagascar
Malawi
Malaysia
Maldives
Malta

63 Martinique
Mauritius
Mexico
Mongolia
Montenegro
Morocco

64 Namibia
Nepal
Netherlands
Neth. Antilles
New Zealand
Nigeria

65 Norway
Oman
Pakistan
Paraguay
Peru
Philippines

66 Poland
Portugal
Puerto Rico
Qatar
Réunion
Romania

67 Russia
St Kitts & Nevis
St Lucia
St Vincent
Samoa
Saudi Arabia

68 Serbia
Seychelles
Singapore
Slovak Rep.
Slovenia
South Africa

69 Spain
Sri Lanka
Sweden
Switzerland
Syria
Taiwan

70 Tanzania
Thailand
Trinidad & T.
Tunisia
Turkey
Uganda

71 Ukraine
UAE
UK
USA
Uruguay
Venezuela

72 Vietnam
Virgin Is., British
Virgin Is., US
Yemen
Zambia
Zimbabwe

AFGHANISTAN

GOVERNMENT Transitional
LANGUAGES Pashtu, Dari/Persian, Uzbek
CURRENCY Afghani = 100 puls
MEDICAL Visitors should protect against yellow fever, polio, typhoid and malaria
TRAVEL Most governments currently advise against all travel to Afghanistan. The security situation remains serious, with danger away from main roads from mines and unexploded ordnance
WEATHER Jun to Aug very hot; Dec to Mar very cold; Jun to Sep scanty rainfall; mild at other times
BANKING 0800–1200 and 1300–1630 Sat to Wed; 0830–1330 Thu. However, at the time of writing, many banks are closed
EMERGENCY Unavailable
TIME ZONE GMT +4.30
INTERNATIONAL DIALING CODE Unavailable

ALBANIA

GOVERNMENT Multiparty republic
LANGUAGES Albanian (official)
CURRENCY Lek = 100 qindars
MEDICAL Water is untreated and not safe to drink. Medical facilities in the country are poor
TRAVEL Crime is high throughout parts of the country and visitors should remain vigilant at all times. It is advisable to dress down and avoid carrying expensive items. Street demonstrations against the government are common
WEATHER Jun to Sep warm and dry; Oct to May cool and wet
BANKING 0700–1500 Mon to Fri
EMERGENCY Police 24445; Fire 23333; Ambulance 22235
TIME ZONE GMT +1
INTERNATIONAL DIALING CODE 355

ALGERIA

GOVERNMENT Socialist republic
LANGUAGES Arabic and Berber (both official), French
CURRENCY Algerian dinar = 100 centimes
MEDICAL There is a risk of yellow fever, malaria, hepatitis A, typhoid, and polio
TRAVEL Most governments currently advise against all tourist and non-essential travel to Algeria. Travel by public transport should be avoided and only secure accommodation used
WEATHER Jun to Sep in the north is usually hot with high humidity along the coast; Oct to Feb wet and mild
BANKING 0900–1630 Sun to Thu
EMERGENCY Unavailable
TIME ZONE GMT +1
INTERNATIONAL DIALING CODE 213

AMERICAN SAMOA

GOVERNMENT US overseas territory
LANGUAGES Samoan, English
CURRENCY US dollar = 100 cents
MEDICAL Water is untreated and is unsafe to drink. Vaccination against polio and typhoid is recommended
TRAVEL Most visits to American Samoa are trouble-free and crime is low. Tourists should respect local culture and take usual precautions, especially in the towns
WEATHER Hot, tropical climate with heavy rainfall from Dec to Apr. The most comfortable time to visit is May to Sep
BANKING 0900–1500 Mon to Fri
EMERGENCY All services 911
TIME ZONE GMT –11
INTERNATIONAL DIALING CODE 1 684

ANDORRA

GOVERNMENT Parliamentary co-princedom
LANGUAGES Catalan, Spanish, French
CURRENCY Euro = 100 cents
MEDICAL There are no specific health risks
TRAVEL In Andorra, visitors will find some of the most stunning scenery and the best skiing in the Pyrenees. Shopping around, prices may often be up to 30% below those in France and Spain
WEATHER Jun to Sep warm and pleasant; Dec to Apr sunny but cold with abundant snow; rain falls throughout the year; snow often remains on the peaks of mountains until July
BANKING 0900–1300 and 1500–1700 Mon to Fri; 0900–1200 Sat
EMERGENCY Police 110; Fire/Ambulance 118
TIME ZONE GMT +1
INTERNATIONAL DIALING CODE 376

ANGOLA

GOVERNMENT Multiparty republic
LANGUAGES Portuguese (official), many others
CURRENCY Kwanza = 100 lwei
MEDICAL There is a risk of yellow fever, hepatitis A, polio, typhoid, and malaria
TRAVEL Most governments currently advise against tourist and non-essential travel to Angola due to the aftermath of civil war. Visitors should remain vigilant, particularly after dark. Crime levels are high and land mines are widely distributed and unmarked
WEATHER Warm to hot all year; Nov to Apr wet; cooler and wetter climate in the south
BANKING 0845–1600 Mon to Fri
EMERGENCY Unavailable
TIME ZONE GMT +1
INTERNATIONAL DIALING CODE 244

ANGUILLA

GOVERNMENT UK overseas territory
LANGUAGES English (official)
CURRENCY East Caribbean dollar = 100 cents
MEDICAL There are no specific health risks, but medical facilities are limited on the island
TRAVEL Most visits are trouble-free, but beachwear should be confined to resort areas. Travelers should take normal precautions, such as locking doors and securing valuables
WEATHER Tropical climate. Hurricane risk from Jun to Nov; Oct to Dec is the rainy season. Optimum diving conditions in summer months
BANKING 0800–1500 Mon to Thu; 0800–1700 Fri
EMERGENCY All services 911
TIME ZONE GMT –4
INTERNATIONAL DIALING CODE 1 264

ANTIGUA & BARBUDA

GOVERNMENT Constitutional monarchy
LANGUAGES English (official), English patois
CURRENCY East Caribbean dollar = 100 cents
MEDICAL Visitors should take normal precautions against mosquito bites. Vaccinations recommended against polio and typhoid
TRAVEL Generally trouble-free, but visitors should avoid isolated areas, including beaches, after dark
WEATHER Tropical with little variation between the seasons; rainfall is minimal. The islands are at risk from hurricanes from Jun to Nov
BANKING 0800–1400 Mon to Thu; 0800–1700 Fri
EMERGENCY All services 999/911
TIME ZONE GMT –4
INTERNATIONAL DIALING CODE 1 268

ARGENTINA

GOVERNMENT Federal republic
LANGUAGES Spanish (official)
CURRENCY Argentine peso = 10,000 australs
MEDICAL Cholera is a risk in the subtropical northern region
TRAVEL Occasional outbreaks of social unrest. It is inadvisable to walk in isolated, poorly-lit areas. Visitors should avoid carrying too much cash or wearing jewelry. Avoid military areas, which usually allow no stopping
WEATHER Jun to Aug cool in Buenos Aires area; Dec to Feb hot and humid; rain falls all year round
BANKING 1000–1500 Mon to Fri
EMERGENCY Police 101/107
TIME ZONE GMT –3
INTERNATIONAL DIALING CODE 54

ARMENIA

GOVERNMENT Multiparty republic
LANGUAGES Armenian (official)
CURRENCY Dram = 100 couma
MEDICAL Visitors should protect against hepatitis and bacterial infection
TRAVEL The border areas with Azerbaijan should be avoided at all times. Crime remains relatively low in Armenia, but occasional thefts from cars and pickpocketing may occur. The local standard of driving is poor, but most visits are generally trouble-free
WEATHER Apr to Oct hot and sunny; Jul to Sep little rainfall; Dec to Feb cold with heavy snow
BANKING 0930–1730 Mon to Fri
EMERGENCY Unavailable
TIME ZONE GMT +4
INTERNATIONAL DIALING CODE 374

ARUBA

GOVERNMENT Parliamentary democracy
LANGUAGES Dutch, English, Spanish, Papiamento
CURRENCY Aruba florin = 100 cents
MEDICAL Water is purified and should be safe; normal precautions should be taken with food
TRAVEL Beachwear should be confined to the beach. Travelers should take normal precautions, such as avoiding isolated areas after dark
WEATHER Tropical marine climate, warm and dry with average temperatures of 82°F [28°C]. Nov and Dec experience short showers
BANKING 0800–1200 and 1300–1600 Mon to Fri
EMERGENCY Police 11 000; Ambulance 74 300; Fire 115
TIME ZONE GMT –4
INTERNATIONAL DIALING CODE 297

AUSTRALIA

GOVERNMENT Federal constitutional monarchy
LANGUAGES English (official)
CURRENCY Australian dollar = 100 cents
MEDICAL No vaccinations required. There are few health hazards, but visitors should protect against sunburn, spider, and snake bites
TRAVEL Visitors should exercise caution in major urban areas, particularly after dark
WEATHER Tropical to temperate; Nov to Mar warm or hot in all areas; Jun to Aug mild in south-eastern region; Sep to May warm to hot; rain falls all year round and is heaviest Mar to Jul
BANKING 0930–1600 Mon to Thu; 0930–1700 Fri, but hours vary throughout the country
EMERGENCY Emergency Services 000
TIME ZONE East GMT +10; Cen. +9.30; West +8
INTERNATIONAL DIALING CODE 61

AUSTRIA

GOVERNMENT Federal republic
LANGUAGES German (official)
CURRENCY Euro = 100 cents
MEDICAL There are no specific health risks in Austria
TRAVEL Visitors to the Alps should contact the Austrian Tourist Agency for advice on safety. Austria benefits all year round by providing summer sightseeing and winter sports
WEATHER Jun to Aug warm and pleasant; Oct to Apr cold; Mar to Aug higher rainfall
BANKING 0800–1230 and 1330–1500 Mon, Tue, Wed and Fri; Thu 0800–1230 and 1330–1730
EMERGENCY Emergency Services 112; Police 133; Ambulance 144
TIME ZONE GMT +1
INTERNATIONAL DIALING CODE 43

AZORES

GOVERNMENT Portuguese autonomous region
LANGUAGES Portuguese
CURRENCY Euro = 100 cents
MEDICAL There are no specific health risks in the Azores
TRAVEL Most visits to the Azores are trouble-free. The nine large islands and numerous small ones are situated in the middle of the Atlantic Ocean and offer the traveler a wealth of stunning scenery
WEATHER Mild throughout the year; Jun to Sep sunny and warm; Jan to Apr changeable; Oct to Mar wet
BANKING Visitors should check at their hotel
EMERGENCY Unavailable
TIME ZONE GMT –1
INTERNATIONAL DIALING CODE Unavailable

BAHRAIN

GOVERNMENT Monarchy (emirate) with a cabinet appointed by the Emir
LANGUAGES Arabic (official), English, Farsi, Urdu
CURRENCY Bahrain dinar = 1,000 fils
MEDICAL There are no specific health risks
TRAVEL Generally calm, but any increase in regional tension may affect travel advice. Visitors should avoid village areas, particularly after dark. Keep cash and valuables out of sight at all times
WEATHER Jun to Sep very hot; Nov to Mar milder and pleasant
BANKING 0800–1200 and 1600–1800 Sat to Wed; 0800–1100 Thu
EMERGENCY All Services 999
TIME ZONE GMT +3
INTERNATIONAL DIALING CODE 973

AZERBAIJAN

GOVERNMENT Federal multiparty republic
LANGUAGES Azerbaijani (official), Russian
CURRENCY Azerbaijani manat = 100 gopik
MEDICAL Visitors should protect against malaria, yellow fever, diptheria, tick-borne encephalitis, hepatitis, rabies, and typhoid fever
TRAVEL Travel to the western region of Nagorno-Karabakh and surrounding occupied area should be avoided. Passport photocopies should be carried at all times. Do not enter or leave the country via the land borders with Russia
WEATHER May to Sep sunny, warm, and dry; Oct to Apr mild with some rain
BANKING 0930–1730 Mon to Fri
EMERGENCY Unavailable
TIME ZONE GMT +4
INTERNATIONAL DIALING CODE 994

BAHAMAS

GOVERNMENT Constitutional parliamentary democracy
LANGUAGES English (official), Creole
CURRENCY Bahamian dollar = 100 cents
MEDICAL Visitors should protect against dehydration, sunburn, tetanus, and jellyfish
TRAVEL Most visits are trouble-free, but crime exists in the cities of Nassau and Freeport. Keep valuables hidden and avoid walking alone
WEATHER Mild throughout the year; May to Oct warm and wet; Dec to Mar cooler and drier; Jun to Nov hurricanes occur
BANKING 0930–1500 Mon to Thu; 0930–1700 Fri, but hours on each island vary
EMERGENCY All Services 911
TIME ZONE GMT –5
INTERNATIONAL DIALING CODE 1 242

BANGLADESH

GOVERNMENT Multiparty republic
LANGUAGES Bengali (official), English
CURRENCY Taka = 100 paisas
MEDICAL Visitors should protect against cholera, dysentery, hepatitis, malaria, and meningitis
TRAVEL Avoid political gatherings. Driving conditions are very poor. Visitors should keep valuables hidden and avoid travel after dark
WEATHER Jun to Sep monsoon with heavy rain and very high humidity; Nov to Feb sunny and cool; Mar to Jun hot with thunderstorms
BANKING 0830–1430 Sun to Wed; 0830–1300 Thu. Closed Fri and Sat
EMERGENCY Police Dhaka 866 551–3; Fire and Ambulance Service Dhaka 9 555 555
TIME ZONE GMT +6
INTERNATIONAL DIALING CODE 880

BARBADOS

GOVERNMENT Parliamentary democracy
LANGUAGES English (local Bajan dialect also spoken)
CURRENCY Barbados dollar = 100 cents
MEDICAL The sun is intense and visitors should wear strong sunscreen at all times. Other health risks include dengue fever
TRAVEL Travel is generally risk-free, but visitors should avoid deserted beaches at night
WEATHER Warm all year round; Jun to Dec wet season; Feb to May cooler and drier
BANKING 0800–1500 Mon to Thu; 0800–1300 and 1500–1700 Fri
EMERGENCY Police 112; Ambulance 115; All Services 119
TIME ZONE GMT –4
INTERNATIONAL DIALING CODE 1 246

BELARUS

GOVERNMENT Multiparty republic
LANGUAGES Belarusian and Russian (both official)
CURRENCY Belarusian rouble = 100 kopecks
MEDICAL Visitors should avoid eating dairy produce, mushrooms, and fruits of the forests which can carry high levels of radiation. Other health risks include hepatitis A and B, and typhoid
TRAVEL Pickpocketing and theft from vehicles or hotel rooms is common. Visitors should avoid demonstrations and rallies, and remain vigilant at all times
WEATHER May to Aug mild; Oct to Apr cold; Jan to Mar snow cover; rain falls all year round
BANKING 0900–1730 Mon to Fri
EMERGENCY Police 02; Ambulance 03
TIME ZONE GMT +2
INTERNATIONAL DIALING CODE 375

BELGIUM

GOVERNMENT Federal constitutional monarchy
LANGUAGES Dutch, French, German (all official)
CURRENCY Euro = 100 cents
MEDICAL There are no specific health risks, but medical care is expensive
TRAVEL Most visits are trouble-free, but visitors should take sensible precautions to avoid the increasing threat of mugging, bag-snatching, and pickpocketing, particularly in Brussels
WEATHER May to Sep mild; Nov to Mar cold; rain falls all year round, often as snow in winter
BANKING 0900–1200 and 1400–1600 Mon to Fri. Some banks open 0900–1200 Sat
EMERGENCY Police 101; Emergency Services 112 Fire/Ambulance 100 (112 from a mobile phone)
TIME ZONE GMT +1
INTERNATIONAL DIALING CODE 32

BELIZE

GOVERNMENT Constitutional monarchy
LANGUAGES English (official), Spanish, Creole
CURRENCY Belizean dollar = 100 cents
MEDICAL Precautions should be taken against polio, typhoid, and cholera. Malaria is present throughout the year, excluding urban areas
TRAVEL Nov to May is the best time to visit, but this is the busy tourist season when prices rise and hotels fill up. Belize has one of the longest barrier reefs in the world
WEATHER Hot and humid climate. Monsoon and hurricane season runs from Jun to Sep
BANKING 0800–1300 Mon to Thu; 0800–1200 and 1500–1800 Fri
EMERGENCY All services 911
TIME ZONE GMT –6
INTERNATIONAL DIALING CODE 501

BENIN

GOVERNMENT Multiparty republic
LANGUAGES French (official), Fon, Adja, Yoruba
CURRENCY CFA franc = 100 centimes
MEDICAL Visitors should protect against cholera and malaria. Yellow fever vaccination certificates are required for entry. Water is unsafe to drink
TRAVEL Travel is generally safe, but driving out of towns at night should be avoided due to poor street lighting. Occasional incidents of mugging and armed robberies occur in Cotonou
WEATHER Warm to hot all year round; Mar to Jul and Sep to Oct are rainy seasons in the south
BANKING 0800–1100 and 1500–1600 Mon to Fri
EMERGENCY Consult foreign embassy
TIME ZONE GMT +1
INTERNATIONAL DIALING CODE 229

BERMUDA

GOVERNMENT Self-governing British dependency
LANGUAGES English (some Portuguese is also spoken)
CURRENCY Bermuda dollar = 100 cents
MEDICAL There are no specific health risks
TRAVEL Most visits to Bermuda are trouble-free. Accommodation can be up to 40% cheaper between Nov and Mar, but events and entertainment are less plentiful at this time
WEATHER Jun to Sep very warm; Nov to Apr mild; rainfall is abundant and evenly distributed all year round
BANKING 0930–1500 Mon to Thu; 0930–1500 and 1630–1730 Fri
EMERGENCY All Services 911
TIME ZONE GMT –4
INTERNATIONAL DIALING CODE 1 441

BOLIVIA

GOVERNMENT Multiparty republic
LANGUAGES Spanish, Aymara, Quechua (official)
CURRENCY Boliviano = 100 centavos
MEDICAL Altitude sickness is common. Visitors should drink plenty of water and protect against cholera, hepatitis, malaria, polio, and tetanus
TRAVEL Pickpocketing is common and visitors are advised to remain vigilant at all times. The country is going through a period of unrest
WEATHER Average max. daily temperature of 62–66°F [17–19°C] all year round; low annual rainfall, most falling Dec to Mar
BANKING 0930–1500 Mon to Thu; 0930–1500 and 1630–1730 Fri
EMERGENCY All Services 911
TIME ZONE GMT –4
INTERNATIONAL DIALING CODE 591

BOSNIA-HERZEGOVINA

GOVERNMENT Federal republic
LANGUAGES Bosnian, Serbian, Croatian
CURRENCY Convertible marka = 100 convertible pfenniga
MEDICAL Medical facilities are limited. There is a risk of hepatitis and typhoid fever
TRAVEL Crime level is generally low, but isolatec incidents of violence can flare up. Unexploded land mines and other ordnance still remain in certain areas
WEATHER Jun to Sep warm; Dec to Feb cold; spring and fall mild; rain falls all year round
BANKING 0730–1530 Mon to Fri
EMERGENCY Consult foreign office in country of residence before departure
TIME ZONE GMT +1
INTERNATIONAL DIALING CODE 387

BOTSWANA

GOVERNMENT Multiparty republic
LANGUAGES English (official), Setswana
CURRENCY Pula = 100 thebe
MEDICAL There are no specific health risks, but visitors should protect against malaria
TRAVEL Most visits are trouble-free, but there is an increasing incidence of crime. Prolonged rainfall may cause flooding and block roads from Dec to Apr
WEATHER In the east, May to Sep mild with little rainfall; Nov to Mar warm, rainy season but nights can be cold
BANKING 0900–1430 Mon, Tue, Thu and Fri; 0815–1200 Wed; 0815–1045 Sat
EMERGENCY Police 351161
TIME ZONE GMT +2
INTERNATIONAL DIALING CODE 267

BRAZIL

GOVERNMENT Federal republic
LANGUAGES Portuguese (official)
CURRENCY Real = 100 centavos
MEDICAL Visitors should take precautions against AIDS, malaria, meningitis, and yellow feve
TRAVEL High crime rate in major cities of Rio de Janeiro and São Paulo. Dress down and avoic wearing jewelry
WEATHER Jun to Sep pleasant in southeast; Dec to Mar hot and humid with high rainfall
BANKING 1000–1630 Mon to Fri
EMERGENCY All Services 0
TIME ZONE Eastern GMT –3; North East and East Pará –3; Western –4; Amapa and West Para –4; Acre State –5; Fernando de Noronha Archipelago –2
INTERNATIONAL DIALING CODE 55

BULGARIA

GOVERNMENT Multiparty republic
LANGUAGES Bulgarian (official), Turkish
CURRENCY Lev = 100 stotinki
MEDICAL There are no specific health risks
TRAVEL Most visits to Bulgaria are trouble-free, but there is a risk of robbery. Pickpockets operate in downtown Sofia and in the Black Sea resorts. Car theft is commonplace
WEATHER May to Sep warm with some rainfall; Nov to Mar cold with snow; rain falls frequently during spring and fall
BANKING 0800–1130 and 1400–1800 Mon to Fri; 0830–1130 Sat
EMERGENCY Police 166; Fire 160; Ambulance 150
TIME ZONE GMT +2
INTERNATIONAL DIALING CODE 359

BURMA (= MYANMAR)

GOVERNMENT Military regime
LANGUAGES Burmese (official); minority ethnic groups have their own languages
CURRENCY Kyat = 100 pyas
MEDICAL Visitors should protect against choler dysentery, hepatitis, malaria, rabies, and typhoid
TRAVEL Politically unsettled. Visitors should avoi large crowds and should not visit Aung San Suu Kyi without prior arrangement. Terrorist attacks have been reported in some areas
WEATHER Monsoon climate; Feb to May hot with very little rain; May to Oct wet; Nov to Fe cooler and drier
BANKING 1000–1400 Mon to Fri
EMERGENCY Unavailable
TIME ZONE GMT +6.30
INTERNATIONAL DIALING CODE 95

CAMBODIA

GOVERNMENT Constitutional monarchy
LANGUAGES Khmer (official), French, English
CURRENCY Riel = 100 sen
MEDICAL Visitors should protect against cholera, hepatitis, malaria, typhoid, and rabies
TRAVEL Visitors should seek advice before traveling. The greatest risks are from traffic accidents and armed robbery after dark. Land mines exist in certain rural areas
WEATHER Tropical monsoon climate; May to Oct monsoon; Dec to Jan lower humidity and little rainfall; Feb to Apr hot; temperatures are constant throughout the country
BANKING 0800–1500 Mon to Fri
EMERGENCY Unavailable
TIME ZONE GMT +7
INTERNATIONAL DIALING CODE 855

CANADA

GOVERNMENT Federal multiparty constitutional monarchy
LANGUAGES English and French (both official)
CURRENCY Canadian dollar = 100 cents
MEDICAL Medical treatment is expensive and it is essential that visitors have travel insurance. Blackfly and mosquitoes can cause problems in areas near water
TRAVEL Most visits to Canada are trouble-free
WEATHER Varies considerably; Jul to Aug tend to be warm all round the country; Nov to Mar very cold everywhere except west coast
BANKING 1000–1500 Mon to Fri
EMERGENCY Emergency Services 911 or 0
TIME ZONE Six zones exist from GMT –3.30 in Newfoundland to –8 on the Pacific coast
INTERNATIONAL DIALING CODE 1

CANARY ISLANDS

GOVERNMENT Spanish autonomous region
LANGUAGES Spanish
CURRENCY Euro = 100 cents
MEDICAL The Canary Islands are part of Spain and there are no specific health risks
TRAVEL The islands are volcanic and the landscape is varied. Many resorts suffer the effects of mass tourism, but beyond these areas there are stunning, peaceful regions to be enjoyed
WEATHER Subtropical climate; generally hot and sunny all year round, but Dec to Feb slightly cooler than rest of year
BANKING Visitors should enquire at hotel
EMERGENCY Unavailable
TIME ZONE GMT
INTERNATIONAL DIALING CODE 34

CAPE VERDE

GOVERNMENT Multiparty republic
LANGUAGES Portuguese, Creole
CURRENCY Cape Verde escudo = 100 centavos
MEDICAL Water is untreated and unsafe to drink. Avoid dairy products as they are unpasteurized. Polio and typhoid vaccinations are recommended; there is a risk of cholera and malaria
TRAVEL Most visits to Cape Verde are trouble-free. Visitors should avoid carrying valuables in public and remain vigilant at all times
WEATHER Warm and temperate climate with a dry summer. The islands suffer periodically from drought
BANKING 0800–1400 Mon to Fri
EMERGENCY All services 87
TIME ZONE GMT –1
INTERNATIONAL DIALING CODE 238

CAYMAN ISLANDS

GOVERNMENT British crown colony
LANGUAGES English (local dialects also spoken)
CURRENCY Cayman Islands dollar = 100 cents
MEDICAL There is a risk of sunburn and poisonous plants are present
TRAVEL Most visits to the Cayman Islands are trouble-free. Car hire is a good way to move around the islands
WEATHER Warm tropical climate all year round; May to Oct wet season with usually brief showers
BANKING 0900–1600 Mon to Thu; 0900–1630 Fri
EMERGENCY Police 911; Ambulance 555; All Services 911
TIME ZONE GMT –5
INTERNATIONAL DIALING CODE 1 345

CHAD

GOVERNMENT Multiparty republic
LANGUAGES French and Arabic (both official)
CURRENCY CFA franc = 100 centimes
MEDICAL Visitors should be vaccinated against yellow fever, tetanus, cholera, and hepatitis A
TRAVEL Visitors to Chad should remain vigilant at all times especially in the southwest region along the border with Cameroon. Areas to avoid include the Aozou Strip and the Tibesti area on the border with Libya, where minefields exist
WEATHER Hot tropical climate; Mar to May very hot; May to Oct wet in south; Jun to Sep wet in central areas; little rain in northern regions
BANKING 0900–1400 Mon to Fri
EMERGENCY Unavailable
TIME ZONE GMT +1
INTERNATIONAL DIALING CODE 235

CHILE

GOVERNMENT Multiparty republic
LANGUAGES Spanish (official)
CURRENCY Chilean peso = 100 centavos
MEDICAL Visitors should protect themselves against cholera
TRAVEL Most visits are trouble-free, but visitors are advised to keep in groups and avoid walking alone, particularly after dark. Pickpockets and muggers are active in cities. Passport photocopies should be carried at all times
WEATHER Variable climate; Sep to Nov and Feb to Apr pleasant temperatures; Dec to Mar hotter; skiing is popular from Jun to Aug
BANKING 0900–1400 Mon to Fri
EMERGENCY Police 133; Fire 132
TIME ZONE GMT –4; Easter Island –6
INTERNATIONAL DIALING CODE 56

CHINA

GOVERNMENT Single-party Communist republic
LANGUAGES Mandarin Chinese (official)
CURRENCY Renminbi yuan = 10 jiao = 100 fen
MEDICAL Rabies is widespread. A virulent strain of viral pneumonia has emerged in the southeast and malaria is common in southern areas
TRAVEL Violent crimes are rare. Crime occurs in cities, and extra care should be taken around street markets and popular bar areas at night
WEATHER Climate varies; Apr to Sep humid and hot; Jan to Mar very cold; rainfall high in central areas; Jul to Sep typhoon season in the south
BANKING 0930–1200 and 1400–1700 Mon to Fri; 0900–1700 Sat
EMERGENCY Police 110; Fire 119
TIME ZONE GMT +8
INTERNATIONAL DIALING CODE 86

COLOMBIA

GOVERNMENT Multiparty republic
LANGUAGES Spanish (official)
CURRENCY Colombian peso = 100 centavos
MEDICAL Visitors should protect against altitude sickness, cholera, hepatitis A, B and D, and malaria
TRAVEL Guerrilla and criminal attacks close to Bogota are increasing. Violence and kidnapping are serious problems in Colombia. The border area with Panama and the Uraba region of Antioquia are particularly dangerous
WEATHER Hot and humid; May to Nov rainy season; cooler in upland areas
BANKING 0900–1500 Mon to Fri
EMERGENCY All Services 112 (01 in smaller towns and rural areas)
TIME ZONE GMT –5
INTERNATIONAL DIALING CODE 57

COMOROS

GOVERNMENT Multiparty republic
LANGUAGES Arabic and French (both official)
CURRENCY CFA franc = 100 centimes
MEDICAL Strict food hygiene precautions are essential. Cholera and malaria are prevalant and medical facilities are basic and limited
TRAVEL Generally crime-free, but be aware of pickpockets. Visitors should not walk around town centres unaccompanied at night
WEATHER Tropical climate with average temperatures of 77°F [25°C]. Cyclone risk between Jan and Apr
BANKING 0730–1300 Mon to Thu; 0730–1100 Fri
EMERGENCY Unavailable
TIME ZONE GMT +3
INTERNATIONAL DIALING CODE 269

COSTA RICA

GOVERNMENT Multiparty republic
LANGUAGES Spanish (official), English
CURRENCY Costa Rican colón = 100 céntimos
MEDICAL Cases of dengue fever have been confirmed. Visitors should protect themselves against malaria, cholera, and hepatitis
TRAVEL Daylight muggings can occur. Do not wear jewelry or carry large amounts of cash. Riptides are very common on all beaches
WEATHER Coastal areas warmer than inland low-lying regions; Dec to Apr warm and dry; May to Nov rainy season; landslides can occur
BANKING 0900–1500 Mon to Fri
EMERGENCY Police 104; Fire 103; Ambulance 225/1436 and 228/2187
TIME ZONE GMT –7
INTERNATIONAL DIALING CODE 506

CROATIA

GOVERNMENT Multiparty republic
LANGUAGES Croatian
CURRENCY Kuna = 100 lipas
MEDICAL No specific health risks, although the health system is severely stretched at present
TRAVEL Exercise caution in the areas bordering Bosnia-Herzegovina, Serbia, and Montenegro. There continue to be incidents of violence and many unexploded land mines remain undetected. It is inadvisable to use the Debelli Brijeg crossing-points into Montenegro
WEATHER Continental climate in the north and Mediterranean on the Adriatic Coast
BANKING 0700–1500 Mon to Fri
EMERGENCY Police 92; Fire 93; Ambulance 94
TIME ZONE GMT +1
INTERNATIONAL DIALING CODE 385

CUBA

GOVERNMENT Socialist republic
LANGUAGES Spanish (official)
CURRENCY Cuban peso = 100 centavos
MEDICAL Tap water is unsafe to drink, with a risk of contracting hepatitis A
TRAVEL Street theft occurs, especially in Old Havana and major tourist sites. Do not carry large amounts of cash or jewelry. Do not travel with anyone other than your recognized tour operator. Avoid military zones
WEATHER May to Oct hot rainy season; Aug to Nov hurricane season; Dec to Apr cooler
BANKING 0830–1200 and 1330–1500 Mon to Fri; 0830–1030 Sat
EMERGENCY All Services 26811
TIME ZONE GMT –4
INTERNATIONAL DIALING CODE 53

CYPRUS

GOVERNMENT Multiparty republic
LANGUAGES Greek and Turkish (both official)
CURRENCY Euro = 100 cents
MEDICAL There are no specific health risks, but visitors should be protected against hepatitis
TRAVEL Travel is generally trouble-free, but attempts to pass overland from the northern Turkish sector into the southern Greek region are not recommended
WEATHER Apr to May and Sep to Oct cool and pleasant; Jun to Aug hot and dry; Nov to Mar rainfall is heavier, but temperatures remain warm
BANKING 0815–1230 in tourist areas; 1530–1730 in winter; 1630–1830 in summer
EMERGENCY All Services 199
TIME ZONE GMT +2
INTERNATIONAL DIALING CODE 357

CZECH REPUBLIC

GOVERNMENT Multiparty republic
LANGUAGES Czech (official)
CURRENCY Czech koruna = 100 haler
MEDICAL Visitors to forested areas should seek advice about immunization against tick-borne encephalitis and lyme disease
TRAVEL Most visits are trouble-free, but petty theft is a growing problem, particularly in Prague. Pickpocketing is very common at tourist attractions
WEATHER May to Sep mild; Apr and Oct much cooler
BANKING 0800–1800 Mon to Fri
EMERGENCY Police 158; Fire 150; Ambulance 155
TIME ZONE GMT +1
INTERNATIONAL DIALING CODE 42

DENMARK

GOVERNMENT Parliamentary monarchy
LANGUAGES Danish (official), English
CURRENCY Danish krone = 100 øre
MEDICAL There are no specific health risks in Denmark
TRAVEL Visits to Denmark are generally trouble-free. Visitors will enjoy relatively low prices compared to other European countries
WEATHER Jun to Aug warm summer season; Oct to Mar cold and wet with chance of frost; spring and fall are usually mild and pleasant
BANKING 0930–1700 Mon, Tue, Wed and Fri; 0930–1800 Thu. Some foreign exchange bureaux remain open until midnight
EMERGENCY Emergency Services 112
TIME ZONE GMT +1
INTERNATIONAL DIALING CODE 45

DOMINICA

GOVERNMENT Parliamentary democracy
LANGUAGES English (official), Creole, French
CURRENCY East Caribbean dollar = 100 cents
MEDICAL Dengue fever is prevalent and visitors should guard against mosquito bites
TRAVEL Most visits are trouble-free. Visitors are advised to take sensible precautions and be vigilant at all times
WEATHER Tropical climate with heavy rainfall, particularly in Jun to Oct, which is also the hottest period. Tropical storms and hurricanes can occur between Jun and Nov
BANKING 0800–1500 Mon to Thu; 0800–1700 Fri
EMERGENCY All services 999
TIME ZONE GMT –4
INTERNATIONAL DIALING CODE 1 767

DOMINICAN REPUBLIC

GOVERNMENT Multiparty republic
LANGUAGES Spanish (official)
CURRENCY Dominican peso = 100 centavos
MEDICAL Tourists should protect against polio and typhoid. There are occasional outbreaks of malaria and dengue fever; anti-mosquito skin repellants are recommended
TRAVEL Border areas should be avoided while the political unrest in neighbouring Haiti continues. Avoid any excursions that are not recommended by tour operators
WEATHER Hot tropical climate; Jun to Nov rainy season with the risk of hurricanes
BANKING 0800–1600 Mon to Fri
EMERGENCY Emergency Services 711
TIME ZONE GMT –4
INTERNATIONAL DIALING CODE 1 809

ECUADOR

GOVERNMENT Multiparty republic
LANGUAGES Spanish (official), Quechua
CURRENCY US dollar = 100 cents
MEDICAL There is a risk of dengue fever, hepatitis, malaria, typhoid, diptheria, and rabies
TRAVEL Street crimes such as muggings and pickpocketing are common in the cities. Visitors should avoid travel to the provinces bordering Colombia due to incidents of kidnapping
WEATHER Jan to Apr warm and rainy on mainland and Galapagos; Jun to Aug cold; Jun to Aug dry in Highlands; Aug to Feb dry in Oriente
BANKING 0900–1330 and 1430–1830 Mon to Fri
EMERGENCY Police 101; Ambulance 131
TIME ZONE GMT –5; Galapagos Islands –6
INTERNATIONAL DIALING CODE 593

EL SALVADOR

GOVERNMENT Republic
LANGUAGES Spanish (official)
CURRENCY US dollar = 100 cents
MEDICAL Tourists should protect against cholera, hepatitis, malaria, rabies, and typhoid
TRAVEL El Salvador is more politically stable than ever, but has high levels of violent crime. Visitors traveling alone should be vigilant at all times
WEATHER Hot subtropical climate; Nov to Apr dry season; May to Oct rainy season with cooler evenings
BANKING 0900–1300 and 1345–1600 Mon to Fri
EMERGENCY All Services 123/121
TIME ZONE GMT –6
INTERNATIONAL DIALING CODE 503

ETHIOPIA

GOVERNMENT Federation of nine provinces
LANGUAGES Amharic (official), many others
CURRENCY Birr = 100 cents
MEDICAL Water-borne diseases and malaria are prevalent. Medical facilities outside the capital are extremely poor
TRAVEL Most governments advise against travel to the Gambella region and the Eritrean border. There is currently a high risk of terrorism throughout the country
WEATHER Lowlands are hot and humid, it is warm in the hills and cool in the upland areas
BANKING 0800–1200 and 1300–1700 Mon to Thu; 0830–1100 and 1300–1700 Fri
EMERGENCY Not available
TIME ZONE GMT +3
INTERNATIONAL DIALING CODE 251

EGYPT

GOVERNMENT Republic
LANGUAGES Arabic (official), French, English
CURRENCY Egyptian pound = 100 piastres
MEDICAL There are no specific health risks in Egyptian
TRAVEL Due to continuing tensions, visitors should keep in touch with developments in the Middle East and remain vigilant at all times. Particular care should be taken when traveling in Luxor and beyond in the Nile Valley
WEATHER Jun to Aug very hot and dry; Sep to May dry and cooler; spring and fall months are pleasant; dusty Saharan winds during Apr
BANKING 0830–1400 Sun to Thu
EMERGENCY Unavailable
TIME ZONE GMT +2
INTERNATIONAL DIALING CODE 20

ESTONIA

GOVERNMENT Multiparty republic
LANGUAGES Estonian (official), Russian
CURRENCY Estonian kroon = 100 senti
MEDICAL There are no specific health risks
TRAVEL Most visits are trouble-free. Despite independence in 1991, much tradition exists in Estonia. Skiing, skating, and ice fishing are popular during the winter months
WEATHER Large temperature variations; Apr to May warm and pleasant; Jun to Sep hot.; Dec to Mar very cold with heavy snowfall; rain falls all year round
BANKING 0930–1630 Mon to Fri
EMERGENCY Police 02; Fire 01; Ambulance 03 (dial an extra 0 first if in Tallinn)
TIME ZONE GMT +2
INTERNATIONAL DIALING CODE 372

FIJI ISLANDS

GOVERNMENT Transitional
LANGUAGES English (official), various Fijian dialects
CURRENCY Fijian dollar = 100 cents
MEDICAL Visitors should protect against dengue fever and should avoid mosquito bites
TRAVEL There has been an increase in petty crime due to the unsettled economic and political situations
WEATHER Tropical climate; Dec to Apr humid, rainy season with a risk of tropical cyclones; May to Oct cooler, dry season
BANKING 0930–1500 Mon to Thu; 0930–1600 Fri
EMERGENCY All Services 000
TIME ZONE GMT +12
INTERNATIONAL DIALING CODE 679

FINLAND

GOVERNMENT Multiparty republic
LANGUAGES Finnish and Swedish (both official)
CURRENCY Euro = 100 cents
MEDICAL There are no specific health risks, but if mushroom-picking/eating, seek advice on safety
TRAVEL Visits to Finland are generally trouble-free
WEATHER Temperate climate; May to Sep warm with midnight sun; Oct to Mar very cold; Nov to May snow cover in the north; skiing starts in Feb, the coldest month, and continues until Jun in Lapland
BANKING 0915–1615 Mon to Fri
EMERGENCY Police 002; Fire/Ambulance 000; Emergency Services 112; Doctor 008
TIME ZONE GMT +2
INTERNATIONAL DIALING CODE 358

FRENCH POLYNESIA

GOVERNMENT French overseas territory
LANGUAGES French and Polynesian (both official)
CURRENCY French Pacific franc = 100 cents
MEDICAL Water is untreated and dairy foods are unpasteurized. Vaccinations against polio and typhoid are recommended
TRAVEL Most visits are trouble-free, but visitors should remain vigilant at al times. French Polynesia is made up of 130 islands, Tahiti being the most popular
WEATHER Tropical but moderate climate with occasional cyclonic storms in Jan. Cool and dry Mar to Nov
BANKING 0745–1530 Mon to Fri
EMERGENCY Dial operator
TIME ZONE GMT –9 to GMT –10
INTERNATIONAL DIALING CODE 689

GEORGIA

GOVERNMENT Multiparty republic
LANGUAGES Georgian (official), Russian
CURRENCY Lari = 100 tetri
MEDICAL Diptheria and rabies cases have been reported. Tap water is unsafe to drink. Anthrax has been reported in the east. Medical care is poor and visitors should carry their own syringes
TRAVEL The regions of Abkhazia and South Ossetia should be avoided. Do not attempt access across the land borders with Russia
WEATHER Jul to Sep hot; Dec to Mar mild, especially in the southwest; low temperatures in alpine areas; rainfall heavy in southwest
BANKING 0930–1730 Mon to Fri
EMERGENCY Police 02; Fire 01; Ambulance 03
TIME ZONE GMT +4
INTERNATIONAL DIALING CODE 995

FRANCE

GOVERNMENT Multiparty republic
LANGUAGES French (official)
CURRENCY Euro = 100 cents
MEDICAL There are no specific health risks
TRAVEL Most visits to France are trouble-free. There have been sporadic bomb attacks on the island of Corsica and care should be exercised
WEATHER Temperate climate in the north; rain falls all year round; Mediterranean climate in the south; mild in the west; May to Sep hot and sunny; Oct to Nov pleasant temperatures
BANKING 0900–1200 and 1400–1600 Mon to Fri. Some banks close on Mondays
EMERGENCY Police 17; Fire 18; Ambulance 15; Emergency Services 112
TIME ZONE GMT +1
INTERNATIONAL DIALING CODE 33

GAMBIA, THE

GOVERNMENT Military regime
LANGUAGES English (official), Mandinka, Wolof
CURRENCY Dalasi = 100 butut
MEDICAL Water-borne diseases and malaria are common. Other health risks include yellow fever, hepatitis, rabies, and typhoid
TRAVEL Exercise caution when walking at night. Do not travel with valuables and dress modestly
WEATHER Nov to Mar dry and cool with winds from the Sahara; Jun to Oct rainy season; inland the cool season is shorter and temperatures are hot from Mar to Jun
BANKING 0800–1330 Mon to Thu; 0800–1100 Fri
EMERGENCY Consult foreign embassy
TIME ZONE GMT
INTERNATIONAL DIALING CODE 220

GERMANY

GOVERNMENT Federal multiparty republic
LANGUAGES German (official)
CURRENCY Euro = 100 cents
MEDICAL There are no specific health risks, but medical care is expensive
TRAVEL Visits to Germany are generally trouble-free. Travelers are able to enjoy a wealth of arts and culture, plus stunning natural scenery
WEATHER Very variable, temperate climate throughout the country; May to Oct warm; Nov to Apr cold; rain falls all year round
BANKING 0830–1300 and 1400/30–1600 Mon to Fri
EMERGENCY Police 110; Fire 112; Emergency Services 112
TIME ZONE GMT +1
INTERNATIONAL DIALING CODE 49

GIBRALTAR

GOVERNMENT UK overseas territory
LANGUAGES English and Spanish
CURRENCY Gibraltar pound = 100 pence
MEDICAL There are no specific health risks in Gibraltar
TRAVEL Most visits to Gibraltar are trouble-free. The country was recognized as a British possession in 1713, and despite Spanish claims, its population has consistently voted to retain its contacts with Britain
WEATHER Warm all year round; Jun to Sep hot and can be humid; Nov to Mar mild
BANKING 0900–1530 and 1630–1800 Mon to Fri
EMERGENCY All Services 999
TIME ZONE GMT +1
INTERNATIONAL DIALING CODE 350

GREECE

GOVERNMENT Multiparty republic
LANGUAGES Greek (official)
CURRENCY Euro = 100 cents
MEDICAL There is a risk of sunburn
TRAVEL Visitors should exercise normal precautions regarding safety and security. Tourists are strongly advised not to hire motorcycles, scooters, or mopeds
WEATHER Mediterranean climate; Aug to Nov pleasant temperatures; Nov to Mar heavy rainfall; Apr to Jun hot
BANKING 0800–1400 Mon to Fri
EMERGENCY Police 100; Fire 199; Ambulance 166; Emergency Services 112
TIME ZONE GMT +2
INTERNATIONAL DIALING CODE 30 + 1 for Athens; 31 Thessaloniki; 81 Heraklion; 661 Corfu

GRENADA

GOVERNMENT Constitutional monarchy
LANGUAGES English (official)
CURRENCY East Caribbean dollar = 100 cents
MEDICAL Tourists should protect against polio and typhoid. Anti-mosquito repellants are recommended
TRAVEL Trips are mostly trouble-free; however, tourists should remain vigilant at all times
WEATHER Tropical climate, rainy season is Jun to Sep when tropical storms and hurricanes occur. Jan to May is drier and less humid
BANKING 0800–1400 Mon to Thu; 0800–1300 and 1400–1700 Fri
EMERGENCY Police 112; Ambulance 434; Emergency services 911
TIME ZONE GMT –4
INTERNATIONAL DIALING CODE 1 473

GUADELOUPE

GOVERNMENT French overseas territory
LANGUAGES French (official), Creole
CURRENCY Euro = 100 cents
MEDICAL Polio and typhoid vaccinations are recommended. Water is untreated and unsafe to drink
TRAVEL Visits to Guadeloupe are generally trouble-free, and the French culture and influence is clearly evident. Soufriere de Guadeloupe is an active volcano
WEATHER Warm, humid weather all year round. Rainy season from Jun to Oct, when there is a risk of hurricanes
BANKING 0800–1600 Mon to Fri
EMERGENCY Police 17; Fire and Ambulance 18
TIME ZONE GMT –4
INTERNATIONAL DIALING CODE 590

HONG KONG

GOVERNMENT Special administrative region of China
LANGUAGES Chinese and English; Cantonese is most widely spoken
CURRENCY Hong Kong dollar = 100 cents
MEDICAL Visitors should protect against polio and typhoid. Slight risk of malaria in rural areas
TRAVEL Most visits are trouble-free
WEATHER Nov to Dec warm with pleasant breeze; Jan to Feb much cooler; Mar to Apr warmer; May to Sep very humid and uncomfortable, with a risk of cyclones in Sep
BANKING 0900–1630 Mon to Fri; 0900–1330 Sat
EMERGENCY All Services 999
TIME ZONE GMT +8
INTERNATIONAL DIALING CODE 852

HUNGARY

GOVERNMENT Multiparty republic
LANGUAGES Hungarian (official)
CURRENCY Forint = 100 fillér
MEDICAL There are no specific health risks in Hungary
TRAVEL Street theft is common in tourist areas, particularly in Budapest. It is illegal to drive having consumed alcohol. Passports to be carried at all times. Do not take photographs of anything connected with the military
WEATHER Jun to Aug very warm and sunny; spring and fall mild and pleasant; Jan to Mar very cold
BANKING 0900–1400 Mon to Fri
EMERGENCY Police 107; Fire/Ambulance 104
TIME ZONE GMT +1
INTERNATIONAL DIALING CODE 36

ICELAND

GOVERNMENT Multiparty republic
LANGUAGES Icelandic (official)
CURRENCY Icelandic króna = 100 aurar
MEDICAL There is a risk of hypothermia if trekking during the winter months
TRAVEL Visitors planning to travel off-road do so at their own risk and must contact the local authorities (Vegagerdin) prior to departure. Interior roads are closed in winter
WEATHER Weather is highly changeable all year round; May to Aug is mild with nearly 24 hours of daylight in Reykjavik; Sep to Apr is cold
BANKING 0915–1600 Mon to Fri
EMERGENCY Unavailable
TIME ZONE GMT
INTERNATIONAL DIALING CODE 354

INDIA

GOVERNMENT Multiparty federal republic
LANGUAGES Hindi, English, Telugu, Bengali, Marathi, Tamil, Urdu, Gujarati, Malayalam, Kannada, Oriya, Punjabi, Assamese, Kashmiri, Sindhi and Sanskrit (all official)
CURRENCY Indian rupee = 100 paisa
MEDICAL There is a risk of malaria, AIDS, and intestinal problems. Precautions should be taken
TRAVEL Visitors are advised to avoid the Pakistan border areas, as well as Jammu and Kashmir
WEATHER Hot tropical climate that varies from region to region; Apr to Sep very hot with monsoon rains
BANKING 1000–1400 Mon to Fri
EMERGENCY Unavailable
TIME ZONE GMT +5.30
INTERNATIONAL DIALING CODE 91

INDONESIA

GOVERNMENT Multiparty republic
LANGUAGES Bahasa Indonesian (official)
CURRENCY Indonesian rupiah = 100 sen
MEDICAL There is a risk of polio, typhoid, hepatitis B, yellow fever, and TB. Unpasteurized dairy produce should be avoided
TRAVEL Non-essential travel to Indonesia is not recommended due to the risk of terrorism against Western interests
WEATHER Tropical, varying climate; May to Oct dry weather from eastern monsoon; Nov to Apr rains from western monsoon. In northern Sumatra this pattern is reversed
BANKING 0800–1500 Mon to Fri
EMERGENCY Police 110; Ambulance 118
TIME ZONE West GMT +7; Central +8; East +9
INTERNATIONAL DIALING CODE 62

IRAN

GOVERNMENT Islamic republic
LANGUAGES Persian, Turkic, Kurdish
CURRENCY Iranian rial = 100 dinars
MEDICAL There is a risk of polio, typhoid, malaria and cholera
TRAVEL Visitors should monitor media reports before traveling. Any increase in regional tension will affect travel advice. Visitors should exercise caution and avoid carrying large sums of money since robbery and bag-snatching are common
WEATHER Dec to Mar very cold; Apr to Jun and Sep to Nov warm; Jun to Sep extremely hot
BANKING 0900–1600 Sat to Wed; 0900–1200 Thu. Closed on Fri
EMERGENCY Unavailable
TIME ZONE GMT +3.30
INTERNATIONAL DIALING CODE 98

IRELAND

GOVERNMENT Multiparty republic
LANGUAGES Irish (Gaelic) and English (both official)
CURRENCY Euro = 100 cents
MEDICAL There are no specific health risks
TRAVEL The Irish usually have close community bonds. Visitors should find people very friendly. Strong economic growth continues
WEATHER Rain falls all year round; Jul to Sep warm; Nov to Mar wet and cold; spring and fall mild
BANKING 1000–1600 Mon to Fri. Banks may open later in Dublin
EMERGENCY Emergency Services 112; All Services 999
TIME ZONE GMT
INTERNATIONAL DIALING CODE 353

ISRAEL

GOVERNMENT Multiparty republic
LANGUAGES Hebrew and Arabic (both official)
CURRENCY New Israeli shekel = 100 agorat
MEDICAL There are no specific health risks
TRAVEL Most governments currently strongly advise against travel to the West Bank, Gaza, and Jerusalem, or near their border areas with Israel. Visitors should keep car doors locked when traveling and avoid carrying large sums of cash
WEATHER Jul to Sep hot and windy; Dec to Mar cool in the north; spring and fall are warm and pleasant
BANKING 0830–1230 and 1600–1730 Mon, Tue and Thu; 0830–1230 Wed; 0830–1200 Fri
EMERGENCY Police/Fire 100; Ambulance 101
TIME ZONE GMT +2
INTERNATIONAL DIALING CODE 972

ITALY

GOVERNMENT Multiparty republic
LANGUAGES Italian (official), German, French, Slovene
CURRENCY Euro = 100 cents
MEDICAL There are no specific health risks
TRAVEL Crime is rare, but visitors in tourist areas and city centres should remain vigilant after dark
WEATHER Apr to May and Oct to Nov warm and pleasant; Jun to Sep hot; Dec to Mar colder temperatures with heavy snow in mountain areas; warmer in the south
BANKING Generally 0830–1330 and 1530–1930 Mon to Fri
EMERGENCY Police 112; Fire 115; Ambulance 113; Emergency Services 112
TIME ZONE GMT +1
INTERNATIONAL DIALING CODE 39

JAPAN

GOVERNMENT Constitutional monarchy
LANGUAGES Japanese (official)
CURRENCY Yen = 100 sen
MEDICAL Health and hygiene standards are high and visitors are not required to have vaccinations
TRAVEL Most visits remain trouble-free. There is a high risk of earthquakes and typhoons which often hit the country
WEATHER Sep to Nov typhoons and rain; Jun to Sep warm/very hot with rain in Jun; Mar to May pleasant; Dec to Feb cold winds and snow in western areas, but dry and clear on Pacific coast
BANKING 0900–1500 Mon to Fri
EMERGENCY Tokyo English Life Line 3403 7106; Japan Helpline 0120 461 997
TIME ZONE GMT +9
INTERNATIONAL DIALING CODE 81

KENYA

GOVERNMENT Multiparty republic
LANGUAGES Kiswahili and English (both official)
CURRENCY Kenyan shilling = 100 cents
MEDICAL Malaria is endemic and AIDS is widespread. Water is unsafe to drink
TRAVEL Be alert at all times, particularly in Nairobi and Mombasa. Avoid traveling after dark and in isolated areas
WEATHER Complex and changeable; Jan to Feb hot and dry; Mar to May hot and wet; Jun to Oct warm and dry; Nov to Dec warm and wet; Cooler with rain at any time at higher altitudes
BANKING 0900–1500 Mon to Fri; 0900–1100 on first and last Sat of each month
EMERGENCY All Services 336886/501280
TIME ZONE GMT +3
INTERNATIONAL DIALING CODE 254

JAMAICA

GOVERNMENT Constitutional monarchy
LANGUAGES English (official), patois English
CURRENCY Jamaican dollar = 100 cents
MEDICAL There are no specific health risks
TRAVEL Most visits are trouble-free, but violent crime does exist, mainly in Kingston. Visitors should avoid walking alone in isolated areas, and be particularly alert after dark and using public transport
WEATHER Tropical climate; temperatures remain high all year round; May to Oct rainy season, but showers can occur at any time
BANKING 0900–1400 Mon to Thu; 0900–1500 Fri
EMERGENCY Police 119; Fire/Ambulance 110
TIME ZONE GMT –5
INTERNATIONAL DIALING CODE 1 876

JORDAN

GOVERNMENT Constitutional monarchy
LANGUAGES Arabic (official)
CURRENCY Jordan dinar = 1,000 fils
MEDICAL There are no specific health risks, but visitors should consider vaccination against hepatitis, polio, tetanus, typhoid, and diptheria
TRAVEL Before traveling, visitors should monitor media reports for any increase in regional tension. Crime is low, but visitors should dress modestly and respect local customs
WEATHER Jun to Sep hot and dry with cool evenings; Nov to Mar cooler with rainfall
BANKING 0830–1230 and 1530–1730 Sat to Thu; 0830–1000 during Ramadan
EMERGENCY Police 192; Fire/Ambulance 193
TIME ZONE GMT +2
INTERNATIONAL DIALING CODE 962

KOREA, SOUTH

GOVERNMENT Multiparty republic
LANGUAGES Korean (official)
CURRENCY South Korean won = 100 chon
MEDICAL There are no specific health risks, but medical and dental treatment can be expensive
TRAVEL Travel to South Korea is generally trouble-free, but some form of identification should be carried at all times
WEATHER Jul to Aug hot with heavy rainfall and a chance of typhoons; Sep to Nov and Apr to May mild and dry; Dec to Mar cold but dry, with good skiing
BANKING 0930–1630 Mon to Fri; 0930–1330 Sat
EMERGENCY Unavailable
TIME ZONE GMT +9
INTERNATIONAL DIALING CODE 82

KUWAIT

GOVERNMENT Constitutional monarchy
LANGUAGES Arabic (official), English
CURRENCY Kuwaiti dinar = 1,000 fils
MEDICAL Vaccinations against polio, typhoid, and cholera are recommended
TRAVEL Visitors should monitor media reports before traveling. Any increase in regional tension will affect travel advice. There is a danger from unexploded bombs and land mines on beaches and in rural areas. All Islamic laws should be respected. Photography permits are required
WEATHER Apr to Oct hot, humid with little rain; Nov to Mar cool and dry
BANKING 0800–1200 Sun to Thu
EMERGENCY Unavailable
TIME ZONE GMT +3
INTERNATIONAL DIALING CODE 965

LEBANON

GOVERNMENT Multiparty republic
LANGUAGES Arabic (official), French, English
CURRENCY Lebanese pound = 100 piastres
MEDICAL Protection against polio and typhoid is recommended
TRAVEL Visitors should remain alert to international developments in the Middle East. Most governments currently advise against travel to areas within the Israeli Occupied Zone
WEATHER Jun to Sep hot and dry, but humid along the coast; Dec to May high rainfall with snow in mountains; spring and fall pleasant
BANKING 0830–1200 Mon to Sat
EMERGENCY Police 386 440 425; Fire 310 105; Ambulance 386 675
TIME ZONE GMT +2
INTERNATIONAL DIALING CODE 961

LIECHTENSTEIN

GOVERNMENT Hereditary constitutional monarchy
LANGUAGES German (official)
CURRENCY Swiss franc = 100 centimes
MEDICAL There is a risk of altitude sickness, sunburn, and hypothermia in the Alps
TRAVEL Most visits to Liechtenstein are trouble-free. The country is culturally and economically extremely similar to Switzerland. Winter sports are very popular in the Alps from Nov to Apr
WEATHER Temperate climate; Nov to Apr cool or cold; Jun to Sep warm with high rainfall
BANKING 0800–1630 Mon to Fri
EMERGENCY Police 117; Ambulance 144
TIME ZONE GMT +1
INTERNATIONAL DIALING CODE 41 75

LATVIA

GOVERNMENT Multiparty republic
LANGUAGES Latvian (official), Lithuanian, Russian
CURRENCY Latvian lat = 10 santimi
MEDICAL Visitors should protect themselves against tick-borne encephalitis, particularly if visiting forested areas
TRAVEL Most visits are trouble-free, but tourists should exercise caution since muggings and pickpocketing have increased recently. Use guarded car parks and keep valuables hidden
WEATHER Temperate climate; Apr to Sep warm and clear; Nov to Mar extremely cold; spring and fall mild
BANKING 1000–1800 Mon to Fri
EMERGENCY Police 02; Fire 01; Ambulance 03
TIME ZONE GMT +2
INTERNATIONAL DIALING CODE 371

LIBYA

GOVERNMENT Single-party socialist state
LANGUAGES Arabic (official), Berber
CURRENCY Libyan dinar = 1,000 dirhams
MEDICAL There is a slight risk of malaria, cholera, and hepatitis
TRAVEL Most visits to Libya are trouble-free, but any increase in regional tension will affect travel advice
WEATHER Warm all year round; Nov to Mar occasional rainfall; Apr to Sep can be very hot; May to Jun severe sandstorms from the south
BANKING 0800–1200 Sat to Wed (during winter); 0800–1200 Sat to Thu; 1600–1700 Sat and Wed (during summer)
EMERGENCY Unavailable
TIME ZONE GMT +1
INTERNATIONAL DIALING CODE 218

LITHUANIA

GOVERNMENT Multiparty republic
LANGUAGES Lithuanian (official), Russian, Polish
CURRENCY Litas = 100 centai
MEDICAL Travelers to forested areas should seek advice about protection against rabies and tick-borne encephalitis
TRAVEL There is a risk of pickpocketing, mugging, and bag-snatching, particularly on public transport. Be alert at all times and avoid quiet areas after dark
WEATHER Temperate climate; May to Sep warm; Oct to Nov mild; Nov to Mar can be very cold with snowfall common
BANKING 0900–1700 Mon to Fri
EMERGENCY Police 02; Fire 01; Ambulance 03
TIME ZONE GMT +2
INTERNATIONAL DIALING CODE 370

LUXEMBOURG

GOVERNMENT Constitutional monarchy (Grand Duchy)
LANGUAGES Luxembourgish (official), French, German
CURRENCY Euro = 100 cents
MEDICAL There are no specific health risks
TRAVEL Most travel to Luxembourg is trouble-free. The country is prosperous with a very high quality of life. Visitors may find it expensive compared to other European countries
WEATHER May to Sep warm with rainfall; Oct to Apr cold with snow
BANKING Varies greatly but generally 0900–1200 and 1330–1630 Mon to Fri
EMERGENCY Police 113; Fire/Ambulance 112
TIME ZONE GMT +1
INTERNATIONAL DIALING CODE 352

MALAWI

GOVERNMENT Multiparty republic
LANGUAGES Chichewa and English (both official)
CURRENCY Malawian kwacha = 100 tambala
MEDICAL AIDS and malaria are very common. Outbreaks of cholera do occur, particularly during the rainy season
TRAVEL Be alert at all times, particularly after dark. Avoid travel out of town at night since the condition of roads is poor. Cases of muggings and bag-snatching are increasing. Do not resist demands since attacks can be very violent
WEATHER Apr to Oct hot and dry; May to Jul cool and cold at night; Nov to Apr rainy season
BANKING 0800–1300 Mon to Fri
EMERGENCY Unavailable
TIME ZONE GMT +2
INTERNATIONAL DIALING CODE 265

MALDIVES

GOVERNMENT Republic
LANGUAGES Maldivian Dhivehi, English
CURRENCY Rufiyaa = 100 laari
MEDICAL There is a high risk of sunburn all year round
TRAVEL Travel to the Maldives is generally trouble-free, but visitors should be aware that there are very harsh penalties for drug offences. Visitors should respect the Islamic religion and act accordingly
WEATHER Hot, tropical climate; May to Oct warm, but humid and wet from the southwest monsoon; Nov to Apr hot and dry
EMERGENCY Police 119; Fire 118; Ambulance 102
TIME ZONE GMT +5
INTERNATIONAL DIALING CODE 960

MADAGASCAR

GOVERNMENT Republic
LANGUAGES Malagasy and French (both official)
CURRENCY Malagasy franc = 100 centimes
MEDICAL There is a risk of polio, typhoid, bilharzia, cholera, rabies, and hepatitis. Precautions should be taken. Water is unsafe to drink and unpasteurized dairy products should be avoided
TRAVEL Locals are very welcoming and have a relaxed attitude toward time. Local culture should be respected
WEATHER Generally hot and subtropical with varying temperatures. Inland is more temperate, and the south is dry and arid
BANKING 0800–1300 Mon to Fri
EMERGENCY Unavailable
TIME ZONE GMT +3
INTERNATIONAL DIALING CODE 261

MALAYSIA

GOVERNMENT Federal constitutional monarchy
LANGUAGES Malay (official), Chinese, English
CURRENCY Ringgit (Malaysian dollar) = 100 cents
MEDICAL No vaccinations required, but visitors should be up-to-date with typhoid, tetanus, and hepatitis B. Also check malarial status of region
TRAVEL The penalty for all drug offences is harsh. There has been a recent increase in street crime in Kuala Lumpur
WEATHER Nov to Feb heavy rains in eastern areas; Apr to May and Oct thunderstorms in western areas; showers can occur all year round
BANKING 1000–1500 Mon to Fri
EMERGENCY All Services 999
TIME ZONE GMT +8
INTERNATIONAL DIALING CODE 60

MALTA

GOVERNMENT Multiparty republic
LANGUAGES Maltese and English (both official)
CURRENCY Euro = 100 cents
MEDICAL There are no specific health risks
TRAVEL Most visits are trouble-free and crime is rare. However, bag-snatching and pickpocketing can occur. Caution should be exercised when traveling by car since many roads are poorly maintained. Visitors should dress modestly when visiting churches
WEATHER Jul to Sep hot with cool breezes; Feb to Jun mild; occasional sudden bursts of rain
BANKING 0800–1200 Mon to Thu; 0800–1200 and 1430–1600 Fri; 0800–1130 Sat
EMERGENCY Police 191; Ambulance 196
TIME ZONE GMT +1
INTERNATIONAL DIALING CODE 356

MARTINIQUE

GOVERNMENT Overseas department of France
LANGUAGES French, French Creole patois, English
CURRENCY Euro = 100 cents
MEDICAL There is a risk of sunburn and intestinal parasites. Bilharzia (schistosomiasis) may be present in fresh water
TRAVEL Travel to Martinique is generally trouble-free
WEATHER Warm all year round; Sep can be very humid; Feb to May cooler and dry; Oct to Dec higher rainfall; upland areas are cooler than lowlands
BANKING 0800–1600 Mon to Fri
EMERGENCY Police 17; Fire/Ambulance 18
TIME ZONE GMT –4
INTERNATIONAL DIALING CODE 596

MEXICO

GOVERNMENT Federal republic
LANGUAGES Spanish (official)
CURRENCY Mexican peso = 100 centavos
MEDICAL Visitors should protect themselves against polio, tetanus, typhoid, and hepatitis A
TRAVEL Most visits are trouble-free, but visitors should remain aware of incidents of armed robbery in urban areas, particularly Mexico City, and should dress down accordingly
WEATHER May to Oct humid, rainy season; Oct to May warm and dry; lowland areas are warmer and upland areas are cooler all year round
BANKING 0900–1330 Mon to Fri
EMERGENCY All Services 08
TIME ZONE Spans three time zones from GMT –6 to –8
INTERNATIONAL DIALING CODE 52

MONTENEGRO

GOVERNMENT Republic
LANGUAGES Serbian
CURRENCY Euro = 100 cents
MEDICAL There are no specific health risks, but the health system suffers from widespread shortages of medicines and other essentials
TRAVEL Most visits to Montenegro are trouble free but sensible precautions should be taken. Visitors should be vigilant for pickpocketing in public places and on public transport.
WEATHER Montenegro has a continental climate; Nov to Mar very cold; Jun to Sep warm with colder conditions in the mountain regions
BANKING 0700–1500 Mon to Fri; 0800-1400 Sat
EMERGENCY Police 92; Fire 93; Ambulance 94
TIME ZONE GMT +1
INTERNATIONAL DIALING CODE 382

MAURITIUS

GOVERNMENT Multiparty democracy
LANGUAGES French (official), Creole, English
CURRENCY Mauritian rupee = 100 cents
MEDICAL Malaria exists in the northern rural areas and there is a risk of bilharzia
TRAVEL Visitors should always respect local customs and traditions. Most visits are trouble-free, crime levels are low, but sensible precautions should be taken
WEATHER The weather is warm with a year-round sea breeze. Jan to May are the best months to visit. Tropical storms are likely to occur from Dec to Mar
BANKING 0930–1430 Mon to Fri; 0930–1130 Sat
EMERGENCY Unavailable
TIME ZONE GMT +4
INTERNATIONAL DIALING CODE 230

MONGOLIA

GOVERNMENT Multiparty republic
LANGUAGES Khalkha Mongolian (official), Turkic, Russian
CURRENCY Tugrik = 100 möngös
MEDICAL Visitors should protect against brucellosis, cholera, and meningitis
TRAVEL Petty street crime is increasing. Visitors should avoid traveling alone after dark. In rural areas always carry a GPS and satellite phone
WEATHER May to Oct dry and mild; Nov to Apr bitterly cold. Note that between Oct and May sudden snowstorms can block roads and bring transport systems to a standstill
BANKING 1000–1500 Mon to Fri
EMERGENCY Unavailable
TIME ZONE GMT +9
INTERNATIONAL DIALING CODE 976

MOROCCO

GOVERNMENT Constitutional monarchy
LANGUAGES Arabic (official), Berber, French
CURRENCY Moroccan dirham = 100 centimes
MEDICAL There are no specific health risks, but malaria is present in northern coastal areas
TRAVEL Visits are usually trouble-free, but visitors should only use authorized guides. Theft is increasing in major cities and valuables should be hidden at all times
WEATHER Winter cool and wet in north; Oct to Apr warm to hot in lowlands; Dec to Mar very cold in upland areas
BANKING 0830–1130 and 1430–1700 Mon to Fri (winter); 0800–1530 Mon to Fri (summer)
EMERGENCY Police 19; Fire/Ambulance 15
TIME ZONE GMT
INTERNATIONAL DIALING CODE 212

NAMIBIA

GOVERNMENT Multiparty republic
LANGUAGES English (official), Afrikaans, German
CURRENCY Namibian dollar = 100 cents
MEDICAL Malaria and bilharzia are endemic in the north and east respectively
TRAVEL Most visits are trouble-free. The Angola border should be avoided because of land mines left undetected after the civil war. Visitors should seek advice before traveling to townships
WEATHER Oct to Apr rain inland; May to Oct hot and dry; the coast is cool and relatively free of rain all year round
BANKING 0900–1530 Mon to Fri
EMERGENCY Police 1011; Fire 2032270; Ambulance 2032276
TIME ZONE GMT +2
INTERNATIONAL DIALING CODE 264

NEPAL

GOVERNMENT Multiparty republic
LANGUAGES Nepali (official), local languages
CURRENCY Nepalese rupee = 100 paisa
MEDICAL There is a risk of altitude sickness, hepatitis A, malaria (in lowland areas), and typhoid
TRAVEL Trekkers are advised to use professional guides and should obtain up-to-date advice regarding the safety of their chosen route
WEATHER Oct to Nov clear and dry, and not too cold at higher altitudes; Dec to Jan cool; Feb to Apr warm; Jun to Sep monsoon season
BANKING 1000–1450 Sun to Thu; 1000–1230 Fri
EMERGENCY Unavailable
TIME ZONE GMT +5.45
INTERNATIONAL DIALING CODE 977

NETHERLANDS

GOVERNMENT Constitutional monarchy
LANGUAGES Dutch (official), Frisian
CURRENCY Euro = 100 cents
MEDICAL There are no specific health risks in the Netherlands
TRAVEL Most visits to the Netherlands are trouble-free. Attitudes here are very liberal. Locals are extremely welcoming and speak very good English
WEATHER Jun to Sep usually warm but changeable; Nov to Mar can be bitterly cold with some snow; rain falls all year round; Apr is best for daffodils and May is best for tulips
BANKING 0900–1600 Mon to Fri
EMERGENCY Emergency Services 112
TIME ZONE GMT +1
INTERNATIONAL DIALING CODE 31

NETHERLANDS ANTILLES

GOVERNMENT Parliamentary democracy
LANGUAGES Dutch (official), French, English, Spanish, many others
CURRENCY Netherlands Antillean gilder = 100 cents
MEDICAL Polio and typhoid vaccinations are recommended. Water is considered drinkable and normal precautions should be taken with food
TRAVEL Most visits to the Netherlands Antilles are trouble-free
WEATHER Hot and tropical climate with cool sea breezes
BANKING 0830–1530 Mon to Fri
EMERGENCY Police 599/5/22222; Ambulance 599/5/22111
TIME ZONE GMT –4
INTERNATIONAL DIALING CODE 599

NEW ZEALAND

GOVERNMENT Constitutional monarchy
LANGUAGES English and Maori (both official)
CURRENCY New Zealand dollar = 100 cents
MEDICAL There are no specific health risks
TRAVEL Most visits are trouble-free, but visitors should take precautions against street crime in urban areas after dark. Travel within the country is relatively cheap and efficient, and accommodation is varied and affordable
WEATHER Subtropical climate in North Island; no extremes of heat or cold, but Nov to Apr warmer; temperate in South Island with cool temperatures; rainfall occurs all year round
BANKING 0900–1630 Mon to Fri
EMERGENCY All Services 111
TIME ZONE GMT +12
INTERNATIONAL DIALING CODE 64

NIGERIA

GOVERNMENT Federal multiparty republic
LANGUAGES English (official), Hausa, Yoruba, Ibo
CURRENCY Naira = 100 kobo
MEDICAL Visitors must have a yellow fever vaccination and protect against cerebral malaria
TRAVEL Incidences of kidnapping are increasing. Violent street crime, armed robberies, and car theft are common throughout the country. Visitors should avoid using public transport and traveling after dark outside tourist areas
WEATHER Mar to Nov hot, humid and wet; Apr to Sep wet; Dec to Mar dusty winds, but cooler
BANKING 0800–1500 Mon; 0800–1330 Tue to Fri
EMERGENCY Unavailable
TIME ZONE GMT +1
INTERNATIONAL DIALING CODE 234

NORWAY

GOVERNMENT Constitutional monarchy
LANGUAGES Norwegian (official)
CURRENCY Norwegian krone = 100 ore
MEDICAL There are no specific health risks in Norway
TRAVEL Most visits to Norway remain trouble-free. The country offers beautiful mountain scenery and year-round skiing
WEATHER May to Sep sunny and warm with long daylight hours; Dec to Mar very cold and dark; midnight sun occurs from 13 May to 29 Jul, and from 28 May to 14 Jul in the Lofoten Islands
BANKING 0900–1700 Mon to Thu; 0900–1530 Fri
EMERGENCY Police (Oslo) 002; Ambulance 003
TIME ZONE GMT +1
INTERNATIONAL DIALING CODE 47

OMAN

GOVERNMENT Monarchy with consultative council
LANGUAGES Arabic (official), Baluchi, English
CURRENCY Omani rial = 100 baizas
MEDICAL Visitors should protect against malaria
TRAVEL Most visits to Oman are trouble-free, but visitors should remain informed of developments in the Middle East. There are harsh penalties, including the death penalty, for drug offences. Driving conditions are hazardous
WEATHER Jun to Sep very hot; Oct to Mar pleasant; the rest of the year is cooler
BANKING 0800–1200 Sat to Wed; 0800–1130 Thu
EMERGENCY All Services 999
TIME ZONE GMT +4
INTERNATIONAL DIALING CODE 698

PAKISTAN

GOVERNMENT Military regime
LANGUAGES Urdu (official), many others
CURRENCY Pakistan rupee = 100 paisa
MEDICAL Visitors should protect against dengue fever, hepatitis A, and malaria. There is also a risk of encephalitis in rural regions
TRAVEL Due to the threat from terrorism, most Western governments advise against all travel to Pakistan, except for their nationals of Pakistan origin
WEATHER Nov to Apr warm; Apr to Jul hot; Jul to Sep monsoon with high rainfall in upland areas
BANKING 0900–1300 and 1500–2000 Sun to Thu; closed on Fri. Some banks open on Sat
EMERGENCY Unavailable
TIME ZONE GMT +5
INTERNATIONAL DIALING CODE 92

PARAGUAY

GOVERNMENT Multiparty republic
LANGUAGES Spanish and Guaraní (both official)
CURRENCY Guaraní = 100 céntimos
MEDICAL There is a risk of cholera, hepatitis, hookworm, typhoid, malaria, and tuberculosis
TRAVEL Most visits to Paraguay are trouble-free, but there is economic recession and some political instability. Attractions include several national parks, including the Chaco – South America's great wilderness
WEATHER Subtropical climate; Dec to Mar is the hottest and wettest season, but rain falls all year round
BANKING 0845–1215 Mon to Fri
EMERGENCY All Services 00
TIME ZONE GMT +5
INTERNATIONAL DIALING CODE 595

PERU

GOVERNMENT Transitional republic
LANGUAGES Spanish and Quechua (both official), Aymara
CURRENCY New sol = 100 centavos
MEDICAL Visitors should protect against altitude sickness, cholera, typhoid, hepatitis, and malaria
TRAVEL Tourist areas are generally safe, but visitors should exercise caution, particularly in Lima and Cuzco, where crime has become a serious problem for foreign visitors
WEATHER Oct to Apr hot and dry in coastal areas, but much rainfall in highlands; May to Sep is dry and the best time to visit the highlands
BANKING 0930–1600 Mon to Fri
EMERGENCY All Services 011/5114
TIME ZONE GMT –5
INTERNATIONAL DIALING CODE 51

PHILIPPINES

GOVERNMENT Multiparty republic
LANGUAGES Filipino (Tagalog) and English (both official), Spanish, many others
CURRENCY Philippine peso = 100 centavos
MEDICAL Visitors should protect against cholera, malaria, rabies and hepatitis
TRAVEL Visitors should check developments before traveling. Bomb explosions and kidnapping by organized gangs or terrorists have occurred in Manila and Mindanao
WEATHER Tropical climate with sea breeze; Jun to Sep wet; Oct to Feb cool and dry; Mar to May hot and dry; Jun to Sep typhoons occur
BANKING 0900–1600 Mon to Fri
EMERGENCY Unavailable
TIME ZONE GMT +8
INTERNATIONAL DIALING CODE 63

POLAND

GOVERNMENT Multiparty republic
LANGUAGES Polish (official)
CURRENCY Zloty = 100 groszy
MEDICAL Medical care is generally poor, particularly in rural regions
TRAVEL Most visits to Poland are trouble-free, but there is a serious risk of robbery when using public transport. Locals are very hospitable and welcoming
WEATHER Temperate climate; May to Sep warm; Nov to Mar cold and dark; spring and fall are warm and pleasant; rain falls all year round
BANKING 0800–1800 Mon to Fri
EMERGENCY Police 997; Ambulance 999
TIME ZONE GMT +1
INTERNATIONAL DIALING CODE 48

PORTUGAL

GOVERNMENT Multiparty republic
LANGUAGES Portuguese (official)
CURRENCY Euro = 100 cents
MEDICAL Sunburn is a risk during summer
TRAVEL Most visits are trouble-free. Children under 18 years traveling to Portugal should be accompanied by parents/guardians, or someone in the country should be authorized to have responsibility for them
WEATHER Apr to Oct hot and sunny; Nov to Mar wetter, particularly in the north; summers are hotter and winters are longer in the north
BANKING 0830–1500 Mon to Fri
EMERGENCY Emergency Services 112; All Services 115
TIME ZONE GMT
INTERNATIONAL DIALING CODE 351

PUERTO RICO

GOVERNMENT Commonwealth of the United States
LANGUAGES Spanish and English (both official)
CURRENCY US dollar = 100 cents
MEDICAL There is a risk of sunburn and a slight risk of hepatitis and bilharzia
TRAVEL Most visits to Puerto Rico are trouble-free
WEATHER Tropical climate with little variation in temperature all year round; May to Nov hurricane season; cooler in upland regions
BANKING 0900–1430 Mon to Thu; 0900–1430 and 1530–1700 Fri
EMERGENCY Police 787 343 2020; Fire 787 343 2330; All Services 911
TIME ZONE GMT –4
INTERNATIONAL DIALING CODE 1 787

QATAR

GOVERNMENT Constitutional absolute monarchy
LANGUAGES Arabic (official), English,
CURRENCY Qatari riyal = 100 dirhams
MEDICAL There are no specific health risks
TRAVEL Visitors should keep informed of international developments before traveling. It is prohibited to bring drugs, alcohol, religious material, or pork products into the country; videos may be censored. Visitors should dress modestly and respect local customs
WEATHER Jun to Sep very hot and dry; Apr to May and Dec to Feb frequent sandstorms; Nov and Feb to Mar warm with little wind
BANKING 0730–1130 Sat to Thu
EMERGENCY All Services 999
TIME ZONE GMT +3
INTERNATIONAL DIALING CODE 974

RÉUNION

GOVERNMENT Overseas department of France
LANGUAGES French (official), Creole
CURRENCY Euro = 100 cents
MEDICAL Precautions should be taken against typhoid and rabies. Water is unsafe to drink and dairy products should be avoided as they are unpasteurized
TRAVEL Most trips to Réunion are trouble-free. Its society and culture are similar to Western Europe. Usual precautions should be taken
WEATHER Hot and tropical with cooler temperatures in the hills. Cool and dry from May to Nov; hot and wet from Dec to Apr
BANKING 0800–1600 Mon to Fri
EMERGENCY Police 17; Fire 18; Ambulance 15
TIME ZONE GMT +4
INTERNATIONAL DIALING CODE 262

ROMANIA

GOVERNMENT Multiparty republic
LANGUAGES Romanian (official), Hungarian
CURRENCY Leu = 100 bani
MEDICAL Visitors should protect against rabies, typhoid, and encephalitis
TRAVEL Petty theft is common in urban areas. It is illegal to exchange money on the street. Corruption is widespread. Roads are poorly maintained
WEATHER May to Oct warm, but coastal areas are cooled by sea breezes; Nov to Apr harsh winter with snow, but milder along the coast
BANKING 0900–1200 Mon to Fri; 1300–1500 Mon to Fri (currency exchange only)
EMERGENCY Police 955; Fire 981; Ambulance 96
TIME ZONE GMT +2
INTERNATIONAL DIALING CODE 40

RUSSIA

GOVERNMENT Federal multiparty republic
LANGUAGES Russian (official), many others
CURRENCY Russian ruble = 100 kopeks
MEDICAL Visitors should protect against diptheria, hepatitis A, typhoid, and encephalitis
TRAVEL Travel to the Chechen Republic and northern Caucasus is inadvisable. Visitors should keep all valuables out of sight
WEATHER Variable climate in north and central regions; Jul to Aug warm and wet; May to Jun and Sep to Oct dry; Nov to Apr very cold with snow
BANKING 0930–1730 Mon to Fri
EMERGENCY Police 02; Fire 01; Ambulance 03
TIME ZONE GMT +3 in Moscow and St Petersburg. Other areas vary
INTERNATIONAL DIALING CODE 7

ST KITTS & NEVIS

GOVERNMENT Constitutional monarchy
LANGUAGES English
CURRENCY East Caribbean dollar = 100 cents
MEDICAL Visitors should protect against mosquito bites as dengue fever is present. Water is untreated and is unsafe to drink
TRAVEL Most visits are trouble-free. The islands are now commercialized and tourists are welcomed. Usual precautions should be taken
WEATHER Hot and tropical with cooling sea breezes. There is little seasonal temperature variation. Hurricane season is Aug to Oct
BANKING 0800–1500 Mon to Thu; 0800-1500/1700 Fri; 0830–1100 Sat
EMERGENCY All Services 911
TIME ZONE GMT –4
INTERNATIONAL DIALING CODE 1 869

ST LUCIA

GOVERNMENT Parliamentary democracy
LANGUAGES English (official), French patois
CURRENCY East Caribbean dollar = 100 cents
MEDICAL Dengue fever is present; precautions should be taken against mosquito bites. Polio and typhoid vaccinations are recommended
TRAVEL Most trips to St Lucia are trouble-free, but sensible precautions should be taken. Beachwear should not be worn in towns
WEATHER Tropical climate moderated by trade winds. Temperatures are uniform at about 79°F [26°C]. St Lucia lies in the hurricane belt
BANKING 0800–1500 Mon to Thu; 0800–1700 Fri; 0800–1200 Sat
EMERGENCY All Services 999
TIME ZONE GMT –4
INTERNATIONAL DIALING CODE 1 758

ST VINCENT & THE GRENADINES

GOVERNMENT Parliamentary democracy
LANGUAGES English
CURRENCY East Caribbean dollar = 100 cents
MEDICAL Protection from polio, typhoid, and mosquito bites are recommended
TRAVEL Sensible precautions should be taken. There is a relaxed society and most visits are trouble-free. Excellent West Indian cuisine can be found on St Vincent
WEATHER Tropical climate with cooling trade winds. Hottest months are Jun and Jul. Tropical storms may occur from Jun to Nov
BANKING 0800–1500 Mon to Thu; 0800–1700 Fri
EMERGENCY All Services 999
TIME ZONE GMT –4
INTERNATIONAL DIALING CODE 1 809

SAMOA

GOVERNMENT Mix of parliamentary democracy and constitutional monarchy
LANGUAGES Samoan (Polynesian), English
CURRENCY Samoan dollar = 100 sene
MEDICAL Vaccination against polio and typhoid are recommended. Water is untreated and is unsafe to drink
TRAVEL Most visits are trouble-free, but traditional moral and religious codes are very important. Beachwear should not be worn outside resorts
WEATHER Tropical climate with cooler temperatures in the evenings. The rainy season is from Dec to Apr
BANKING 0900–1500 Mon to Fri; 0830–1130 Sat
EMERGENCY All services 999
TIME ZONE GMT –11
INTERNATIONAL DIALING CODE 685

SAUDI ARABIA

GOVERNMENT Absolute monarchy with consultative assembly
LANGUAGES Arabic (official)
CURRENCY Saudi riyal = 100 halalas
MEDICAL Cases of cerebral malaria have been reported in Jizan, southwest Saudi Arabia
TRAVEL Visitors should seek advice on recent developments. Islamic customs must be followed. Bombings have occurred in Riyadh and visitors should remain extremely vigilant
WEATHER Desert climate; extremely dry; May to Oct very hot; Nov to Feb mild
BANKING 0830–1200 and 1700–1900 Sat to Wed; 0830–1200 Thu
EMERGENCY Unavailable
TIME ZONE GMT +3
INTERNATIONAL DIALING CODE 966

SERBIA

GOVERNMENT Republic
LANGUAGES Serbian (official), Albanian
CURRENCY New dinar = 100 paras
MEDICAL The medical system is suffering from widespread shortages. Visitors should protect themselves against hepatitis and rabies.
TRAVEL The situation in Serbia is calm at present, though visitors should seek advice on developments before travelling. Travel to Kosovo is still inadvisable
WEATHER Serbia has a continental climate with a gradual transition between the four seasons. Nov to Mar very cold; Jun to Sep warm
BANKING 0700–1500 Mon to Fri; 0800-1400 Sat
EMERGENCY Police 92; Fire 93; Ambulance 94
TIME ZONE GMT +1
INTERNATIONAL DIALLING CODE 381

SEYCHELLES

GOVERNMENT Democratic republic
LANGUAGES English, French, French Creole
CURRENCY Seychelles rupee = 100 cents
MEDICAL There are no specific health risks
TRAVEL Crime is relatively rare, but incidents of theft do occur in tourist areas. Visitors, particularly women, should remain vigilant and avoid walking in quiet areas after dark. Roads often have sheer drops and no barriers
WEATHER Nov to Feb hot, humid monsoon; very warm temperatures all year round; May and Oct breezy at the start and finish of the trade winds
BANKING 0830–1430 Mon to Fri
EMERGENCY Unavailable
TIME ZONE GMT +4
INTERNATIONAL DIALLING CODE 248

SINGAPORE

GOVERNMENT Multiparty republic
LANGUAGES Chinese, Malay, Tamil and English (all official)
CURRENCY Singapore dollar = 100 cents
MEDICAL There are no specific health risks
TRAVEL The crime rate is very low in Singapore and most visits remain trouble-free. There are harsh penalties, including the death penalty, for all drug offences. Smoking is illegal in public places
WEATHER Hot and humid all year round; Nov to Jan cool with most rainfall
BANKING 1000–1500 Mon to Fri; 1100–1600 Sat
EMERGENCY All Services 999
TIME ZONE GMT +8
INTERNATIONAL DIALLING CODE 65

SLOVAK REPUBLIC

GOVERNMENT Multiparty republic
LANGUAGES Slovak (official), Hungarian
CURRENCY Slovak koruna = 100 halierov
MEDICAL There is risk from rabies and tick-borne encephalitis in forested areas during summer months
TRAVEL Pickpockets operate around the main tourist areas, and foreigners are easily identified and targeted. Sensible precautions should be taken
WEATHER A temperate climate with cold winters and mild summers
BANKING 0800–1700 Mon to Fri
EMERGENCY Fire 150; Ambulance 155; Police 15
TIME ZONE GMT +1 in winter; GMT +2 in summer
INTERNATIONAL DIALLING CODE 42

SLOVENIA

GOVERNMENT Multiparty republic
LANGUAGES Slovene (official), Serbo-Croatian
CURRENCY Tolar = 100 stotin
MEDICAL Summer visitors to forested areas should seek advice about protection against tick-borne encephalitis
TRAVEL Harsh fines are given for traffic offences and jaywalking. Passports and international driving licences should be carried at all times
WEATHER Continental climate inland; Jun to Sep warm; Nov to Mar cold; Mediterranean climate in coastal areas; Sep is the best time for hiking and climbing
BANKING 0800–1800 Mon to Fri
EMERGENCY Police 92; Fire 93; Ambulance 94
TIME ZONE GMT +1
INTERNATIONAL DIALLING CODE 386

SOUTH AFRICA

GOVERNMENT Multiparty republic
LANGUAGES Afrikaans, English, Ndebele, Pedi, Sotho, Swazi, Tsonga, Tswana, Venda, Xhosa and Zulu (all official)
CURRENCY Rand = 100 cents
MEDICAL There is a high incidence of HIV/AID Malaria is a risk in certain areas. Hygiene and water standards are high in tourist areas
TRAVEL Violent crime is high in the townships. There is a risk of car-jacking and armed robbery. Visitors should hide valuables and seek advice about which areas to avoid
WEATHER Generally warm and sunny all year
BANKING 0830–1530 Mon to Fri
EMERGENCY Police 1011; Ambulance 10222
TIME ZONE GMT +2
INTERNATIONAL DIALLING CODE 27

SPAIN

GOVERNMENT Constitutional monarchy
LANGUAGES Castilian Spanish (official), Catalan, Galician, Basque
CURRENCY Euro = 100 cents
MEDICAL There are no specific health risks in Spain
TRAVEL Most visits to Spain are trouble-free. The country is rich in arts and culture
WEATHER Temperate in north; Apr to Oct hot and dry, particularly in the south; central plateau can by very cold during winter
BANKING 0900–1400 Mon to Fri; 0900–1300 Sat (but not during summer)
EMERGENCY Police 091; Fire/Ambulance 085; Emergency Services 112
TIME ZONE GMT +1
INTERNATIONAL DIALING CODE 34

SWEDEN

GOVERNMENT Constitutional monarchy
LANGUAGES Swedish (official), Finnish, Sami
CURRENCY Swedish krona = 100 öre
MEDICAL There are no specific health risks
TRAVEL Most visits to Sweden are generally trouble-free. Since devaluation of the Swedish currency, the country has become considerably more affordable
WEATHER May to Jul hot and dry, but Aug can be wet; the midnight sun can be seen from May to Jun above the Arctic Circle; Nov to Apr extremely cold, particularly in the north
BANKING 0930–1500 Mon to Fri
EMERGENCY Emergency Services 112; All Services 90 000/112
TIME ZONE GMT +1
INTERNATIONAL DIALING CODE 46

SYRIA

GOVERNMENT Multiparty republic
LANGUAGES Arabic (official), Kurdish, Armenian
CURRENCY Syrian pound = 100 piastres
MEDICAL Visitors should vaccinate against polio, hepatitis A and B, and tetanus
TRAVEL Visitors should keep informed of developments in the Middle East. They should dress modestly and avoid driving out of main cities at night. Harsh penalties exist for drug offences
WEATHER Apr to Jun mild and dry; Jun to Sep hot; Dec to Mar very cold, particularly in coastal and upland regions
BANKING 0800–1400 Sat and Thu
EMERGENCY Contact hotel operator
TIME ZONE GMT +2
INTERNATIONAL DIALING CODE 963

SRI LANKA

GOVERNMENT Multiparty republic
LANGUAGES Sinhala and Tamil (both official)
CURRENCY Sri Lankan rupee = 100 cents
MEDICAL There is a risk of cholera and malaria. Rabies is widespread
TRAVEL The northern region and the eastern coast remain heavily mined. A cease-fire between the Tamil Tigers and the government was signed in February 2002
WEATHER Tropical climate; May to Jul and Dec to Jan monsoon seasons; coastal regions are cool due to sea breezes
BANKING 0900–1300 Mon to Sat; 0900–1500 Tue to Fri
EMERGENCY All Services 1 691095/699935
TIME ZONE GMT +5.30
INTERNATIONAL DIALING CODE 94

SWITZERLAND

GOVERNMENT Federal republic
LANGUAGES French, German, Italian and Romansch (all official)
CURRENCY Swiss franc = 100 centimes
MEDICAL There is a risk of altitude sickness, sunburn and hypothermia in the Alps
TRAVEL Most visits to Switzerland remain trouble-free
WEATHER Climate varies from region to region; Alpine regions have lower temperatures; Jun to Sep warm and sunny; Nov to Apr cold with snow which starts to melt in Apr
BANKING 0830–1630 Mon to Fri
EMERGENCY Police 117; Fire 118; Ambulance 144
TIME ZONE GMT +1
INTERNATIONAL DIALING CODE 41

TAIWAN

GOVERNMENT Unitary multiparty republic
LANGUAGES Mandarin Chinese (official)
CURRENCY New Taiwan dollar = 100 cents
MEDICAL There are no specific health risks, but visitors should be vaccinated against hepatitis
TRAVEL Most visits to Taiwan are trouble-free. Petty crime exists, but is not common. Some roads in central and southern areas may still be blocked by landslides following the 1999 earthquake
WEATHER Subtropical climate with moderate temperatures in the north; Jun to Sep very hot and humid; Jun to Oct typhoon season
BANKING 0900–1530 Mon to Fri; 0900–1230 Sat
EMERGENCY Police 110
TIME ZONE GMT +8
INTERNATIONAL DIALING CODE 886

TANZANIA

GOVERNMENT Multiparty republic
LANGUAGES Swahili and English (both official)
CURRENCY Tanzanian shilling = 100 cents
MEDICAL There is a risk of yellow fever, malaria, cholera, and hepatitis. AIDS is widespread
TRAVEL Most visits are trouble-free, but crime does occur, particularly on public transport and in tourist areas. There are increased risks in Zanzibar where bomb explosions have occurred
WEATHER Tropical climate; Mar to May rainy season in coastal areas; Jan to Feb hot and dry; Nov to Dec and Feb to May rainy season in highland areas
BANKING 0830–1600 Mon to Fri
EMERGENCY Unavailable
TIME ZONE GMT +3
INTERNATIONAL DIALING CODE 255

TRINIDAD & TOBAGO

GOVERNMENT Parliamentary democracy
LANGUAGES English (official), Spanish
CURRENCY Trinidad & Tobago dollar = 100 cents
MEDICAL Dengue fever has become a problem in recent years. Medical facilities are basic and limited
TRAVEL While most visits are trouble-free, attacks on travelers are on the increase. Visitors should remain vigilant and alert at all times, and take sensible precautions
WEATHER Tropical climate with cooling trade winds. Hottest and wettest time is Jun to Nov
BANKING 0900–1400 Mon to Thu; 0900–1200 and 1500–1700 Fri
EMERGENCY Police 999; Ambulance/Fire 990
TIME ZONE GMT –4
INTERNATIONAL DIALING CODE 1 868

TURKEY

GOVERNMENT Multiparty republic
LANGUAGES Turkish (official), Kurdish, Arabic
CURRENCY New Turkish lira = 100 kurus
MEDICAL Contagious diseases are increasing and visitors should keep inoculations up-to-date
TRAVEL Most visits are trouble-free, but visitors should exercise caution, particularly in the tourist areas of Istanbul where street robbery is common, and seek recent advice before traveling
WEATHER Mediterranean climate; summers are hot and winters are mild
BANKING 0830–1200 and 1300–1700 Mon to Fri
EMERGENCY Police 155; Fire 111; Ambulance 112
TIME ZONE GMT +2
INTERNATIONAL DIALING CODE 90

THAILAND

GOVERNMENT Constitutional monarchy
LANGUAGES Thai (official), English, local dialects
CURRENCY Baht = 100 satang
MEDICAL Visitors should protect against malaria dengue fever, AIDS, and cholera
TRAVEL Harsh penalties exist for drug offences. Tourists should use licensed taxis with yellow number plates. Visitors should seek advice before traveling to border areas with Burma or Cambodia. Riptides occur off the coast of Phuket
WEATHER Jun to Oct hot and rainy monsoon; Nov to Feb dry and pleasant; Mar to May hot; temperatures are more consistent in the south
BANKING 0830–1530 Mon to Fri
EMERGENCY Unavailable
TIME ZONE GMT +7
INTERNATIONAL DIALING CODE 66

TUNISIA

GOVERNMENT Multiparty republic
LANGUAGES Arabic (official), French
CURRENCY Tunisian dinar = 1,000 millimes
MEDICAL There is a risk of yellow fever and malaria
TRAVEL Travel to Tunisia is generally trouble-free but visitors to southern desert areas and to areas close to the Algerian border should exercise caution. Tunisian laws and customs should be respected. Drug offences carry harsh penalties
WEATHER Jun to Aug hot and humid; Jan to Feb cooler; hotter inland; higher rainfall in winter
BANKING 0830–1200 and 1300–1700 Mon to Fri
EMERGENCY Unavailable
TIME ZONE GMT +1
INTERNATIONAL DIALING CODE 216

UGANDA

GOVERNMENT Republic in transition
LANGUAGES English and Swahili (both official)
CURRENCY Ugandan shilling = 100 cents
MEDICAL There is a risk of AIDS, yellow fever, and malaria
TRAVEL Most visits to Uganda are trouble-free, but visitors should seek recent advice before traveling. It is inadvisable to travel to areas bordering the Democratic Republic of the Congo or Sudan, and visitors should remain cautious if traveling to areas bordering Rwanda
WEATHER Dec to Feb and Jun to Aug hot and dry; Mar to May and Oct to Nov heavy rain
BANKING 0830–1400 Mon to Fri
EMERGENCY Unavailable
TIME ZONE GMT +3
INTERNATIONAL DIALING CODE 256

UKRAINE

GOVERNMENT Multiparty republic
LANGUAGES Ukrainian (official), Russian
CURRENCY Hryvnia = 100 kopiykas
MEDICAL There is a risk of diptheria in western Ukraine. Tick-borne encephalitis is common in forested areas. Do not drink tap water without first boiling it
TRAVEL Crime in the Ukraine remains low, but visitors should remain vigilant and keep valuables out of sight, particularly in crowded areas where pickpocketing and bag-snatching can occur
WEATHER Jun to Aug warm; Oct to Nov sunny but cold; Dec to Mar cold with snowfall
BANKING 0900–1600 Mon to Fri
EMERGENCY Unavailable
TIME ZONE GMT +2
INTERNATIONAL DIALING CODE 380

UNITED ARAB EMIRATES

GOVERNMENT Federation of seven emirates, each with its own government
LANGUAGES Arabic (official), English
CURRENCY Dirham = 100 fils
MEDICAL There is a risk of hepatitis A and B
TRAVEL Visitors should remain informed of recent international developments before traveling. They should dress modestly and respect local customs. Penalties for all drug offences are harsh and can include the death penalty
WEATHER Jun to Sep very hot and dry; Oct to May cooler and is the best time to visit
BANKING 0800–1200 Sat to Wed and 0800–1100 Thu
EMERGENCY All Services 344 663
TIME ZONE GMT +4
INTERNATIONAL DIALING CODE 971

UNITED KINGDOM

GOVERNMENT Constitutional monarchy
LANGUAGES English (official), Welsh, Gaelic
CURRENCY Pound sterling = 100 pence
MEDICAL No vaccinations are required in the UK and citizens of all EU countries are entitled to free medical treatment at National Health Service hospitals
TRAVEL Most visits are trouble-free, but visitors should exercise caution in urban areas after dark
WEATHER May to Aug warm and wet; Sep to Apr mild and wet
BANKING 0900–1730 Mon to Fri. Some bank branches open on Saturday mornings
EMERGENCY Police/Fire/Ambulance 999; Emergency Services 112
TIME ZONE GMT
INTERNATIONAL DIALING CODE 44

UNITED STATES OF AMERICA

GOVERNMENT Federal republic
LANGUAGES English (official), Spanish, more than 30 others
CURRENCY US dollar = 100 cents
MEDICAL There are no specific health risks, but medical treatment is expensive
TRAVEL Most visits to the USA are trouble-free, but visitors should remain vigilant and avoid wearing valuable jewelry or walking through isolated urban areas after dark
WEATHER Varies considerably; check climate before traveling
BANKING 0900–1500 Mon to Fri
EMERGENCY Emergency Services 911
TIME ZONE USA has six time zones from GMT –5 on East coast to –10 in Hawai'i
INTERNATIONAL DIALING CODE 1

URUGUAY

GOVERNMENT Multiparty republic
LANGUAGES Spanish (official)
CURRENCY Uruguayan peso = 100 centésimos
MEDICAL There are no specific health risks, but medical treatment can be expensive
TRAVEL Most visits to Uruguay are trouble-free, but street crime exists in urban areas, including Montevideo. It is, however, less common than in other Latin American countries
WEATHER Dec to Mar hot, but nights can be cool; Apr to Nov mild
BANKING 1330–1730 Mon to Fri (summer); 1300–1700 Mon to Fri (winter)
EMERGENCY Police 109; Fire 104; Ambulance 105; All Services 999
TIME ZONE GMT –3
INTERNATIONAL DIALING CODE 598

VENEZUELA

GOVERNMENT Federal republic
LANGUAGES Spanish (official), local dialects
CURRENCY Bolívar = 100 céntimos
MEDICAL There is a risk of yellow fever, cholera, dengue fever, and hepatitis
TRAVEL The incidence of violent crime is high and the political situation is volatile. Visitors should take precautions. Terrorist and narcotic gangs are active in areas bordering Colombia, where there is the risk of kidnapping
WEATHER May to Dec rainy season; Jan to Apr pleasant temperatures
BANKING 0830–1130 and 1400–1630 Mon to Fri
EMERGENCY Doctor 02 483 7021; Ambulance 02 545 4545
TIME ZONE GMT –4
INTERNATIONAL DIALING CODE 58

VIETNAM

GOVERNMENT Socialist republic
LANGUAGES Vietnamese (official), English, Chinese
CURRENCY Dong = 10 hao = 100 xu
MEDICAL Malaria, dengue fever, and encephalitis are common throughout the country. Visitors should avoid mosquito bites. Typhoid is common in the Mekong Delta
TRAVEL Take care if traveling in border areas. Unexploded mines and bombs still exist in certain areas. Drug smuggling carries the death penalty. Serious flooding can occur in central areas
WEATHER May to Oct tropical monsoons; Nov to Apr hot and dry
BANKING 0800–1630 Mon to Fri
EMERGENCY Police 13; Fire 14; Ambulance 15
TIME ZONE GMT +7
INTERNATIONAL DIALING CODE 84

VIRGIN ISLANDS, BRITISH

GOVERNMENT UK overseas territory
LANGUAGES English (official)
CURRENCY US dollar = 100 cents
MEDICAL Medical facilities are limited. Precautions should be taken against polio, typhoid and dengue fever
TRAVEL There is a low crime rate, but sensible precautions should be taken. Backpacking is discouraged throughout the 60 islands
WEATHER Subtropical and humid climate moderated by trade winds. Hurricanes are a risk from Jul to Oct
BANKING 0900–1500 Mon to Thu; 0900–1700 Fri
EMERGENCY Police 114; Ambulance 112
TIME ZONE GMT –4
INTERNATIONAL DIALING CODE 1 284

VIRGIN ISLANDS, US

GOVERNMENT US overseas territory
LANGUAGES English, Spanish, French, Creole
CURRENCY US dollar = 100 cents
MEDICAL Visitors should protect against typhoid and polio. Water is generally considered drinkable
TRAVEL Most visit are trouble-free and normal precautions should be taken. There is a large selection of hotel accommodation available
WEATHER Hot climate with cool winds. Low humidity with little seasonal temperature variation. The rainy season is Sep to Nov
BANKING 0900–1430 Mon to Thu; 0900–1400 and 1530–1700 Fri
EMERGENCY All services 911
TIME ZONE GMT –4
INTERNATIONAL DIALING CODE 1 340

YEMEN

GOVERNMENT Multiparty republic
LANGUAGES Arabic (official)
CURRENCY Yemeni rial = 100 fils
MEDICAL Visitors should protect against hepatitis A and B
TRAVEL Most governments currently strongly advise against travel to Yemen. Random armed kidnapping is common, and foreigners remain targets for crime and terrorism
WEATHER Varies with altitude; Oct to Mar nights can be very cold in upland regions; Apr to Sep very hot; Oct to Apr cool, dry and dusty
BANKING 0800–1200 Sat to Wed; 0800–1100 Thu. Closed on Fridays
EMERGENCY Unavailable
TIME ZONE GMT +3
INTERNATIONAL DIALING CODE 967

ZAMBIA

GOVERNMENT Multiparty republic
LANGUAGES English (official), Bemba, Nyanja
CURRENCY Zambian kwacha = 100 ngwee
MEDICAL Outbreaks of cholera and dysentery are common. Malaria is endemic, and cases of AIDS and tuberculosis are very high
TRAVEL Visitors should avoid traveling to areas bordering Angola and the Democratic Republic of the Congo. Armed robbery, bag-snatching and mugging are increasing, particularly in downtown areas. Keep valuables out of sight
WEATHER May to Sep very cool and dry; Oct to Nov hot and dry; Dec to Apr hot and wet
BANKING 0815–1430 Mon to Fri
EMERGENCY All Services 1 2 25067/254798
TIME ZONE GMT +2
INTERNATIONAL DIALING CODE 260

ZIMBABWE

GOVERNMENT Multiparty republic
LANGUAGES English (official), Shona, Ndebele
CURRENCY Zimbabwean dollar = 100 cents
MEDICAL There is a risk of bilharzia, cholera, malaria, yellow fever, and rabies. Incidences of HIV/AIDS are very high
TRAVEL There is currently political and social unrest throughout the country, in both rural and urban areas. Visitors should exercise caution and avoid large crowds and demonstrations
WEATHER May to Oct warm and dry, but cold at night; Nov to Apr wet and hot
BANKING 0800–1500 Mon, Tue, Thu and Fri. 0800–1300 Wed and 0800–1130 Sat
EMERGENCY Police 995; Ambulance 994
TIME ZONE GMT +2
INTERNATIONAL DIALING CODE 263

WORLD MAPS – GENERAL REFERENCE

Settlements

Capital cities have red infills

Settlement symbols and type styles vary according to the scale of each map and indicate the importance of towns rather than specific population figures.

PACIFIC OCEAN
ARCTIC OCEAN
ATLANTIC OCEAN
North America
Asia
Europe
RUSSIA
CHINA
INDIA
UNITED STATES
CANADA
MEXICO
GREENLAND (Denmark)
ICELAND
JAPAN
Tokyo
Osaka
Seoul
Pyongyang
Beijing
Tianjin
Shenyang
Ulan Bator
Shanghai
Wuhan
Hong Kong
Xi'an
Chongqing
Hanoi
Bangkok
Rangoon
Dhaka
Kolkata (Calcutta)
Chennai (Madras)
Colombo
Mumbai (Bombay)
Bangalore
Hyderabad
New Delhi
Islamabad
Lahore
Kabul
Kandahar
Karachi
Tehran
Baghdad
Muscat
Riyadh
Tashkent
Astana
Moscow
St. Petersburg
Kyiv
Warsaw
Berlin
Paris
London
Madrid
Rome
Athens
Cairo
Jerusalem
Beirut
Ankara
Tunis
Algiers
Rabat
Casablanca
Lisbon
Gibraltar
Reykjavik
Nuuk
Oslo
Copenhagen
Stockholm
Helsinki
Vancouver
Seattle
San Francisco
Los Angeles
San Diego
Phoenix
Dallas
Houston
Chicago
Detroit
Toronto
Ottawa
Montreal
New York
Boston
Philadelphia
Washington
Atlanta
Miami
Havana
Kingston
Santo Domingo
Caracas
Bogotá
Quito
Medellín
Lima
Port of Spain
Guatemala
Guadalajara
Monterrey
Mexico City
Anchorage
Alaska (USA)
Arctic Circle
North Pole
Magnetic Pole
Tropic of Cancer
Equator
PROJECTION CENTRED ON LONDON

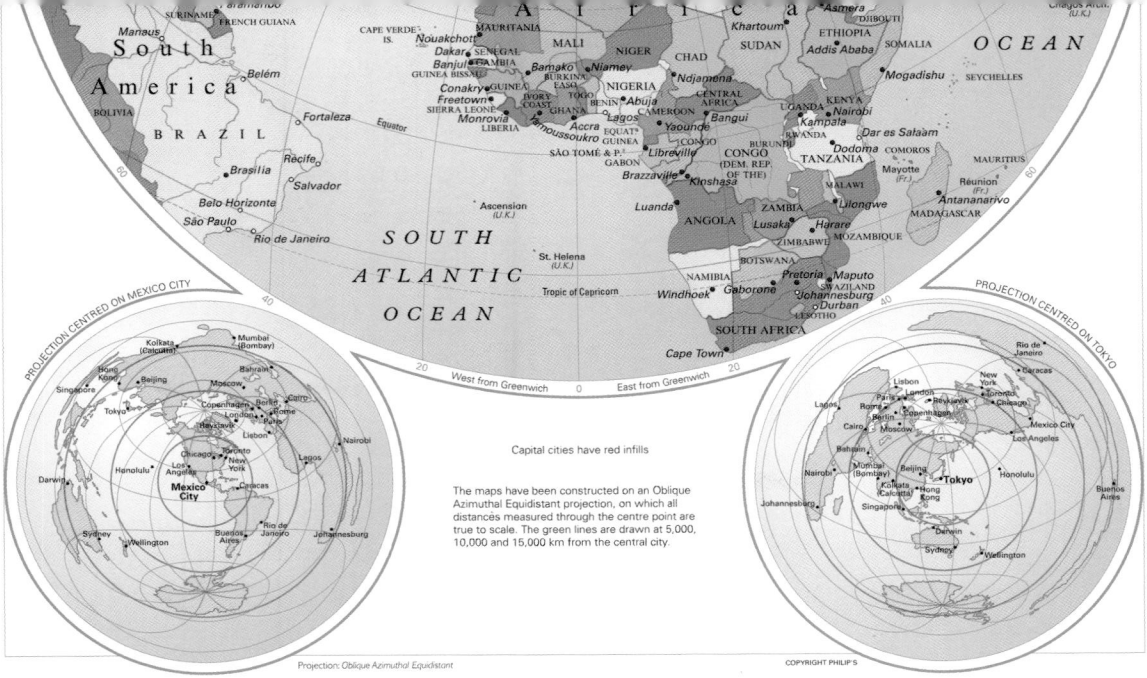

Capital cities have red infills

The maps have been constructed on an Oblique Azimuthal Equidistant projection, on which all distances measured through the centre point are true to scale. The green lines are drawn at 5,000, 10,000 and 15,000 km from the central city.

Projection: *Oblique Azimuthal Equidistant*

COPYRIGHT PHILIP'S

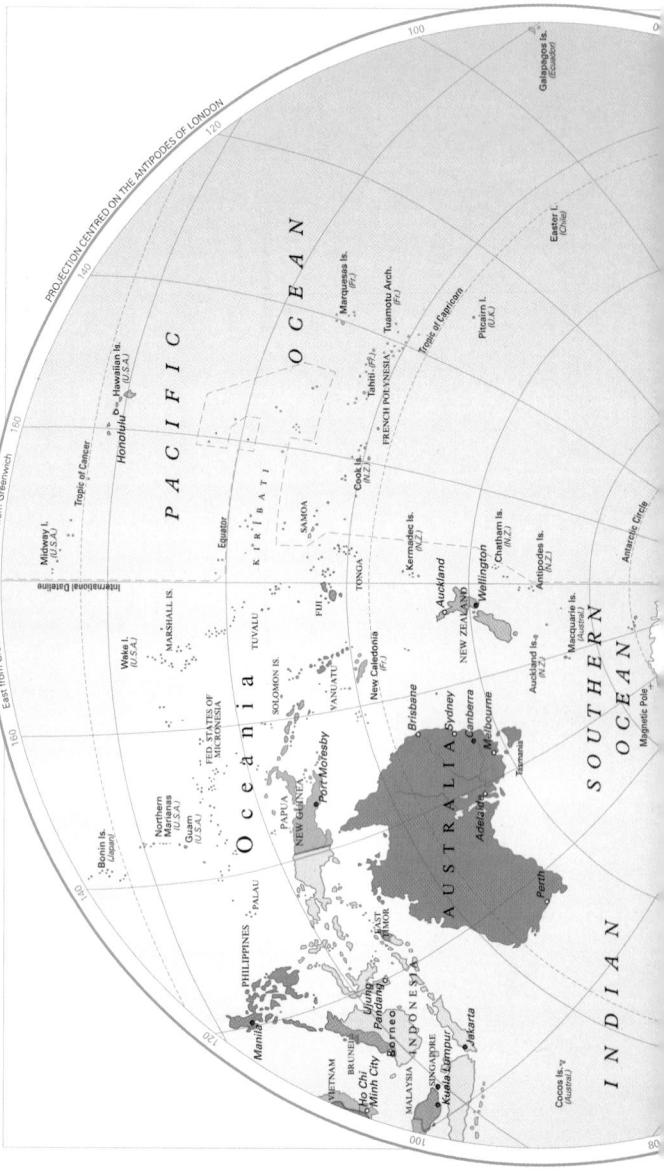
PROJECTION CENTRED ON THE ANTIPODES OF LONDON
East from Greenwich
West from Greenwich
International Dateline
Tropic of Cancer
Equator
Tropic of Capricorn
Antarctic Circle
Magnetic Pole
PACIFIC OCEAN
INDIAN OCEAN
SOUTHERN OCEAN
Oceania
AUSTRALIA
Honolulu
Hawaiian Is. (U.S.A.)
Midway I. (U.S.A.)
Wake I. (U.S.A.)
MARSHALL IS.
KIRIBATI
TUVALU
SAMOA
TONGA
FIJI
Cook Is. (N.Z.)
Tahiti (Fr.)
FRENCH POLYNESIA
Marquesas Is. (Fr.)
Tuamotu Arch. (Fr.)
Pitcairn I. (U.K.)
Easter I. (Chile)
Galapagos Is. (Ecuador)
Kermadec Is. (N.Z.)
Chatham Is. (N.Z.)
Antipodes Is. (N.Z.)
Macquarie Is. (Australia)
Auckland Is. (N.Z.)
Auckland
Wellington
NEW ZEALAND
Tasmania
Cocos Is. (Australia)
Bonin Is. (Japan)
Northern Mariana Is. (U.S.A.)
Guam (U.S.A.)
FED. STATES OF MICRONESIA
PALAU
PHILIPPINES
Manila
SOLOMON IS.
VANUATU
New Caledonia (Fr.)
PAPUA NEW GUINEA
Port Moresby
EAST TIMOR
BRUNEI
Bandar Seri Begawan
Bintulu
Kuching
Sandakan
Borneo
INDONESIA
Jakarta
MALAYSIA
Kuala Lumpur
SINGAPORE
VIETNAM
Ho Chi Minh City
Brisbane
Sydney
Canberra
Melbourne
Adelaide
Perth
160
140
120
100
80
180
160
140
120
100
0

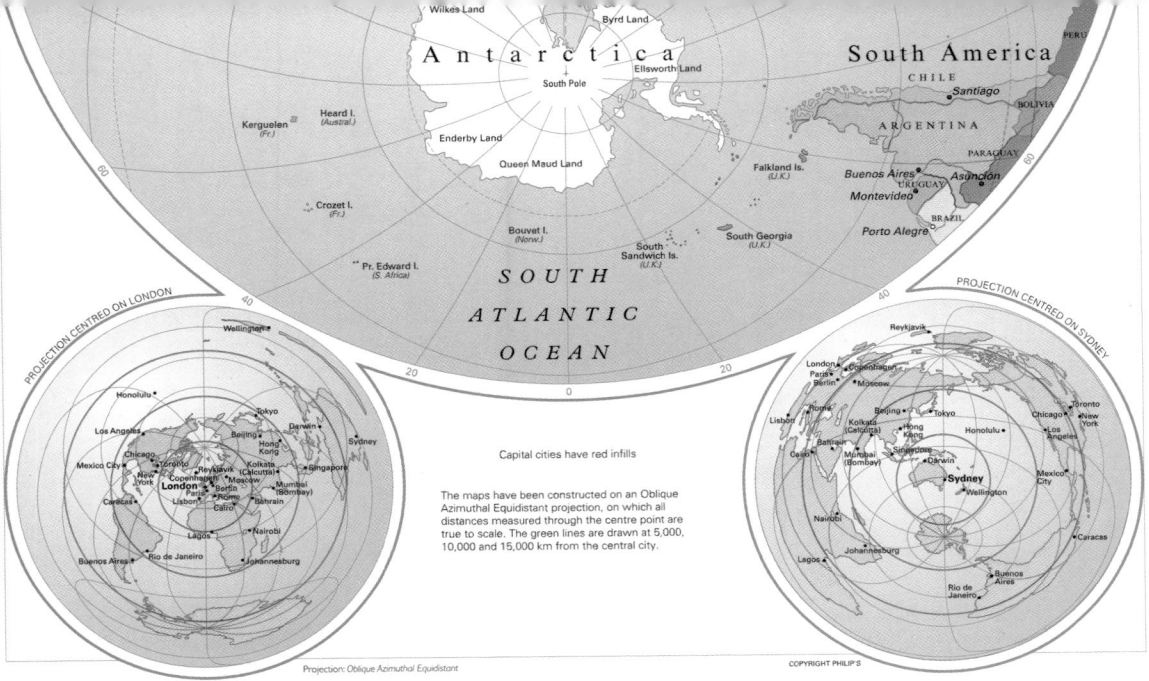

Capital cities have red infills

The maps have been constructed on an Oblique Azimuthal Equidistant projection, on which all distances measured through the centre point are true to scale. The green lines are drawn at 5,000, 10,000 and 15,000 km from the central city.

Projection: *Oblique Azimuthal Equidistant*

COPYRIGHT PHILIP'S

6 EUROPE

ICELAND
Reykjavik
Arctic Circle
Norwegian Sea
Faroe Is. (Den.)
Shetland Is.
Orkney Is.
Hebrides
ATLANTIC OCEAN
UNITED KINGDOM
SCOTLAND
Aberdeen
Glasgow
Dundee
Edinburgh
N. IRELAND
Belfast
IRELAND
Dublin
Cork
Manchester
Liverpool
Newcastle-upon-Tyne
Leeds
Sheffield
Birmingham
WALES
Cardiff
ENGLAND
LONDON
Bristol
Southampton
Plymouth
English Channel
Channel Is.
Le Havre
Brest
Rouen
PARIS
Seine
Amsterdam
The Hague
Rotterdam
Antwerp
NETHERLANDS
BELGIUM
Brussels
Lille
Luxembourg
Essen
Dortmund
Cologne
Bonn
Frankfurt am Main
Nuremberg
Rhine
GERMANY
Hamburg
Kiel
Bremen
Hannover
Magdeburg
Berlin
Leipzig
Halle
Chemnitz
Dresden
Prague
CZECH REP.
Ostrava
Katowice
Szczecin
Gdańsk
Bydgoszcz
Poznań
Łódź
Wrocław
Oder
POL
FRANCE
Nantes
Loire
Bay of Biscay
Gironde
Limoges
Dijon
Strasbourg
Stuttgart
Munich
Zurich
LIECH.
SWITZERLAND
Geneva
Lyons
St-Etienne
Bordeaux
Garonne
Toulouse
Grenoble
Milan
Turin
Venice
Trieste
Genoa
Bologna
Nice
MONACO
Marseilles
Toulon
Florence
SAN MARINO
Rome
Naples
Bari
Taranto
Vienna
Linz
Salzburg
Innsbruck
Graz
AUSTRIA
Budapest
HUN
Ljubljana
SLOVENIA
Zagreb
CROATIA
BOSNIA-HERZ.
Sarajevo
MONTENEGRO
Podgorica
Adriatic Sea
ITALY
Corsica
Ajaccio
Sardinia
Cagliari
Tyrrhenian Sea
Palermo
Messina
Sicily
Catania
Ionia Sea
Malta
Valletta
Pantelleria (Italy)
Tunis
TUNISIA
Oslo
Bergen
Stavanger
Trondheim
Tromsø
Norway
Skagerrak
Kattegat
Aalborg
Aarhus
Copenhagen
Malmö
Gothenburg
Jönköping
Uppsala
Stockholm
Örebro
Vättern
Vänern
Gotland
Gdańsk
Baltic Sea
Lisbon
Tagus
PORTUGAL
Porto
Douro
La Coruña
Vigo
Bilbao
Valladolid
Madrid
Guadiana
SPAIN
Zaragoza
Barcelona
Ebro
Valencia
Alicante
Murcia
Balearic Is.
Palma
Minorca
Ibiza
Majorca
Seville
Guadalquivir
Córdoba
Granada
Málaga
Cádiz
Gibraltar (U.K.)
Str. of Gibraltar
Tangier
Ceuta
Melilla
Mediterranean Sea
Algiers
Annaba
Constantine
ALGERIA
MOROCCO
Africa
Projection: Bonne
West from Greenwich
East from Greenwich
m ft
0 200 1000 2000 4000
0 600 3000 6000 12 000
LONDON Capital Cities

7
100 0 100 200 300 400 500 600 700 800 km
100 0 100 200 300 400 500 miles
Murmansk
White Sea
Arkhangelsk
KOMI
Ob
KARELIA
N. Dvina
FINLAND
Kotlas
Perm
Nizhny Tagil
Yekaterinburg
L. Onega
Vyborg
L. Ladoga
Kirov
Turku
Helsinki
Velogda
Cheboksary
ST. PETERSBURG
Rybinsk Res.
Kostroma
UDMURTIA
Ufa
Tallinn
ESTONIA
L. Chudskoye
Yaroslavl
Ivanovo
Nizhny Novgorod
MARI EL
Kazan
TATARSTAN
BASHKORTOSTAN
Magnitogorsk
CHUVASHIA
LATVIA
Riga
MOSCOW
Saransk
Samara
Orenburg
MORDVINIA
Penza
Volga
Vitebsk
W. Dvina
Tula
Uralsk
LITHUANIA
Kaunas
Smolensk
Vilnius
Mahilyow
Tambov
Orel
Saratov
Minsk
BELARUS
Gomel
Voronezh
Kursk
KAZAKHSTAN
Ural
Atyrau
Brest
Pripet
Chernihiv
Warsaw
Lublin
Volgograd
Kharkov
Kiev
Dnieper
Zhytomyr
Lviv
UKRAINE
Donetsk
Don
Astrakhan
Taganrog
Rostov
Dnepropetrovsk
Dniester
Zaporozhye
Krivoy Rog
Kherson
KALMYKIA
Caspian Sea
Debrecen
MOLDOVA
Nikolayev
Odessa
Stavropol
NORTH OSSETIA
CHECHNIA
Makhachkala
Cluj-Napoca
Kishinev
CRIMEA
Krasnodar
Maykop
ROMANIA
Timisoara
Galati
Brasov
Ploiesti
Sevastopol
KARACHAI-CHERKESSIA
KABARDINO-BALKARIA
NORTH OSSETIA
DAGESTAN
GEORGIA
Tbilisi
Baku
Black Sea
Bucharest
Constanta
Varna
Danube
AZERBAIJAN
ARMENIA
Yerevan
Sofia
Pristina
Samsun
Erzerum
Tabriz
BULGARIA
Plovdiv
Bosporus
Skopje
ISTANBUL
Thessaloniki
Bursa
Ankara
Kayseri
Diyarbakir
IRAN
GREECE
Izmir
Konya
Adana
Patra
Athens
Antalya
Aleppo
Euphrates
IRAQ
Tigris
SYRIA
Baghdad
CYPRUS
Nicosia
Rhodes
Crete
COPYRIGHT PHILIP'S

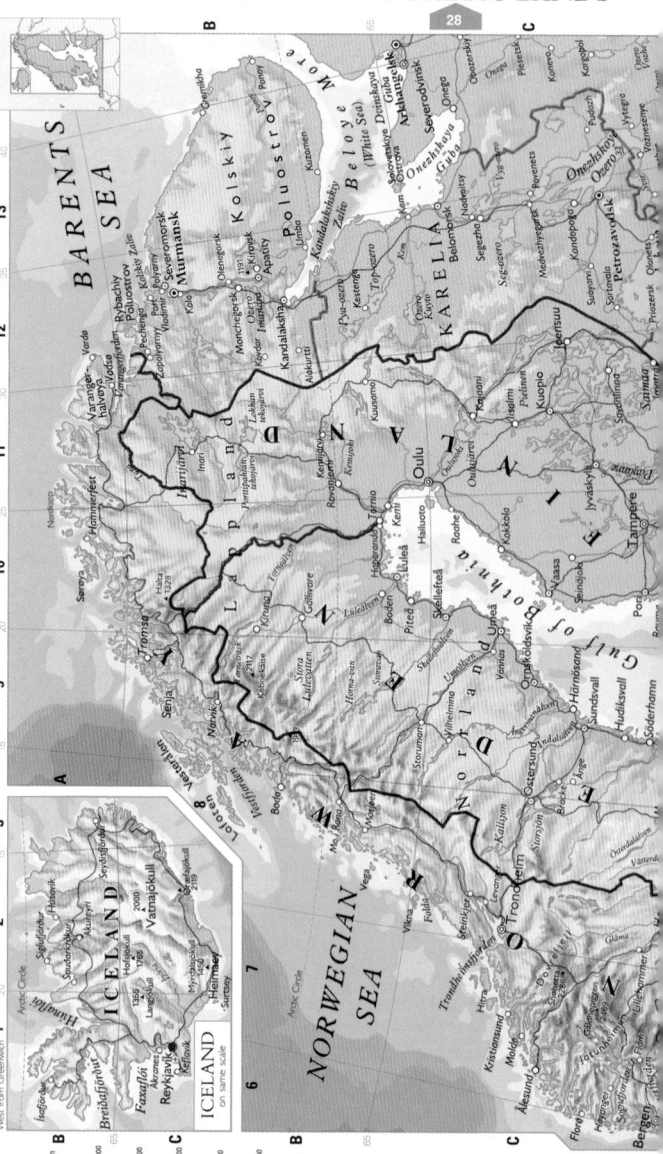
BARENTS SEA
NORWEGIAN SEA
White Sea (Beloye More)
Gulf of Bothnia
Murmansk
Kolskiy Poluostrov
Kandalakshskiy Zaliv
Belomorsk
Kem
Solovetskie Ostrova
Onezhskoye Ozero
Onezhskaya Guba
Petrozavodsk
Severodvinsk
Arkhangel'sk
Kirovsk
Apatity
Monchegorsk
Kandalaksha
Kuusamo
Oulu
Kajaani
Joensuu
Kuopio
Jyväskylä
Tampere
Pori
Vaasa
Kokkola
Rovaniemi
Kemi
Tornio
Luleå
Piteå
Skellefteå
Umeå
Hudiksvall
Sundsvall
Hämösand
Söderhamn
Kristiansand
Bergen
Ålesund
Molde
Kristiansund
Trondheim
Narvik
Tromsø
Hammerfest
Murmansk
Vardø
Nordkapp
Lofoten
Vesterålen
Lofoten
Arctic Circle
West from Greenwich
ICELAND
on same scale
Reykjavík
Akureyri
Vatnajökull
Hofsjökull
Langjökull
Myrdalsjökull
Heimaey
Surtsey
Þjórsá
Vatnajökull
Myrdalsjökull
Hofsjökull
Langjökull

24
Gulf of Finland
SANKT PETERBURG
(St. Petersburg)
Kolpino
Helsinki
Espoo
Tallinn
Narva
Kohtla-Järve
ESTONIA
Tartu
Pärnu
Hiiumaa (Dagö)
Saaremaa (Ösel)
Gulf of Riga
Riga
LATVIA
Jelgava
Rēzekne
Daugavpils
Pskov
Ozero Chudskoye
Gdov
Movgorod
Staraya Russa
Valdayskaya Vozvyshennost'
Tver
Kimry
Zelenograd
MOSKVA
(Moscow)
Odintsovo
Rzhev
Vyazma
Kaluga
Smolensk
Roslavl
Bryansk
Orel
Belev
Sevsk
Velikiye Luki
Nevel
Polotsk
Vitsyebsk
Lyepyel
Orsha
Mahilyow
Babruysk
Zhlobin
Homyel
Novhorod-Siversky
Chernihiv
Konotop
Sumy
Okhtyrka
Nizhyn
Pryluky
Chornobyl
Korosten
Kovel
Rivne
Zhytomyr
KYYIV
(Kiev)
Pereyaslav-Khmelnytskyy
Berdychiv
Bila Tserkva
Cherkasy
Poltava
Lutsk
Chervonohrad
Lviv
Rzeszów
Przemyśl
Tarnów
Ostrava
Cieszyn
Žilina
2655
Katowice
Kraków
Tychy
Chorzów
Częstochowa
Hradec Králové
Pardubice
Opole
Kielce
Lublin
Wałbrzych
Wrocław
Legnica
Radom
Łódź
Kalisz
Poznań
Toruń
Płock
Białystok
Łomża
Suwałki
Olsztyn
Elbląg
Gdańsk
Gdynia
Koszalin
Świnoujście
Szczecin
Bydgoszcz
Kaliningrad
(Russia)
Kaunas
Vilnius
Šiauliai
Panevėžys
Klaipėda
Sovetsk
Liepāja
Ventspils
Gotland
Visby
Oland
Karlskrona
Kalmar
Vastervik
Oskarshamn
Linköping
Norrköping
Jonköping
Borås
Varberg
Halmstad
Helsingborg
Malmö
Lund
(Copenhagen)
KØBENHAVN
Sjælland
Odense
Fyn
Esbjerg
Aarhus
Randers
Aalborg
Frederikshavn
Skagen
Kattegat
Holstebro
Djylland
DENMARK
Göteborg
(Gothenburg)
Trollhättan
Göta land
Vänern
Vättern
Skagerrak
Kristiansand
Arendal
Mandal
Stavanger
Karlstad
Fredrikstad
Drammen
Skien
Orebro
Eskilstuna
Uppsala
Åland
(Ahvenanmaa)
Hanko
STOCKHOLM
Vasteras
Malmo
Hiiumaa
Bornholm
Rügen
Gedser
Stralsund
Sassnitz
Rostock
Lübeck
Kiel
Flensburg
Helgoland
Emden
Bremen
HAMBURG
Osnabrück
Hannover
Braunschweig
Magdeburg
Potsdam
BERLIN
Frankfurt
Münster
Dortmund
Kassel
Halle
Erfurt
Leipzig
Chemnitz
Plauen
Gaelitz
Dresden
Legnica
Wrocław
Walbrzych
Opole
Częstochowa
Katowice
Kraków
Tychy
Chorzów
Hradec Králové
Pardubice
Kielce
Lublin

m 2000 1000 500 200 100 50 0
ft 6000 3000 1500 600 300 150 0
ft 600 1500 3000
0 200 500 1000 m
2 3 4 5 6 7 8 9
A B C
10
BRITISH ISLES
9
ATLANTIC OCEAN
NORTH SEA
Shetland Is. (U.K.)
Yell
Unst
Fetlar
Mainland
Lerwick
Foula
Fair Isle
Orkney Is.
Westray
Sanday
Stronsay
Mainland
Kirkwall
Hoy
South Ronaldsay
Pentland Firth
Thurso
Wick
C. Wrath
Helmsdale
Lewis
Stornoway
Harris
North Uist
Benbecula
South Uist
Barra
St. Kilda (U.K.)
Outer Hebrides
Inner Hebrides
Sea of the Hebrides
North Minch
North West Highlands
Ullapool
Lairg
Golspie
Tain
Invergordon
Dingwall
Moray Firth
Buckie
Banff
Fraserburgh
Peterhead
Nairn
Elgin
Inverness
Huntly
Portree
Skye
Glen More
Aviemore
L. Ness
CAIRNGORMS
Dee
Don
Inverurie
Aberdeen
Mallaig
Rhum
Eigg
Fort William
Ben Nevis
1343
SCOTLAND
Grampian Mts.
Ballater
Stonehaven
Coll
Tobermory
Tiree
Mull
Oban
Forfar
Montrose
Arbroath
Dundee
St. Andrews
Perth
L. Lomond
L. Arkaig
Glenrothes
Stirling
Kirkcaldy
Colonsay
L. Fyne
Jura
Islay
Dumbarton
Greenock
Dunfermline
Dunbar
Glasgow
Paisley
Motherwell
Edinburgh
East Kilbride
Hamilton
Irvine
Galashiels
Berwick-upon-Tweed
Askøyna
Bergen
Osøyro
Stord
Bømlo
Leirvik
NORWAY
Haugesund
Kopervik
Åkrahamn
Boknafjorden
Stavanger
Sandnes
Bryne
Nærbø
1224
336
789
1182
1311
1214
238

UNITED KINGDOM
IRELAND
NORTHERN IRELAND
IRISH SEA
ENGLAND
WALES
CELTIC SEA
English Channel
St. George's Channel
Bristol Channel
Cardigan Bay
Irish Sea
Belfast
Dublin
Dun Laoghaire
Cork
Limerick
Waterford
Galway
Sligo
Londonderry
Enniskillen
Armagh
Newry
Dundalk
Drogheda
Wicklow Mts
Cambrian Mts
Snowdonia
Pembrokeshire Coast
Exmoor
Dartmoor
Brecon Beacons
Cotswolds
Peak District
Lake District
Yorkshire Dales
North York Moors
Pennines
Isle of Man
Douglas
Liverpool
MANCHESTER
Leeds
Sheffield
Bradford
Kingston upon Hull
Nottingham
Derby
Stoke-on-Trent
Birmingham
Coventry
Leicester
Norwich
Peterborough
Cambridge
Ipswich
Colchester
Southend-on-Sea
Chelmsford
Luton
Milton Keynes
Northampton
Oxford
Reading
Slough
LONDON
Southampton
Portsmouth
Brighton
Bournemouth
Exeter
Plymouth
Torbay
Swansea
Cardiff
Newport
Bristol
Gloucester
Cheltenham
Worcester
Hereford
Shrewsbury
Wolverhampton
Telford
Stoke-on-Trent
Chester
Wrexham
Blackpool
Preston
Lancaster
Carlisle
Sunderland
Durham
Hartlepool
Middlesbrough
Darlington
Scarborough
Bridlington
Hull
Lincoln
Grimsby
Boston
Skegness
Cromer
King's Lynn
Great Yarmouth
Lowestoft
Ely
Bury St. Edmunds
Thetford
Harwich
Felixstowe
Southampton
Isle of Wight
Channel Is.
Guernsey
Jersey
Alderney
Sark
Cherbourg
Le Havre
Rouen
Caen
Lisieux
Bayeux
Trouville-sur-Mer
Fécamp
Dieppe
Le Tréport
Abbeville
Amiens
Calais
Boulogne-sur-Mer
Dunkerque
Lille
Tourcoing
Tournai
Antwerpen
Gent
Brugge
Oostende
Zeebrugge
Mechelen
Brussel (Bruxelles)
Vlissingen
Texel
Den Helder
Alkmaar
Haarlem
Rotterdam
Dordrecht
Den Haag (Hoek van Holland)
's-Gravenhage
NETHERLANDS
BELGIUM
FRANCE
Pays de Caux
Picardie
Str. of Dover
Seine
Caen
Elbeuf
Le Havre
Le Touquet-Paris-Plage
Boulogne-sur-Mer
Calais
St-Omer
Béthune
Bruay-la-Buissière
Valenciennes
Cambrai
St-Quentin
Laon
Münster
Caen
Rouen
Le Havre
Dieppe
Amiens
Lille
Calais
Boulogne

12 FRANCE

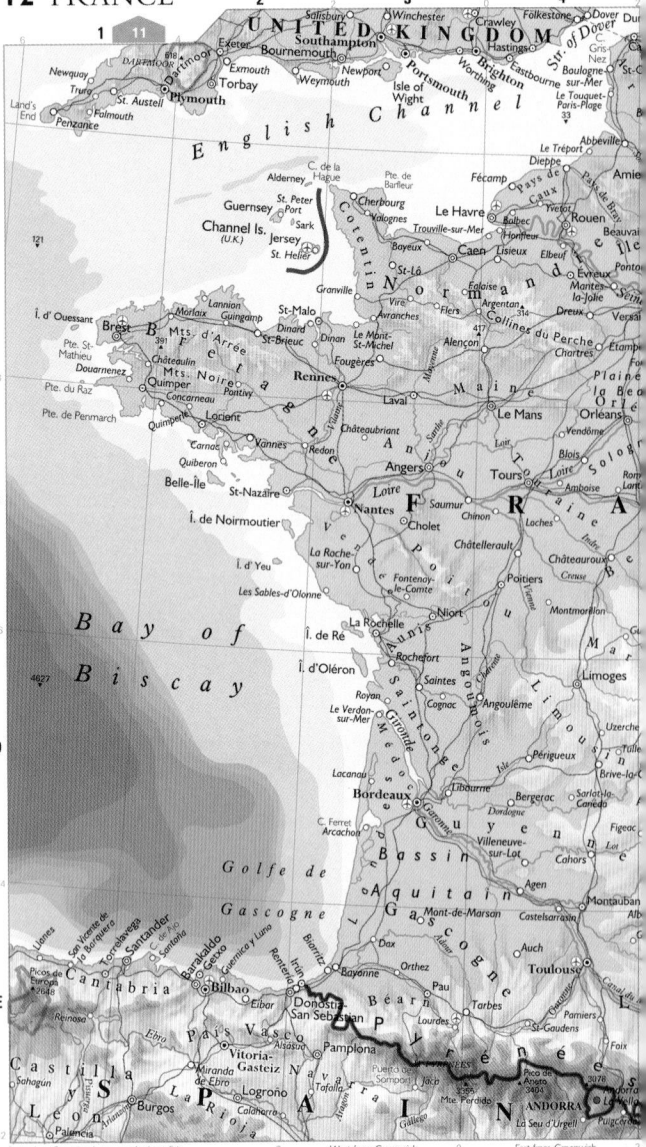
UNITED KINGDOM
English Channel
Str. of Dover
Bay of Biscay
Golfe de Gascogne
Bassin Aquitain
Normandie
Bretagne
Pays de la Loire
Poitou-Charentes
Limousin
Aquitaine
Île de France
Cantabria
Castilla y León
Pays Vasco
Navarra
La Rioja
Aragón
ANDORRA
Pyrénées
Plaine de la Beauce
Salisbury
Winchester
Crawley
Folkestone
Dover
Southampton
Bournemouth
Exeter
Exmouth
Torbay
Plymouth
Newquay
Truro
St. Austell
Land's End
Penzance
Falmouth
Newport
Weymouth
Isle of Wight
Portsmouth
Brighton
Worthing
Hastings
Eastbourne
Boulogne-sur-Mer
Le Touquet-Paris-Plage
Gris-Nez
Le Tréport
Abbeville
Dieppe
Fécamp
Amiens
Le Havre
Rouen
Beauvais
Evreux
Mantes-la-Jolie
Versailles
Dreux
Chartres
Etampes
Orléans
Blois
Vendôme
Tours
Amboise
Loches
Saumur
Chinon
Chatellerault
Châtelleraudon
Poitiers
Niort
Montmorillon
Limoges
Uzerche
Brive-la-Gaillarde
Périgueux
Bergerac
Sarlat-la-Canéda
Figeac
Cahors
Agen
Montauban
Castelsarrasin
Mont-de-Marsan
Dax
Auch
Toulouse
Pamiers
Foix
St-Gaudens
Lourdes
Tarbes
Pau
Orthez
Bayonne
Biarritz
Donostia San Sebastián
Irún
Pamplona
Vitoria-Gasteiz
Miranda de Ebro
Logroño
Burgos
Palencia
Bilbao
Eibar
Santander
Torrelavega
Barakaldo
Getxo
Guernica y Luno
Los Viveros de la Barquera
Llanes
Picos de Europa
Reinosa
Sahagún
Tafalla
Calahorra
Jaca
Gallego
Sorport
Pico de Aragón
Mte. Perdido
Pico de Aneto
La Seu d'Urgell
Puigcerdá
Ebro
Garonne
Dordogne
Lot
Tarn
Adour
Loire
Cher
Vienne
Creuse
Indre
Charente
Sarthe
Mayenne
Seine
Somme
Marne
Dordogne
Lot
Tarn
Ile de Ré
Ile d'Oléron
Ile d'Yeu
Ile de Noirmoutier
Belle-Île
Ile d'Ouessant
Pte. de Penmarch
Pte. St-Mathieu
Pte. du Raz
Douarnenez
Quimper
Concarneau
Lorient
Quiberon
Carnac
Vannes
Redon
St-Nazaire
Nantes
Cholet
Angers
Le Mans
Laval
Rennes
Fougères
Dinan
St-Brieuc
Dinard
St-Malo
Granville
Avranches
Fougères
Le Mont-St-Michel
Alençon
Argentan
Lisieux
Caen
Bayeux
St-Lô
Cherbourg
Valognes
Trouville-sur-Mer
Honfleur
Bolbec
Yvetot
Elbeuf
Falaise
Vire
Fécamp
Pte. de Barfleur
C. de la Hague
Alderney
Guernsey
St. Peter Port
Sark
Channel Is. (U.K.)
Jersey
St. Helier
Morlaix
Lannion
Guingamp
Brest
Châteaulin
Pontivy
Quimperlé
Vannes
Redon
Châteaubriant
Saumur
Chinon
Loches
Cognac
Angoulême
Saintes
Rochefort
La Rochelle
Royan
Le Verdon-sur-Mer
Lacanau
Arcachon
C. Ferret
Bordeaux
Libourne
Villeneuve-sur-Lot
Castelsarrasin
Montauban
Figeac
Lacaune
Fontenay-le-Comte
La Roche-sur-Yon
Les Sables-d'Olonne
Cholet
Saumur
Chinon
Loches
Châtellerault

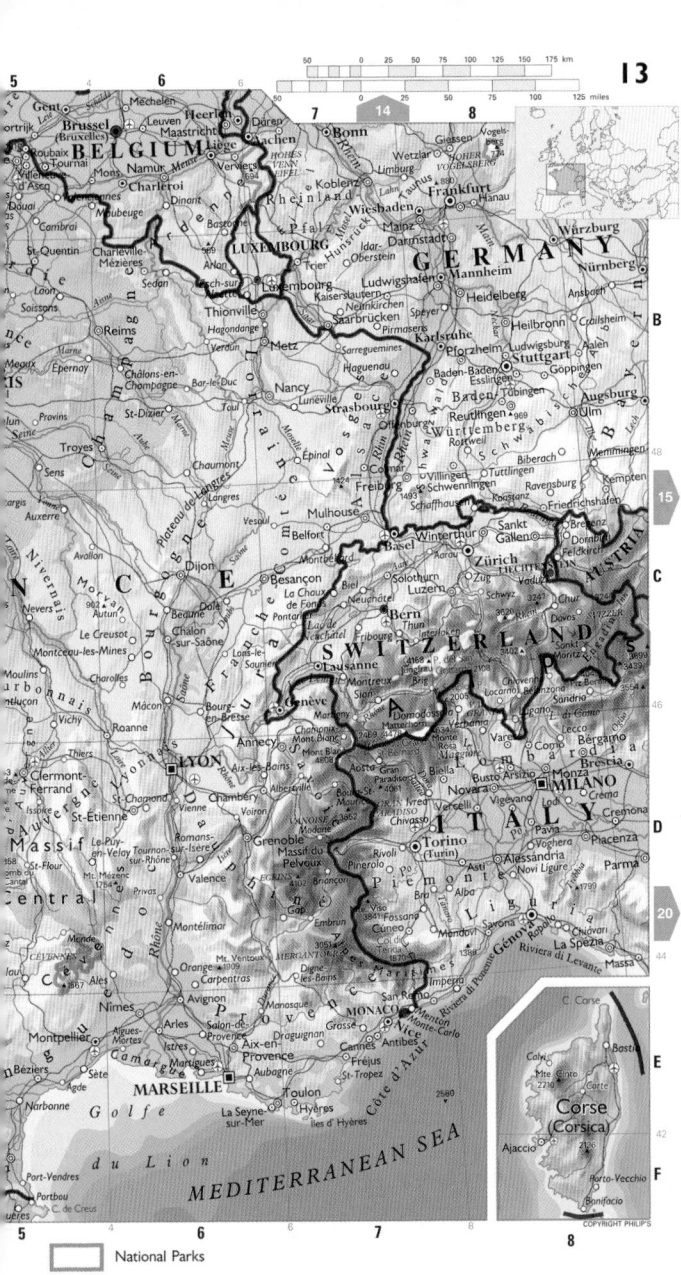
13
50 0 25 50 75 100 125 150 175 km
50 0 25 50 75 100 125 miles
BELGIUM
LUXEMBOURG
GERMANY
SWITZERLAND
AUSTRIA
FRANCE
ITALY
MONACO
MEDITERRANEAN SEA
Golfe du Lion
Côte d'Azur
Riviera di Levante
Riviera di Ponente
Corse (Corsica)
Brussel (Bruxelles)
Gent
Mechelen
Leuven
Maastricht
Aachen
Bonn
Koblenz
Frankfurt
Wiesbaden
Mainz
Darmstadt
Mannheim
Heidelberg
Karlsruhe
Stuttgart
Ulm
Augsburg
Würzburg
Nürnberg
Heilbronn
Ludwigshafen
Speyer
Saarbrücken
Trier
Luxembourg
Metz
Nancy
Strasbourg
Colmar
Mulhouse
Freiburg
Basel
Zürich
Bern
Luzern
Lausanne
Genève
Lyon
Dijon
Besançon
Reims
Lille
Le Mans
Clermont-Ferrand
St-Etienne
Grenoble
Valence
Montpellier
Nîmes
Avignon
Marseille
Toulon
Nice
Cannes
Antibes
Aix-en-Provence
Arles
Perpignan
Milano
Torino
Genova
Brescia
Bergamo
Ajaccio
Bastia
Porto-Vecchio
Bonifacio
Corte
Calvi
Mte. Cinto 2706
Mt. Ventoux 1909
Mt. Mezenc 1754
Massif Central
Massif du Pelvoux
Massif des Vosges
Massif Central
Jura
Alps
Rhine
Rhône
Loire
Seine
Moselle
Saône
Marne
Meuse
Scheldt
Elbe
Inn
Po
Durance
Aude
Vienne
Loire
Allier
Vienne
Aisne
Marne
Meuse
Moselle
Saône
Doubs
Isère
Aude
Seine-Maritime
Aisne
Ardennes
Marne
Meuse
Moselle
Vosges
Doubs
Jura
Savoie
Isère
Cantal
Puy-de-Dôme
Allier
Yonne
Côte-d'Or
Saône-et-Loire
Seine-Maritime
Aisne
Ardennes
Marne
Meuse
Moselle
Vosges
Doubs
Jura
Savoie
Isère
Cantal
Puy-de-Dôme
Allier
Yonne
Côte-d'Or
Saône-et-Loire

14 GERMANY AND BENELUX

NORTH SEA
UNITED KINGDOM
NETHERLANDS
AMSTERDAM
's-Gravenhage (Den Haag)
ROTTERDAM
BELGIUM
Brussel (Bruxelles)
LUXEMBOURG
Luxembourg
PARIS
FRANCE
SWITZERLAND
LYON
Nordfriesische Inseln
Ost-friesische Inseln
Deutsche Bucht
Niedersachsen
Nordrhein-Westfalen
Hessen
Rheinland-Pfalz
Baden-Württemberg
Picardie
Ile-de-France
Champagne-Ardenne
Lorraine
Franche-Comté
Bourgogne
Auvergne
Aachen
Köln (Cologne)
Bonn
Düsseldorf
Dortmund
Essen
Bremen
Hamburg
Hannover
Frankfurt
Wiesbaden
Mainz
Mannheim
Stuttgart
Karlsruhe
Freiburg
Basel
Zürich
Bern
Lausanne
Genève
Strasbourg
Metz
Nancy
Reims
Lille
Amiens
Clermont-Ferrand
Dijon
Besançon
Mulhouse
Belfort
Grenoble
Annecy
Chambéry
Marseille
Lille
Antwerpen
Gent
Brugge
Leuven
Mechelen
Charleroi
Namur
Liège
Mons
Maastricht
Eindhoven
Arnhem
Nijmegen
Utrecht
Groningen
Leeuwarden
Amsterdam
Rotterdam
Den Haag
Leiden
Haarlem
Zwolle
Enschede
Osnabrück
Hannover
Hamburg
Kiel
Flensburg
Aachen
Koblenz
Trier
Saarbrücken
Karlsruhe
Heidelberg
Mannheim
Würzburg
Nürnberg
Regensburg
Ulm
Augsburg
Kempten
Hannover
Kassel
Fulda
Eisenach
Gotha
Ansbach
Aschaffenburg
Darmstadt
Offenbach
Hanau
Giessen
Marburg
Siegen
Paderborn
Detmold
Bielefeld
Münster
Osnabrück
Oldenburg
Bremerhaven
Wilhelmshaven
Emden
Aurich
Cuxhaven
Helgoland
Sylt
Föhr
Lüneburg
Hamburg
Kiel
Flensburg
Schleswig
Rendsburg
Holstein
Braunschweig
Hannover
Hildesheim
Göttingen
Kassel
Fulda
Würzburg
Regensburg
Augsburg
Ulm
Stuttgart
Karlsruhe
Freiburg
Basel
Zürich
Bern
Lausanne
Genève

15
BALTIC SEA
Zatoka Gdańska
Zalew Wiślany
Rügen
Stralsund
Greifswald
Rostock
Wismar
Usedom
Wolin
Świnoujście
Szczecin
Stettiner Haff
Mecklenburg
Schwerin
Neubrandenburg
Brandenburg
Wittenberge
Neuruppin
Salzwedel
Stendal
Eberswalde
Finow
BERLIN
Potsdam
Magdeburg
Luckenwalde
Sachsen-Anhalt
Lutherstadt Wittenberg
Dessau
Bernburg
Halle
Leipzig
Merseburg
Naumburg
Weimar
Gera
Zwickau
Chemnitz
Dresden
Meissen
Bautzen
Görlitz
Zgorzelec
Cottbus
Forst
Lauchhammer
Hoyerswerda
Erzgebirge
Plauen
Reichenbach
Karlovy Vary
Cheb
Bayreuth
Weiden
Amberg
Regensburg
Straubing
Deggendorf
Landshut
Passau
Freising
MÜNCHEN (Munich)
Braunau
Ried
Wels
Linz
Salzburg
Bad Ischl
Kufstein
Innsbruck
Steyr
Amstetten
Melk
Gmunden
Leoben
Kapfenberg
Bruck an der Mur
Graz
Wolfsberg
Klagenfurt
Villach
Karnische Alpen
Udine
Vittorio Veneto
Pordenone
Conegliano
Gorizia
Kobarid
Kranj
Ljubljana
SLOVENIA
Celje
Maribor
ZAGREB
Varaždin
Koprivnica
Bjelovar
Virovitica
Drava
Sava
Mürzzuschlag
Semmering
Eisenerz
Zalaegerszeg
Nagykanizsa
Kaposvár
Szekszárd
Pécs
Mohács
Baja
Kalocsa
Dunaújváros
Siófok
Balaton
Veszprém
Székesfehérvár
Tatabánya
Esztergom
Győr
Komárno
Dunaújváros
Szombathely
Pápa
Ajka
Sopron
Neusiedler See
Wiener Neustadt
Baden
Bruck an der Leitha
Mosonmagyaróvár
Bratislava
Nové Zámky
Nitra
Levice
Trnava
Hodonín
Znojmo
Brno
Jihlava
Třebíč
Tábor
Pardubice
Hradec Králové
Kolín
Sumperk
Olomouc
Prostějov
Přerov
Vyškov
Zlín
Frýdek Místek
Ostrava
Karviná
Opava
Bielsko-Biała
Cieszyn
Žywiec
Katowice
Tychy
Oświęcim
Tarnów
Lublin
Chełm
Pécs
Mohács
Baja
Kaposvár
Szekszárd
Budapest
Vác
Dunakeszi
Komárno
Nové Zámky
Levice
Banská Bystrica
Prievidza
Trenčín
Žilina
Martin

16 CENTRAL EUROPE

Zatoka Gdańska
Kaliningrad (Russ
Baltiysk
Gdańsk
Gdynia
Sopot
Elbląg
Słupsk
Koszalin
Szczecin
Stettin Haff
Usedom
Wolin
Świnoujście
Stargard Szczeciński
Gorzów Wielkopolski
Bydgoszcz
Toruń
Włocławek
Plock
Olsztyn
Ostrołęka
Łomża
Ostrów Mazowiecki
Chełm
Lublin
Kielce
Radom
Ostrowiec-Świętokrzyski
Legionowo
Mińsk Mazowiecki
WARSZAWA (Warsaw)
Łódź
Piotrków Trybunalski
Skierniewice
Żyrardów
Pruszków
Otwock
Tomaszów Mazowiecki
Skarżysko-Kamienna
Starachowice
Radomsko
Częstochowa
Kalisz
Konin
Poznań
Gniezno
Leszno
Zielona Góra
Frankfurt
Eberswalde-Finow
BERLIN
Cottbus
Forst
Nowa Sól
Żagań
Głogów
Legnica
Wrocław
Oława
Świdnica
Jelenia Góra
Wałbrzych
Opole
Tarnowskie Góry
Gliwice
Zabrze
Bytom
Katowice
Chorzów
Tychy
Racibórz
Oświęcim
Kraków
Tarnów
Bochnia
Nowy Sącz
Zakopane
Nowy Targ
Bielsko-Biała
Cieszyn
Frydek Mistek
Ostrava
Havířov
Karviná
Opava
Olomouc
Prostějov
Přerov
Zlín
Vyškov
Brno
Znojmo
Hodonín
Trenčín
Prievidza
Banská Bystrica
Zvolen
Topoľčany
Trnava
Nitra
Levice
Lučenec
Košice
Miskolc
Eger
Gyöngyös
Debrecen
Vác
Hatvan
Jászberény
Komárno
Esztergom
Dunakeszi
BUDAPEST
Érd
Cegléd
Szolnok
Mezőtúr
Nagykőrös
Kecskemét
Kiskunfélegyháza
Csongrád
Békéscsaba
Szentes
Gyula
Orosháza
Hódmezővásárhely
Makó
Arad
Szeged
Kiskunhalas
Kiskőrös
Kalocsa
Baja
Subotica
Senta
Kikinda
Timiș
Sombor
Novi Sad
Zrenjanin
Vukovar
Osijek
Sisak
Karlovac
Virovitica
Bjelovar
Varaždin
Koprivnica
Pécs
Mohács
Kaposvár
Nagykanizsa
Szekszárd
Tatabánya
Pápa
Szombathely
Ajka
Veszprém
Balaton
Siófok
Zalaegerszeg
Maribor
Celje
Ljubljana
Kranj
Trieste
Rijeka
Linz
Wels
Steyr
Amstetten
Wiener Neustadt
Baden
Bruck an der Leitha
Neusiedler See
Sopron
Graz
Leoben
Bruck an der Mur
Murzzuschlag
Eisenerz
Kapfenberg
Wolfsberg
Klagenfurt
Trieste
Rijeka
Karlovac
Sisak
Zagreb
Varaždin
Koprivnica
Bielovar
Virovitica
Osijek
Vukovar
Novi Sad
Zrenjanin
Subotica
Senta
Kikinda
Timiș
Sombor
Szolnok
Mezőtúr
Nagykőrös
Kecskemét
Kiskunfélegyháza
Csongrád
Szentes
Gyula
Orosháza
Hódmezővásárhely
Makó
Arad
Szeged
Kiskunhalas
Kiskőrös
Kalocsa
Baja

17
50 0 25 50 75 100 125 150 175 km
50 0 25 50 75 100 125 miles
B E L A R U S
MINSK
Hrodna
Lida
Baranavichy
Pinsk
Brest
Mazyr
Homyel
Babruysk
Bialystok
Chernobyl
Pripyat
Desna
Dnestr
Prut
Danube
U K R A I N E
KYIV (Kiev)
Zhytomyr
Rivne
Lutsk
Lviv (Lvov)
Ternopil
Khmelnytskyy
Vinnytsya
Bila Tserkva
Ivano-Frankivsk
Chernivtsi
Kamyanets-Podilskyy
Uzhhorod
Chisinau
Tiraspol
Iasi
Suceava
Botosani
Galati
Braila
Brasov
Sibiu
Cluj-Napoca
Oradea
Satu Mare
Baia Mare
Bacau
Piatra Neamt
Focsani
Buzau
Tulcea
Reni
Izmayil
Kilija
Ozero Katyk
Sulina
Bilhorod-Dnistrovskyy
Cahul
Vulcanesti
Balti
Soroca
Edineti
Orhei
Ungheni
Falticeni
Pascani
Roman
Husi
Vaslui
Tecuci
Galati
Braila
Deva
Hunedoara
Petroseni
Vulcan
Curtea de Arges
Campulung
Campina
Sibiu
Fagaras
Sacele
Sighisoara
Medias
Aiud
Alba-Iulia
Turda
Cluj-Napoca
Dej
Bistrita
Zalau
Oradea
Satu Mare
Baia Mare
Borsa
Sighetu Marmatiei
Vatra Dornei
Radauti
Suceava
Botosani
Dorohoi
Siret
Prut
Dniester
Nistru
Pripyat
Gomel
Zhytomyr
Kyiv
Uman
Vinnytsya
Khmelnytskyy
Ternopil
Lviv
Ivano-Frankivsk
Chernivtsi
Uzhhorod
Mukacheve
Berehove
Khust
Tyachiv
Rakhiv
Sighetu Marmatiei
Satu Mare
Baia Mare
Borsa
Vatra Dornei
Bistrita
Zalau
Oradea
Cluj-Napoca
Turda
Dej
Reghin
Târgu Mureş
Odorheiu Secuiesc
Miercurea-Ciuc
Onesti
Târnăveni
Sighisoara
Mediaş
Aiud
Alba-Iulia
Deva
Hunedoara
Petroseni
Vulcan
Curtea de Arges
Campulung
Campina
Sibiu
Fagaras
Sacele
Brasov
Focsani
Buzau
Rimnicu Sarat
Braila
Galati
Tulcea
Reni
Izmayil
Kilija
Ozero Katyk
Sulina
Bilhorod-Dnistrovskyy
Cahul
Vulcanesti
Balti
Soroca
Edineti
Orhei
Ungheni
Falticeni
Pascani
Roman
Husi
Vaslui
Tecuci
Galati
Braila
Deva
Hunedoara
Petroseni
Vulcan
Curtea de Arges
Campulung
Campina
Sibiu
Fagaras
Sacele
Sighisoara
Mediaş
Aiud
Alba-Iulia
Turda
Cluj-Napoca
Dej
Bistrita
Zalau
Oradea
Satu Mare
Baia Mare
Borsa
Sighetu Marmatiei
Vatra Dornei
Radauti
Suceava
Botosani
Dorohoi
Siret
Prut
Dniester
Nistru
Pripyat
Gomel
Zhytomyr
Kyiv
Uman
Vinnytsya
Khmelnytskyy
Ternopil
Lviv
Ivano-Frankivsk
Chernivtsi
Uzhhorod
Mukacheve
Berehove
Khust
Tyachiv
Rakhiv
Sighetu Marmatiei
Satu Mare
Baia Mare
Borsa

18 SPAIN AND PORTUGAL

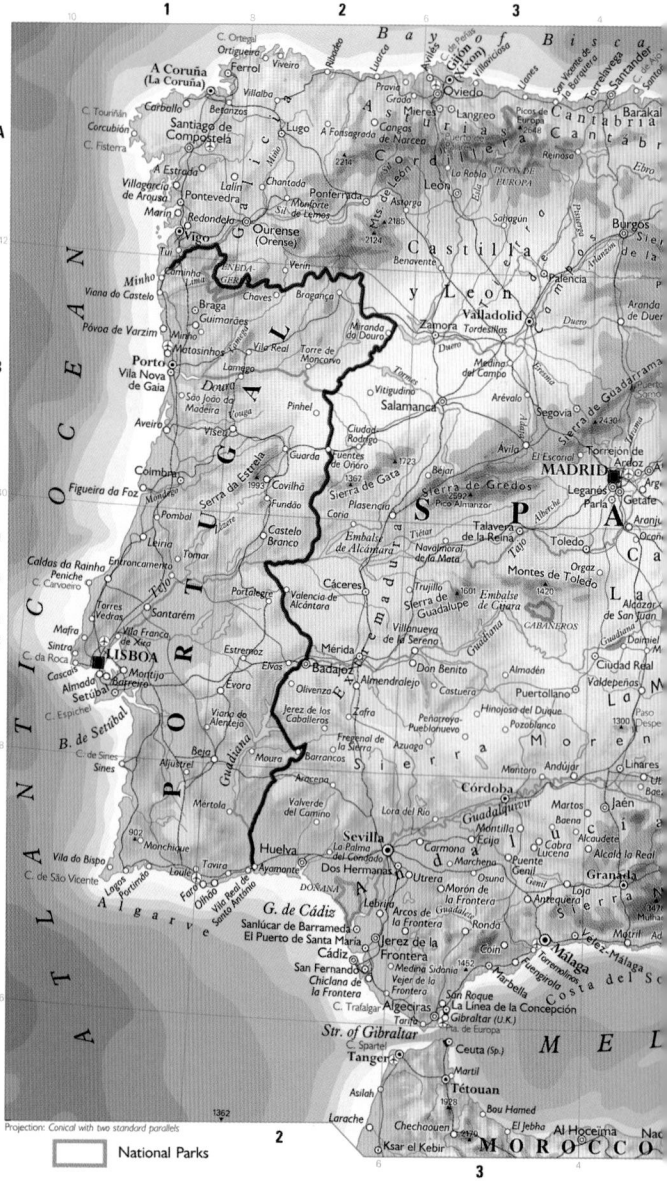
Bay of Biscay
A Coruña (La Coruña)
Ferrol
Viveiro
Ortigueira
Rinlodo
Lugo
Santiago de Compostela
Carballo
Betanzos
C. Tourinán
Corcubión
C. Finisterra
Villagarcía de Arousa
Pontevedra
Marín
Redondela
Vigo
Ourense (Orense)
Lalín
Chantada
Ponferrada
Monforte de Lemos
Astorga
León
La Robla
Sahagún
Palencia
Burgos
Valladolid
Zamora
Tordesillas
Medina del Campo
Arévalo
Segovia
Sierra de Guadarrama
Avila
El Escorial
Torrejón de Ardoz
MADRID
Leganés
Getafe
Parla
Aranjuez
Toledo
Talavera de la Reina
Navalmoral de la Mata
Montes de Toledo
Orgaz
Ciudad Real
Valdepeñas
Puertollano
Almadén
Don Benito
Mérida
Badajoz
Almendralejo
Zafra
Jerez de los Caballeros
Fregenal de la Sierra
Azuaga
Barranco
Aracena
Valverde del Camino
Lora del Río
Sevilla
La Palma del Condado
Dos Hermanas
Carmona
Marchena
Osuna
Utrera
Morón de la Frontera
Huelva
Ayamonte
Lebrija
Arcos de la Frontera
Ronda
Jerez de la Frontera
Medina Sidonia
Vejer de la Frontera
Chiclana de la Frontera
San Fernando
Cádiz
Sanlúcar de Barrameda
El Puerto de Santa María
G. de Cádiz
Algeciras
La Línea de la Concepción
Gibraltar (U.K.)
Tarifa
Str. of Gibraltar
Tanger
Ceuta (Sp.)
Tétouan
Larache
Chechaouen
Ksar el Kebir
Al Hoceima
MOROCCO
Málaga
Marbella
Fuengirola
Torremolinos
Vélez-Málaga
Motril
Granada
Jaén
Linares
Baeza
Alcaudete
Alcalá la Real
Lucena
Cabra
Montilla
Baena
Martos
Puente Genil
Lojá
Antequera
Sierra Nevada
Sierra Morena
Sierra de Gredos
Sierra de Guadalupe
Sierra de Cáceres
Sierra de Gata
Sierra de Aracena
Sierra de Ronda
Sierra de Gredos
Sierra de Guadarrama
Sierra de Aitana

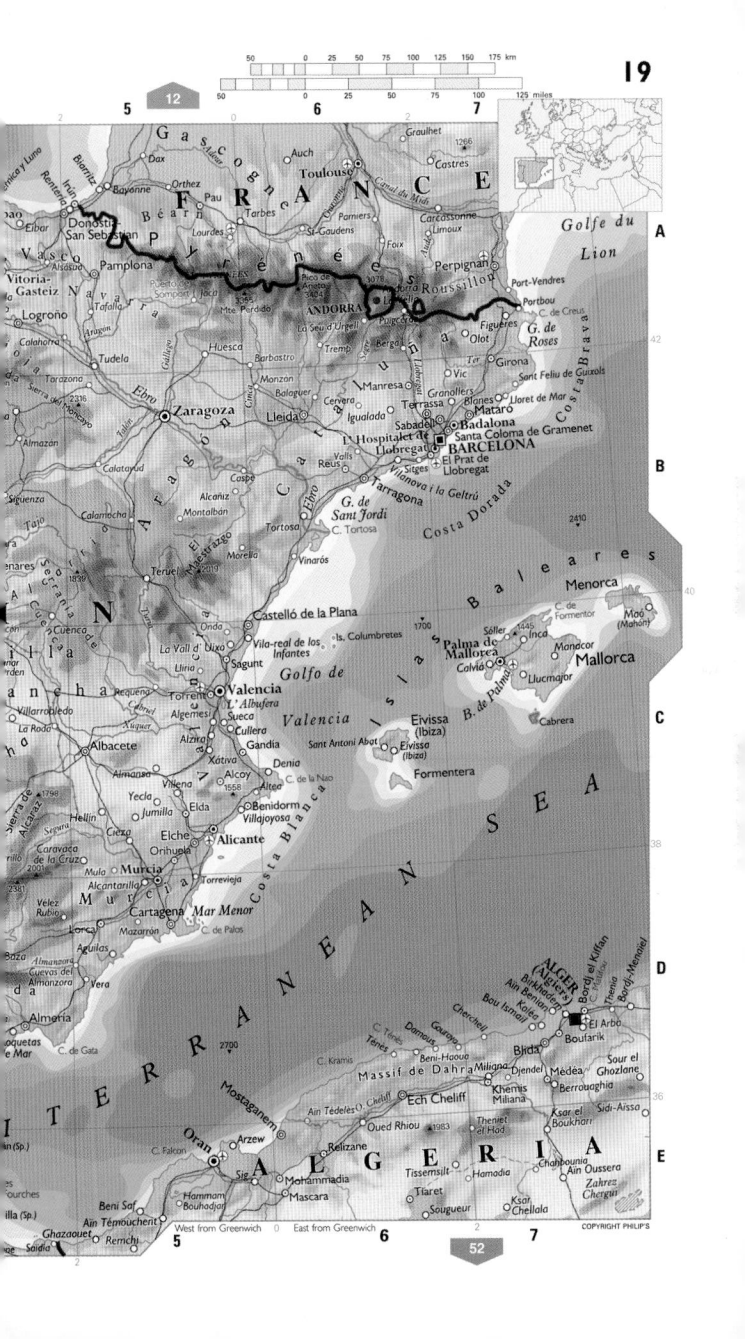
50 0 25 50 75 100 125 150 175 km
50 0 25 50 75 100 125 miles
12
5
6
7
A
B
C
D
E
42
40
38
36
2
0
2
Graulhet
Castres
Auch
Toulouse
Dax
Orthez
Bayonne
Pau
Tarbes
Lourdes
St-Gaudens
Pamiers
Carcassonne
Limoux
Foix
Perpignan
Port-Vendres
Portbou
C. de Creus
Roussillon
Figueres
G. de Roses
Olot
Girona
Sant Feliu de Guixols
Vic
Ter
Manresa
Granollers
Terrassa
Mataró
Blanes
Lloret de Mar
Sabadell
Badalona
Santa Coloma de Gramenet
BARCELONA
L'Hospitalet de Llobregat
El Prat de Llobregat
Vilanova i la Geltrú
Sitges
Tarragona
Reus
Valls
Cospe
Alcaniz
Montalbán
Tortosa
C. Tortosa
Vinarós
Morella
Teruel
Cuenca
Castelló de la Plana
Onda
Vila-real de los Infantes
Is. Columbretes
La Vall d'Uixó
Llíria
Sagunt
Valencia
Torrent
Algemesí
Sueca
Cullera
L'Albufera
Gandia
Xátiva
Alzira
Albacete
Almansa
Villena
Alcoy
Altea
C. de la Nao
Denia
Yecla
Jumilla
Elda
Benidorm
Villajoyosa
Hellín
Cieza
Elche
Alicante
Orihuela
Caravaca de la Cruz
Mula
Murcia
Alcantarilla
Torrevieja
Cartagena
Mar Menor
C. de Palos
Lorca
Mazarrón
Aguilas
Almanzora
Cuevas del Almanzora
Vera
Almería
C. de Gata
Zaragoza
Lleida
Huesca
Tudela
Pamplona
Vitoria
Gasteiz
Logroño
Donostia San Sebastián
Bilbao
Biarritz
Baiona
Irún
Vascos
Navarra
Aragón
Cataluña
Valencia
Baleares
Menorca
Mahón
C. de Formentor
Mallorca
Palma de Mallorca
Sóller
Inca
Manacor
Llucmajor
Colònia
B. de Palma
Cabrera
Eivissa (Ibiza)
Sant Antoni Abat
Formentera
Costa Dorada
Costa Brava
Costa Blanca
Costa del Sol
Golfe du Lion
Golfo de Valencia
MEDITERRANEAN SEA
Massif de Dahra
Ech Cheliff
Mostaganem
Oran
Arzew
Relizane
Sig
Mohammadia
Mascara
Tiaret
Tissemsilt
Hamadia
Sougueur
Ksar Chellala
Ksar el Boukhari
Sidi-Aissa
Chahbounia
Ain Oussera
Zahrez Chergui
Djelfa
Médea
Berrouaghia
Sour el Ghozlane
Boulaiik
El Arbo
Bordj el Kiffan
Bordj-Menaiel
Tizi Ouzou
Thenia
ALGER (Algiers)
Blida
Bou Ismail
Koléa
Cherchell
Tenès
Damous
Gouraya
C. Tenès
C. Kramis
Beni-Haoua
Miliana
Djendel
Khemis Miliana
Aïn Tédeles
Chlef
Oued Rhiou
Thenet el Hod
Aïn Bénian
Aïn Bouhdjar
Bou Saf
Aïn Témouchent
Ghazaouet
Remchi
Hammam Bouhadjar
C. Falcon
ALGERIA
West from Greenwich 0 East from Greenwich
COPYRIGHT PHILIP'S
52

SWITZERLAND
AUSTRIA
HUNGARY
SLOVENIA
CROATIA
BOSNIA-
HERZEGOVINA
FRANCE
MONACO
SAN MARINO
VATICAN CITY
ADRIATIC SEA
LIGURIAN SEA
Golfo di Venezia
Golfo di Genova
Golfo dell' Asinara
Bonifacio
Corse (Corsica)
Lombardia
Piemonte
Liguria
Emilia
Toscana
Marche
Lazio
Abruzzi
Istria
Dalmazia
Slavonia
Bosnia
Herzegovina
Milano
Torino (Turin)
Genova
Venezia (Venice)
Trieste
Ljubljana
Zagreb
Rijeka
Sarajevo
Roma
Firenze (Florence)
Bari
Ancona
Pescara
Foggia
Bologna
Verona
Padova
Trento
Bolzano
Graz
Klagenfurt
Nice
Split
Dubrovnik
Mostar
Banja Luka
Osijek
Pécs
Szekszárd
Maribor
Celje
Varaždin
Bjelovar
Karlovac
Sisak
Novska
Slavonski Brod
Vinkovci
Vukovar
Brčko
Tuzla
Zenica
Travnik
Konjic
Goražde
Trebinje
Niksić
Herceg Novi
Dubrovnik
Korčula
Lastovo
Mljet
Pelješac
Hvar
Vis
Brač
Šolta
Šibenik
Zadar
Pag
Krk
Cres
Lošinj
Pula
Rovinj
Koper
Ljubljana
Kranj
Maribor
Nagykanizsa
Kaposvár
Szekszárd
Mohács
Osijek
Vukovar
Novi Sad
Bolzano
Trento
Verona
Padova
Venezia
Trieste
Udine
Gorizia
Pordenone
Treviso
Vicenza
Mantova
Cremona
Brescia
Bergamo
Como
Lecco
Varese
Milano
Torino
Alessandria
Asti
Cuneo
Savona
Genova
La Spezia
Massa
Carrara
Lucca
Pisa
Livorno
Siena
Arezzo
Perugia
Terni
Rieti
Viterbo
Grosseto
Orbetello
Civitavecchia
Latina
Frosinone
Cassino
Campobasso
Foggia
Bari
Olbia
Ajaccio
Bastia
Porto-Vecchio
Bonifacio
Asinara
Porto
Cannes
Grenoble
Chambéry
Annecy
Cannes
Grenoble
Chambéry
Annecy
Cannes
Grenoble
Chambéry
Annecy

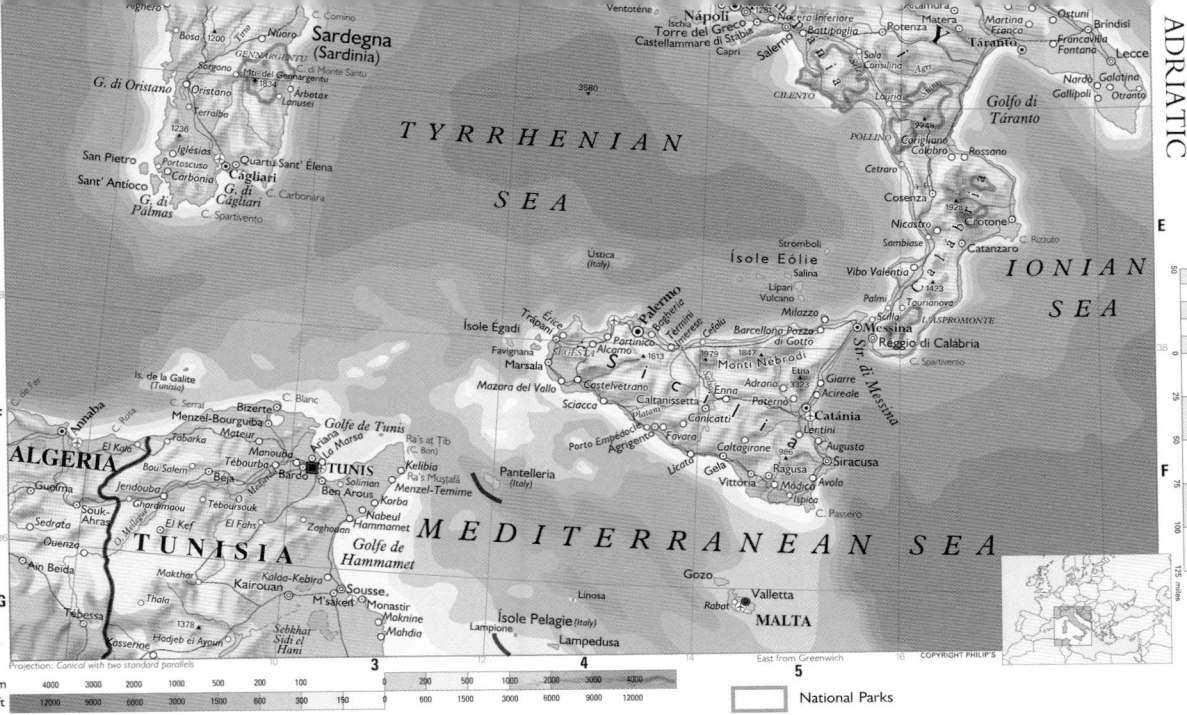
Sardegna
(Sardinia)
Nuoro
Oristano
G. di Oristano
Cagliari
G. di Cagliari
San Pietro
Sant' Antioco
Quartu Sant' Élena
Carbonara
Spartivento
Alghero
Bosa
Terralba
Iglesias
Portoscuso
Carbonia
G. di Palmas
TYRRHENIAN
SEA
Napoli
Ischia
Torre del Greco
Castellammare di Stabia
Capri
Salerno
Potenza
Matera
Taranto
Brindisi
Lecce
Golfo di Táranto
Cosenza
Crotone
Catanzaro
Rossano
Corigliano Calabro
Cetraro
Sambiase
Rizzuto
IONIAN
SEA
Ústica
(Italy)
Ísole Eólie
Stromboli
Salina
Lipari
Vulcano
Milazzo
Vibo Valentia
Palmi
Scilla
Tauriánova
Messina
Reggio di Calábria
Str. di Messina
Palermo
Trápani
Ísole Égadi
Marsala
Mazara del Vallo
Sciacca
Castelvetrano
Caltanissetta
Canicattì
Agrigento
Porto Empedocle
Licata
Gela
Ragusa
Vittoria
Módica
Ispica
Avola
Siracusa
Augusta
Catánia
Lentini
Caltagirone
Enna
Adrano
Paterno
Giarre
Acireale
Etna
Monti Nebrodi
Cefalù
Barcellona Pozzo di Gotto
Pantelleria
(Italy)
Linosa
Ísole Pelagie (Italy)
Lampedusa
Lampione
Gozo
Valletta
MALTA
Rabat
ALGERIA
TUNISIA
Annaba
Bizerte
Menzel-Bourguiba
Golfe de Tunis
TUNIS
Bárdo
Ben Arous
Golfe de Hammamet
Nabeul
Hammamet
Kairouan
Sousse
Monastir
Mahdia
Tébessa
Kasserine
MEDITERRANEAN SEA
Projection: Conical with two standard parallels
East from Greenwich
COPYRIGHT PHILIP'S
National Parks

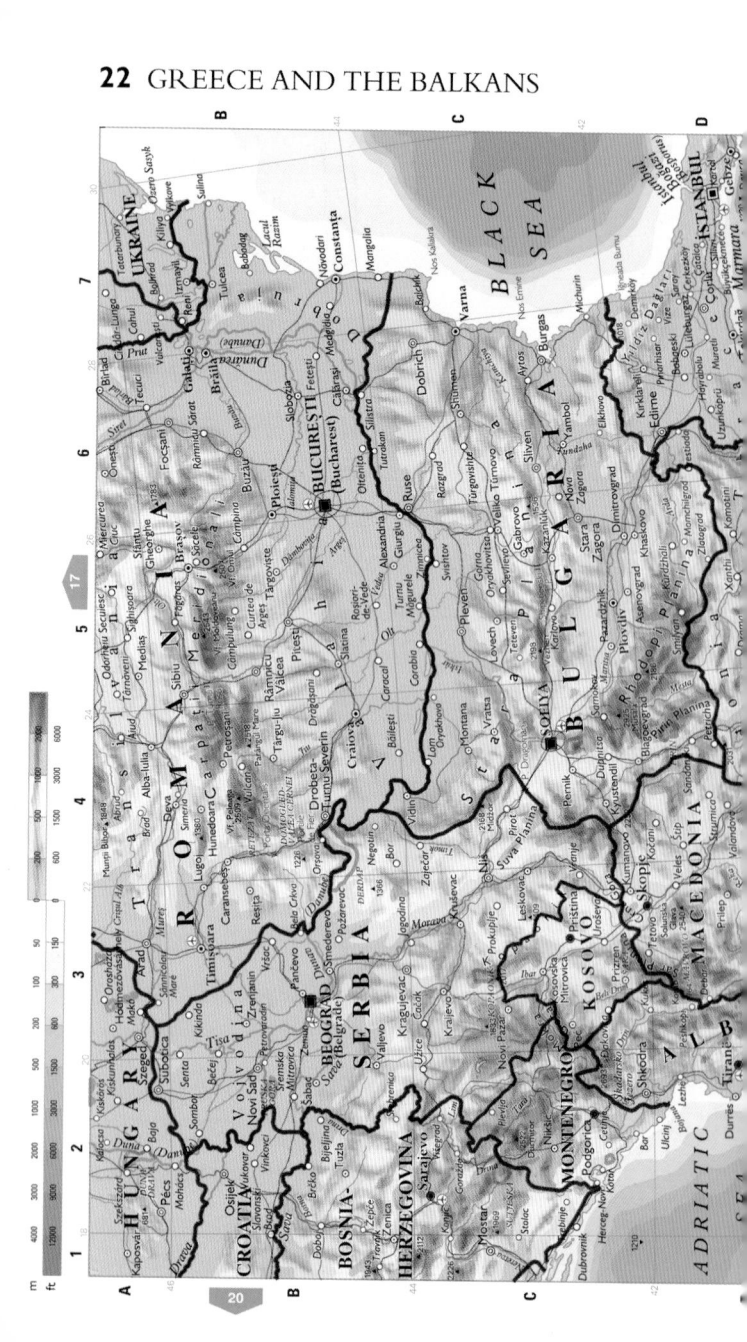
UKRAINE
HUNGARY
ROMANIA
CROATIA
BOSNIA-HERZEGOVINA
SERBIA
MONTENEGRO
KOSOVO
MACEDONIA
BULGARIA
BLACK SEA
ADRIATIC SEA
BUCUREŞTI (Bucharest)
BEOGRAD (Belgrade)
SOFIA
ISTANBUL
Marmara Denizi
Constanta
Varna
Burgas
Dobrich
Ruse
Plovdiv
Stara Zagora
Pleven
Veliko Tŭrnovo
Edirne
Tekirdağ
Kırklareli
Istanbul
Bosphorus
Danube
Prut
Tisza
Sava
Morava
Maritsa
Iskŭr
Ibar
Drina
Tiza
Mureş
Olt
Siret
Dunărea (Danube)
Pirin Planina
Rhodope Mts
Sarajevo
Mostar
Podgorica
Tirana
Durrës
Skopje
Prishtina
Niš
Novi Sad
Osijek
Szeged
Galaţi
Brăila
Tulcea
Constanţa
Craiova
Ploieşti
Braşov
Sibiu
Timişoara
Arad

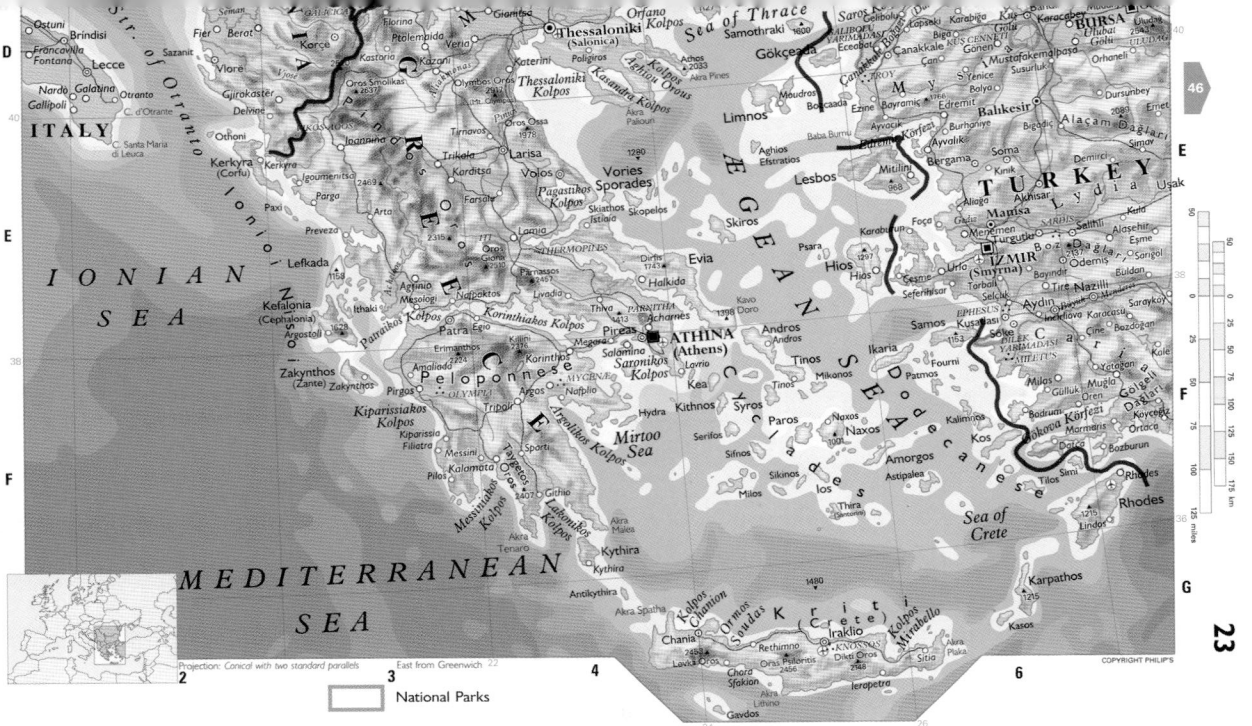
ITALY
IONIAN SEA
MEDITERRANEAN SEA
Sea of Thrace
AEGEAN SEA
Sea of Crete
TURKEY
GREECE
Thessaloniki (Salonica)
ATHINA (Athens)
Peloponnese
Crete
Rhodes
Dodecanese
Cyclades
Mirtoo Sea
Samothraki
Gökçeada
Limnos
Lesbos
Skiros
Evia
Andros
Tinos
Mykonos
Naxos
Paros
Kythira
Karpathos
Kasos
Lefkada
Kefalonia (Cephalonia)
Zakynthos (Zante)
Corfu
Kerkyra
Ionian Sea
Str. of Otranto
Gulf of Thessaloniki
Gulf of Rethimno
Gulf of Mirabello
Gulf of Kiparissia
Gulf of Messinia
Gulf of Antikythira
Gulf of Sporades
Gulf of Rethimno
Gulf of Mirabello
Gulf of Kiparissia
Gulf of Messinia
Gulf of Antikythira
Gulf of Sporades
Gulf of Rethimno
Gulf of Mirabello
Gulf of Kiparissia
Gulf of Messinia
Gulf of Antikythira
Gulf of Pagasitikos
Gulf of Sporades
Gulf of Kyparissia
Gulf of Orfanos
Gulf of Gökova
Projection: Conical with two standard parallels
East from Greenwich
National Parks
COPYRIGHT PHILIP'S
23

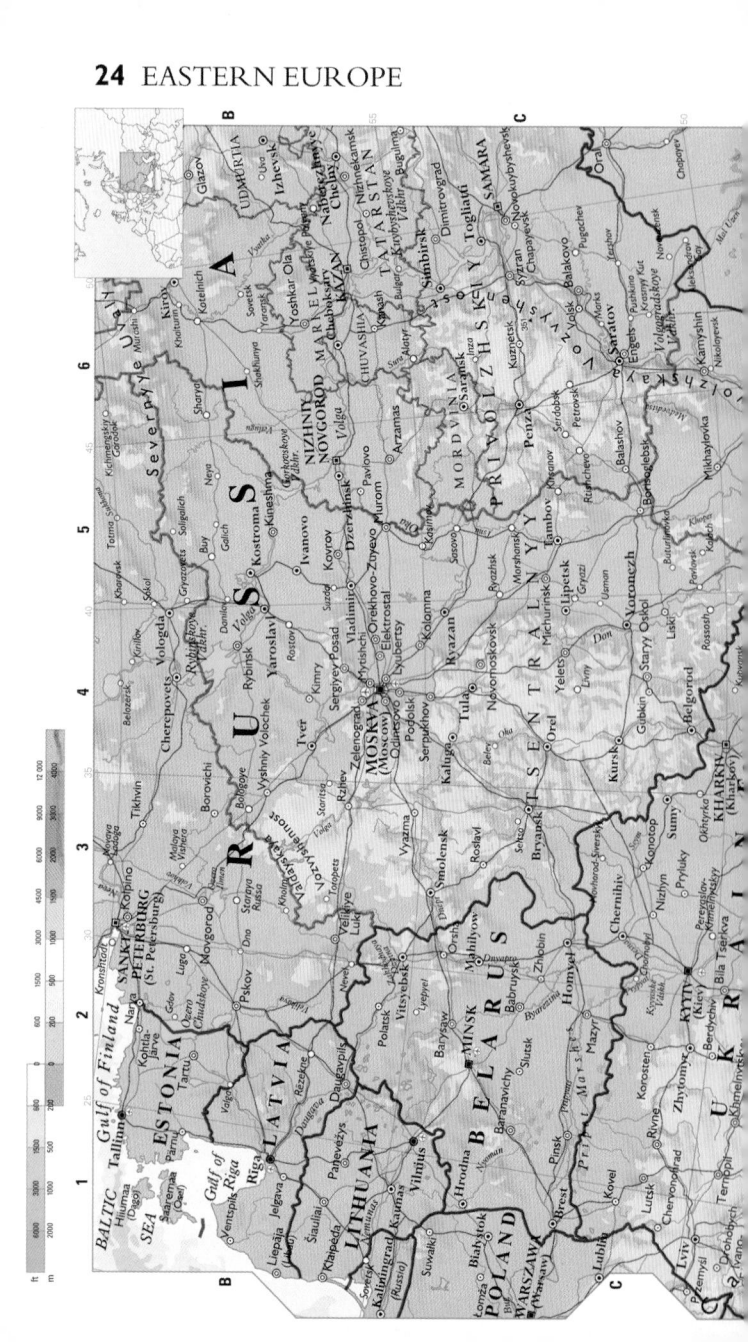
ft
m
6000
3000
1500
600
0
600
1500
3000
6000
9000
12 000
2000
1000
500
200
0
200
500
1000
2000
3000
4000
1
2
3
4
5
6
B
C
BALTIC SEA
Gulf of Finland
Gulf of Riga
Tallinn
Hiiumaa (Dagö)
Saaremaa (Ösel)
Kohtla-Järve
Narva
Pärnu
Tartu
ESTONIA
Riga
Jelgava
Liepāja
Daugavpils
LATVIA
Šiauliai
Panevėžys
Klaipėda
Kaunas
Vilnius
LITHUANIA
Kaliningrad (Russia)
Suwałki
Białystok
POLAND
WARSZAWA (Warsaw)
Lublin
Lwów
Przemyśl
Ivano-Frankivsk
Chernivtsi
Ternopil
Khmelnytskyi
Zhytomyr
Rivne
Lutsk
Brest
Pinsk
Kovel
Hrodna
Baranavichy
Slutsk
Mazyr
Homyel
MINSK
Bayrysaw
Polatsk
Vitsyebsk
Mahilyow
Babruysk
Zhlobin
Smolensk
Vyazma
Roslavl
Bryansk
Chernihiv
Nizhyn
Pryluky
Sumy
Konotop
KYIV (Kiev)
Bila Tserkva
Berdychiv
Korosten
Novgorod-Sivetskiy
Belgorod
Kursk
Gubkin
Staryy Oskol
Liski
Voronezh
Lipetsk
Yelets
Orel
Kaluga
Tula
Ryazan
Kolomna
Podolsk
Serpukhov
Zelenograd
MOSKVA (Moscow)
Orekhovo-Zuyevo
Elektrostal
Dzerzhinsk
Vladimir
Sergiyev Posad
Ryazhsk
Novoposkovsk
Michurinsk
Tambov
Ivanovo
Kostroma
Yaroslavl
Rybinsk
Cherepovets
Vologda
Belozersk
Tikhvin
Borovichi
Novgorod
Pskov
Velikiye Luki
Tver
Kimry
Rostov

ROMANIA
MOLDOVA
Chişinău
Iaşi
Botoşani
Bălţi
Tiraspol
Tighina
Bacău
Braşov
Focşani
Galaţi
Buzău
Brăila
Piteşti
Ploieşti
BUCUREŞTI
(Bucharest)
Ruse
Silistra
Constanţa
Dobrich
Veliko Tŭrnovo
Varna
BULGARIA
Sliven
Burgas
Khaskovo
Edirne
İSTANBUL
Tekirdağ
Gebze
Kocaeli
(Izmit)
Çanakkale
Marmara Denizi
Bandırma
BURSA
Balıkesir
Ayvalık
Akhisar
Manisa
İZMİR
(Smyrna)
Aydın
Samos
Uşak
Afyon
Eskişehir
Kütahya
ANKARA
Kırşehir
Kırıkkale
Sivrihisar
Yozgat
Çankırı
Karabük
Kastamonu
Zonguldak
Ereğli
Sakarya
Bolu
Sinop
Samsun
Bafra
Ordu
Giresun
Trabzon
Rize
Amasya
Tokat
Çorum
Sebinkarahisar
Erzincan
Erzurum
Sivas
Tuz Gölü
Kayseri
Aksaray
Malatya
Elazığ
Keban
Van
Tatvan
Van Gölü
Muş
Malatya
Erzincan
Tokat
Amasya
Sinop
Kastamonu
Çankırı
Karabük
Zonguldak
Bolu
Sakarya
Kocaeli
Bilecik
Eskişehir
Afyon
Denizli
Aydın
Malatya
Elazığ
Muş
Van
Erzurum
Kars
Artvin
Rize
Trabzon
Giresun
Ordu
Samsun
Karabük
Zonguldak
Bolu
Çankırı
Kastamonu
Sinop
Çorum
Yozgat
Kırıkkale
Kırşehir
Aksaray
Kayseri
Sivas
Tokat
Amasya
Erzincan
Ağrı
Van
Muş
Malatya
Elazığ
Muş
Van

26 ASIA

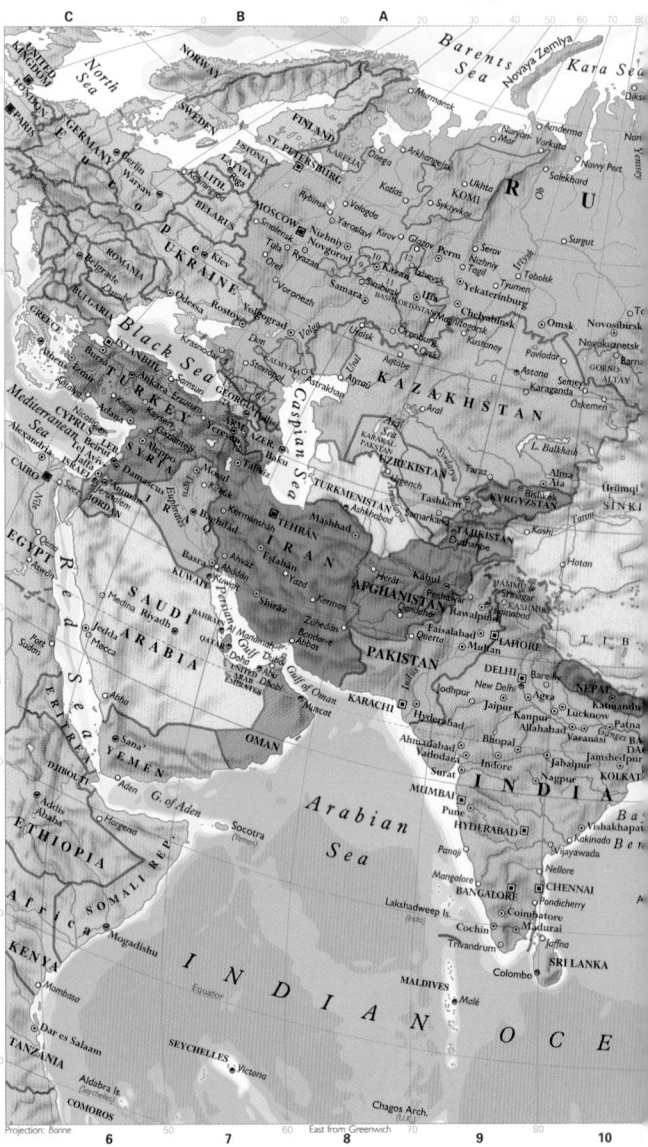
100 0 200 400 600 800 1000 1200 1400 km
100 0 200 400 600 800 1000 miles
Barents Sea
Novaya Zemlya
Kara Sea
North Sea
NORWAY
SWEDEN
FINLAND
ESTONIA
LATVIA
LITHUANIA
BELARUS
UKRAINE
ROMANIA
BULGARIA
GREECE
TURKEY
Black Sea
Caspian Sea
KAZAKHSTAN
UZBEKISTAN
TURKMENISTAN
KYRGYZSTAN
TAJIKISTAN
IRAN
AFGHANISTAN
PAKISTAN
INDIA
NEPAL
SAUDI ARABIA
YEMEN
OMAN
Persian Gulf
Gulf of Oman
Red Sea
Mediterranean Sea
EGYPT
LIBYA
SUDAN
ERITREA
DJIBOUTI
ETHIOPIA
SOMALI REP.
KENYA
TANZANIA
SEYCHELLES
COMOROS
MALDIVES
SRI LANKA
Arabian Sea
INDIAN OCEAN
Socotra (Yemen)
Chagos Arch. (U.K.)
Aldabra Is. (Seychelles)
Lakshadweep Is. (India)
Equator
Projection: Bonne
East from Greenwich
m ft

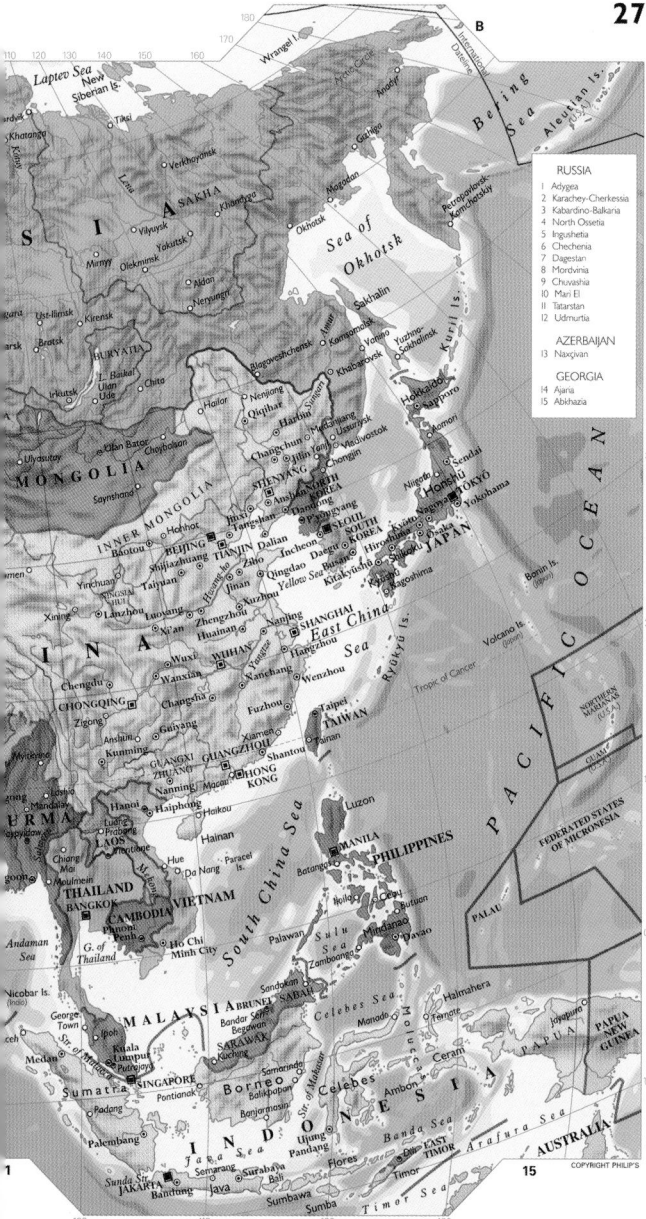
RUSSIA
1 Adygea
2 Karachey-Cherkessia
3 Kabardino-Balkaria
4 North Ossetia
5 Ingushetia
6 Chechenia
7 Dagestan
8 Mordvinia
9 Chuvashia
10 Mari El
11 Tatarstan
12 Udmurtia
AZERBAIJAN
13 Naxçivan
GEORGIA
14 Ajaria
15 Abkhazia
Laptev Sea
New Siberian Is.
Wrangel I.
Bering Sea
Aleutian Is.
Sea of Okhotsk
Sakhalin
Kuril Is.
Hokkaido
Honshu
Shikoku
Kyushu
Ryukyu Is.
Volcano Is.
Bonin Is.
Tropic of Cancer
PACIFIC OCEAN
NORTHERN MARIANA (USA)
GUAM (USA)
FEDERATED STATES OF MICRONESIA
PALAU
PHILIPPINES
MANILA
Luzon
Mindanao
Davao
Palawan
Sulu Sea
Celebes Sea
Molucca Sea
Halmahera
Ternate
Manado
Ambon
Ceram
Banda Sea
Arafura Sea
Timor Sea
Timor
Flores
Sumba
Sumbawa
Java Sea
Sunda Str.
JAKARTA
Bandung
Jaya
Semarang
Surabaya
Bali
Pontianak
Palembang
Padang
Pandang
Ujung
Banjarmasin
Balikpapan
Samarinda
Sumatra
Borneo
Celebes
INDONESIA
Sarawak
Kuching
Sabah
Kota Kinabalu
Bandar Seri Begawan
BRUNEI
Sandakan
Zamboanga
Batangas
Iloilo
Cebu
Butuan
Tawau
MALAYSIA
Kuala Lumpur
Putrajaya
Ipoh
George Town
Medan
SINGAPORE
Johor Bahru
Melaka
Kuantan
Kota Bharu
Alor Setar
Pattani
Phuket
Ranong
Chumphon
Nakhon Si Thammarat
Surat Thani
Phangnga
Andaman Sea
G. of Thailand
Nicobar Is. (India)
Phnom Penh
CAMBODIA
Ho Chi Minh City
VIETNAM
Da Nang
Paracel Is.
Hue
Vientiane
LAOS
Luang Prabang
Mandalay
Myitkyina
Lashio
BURMA
Chiang Mai
Moulmein
Mae Sot
Nan
Phitsanulok
Ubon Ratchathani
Khon Kaen
Nakhon Ratchasima
Chanthaburi
Bangkok
THAILAND
Hanoi
Haiphong
Hainan
Haikou
South China Sea
Macao
HONG KONG
Nanning
GUANGXI ZHUANG
Kunming
Shantou
Xiamen
Fuzhou
Taipei
TAIWAN
Tainan
Nanchang
Wenzhou
Hangzhou
Changsha
Guiyang
Chongqing
CHONGQING
Chengdu
Zigong
Wanxian
Wuxi
Nanjing
Wuhan
Yangtze
Shanghai
East China Sea
Zhengzhou
Luoyang
Kuzhou
Yellow Sea
Lanzhou
Xining
Yinchuan
Xi'an
Taiyuan
Shijiazhuang
Zhao
Qingdao
Dalian
Jinan
Tianjin
Beijing
Baotou
Hohhot
INNER MONGOLIA
Shenyang
Changchun
Jilin
Harbin
Qiqihar
Hailar
Nenjiang
Mudanjiang
Ussuriysk
Vladivostok
Chongjin
Pusan
Taegu
Inchon
Kitakyushu
Hiroshima
Kyoto
Osaka
Nagoya
Niigata
Sendai
Sapporo
Tokyo
Yokohama
Chita
Irkutsk
Ulan Bator
Choybalsan
Sayntsagaan
Ulyasutay
MONGOLIA
Ust-Ilimsk
Bratsk
Kirensk
BURYATIA
L. Baikal
Ulan Ude
Yakutsk
Vilyuyrsk
Verkhoyansk
Tiksi
Khatanga
Olekminsk
Aldan
Nerungri
Mirny
SAKHA
Magadan
Okhotsk
Petropavlovsk Kamchatskiy
Anadyr
Khabarovsk
Komsomolsk
Vanino
Yuzhno Sakhalinsk
Amur
Lena
Ob
Mekong
Salween
Chao Phraya
Tonle Sap
Yangtze
Huang He
Amur
Lena
Ob

28 WESTERN RUSSIA AND CENTRAL ASIA

RUSSIA
1 Adygea
2 Karachay-Cherkessia
3 Kabardino-Balkaria
4 North Ossetia
5 Ingushetia
6 Chechenia
7 Dagestan
8 Kalmykia
9 Stavropolia
10 Mari El
11 Tatarstan
12 Udmurtia
13 Khakassia
AZERBAIJAN
14 Nakhichevan
GEORGIA
15 Ajaria
16 Abkhazia
UKRAINE
17 Crimea
ARCTIC OCEAN
Barents Sea
Kara Sea
Zemlya Franza Iosifa
Zemlya Georga
Ostrov Rudolfa
Ostrov Green-Bell
Novaya Zemlya
Ostrov Bely
Ostrov Vaygach
Pechorskaya Guba
Ob'skaya Guba
Yenisey
Dikson
Yuzhnyy Zaliv
Gydanskiy
Poluostrov Yamal
Poluostrov Gydan
Poluostrov Kanin
Poluostrov Kola
Ostrov Kolguyev
Mys Kanin Nos
Mys Sporiy Navolok
Murmansk
Nordkapp
Hammerfest
Vardø
Pechenga
Murmashi
Gremikha
Kolskiy
Apatity
Kandalaksha
Kem
Belomorsk
Kotlas
Kotlas
Kuzomen
Mezen
Arkhangelsk
Belomorskaya Guba
Onezhskoye Ozero
Onega
Onezhskaya Guba
Severodvinsk
Severnaya Dvina
Vologda
Cherepovets
Vyshnyy Volochek
Tver
Novgorod
Pskov
Rybinsk
Yaroslavl
Kostroma
Kirov
Volga
Ob
Yenisey
Irtysh
Ust'-Port
Igarka
Tazovskiy
Yenisey
Nyda
Nyda
Nadym
Nadym
Ob
Ob'
Ob'
Ob'

Black Sea
Caspian Sea
Aral Sea
Sea of Azov
ROSTOV
YUZHNYY
SAMARA
YEKATERINBURG
CHELYABINSK
KOLOGRAD
Astrakhan
KALMYKS
Volgograd
Orenburg
Orsk
Aktyubinsk
Uralsk
Atyrau
Makhachkala
Derbent
Grozny
Stavropol
Krasnodar
Sochi
Sukhumi
Batumi
Kutaisi
Tbilisi
Rustavi
Yerevan
Nakhichevan
Gyumri
Kars
Erzurum
Trabzon
Samsun
Sinop
Ordu
Giresun
Rize
Ankara
Eskisehir
Adana
Sivas
Zonguldak
Kastamonu
Sinop
Samsun
Trabzon
Giresun
Rize
Kars
Artvin
Erzurum
Yozgat
Karabuk
Kastamonu
Sinop
Samsun
Corum
Erzincan
Adana
Karaman
Kutahya
Eskisehir
Bilecik
Bolu
Manisa

30 EASTERN SIBERIA

31
100 0 100 200 300 400 500 600 700 800 km
0 100 200 300 400 500 miles
B
C
D
E
14
15
16
9
10
11
Mys Dezhneva (East C.)
Ostrov Vrangelya
East Siberian Sea
Chukotskoye Nagorye
Sk. Lawrence I. (USA)
Bering Sea
Anadyrskiy Zaliv
Penzhinskaya Guba
Ambarchik
Chersky
Bilibino
Anadyr
Egvekinot
Beringovskiy
Nizhne Kolymsk
Omolon
Magadan
Okhotsk
Sea of Okhotsk
Kolymskoye Nagorye
Koryakskoye Nagorye
Poluostrov Kamchatka
Petropavlovsk-Kamchatskiy
Ust-Kamchatsk
Ust-Bolsheretsk
Kirovskiy
Ust-Khoyrynovo
Tigil'
Ust-Maya
Yakutsk
Aldan
Neryungri
Tommot
Ust-Mil'
Ust-Aldan
Ayan
Okha
Sakhalin
Nikolayevsk-na-Amure
Komsomol'sk
Khabarovsk
Birobidzhan
Blagoveshchensk
Zeya
Nerchinsk
Zabaykal'sk
Hailar
Hulun Nur
Beijing
Tianjin
Qiqihar
Harbin
Jiamusi
Mudanjiang
Changchun
Dalian
Shenyang
Hegang
Yichun
Daqing
Nenjiang
Beian
Bacheng
Yanji
Nakhodka
Vladivostok
Nakhodka
Kraskino
Ussuriysk
Dalnerechensk
Olgo
Dalnegorsk
Terney
Rumoi
Sapporo
Hokkaido
Hakodate
Aomori
Hachinohe
JAPAN
CHINA
Sea of Japan
Kurilskiye Ostrova
Ostrov Iturup
Ostrov Kunashir
Ostrov Paramushir
Ostrov Onekotan
Ostrov Kamchatka
Ostrov Bolshoy Lyakhovskiy
Ostrov Zhokhova
Ostrov Faddeyevskiy
Ostrov Ayon
Ostrova Medvezhiy

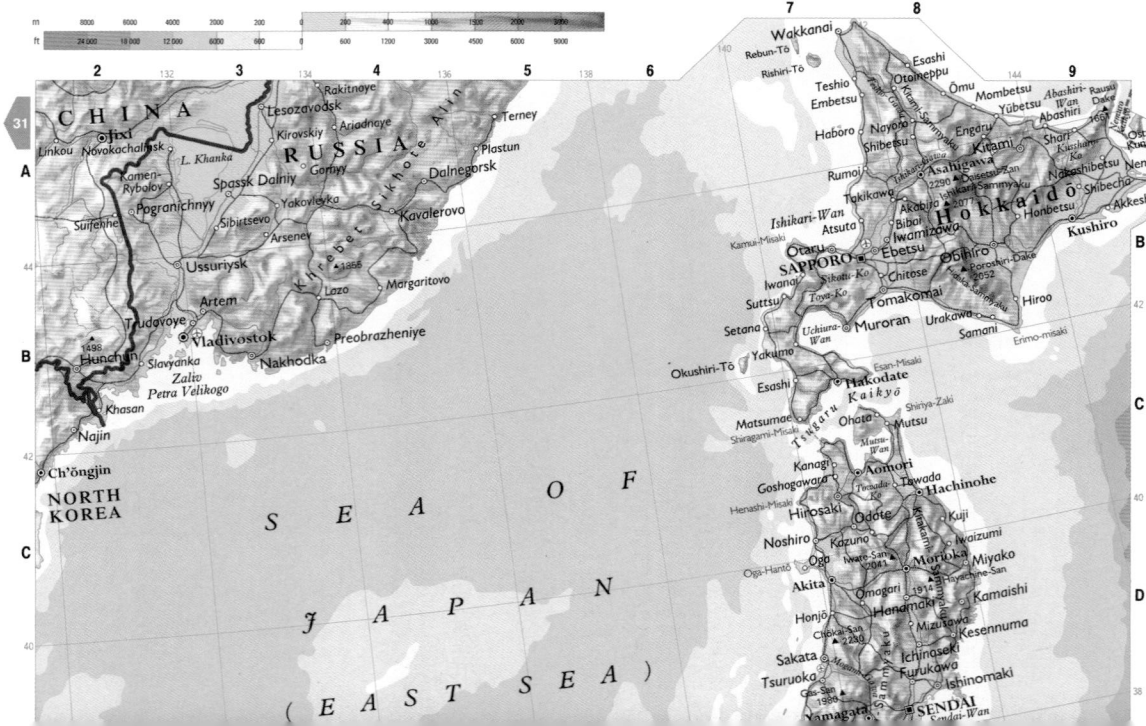
m 8000 6000 4000 2000 200 0
ft 24 000 18 000 12 000 6000 600 0
200 400 1000 1500 2000 3000
600 1200 3000 4500 6000 9000
CHINA
RUSSIA
Jilin
Linkou
Novokachalinsk
L. Khanka
Kamen-Rybalov
Pogranichnyy
Suifenhe
Spassk Dalniy
Sibirtsevo
Arseniev
Ussuriysk
Artem
Vladivostok
Nakhodka
Preobrazheniye
Hunchun
Slavyanka
Zalivo Petra Velikogo
Khasan
Najin
Ch'ongjin
NORTH KOREA
Rakitnoye
Lesozavodsk
Kirovskiy
Ariadnoye
Gornyy
Yakovlevka
Kavalerovo
Dalnegorsk
Plastun
Terney
Sikhote Alin
Kirgbet
Lazo
Margaritovo
SEA OF JAPAN
(EAST SEA)
Wakkanai
Rebun-Tō
Rishiri-Tō
Esashi
Teshio
Embetsu
Haboro
Otoineppu
Ōmu
Mombetsu
Yubetsu
Engaru
Abashiri
Shibetsu
Kitami
Rumoi
Asahigawa
Tokikawa
Ishikari-Wan
Atsuta
Bibai
Iwamizawa
Hokkaidō
Nakashibetsu
Nemuro
Shibecha
Akkeshi
Kushiro
Honbetsu
Otaru
SAPPORO
Ebetsu
Obihiro
Iwanai
Chitose
Tomakomai
Hiroo
Suttsu
Muroran
Urakawa
Samani
Setana
Yakumo
Okushiri-Tō
Esashi
Hakodate
Kaikyō
Matsumae
Ōhata
Mutsu
Tsugaru Kaikyō
Aomori
Kanagi
Goshogawara
Tawada
Hachinohe
Hirosaki
Odate
Kuji
Noshiro
Kazuno
Iwaizumi
Ōga
Morioka
Miyako
Akita
Ōmagari
Kamaishi
Honjō
Hanamaki
Mizusawa
Kesennuma
Sakata
Ichinoseki
Tsuruoka
Furukawa
Ishinomaki
Yamagata
SENDAI
Sendai-Wan

JAPAN
Honshū
Shikoku
Kyūshū
SOUTH KOREA
Korea Strait
PACIFIC OCEAN
Nampō Shotō
Ulleungdo (S. Korea)
Liancourt Rocks (Dokdo, Takeshima)
Oki-Shotō (Japan)
Tsushima (Japan)
Yeongdeok
Pohang
ULSAN
Wajima
Suzu
Nanao
Hakui
Himi
Toyama
Takaoka
Kanazawa
Komatsu
Fukui
Takefu
Tsuruga
Gifu
Ōgaki
Ichinomiya
Toyota
Okazaki
Toyohashi
Iwata
Hamamatsu
Tottori
Yonago
Matsue
Izumo
Ōda
Hamada
Masuda
Fukuchiyama
Maizuru
Tsuyama
Miyoshi
Fuchū
Okayama
Himeji
Nishinomiya
KOBE
OSAKA
Higashiosaka
Matsusaka
Amagasaki
Izumi-Sano
Wakayama
Tokushima
Naruto
Takamatsu
Marugame
Fukuyama
Kure
Hiroshima
Iwakuni
Yamaguchi
Ube
Tokuyama
Hofu
Shimonoseki
Matsuyama
Imabari
Ikeda
Anan
Gobō
Tanabe
Shingū
Kushimoto
Muroto
Muroto-Misaki
Kōchi
Nankoku
Mugi
Tosa-Wan
Shikoku
Uwajima
Yawatahama
Nakamura
Sukumo
Ashizuri-Zaki
Owase
Daiō-Misaki
Shio-no-Misaki
Kitakyūshū
Fukuoka
Nōgata
Buzen
Beppu
Ōita
Kurume
Saga
Karatsu
Imari
Omuta
Kumamoto
Saiki
Nobeoka
Hyūga
Sasebo
Gotō-Rettō
Nagasaki
Yatsushiro
Hondo
Amakusa-Shotō
Ushibuka
Minamata
Kurino
Miyazaki
Miyakonojō
Sendai
Koshiki-Rettō
Kagoshima
Makurazaki
Nichinan
Kanoya
Ibusuki
Sata-Misaki
Bungo-Suidō
Tōkyō
KAWASAKI
YOKOHAMA
Chiba
Mito
Hitachi
Kitaibaraki
Iwaki
Sendai
Akita
Niigata
Nagaoka
Kōriyama
Fukushima
Tsuchiura
Kawagoe
Kumagaya
Maebashi
Takasaki
Utsunomiya
Oyama
Kofu
Fuji
Numazu
Atami
Odawara
Yokosuka
Tateyama
Ito
Ō-Shima
Izu-Shotō
Nii-Jima
Miyake-Jima
Hachijō-Jima
Aoga-Shima
Sunaga-Wan
Suruga-Wan
Ise-Wan
Tokyo-Wan
Ise-Shima
Fuji-San
Kyō-gai-Saki
Echizen-Misaki
Wakasa-Wan
Biwa-Ko
Kyōto
Nagoya
Ōsaka
Kōbe
Yokkaichi
Ōsaka-Wan
Kii-Suidō
Bungo-Suidō
Suzu-Misaki
Tōkyō-Wan
Sanjo
Aizuwakamatsu
Niitsu
Tajima
Sukagawa
Iwaki
Kitaibaraki
Hitachi
Tanakura
Yaita
Shirane-San
Kusatsu
Kiryū
Utsunomiya
Mito
Oyama
Tsuchiura
Kawagoe
Kawaguchi
Funabashi
Chiba
Tchihara
YOKOHAMA
Yokosuka
Tateyama
Numazu
Itō
Ō-Shima
Nojima-Zaki
Nii-Jima
Miyake-Jima
Hachijō-Jima
Aoga-Shima
Izu-Shotō
Nampō Shotō
Suruga-Wan
Ise-Wan
Tokyo-Wan
Ise-Shima
Fuji-San
Kyō-gai-Saki
Echizen-Misaki
Wakasa-Wan
Biwa-Ko
Kyōto
Nagoya
Ōsaka
Kōbe
Yokkaichi
Ōsaka-Wan
Kii-Suidō
Bungo-Suidō
Suzu-Misaki
Tōkyō-Wan
8412
9076
Projection: Conical with two standard parallels
East from Greenwich
COPYRIGHT PHILIP'S
33

34 CHINA

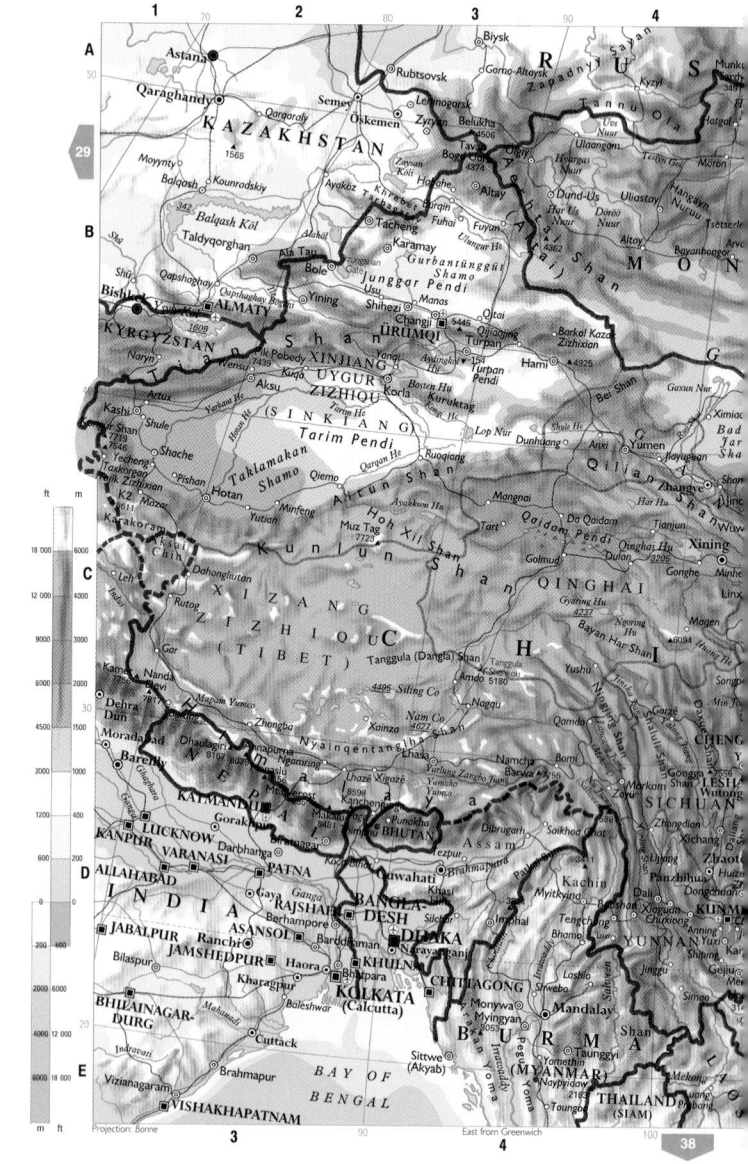
Astana
Qaraghandy
KAZAKHSTAN
Semey
Öskemen
Rubtsovsk
Biysk
Gorno-Altaysk
RUSSIA
Zapadnyy Sayan
Tannu Ola
Kyzyl
Munku Sardyk
Hatgal
Moyynty
Balqash
Kounrodskiy
Balqash Köl
Taldyqorghan
Ala Tau
Bole
Yining
Usu
Shihezi
Changji
Manas
Urumqi
Turpan
Hami
Altay
Tacheng
Fuhai
Fuyun
Karamay
Junggar Pendi
Gurbantünggüt Shamo
Altai Shan
MONGOLIA
Bishkek
ALMATY
KYRGYZSTAN
Naryn
Tian Shan
Pobeda
Aksu
Kuqa
XINJIANG UYGUR ZIZHIQU (SINKIANG)
Korla
Bosten Hu
Kuruktag
Tarim Pendi
Turpan Pendi
Barkol Kazak Zizhixian
Bei Shan
Gaxun Nur
Ximiao
Kashi
Shule
Shache
Taklamakan Shamo
Qiemo
Ruoqiang
Dunhuang
Anxi
Yumen
Qilian Shan
Zhangye
Xining
Tianjun
Altun Shan
Mangnai
Qaidam Pendi
Da Qaidam
Golmud
Dulan
Qinghai Hu
Gonghe
Hoh Xil Shan
Kunlun Shan
Hotan
Minfeng
Yutian
Muz Tag
Karakoram Pass
Leh
Dzhongliutan
Rutog
XIZANG ZIZHIQU (TIBET)
Tanggula (Dangla) Shan
Amdo
Siling Co
Nagqu
Nam Co
Kainza
QINGHAI
Yushu
Gyaring Hu
Ngoring Hu
Bayan Har Shan
Magen
Gar
Kathmandu
Dehra Dun
Moradabad
Bareilly
Dhaulagiri
Nyainqentanglha
Lhasa
Lhoze Xigaze
Namcha Barwa
Bomi
Qamdo
Gaze
Nagqu
Nujiang
Salween
Mekong
Min
Songpan
CHENGDU
LESHAN
SICHUAN
Maykum
Gongga Shan
Zhongdian
Xichang
Zhaotong
Huize
Panzhihua
Dongchuan
KUNMING
Dali
Xiaguan
Chuxiong
Anning
Yuxi
Kai
YUNNAN
Shiping
Geejiu
Simao
Lashio
Shweba
Mandalay
Shan
BURMA (MYANMAR)
Monywa
Myingyan
Irrawaddy
Yoma
Taungoo
Naypyidaw
Sittwe (Akyab)
THAILAND (SIAM)
Mekong
Lao
Lucknow
KANPUR
Darbhanga
VARANASI
PATNA
Gaya
Ganga
ALLAHABAD
INDIA
RAJSHAHI
BANGLADESH
DHAKA
Narayanganj
Berhampore
Barddhaman
ASANSOL
JABALPUR
Ranchi
JAMSHEDPUR
Haora
KHULNA
Kharagpur
Baleshwar
KOLKATA (Calcutta)
CHITTAGONG
BHILAINAGAR-DURG
Mahanadi
Cuttack
Brahmapur
Vizianagaram
VISHAKHAPATNAM
BAY OF BENGAL
Guwahati
Brahmaputra
Dibrugarh
Assam
Saikhoa Ghat
Kachin
Myitkyina
Bhamo
Imphal
Chindwin
Irrawaddy
Salween
Tenchong
BHUTAN
Punakha
Thimphu
Gorakhpur
Darbhanga
Kathmandu
Ganges
Mahanadi
Indravati
Ghaghara
Brahmaputra
Ft
m
18 000
12 000
9000
6000
4500
3000
1200
600
0
200
400
2000
6000
12 000
18 000
Projection: Bonne
East from Greenwich
29
30
20
38

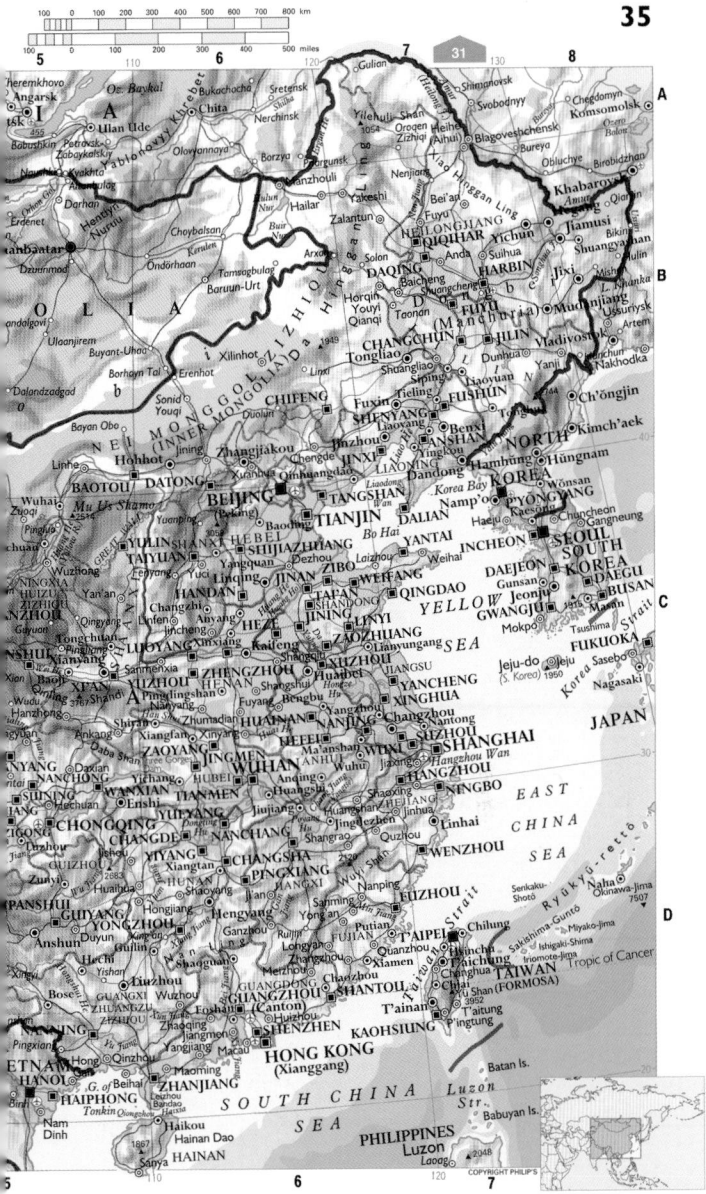
100 0 100 200 300 400 500 600 700 800 km
100 0 100 200 300 400 500 miles
31
5
6
7
8
A
B
C
D
Oz. Baykal
Angarsk
Bukachacha
Sretensk
Chita
Ulan Ude
Nerchinsk
Olovyannaya
Borzya
Gurgunsk
Manzhouli
Hailar
Yakeshi
Zalantun
Arxan
Choybalsan
Ondörhaan
Baruun-Urt
Tarnsagbulag
Dzuunmod
Erdenet
Darhan
Hentiy Nuruu
Yilehuli Shan
Oroqen Zizhiqi
Heihe
Aihui
Blagoveshchensk
Bureya
Obluchye
Birobidzhan
Khabarovsk
Qiqihar
Jamusi
Bikin
Shuangyashan
Mishan
Jixi
Harbin
Daqing
Baicheng
Changchun
Jilin
Tonghua
Dunhua
Yanji
Vladivostok
Ussuriysk
Artem
Nakhodka
Ch'ongjin
Kimch'aek
Hungnam
Wonsan
Kaesong
Gangneung
Chuncheon
Seoul
Incheon
Daejeon
Daegu
Busan
Masan
Gwangju
Jeonju
Gunsan
Mokpo
Tsushima
Fukuoka
Sasebo
Nagasaki
Jeju-do
(S. Korea)
Korea Strait
Korea Bay
Liaodong Wan
Bo Hai
Yellow Sea
East China Sea
Ryukyu-retto
Senkaku-Shoto
Naha
Okinawa-Jima
Miyako-Jima
Ishigaki-Shima
Iriomote-Jima
Taiwan Strait
Taipei
Chilung
Hsinchu
Taichung
Changhua
Chiai
Tainan
T'aitung
P'ingtung
Kaohsiung
Taiwan (Formosa)
Tropic of Cancer
Shantou
Chaozhou
Xiamen
Quanzhou
Fuzhou
Wenzhou
Ningbo
Hangzhou
Shanghai
Suzhou
Nanjing
Changzhou
Yangzhou
Nantong
Xuzhou
Lianyungang
Yantai
Weihai
Qingdao
Weifang
Jinan
Zibo
Tianjin
Dalian
Beijing
Tangshan
Qinhuangdao
Shenyang
Anshan
Fushun
Benxi
Liaoyang
Dandong
Hunan
Changsha
Pingxiang
Nanchang
Jingdezhen
Jiujiang
Wuhan
Huangshi
Yichang
Xiangfan
Zhengzhou
Kaifeng
Luoyang
Anyang
Handan
Shijiazhuang
Taiyuan
Datong
Hohhot
Baotou
Yinchuan
Lanzhou
Xi'an
Baoji
Xining
Chengdu
Chongqing
Guiyang
Nanning
Guangzhou (Canton)
Shenzhen
Hong Kong (Xianggang)
Macau
Zhanjiang
Haikou
Hainan Dao
Sanya
Haiphong
Hanoi
Nam Dinh
Tonkin
Gulf of Tonkin
Hainan
Philippines
Luzon
Luzon Str.
Batan Is.
Babuyan Is.
Laoag

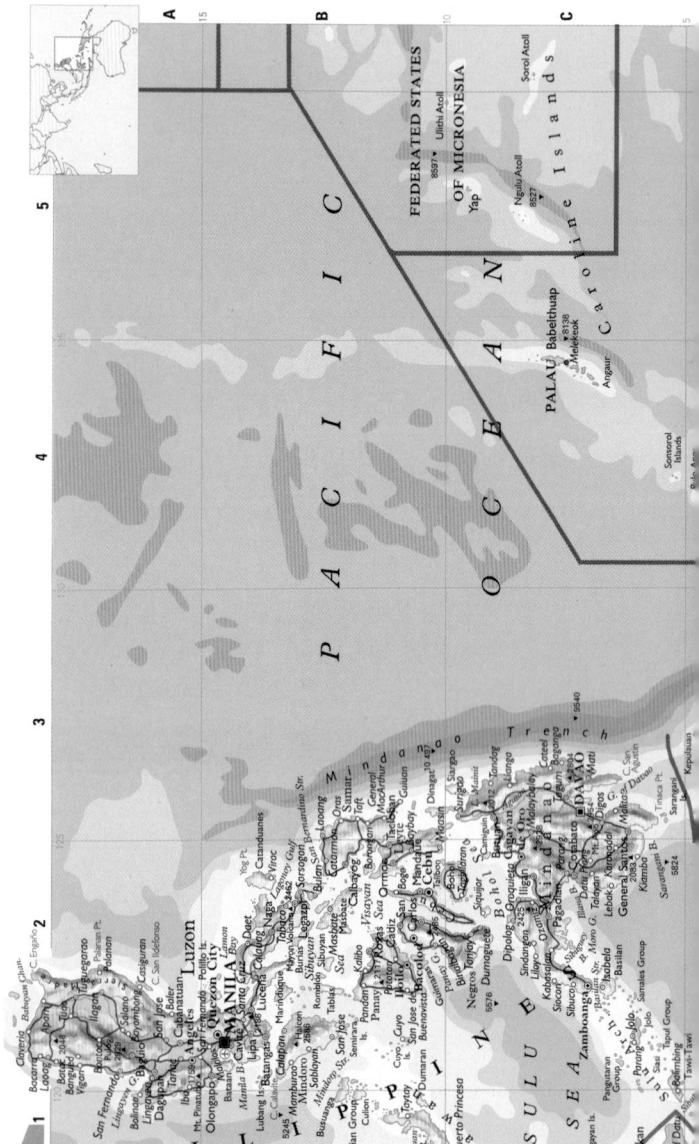
PHILIPPINES
Luzon
MANILA
Quezon City
Cebu
Mindanao
DAVAO
Zamboanga
SULU SEA
PACIFIC OCEAN
FEDERATED STATES OF MICRONESIA
Yap
Ulithi Atoll
Ngulu Atoll
Sorol Atoll
Caroline Islands
PALAU
Babelthuap
Angaur
Sonsorol Islands
Tawi-Tawi
Jolo
Basilan
Samales Group
Tapul Group
Sibutu
Cagayan Is.
Pangutaran Group
Tawitawi
Sibutu Passage
Sulu Sea
Kepulauan
Palau Arch.
Ulithi
Sorol
Angaur
Ngulu
Volcano Is.
Philippine Sea
Philippine Trench
Yap Trench
Palau Trench
Ulithi Atoll
Sonsorol Islands

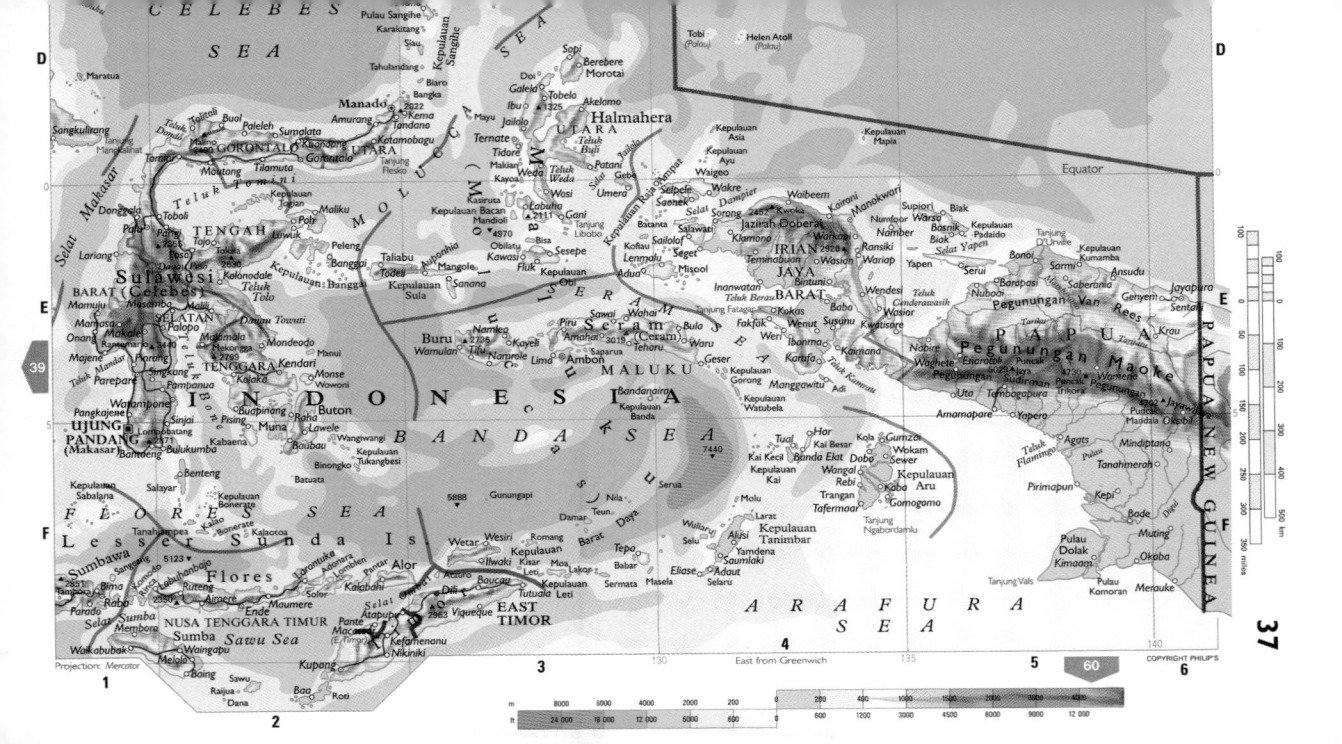
CELEBES SEA
Pulau Sangihe
Kepulauan Sangihe
Karakitang
Siau
Tahuhandang
Biaro
Bangka
Maratua
Manado
2022
Amurang
Tondano
Katamobagu
Sangkulirang
Tanjung Manakinat
Tolitoli
Buol
Paleleh
Sumalata
Gorontalo
Kabandang
Gorontalo
Moutong
Tilamuta
Teluk Tomini
Teluk Palu
Dongala
Toboli
Palu
Parigi
2351
Tojo
Poso
Tokasa
2440
Lariang
Kepulauan Togian
Poso
Maliku
Peleng
Banggai
Taliabu
Todeli
Kepulauan Banggai
Kepulauan Sula
Mangole
Sanana
Sulawesi (Celebes)
BARAT (Celebes)
Mamuju
Masamba
Malili
Mamasa
Palopo
Mikale
Onang
Rantemario
3440
Mamuju
Makassar
2789
Majene
Parepare
Pangkajene
Watampone
UJUNG PANDANG (Makasar)
2171
Bantaeng
Bulukumba
Benteng
Kepulauan Sabalana
Salayar
Selat Makassar
Selat Mandar
Teluk Bone
Selat Buton
Selat Peleng
Selat Sangihe
Selat Molucca
Selat Ternate
Selat Obi
Selat Bacan
Selat Dampier
Selat Salawati
Selat Sele
Selat Yapen
Selat Sumba
Selat Makassar
Selat Bangka

BURMA
RANGOON (Yangon)
(MYANMAR)
THAILAND
BANGKOK
LAOS
VIETNAM
CAMBODIA
PHNOM PENH
THANH PHO HO CHI MINH (Saigon)
Da Nang
Hue
Hoi An
Quang Ngai
Qui Nhon
Nha Trang
Cam Ranh
Da Lat
Buon Ma Thuot
Bien Hoa
My Tho
Can Tho
Soc Trang
Bac Lieu
Ca Mau
Vung Tau
Paracel Is.
Spratly Is.
Spratly I.
Amboyna Cay
Loaita I.
Itu Aba I.
Sin Cowe I.
Nanshan I.
PHILIPPINES
Palawan
Mt. Mantalingajan
C. Bulluyan
Bugsuk
Balabac I.
Balabac Str.
P. Banggi
Kudat
Langkon
P. Jambongan
Cagayan Is.
Kota Belud
Kota Kinabalu
Gunung Kinabalu
Sandakan
Bandar Labuan
Beaufort
Papar
Beluran
SABAH
LABUAN
Melalap
Tenom
Lahad Datu
Bandar Seri Begawan
BRUNEI
Tutong
Miri
Limbang
Lawas
Kuala Terengganu
Kota Bharu
Malacca
Lhokseumawe
Banda Aceh
Sabang
Ambon
Kotabaru
Tawau
Sandakan
Kota Kinabalu
Miri
Limbang
Lawas
Kuala Terengganu
Kota Bharu
Alor Setar
George Town
Butterworth
Ipoh

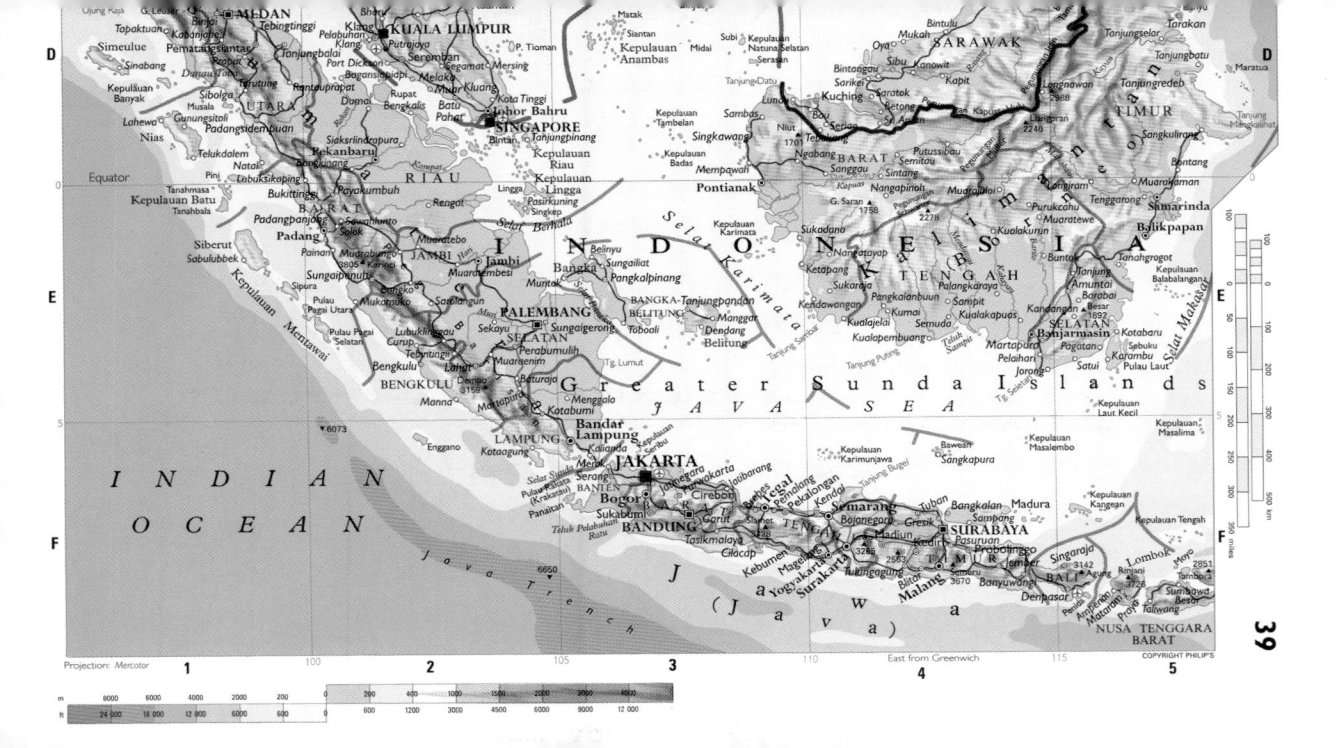
MEDAN
KUALA LUMPUR
SINGAPORE
Johor Bahru
Pontianak
Palembang
Bandar Lampung
JAKARTA
Bogor
BANDUNG
Semarang
SURABAYA
Malang
Yogyakarta
Surakarta
Cirebon
Pekanbaru
Padang
Jambi
Bengkulu
Banjarmasin
Balikpapan
Samarinda
Kuala Lumpur
Kota Bharu
Kuantan
Kuching
Sibu
Bintulu
Kuala Belait
Bintan
Tanjungpinang
Pulau Natuna Selatan
Pulau Natuna Utara
Kepulauan Anambas
Kepulauan Tambelan
Kepulauan Badas
Kepulauan Karimata
Kepulauan Riau
Kepulauan Lingga
Kepulauan Bangka Belitung
Kepulauan Mentawai
Kepulauan Batu
Kepulauan Banyak
Kepulauan Karimunjawa
Kepulauan Masalembo
Kepulauan Laut Kecil
Kepulauan Masaliman
Kepulauan Kangean
Kepulauan Tengah
Kepulauan Aru
Kepulauan Sula
Kepulauan Seribu
Kepulauan Natuna Selatan
Kepulauan Natuna Utara
Selat Karimata
Selat Makassar
Selat Bangka
Selat Sunda
Selat Lombok
Selat Bali
Selat Singapore
Selat Bintan
Selat Riau
Selat Berhala
Selat Mentawai
Selat Sumba
Selat Bali
Selat Lombok
Selat Sunda
Selat Bangka
Selat Karimata
Selat Makassar

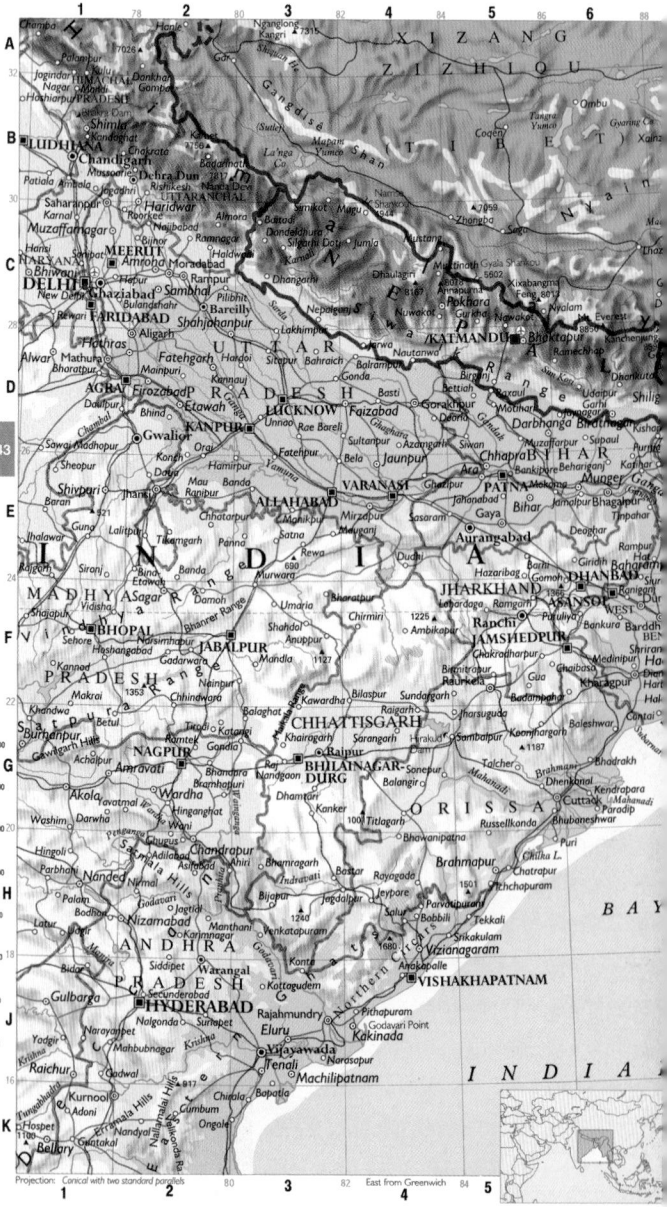
X I Z A N G
Z I Z H L Q U
T I B E T
Y a r l u n g
Y a r u
N y a n
Ganglise
Gangdisê
Shan
Mabam Yumco
La'nga Co
Gangdise
Himalaya
Indus
Sutlej
Chenab
Ravi
Jhelum
Chenab
Yamuna
Brahmaputra
Kosi
Gandak
Ghaghara
Chambal
Narmada
Tapti
Godavari
Krishna
Tungabhadra
Mahanadi
Brahmaputra
Indus
Sutlej
Ravi
Chenab
Jhelum
Yamuna
Chambal
Narmada
Tapti
Godavari
Krishna
Tungabhadra
Mahanadi
Brahmaputra

50 0 100 200 300 400 km
50 0 50 100 150 200 250 miles
34
38
CHINA
Bagen
Nangqen
Gamtog
Gorze
Dengqen
Bayu
Nagqu
Damdo
Xinlong
SICHUAN
Yajiang
Nam Co
Lhorong
Yidun
Litang
Lhari
Zhaxizé
Ningjing
Gongbo'gyamda
Lhünzub
Nyainqentanglha Shan
Namcha Barwa 7756
Rigé
Lhasa
Nang Xian
Mainkung
Muli Zangzu Zizhixian
Lhunze
Zhongdian
Cona
Mukangselek
Dunri Dumo
Sriokhoa Ghat
Tsinsukha
Putao
Kanglu
Weixi
Lijiang
Punakha
Tongsa Dzong
Rupa
Lakhimpur
North Dibrugarh
Sibsagar
Jianchuan
BHUTAN
Tuna Dzong
Tezpur
Hukawng Valley
Mainglawan
KACHIN
Yunlong
Jayanti
Sibsagar
Sylhet
Mogok
Myitkyina
Kohima
NAGALAND
Sinekaling Hkamti
Mogaung
Bhamo
Kochi Bihar
Gauripara
Guwahati
Brahmaputra
Shillong
Dhubri
Tura
MEGHALAYA
Cherrapunji
Barail Range
Ukhrul
Homalin
Tengchong
Longling
Changning
Rangpur
Jamalpur
Mohangonj
Mymensingh
Sylhet
Silchar
Imphal
MANIPUR
Churachandpur
Thaungdut
Katha
Indaw
Shwegu
Tamu
Wuntho
Tigyaing
Myitkyina
Bhamo
Lalaghat
Kohima
Sairang
Aizawl
MIZORAM
Tiddim
Kalewa
SAGAING
Mawlaik
Kyunhla
Mawlaik
Hsenwi
Pang-Long
Kunlong
Kawng
Narayanganj
Chandpur
Comilla
Dhaka
Lunglei
Kaptai
Falam
Mingin
Shwebo
Budalin
Bawdwine
Mogok
Nantu
Lashio
Mong Yai
Mong Hsu
Mong Pawk
Khulna
Barisal
Bhola
Patuakhali
Hatia
Chittagong
Dohazari
Gongaw
Alon
Yinmabin
Sagaing
Mandalay
Mogaung
Kyaukse
Mong Kung
Mong Nai
Keng Tung
Mong Tan
Cox's Bazar
Kanpetlet
Pauk
Pakokku
Myingyan
Meiktila
Thazi
Taunggyi
Heho
Keng Tawng
Mong Pan
Mawk Mai
Muang Chiang Rai
Sittwe (Akyab)
Kyaukpadaung
Yenangyaung
Minbu
Magwe
Taungdwingyi
Loikaw
Mae Hong Son
Chiang Mai
ARAKAN
Kyaukpyu
Ramree I.
Letpan
Taungup
Prome
Pyinmana
Bawlake
Taungoo
KAYAH
KAYIN
THAILAND
Mugang
Lamphun
Lampang
Cheduba I.
Sandoway
Myanaung
Pyu
Moulmein
Tak
Letpadan
Tharawadey
Pegu
Gwa
Henzada
Kyongpyaw
Yendoon
PEGU
Insein
RANGOON
Thaton
Pa-an
Martaban
MON
Bassein
Maubin
Myaungmya
IRRAWADDY
Pyapon
G. of Martaban
Amherst
Kalegauk
Lamaing
Ye
Sangkhla Buri
Sangkhla
Nam Tok
Natkyizin
Yebyu
Tavoy
Maungmagan Is.
Launglon Bok
Moscos Is.
Mouths of the Irrawaddy
Maudin Sun
Preparis North Channel
Pariparit Kyun (Burma)
Preparis South Channel
Koko Kyunzu (Burma)
BENGAL
OCEAN
Arakan Coast
Irrawaddy
Sittang
Salween
Mekong
Chindwin
Mu
Kaladan
Chin Hills
Brahmaputra
Ganges
Dibang
Nu Jiang
Yarlung Zangbo Jiang
Mekong
Salween
Chindwin
Mu
Kaladan
Chin Hills
Brahmaputra
Ganges
Meghna
Dibang
Nu Jiang
Yarlung Zangbo Jiang
COPYRIGHT PHILIP'S

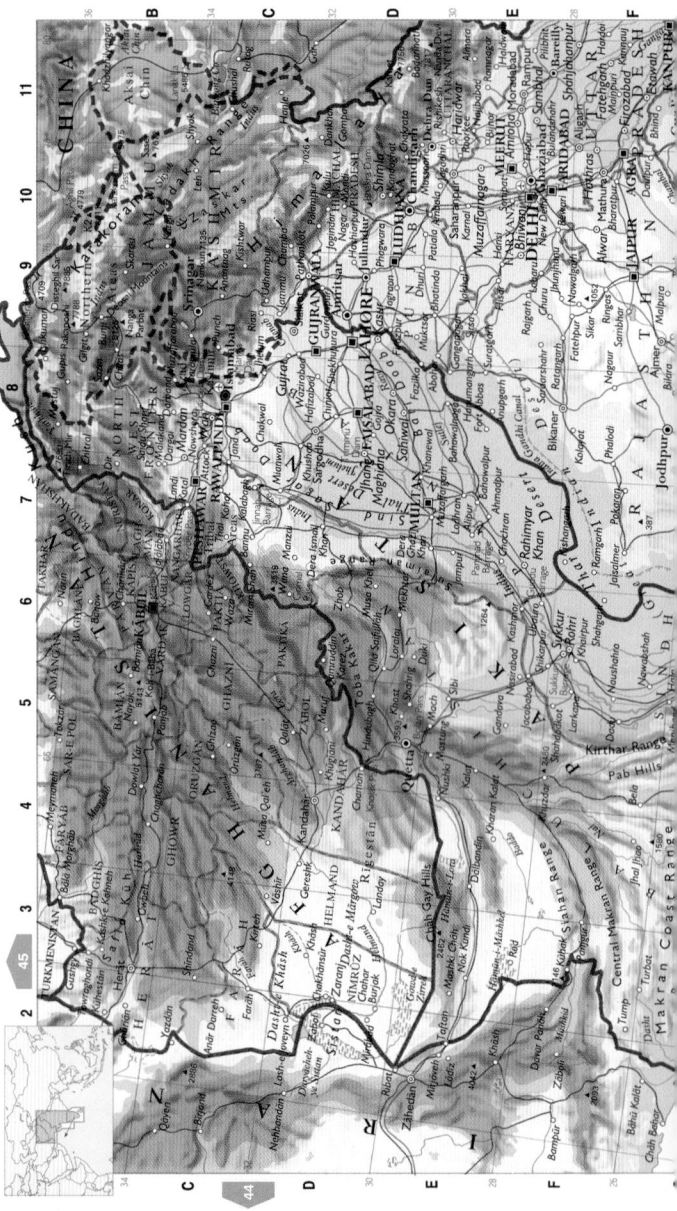
CHINA
TURKMENISTAN
AFGHANISTAN
PAKISTAN
INDIA
Kirthar Range
Pab Hills
Makran Coast Range
Central Makran Range
Sulaiman Range
Khyber Pass
Bolan Pass
Gomal Pass
Zhob Pass
Dasht-i-Margan
Dasht-i-Khash
Dasht-i-Margo

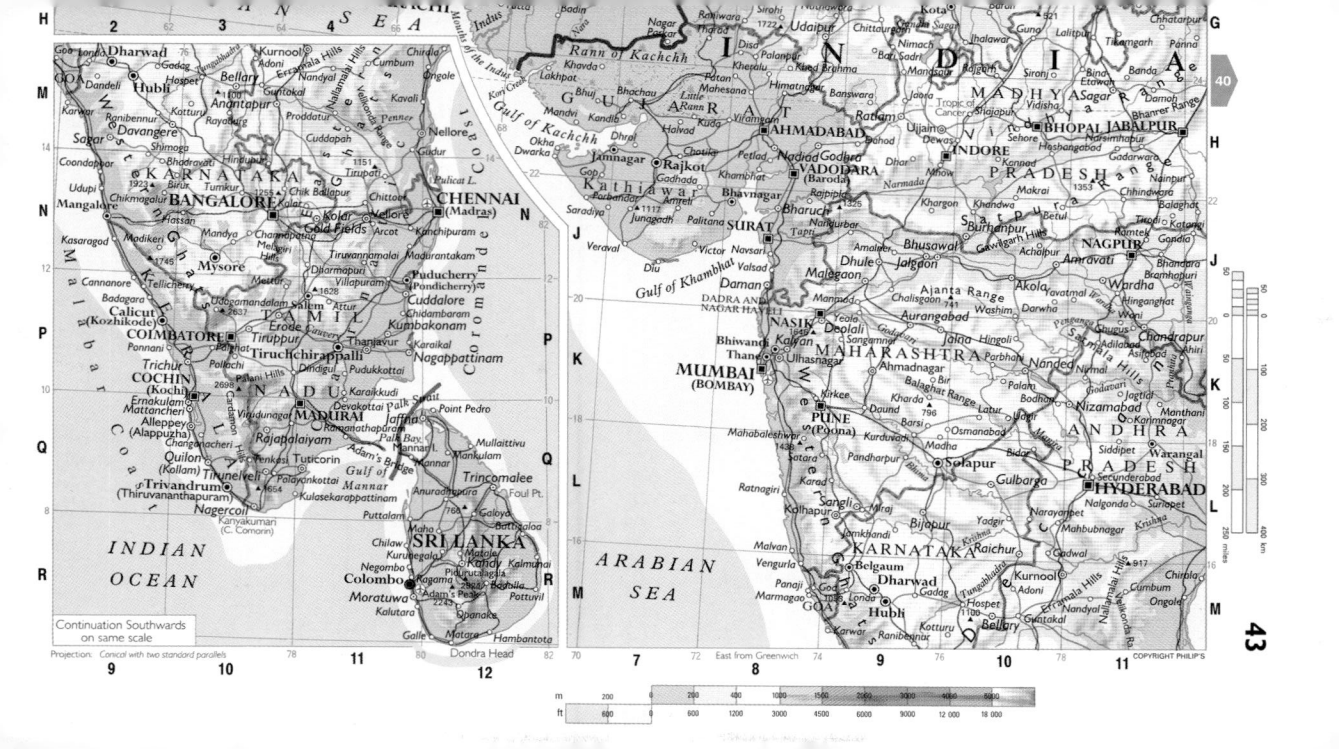
INDIA
ARABIAN SEA
INDIAN OCEAN
SRI LANKA
Continuation Southwards on same scale
Projection: Conical with two standard parallels
East from Greenwich
COPYRIGHT PHILIP'S
43
40
Gulf of Kachchh
Gulf of Khambhat
Rann of Kachchh
Kathiawar
GUJARAT
MADHYA PRADESH
MAHARASHTRA
KARNATAKA
TAMIL NADU
ANDHRA PRADESH
Western Ghats
Eastern Ghats
Malabar Coast
Coromandel Coast
Indus
Narmada
Tapti
Godavari
Krishna
Tungabhadra
Kaveri
Palk Strait
Palk Bay
Gulf of Mannar
Adam's Bridge
Mouths of the Indus
Kori Creek
Okha
Dwarka
Jamnagar
Rajkot
AHMADABAD
VADODARA (Baroda)
SURAT
MUMBAI (BOMBAY)
PUNE (Poona)
NAGPUR
INDORE
BHOPAL
JABALPUR
HYDERABAD
BANGALORE
CHENNAI (Madras)
COIMBATORE
MADURAI
Trivandrum (Thiruvananthapuram)
Colombo
Dondra Head
Point Pedro
Trincomalee
Foul Pt.
Kanyakumari (C. Comorin)
Dharwad
Hubli
Belgaum
Bellary
Raichur
Solapur
Gulbarga
Aurangabad
Nagpur
Amravati
Udaipur
Kota
Ratlam
Ujjain
Bhopal
Jabalpur
Indore
Surat
Bhavnagar
Jamnagar
Rajkot
Vadodara
Ahmadabad
Mumbai
Pune
Solapur
Hyderabad
Bangalore
Chennai
Coimbatore
Madurai
Trivandrum
Colombo
Moratuwa
Kalutara
Galle
Matara
Hambantota
Dondra Head
Trincomalee
Jaffna
Point Pedro
Puttalam
Anuradhapura
Kandy
Kalmunai
Batticaloa
Negombo
Kurunegala
Matale
Badulla
Galoya

44 PERSIAN GULF, IRAN AND AFGHANISTAN

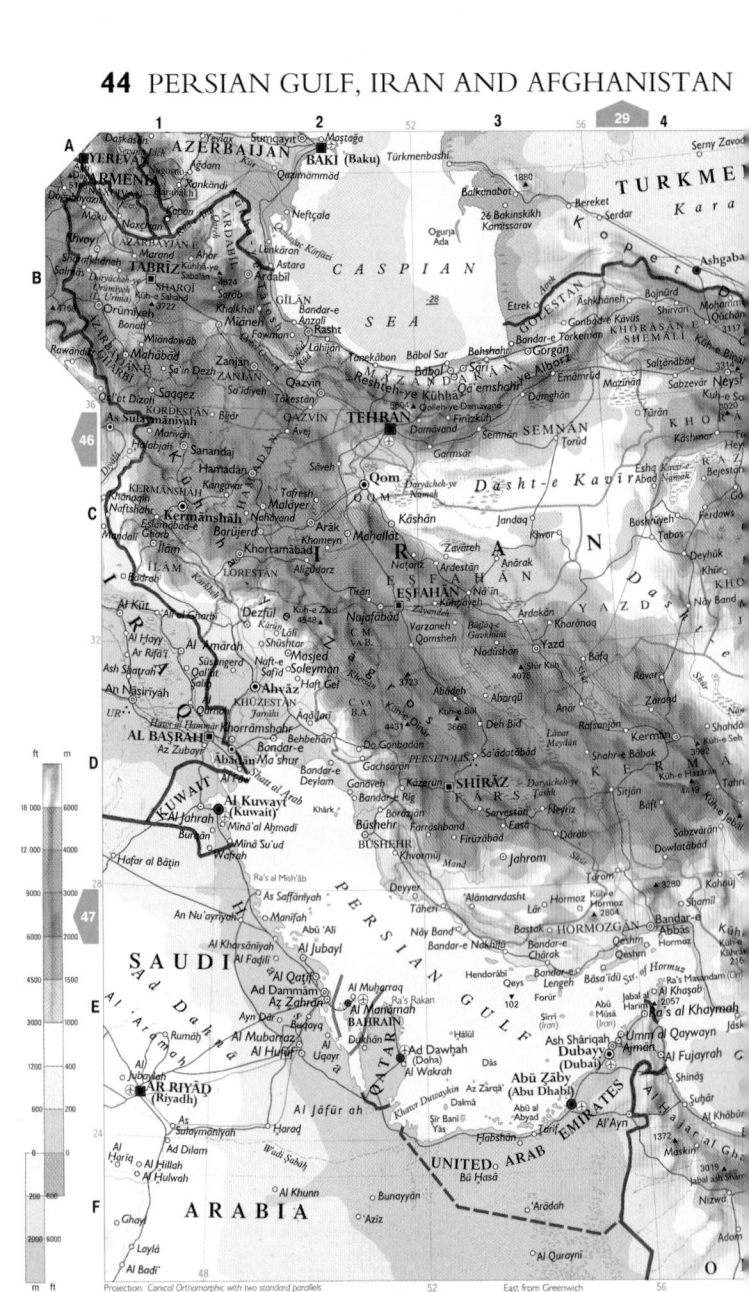
AZERBAIJAN
YEREVAN
ARMENIA
BAKI (Baku)
Türkmenbashi
Ashgabat
TABRIZ
CASPIAN SEA
GILAN
Bandar-e Anzali
Rasht
Lahijan
Qazvin
ZANJAN
Zanjan
Mahabad
Saqqez
KORDESTAN
As Sulaymaniyah
Bijar
QAZVIN
TEHRAN
Damavand
Semnan
SEMNAN
Garmsar
Qom
QOM
Kashan
Kermanshah
KERMANSHAH
Hamadan
Malayer
Arak
Khomeyni
Mahallat
Khorramabad
LORESTAN
ILAM
Ilam
Dezful
Ahvaz
KHUZESTAN
Masjed Soleyman
Haft Gel
AL BAŞRAH
Az Zubayr
Al Kuwayt (Kuwait)
KUWAYT
Al Jahrah
Hafar al Bāṭin
Ra's al Mish'āb
As Saffaniyah
An Nu'ayriyah
Al Jubayl
SAUDI
Al Qatif
Ad Dammam
Az Zahran
Al Mubarraz
Al Hufuf
Al Hofuf
Al Kharsaniyah
Al Ḥarīq
Al Hillah
Al Hulwah
Al Khunn
Ghayl
Layla
Al Badi'
AR RIYAD (Riyadh)
Al Jafūr ah
Ad Dilam
Al Ḥaraq
Wadi Sahba
Al Ḥasā
Al Ḥufūf
Al Muḥarraq
Ra's Rakan
Al Manamah
BAHRAIN
Dukhan
Ad Dawḥah (Doha)
Al Wakrah
QATAR
Khawr Dimsyahin
Az Zarqa
Dalma
Abū al Abyad
Yas
Ḥabshān
Abū Ẓāby (Abu Dhabi)
UNITED ARAB EMIRATES
Al 'Ayn
Ash Shāriqah
Dubayy (Dubai)
Umm al Qaywayn
Al Fujayrah
Ra's al Khaymah
Bū Ḥasā
Bunayyān
'Arādah
Al Quroyni
'Aziz
Nizwa
Bandar-e Lengeh
Bandar-e Chārak
Qeshm
Bandar-e Abbas
HORMOZGAN
Jahrom
Shiraz
SHIRAZ
Bushehr
BUSHEHR
Bandar-e Rig
Bandar-e Deylam
Gachsaran
Behbahan
Bandar-e Ma'shur
Khorramshahr
Abadan
Masjed Soleyman
Yazd
Kerman
Bandar-e Nakhilu
Bandar-e Lengeh
Bandar-e Chārak
Bandar-e Ḥormoz
Bandar-e Abbas
Ra's Musandam
Al Khaṣab
Ra's al Khaymah
Ash Shāriqah
Dubayy (Dubai)
Umm al Qaywayn
Al Fujayrah
Shinās
Suḥār
Al Khābūr
Al 'Ayn
Maskat
Jabal ash Shams
Nizwa
Adam
Ashgabat
Mashhad
Neyshabur
Sabzevar
Tehran
Qom
Esfahan
Yazd
Kerman
Bandar-e Bushehr
Bandar-e Lengeh
Bandar-e Chārak
Qeshm
Bandar-e Abbas
Hormoz
Ra's al Khaymah
Ra's al Khaṣab
Al Fujayrah
Ash Shāriqah
Dubayy (Dubai)
Abū Ẓāby (Abu Dhabi)
Al 'Ayn
Al Khābūr
Suḥār
Shinās
Al Quroyni
'Arādah
Bū Ḥasā
Bunayyān
Al Ḥufūf
Al Hofuf
Al Ḥarīq
Al Hillah
Al Hulwah
Al Khunn
Ghayl
Layla
Al Badi'
Al Jafūr ah
Ad Dilam
Al Ḥaraq
Wadi Sahba
Al Ḥasā
Al Ḥufūf
Al Muḥarraq
Ra's Rakan
Al Manamah
BAHRAIN
Dukhan
Ad Dawḥah (Doha)
Al Wakrah
QATAR
Khawr Dimsyahin
Az Zarqa
Dalma
Abū al Abyad
Yas
Ḥabshān
Abū Ẓāby (Abu Dhabi)
UNITED ARAB EMIRATES
Al 'Ayn
Ash Shāriqah
Dubayy (Dubai)
Umm al Qaywayn
Al Fujayrah
Ra's al Khaymah
Ra's al Khaṣab

50 0 100 200 300 400 km
50 0 50 100 150 200 250 miles
UZBEKISTAN
TAJIKISTAN
AFGHANISTAN
PAKISTAN
INDIA
IRAN
ARABIAN SEA
Gulf of Kachchh
Tropic of Cancer
Oman
Bukhara
Dushanbe
Qarshi
Türkmenabat
Mary
Herat
Kabul
Jalalabad
Peshawar
Islamabad
RAWALPINDI
Lahore
Multan
Quetta
Zahedan
Kandahar
Zaranj
Chaman
Mashkel
Panjgur
Turbat
Gwadar
Pasni
Ormara
Karachi
Hyderabad
Jaisalmer
Jamnagar
Porbandar
Bhuj
Khyber Pass
Bolan Pass
Mouths of the Indus
Rann of Kachchh
Central Makran Range
Makran Coast Range
Kirthar Range
Pab Hills
Great Indian Desert
Thal Desert
Sulaiman Range
Hindu Kush
Pamir
COPYRIGHT PHILIP'S

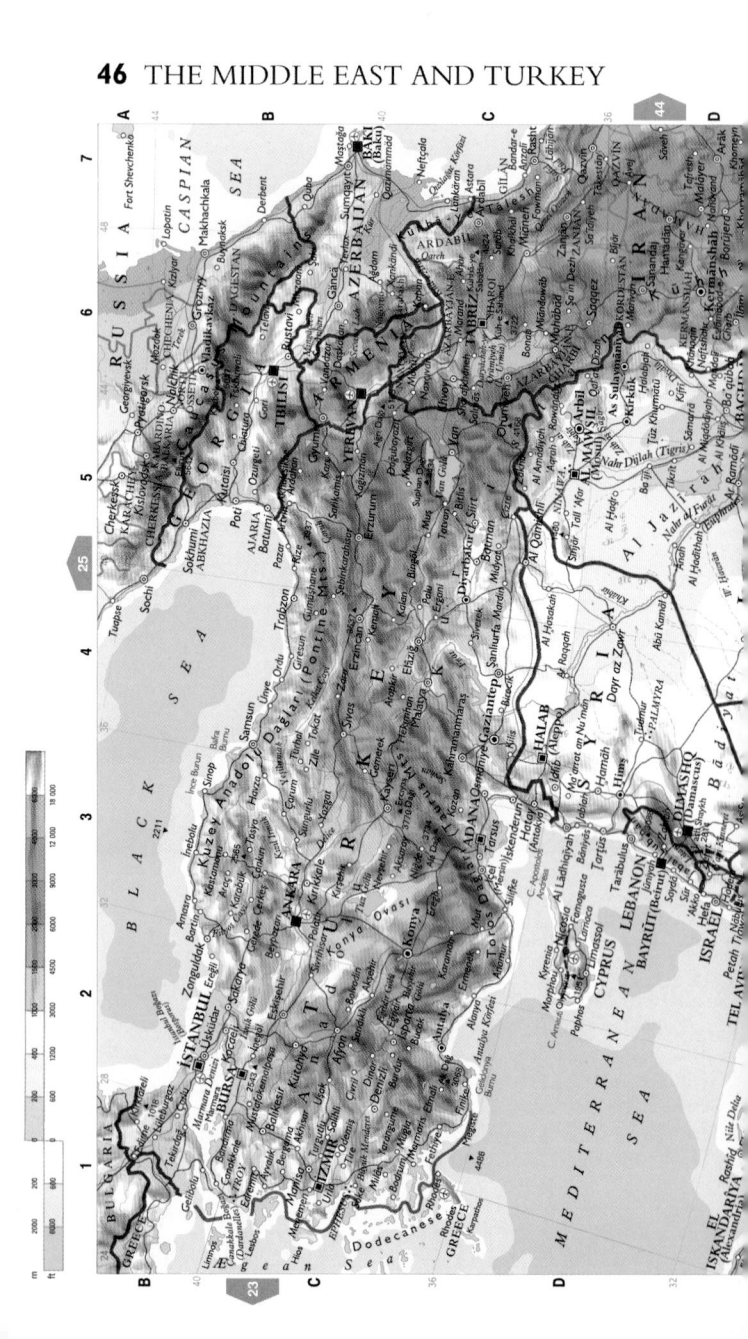
RUSSIA
CASPIAN SEA
BLACK SEA
MEDITERRANEAN SEA
Æ g e a n S e a
Dodecanese
GREECE
BULGARIA
CYPRUS
GEORGIA
ARMENIA
AZERBAIJAN
IRAN
IRAQ
SYRIA
LEBANON
ISRAEL
TURKEY
Anadolu
Kuzey Anadolu Dağları (Pontine Mts.)
Doğu Anadolu Dağları
Al Jazira
Bādiyat
İSTANBUL
ANKARA
İZMIR
BURSA
Konya Ovası
Tuz Gölü
Van Gölü
Urmia
Caspian Sea
Black Sea
Mediterranean Sea
Nahr Dijlah (Tigris)
Nahr al Furāt (Euphrates)
Al Ḥadīthah
Al Ramādī
Al Ḥasakah
Al Qāmishlī

EL QAHIRA (Cairo)
El Giza
PYRAMIDS
Bekhta
Zagazig
Ismailiyya
El Suweis (Suez)
Nakhl
Birket Qarun
El Fayyum
Beni Suef
Helwan
Shibin al Kawm
Al Minyā
Mallawi
Dairūt
Manfalūt
Asyūt
Tahta
Sūhāg
Akhmim
Girga
Qena
Qūs
THEBES
Nag Hammādi
El Khārga
Bārīs
El Uqsur
Idfū
Kōm Ombo
Aswān
El Shallal
Sadd el Ali (Aswan High Dam)
Dunqul
Buheirat en Nasir (Lake Nasser)
Wadi Halfa
HALAIB TRIANGLE
Halaib
Ras Hadarba
SUDAN
Es Sahrā' en Nūbiya
Gebeit
Muhammad Qol
Ras al Aswad
Ras al Hājibah
Dhahabān
JIDDAH (Jedda)
Makkah (Mecca)
Aṭ Ṭā'if
Zaymah
Uthmayrah
Harrat Nawāsif
Usfān
Sahl Rakbah
As Sūq
Al Qadīmah
Rābigh
Mastūrah
Ra's Abū Madd
Ra's Bārūd
Ra's Bālās
Ra's Banās
Ra's Ba'ir
Ra's Ba'ir
Ra's Ba'ir

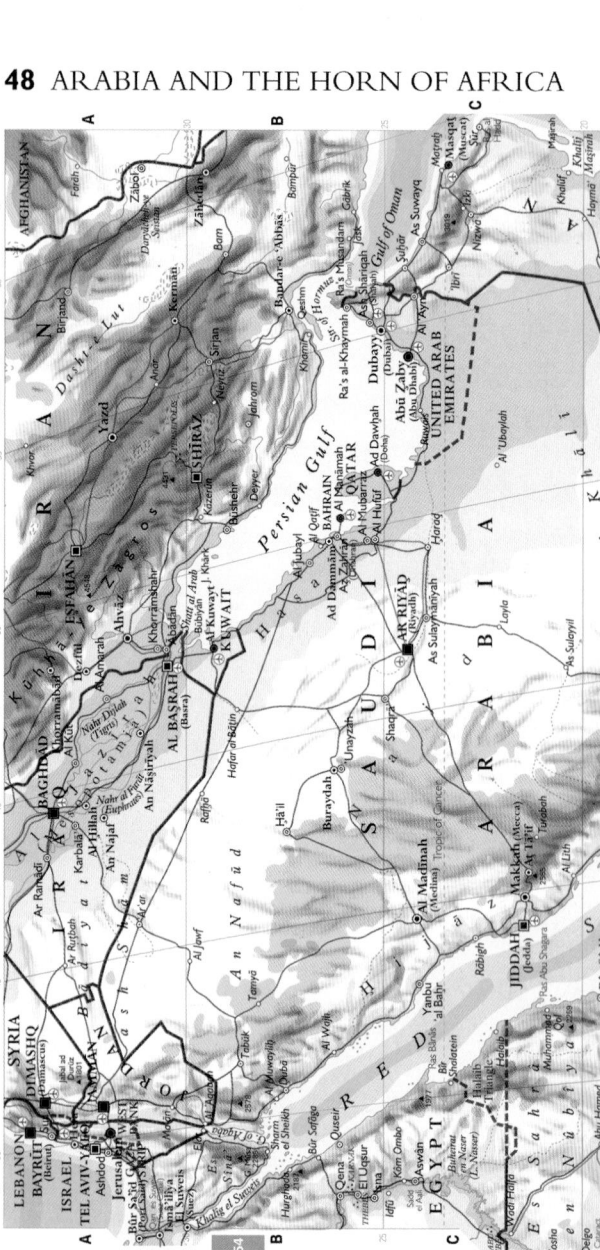
AFGHANISTAN
IRAN
Persian Gulf
Gulf of Oman
SHIRAZ
ESFAHAN
TEHRAN
BAGHDAD
AL BAṢRAH (Basra)
KUWAIT
BAHRAIN
QATAR
Dubayy (Dubai)
Abū Ẓaby (Abu Dhabi)
UNITED ARAB EMIRATES
AR RIYĀḌ (Riyadh)
SAUDI ARABIA
Al Madīnah (Medina)
Makkah (Mecca)
JIDDAH (Jedda)
Muscat
OMAN
Port Sudan
Jerusalem
Amman
Damascus
DAMASHQ
Beirut
BAYRŪT
LEBANON
SYRIA
ISRAEL
TEL AVIV-YAFO
Ashdod
Ashqelon
Gaza
Suez
EGYPT
Port Said
Bur Said
Ismailia
Al Ismā'īlīyah
Sharm el Sheikh
Ash Sharm
Hurghada
Qena
Aswan

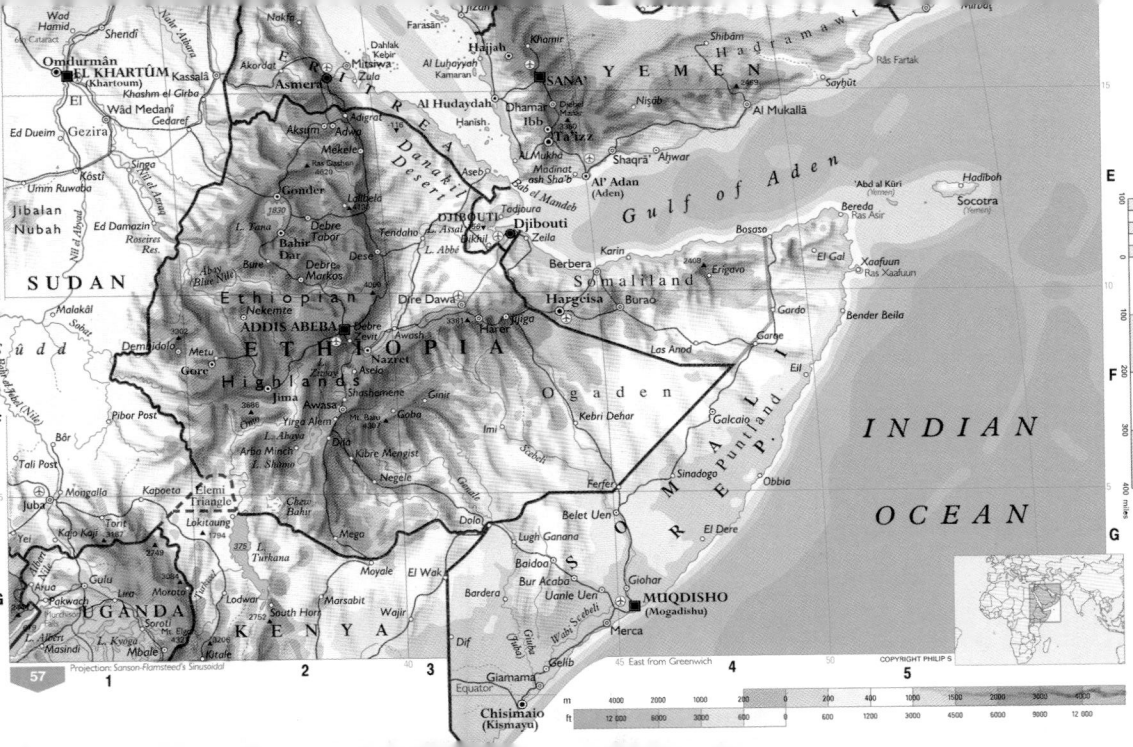
INDIAN
OCEAN
Gulf of Aden
Danakil Desert
Hadramawt
Ras Fartak
Socotra
(Yemen)
Hadiboh
Bereda
Ras Asir
Bosaso
Xaafuun
Ras Xaafuun
Bender Beila
Garoe
Las Anod
Eil
Obbia
El Dere
Hobyo
Galcaio
Sinadogo
Ferfer
Belet Uen
Kebri Dehar
Gaalkacyo
Ogaden
Somaliland
Puntland
Somalia
Berbera
Hargeisa
Burao
Erigavo
Karin
Zeila
Tadjoura
Dikhil
Djibouti
DJIBOUTI
Tendaho
Dese
Dire Dawa
Harar
Jijiga
Kebri Dehar
Imi
Goba
Ginir
Shashamene
Asela
Nazret
Debre Zeyit
ADDIS ABEBA
Awash
Zeway
Jima
Awasa
Yirga Alem
L. Abaya
L. Chamo
Arba Minch
Dila
Kibre Mengist
Negele
Dolo
Mega
Moyale
El Wak
Wajir
Bardera
Baidoa
Bur Acaba
Uanle Uen
Giohar
MUQDISHO
(Mogadishu)
Merca
Gelib
Giamama
Equator
Chisimaio
(Kismayu)
Dif
Lugh Ganana
Ethiopian
Highlands
ETHIOPIA
Gondar
Lalibela
Debre Tabor
Bahir Dar
L. Tana
Debre Markos
Bure
Nekemte
Dembidolo
Metu
Gore
Malakâl
Sûdd
Bor
Pibor Post
Tali Post
Juba
Mongalla
Kapoeta
Elemi Triangle
Lokitaung
Kajo Kaji
Yei
Torit
L. Turkana
Gulu
Lira
Pakwach
Arua
Moroto
Lodwar
Marsabit
South Horr
Soroti
Mt. Elgon
L. Albert
Masindi
L. Kyoga
Mbale
Kitale
UGANDA
KENYA
SUDAN
Jibalan
Nubah
Ed Dueim
Gezira
Kosti
Umm Ruwaba
Ed Damazin
Roseires Res.
Singa
Gedaref
Wad Medani
Khashm el Girba
Kassalâ
Omdurmân
EL KHARTÛM
(Khartoum)
Wad Hamid
Shendi
Atbara
Nile
Blue Nile
Sobat
Asmera
Massawa
Mitsiwa
Zula
Dahlak Kebir
Nakfa
Farasan
Jizan
Hajjah
Khamir
Al Luhayyah
Kamaran
SANA'
YEMEN
Al Hudaydah
Dhamar
Ibb
Ta'izz
Al Mukhâ
Madinat ash Sha'b
Bab al Mandeb
Aden
Al' Adan
(Aden)
Shaqrâ'
Ahwar
Al Mukallâ
Nisab
Shibam
Saybut
'Abd al Kuri
(Yemen)
Aseb
Hanish
Adigrat
Adwa
Aksum
Mekele
Ras Dashen
4620
Akordat
Atbara
Blue Nile
Rosaires Res.
Kosti
Ed Dueim
Gezira
Wad Medani
Khashm el Girba
Kassalâ
Omdurmân
EL KHARTÛM
(Khartoum)
Wad Hamid
Shendi
Atbara
Nile
Sobat
Asmera
Massawa
Mitsiwa
Zula
Dahlak Kebir
Nakfa
Farasan
Jizan
Hajjah
Khamir
Al Luhayyah
Kamaran
SANA'
YEMEN
Al Hudaydah
Dhamar
Ibb
Ta'izz
Al Mukhâ
Madinat ash Sha'b
Bab al Mandeb
Aden
Al' Adan
(Aden)
Shaqrâ'
Ahwar
Al Mukallâ
Nisab
Shibam
Saybut
Ras Fartak
Hadramawt
Aksum
Adwa
Adigrat
Mekele
Ras Dashen
4620
Gondar
Lalibela
Debre Tabor
Bahir Dar
L. Tana
Debre Markos
Bure
Nekemte
Dembidolo
Metu
Gore
Malakâl
Sûdd
Bor
Pibor Post
Tali Post
Juba
Mongalla
Kapoeta
Elemi Triangle
Lokitaung
Kajo Kaji
Yei
Torit
L. Turkana
Gulu
Lira
Pakwach
Arua
Moroto
Lodwar
Marsabit
South Horr
Soroti
Mt. Elgon
L. Albert
Masindi
L. Kyoga
Mbale
Kitale
UGANDA
KENYA
SUDAN
Jibalan
Nubah
Ed Dueim
Gezira
Kosti
Umm Ruwaba
Ed Damazin
Roseires Res.
Singa
Gedaref

NORTH ATLANTIC OCEAN
Mediterranean Sea
Black Sea
Caspian Sea
Red Sea
Persian Gulf
Sahara
RUSSIA
KAZAKHSTAN
UKRAINE
POLAND
GERMANY
FRANCE
SPAIN
PORTUGAL
ITALY
TURKEY
IRAN
SAUDI ARABIA
EGYPT
LIBYA
ALGERIA
TUNISIA
MOROCCO
MAURITANIA
MALI
NIGER
CHAD
SUDAN
YEMEN
NIGERIA
GHANA
IVORY COAST
GUINEA
SENEGAL
GAMBIA
CAPE VERDE IS.
Madeira (Port.)
Canary Is. (Sp.)
Azores (Port.)
Sicily
Sardinia
Corsica
Crete
CYPRUS
MALTA
Socotra
Addis Ababa
Asmara
Khartoum
Omdurman
Port Said
Suez
Alexandria
CAIRO
Tripoli
Benghazi
Algiers
Tunis
Rabat
Casablanca
Fez
Marrakesh
Madrid
Lisbon
Paris
LONDON
Rome
Athens
Vienna
Prague
Warsaw
Kiev
Volgograd
Odessa
Ankara
Aleppo
Damascus
Baghdad
Basra
Mecca
Medina
Riyadh
Jeddah
Tehran
Isfahan
Dakar
Bamako
Abidjan
Accra
Lagos
Abuja
Kano
Maiduguri
Ndjamena
Abéché
Djibouti
Berbera
Port Louis
Tripoli
Sebha
Murzuq
Al Jawf
Aswan
Port Sudan
Wadi Halfa
Tel Aviv
Jerusalem
Damascus
Nile
White Nile
Blue Nile
Tigris
Euphrates
Niger
Tropic of Cancer
Tropic of Capture
B. of Biscay
Gulf of Aden
G. of Aden
Socotra
Pas Aer
Berbera
Djibouti
Addis Ababa
Asmara
Port Sudan
Khartoum
Omdurman

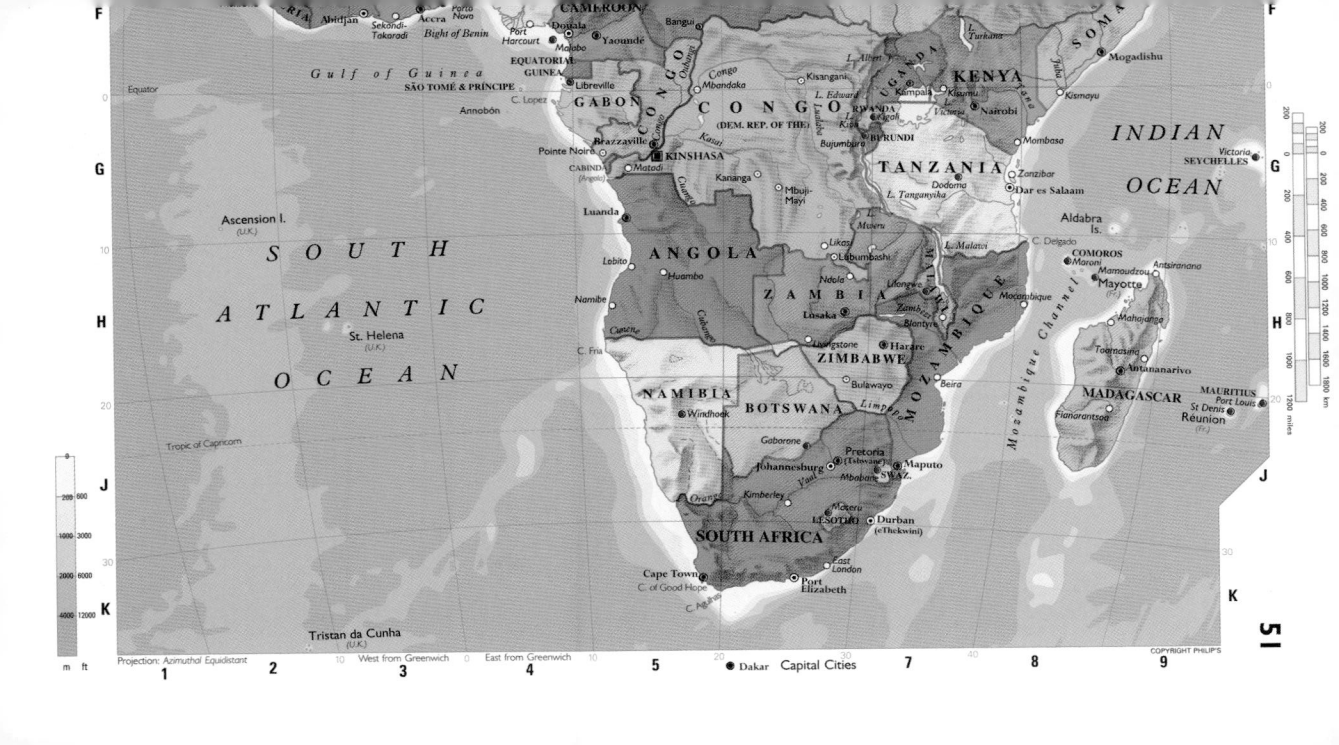
Abidjan
Sekondi-Takoradi
Accra
Porto Novo
Bight of Benin
Port Harcourt
Douala
CAMEROON
Malabo
EQUATORIAL GUINEA
Yaoundé
Bangui
Gulf of Guinea
SÃO TOMÉ & PRÍNCIPE
Libreville
GABON
Annobón
C. Lopez
Equator
Congo
Mbandaka
CONGO
(DEM. REP. OF THE)
Kisangani
L. Albert
L. Edward
UGANDA
Kampala
RWANDA
Kigali
BURUNDI
Bujumbura
KENYA
Kisumu
Nairobi
Kismayu
Mogadishu
SOMALIA
L. Turkana
Mombasa
Pointe Noire
Brazzaville
KINSHASA
Matadi
CABINDA
(Angola)
Kananga
Mbuji-Mayi
Luanda
TANZANIA
Zanzibar
Dar es Salaam
Dodoma
L. Tanganyika
L. Mweru
INDIAN
OCEAN
Victoria
SEYCHELLES
Aldabra Is.
Ascension I.
(U.K.)
SOUTH
ATLANTIC
OCEAN
St. Helena
(U.K.)
Lebito
Huambo
ANGOLA
Likasi
Lubumbashi
L. Malawi
C. Delgado
COMOROS
Moroni
Mamoudzou
Antsiranana
Mayotte
(Fr.)
Namibe
ZAMBIA
Ndola
Lusaka
Lilongwe
MALAWI
Zambezi
Blantyre
Mozambique
Cuanza
Cunene
Cubango
Harare
Livingstone
ZIMBABWE
Mahajanga
Toamasina
Antananarivo
C. Frio
Bulawayo
Beira
MOZAMBIQUE
Mozambique Channel
MADAGASCAR
Fianarantsoa
MAURITIUS
Port Louis
St Denis
Réunion
(Fr.)
NAMIBIA
BOTSWANA
Windhoek
Limpopo
Tropic of Capricorn
Gaborone
Pretoria
(Tshwane)
Johannesburg
Maputo
Vaal
Mbabane
SWAZ.
Orange
Kimberley
Maseru
LESOTHO
Durban
(eThekwini)
SOUTH AFRICA
East London
Cape Town
C. of Good Hope
Port Elizabeth
C. Agulhas
Tristan da Cunha
(U.K.)
F
G
H
J
K
0
10
20
30
1
2
3
4
5
7
8
9
West from Greenwich
East from Greenwich
Dakar Capital Cities
Projection: Azimuthal Equidistant
m ft
0
200 600
1000 3000
2000 6000
4000 12000
miles
kms
COPYRIGHT PHILIP'S
51

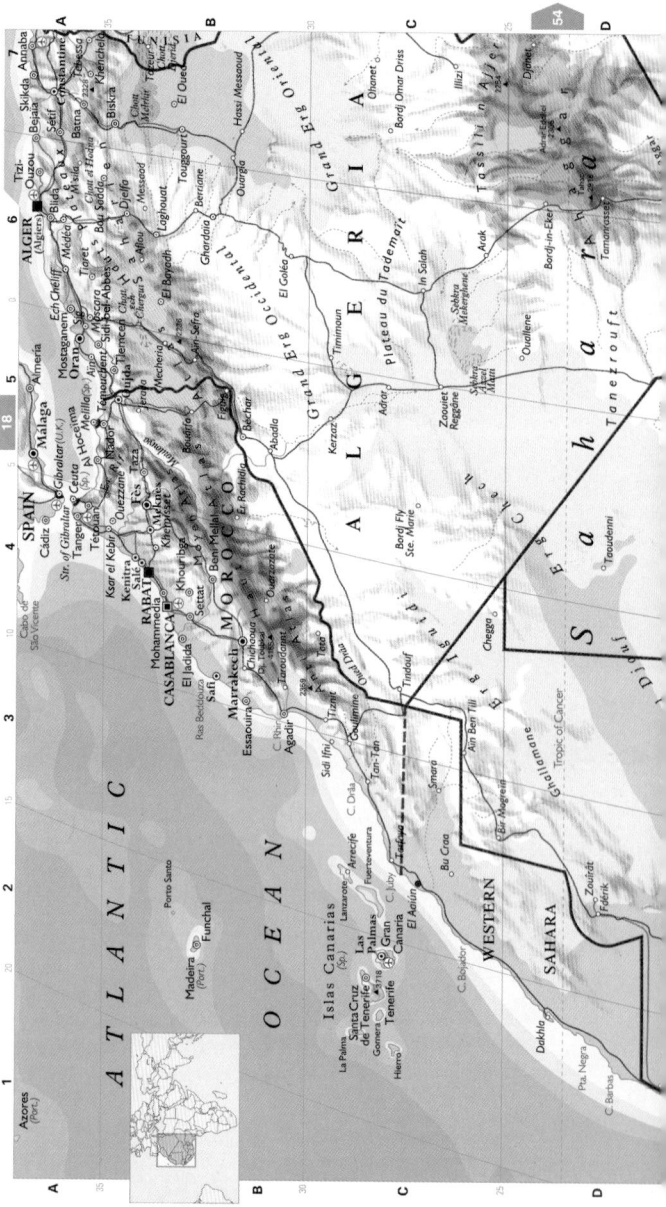
ATLANTIC
OCEAN
SPAIN
MOROCCO
ALGERIA
WESTERN
SAHARA
Sahara
Azores (Port.)
Madeira (Port.)
Porto Santo
Funchal
Islas Canarias
Santa Cruz de Tenerife
Las Palmas
Gran Canaria
Tenerife
La Palma
Gomera
Hierro
Lanzarote
Fuerteventura
Arrecife
Malaga
Gibraltar (U.K.)
Ceuta
Melilla
Almeria
Mostaganem
Oran
Tlemcen
ALGIER (Algiers)
Annaba
Skikda
Bejaia
Constantine
Tiaret
Mascara
Sidi Bel Abbes
Biskra
Touggourt
Ghardaia
Laghouat
Bechar
Tindouf
Tan-Tan
Agadir
Essaouira
Marrakech
CASABLANCA
RABAT
Tangier
Tetouan
Fez
Meknes
Oujda
Ouarzazate
Tiznit
Dakhla
Zouérat
Tamanrasset
Djanet
Tunis
Cabo de São Vicente
C. Bojador
C. Barbas
Pta. Negra
Grand Erg Oriental
Grand Erg Occidental
Tanezrouft
Tassili n Ajjer
Tropic of Cancer
Str. of Gibraltar
Strait of Gibraltar

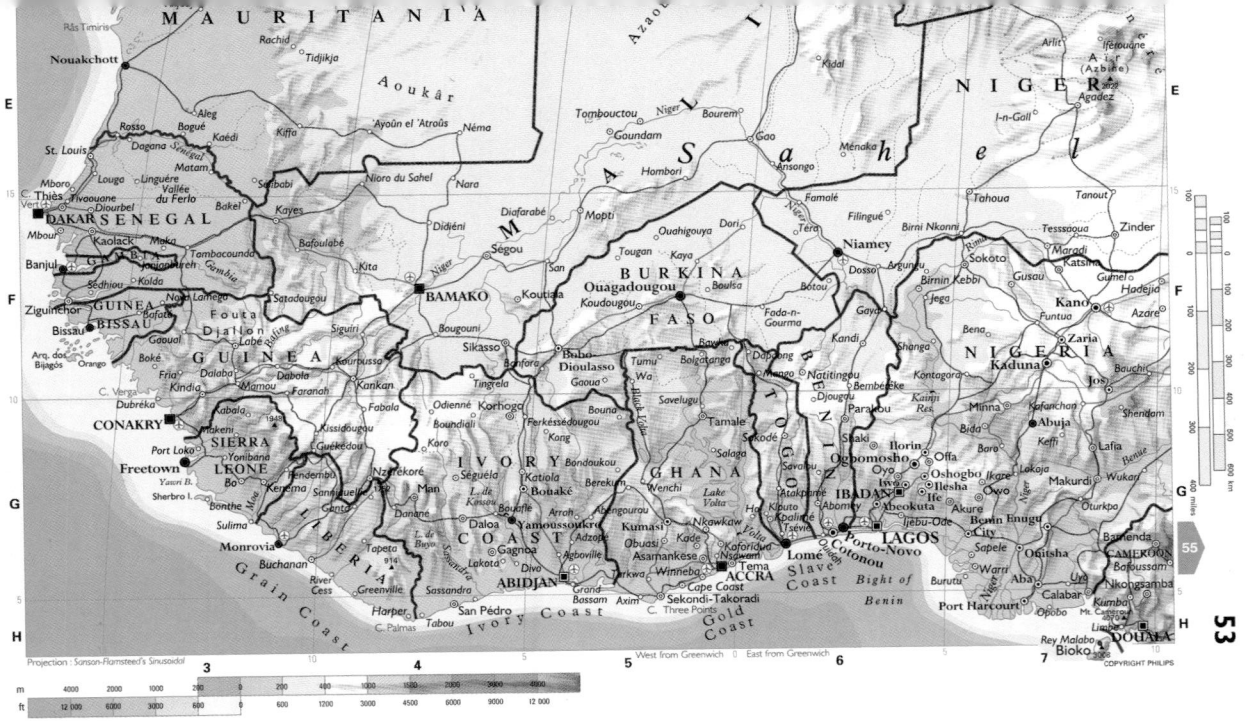
MAURITANIA
Ras Timiris
Nouakchott
Rachid
Tidjikja
Aoukâr
Azaouad
MALI
Kidal
NIGER
Arlit
Iférouane
Air (Azbine)
Agadez
I-n-Gall
Sahel
Tombouctou
Niger
Bourem
Gao
Goundam
Ménaka
Hombori
Ansongo
Aleg
Rosso
Bogué
Kaédi
Kiffa
Ayoûn el 'Atroûs
Néma
St. Louis
Dagana
Sénégal
Matam
Louga
Linguère
Vallée du Ferlo
Mboro
Thiès
Tivaouane
Diourbel
Bakel
Selibabi
Nioro du Sahel
Nara
Kayes
Mopti
Diafarabé
Didiéni
Ségou
Famolé
Tera
Filingué
Niamey
Tahoua
Tanout
Birni Nkonni
Tessaoua
Zinder
Maradi
Katsina
Gumel
Hadejia
Kano
Azare
Funtua
Zaria
Kaduna
Jos
Bauchi
Shendam
Abuja
Kafanchan
Keffi
Lafia
Benue
Makurdi
Wukari
Otukpa
Sokoto
Gusau
Birnin Kebbi
Jega
Argungu
Dosso
Botou
Gaya
Kandi
Shinga
Kontagora
Bena
Kainji Res.
Minna
Bida
Bare
Lokoja
Ikare
Owo
Ilesha
Ife
Akure
Ijebu-Ode
Benin City
Enugu
Sapele
Onitsha
Warri
Aba
Uyo
Calabar
Port Harcourt
Opobo
Bamenda
Bafoussam
Nkongsamba
Kumba
Mt. Cameroon
Douala
Rey Malabo
Bioko
CAMEROON
DAKAR
SENEGAL
Kaolack
Mbour
Tambacounda
Gambia
Banjul
Sédhiou
Kolda
Ziguinchor
GUINEA-BISSAU
Bissau
Bissagos
Arq. dos Bijagós
Orango
Bafatá
Boké
Fria
Kindia
Dalaba
Mamou
Dubréka
CONAKRY
Kankan
Faranah
Kissidougou
Guéckédou
Kouroussa
Siguiri
Kita
Bafoulabé
Satadougou
Nioro
Kaédi
Fouta Djallon
GUINEA
Labé
Dabola
Siguiri
Bamako
Koutiala
Sikasso
Bougouni
Bobo-Dioulasso
Banfora
Gaoua
Tingrela
Korhogo
Odienné
Boundiali
Ferkéssédougou
Bouna
Kong
Bondoukou
Séguéla
Katiola
Bouaké
Bérékum
Wenchi
Savelugu
Tamale
Salaga
Sokodé
Atakpamé
Kpalimé
Tsévié
Lomé
Kumasi
Nkawkaw
Kade
Koforidua
Nsawam
Obuasi
Asamankese
Winneba
Tema
ACCRA
Cape Coast
Sekondi-Takoradi
Axim
Tarkwa
Grand Bassam
Abidjan
Adzopé
Agboville
Divo
Gagnoa
Lakota
Yamoussoukro
Daloa
Bouaflé
Arrah
Abengourou
Danané
Man
Bonthe
Sulima
Monrovia
Buchanan
Topeta
River Cess
Greenville
Sassandra
Harper
C. Palmas
San Pedro
Tabou
Ouagadougou
Koudougou
Boulsa
Tougan
Kaya
Ouahigouya
Dori
Dapong
Mango
Bolgatanga
Tumu
Wa
Nalitingou
Djougou
Parakou
Bembereke
Savalou
Abomey
Porto-Novo
Cotonou
LAGOS
Ilorin
Offa
Oyo
Iwo
Ibadan
Abeokuta
Ogbomosho
Oshogbo
Ilesha
Ife
Owo
Ikare
Lokoja
Benin
Bight of Benin
Slave Coast
Gold Coast
Ivory Coast
Grain Coast
C. Three Points
C. Verga
Dubréka
Port Loko
Freetown
Sierra Leone
Bo
Kenema
Sherbro I.
Yaxuri B.
Henderiba
Sanquelle
Ganta
Nzérékoré
Man
Danané
Tabou
Sassandra
Harper
Greenville
Topeta
Buchanan
Monrovia
Sulima
Bonthe
Port Harcourt
Calabar
Douala
Bioko
Rey Malabo
Mt. Cameron
Kumba
Nkongsamba
Bamenda
Bafoussam
Uyo
Aba
Warri
Onitsha
Sapele
Benin City
Enugu
Ilorin
Offa
Oyo
Iwo
Ibadan
Abeokuta
Ogbomosho
Oshogbo
Ilesha
Ife
Owo
Ikare
Lokoja
Akure
Ijebu-Ode
Porto-Novo
Cotonou
Lomé
Tsévié
Kpalimé
Atakpamé
Kouto
Abomey
Savalou
Bembereke
Parakou
Djougou
Natitingou
Mango
Dapong
Bolgatanga
Tumu
Wa
Savelugu
Tamale
Salaga
Sokodé
Kumasi
Nkawkaw
Kade
Koforidua
Nsawam
Obuasi
Asamankese
Winneba
Tema
ACCRA
Cape Coast
Sekondi-Takoradi
Axim
Tarkwa
Grand Bassam
Abidjan
Adzopé
Agboville
Divo
Gagnoa
Lakota
Yamoussoukro
Daloa
Bouaflé
Arrah
Abengourou
Danané
Man
Bonthe
Sulima
Monrovia
Buchanan
Topeta
River Cess
Greenville
Sassandra
Harper
C. Palmas
San Pedro
Tabou
Ouagadougou
Koudougou
Boulsa
Tougan
Kaya
Ouahigouya
Dori
Dapong
Mango
Bolgatanga
Tumu
Wa
Nalitingou
Djougou
Parakou
Bembereke
Savalou
Abomey
Porto-Novo
Cotonou
Lomé
Tsévié
Kpalimé
Atakpamé
Kouto
Abomey
Savalou
Bembereke
Parakou
Djougou
Natitingou
Mango
Dapong
Bolgatanga
Tumu
Wa
Savelugu
Tamale
Salaga
Sokodé
Kumasi
Nkawkaw
Kade
Koforidua
Nsawam
Obuasi
Asamankese
Winneba
Tema
ACCRA
Cape Coast
Sekondi-Takoradi
Axim
Tarkwa
Grand Bassam
Abidjan
Adzopé
Agboville
Divo
Gagnoa
Lakota
Yamoussoukro
Daloa
Bouaflé
Arrah
Abengourou
Danané
Man
Bonthe
Sulima
Monrovia
Buchanan
Topeta
River Cess
Greenville
Sassandra
Harper
C. Palmas
San Pedro
Tabou
Port Harcourt
Calabar
Douala
Bioko
Rey Malabo
Mt. Cameron
Kumba
Nkongsamba
Bamenda
Bafoussam
Uyo
Aba
Warri
Onitsha
Sapele
Benin City
Enugu
Ilorin
Offa
Oyo
Iwo
Ibadan
Abeokuta
Ogbomosho
Oshogbo
Ilesha
Ife
Owo
Ikare
Lokoja
Akure
Ijebu-Ode

MEDITERRANEAN SEA
GREECE
Peloponnese
Cyclades
Rhodes
Crete
Kriti
Iraklio
Chania
TURKEY
Antalya
Alanya
Sifke
Anamur
ADANA
HALAB (Aleppo)
Nahr al Furāt (Euphrates)
Hatay
CYPRUS
Nicosia
Al Lādhiqiyah
Paphos
Limassol
Tarābulus
SYRIA
Hamah
Hims
LEBANON
BAYRŪT (Beirut)
DIMASHQ (Damascus)
Sūr
Jabal ad Dūrūz
ISRAEL
TEL AVIV-YAFO
Ashdod
Jerusalem
AMMAN
IRAQ
Ar Rutbah
Rādiyat
ash Shām
JORDAN
Al Jawf
SAUDI ARABIA
Tabūk
Al Muwaylih
Sharm el Sheikh
Hurghada
Al 'Aqabah
Ma'ān
Elat
Bir Safāga
Al Wajh
Quseir
Qena
Dumyāt
Damanhūr
Al Mahalla el Kubra
EL ISKANDARIYA (Alexandria)
Marsa Matrūh
El Alamein
Tanta
Zagazig
El Mansūra
Ismā'īlīya
El Giza
PYRAMIDS
Helwān
El Fayyūm
Beni Suef
Maghāghar
El Minyā
Mallawi
Asyūt
Manfalūt
Tahta
Sohāg
Girga
THEBES
KARNAK
El Khārga
El Uqsur
Isnā
Idfū
Kōm Ombo
Aswān
Ras Bānās
Yanbu al Bahr
Bir Shalatein
Halaib Triangle
Halaib
Ras Hadarba
Rābigh
RED SEA
Wādī Hafra
Toshka Lakes
Buhayrat en Nasser (L. Nasser)
ABU SIMBEL
Hadabat el Gilf el Kebīr
Ma'ţan as Sarra
Tropic of Cancer
Sahrā' Libīya
Sahrā' Rebiana
Sarīr Calanscio
Sarīr Nerastro
Sarīr Tibasti
Sahrā' Egypt
Es Sahrā' Esh Sharqīya
El Wāhāt el-Dakhla
El Wāhāt el-Khārga
Qasr Farāfra
Mūt
Al Jawf
Al Kufrah
Ajdābiya
Cyrenaica
Al Jaghbūb
Awjilah
Zillah
Dahra
Hūn
Munkhafed el Qattāra
Siwa
Marsā Susah
Al Marj
Darnah
Tubruq
Bardiyah
Salūm
Khalij Sirte
Khalij Burbah
Banghāzī
Zāwiyat al Baydā
CYRENE
Suluq
Surt
Khalij Surt
Mizdah
Tripolitania
Al Khums
Misrātah
TARĀBULUS (Tripoli)
Zuwārah
Zawiyah
Gharyān
LEPTIS MAGNA
Dehibat
Tatouine
Ben Gardane
Zarzis
Ile de Djerba
Médenine
Gabès
Golfe de Gabès
Gafsa
Chott Djerid
Tozeur
Sfax
Monastir
Mahdia
Sousse
Nabeul
Kairouan
Tebessa
Bizerte
CARTHAGE
Ariana
TUNIS
Bejaa
El Kef
Sicilia
ITALY
MALTA
Valletta
Idehan Awbārī
Awbārī
Sabhā
Brach
Al Hārūj
Al Asrad
Idehan Murzuq
Murzuq
W. Barjūj
Fezzan
Ghāt
Al Qaţrūn
Wāw al Kabīr
Tummo
Madama
Bardai
Aozou
Tibesti
Tarso Emissi
Tarso Toussidé
Aazou
Ma'ţan as Sarra
J. Uweinat
Hūn
ALGERIA
LIBYA
EGYPT
Sahara
Sahara
Sahara
Sahara
46
52
48
1
2
3
4
5
6
7
A
B
C
D

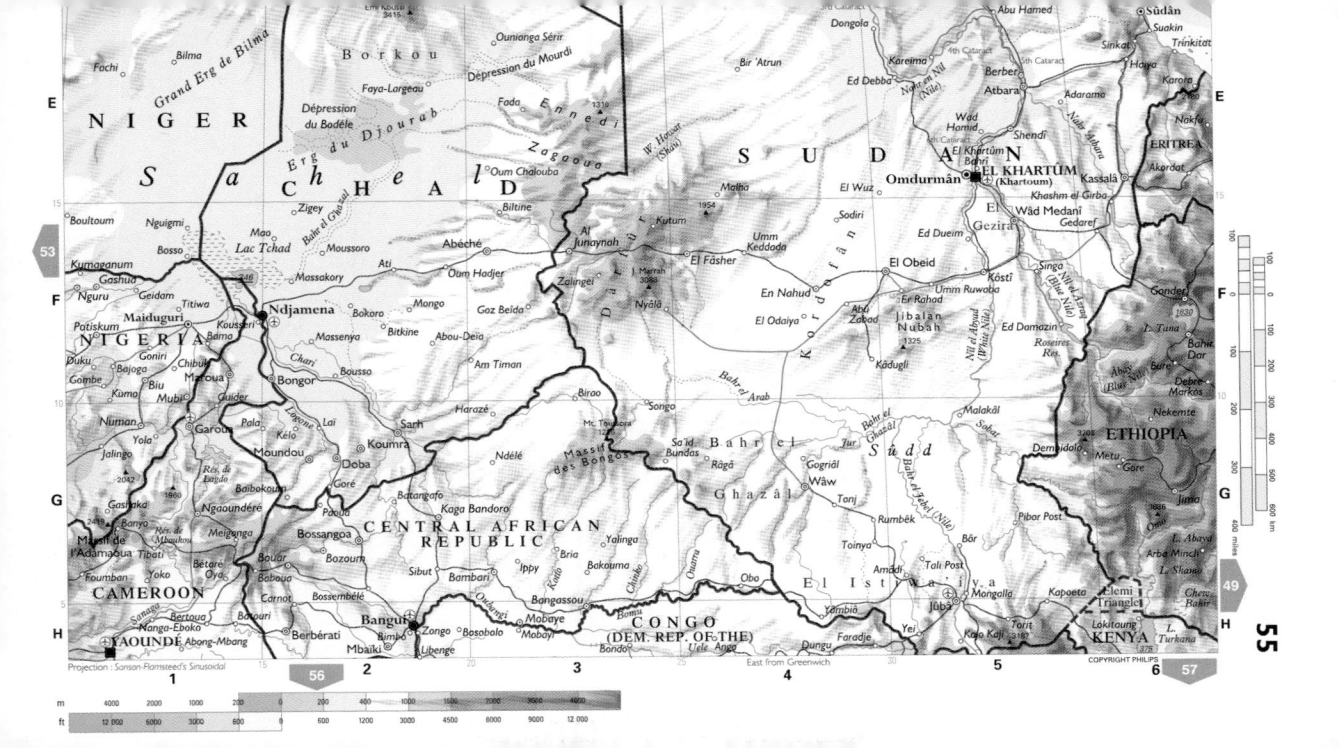
NIGER
Borkou
Grand Erg de Bilma
Bilma
Fachi
Ouniang Sérir
Dépression du Mourdi
Faya-Largeau
Dépression du Bodélé
Erg du Djourab
Fada
Ennedi
Zagaoua
Oum Chalouba
Biltine
Lac Tchad
Bahr el Ghazal
Zigey
Boultoum
Nguigmi
Mao
Moussoro
Abéché
Ati
Massakory
Oum Hadjer
Ndjamena
Kousseri
Maiduguri
NIGERIA
Bokoro
Mongo
Goz Beïda
Bitkine
Abou-Deïa
Massenya
Am Timan
Bongor
Bousso
Guider
Garoua
Pala
Lai
Koumra
Moundou
Doba
Goré
Sarh
Harazé
Ndélé
Baibokoum
Ngaoundéré
Meiganga
Bossangoa
Bouar
Bozoum
Bétaré Oya
Bossembélé
Carnot
Berbérati
Bangui
Mbaïki
Bimbo
Zongo
Bosobolo
Libenge
Mobaye
Bangassou
Bambari
Sibut
Ippy
Bria
Yalinga
Bakouma
Obo
Dungu
Faradje
Yei
Yambio
Tonj
Wāw
Rumbēk
Toinya
Bōr
Pibor Post
Malakāl
Kōstī
Ed Damazīn
Singa
Gondar
Bahr el Ghazāl
Bahr el Jabal (Nile)
Bahr el Arab
Bahr el Ghazāl
Sudd
Ghazāl
Kordofān
Dārfūr
Jebel Marra
Mt. Tembura
Massif des Bongos
Sa'id Bundas
Rāgā
Gogriāl
Ndjamena
Maiduguri
Kousseri
Bama
Gashua
Nguru
Geidam
Titiwa
Patiskum
Biu
Mubi
Numan
Yola
Jalingo
Gashaka
Banyo
Mont de l'Adamaoua
Tibati
Foumban
Yoko
Bertoua
Nanga-Eboko
Abong-Mbang
YAOUNDÉ
CAMEROON
CENTRAL AFRICAN REPUBLIC
CONGO (DEM. REP. OF THE)
SUDAN
EL KHARTŪM (Khartoum)
Omdurmān
Kassalā
Atbara
Berber
Ed Debba
Kareima
Dongola
Abu Hamed
Sūdān
Suakin
Trinkitat
Sinkat
Hayā
Karora
Nakfa
ERITREA
Akordat
Adaroma
Shendī
Wād Hamid
Khashm el Girba
Wād Madanī
Gedaref
Gezira
Ed Dueim
El Obeid
Umm Ruwaba
En Nahud
Ed Rahad
Abū Zabad
Jibalan Nubah
El Odaiya
Kādugli
Umm Keddada
El Fāsher
Nyālā
Zalingei
Merrah
Kutum
Al Junaynah
Matha
El Wuz
Sodiri
Gondar
L. Tana
Bahir Dar
Debre Markos
Nekemte
ETHIOPIA
Dembidolo
Metu
Gore
Jimma
Omo
L. Abaya
Arba Minch
L. Stiama
Kapoeta
Lokitaung
KENYA
L. Turkana
Torit
Kajo Kaji
Juba
Mongalla
Amadi
Tali Post
Gogrial
Malakal
Nile
Blue Nile
White Nile
Atbara
Sobat
Tana
Jebel Marra
Ennedi
Tchad
Chari
Logone
Shari
Ubangi
Mbomou
Uele
Turkana
Sobat
Atbara
Blue Nile
White Nile
Nile
Lake Turkana
Lake Tana
Lake Abaya
Lake Stiama
Lake Tana

56 CENTRAL AFRICA

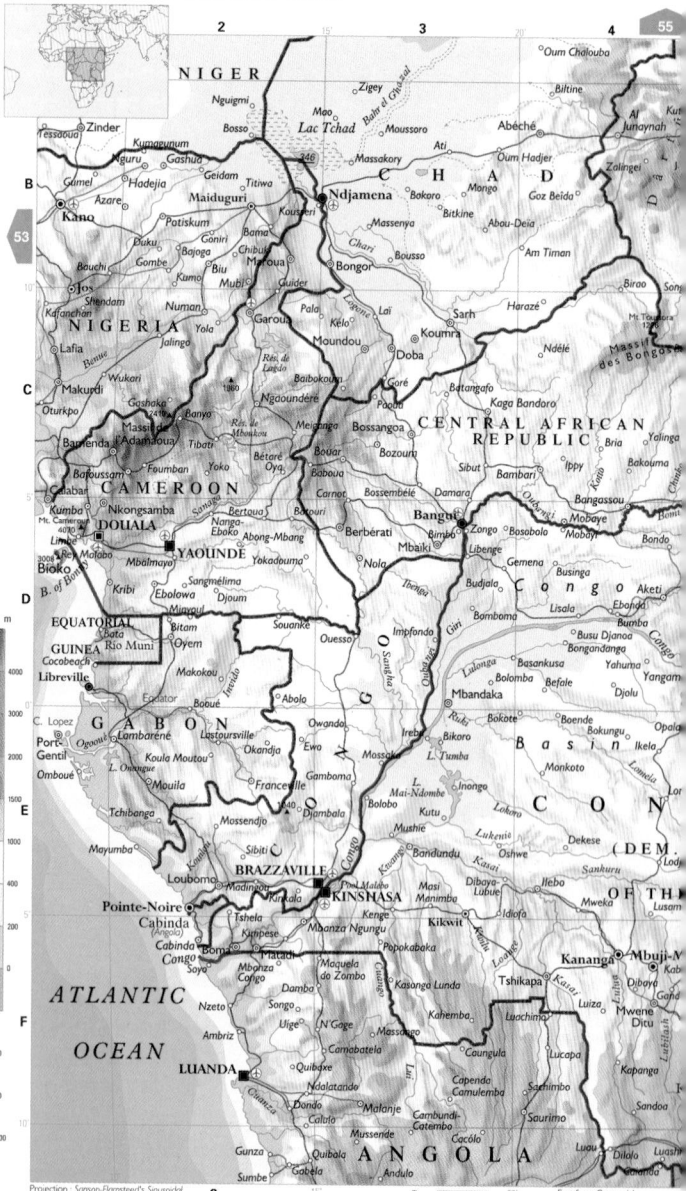

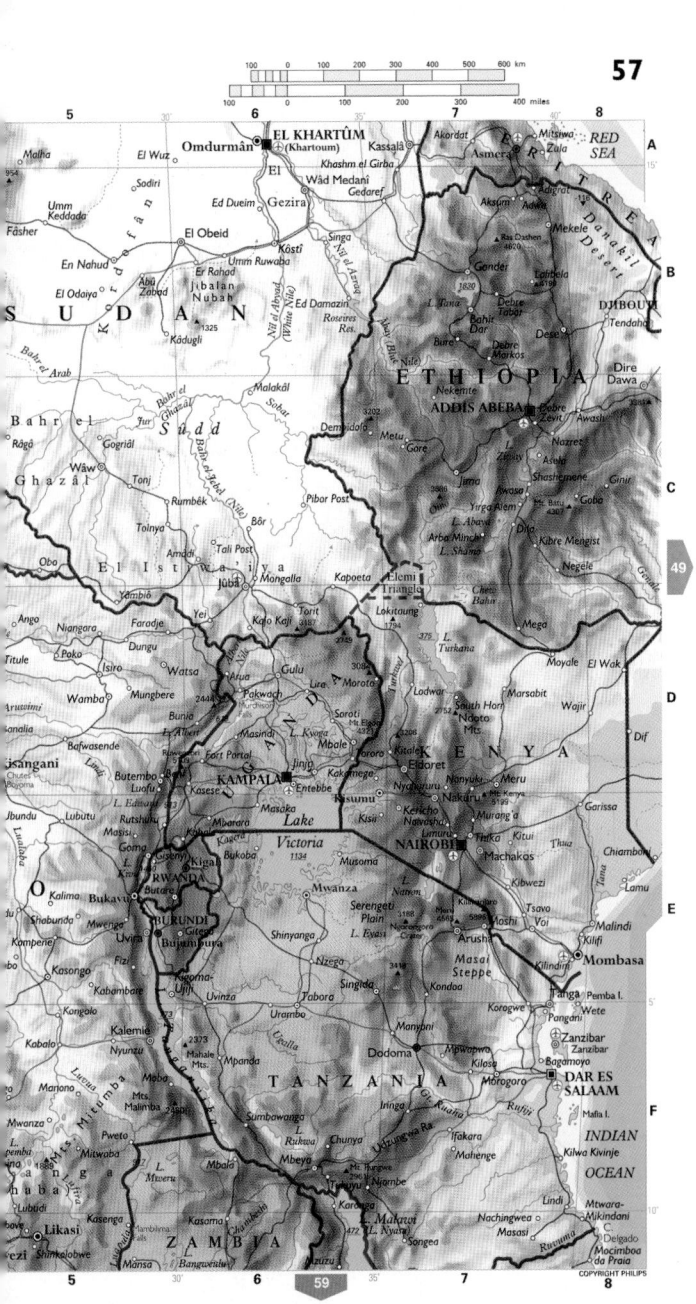
100 0 100 200 300 400 500 600 km
100 0 100 200 300 400 miles
5 6 7 8
A B C D E F
EL KHARTÚM (Khartoum)
Omdurmān
Kassalā
Akordat
Asmera
Massawa
Zula
RED SEA
ERITREA
Danakil Desert
Adigrat
Adwa
Aksum
Mekele
Ras Dashen 4620
Gondar
Lalibela
Lake Tana
Debre Tabor
Bahir Dar
Dessie
Debre Markos
DJIBOUTI
Tendaha
Dire Dawa
ETHIOPIA
Nekemte
ADDIS ABEBA
Debre Zeit
Awasa
Nazret
L. Zeway
Asela
Shashemene
Ginir
Jima
Kwasa
Yirga Alem
Mt. Batu 4307
Goba
L. Abaya
L. Shala
Arba Minch
Dila
Kibre Mengist
Negele
Gonale
Omdurman
El Wuz
Sodiri
Umm Keddada
Fāsher
El Obeid
Gezira
Ed Dueim
Wād Medanī
Gedaref
Kōstī
Singa
Umm Ruwaba
En Nahud
Er Rahad
Jibalān
Nubah
Abū Zabad
El Odaiya
Ed Damazin
Roseires Res.
SUDAN
Kordofān
Kādugli
Nile
Blue Nile
White Nile
Bahr el Ghazal
Bahr el Arab
Malakāl
Sobat
Bahr el Jebel
Sudd
Rāgā
Gogriāl
Wāw
Ghazāl
Tonj
Rumbēk
Pibor Post
Bōr
Tolnya
Tali Post
Amadi
El Istwa'iya
Oba
Yambio
Juba
Mongalla
Kapoeta
Elemi Triangle
Lokitaung
Ango
Niangara
Faradje
Yei
Torit
Kato Kaji
Dungu
Poko
Isiro
Watsa
Titule
Gulu
Arua
Pakwach
Lira
Moroto
Tororo
Lodwar
Marsabit
Moyale
El Wak
Wambo
Mungbere
Bunia
Masindi
L. Kyoga
Sorati
Mt. Elgon 4321
Mbale
Kitale
Eldoret
South Horn
Nadoto Mts.
Wajir
Dif
Bafwasende
Fort Portal
Butembo
Kasese
KAMPALA
Entebbe
Jinja
Kakamega
Nyahururu
Nanyuki
Meru
Nakuru
Mt. Kenya 5199
Kisumu
Kericho
Nanyuki
Murang'a
Garissa
Lubutu
Rutshuru
Masisi
Goma
Kigali
RWANDA
Butare
Bukavu
BURUNDI
Gitega
Bujumbura
Uvira
Kalima
Shabunda
Mwenge
Kampene
Kasongo
Fizi
Kabambare
Kongolo
Kalemie
Nyunza
Kabalo
Mahale Mts.
Mpanda
Moba
Mariano
Mts. Mitumba
Mts. Malimba
Pweto
Mitwaba
Mbala
Mwanza
Victoria
Lake
Musoma
Bukoba
Serengeti Plain
Shinyanga
Nzega
Singida
Tabora
Uvinza
Urambo
Kondoa
Masai Steppe
Arusha
Moshi
Tsavo
Voi
Kilimanjaro 5895
Mombasa
Kilindini
Malindi
Yilifi
Lamu
Chiambani
Kibwezi
Kitui
Machakos
Thika
Nairobi
Naivasha
Lake Nakuru
Kisii
Muranga
Kericho
Eldoret
Tanga
Pemba I.
Wete
Pangani
Zanzibar
Bagamoyo
Kilosa
Morogoro
DAR ES SALAAM
Mafia I.
Kilwa Kivinje
INDIAN OCEAN
Mtwara-Mikindani
Delgado
Mocimboa da Praia
Manyoni
Dodoma
Mpwapwa
Iringa
Kilombero
Rufiji
Ifakara
Mahenge
Sumbawanga
Mbeya
Mt. Ihanga 2960
Mt. Nyambe
Kasama
Kasenga
Mbala
Mweru
Kabanga
L. Mukazi
L. Kyela
Songea
Nachingwea
Masasi
Lindi
Likasi
Shinkolobwe
Mansa
Bangweulu
Luzuru
ZAMBIA
TANZANIA
Kigoma
Ujiji
Bujumbura
Tabora
Kondoa
Korogwe
Pangani
Kilosa
Morogoro
Kilindini
Mafia I.
Kilwa Kivinje
Lindi
Nachingwea
Masasi
Songea
Mtwara-Mikindani
Delgado
Mocimboa da Praia
COPYRIGHT PHILIPS

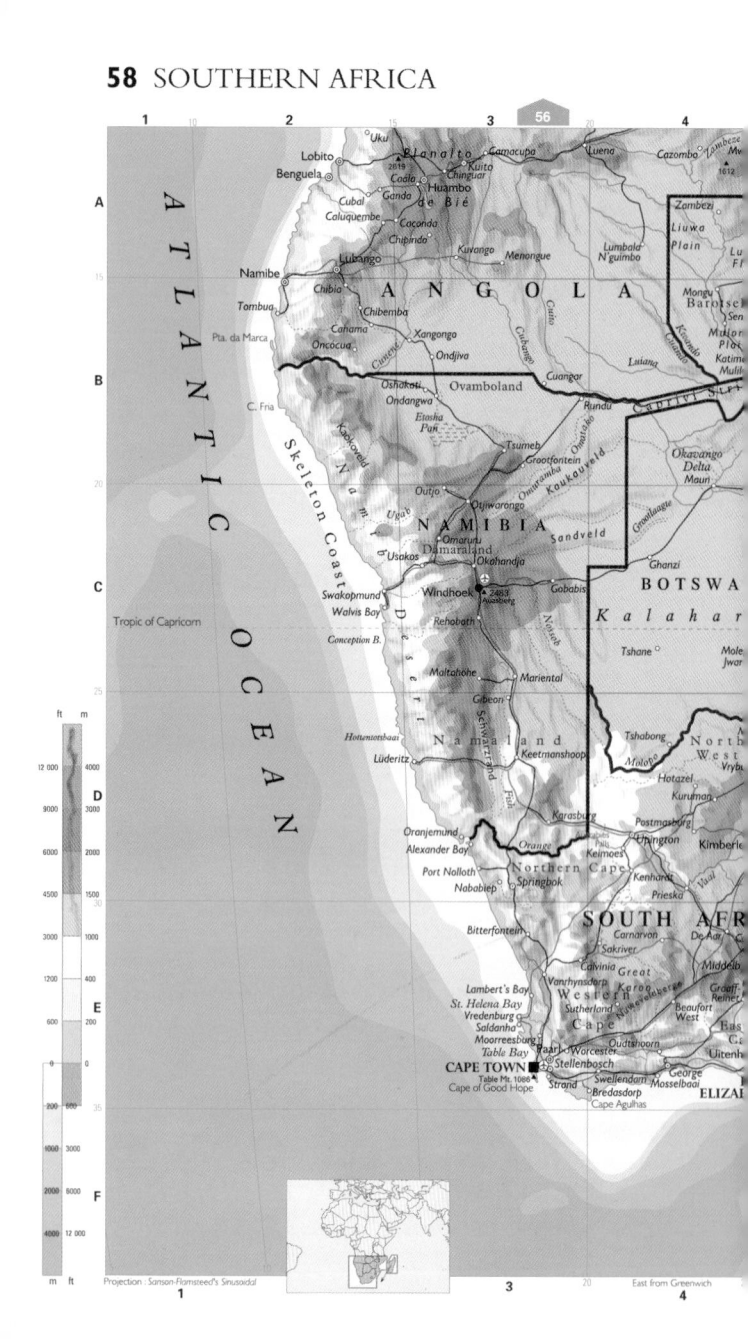
56
ATLANTIC OCEAN
ANGOLA
NAMIBIA
BOTSWA
SOUTH AFR
Lobito
Benguela
Namibe
Lubango
Huambo
Kuito
Luena
Cazombo
Zambezi
Liuwa Plain
Lumbala N'guimbo
Menongue
Kuvango
Cubal
Caluquembe
Caconda
Chipindo
Chibia
Tombua
Chibemba
Cahama
Oncocua
Xangongo
Ondjiva
Pta. da Marca
C. Fria
Ovamboland
Oshakati
Ondangwa
Etosha Pan
Tsumeb
Grootfontein
Rundu
Cuangar
Lutana
Okavango Delta
Maun
Outjo
Otjiwarongo
Omaruru
Damaraland
Usakos
Okahandja
Windhoek
2483 Jacobsberg
Swakopmund
Walvis Bay
Rehoboth
Gobabis
Ghanzi
Kalahar
Tshane
Mariental
Maltahohe
Gibeon
Namaland
Keetmanshoop
Hottentotbaai
Lüderitz
Tshabong
Hotazel
Kuruman
Karasburg
Postmasburg
Upington
Kimberle
Oranjemund
Alexander Bay
Port Nolloth
Nababiep
Springbok
Kenhardt
Prieska
Bitterfontein
Carnarvon
Sakrivier
Calvinia
Great Karoo
Vanrhynsdorp
Lambert's Bay
St. Helena Bay
Vredenburg
Saldanha
Moorreesburg
Table Bay
Beaufort West
Sutherland
Oudtshoorn
Worcester
Stellenbosch
CAPE TOWN
Table Mt. 1086
Cape of Good Hope
Strand
Swellendam
Bredasdorp
Cape Agulhas
George
Mossel Bay
Tropic of Capricorn
Conception B.
Skeleton Coast
Namib Desert
Kaokoveld
Kaukauveld
Sandveld
Kalahari
Cuando
Cubango
Cuito
Kunene
Okavango
Zambezi
Orange
Fish
Nossob
Molopo
Vaal
Gamacupa
Chinguar
Ganda
Cadia
Ukui
Mongu
Barotse
Sen
Mulor
Plai
Katime
Mulib
Lu
Fl
Mo
Tshabong
Mole
Jwar
Northern Cape
Kimberley
Prieska
Middelb
Graaff-Reinet
Beaufort West
Bas
Ca
Uitenh
George
Mossel Bay
ELIZAB
Cape Agulhas
Projection : Sanson-Flamsteed's Sinusoidal
East from Greenwich
ft
m
12 000
9000
6000
4500
3000
1200
600
0
200
1000
2000
4000
4000
3000
2000
1500
1000
400
200
0
600
3000
6000
12 000
A
B
C
D
E
F
1
2
3
4

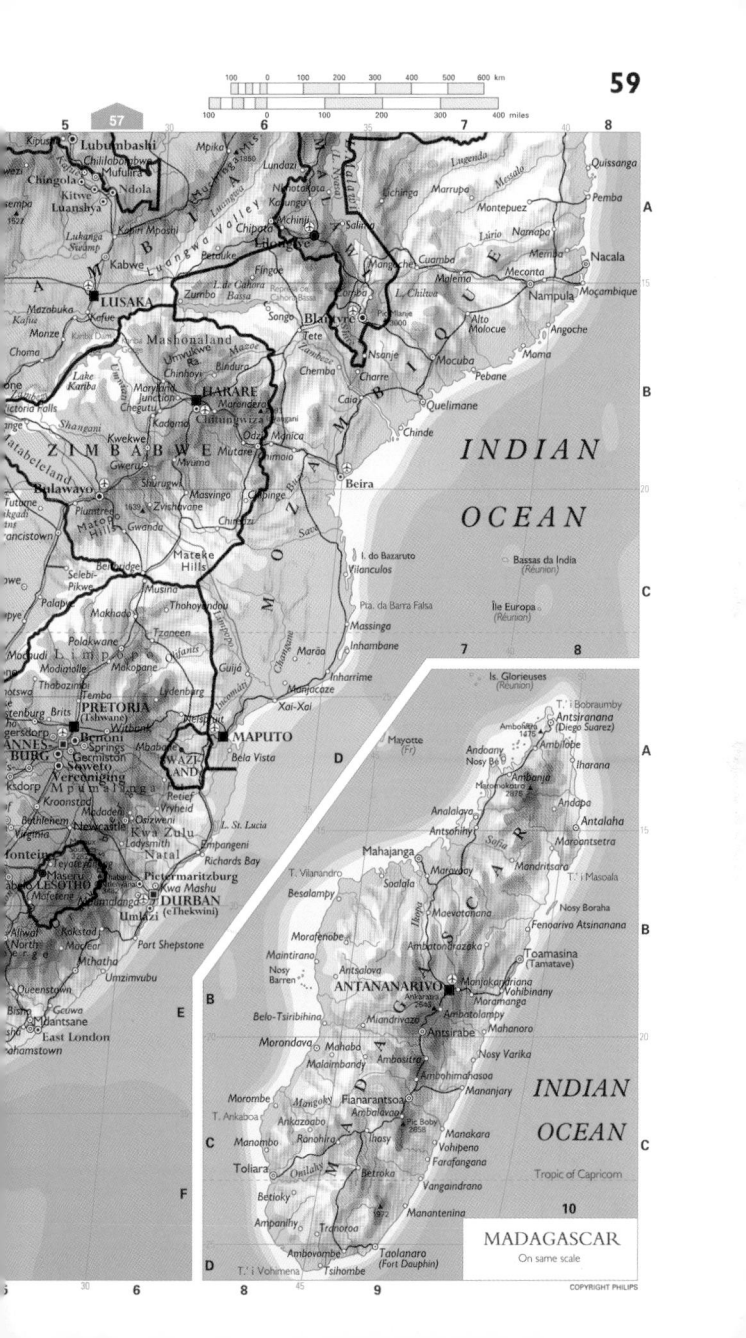
100 0 100 200 300 400 500 600 km
100 0 100 200 300 400 miles
57
Lubumbashi
Chililabombwe
Mufulira
Chingola
Ndola
Kitwe
Luanshya
Mpika
Lundazi
Kasungu
Lilongwe
Chipata
Mchinji
Salima
Lake Malawi
Nampula
Quissanga
Pemba
Montepuez
Marrupa
Lichinga
Mesalo
Lugenda
Namapa
Nacala
Cuamba
Mandimba
Malema
Meconta
Moçambique
Lake Chilwa
Alto Molocue
Angoche
Mocuba
Mocuba
Pebane
Quelimane
Chinde
Beira
Nsanje
Chemba
Charre
Caia
Tete
Blantyre
Zomba
Songo
Lake Chirwa
Fingoe
Lake Cahora Bassa
Tete
Zambezi
Lusaka
Kafue
Mazabuka
Kafue
Monze
Choma
Kariba
Lake Kariba
Victoria Falls
Shangani
Matabeleland
Bulawayo
Gwanda
Plumtree
Matopo Hills
Francistown
Tutume
Selebi-Pikwe
Palapye
Mashonaland
Umvukwe Range
Bindura
Chinhoyi
Mazowe
Harare
Marondera
Chimoio
Mutare
Masvingo
Chipinge
Zvishavane
Chiredzi
Gwelo
Shurugwi
Kwekwe
Gweru
Mvuma
Kadoma
Odzi
Mpika
Zimbabwe
Mozambique
Mateke Hills
Bell Ridge
Musina
Thohoyandou
Makhado
Tzaneen
Polokwane
Mokopane
Lydenburg
Thabazimbi
Temba
Pretoria
(Tshwane)
Witbank
Brits
Bethlehem
Vryheid
Ladysmith
Kwa Zulu
Natal
Richards Bay
Empangeni
Pietermaritzburg
Kwa Mashu
Durban
(eThekwini)
Umlazi
Maseru
Lesotho
Maputo
Bela Vista
Swaziland
Nelspruit
Xai-Xai
Inhambane
Inharrime
Manjacaze
Gujá
Marão
Massinge
Pta. da Barra Falsa
I. do Bazaruto
Vilanculos
Bassas da India
(Réunion)
Île Europa
(Réunion)
Indian Ocean
Is. Glorieuses
(Réunion)
Mayotte
(Fr)
Antsiranana
(Diego Suarez)
Ambohitra
1475
Ambilobe
Andoany
Nosy Be
Ambanja
Mahajanga
Mananjary
Fianarantsoa
Ambalavao
Ankazoabo
Ranohira
Ihosy
Manakara
Vohipeno
Farafangana
Toliara
Betroka
Betioky
Ampanihy
Tranoroa
Ambovombe
Taolanaro
(Fort Dauphin)
Tsihombe
Vangaindrano
Manantenina
Tropic of Capricorn
Madagascar
On same scale
COPYRIGHT PHILIPS

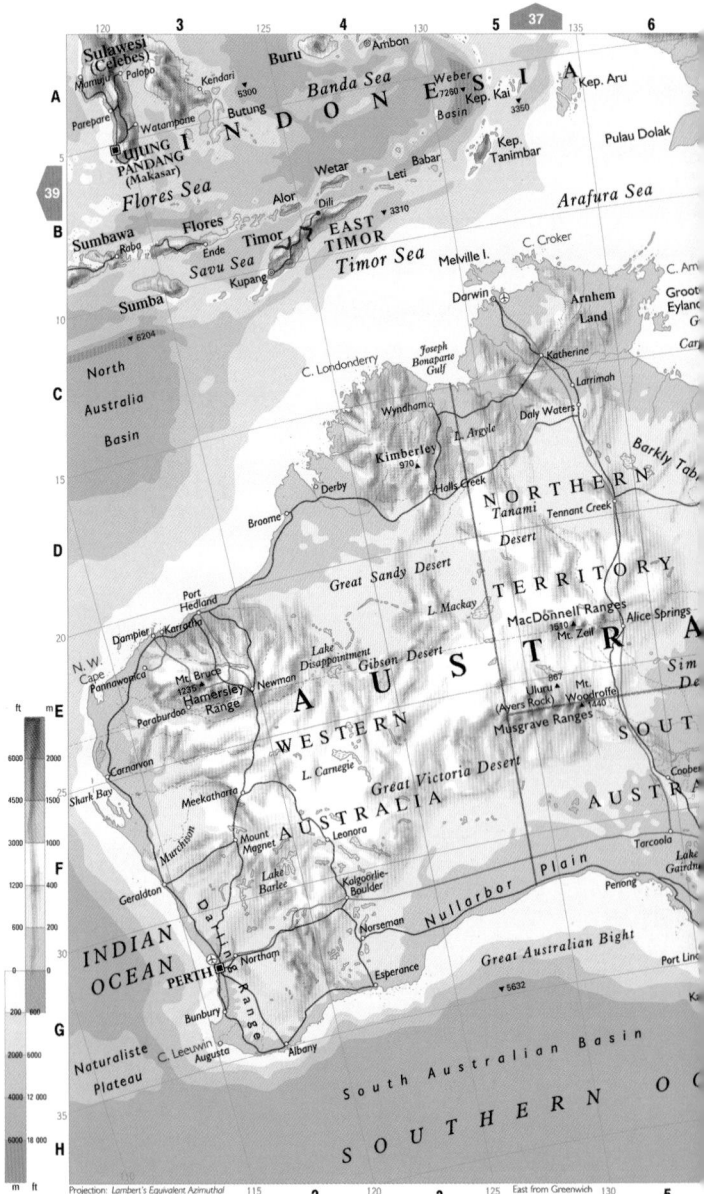
Sulawesi (Celebes)
Ambon
Buru
Banda Sea
Weber Basin
Kep. Aru
Kep. Kai
Kendari
Palopo
Mamuju
Parepare
Watampone
Butung
UJUNG PANDANG (Makasar)
Kep. Tanimbar
Pulau Dolak
Flores Sea
Wetar
Leti
Babar
Alor
Dili
Arafura Sea
Sumbawa
Flores
Ende
Savu Sea
Timor
EAST TIMOR
Timor Sea
Melville I.
C. Croker
Kupang
Sumba
Darwin
Arnhem Land
Joseph Bonaparte Gulf
Katherine
Larrimah
C. Londonderry
North Australia Basin
Wyndham
Doly Waters
L. Argyle
Kimberley
Hells Creek
Derby
Broome
NORTHERN TERRITORY
Tanami Desert
Tennant Creek
Barkly Tabl
Great Sandy Desert
L. Mackay
MacDonnell Ranges
Alice Springs
Mt. Zeil
Port Hedland
Dampier
Karratha
N.W. Cape
Pannawonica
Mt. Bruce
Hamersley Range
Newman
Lake Disappointment
Gibson Desert
Uluru (Ayers Rock)
Mt. Woodroffe
Musgrave Ranges
Paraburdoo
WESTERN AUSTRALIA
L. Carnegie
Great Victoria Desert
Carnarvon
Shark Bay
Meekatharra
Mount Magnet
Leonora
Marchison
Geraldton
Lake Barlee
Kalgoorlie-Boulder
Tarcoola
Penong
Nullarbor Plain
Norseman
Great Australian Bight
INDIAN OCEAN
PERTH
Darling Range
Northam
Esperance
Bunbury
Augusta
C. Leeuwin
Albany
Naturaliste Plateau
South Australian Basin
SOUTHERN OCEAN
Projection: Lambert's Equivalent Azimuthal
East from Greenwich

61
100 0 100 200 300 400 500 600 700 800 km
100 0 100 200 300 400 500 miles
New Britain
Trench
Bougainville
SOLOMON ISLANDS
Mount Hagen
Mt. Wilhelm
Lae
New Britain
Mt. Balbi
Shortland Is.
Choiseul
Santa Isabel
Vella Lavella
PAPUA NEW GUINEA
Solomon Sea
New Georgia Is.
Vangunu
Russell Is.
Florida Is.
Malaita
Fly
Gulf of Papua
Owen Stanley Range
Port Moresby
D'Entrecasteaux Islands
Honiara
Guadalcanal
Torres Strait
Badu I.
Moa I.
Prince of Wales I.
C. York
Louisiade Archipelago
Pocklington Reef
Bellona
Rennell
San Cristóbal (Makira)
Coral Sea Basin
Coral Sea
Great Barrier Reef
Cape York Peninsula
Weipa
Queensland Plateau
PACIFIC
Cooktown
Cairns
Mitchell
Normanton
Forsayth
CORAL SEA ISLANDS TERRITORY
Îles D'Entrecasteaux (Fr.)
Îles Chesterfield (Fr.)
OCEAN
Townsville
Charters Towers
Flinders
Whitsunday Is.
Mackay
Lord Howe Seamount Chain
Cloncurry
Hughenden
Great Dividing Range
Tropic of Capricorn
Winton
Emerald
Rockhampton
Gladstone
QUEENSLAND
Longreach
Bundaberg
Yaraka
Maryborough
Sunshine Coast
Charleville
Roma
Gympie
Quilpie
BRISBANE
Grey Range
Toowoomba
Ipswich
Cunnamulla
Gold Coast
Thargomindah
Dirranbandi
Lismore
Grafton
Moree
Bourke
Walgett
Tamworth
Round Mt.
Port Macquarie
Taree
NEW SOUTH WALES
Lord Howe I. (Austral.)
Broken Hill
Cobar
Dubbo
Newcastle
Bathurst
Orange
SYDNEY
Wollongong
Murray
Mildura
Hay
Griffith
Goulburn
Wagga Wagga
Canberra A.C.T.
ADELAIDE
Swan Hill
Murray
Mt. Kosciuszko
Sheppaston
Albury
Bendigo
Wodonga
Bombala
Tasman Sea
Horsham
Ballarat
VICTORIA
MELBOURNE
C. Howe
Mount Gambier
Warrnambool
Geelong
Sale
Tasman Abyssal Plain
Bass Strait
Flinders I.
King I.
Furneaux Group
Burnie
Launceston
Mt. Ossa
TASMANIA
Hobart
S.E. Cape
COPYRIGHT PHILIP'S

SOUTH AUSTRALIA
ADELAIDE
Port Augusta
Port Pirie
Whyalla
Port Lincoln
Kangaroo I.
Mount Gambier
Broken Hill
Mildura
Lake Eyre (North)
Lake Eyre (South)
LAKE EYRE
Lake Torrens
Lake Gairdner
Lake Frome
Strzelecki Desert
Sturt Stony Desert
Murray Bridge
Salisbury
Elizabeth
Gawler
Victor Harbor
Leigh Creek
Coober Pedy
William Creek
Marree
Innamincka
Cooper Cr.
Flinders Ranges
Spencer Gulf
Eyre Peninsula
Yorke Pen.
Fleurieu Pen.
Murray R.
Darling R.
Bass Strait
King Island
Flinders Island
Furneaux Group
Cape Barren I.
Devonport
Launceston
Hobart
TASMANIA
Bass
SOUTHERN OCEAN
MELBOURNE
Horsham
Warrnambool
Portland
Port Fairy
Port Campbell
Port Pirie
Port Augusta
Port Lincoln
Port Adelaide
Port Arthur
Port Davey
Port Cygnet
Port Sandy
Port Cygnet
Port Sandy
Port Davey
Port Arthur
Port Pirie
Port Augusta
Port Lincoln
Port Adelaide
Port Fairy
Port Campbell
Port Pirie
Port Augusta
Port Lincoln
Port Adelaide
Port Arthur
Port Davey

61
50 0 50 100 150 200 250 300 km
50 0 50 100 150 200 miles
4
5
145
150
QUEENSLAND
NEW SOUTH WALES
TASMAN SEA
Great Dividing Range
Darling Downs
Bundaberg
Fraser I.
Hervey Bay
Maryborough
Gympie
Tewantin
Sunshine Coast
Maroochydore
Caloundra
Nambour
Caboolture
Redcliffe
Deception Bay
Toowoomba
Ipswich
BRISBANE
Beenleigh
Gold Coast
Southport
Nerang
Surfers Paradise
Warwick
Tweed Hds.
Murwillumbah
Byron Bay
Lismore
Ballina
Casino
Grafton
Coffs Harbour
Nambucca Heads
South West Rocks
Kempsey
Port Macquarie
Taree
Tuncurry
Forster
Nelson Bay
Raymond Terrace
Newcastle
Gosford
Maitland
Cessnock
Singleton
Muswellbrook
Dubbo
Bathurst
Orange
Parkes
Forbes
Penrith
Windsor
Blacktown
SYDNEY
Campbelltown
Wollongong
Shellharbour
Kiama
Nowra
Goulburn
Queanbeyan
Canberra
Wagga Wagga
Griffith
Albury
Wodonga
Shepparton
Bendigo
Ballarat
Geelong
Melbourne
Warrnambool
Mildura
Swan Hill
Echuca
Bairnsdale
Sale
Traralgon
Moe
Morwell
Dandenong
Cranbourne
Hogan Group
Kent Group
Deal I.
Flinders Island
Furneaux Group
Prime Seal I.
Cape Barren I.
Clarke I.
Banks Strait
Freeways
National Parks
COPYRIGHT PHILIP'S

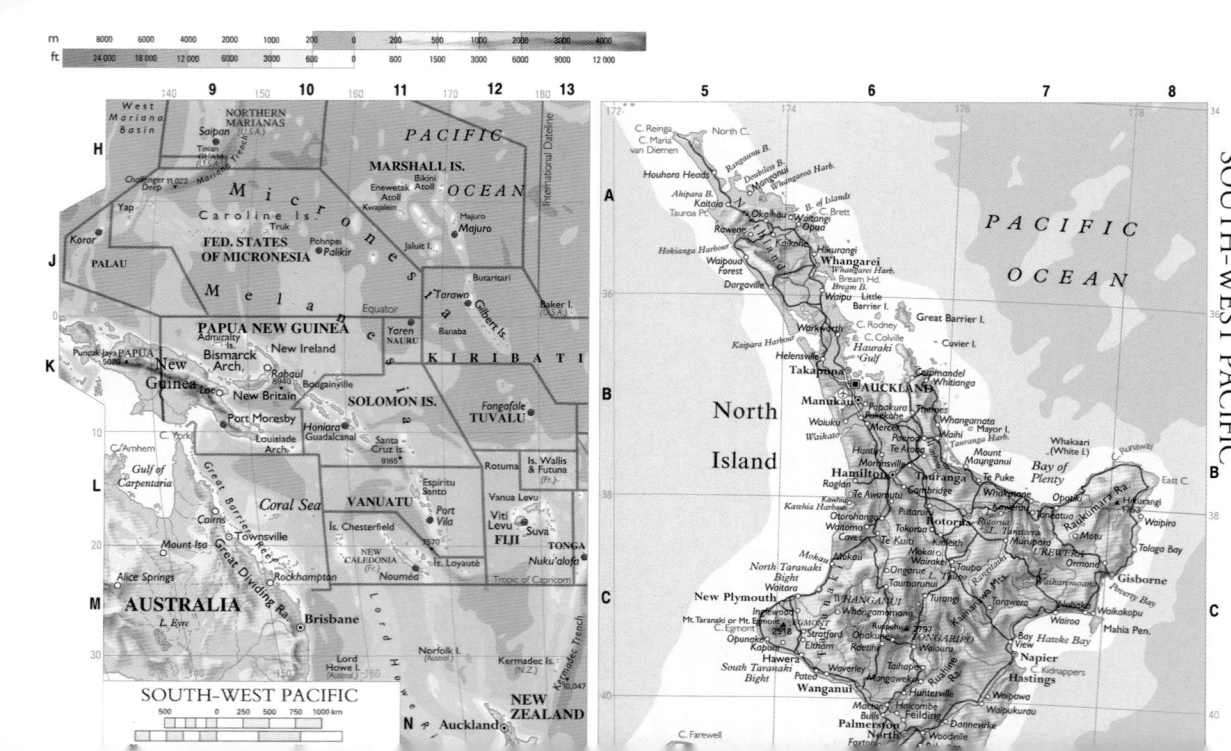
m 8000 6000 4000 2000 1000 200 0 200 500 1000 2000 3000 4000
ft 24 000 18 000 12 000 6000 3000 600 0 600 1500 3000 6000 9000 12 000
PACIFIC OCEAN
NORTHERN MARIANAS (U.S.A.)
Saipan
Tinian
Guam (U.S.A.)
Mariana Trench
Challenger Deep 11,022
MARSHALL IS.
Enewetak Atoll
Bikini Atoll
Kwajalein
Majuro
Micronesia
Caroline Is.
Truk
Yap
Koror
PALAU
FED. STATES OF MICRONESIA
Pohnpei
Palikir
Jaluit I.
Melanesia
Butaritari
Tarawa
Gilbert Is.
Baker I. (U.S.A.)
Equator
Yaren
NAURU
Banaba
KIRIBATI
International Dateline
PAPUA NEW GUINEA
Admiralty Is.
Bismarck Arch.
New Ireland
Puncak Jaya 5030
PAPUA
New Guinea
Rabaul
Bougainville
New Britain
Port Moresby
Honiara
Guadalcanal
Santa Cruz Is.
SOLOMON IS.
Fongafale
TUVALU
Louisiade Arch.
C. York
C. Arnhem
Gulf of Carpentaria
Great Barrier Reef
Coral Sea
Cairns
Townsville
Mount Isa
Espiritu Santo
VANUATU
Port Vila
Rotuma
Is. Wallis & Futuna (Fr.)
Vanua Levu
Is. Chesterfield
Viti Levu
Suva
FIJI
TONGA
NEW CALEDONIA (Fr.)
Noumea
Is. Loyauté
Nuku'alofa
Tropic of Capricorn
Alice Springs
Great Dividing Ra.
Rockhampton
AUSTRALIA
L. Eyre
Brisbane
Lord Howe I. (Austral.)
Norfolk I. (Austral.)
Kermadec Is. (N.Z.)
Kermadec Trench
NEW ZEALAND
Auckland
SOUTH-WEST PACIFIC
500 0 250 500 750 1000 km
C. Reinga
C. Maria van Diemen
North C.
Houhora Heads
Rangaunu B.
Doubtless B.
Mangonui
Whangaroa Harb.
Aliipara B.
Kaitaia
Tauroa Pt.
Okaihau
Waitangi
Opua
B. of Islands
C. Brett
Rawene
Kaikohe
Hokianga Harbour
Waipoua Forest
Dargaville
Hikurangi
Whangarei
Whangarei Harb.
Bream Hd.
Bream B.
Waipu
Little Barrier I.
Great Barrier I.
C. Rodney
C. Colville
Cavier I.
Warkworth
Kaipara Harbour
Hauraki Gulf
Helensville
Takapuna
Coromandel
Whitianga
AUCKLAND
Manukau
Papakura
Pukekohe
Thames
Whangamata
Mayor I.
Waiuku
Waikato
Mercer
Raglan
Waitomo
Waikohi
Tauranga Harb.
Mount Maunganui
Whakaari (White I.)
Runaway
Bay of Plenty
East C.
North Island
Hunter
Morrinsville
Hamilton
Tauranga
Te Puke
Te Awamutu
Sanbridge
Whakatane
Opotiki
Kawhia Harbour
Otorohanga
Putaruru
Rotorua
Tarawera
Hikurangi
Waipiro
Waitomo Caves
Tokoroa
Te Kuiti
Taupo
Motu
Taloga Bay
Mokau
Moeakau
Waitara
Ongarue L.
Taumarunui
Turangi
Gisborne
North Taranaki Bight
Tolaga Bay
Ormond
Waikaremoana
Tiverton Bay
New Plymouth
WHANGANUI
Tangiwai
Tangiwai Ra.
Tangiwai
Waikokopu
Mt. Taranaki or Mt. Egmont 2518
C. Egmont
Stratford
Ohakune
Raetihi
Wairoa
Mahia Pen.
Opunake
Kapuni
Hawera
Eltham
Waverley
Taihape
Waiouru
Bay of Hawke Bay
Napier
Kidnappers
Hastings
South Taranaki Bight
Pateo
Wanganui
Mangaweka
Hunterville
Waipawa
Waipukurau
Marton
Bulls
Feilding
Dannevirke
Palmerston North
Woodville
Foxton
C. Farewell

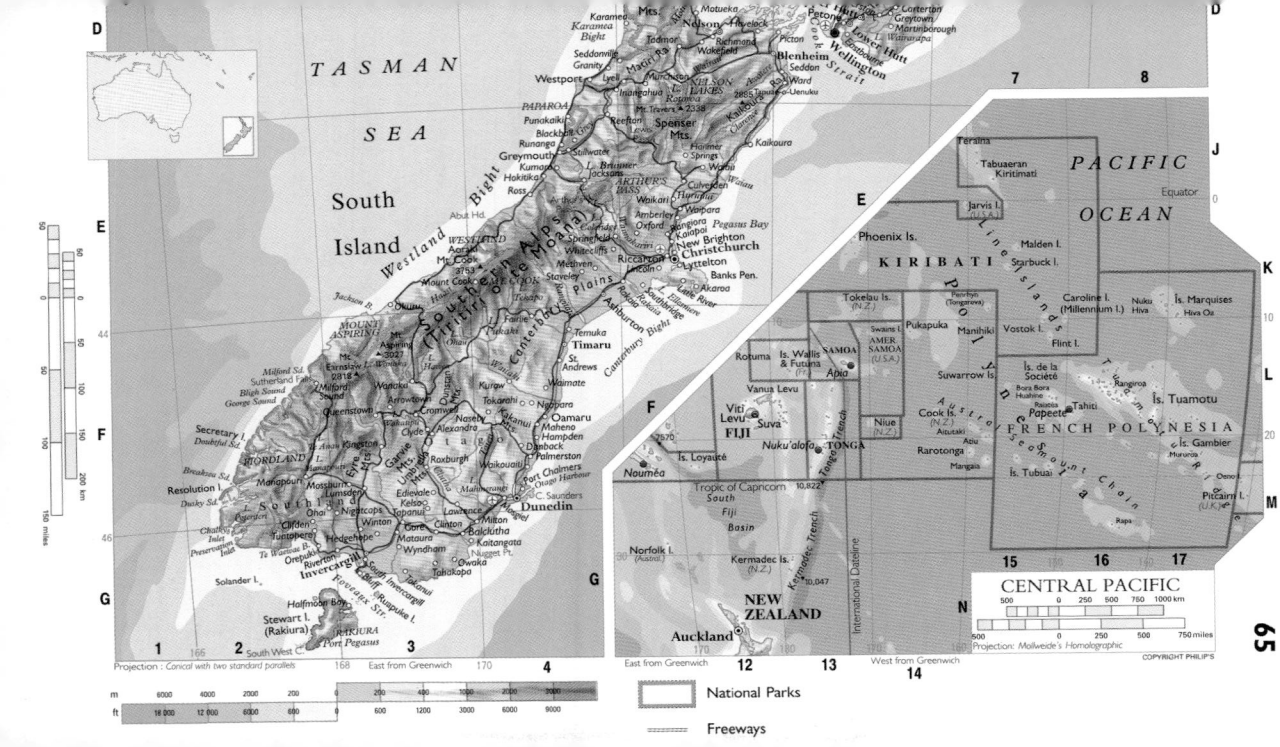
TASMAN SEA
South Island
Westland Bight
Canterbury Bight
Southern Alps (Kaikoura Mountains)
Canterbury Plains
Nelson
Blenheim
Wellington
Hutt
Kapiti I.
Cook Strait
Westport
Greymouth
Hokitika
Ross
Mt. Cook 3753
Mt. Aspiring 3027
Mt. Earnslaw 2819
Mt. Cook
Timaru
Oamaru
Dunedin
Invercargill
Queenstown
Wanaka
Alexandra
Cromwell
Milford Sound
Stewart I. (Rakiura)
Halfmoon Bay
Bluff
Port Pegasus
Foveaux Str.
Solander I.
Secretary I.
Resolution I.
Preservation Inland
Pegasus Bay
Banks Pen.
Akaroa
Lyttelton
New Brighton
Christchurch
Kaikoura
Hanmer Springs
Nelson Lakes
Abt Hd
Jackson B.
Milford Sd
Sutherland Falls
Bligh Sound
George Sound
Dusky Sd
Breaksea Sd
Doubtful Sd
Chalmers
Port Chalmers
Otago Harbour
Clutha R.
Waitaki R.
Rangitata R.
Rakaia R.
Waimakariri R.
Waipara R.
Kaikoura Mts.
Spenser Mts.
Alps
Mt. Aspiring
Mt. Tasman
Mt. Cook
Mt. Earnslaw
Mt. Travers
Mt. Tapuae-o-Uenuku
Lake Ellesmere
Lake Wanaka
Lake Hawea
Lake Manapouri
Lake Ellesmere
Lake Rotoroa
Lake Ellesmere
Lake Wanaka
Lake Hawea
Lake Manapouri
Lake Ellesmere
Lake Rotoroa
Lake Ellesmere
Lake Manapouri
Projection : Conical with two standard parallels
East from Greenwich
South West
PACIFIC OCEAN
Equator
Tarawa
Tabuaeran
Kiritimati
Jarvis I. (U.S.A.)
Phoenix Is.
KIRIBATI
Malden I.
Starbuck I.
Line Is.
Tokelau Is. (N.Z.)
Penrhyn (Tongareva)
Pukapuka
Manihiki
Caroline I. (Millennium I.)
Nukuhiva
Is. Marquises
Hiva Oa
Vostok I.
Flint I.
Swains I.
AMER. SAMOA (U.S.A.)
SAMOA
Apia
Rotuma
Is. Wallis & Futuna (Fr.)
Is. de la Société
Bora Bora
Huahine
Raiatea
Rangiroa
Suwarrow Is.
Tahiti
Papeete
Is. Tuamotu
Vanua Levu
Viti Levu
Suva
FIJI
Niue (N.Z.)
Cook Is. (N.Z.)
Aitutaki
Atiu
Rarotonga
Mangaia
Nuku'alofa
TONGA
Tonga Trench
Is. Gambier
Mururoa
Is. Loyauté
Noumea
Is. Tubuai
Rapa
Pitcairn I. (U.K.)
Tropic of Capricorn
South Fiji Basin
Norfolk I. (Aust.)
Kermadec Is. (N.Z.)
Kermadec Trench
10,047
NEW ZEALAND
Auckland
International Dateline
CENTRAL PACIFIC
Projection: Mollweide's Homalographic
COPYRIGHT PHILIP'S
National Parks
Freeways
65

ICELAND
Reykjavik
Denmark Strait
GREENLAND
(Denmark)
Nuuk
Davis Strait
Baffin Bay
Baffin Island
Hudson Strait
Ellesmere I.
Queen Elizabeth Is.
Victoria I.
ARCTIC OCEAN
Beaufort Sea
NUNAVUT
Hudson Bay
LABRADOR
NEWFOUNDLAND
QUEBEC
Quebec
Montreal
Ottawa
ONTARIO
Toronto
Winnipeg
MANITOBA
Churchill
SASKATCHEWAN
Regina
Saskatoon
ALBERTA
Edmonton
Calgary
BRITISH COLUMBIA
Vancouver
Victoria
Yellowknife
NORTHWEST TERRITORIES
Great Slave L.
Great Bear L.
Mackenzie
YUKON TERRITORY
Whitehorse
Dawson
ALASKA
Fairbanks
Anchorage
Juneau
Kodiak I.
Gulf of Alaska
Bering Sea
St. Lawrence I.
RUSSIA
Asia
Bering Strait
Date line (approximate)

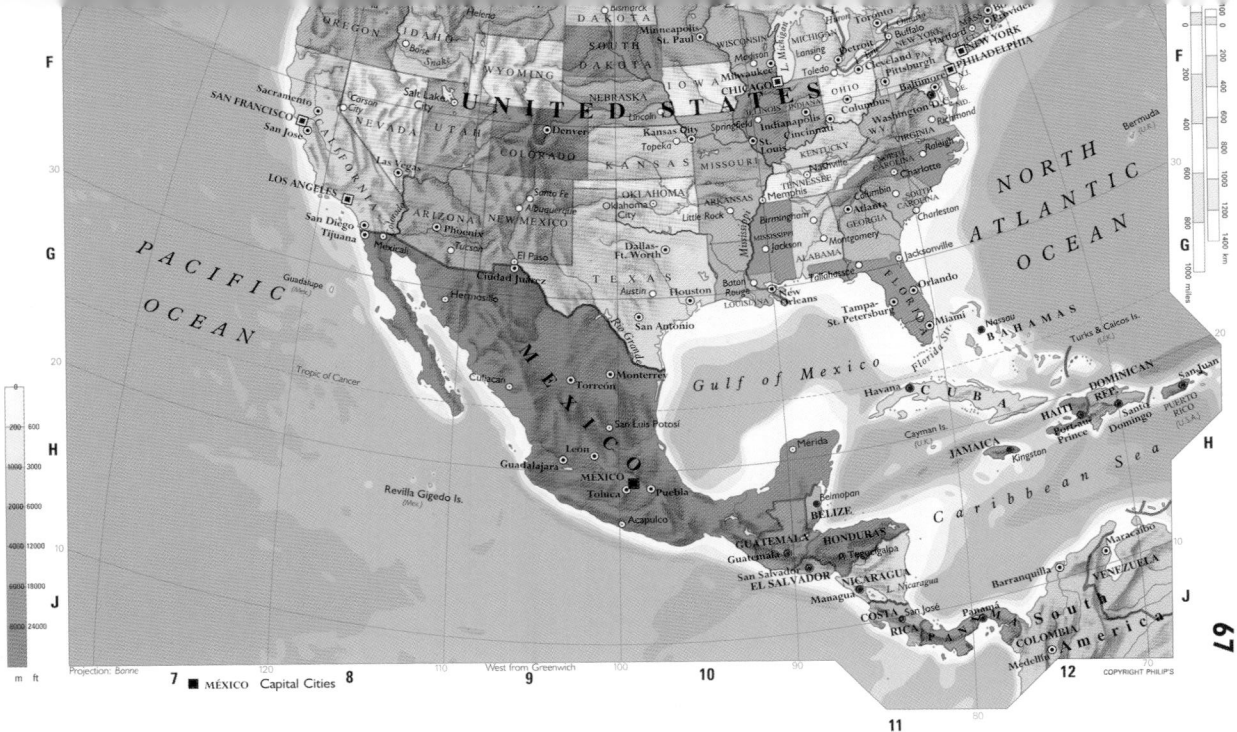
UNITED STATES
MEXICO
CANADA
PACIFIC OCEAN
NORTH ATLANTIC OCEAN
Gulf of Mexico
Caribbean Sea
South America
CUBA
HAITI
DOMINICAN REP.
JAMAICA
BAHAMAS
PUERTO RICO (U.S.A.)
GUATEMALA
BELIZE
HONDURAS
NICARAGUA
COSTA RICA
PANAMA
COLOMBIA
VENEZUELA
EL SALVADOR
Tropic of Cancer
Revilla Gigedo Is.
Bermuda
Turks & Caicos Is.
Cayman Is.
Projection: Bonne
West from Greenwich
m ft
■ MÉXICO Capital Cities
COPYRIGHT PHILIP'S

PACIFIC
Hudson Bay
NUNAVUT
NORTHWEST TERRITORIES
YUKON TERRITORY
ALASKA
BRITISH COLUMBIA
Victoria Island
Banks Island
Prince of Wales I.
Somerset Island
Prince Albert Pen.
Boothia Pen.
Melville Peninsula
M'Clintock Channel
Amundsen Gulf
Coronation Gulf
Great Bear L.
Great Slave L.
Lake Athabasca
Mackenzie Mountains
Selwyn Mts.
Cassiar Mountains
Rocky Mountains
Wrangell Mts.
St. Elias Mts.
Alexander Archipelago
Queen Charlotte Is.
Anchorage
Yellowknife
Whitehorse
Dawson
Fairbanks
Inuvik
Churchill
Baker Lake
Fort Smith
Fort Nelson
Prince Rupert
Ketchikan
Juneau
Skagway
Haines
Yakutat
Cordova
Arctic Circle
Mt. Logan 5959
Mt. Fairweather 4663
Mt. Sanford 4949
Mt. Lucania 5226
Mt. Fairweather 4663
Mt. Logan 5959

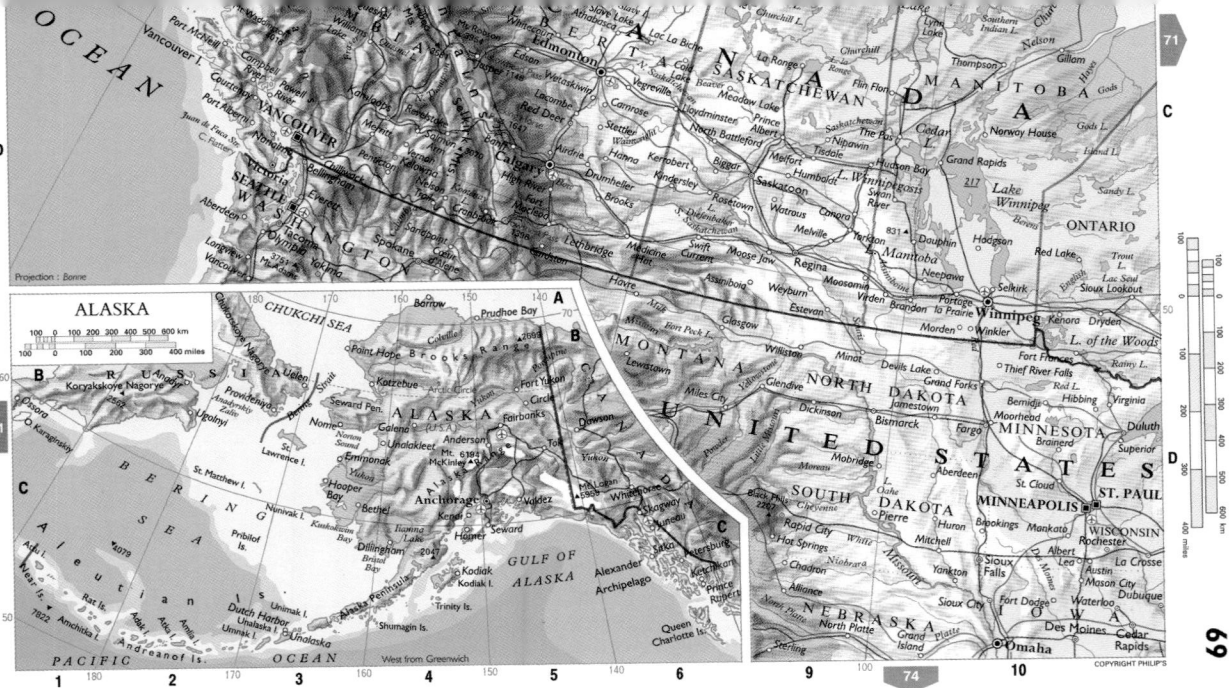
ALASKA
CHUKCHI SEA
BERING SEA
PACIFIC OCEAN
GULF OF ALASKA
Aleutian Is.
Alexander Archipelago
Queen Charlotte Is.
Anchorage
Fairbanks
Juneau
Kodiak I.
Kodiak
Dutch Harbor
Unalaska
Nome
Kotzebue
Barrow
Prudhoe Bay
Bethel
Seward
Homer
Valdez
Whitehorse
Dawson
Yukon
Alaska Pennsula
Shumagin Is.
Trinity Is.
Pribilof Is.
Kuskokwim Bay
Norton Sound
Brooks Range
Alaska Range
Mt. McKinley 6194
Mt. Logan 5959
Dillingham
Ketchikan
Prince Rupert
Sitka
Petersburg
Wrangell
Skagway
West from Greenwich
Projection : Bonne
OCEAN
VANCOUVER I.
Victoria
SEATTLE
WASHINGTON
Vancouver
Calgary
Edmonton
Saskatoon
Regina
Winnipeg
Lake Winnipeg
Lake Manitoba
Lake Saskatchewan
SASKATCHEWAN
MANITOBA
ONTARIO
MONTANA
NORTH DAKOTA
SOUTH DAKOTA
MINNESOTA
UNITED STATES
MINNEAPOLIS
ST. PAUL
WISCONSIN
NEBRASKA
IOWA
Omaha
Des Moines
Cedar Rapids
Duluth
Superior
Fargo
Bismarck
Minot
Williston
Lethbridge
Medicine Hat
Swift Current
Moose Jaw
Prince Albert
Flin Flon
Thompson
Churchill
Norway House
Grand Rapids
Hudson Bay
Dauphin
Brandon
Portage la Prairie
Selkirk
Winnipeg
Kenora
Dryden
Sioux Lookout
Red Lake
Hodgson
Kamloops
Prince Rupert
Port Alberni
Nanaimo
Victoria
Vancouver
Kelowna
Penticton
Cranbrook
Kamloops
Fort Nelson
Edmonton
Calgary
Lethbridge
Medicine Hat
Swift Current
Moose Jaw
Regina
Saskatoon
Prince Albert
North Battleford
Lloydminster
Meadow Lake

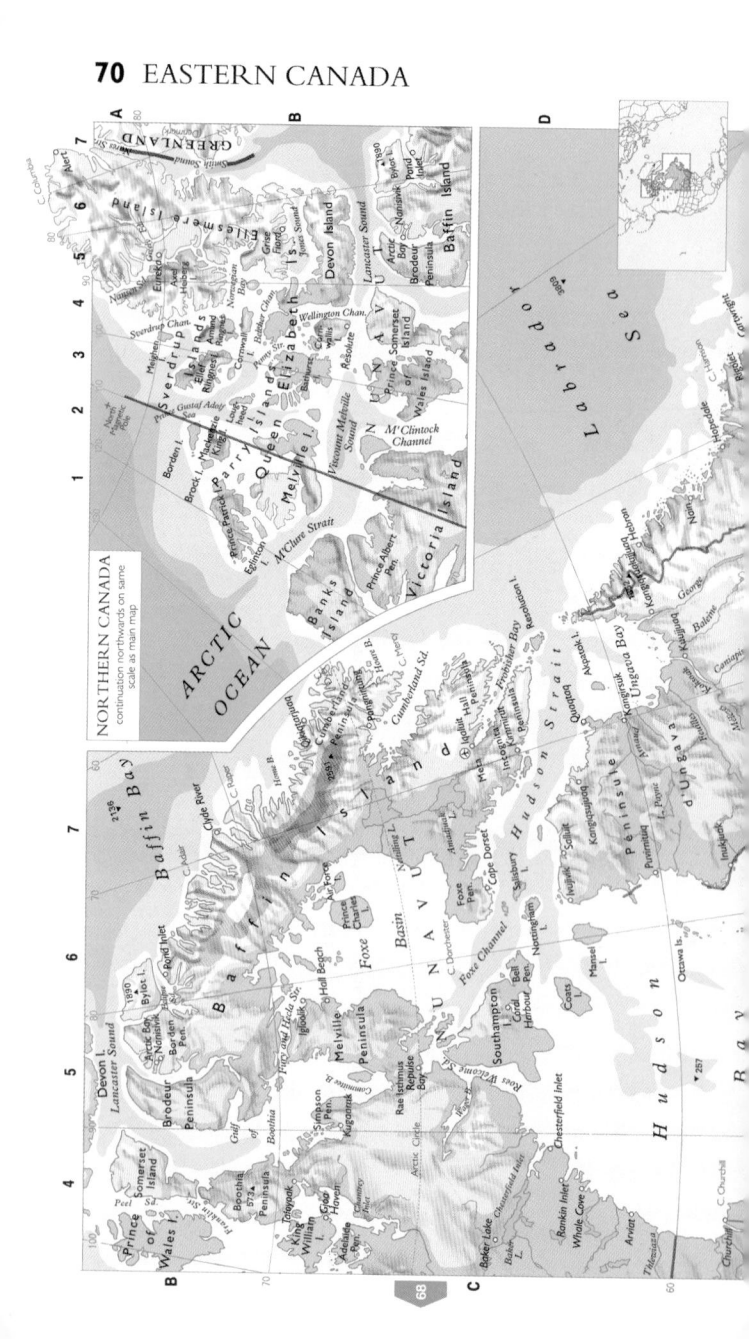
NORTHERN CANADA
continuation northwards on same scale as main map
ARCTIC OCEAN
GREENLAND
Ellesmere Island
Axel Heiberg I.
Ellef Ringnes I.
Sverdrup Islands
Queen Elizabeth Is.
Devon Island
Lancaster Sound
Baffin Island
Arctic Bay
Brodeur Peninsula
Prince of Wales I.
Somerset Island
Victoria Island
Banks Island
Melville I.
Parry Islands
Borden I.
Brock I.
Prince Patrick I.
Eglinton
Lougheed I.
Bathurst I.
Cornwallis I.
Bylot I.
Baffin Bay
Pond Inlet
Clyde River
Cape Dyer
Home B.
Cumberland Sd.
Frobisher Bay
Baffin Island
Foxe Basin
Foxe Channel
Hudson Strait
Ungava Peninsula
Ungava Bay
Labrador Sea
Hudson Bay
Southampton I.
Coats I.
Mansel I.
Nottingham I.
Salisbury I.
Cape Dorset
Iqaluit
Kangiqsujuaq
Kangiqsualujjuaq
Kuujjuaq
Inukjuak
Puvirnituq
Churchill
Churchill R.
Churchill Inlet
Chesterfield Inlet
Rankin Inlet
Whale Cove
Baker Lake
Arviat
Repulse Bay
Ross Welcome Sd.
Simpson Pen.
Ras Isthmus
Melville Peninsula
Foxe Pen.
Prince Charles I.
Hall Beach
Igloolik
Pond Inlet
Nanisivik
Arctic Bay
Brodeur Peninsula
Bylot I.
Borden Pen.
Lancaster Sound
Devon I.
Resolute
Grise Fiord
Eureka
Alert
Cape Columbia
Ellesmere Island
Axel Heiberg I.
Ellef Ringnes I.
Sverdrup Islands
Queen Elizabeth Is.
Devon Island
Lancaster Sound
Baffin Island
Arctic Bay
Brodeur Peninsula
Prince of Wales I.
Somerset Island
Victoria Island
Banks Island
Melville I.
Parry Islands
Borden I.
Brock I.
Prince Patrick I.
Eglinton
Lougheed I.
Bathurst I.
Cornwallis I.
Bylot I.
Baffin Bay
Pond Inlet
Clyde River
Cape Dyer
Home B.
Cumberland Sd.
Frobisher Bay
Baffin Island
Foxe Basin
Foxe Channel
Hudson Strait
Ungava Peninsula
Ungava Bay
Labrador Sea
Hudson Bay
Southampton I.
Coats I.
Mansel I.
Nottingham I.
Salisbury I.
Cape Dorset
Iqaluit
Kangiqsujuaq
Kangiqsualujjuaq
Kuujjuaq
Inukjuak
Puvirnituq
Churchill
Churchill R.
Churchill Inlet
Chesterfield Inlet
Rankin Inlet
Whale Cove
Baker Lake
Arviat
Repulse Bay
Ross Welcome Sd.
Simpson Pen.
Ras Isthmus
Melville Peninsula
Foxe Pen.
Prince Charles I.
Hall Beach
Igloolik
Pond Inlet
Nanisivik
Arctic Bay
Brodeur Peninsula
Bylot I.
Borden Pen.
Lancaster Sound
Devon I.
Resolute
Grise Fiord
Eureka
Alert
Cape Columbia
68

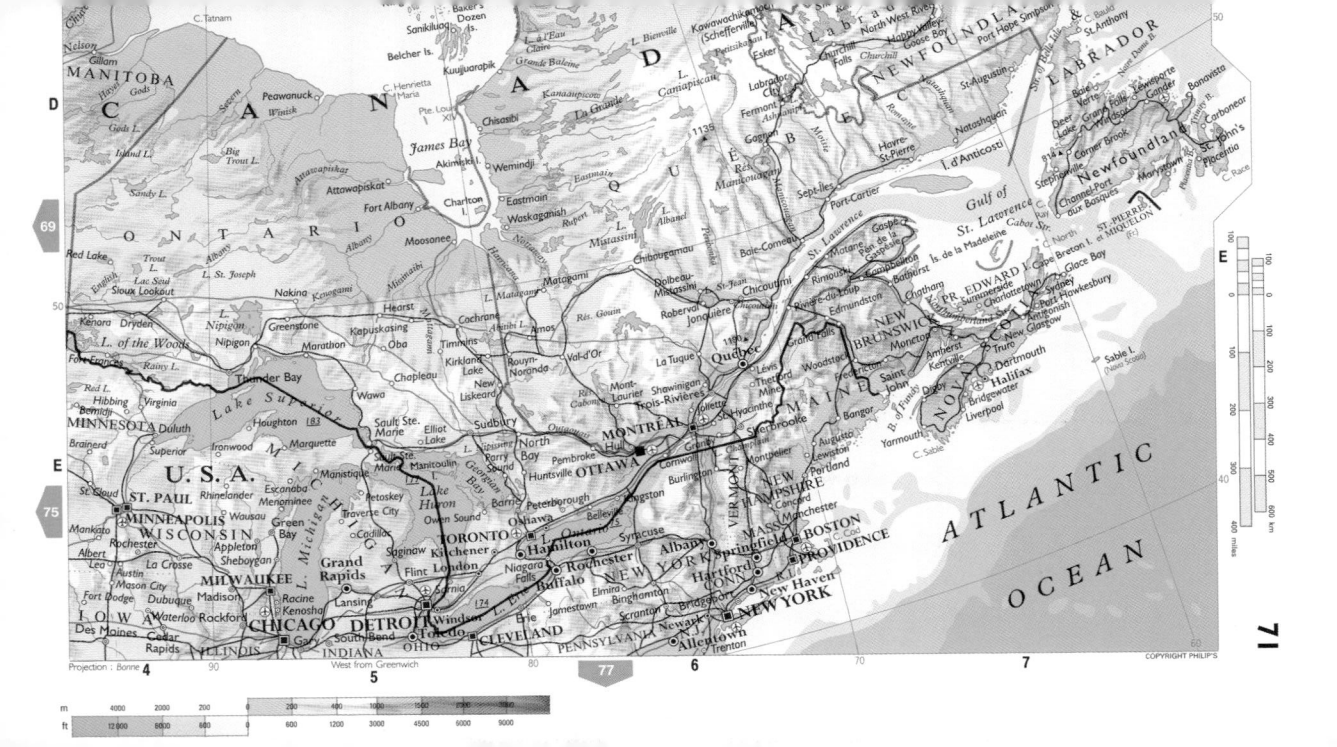
CANADA
U.S.A.
ATLANTIC OCEAN
MANITOBA
ONTARIO
QUÉBEC
NEWFOUNDLAND & LABRADOR
NEW BRUNSWICK
NOVA SCOTIA
PR. EDWARD I.
MAINE
VERMONT
NEW HAMPSHIRE
MASSACHUSETTS
CONN.
R.I.
NEW YORK
PENNSYLVANIA
NJ
OHIO
INDIANA
ILLINOIS
WISCONSIN
MINNESOTA
IOWA
MICHIGAN
Lake Superior
Lake Michigan
Lake Huron
Lake Erie
James Bay
Gulf of St. Lawrence
Newfoundland
Thunder Bay
Sault Ste. Marie
Sudbury
North Bay
Timmins
Moosonee
Kapuskasing
Hearst
Cochrane
Chibougamau
Chicoutimi
Roberval
Quebec
Trois-Rivières
Montréal
Ottawa
Toronto
Hamilton
Kitchener
London
Windsor
Sarnia
Sault Ste. Marie
Thunder Bay
Duluth
Minneapolis
St. Paul
Milwaukee
Chicago
Detroit
Cleveland
Buffalo
Rochester
Albany
Boston
Providence
New Haven
Hartford
Springfield
New York
Newark
Allentown
Scranton
Binghamton
Syracuse
Toronto
Kingston
Ottawa
Montreal
Quebec
Saint John
Halifax
Moncton
Charlottetown
St. John's
Corner Brook
Stephenville
Gander
Grand Falls
Goose Bay
Happy Valley
Churchill Falls
Schefferville
Kuujjuarapik
Chisasibi
Wemindji
Akimiski I.
Attawapiskat
Fort Albany
Moosonee
Moosonee
Kenora
Dryden
Red Lake
Sioux Lookout
Nipigon
Marathon
Wawa
Chapleau
Timmins
Kirkland Lake
Rouyn-Noranda
Val-d'Or
Chibougamau
Matagami
Chicoutimi
Roberval
Jonquière
Rimouski
Gaspé
Baie-Comeau
Sept-Îles
Port-Cartier
Natashquan
St-Augustin
Port Hope Simpson
Cape Breton I.
Sydney
Charlottetown
Moncton
Saint John
Halifax
Yarmouth
Liverpool
Bridgewater
Dartmouth
Truro
Amherst
Kentville
Sable I.
Bangor
Augusta
Portland
Lewiston
Montpelier
Burlington
Concord
Manchester
Boston
Providence
Hartford
New Haven
New York
Newark
Allentown
Trenton
Scranton
Binghamton
Albany
Syracuse
Rochester
Buffalo
Niagara Falls
Toronto
Hamilton
Kingston
Ottawa
Montreal
Quebec
Saint John
Halifax

NORTH-WEST USA

VANCOUVER
Nanaimo
Coquitlam
Surrey
New Westminster
Chilliwack
Victoria
Bellingham
Anacortes
Mt. Baker 3285
Mt. Vernon
Arlington
Everett
Snohomish
Darrington
Glacier Peak 3213
Chelan
Omak
Okanogan
Brewster
Oroville
Tonasket
Republic
Nelson
Trail
Kootenay L.
Cranbrook
Bonners Ferry
Sandpoint
Kootenay Nat. Park
Yoho Nat. Park
Glacier Nat. Park
Revelstoke
Golden
Cranbrook
Bonners Ferry
Sandpoint
Kootenay Nat. Park
Yoho Nat. Park
Glacier Nat. Park
Revelstoke
Golden
Port Angeles
Port Townsend
Olympic Nat. Park
Olympic Mts.
Bremerton
Shelton
Hoquiam
Aberdeen
Grays Harbor
Westport
Ocean Park
Long Beach
Astoria
Warrenton
Cathlamet
Longview
Kelso
Ketchikan
Seattle
Bellevue
Renton
Kent
Puyallup
Tacoma
Lacey
Tumwater
Olympia
Centralia
Chehalis
Mt. Rainier 4392
Mt. St. Helens 2549
Mt. Adams 3742
Yakima
Toppenish
Sunnyside
Prosser
Kennewick
Richland
Pasco
Walla Walla
Dayton
Pullman
Moscow
Lewiston
Clarkston
Spokane
Post Falls
Coeur d'Alene
Ritzville
Moses Lake
Ephrata
Quincy
Odessa
Cheney
Spokane
Newport
Kettle Falls
Chewelah
Deer Park
Colfax
Pomeroy
Dayton
Columbia Basin
Columbia
Snake
Pend Oreille
Salmon
Salmon River

50 0 50 100 150 200 km
50 0 50 100 150 miles
69
6
7
8
9
10
11
112
114
110
108
B
C
D
E
F
G
74
79
ALBERTA
SASKATCHEWAN
MONTANA
IDAHO
WYOMING
COLORADO
UTAH
Lethbridge
Medicine Hat
Great Falls
Missoula
Helena
Butte
Bozeman
Billings
Idaho Falls
Pocatello
Casper
Ogden
Salt Lake City
Laramie
Green River
Rock Springs
Evanston
Uinta Mountains
Roan Plateau
Great Salt Lake
Salt Lake
Yellowstone
Glacier
Bighorn Mountains
Medicine Bow Mts.
Wind River Range
Snake River
Bitterroot Range
Lemhi Range
Lemhi Plain
Big Belt Mts.
Little Belt Mts.
Crazy Mts.
Absaroka Range
Teton
Swan Range
Swan Peak
Mt. Cleveland
Bears Paw Mts.
Big Sandy Pk.
Upper Missouri River Breaks Nat. Mon.
Fort Peck Lake
Bighorn Canyon Nat. Recreation Area
Big Horn Battlefield Nat. Mon.
Yellowstone Nat. Park
Grand Teton Nat. Park
Jackson L.
Yellowstone L.
Flaming Gorge Reservoir
Flaming Gorge Nat. Recreation Area
Dinosaur Nat. Mon.
Rocky Mountain Nat. Park
Grand Lake
Grassland Nat. Park
Glacier Nat. Park
Waterton Lakes Nat. Park
Red Deer
Lethbridge
Medicine Hat

74 NORTH-CENTRAL USA

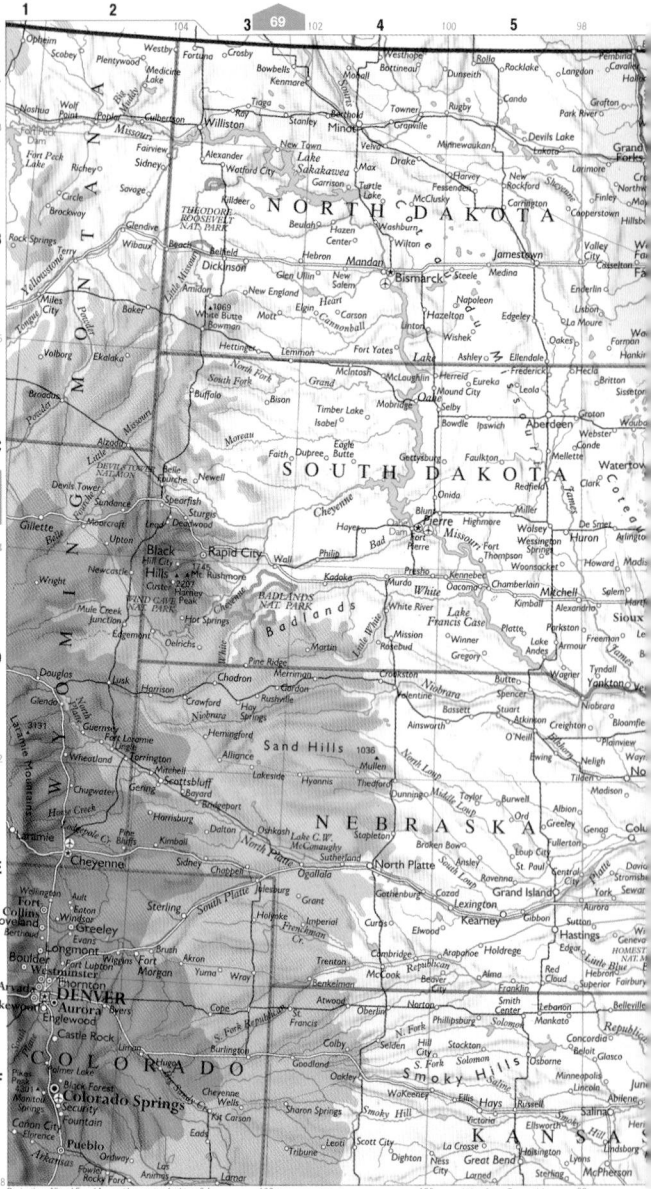

50 0 50 100 150 200 km
50 0 50 100 150 miles
CANADA
Lake of the Woods
Rainy Lake
Rainy River
Fort Frances
International Falls
Warroad
Baudette
Greenbush
Thunder Bay
Northern Light L.
Cloud Bay
Isle Royale
Upper Red L.
Big Falls
Little Fork
Vermilion
Sagaunaga
Grand Portage
ISLE ROYALE NAT. PARK
LAKE SUPERIOR
Grand Marais
Eagle River
Copper Harbor
Keweenaw Pt.
Keweenaw Pen.
Laurium
Hancock
Houghton
Keweenaw B.
Pt. Abbaye
Baraga
L'Anse
Marquette
Negaunee
Ishpeming
Ontonagon
Chippewa R.
APOSTLE ISLANDS NAT. LAKESHORE
Apostle Is.
Two Harbors
Duluth
Superior
Bayfield
Washburn
Ashland
Ironwood
Hurley
Bessemer
Rockland
Gogebic
Watersmeet
Iron River
Crystal Falls
Iron Mountain
Kingsford
Powers
MINNESOTA
MICHIGAN
Pine River
Aitkin
Brainerd
Mille Lacs
Staples
Baxter
Bemidji
Cloquet
Moose Lake
Solon Springs
Hayward
Park Falls
Phillips
Rhinelander
Crandon
Tomahawk
Merrill
Antigo
Menominee
Peshtigo
Oconto Falls
Green Bay
Marinette
Sturgeon Bay
Fergus Falls
Battle Lake
Alexandria
Long Prairie
Little Falls
Mora
Hinckley
Siren
Spooner
Rice Lake
Prentice
Ladysmith
Medford
Bloomer
Chippewa Falls
Wausau
Wisconsin Rapids
Stevens Point
Marshfield
Neenah
Appleton
Kaukauna
Kewaunee
Two Rivers
Manitowoc
Sheboygan
Port Washington
Milwaukee
Waukesha
Racine
Kenosha
Waukegan
North Chicago
Highland Park
Wilmette
Evanston
CHICAGO
Cicero
Oak Park
Elgin
Gary
Hammond
Michigan City
Benton Harbor
Kalamazoo
Battle Creek
Jackson
Ann Arbor
Detroit
Pontiac
Flint
Saginaw
Bay City
Cheboygan
Sault Ste. Marie
Lake Michigan
Sauk Rapids
Coon Rapids
Brooklyn Park
Minneapolis
St. Paul
Hastings
Red Wing
Northfield
Faribault
Owatonna
Rochester
Austin
Albert Lea
Winona
La Crosse
Eau Claire
Menomonie
Hudson
New Richmond
Bloomington
Hutchinson
Glencoe
Burnsville
Lakeville
Redwood Falls
Marshall
New Ulm
St. Peter
Mankato
N. Mankato
Sleepy Eye
Tracy
Windom
Worthington
Jackson
Fairmont
Blue Earth
Waseca
St. James
Sibley
Estherville
Lake Mills
Forest City
Mason City
Clear Lake
Osage
Charles City
Decorah
Waukon
Prairie du Chien
Viroqua
Richland Center
Reedsburg
Baraboo
Portage
Beaver Dam
Fond du Lac
Oconomowoc
Whitewater
Janesville
Beloit
Madison
Watertown
Hartford
Waterloo
Fitchburg
Delavan
Burlington
Lake Geneva
Sheldon
Spencer
Emmetsburg
Algona
Humboldt
Clarion
Hampton
Waverly
Oelwein
Cedar Falls
Dubuque
Monroe
Belvidere
Rockford
Freeport
Woodstock
Arlington Hts.
Elgin
Evanston
Wilmette
Highland Park
Cherokee
Pocahontas
Eagle Grove
Storm Lake
Fort Dodge
Webster City
Eldora
Grundy Center
Waterloo
Manchester
Independence
Monticello
Savanna
Oregon
Rochelle
St. Charles
Elmhurst
Aurora
Joliet
Morris
Sioux City
Rockwell City
Carroll
Jefferson
Boone
Nevada
Marshalltown
Marion
Vinton
Anamosa
Maquoketa
Cedar Rapids
Clinton
Sterling
Rock Falls
Dixon
De Kalb
Mendota
La Salle
Princeton
Streator
Dwight
Kankakee
Ida Grove
Denison
Harlan
Audubon
Perry
Ankeny
Newton
Grinnell
Marengo
Tipton
Bettendorf
Moline
Rock Island
Geneseo
Henry
Pontiac
Lexington
Paxton
Rantoul
Champaign
Urbana
Decatur
Tuscola
Mattoon
Shelbyville
Effingham
Newton
Vandalia
Flora
Centralia
Fairfield
Mount Vernon
McLeansboro
Benton
West Frankfort
Jackson
Paducah
Mt. Vernon
Marion
Du Quoin
Pinckneyville
Chester
Sullivan
Mattoon
Charleston
Terre Haute
Bloomington
Normal
Pekin
Peoria
Galesburg
Monmouth
Macomb
Canton
Havana
Lincoln
Springfield
Jacksonville
Taylorville
Pana
Shelbyville
Litchfield
Carlinville
Alton
Granite City
Belleville
Waterloo
Pinckneyville
Du Quoin
Council Bluffs
Atlantic
Winterset
Greenfield
Red Oak
Creston
Osceola
Corning
Shenandoah
Clarinda
Bedford
Centerville
Chariton
Albia
Oskaloosa
Ottumwa
Fairfield
Mount Pleasant
Burlington
Keokuk
Fort Madison
Kahoka
Canton
Macomb
Carthage
Monmouth
Galesburg
Galva
Aledo
Chillicothe
Pontiac
Streator
Dwight
Kankakee
Rock Island
Moline
Davenport
Iowa City
Grinnell
Marshalltown
Ames
Boone
Nevada
Tama
Belle Plaine
Marion
Vinton
Anamosa
Maquoketa
Monticello
Manchester
Independence
Waverly
Cedar Falls
Waterloo
Dubuque
Clinton
Cedar Rapids
Iowa City
Davenport
Muscatine

NORTH-EAST US

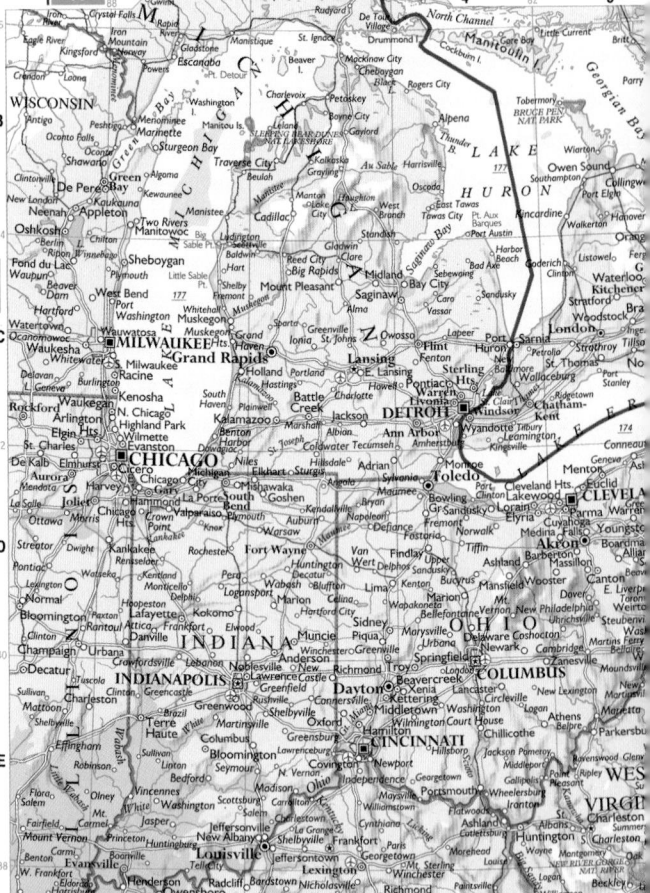
WISCONSIN
MICHIGAN
LAKE HURON
LAKE MICHIGAN
LAKE ERIE
Sault Ste. Marie
Grand Marais
PICTURED ROCKS NAT. LAKESHORE
Munising
Newberry
Rudyard
De Tour Village
Drummond I.
North Channel
Manitoulin I.
Little Current
Cockburn I.
Georgian Bay
Iron Mountain
Kingsford
Escanaba
Gladstone
Menominee
Marinette
Sturgeon Bay
Green Bay
Oconto
Shawano
Green Bay
Algoma
Kewaunee
De Pere
Appleton
Neenah
Oshkosh
Two Rivers
Manitowoc
Sheboygan
Fond du Lac
Port Washington
Milwaukee
Waukesha
Racine
Kenosha
Waukegan
Rockford
Arlington Hts.
Elgin
Wilmette
Evanston
CHICAGO
Cicero
Gary
Joliet
Hammond
Aurora
Elmhurst
Harvey
Orland Park
Ottawa
Streator
Pontiac
Normal
Bloomington
Champaign
Urbana
Decatur
Danville
Terre Haute
Evansville
Henderson
Owensboro
Elizabethtown
Paducah
Mayfield
Murray
Hopkinsville
Clarksville
Nashville
Dickson
Lexington
Columbia
Murfreesboro
Jackson
Henderson
Bowling Green
Glasgow
Somerset
Campbellsville
Lebanon
Cookeville
Crossville
Harriman
Knoxville
Morristown
Greeneville
Johnson City
Elizabethton
Bristol
Abingdon
Kingsport
Asheville
Hendersonville
Marion
Morganton
Lincolnton
Shelby
Grand Rapids
Holland
Muskegon
Lansing
Jackson
Battle Creek
Kalamazoo
Benton Harbor
Niles
Elkhart
Sturgis
Goshen
South Bend
Michigan City
Valparaiso
Gary
Hammond
Crown Point
Kankakee
Rochester
Fort Wayne
Huntington
Decatur
Wabash
Logansport
Marion
Kokomo
Hartford City
Muncie
Anderson
Noblesville
Lafayette
Frankfort
Attica
Rantoul
Danville
Terre Haute
Vincennes
Washington
Jasper
Princeton
Mt. Vernon
Boonville
Tell City
Jeffersonville
New Albany
Salem
Bedford
Seymour
Columbus
Greenfield
Shelbyville
Greenwood
Franklin
Scottsburg
Madison
Lawrenceburg
Greensburg
Rushville
Connersville
Richmond
Muncie
Anderson
Kendallville
Auburn
Warsaw
Elkhart
Goshen
Niles
Hillsdale
Adrian
Tecumseh
Coldwater
Marshall
Albion
Ann Arbor
Jackson
Ionia
St. Johns
Owosso
Flint
Saginaw
Bay City
Midland
Alma
Mount Pleasant
Big Rapids
Reed City
Cadillac
Manistee
Ludington
Traverse City
Petoskey
Alpena
Harbor Beach
Port Huron
Sarnia
Windsor
Chatham
Kent
Wyandotte
Tilbury
Leamington
Kingsville
Amherstburg
Monroe
Toledo
Sandusky
Lorain
Elyria
Cleveland
Akron
Canton
Mansfield
Wooster
Marion
Bucyrus
Lima
Findlay
Tiffin
Fremont
Norwalk
Ashland
Massillon
Barberton
Youngstown
Warren
Kent
Medina
Cuyahoga Falls
Akron
Alliance
Steubenville
Wheeling
Zanesville
Newark
Delaware
Marysville
Urbana
Springfield
Xenia
Dayton
Middletown
Hamilton
Oxford
Lancaster
Circleville
Chillicothe
Athens
Belpre
Parkersburg
Ravenswood
Ripley
Gallipolis
Pomeroy
Jackson
Portsmouth
Wheelersburg
Ironton
Ashland
Huntington
Charleston
Beckley
Hinton
Princeton
Bluefield
Pulaski
Wytheville
Abingdon
Bristol
Johnson City
Elizabethton
Bristol
Kingsport
Morristown
Greeneville
Knoxville
Newport
Asheville
Hendersonville
Morganton
Lincolnton
Shelby
Hickory
Greensboro
Lexington
Shelby
Lenoir
Boone
Danville
Martinsville
Bedford
Salem
Pulaski
Wytheville
Bristol
Abingdon
Big South Fork National River and Recreation Area
Great Smoky Mts. National Park
Appalachian Plateau
Cumberland Plateau
Ft. Knox
Louisville
Lexington
Frankfort
Bowling Green
Owensboro
Paducah
Hopkinsville
Elizabethtown
Radcliff
Richmond
Nicholasville
Harrodsburg
Lexington
Winchester
Paris
Georgetown
Frankfort
Shelbyville
Elizabethtown
Bardstown
Lebanon
Danville
Harrodsburg
Lexington
Richmond
Paintsville
Prestonsburg
Pikeville
Hazard
Manchester
Corbin
London
Somerset
Campbellsville
Lebanon
Danville
Harrodsburg
Lexington
Richmond
Berea
Lancaster
Nicholasville
Lexington
Winchester
Mt. Sterling
Morehead
Louisa

50 0 50 100 150 200 km
50 0 50 100 150 miles
CANADA
ONTARIO
OTTAWA
MONTREAL
TORONTO
LAKE ONTARIO
ADIRONDACK PARK
NEW YORK
Albany
Buffalo
Rochester
Syracuse
Binghamton
Elmira
Jamestown
Utica
Schenectady
Troy
Saratoga Spgs
Plattsburgh
Burlington
Montpelier
Concord
Manchester
Nashua
Lowell
Lawrence
Haverhill
Cambridge
Boston
Worcester
Springfield
Pittsfield
Northampton
Hartford
Bridgeport
Stamford
Norwalk
Yonkers
Poughkeepsie
Newburgh
Kingston
Catskill
Hudson
Albany
Schenectady
Troy
Saratoga Spgs
Glens Falls
Plattsburgh
Burlington
Montpelier
Concord
Manchester
Nashua
Lowell
Lawrence
Haverhill
Cambridge
Boston
Worcester
Springfield
Pittsfield
Northampton
Hartford
Bridgeport
Stamford
Norwalk
Yonkers
Poughkeepsie
Newburgh
Kingston
Catskill
Hudson
PENNSYLVANIA
Pittsburgh
Harrisburg
Lancaster
Reading
Allentown
Easton
Scranton
Williamsport
Erie
Philadelphia
Trenton
Camden
Atlantic City
NEW JERSEY
NEW YORK
ATLANTIC OCEAN
Baltimore
Annapolis
Washington
Alexandria
Arlington
Dover
Wilmington
Newark
Salisbury
Ocean City
Chesapeake Bay
Delaware Bay
VIRGINIA
Richmond
Norfolk
Virginia Beach
Portsmouth
Newport News
Hampton
Williamsburg
Petersburg
Lynchburg
Roanoke
Danville
Charlottesville
Staunton
Harrisonburg
Winchester
Fredericksburg
Chesapeake
Suffolk
Elizabeth City
Edenton
Rocky Mount
Greenville
Kinston
New Bern
Pamlico Sound
Hatteras
Raleigh
Durham
Chapel Hill
Wilmington
Goldsboro
Wilson
Rocky Mount
Henderson
Roanoke Rapids
Greensboro
Burlington
Charlotte
Gulf of Maine
Portland
Bangor
Augusta
Lewiston
Auburn
Brunswick
Bath
Rockland
Belfast
Bar Harbor
Mt. Desert I.
Eastport
Machias
Calais
Sherbrooke
Ottawa
Toronto
Hamilton
London
Windsor
Sudbury
Kingston
Peterborough
Belleville
Cornwall
Brockville
Pembroke
Prince George
St. John's
Fort St John
Cape Hatteras
Cape Cod
Cape Ann
Cape Elizabeth
Cape Ann
Block I.
Nantucket I.
Martha's Vineyard
Montauk Pt.
Long Island Sound
Cape May
Lewes
Ocean City
Assateague Island Nat. Seashore
Cape Hatteras Nat. Seashore
Acadia Nat. Park
Baxter State Park
Katahdin
Chamberlain L.
Eagle L.
Moosehead L.
Millinocket
Greenville
Rangeley
Bangor
Dexter
Old Town
Orono
Brewer
Belfast
Rockland
Camden
Waterville
Augusta
Bath
Brunswick
Lewiston
Auburn
Portland
Saco
Biddeford
Sanford
Rochester
Dover
Kittery
Portsmouth
Newburyport
Gloucester
Salem
Lynn
Newton
Quincy
Brockton
Attleboro
Taunton
Fall River
New Bedford
Cape Cod
Martha's Vineyard
Nantucket I.
Block I.
Montauk Pt.
Long Island Sound
Cape May
Lewes
Ocean City
Assateague Island Nat. Seashore
Cape Hatteras Nat. Seashore
Acadia Nat. Park
Baxter State Park
Katahdin
Chamberlain L.
Eagle L.
Moosehead L.
Millinocket
Greenville
Rangeley
Bangor
Dexter
Old Town
Orono
Brewer
Belfast
Rockland
Camden
Waterville
Augusta
Bath
Brunswick
Lewiston
Auburn
Portland
Saco
Biddeford
Sanford
Rochester
Dover
Kittery
Portsmouth
Newburyport
Gloucester
Salem
Lynn
Newton
Quincy
Brockton
Attleboro
Taunton
Fall River
New Bedford
Cape Cod
Cape Ann
Cape Elizabeth
Cape Ann
Block I.
Nantucket I.
Martha's Vineyard

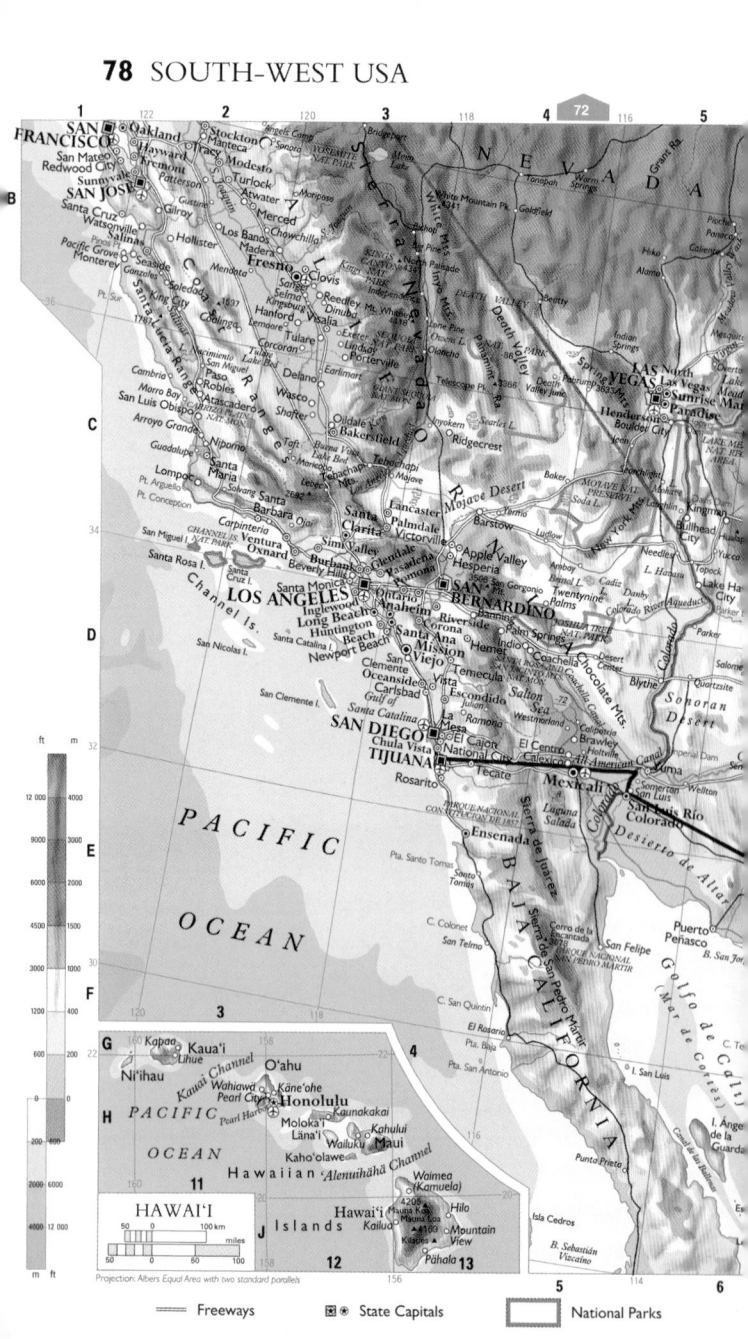
SAN FRANCISCO
Oakland
San Mateo
Redwood City
Hayward
Fremont
Sunnyvale
SAN JOSE
Santa Cruz
Watsonville
Salinas
Pacific Grove
Monterey
Gilroy
Hollister
Stockton
Tracy
Modesto
Turlock
Atwater
Merced
Los Banos
Madera
Chowchilla
Fresno
Clovis
Selma
Kingsburg
Reedley
Dinuba
Visalia
Hanford
Lemoore
Tulare
Corcoran
Delano
Wasco
Shafter
Taft
Bakersfield
Tehachapi
Mojave
Lancaster
Palmdale
Victorville
Barstow
Apple Valley
Hesperia
Yucca Valley
Twentynine Palms
Needles
Bullhead City
Kingman
Lake Havasu City
Parker
Blythe
Quartzsite
Yuma
Mexicali
San Luis Río Colorado
Puerto Peñasco
Ensenada
Tijuana
Tecate
Rosarito
Chula Vista
National City
El Cajon
Escondido
Vista
Oceanside
Carlsbad
Mission Viejo
Santa Ana
Anaheim
Long Beach
Huntington Beach
Newport Beach
Santa Monica
Burbank
Glendale
Pasadena
Ventura
Oxnard
Santa Barbara
Lompoc
Santa Maria
Arroyo Grande
San Luis Obispo
Paso Robles
Atascadero
Cambria
Morro Bay
Guadalupe
Nipomo
Pt. Arguello
Pt. Conception
Santa Rosa I.
San Miguel I.
Santa Cruz I.
Santa Catalina I.
San Nicolas I.
San Clemente I.
Santa Catalina I.
Channel Is.
Gulf of Santa Catalina
PACIFIC OCEAN
Pta. Santo Tomas
C. Colonet
C. San Quintin
El Rosario
Pta. Baja
Pta. San Antonio
I. San Luis
Punta Prieta
Isla Cedros
B. Sebastián Vizcaíno
Golfo de California (Mar de Cortés)
Desierto de Altar
Sonoran Desert
Mojave Desert
Death Valley
Sierra Nevada
Sierra de Juárez
Sierra de San Pedro Mártir
BAJA CALIFORNIA
LAS VEGAS
Las Vegas
Henderson
Boulder City
Sunrise Manor
Paradise
Nevada
Kapaa
Kaua'i
Lihue
Ni'ihau
Kaua'i Channel
O'ahu
Wahiawa
Pearl City
Pearl Harbor
Kāne'ohe
Honolulu
Moloka'i
Kaunakakai
Lāna'i
Kahului
Wailuku
Maui
Kaho'olawe
Hawaiian Islands
'Alenuihāhā Channel
Waimea (Kamuela)
Hawai'i
Kailua
Hilo
Mauna Loa
Mauna Kea
Mountain View
Kīlauea
Pāhala
HAWAI'I
50 0 100 km
miles
Projection: Albers Equal Area with two standard parallels
Freeways
State Capitals
National Parks

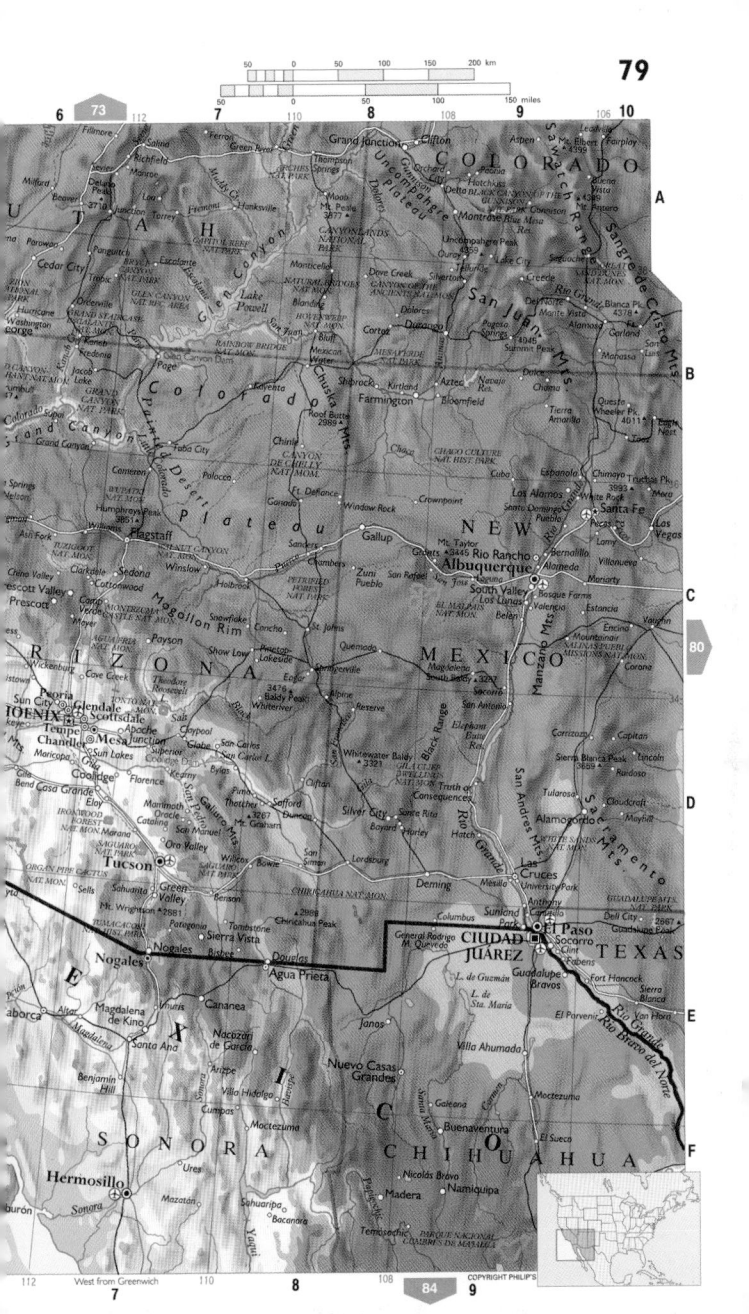
50 0 50 100 150 200 km
50 0 50 100 150 miles
73
80
84
6 7 8 9 10
112 110 108 106
A B C D E F
COLORADO
UTAH
ARIZONA
NEW MEXICO
TEXAS
SONORA
CHIHUAHUA
Grand Junction
Clifton
Aspen
Leadville
Fairplay
Salina
Richfield
Milford
Beaver
Delta
Lake Powell
Cedar City
Parowan
Panguitch
Escalante
Kanab
Page
Jacob Lake
Grand Canyon
Tuba City
Cameron
Polacca
Flagstaff
Williams
Ash Fork
Sedona
Cottonwood
Clarkdale
Chino Valley
Prescott
Cottonwood
Prescott Valley
Payson
Show Low
Pinetop-Lakeside
Springerville
Eagar
Alpine
Safford
Bisbee
Douglas
Agua Prieta
Nogales
Sierra Vista
Tombstone
Benson
Tucson
Green Valley
Sahuarita
Oracle
Catalina
San Manuel
Mammoth
Superior
Globe
Kearny
Florence
Casa Grande
Coolidge
Eloy
Maricopa
Chandler
Tempe
Mesa
Scottsdale
Glendale
Peoria
Sun City
PHOENIX
Apache Junction
Superior
Bylas
San Carlos
Safford
Thatcher
Pima
Willcox
Bowie
San Simon
Lordsburg
Deming
Mesilla
Las Cruces
Anthony
Sunland Park
Columbus
Chiricahua Peak
Tombstone
Sierra Vista
Bisbee
Douglas
Agua Prieta
Nogales
Magdalena de Kino
Santa Ana
Cananea
Nacozari de García
Janos
Nuevo Casas Grandes
Villa Ahumada
Moctezuma
Buenaventura
El Sueco
Galeana
Namiquipa
Madera
Nicolás Bravo
Temósachic
Cumpas
Villa Hidalgo
Arizpe
Benjamín Hill
Hermosillo
Sonora
Ures
Mazatán
Suhuaripa
Bacanora
Navajo
Shiprock
Kirtland
Farmington
Aztec
Bloomfield
Chinle
Canyon de Chelly Nat. Monument
Ganado
Window Rock
Crownpoint
Gallup
Zuni Pueblo
Grants
Mt. Taylor
Rio Rancho
Albuquerque
Los Alamos
Santa Fe
Espanola
Taos
Chimayo
Tierra Amarilla
Chama
Cuba
Los Lunas
Belen
Bernalillo
Alameda
Moriarty
Estancia
Mountainair
Encino
Vaughn
Capitan
Carrizozo
Tularosa
Alamogordo
Cloudcroft
Mayhill
Ruidoso
Lincoln
Sierra Blanca
Truth or Consequences
Silver City
Bayard
Hurley
Hatch
Las Cruces
Mesilla
Deming
Lordsburg
Columbus
Sierra Blanca
Van Horn
El Paso
Socorro
Fort Hancock
Guadalupe Bravos
Ciudad Juárez
Rio Grande
Rio Bravo del Norte
Rio Conchos
Rio Yaqui
Rio Sonora
Rio Bavispe
Rio Casas Grandes
Rio Papigochic
Rio Verde
Rio Gila
Rio Salinas
Rio Pecos
Rio Ruidoso
Rio Tularosa
Rio Sacramento
Rio Grande
Rio Bravo del Norte

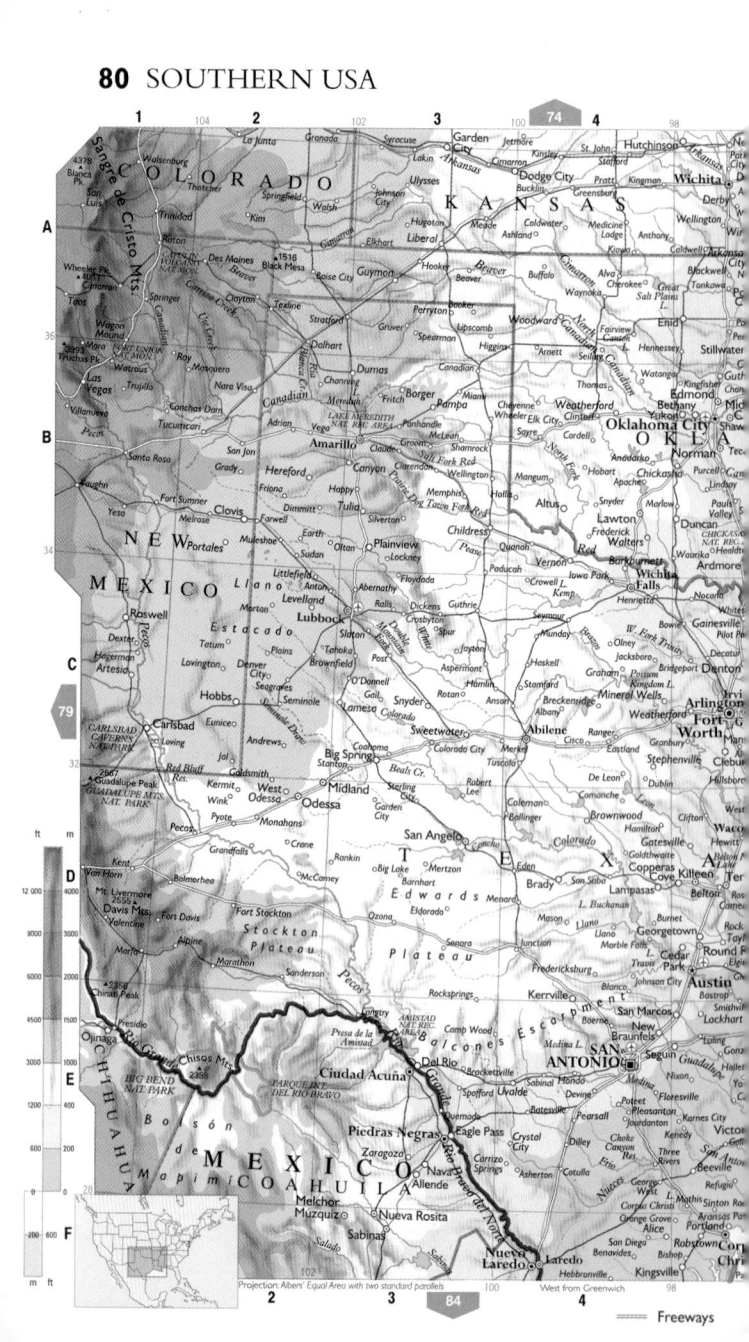
COLORADO
KANSAS
OKLA
NEW MEXICO
TEXAS
CHIHUAHUA
COAHUILA
MEXICO
Sangre de Cristo Mts.
Raton
Trinidad
Colorado Springs
Denver
Cheyenne
Garden City
Dodge City
Wichita
Hutchinson
Kansas City
Oklahoma City
Norman
Lubbock
Amarillo
Hereford
Canyon
Clovis
Portales
Roswell
Carlsbad
Hobbs
Odessa
Midland
Big Spring
Abilene
Sweetwater
Lamesa
Snyder
Wichita Falls
Denton
Arlington
Fort Worth
Waco
Austin
San Antonio
Laredo
Nuevo Laredo
Del Rio
Eagle Pass
Piedras Negras
Ciudad Acuña
Presa de la Amistad
Chisos Mts.
Big Bend National Park
Guadalupe Mts. National Park
Carlsbad Caverns National Park
Rio Grande
Pecos
Canadian
Red
Brazos
Colorado
Llano Estacado
Edwards Plateau
Stockton Plateau
Balcones Escarpment
Bolsón de Mapimí
Nuevo Laredo
Laredo
Kingsville
Corpus Christi
Alice
Mt. Livermore 2555
Davis Mts.
Guadalupe Peak 2667
Chinati Peak 5363
Black Mesa 1516
Ft. Sumner
Tucumcari
Santa Rosa
Las Vegas
Taos
Pecos
Ft. Stockton
Marfa
Alpine
Presidio
Ojinaga
Del Rio
Eagle Pass
Laredo
Kerrville
San Marcos
New Braunfels
Seguin
Brady
San Angelo
Abilene
Lubbock
Amarillo
Pampa
Borger
Dumas
Guymon
Liberal
Garden City
Hutchinson
Wichita
Kansas City
Oklahoma City
Norman
Lawton
Wichita Falls
Denton
Arlington
Fort Worth
Waco
Austin
San Antonio
Laredo
Nuevo Laredo
Kingsville
Corpus Christi
Alice
Ft. Stockton
Marfa
Alpine
Presidio
Ojinaga
Del Rio
Eagle Pass
Piedras Negras
Ciudad Acuña
Presa de la Amistad
Chisos Mts.
Big Bend National Park
Guadalupe Mts. National Park
Carlsbad Caverns National Park
Rio Grande
Pecos
Canadian
Red
Brazos
Colorado
Llano Estacado
Edwards Plateau
Stockton Plateau
Balcones Escarpment
Bolsón de Mapimí
Nuevo Laredo
Laredo
Kingsville
Corpus Christi
Alice
Mt. Livermore 2555
Davis Mts.
Guadalupe Peak 2667
Chinati Peak 5363
Black Mesa 1516
Ft. Sumner
Tucumcari
Santa Rosa
Las Vegas
Taos
Pecos
Ft. Stockton
Marfa
Alpine
Presidio
Ojinaga
Del Rio
Eagle Pass
Laredo
Kerrville
San Marcos
New Braunfels
Seguin
Brady
San Angelo
Abilene
Lubbock
Amarillo
Pampa
Borger
Dumas
Guymon
Liberal
Garden City
Hutchinson
Wichita
Kansas City
Oklahoma City
Norman
Lawton
Wichita Falls
Denton
Arlington
Fort Worth
Waco
Austin
San Antonio
Laredo
Nuevo Laredo
Kingsville
Corpus Christi
Alice
Projection: Albers' Equal Area with two standard parallels
West from Greenwich
Freeways

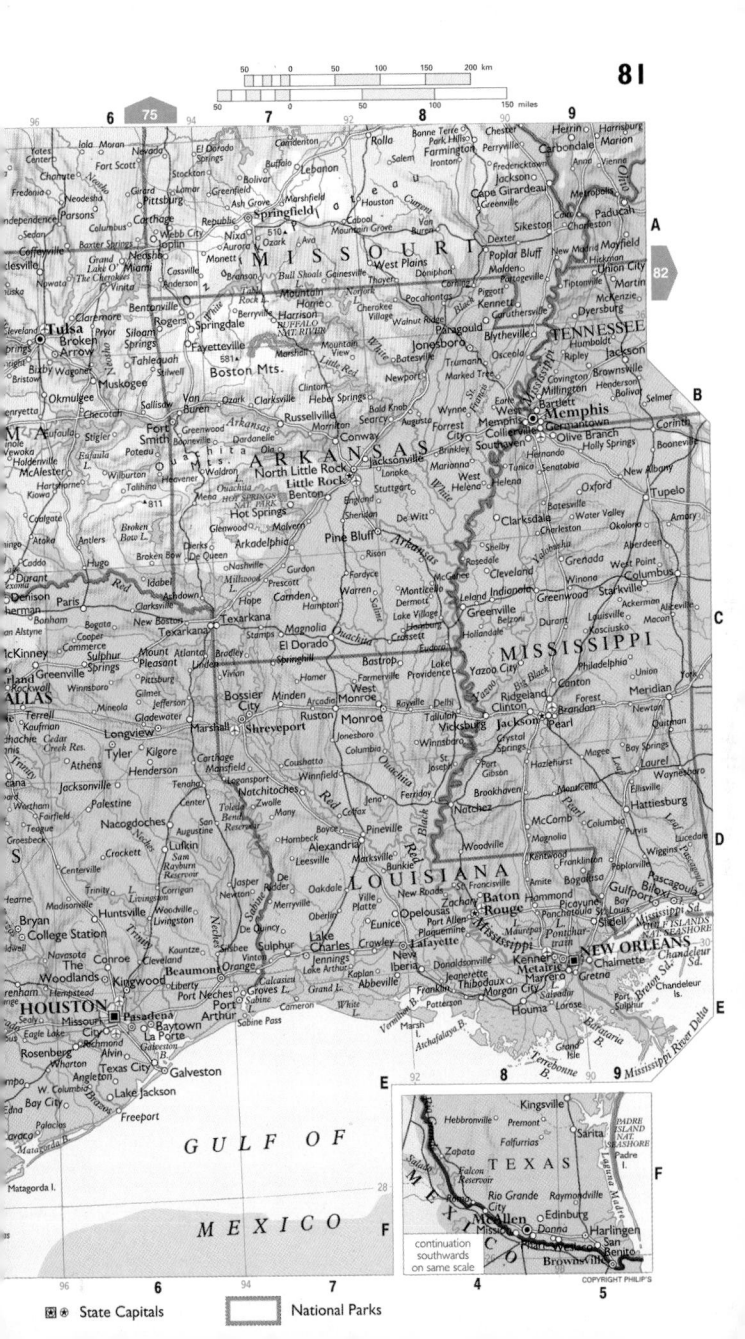
50 0 50 100 150 200 km
50 0 50 100 150 miles
MISSOURI
ARKANSAS
TENNESSEE
MISSISSIPPI
LOUISIANA
OKLAHOMA
TEXAS
GULF OF MEXICO
Springfield
Tulsa
Memphis
Little Rock
North Little Rock
Shreveport
Jackson
Baton Rouge
NEW ORLEANS
HOUSTON
Pasadena
Beaumont
Lake Charles
Monroe
Tupelo
Columbus
Meridian
Hattiesburg
Biloxi
Gulfport
Pascagoula
Natchez
Vicksburg
Hot Springs
Fort Smith
Texarkana
Joplin
Springfield
Cape Girardeau
Paducah
Jonesboro
Pine Bluff
Hot Springs
Boston Mts.
Ozark Mts.
Mississippi River Delta
Mississippi Sd.
Chandeleur Is.
Matagorda I.
Galveston
Corpus Christi
Kingsville
McAllen
Edinburg
Harlingen
Brownsville
Laredo
Eagle Pass
Del Rio
Uvalde
Rio Grande City
Raymondville
Falfurrias
Sarita
Hebbronville
Premont
Zapata
Falcon Reservoir
Laguna Madre
PADRE ISLAND NAT. SEASHORE
Padre I.
continuation southwards on same scale
COPYRIGHT PHILIP'S
State Capitals
National Parks

82 SOUTH-EAST USA

TENNESSEE
ARKANSAS
MISSISSIPPI
ALABAMA
LOUISIANA
GULF OF MEXICO
Nashville
Memphis
Birmingham
Jackson
Montgomery
Baton Rouge
NEW ORLEANS
Mobile
Pensacola
Panama City
Huntsville
Chattanooga
Little Rock
Shreveport
Tupelo
Meridian
Mississippi River Delta
Mississippi Sd.
Chandeleur Sd.
Chandeleur Is.
Breton Sd.
Atchafalaya B.
Terrebonne B.
Barataria B.
Grand Isle
Port St. Joe
C. San Blas
C. St. G
Apalach
Panama City Beach
Fort Walton Beach
Pensacola Bay
Gulf Islands Nat. Seashore
Natchez
Vicksburg
Hattiesburg
Gulfport
Biloxi
Pascagoula
Bogalusa
Hammond
Slidell
Kenner
Metairie
Chalmette
Gretna
Houma
Morgan City
Lafayette
New Iberia
Abbeville
Jeanerette
Franklin
Thibodaux
Marrero
Larose
Donaldsonville
Port Allen
Plaquemine
Zachary
Ponchatoula
Hammond
Covington
Slidell
Pearl
Brandon
Ridgeland
Clinton
Canton
Yazoo City
Greenwood
Grenada
Oxford
Tupelo
Corinth
Columbus
Starkville
Aberdeen
Amory
Hamilton
Fayette
Jasper
Tuscaloosa
Bessemer
Hoover
Alabaster
Northport
Gadsden
Anniston
Talladega
Selma
Prattville
Opelika
Auburn
Phenix City
Tuskegee
Troy
Dothan
Enterprise
Ozark
Eufaula
Greenville
Luverne
Andalusia
Brewton
Atmore
Bay Minette
Fairhope
Foley
Niceville
Milton
Crestview
Fort Walton Beach
Panama City
Port St. Joe
Apalachicola
Dothan
Columbus
Phenix City
Opelika
Auburn
Alexander City
Talladega
Anniston
Gadsden
Attalla
Albertville
Guntersville
Scottsboro
Decatur
Athens
Huntsville
Florence
Muscle Shoals
Tuscumbia
Russellville
Jasper
Fayette
Aberdeen
Amory
Hamilton
Tupelo
Corinth
Columbus
Starkville
Grenada
Oxford
Clarksdale
Greenwood
Yazoo City
Canton
Ridgeland
Clinton
Vicksburg
Natchez
Hattiesburg
Laurel
Meridian
Tuscaloosa
Bessemer
Hoover
Alabaster
Birmingham
Anniston
Gadsden
Talladega
Selma
Prattville
Montgomery
Tuskegee
Auburn
Opelika
Phenix City

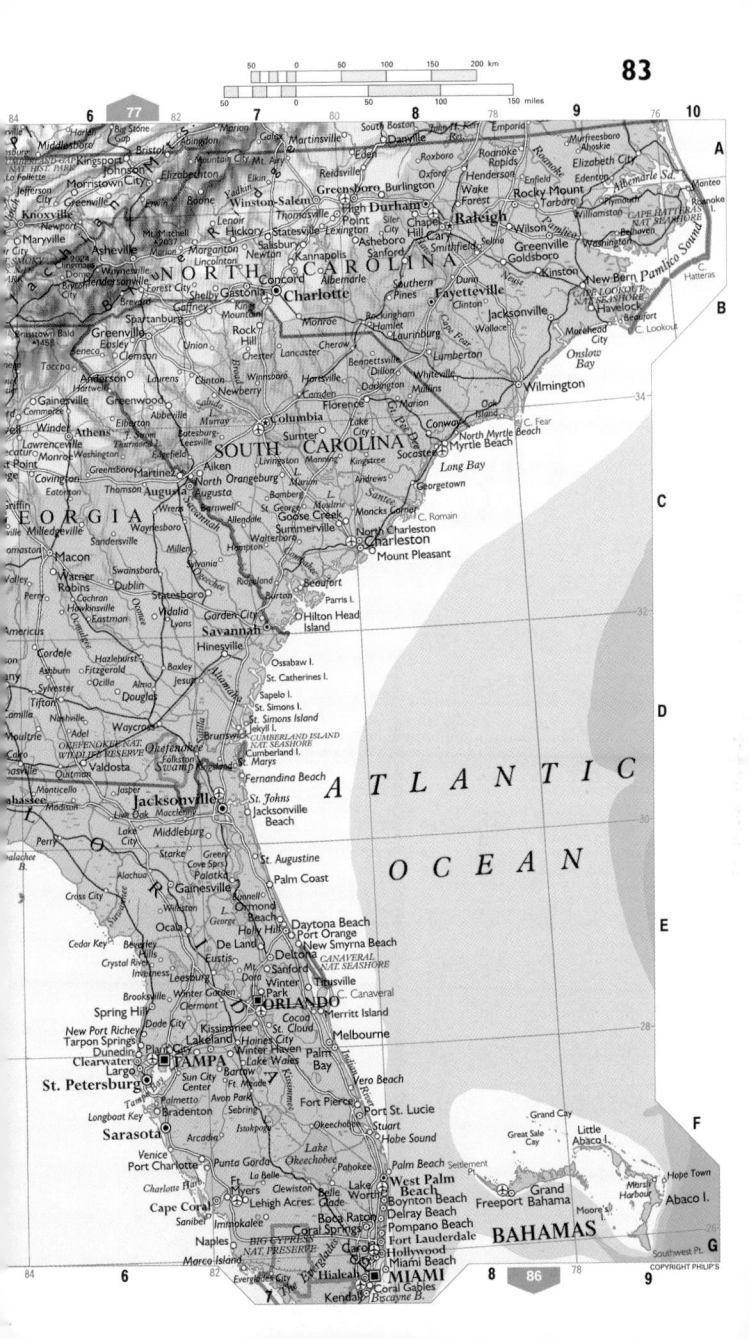
50 0 50 100 150 200 km
50 0 50 100 150 miles
77
86
NORTH CAROLINA
SOUTH CAROLINA
GEORGIA
ATLANTIC OCEAN
BAHAMAS
Charlotte
Raleigh
Durham
Greensboro
Winston-Salem
Fayetteville
Wilmington
Columbia
Charleston
Savannah
Jacksonville
Gainesville
Ocala
Orlando
Tampa
St. Petersburg
Sarasota
Miami
Key West
Cape Coral
Naples
Fort Myers
Fort Lauderdale
Hollywood
West Palm Beach
Freeport
Grand Bahama
Abaco I.
Little Abaco I.
Nassau
Andros I.
Long Bay
Pamlico Sound
Albemarle Sd.
Cape Hatteras
Cape Lookout
Onslow Bay
Cape Fear
Cape Romain
Cape Canaveral
Cape Sable
Southwest Pt.
Okefenokee NAT. WILDLIFE REFUGE
CUMBERLAND ISLAND NAT. SEASHORE
CAPE HATTERAS NAT. SEASHORE
CAPE LOOKOUT NAT. SEASHORE
BIG CYPRESS NAT. PRESERVE
EVERGLADES NAT. PARK
CANAVERAL NAT. SEASHORE
COPYRIGHT PHILIP'S

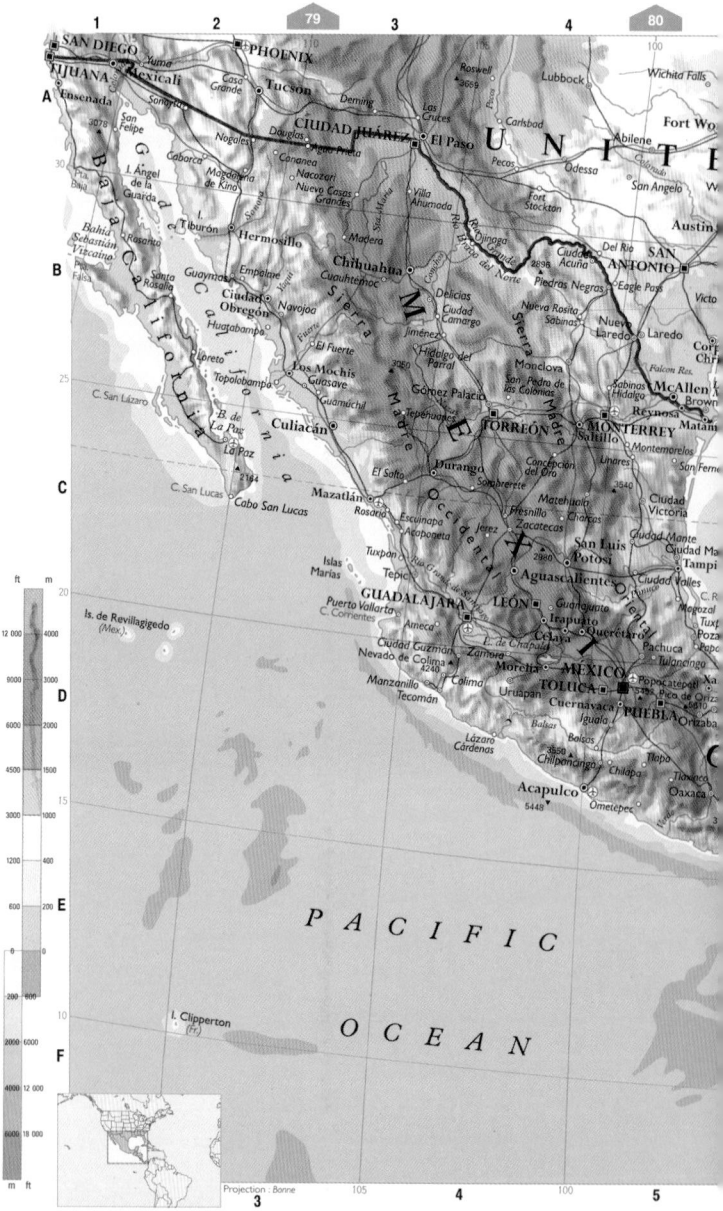
SAN DIEGO
TIJUANA
Mexicali
Ensenada
PHOENIX
Tucson
Sonoita
Nogales
Douglas
Agua Prieta
CIUDAD JUÁREZ
El Paso
Deming
Las Cruces
Roswell
Carlsbad
Lubbock
Wichita Falls
Abilene
Fort Wo
Odessa
San Angelo
Austin
Pecos
Fort Stockton
Del Rio
Ciudad Acuña
SAN ANTONIO
Piedras Negras
Eagle Pass
Nuevo Laredo
Laredo
McAllen
Reynosa
Matam
MONTERREY
Saltillo
Montemorelos
San Fernando
Ciudad Victoria
Ciudad Mante
Tampi
Ciudad Valles
Mogezal
Tuxp
Poza
Papo
Xal
Orizaba
Oaxaca
Tlapa
Chilapa
Iguala
Balsas
Balcas
Chilpancingo
Acapulco
Ometepec
Lázaro Cárdenas
Manzanillo
Tecomán
Colima
Nevado de Colima
4240
Ciudad Guzmán
Zamora
Morelia
Uruapan
Cuernavaca
TOLUCA
MÉXICO
PUEBLA
Pachuca
Tulancingo
Pico de Orizaba
Popocatepetl
Celaya
Irapuato
Querétaro
Guanajuato
LEÓN
GUADALAJARA
Ameca
Puerto Vallarta
C. Corrientes
Tepic
Islas Marías
Aguascalientes
San Luis Potosí
Zacatecas
Fresnillo
Matehuala
Charcas
Durango
Sombrerete
Concepción del Oro
Linares
Mazatlán
Rosario
Escuinapa
Acaponeta
Tuxpan
Culiacán
Los Mochis
Guasave
Guamúchil
Navojoa
Hermosillo
Caborca
Cananea
Nacozari
Nuevo Casas Grandes
Villa Ahumada
Chihuahua
Cuauhtémoc
Delicias
Ciudad Camargo
Jiménez
Hidalgo del Parral
Monclova
San Pedro de las Colonias
Sabinas Hidalgo
Nueva Rosita
Sabinas
Gómez Palacio
TORREÓN
Tepehuanes
Madera
Guaymas
Ciudad Obregón
Huatabampo
Empalme
Santa Rosalía
Loreto
Topolobampo
El Fuerte
B. de La Ruta
La Paz
C. San Lázaro
C. San Lucas
Cabo San Lucas
El Salto
Is. de Revillagigedo (Mex.)
I. Clipperton (Fr.)
I. Ángel de la Guarda
Bahía Sebastián Vizcaíno
Bahía Falsa
Rosarito
I. Tiburón
Sierra Madre Occidental
Sierra Madre Oriental
Río Bravo del Norte
Río Grande
Río Conchos
Río Fuerte
Río Yaqui
Río Sonora
Río Balsas
Río Pecos
Río Colorado
Río Verde
Río Tuxpan
Río Pánuco

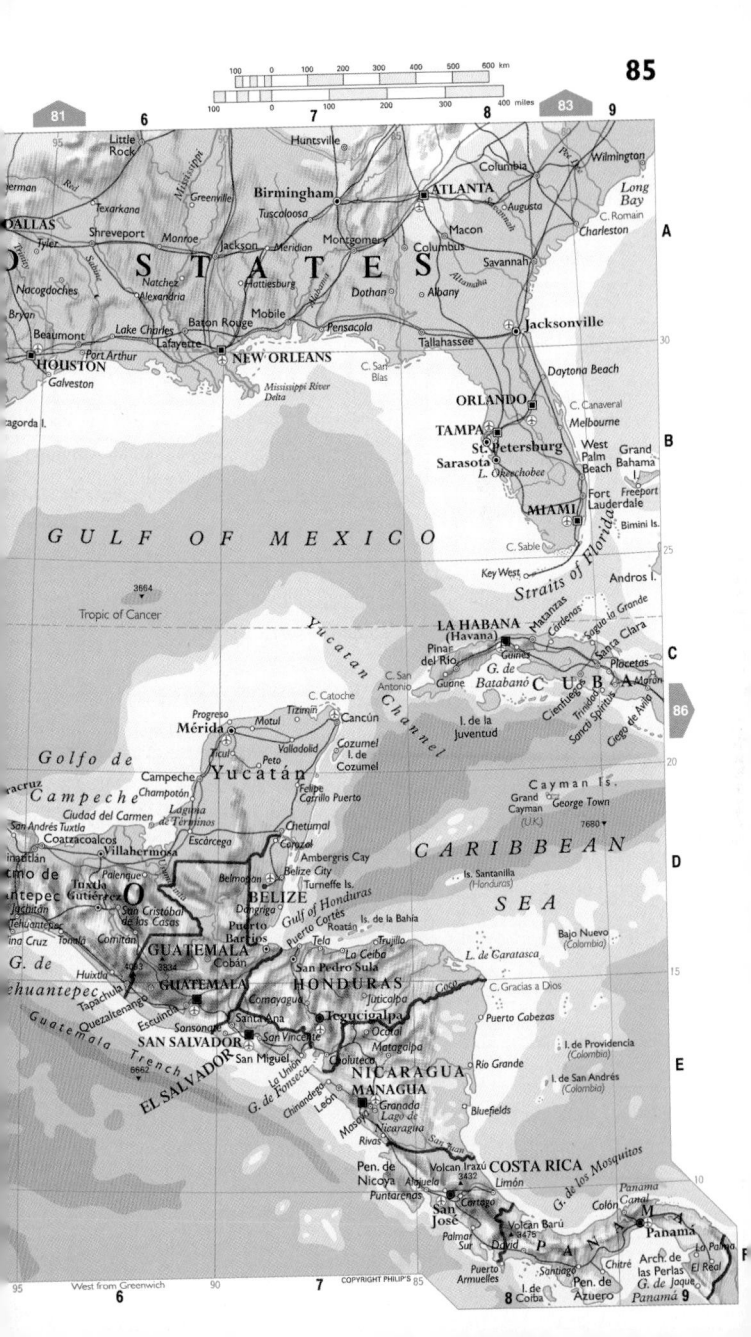
100 0 100 200 300 400 500 600 km
100 0 100 200 300 400 miles
81
83
86
6
7
8
9
A
B
C
D
E
F
Little Rock
Huntsville
Columbia
Wilmington
Long Bay
C. Romain
Charleston
Birmingham
ATLANTA
Augusta
Macon
Columbus
Savannah
Greenville
Tuscaloosa
Montgomery
Meridian
Jackson
Shreveport
Monroe
Texarkana
Tyler
DALLAS
Natchez
Alexandria
Hattiesburg
Mobile
Dothan
Albany
Nacogdoches
Bryan
Beaumont
Lake Charles
Lafayette
Baton Rouge
Pensacola
Tallahassee
Jacksonville
Port Arthur
HOUSTON
Galveston
NEW ORLEANS
C. San Blas
Mississippi River Delta
Daytona Beach
ORLANDO
C. Canaveral
Melbourne
TAMPA
St. Petersburg
Sarasota
L. Okeechobee
West Palm Beach
Grand Bahama I.
Fort Lauderdale
Freeport
MIAMI
Bimini Is.
C. Sable
Key West
Straits of Florida
Andros I.
GULF OF MEXICO
3664
Tropic of Cancer
Yucatan Channel
LA HABANA (Havana)
Matanzas
Cárdenas
Sagua la Grande
Santa Clara
Pinar del Río
Guines
G. de Batabanó
C. San Antonio
Guane
Placetas
Cienfuegos
Trinidad
Sancti Spíritus
Ciego de Avila
C U B A
C. Catoche
Tizimín
Cancún
Progreso
Mérida
Motul
Tizul
Valladolid
Peto
Cozumel
I. de Cozumel
I. de la Juventud
Golfo de Campeche
Campeche
Champotón
Ciudad del Carmen
Laguna de Términos
Yucatán
Felipe Carrillo Puerto
Cayman Is.
Grand Cayman (U.K.)
George Town
7680
Coatzacoalcos
Villahermosa
Palenque
San Andrés Tuxtla
Escárcego
Chetumal
Corozal
Ambergris Cay
CARIBBEAN SEA
Tuxtla Gutiérrez
San Cristóbal de las Casas
Comitán
Belmopan
BELIZE
Belize City
Turneffe Is.
Dangriga
Gulf of Honduras
Puerto Cortés
Roatán
Is. de la Bahía
Is. Santanilla (Honduras)
Puerto Barrios
Tela
Trujillo
Bajo Nuevo (Colombia)
L. de Caratasca
GUATEMALA
Cobán
La Ceiba
San Pedro Sula
HONDURAS
Huixtla
Tapachula
Quetzaltenango
Escuintla
Comayagua
Juticalpa
C. Gracias a Dios
Puerto Cabezas
GUATEMALA
Sonsonate
Santa Ana
Tegucigalpa
Ocotal
Guatemala
SAN SALVADOR
San Vincente
San Miguel
Matagalpa
Trench
6662
Choluteca
Rio Grande
I. de Providencia (Colombia)
EL SALVADOR
La Unión
G. de Fonseca
NICARAGUA
MANAGUA
I. de San Andrés (Colombia)
Chinandega
León
Granada
Lago de Nicaragua
Bluefields
Masaya
Rivas
San Juan
Pen. de Nicoya
Volcan Irazú 3432
COSTA RICA
Alajuela
Limón
G. de los Mosquitos
Puntarenas
Cartago
San José
Panama Canal
Colón
Volcan Barú 3475
Palmar Sur
David
PANAMÁ
Panamá
La Palma
Chitré
Arch. de las Perlas
El Real
Puerto Armuelles
Santiago
I. de Coiba
Pen. de Azuero
G. de Jaque
Panamá
95
90
85
West from Greenwich
COPYRIGHT PHILIP'S

Mississippi River Delta
Daytona Beach
ORLANDO
C. Canaveral
TAMPA
Melbourne
St. Petersburg
West Palm Beach
Grand Bahama I.
Sarasota
L. Okeechobee
Fort Lauderdale
Freeport
Abaco I.
GULF OF MEXICO
U.S.A.
MIAMI
Bimini Is.
New Providence I.
Eleuthera I.
C. Sable
Key West
Straits of Florida
Nassau
Cat I.
Andros I.
BAHAMAS
San Salvador
Tropic of Cancer
Yucatan Channel
LA HABANA (Havana)
Matanzas
Cárdenas
Sagua la Grande
Santa Clara
Great Exuma I.
Long I.
Pinar del Rio
Güines
G. de Batabanó
Placetas
Morón
Camagüey
C. San Antonio
Guane
CUBA
Progreso
Tizimín
C. Catoche
Cancún
Motul
Cienfuegos
Trinidad
Sancti Spíritus
Ciego de Ávila
Nuevitas
Holguín
Great Inagua I.
Mérida
Valladolid
Cozumel
I. de la Juventud
Las Tunas
Bayamo
Bahía de Cuba
Santiago de Cuba
Guantánamo
Yucatán
Peto
I. de Cozumel
Manzanillo
1972
Campeche
Champotón
Felipe Carrillo Puerto
Great Cayman
Cayman Is.
Grand Cayman (U.K.)
George Town
7680
Montego Bay
MEXICO
Chetumal
Escárcega
Carazo
Ambergris Cay
Belmopan
Belize City
Turneffe Is.
Dangriga
BELIZE
Gulf of Honduras
Puerto Barrios
Puerto Cortés
Roatán
Is. de la Bahía
Trujillo
Tela
La Ceiba
Coban
GUATEMALA
San Pedro Sula
HONDURAS
Is. Santanilla (Honduras)
JAMAICA
Mandeville
Spanish Town
Kingston
Pedro Cays (Jamaica)
Jérémie
Les Cayes
L. de Caratasca
Bajo Nuevo (Colombia)
Cobán
Camayagüe
Juticalpa
Tegucigalpa
C. Gracias a Dios
CARI
Santa Ana
SAN SALVADOR
San Vicente
Ocotal
Puerto Cabezas
Sonsonate
EL SALVADOR
San Miguel
Matagalpa
Tegucigalpa
Golfo de Fonseca
Chinandega
León
NICARAGUA
Río Grande
I. de Providencia (Colombia)
I. de San Andrés (Colombia)
MANAGUA
Granada
Lago de Nicaragua
Masaya
Rivas
Bluefields
Santa Marta
BARRANQUILLA
Cartagena
Pen. de Nicoya
Puntarenas
Volcan Irazú 3432
COSTA RICA
Limón
G. de los Mosquitos
Panama Canal
Colón
Sincelejo
G. del Darién
Montería
San José
Cartago
Volcan Barú 3475
Palmar Sur
David
PANAMA
Panamá
Puerto Armuelles
Santiago
Chitré
Arch. de las Perlas
Pen. de Azuero
I. de Coiba
G. de Panamá
Jaque
Quibdó
Antioquia
Bello
MEDELLÍN
PACIFIC
I. del Coco (C. Rica)
C. Corrientes
Manizales
Pereira
Armenia
Ibagué
OCEAN
I. de Malpelo (Colombia)
Buenaventura
Palmira
CALI
Neiva
Popayán
Volcan Puracé 4646
Projection : Bonne
West from Greenwich
ft
m

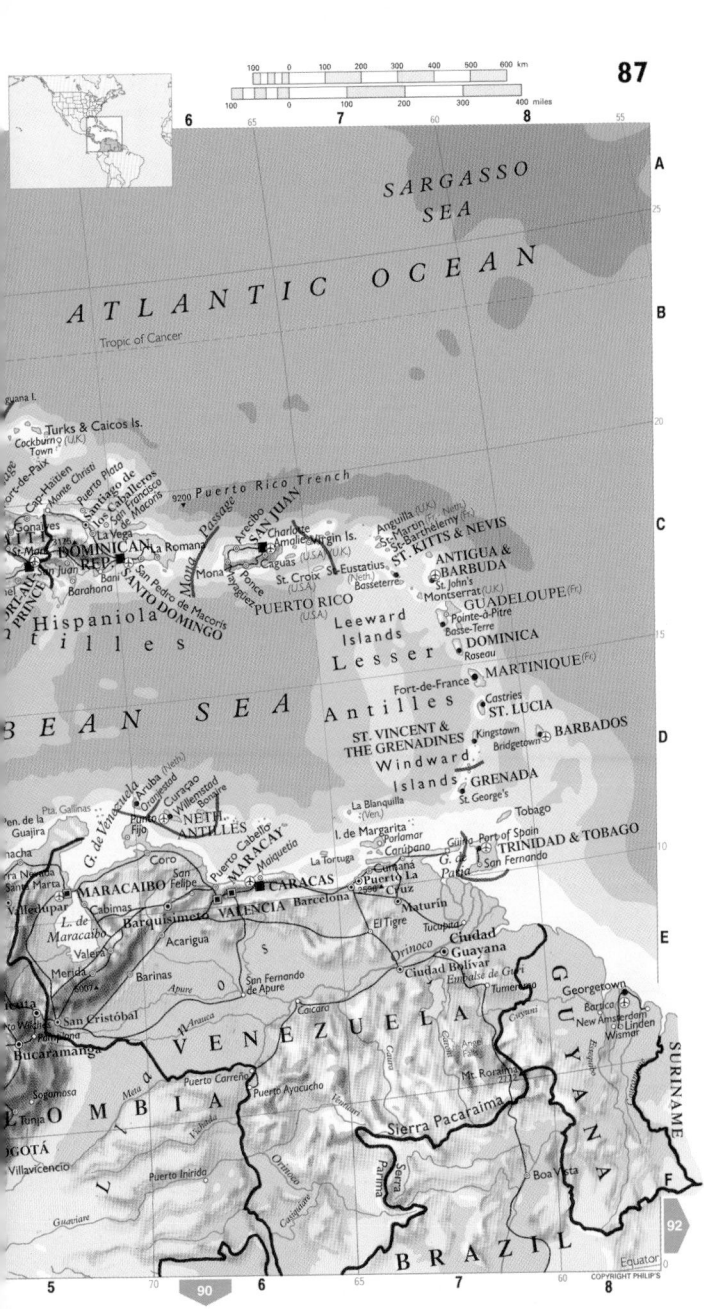
SARGASSO SEA
ATLANTIC OCEAN
Tropic of Cancer
Turks & Caicos Is.
Cockburn Town (UK)
Puerto Rico Trench
9200
Mona Passage
SAN JUAN
Arecibo
Charlotte Amalie
Virgin Is. (USA)
Anguilla (UK)
St. Martin (Neth)
St. Barthélemy (Fr)
ST. KITTS & NEVIS
ANTIGUA & BARBUDA
St. John's
Montserrat (UK)
GUADELOUPE (Fr)
Pointe-à-Pitre
Basse-Terre
DOMINICA
Roseau
MARTINIQUE (Fr)
Fort-de-France
Castries
ST. LUCIA
ST. VINCENT & THE GRENADINES
Kingstown
BARBADOS
Bridgetown
GRENADA
St. George's
Tobago
TRINIDAD & TOBAGO
Port of Spain
San Fernando
Caripito
Cumaná
Puerto La Cruz
Maturín
Ciudad Guayana
Ciudad Bolívar
Tucupita
Tumeremo
Georgetown
Barima
New Amsterdam
Linden
Wismar
Mt. Roraima
Sierra Pacaraima
Boa Vista
Puerto Ayacucho
Puerto Inírida
Puerto Carreño
Puerto Cabello
Puerto Fijo
Coro
Maracaibo
Cabimas
Barquisimeto
Acarigua
Valencia
Barcelona
Caracas
Maracay
San Felipe
Mérida
Barinas
San Cristóbal
Cúcuta
Bucaramanga
Villavicencio
Tunja
Sogamoso
Pamplona
San Fernando de Apure
El Tigre
La Tortuga
La Blanquilla (Ven)
I. de Margarita
Porlamar
Aruba (Neth)
Oranjestad
Curaçao
Willemstad
Bonaire
NETH. ANTILLES
Pta. Gallinas
Ven. de la Guajira
Santa Marta
Valledupar
Dominican Rep.
Hispaniola
Leeward Islands
Lesser Antilles
Windward Islands
VENEZUELA
COLOMBIA
GUYANA
SURINAME
BRAZIL
Equator
COPYRIGHT PHILIP'S

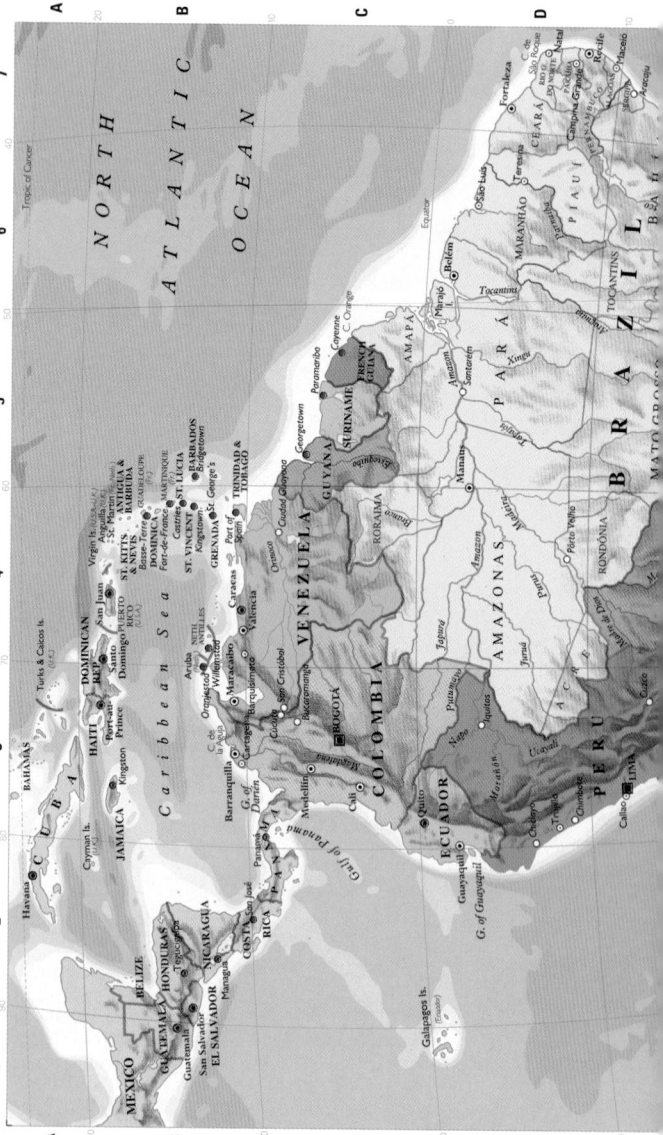
NORTH ATLANTIC OCEAN
Caribbean Sea
Gulf of Panama
Tropic of Cancer
Equator
Havana
CUBA
BAHAMAS
Turks & Caicos Is.
(U.K.)
Cayman Is.
(U.K.)
JAMAICA
Kingston
HAITI
Port-au-Prince
DOMINICAN REPUBLIC
Santo Domingo
San Juan
PUERTO RICO
(U.S.)
Virgin Is.
(U.S.)
Anguilla
(U.K.)
St. Martin
(Fr.)
Sint Maarten
(Neth.)
ANTIGUA & BARBUDA
ST. KITTS & NEVIS
Basse-Terre
Pointe-à-Pitre
GUADELOUPE
(Fr.)
Fort-de-France
MARTINIQUE
(Fr.)
Castries
ST. LUCIA
Kingstown
ST. VINCENT
BARBADOS
Bridgetown
GRENADA
St. George's
Port of Spain
TRINIDAD & TOBAGO
Caracas
Valencia
Oranjestad
Willemstad
Aruba
NETH. ANTILLES
(Neth.)
Maracaibo
Barranquilla
Cartagena
Santa Marta
Riohacha
Maracaibo
San Cristóbal
Cúcuta
Bucaramanga
VENEZUELA
Orinoco
Ciudad Guayana
Georgetown
GUYANA
Paramaribo
SURINAME
Cayenne
FRENCH GUIANA
BOGOTÁ
COLOMBIA
Medellín
Cali
Pasto
Quito
ECUADOR
Guayaquil
G. of Guayaquil
Galápagos Is.
(Ecuador)
Tumbes
Chiclayo
Trujillo
Chimbote
Lima
Callao
PERU
Cuzco
Iquitos
Ucayali
Marañón
Putumayo
Napo
Tapajós
Tocantins
Xingu
Madeira
Purus
Juruá
Negro
Branco
Amazonas
Tapajós
Tocantins
Xingu
Belém
Santarém
Manaus
Porto Velho
Rio Branco
Boa Vista
Fortaleza
Teresina
São Luís
Natal
Recife
Maceió
Aracaju
Salvador
Cabo de São Roque
Cabo de São Roque
Cabo de São Roque

PACIFIC
OCEAN
SOUTH
ATLANTIC
OCEAN
Tropic of Capricorn
Santa Cruz
Sucre
Iquique
Antofagasta
Salta
San Miguel de Tucumán
San Félix (Chile)
San Ambrosio (Chile)
Arch. de Juan Fernández (Chile)
Viña del Mar
Valparaíso
SANTIAGO
Talca
Concepción
Valdivia
Puerto Montt
Cordoba
San Juan
Mendoza
Santa Fe
Rosario
Resistencia
Corrientes
Asunción
PARAGUAY
Pilcomayo
Paraguay
Paraná
Salado
Uruguay
Colorado
Negro
Chubut
Deseado
Santa Cruz
Gulf of Penas
Comodoro Rivadavia
Gulf of San Jorge
Puerto Madryn
Bahía Blanca
Mar del Plata
BUENOS AIRES
La Plata
Rio de la Plata
Montevideo
URUGUAY
Pelotas
Porto Alegre
RIO GRANDE DO SUL
SANTA CATARINA
PARANÁ
Curitiba
SÃO PAULO
Ribeirão Preto
MATO GROSSO DO SUL
Goiânia
MINAS GERAIS
Belo Horizonte
Juiz de Fora
Campos
Niterói
RIO DE JANEIRO
Santos
SÃO PAULO
ESPÍRITO SANTO
Vitória
Punta Arenas
Magellan's Str.
Tierra del Fuego
C. Horn
West Falkland
FALKLAND IS. (U.K.)
Stanley
East Falkland
South Georgia (U.K.)
Projection: Lambert's Azimuthal Equal Area
LIMA Capital Cities
West from Greenwich
COPYRIGHT PHILIP'S
m ft
0 200 1000 2000 4000 6000 8000
600 3000 6000 12000 16000 24000
100 0 200 400 600 800 1000 1200 1400 km
100 0 200 400 600 800 1000 miles

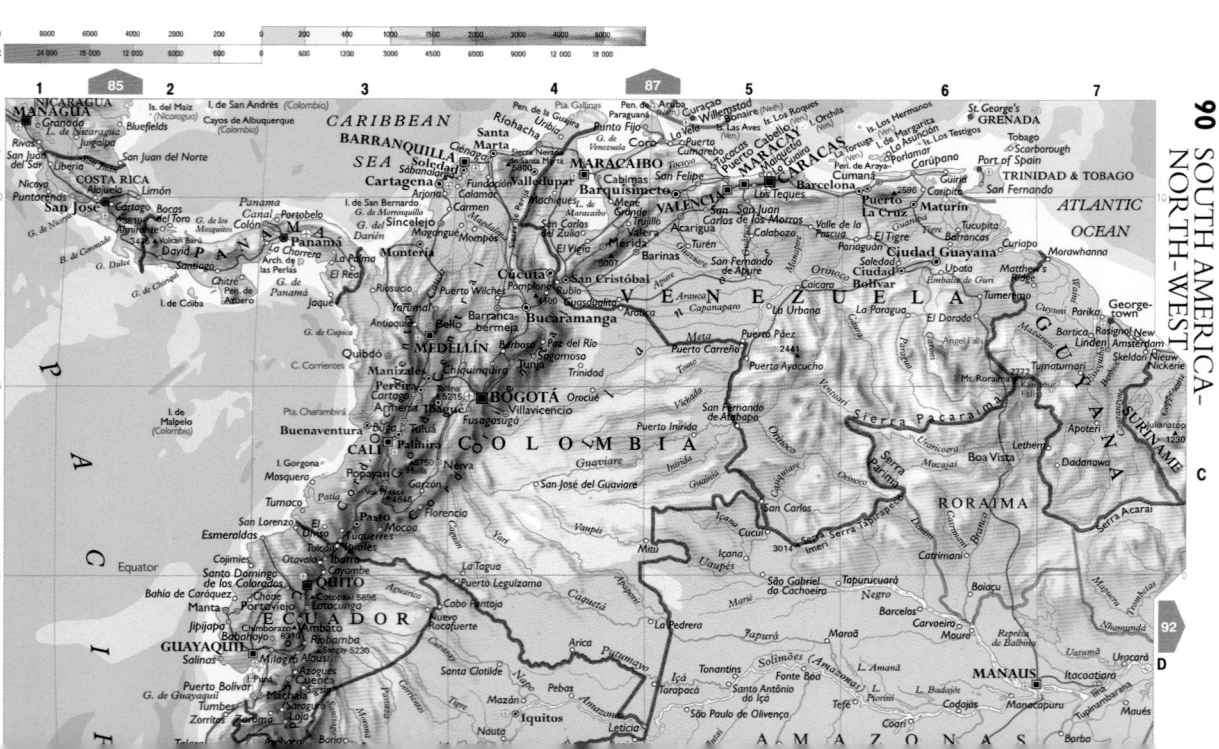
m 8000 6000 4000 2000 200 0 200 400 1000 1500 2000 3000 4000 6000
ft 24 000 18 000 12 000 6000 600 0 600 1200 3000 4500 6000 9000 12 000 18 000
85
87
92
1 2 3 4 5 6 7
A B C D
NICARAGUA
MANAGUA
Granada
L. de Nicaragua
Jugalpa
Bluefields
Rivas
San Juan del Sur
Liberia
San Juan del Norte
Is. del Maíz (Nicaragua)
I. de San Andrés (Colombia)
Cayos de Albuquerque (Colombia)
CARIBBEAN SEA
BARRANQUILLA
Soledad
Sabanalarga
Cartagena
Santa Marta
Riohacha
Ciénaga
Valledupar
Fundación
Calamar
Pen. de la Guajira
Uribia
Pta. Gallinas
Pen. de Paraguaná
Punto Fijo
Coro
Curaçao (Netherlands)
Willemstad
Aruba (Netherlands)
MARACAIBO
Cabimas
Barquisimeto
San Felipe
Tocuyo
Puerto Cumarebo
La Vela
Tucacas
Puerto Cabello
Is. Los Roques (Venezuela)
Is. Los Aves (Venezuela)
Orchila (Venezuela)
La Guaira
CARACAS
Pen. de Araya
Cumaná
Barcelona
Los Teques
Is. Los Hermanos (Venezuela)
Is. de Margarita (Venezuela)
I. de Aves (Venezuela)
Is. Los Testigos
Porlamar
Carúpano
St. George's
GRENADA
Tobago
Scarborough
Port of Spain
TRINIDAD & TOBAGO
San Fernando
ATLANTIC OCEAN
COSTA RICA
Alajuela
Limón
San José
Cartago
Puntarenas
Nicoya
Bocas del Toro
Panama Canal
Portobelo
Colón
Panama
La Chorrera
Arch. de las Perlas
Pen. de Azuero
I. de Coiba
David
PANAMA
Santiago
Chitré
Volcán Barú
I. de San Bernardo
G. de Morrosquillo
G. de Darién
Sincelejo
Montería
Magangué
Carmen
Mompós
Valledupar
Machiques
L. de Maracaibo
Mene Grande
Trujillo
Valera
Barinas
Mérida
El Vigía
San Carlos
San Cristóbal
Cúcuta
Pamplona
Puerto Wilches
Barrancabermeja
Bucaramanga
Guasdualito
Arauca
VENEZUELA
Puerto Cabello
Valencia
San Juan de los Morros
Calabozo
Acarigua
Turén
San Fernando de Apure
Maracay
Caracas
Los Teques
Puerto La Cruz
Maturín
Caripito
Tucupita
Barrancas
Curiapo
Morawhanna
Ciudad Guayana
Upata
Matthews Ridge
Tumeremo
Embarcadero de Guri
Valle de la Pascua
El Tigre
Pariaguán
Soledad
Ciudad Bolívar
Caicara
La Paragua
El Dorado
Angel Falls
La Urbana
Puerto Páez
Puerto Carreño
Puerto Ayacucho
Tumatumari
Mt. Roraima
Kaieteur Falls
Sierra Pacaraima
Sierra Parima
Sierra Tapirapeco
Sierra Imeri
Sierra Acaral
GUYANA
SURINAME
Georgetown
Bartica
Rasignol
New Amsterdam
Linden
Skeldon
Nieuw Nickerie
Apoteri
Lethem
Boa Vista
Dadanawa
RORAIMA
Catrimani
Boiaçu
Barcelos
Carvoeiro
Mouro
Reprêsa de Balbina
Uatumã
Uracará
MANAUS
Itacoatiara
Tapiranbarana
Maués
Manacapuru
Codajás
L. Badajós
L. Amanã
Tefé
Coari
Borba
Fonte Boa
Tonantins
Santo Antônio do Içá
São Paulo de Olivença
Tarapacá
Iquitos
Leticia
Nauta
Mazán
Pebas
Santa Clotilde
Arica
La Pedrera
Mitú
Uaupés
Içana
Cucuí
San Carlos
Tapurucuara
São Gabriel da Cachoeira
Cabo Fantoja
Puerto Leguizamo
La Tagua
Puerto Rico
Puerto Leguizamo
Puerto Inírida
San José del Guaviare
San Fernando de Atabapo
Puerto Ayacucho
Puerto Carreño
Puerto Páez
Puerto Ayacucho
Puerto Inírida
Puerto Leguizamo
Puerto Rico
Puerto Bolívar

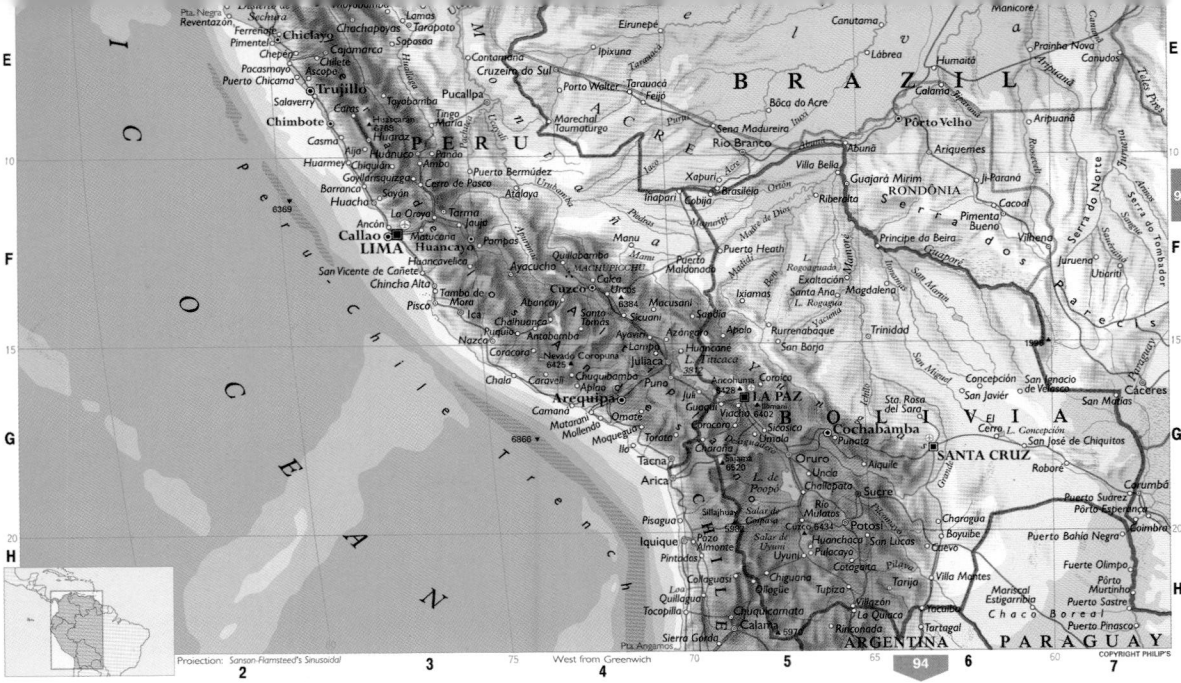
B R A Z I L
P E R U
B O L I V I A
P A R A G U A Y
A R G E N T I N A
C H I L E
P a c i f i c O c e a n
Chile Trench
Pta. Negra
Reventazón
Sechura
Ferreñafe
Pimentel
Chiclayo
Chepén
Cajamarca
Chilete
Pacasmayo
Ascope
Puerto Chicama
Trujillo
Salaverry
Chimbote
Casma
Huarmey
Chiquián
Huánuco
Huaraz
Pucallpa
Tingo María
Tarapoto
Lamas
Chachapoyas
Sapaosa
Tayabamba
Cerro de Pasco
Huancayo
Huancavelica
Ica
Pisco
Nazca
Ayacucho
Abancay
Cuzco
Arequipa
Tacna
Arica
Iquique
Pisagua
Pintados
Tocopilla
Quillagua
Calama
Sierra Gorda
Pta. Angamos
LIMA
Callao
Tarma
Jauja
Pampas
Huancayo
Huancavelica
San Vicente de Cañete
Chincha Alta
Tambo de Mora
Huanuco
Huacho
Ancón
Barranco
Soyón
Huarmey
Casma
Chimbote
Tingo María
Puerto Bermúdez
Atalaya
Quillabamba
MACHU PICCHU
Cuzco
Urcos
Sicuani
Santo Tomás
Chalhuanca
Abancay
Ayacucho
Puerto Maldonado
Puerto Heath
Manu
Iquitos
Pucallpa
Contamana
Cruzeiro do Sul
Ipixuna
Eirunepé
Tarauacá
Feijó
Porto Walter
Marechal Taumaturgo
Sena Madureira
Rio Branco
Xapuri
Brasiléia
Cobijá
Tahapari
Villa Bella
Guajará Mirim
RONDÔNIA
Riberalta
Abunã
Ariquemes
Porto Velho
Humaitá
Lábrea
Canutama
Manicoré
Prainha Nova
Canuto
Aripuanã
Calama
Cacoal
Pimenta Bueno
Vilhena
Juruena
Utiariti
Serra do Norte
Serra do Tombador
Serra dos Parecis
Príncipe da Beira
Guaporé
Magdalena
Exaltación
Santa Ana
Iximiás
Trinidad
San Borja
Rurrenabaque
Apolo
Lampa
Juliaca
Puno
Ancohuma
Coroico
LA PAZ
Viacha
Sicasica
Umala
Oruro
Uncía
Challapata
Sucre
Potosí
Cochabamba
Punata
Aiquile
Sta. Rosa del Sara
Cerro
San Javier
Concepción
San Ignacio de Velasco
San José de Chiquitos
SANTA CRUZ
Roboré
Corumbá
Puerto Suárez
Pórto Esperança
Puerto Bahía Negra
Fuerte Olimpo
Pórto Murtinho
Puerto Sastre
Puerto Pinasco
Mariscal Estigarribia
Chaco Boreal
Villa Montes
Tarija
Tupiza
Villazón
Tartagal
Rinconada
Chuquicamata
Calama
Pulacayo
Uyuni
Huanchaca
San Lucas
Cotagaita
Charagua
Boyuibe
Cuevo
Sillajhuay
Salar de Coipasa
Salar de Uyuni
Pozo Almonte
Chiguana
Tupiza
Tocopilla
Quillagua
Pta. Negra
Reventazón
Projection: Sanson-Flamsteed's Sinusoidal
West from Greenwich
COPYRIGHT PHILIP'S
93
94
91

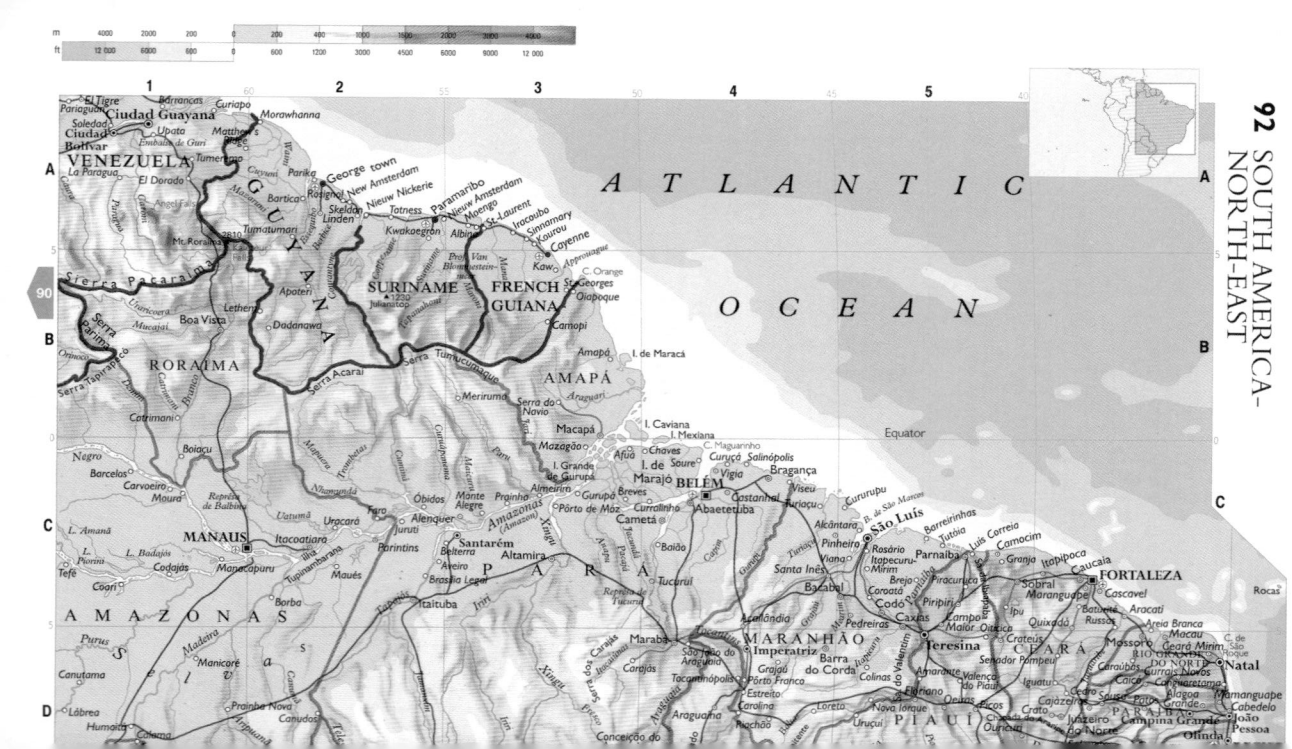
m 4000 2000 200 0 200 400 1000 1500 2000 3000 4000
ft 12 000 6000 600 0 600 1200 3000 4500 6000 9000 12 000
ATLANTIC OCEAN
Equator
VENEZUELA
Ciudad Guayana
Ciudad Bolívar
El Tigre
Pariaguán
Barrancas
Curiapo
Morawhanna
Upata
Matthews
Tumeremo
La Paragua
El Dorado
Angel Falls
Mt. Roraima
2810
Tumatumari
Sierra Pacaraima
Sierra Parima
Sierra Tapirapecó
Boa Vista
Lethem
Apoteri
Dadanawa
RORAIMA
Catrimani
Boiaçu
Barcelos
Carvoeiro
Moura
Negro
Orinoco
Uaricoera
Mucajaí
Serra Acaraí
Serra Tumucumaque
GUYANA
SURINAME
FRENCH GUIANA
George town
New Amsterdam
Rosignol
Nieuw Nickerie
Skeldon
Linden
Tatness
Paramaribo
Nieuw Amsterdam
Moengo
St. Laurent
Albina
Kwakoegron
Sinnamary
Cayenne
Kaw
Approuague
C. Orange
St Georges
Oiapoque
Camopi
1230
Julianatop
Amapá
I. de Maracá
AMAPÁ
Meriruma
Serra do Navio
Macapá
I. Caviana
I. Mexiana
Mazagão
Afuá
Chaves
I. de Marajó
Soure
C. Maguariinho
Curuçá
Salinópolis
Vigia
Bragança
BELÉM
I. Grande de Gurupá
Almeirim
Gurupá
Breves
Pôrto de Moz
Curralinho
Cametá
Castanhal
Abaetetuba
Viseu
Turiaçu
Cururupu
Alcântara
São Luís
Barreirinhas
Tutóia
Pinheiro
Rosário
Itapecuru-Mirim
Viana
Santa Inês
Bacabal
Brejo
Coroatá
Caxias
Parnaíba
Luís Correia
Camocim
Granja
Itapipoca
Caucaia
FORTALEZA
Sobral
Maranguape
Cascavel
Piracuruca
Piripiri
Campo Maior
Ipu
Quixadá
Batuité
Russas
Aracati
Areia Branca
Macau
C. de São Roque
Rocas
Teresina
Senador Pompeu
Crateús
Iguatu
Mossoró
Natal
Caicó
Cajazeiras
Sousa
Campina Grande
João Pessoa
Olinda
Recife
Juazeiro do Norte
Crato
Cedro
Oeiras
Picos
Parnaíba
Pedreiras
Tocantinópolis
Estreito
Carolina
Grajaú
Barra do Corda
Colinas
Caxias
Amarante
Valença do Piauí
Oeiras
Floriano
Nova Iorque
Uruçuí
Paulistana
Oeiras
Picos
Parnaíba
Piracuruca
Sobral
Iguatu
Crato
Cedro
Sousa
Campina Grande
Olinda
Recife
Natal
Caicó
Mossoró
Aracati
Areia Branca
Macau
Rocas
Maranguape
Cascavel
Caucaia
Itapipoca
Granja
Luís Correia
Camocim
Parnaíba
Piracuruca
Piripiri
Campo Maior
Ipu
Quixadá
Batuité
Russ

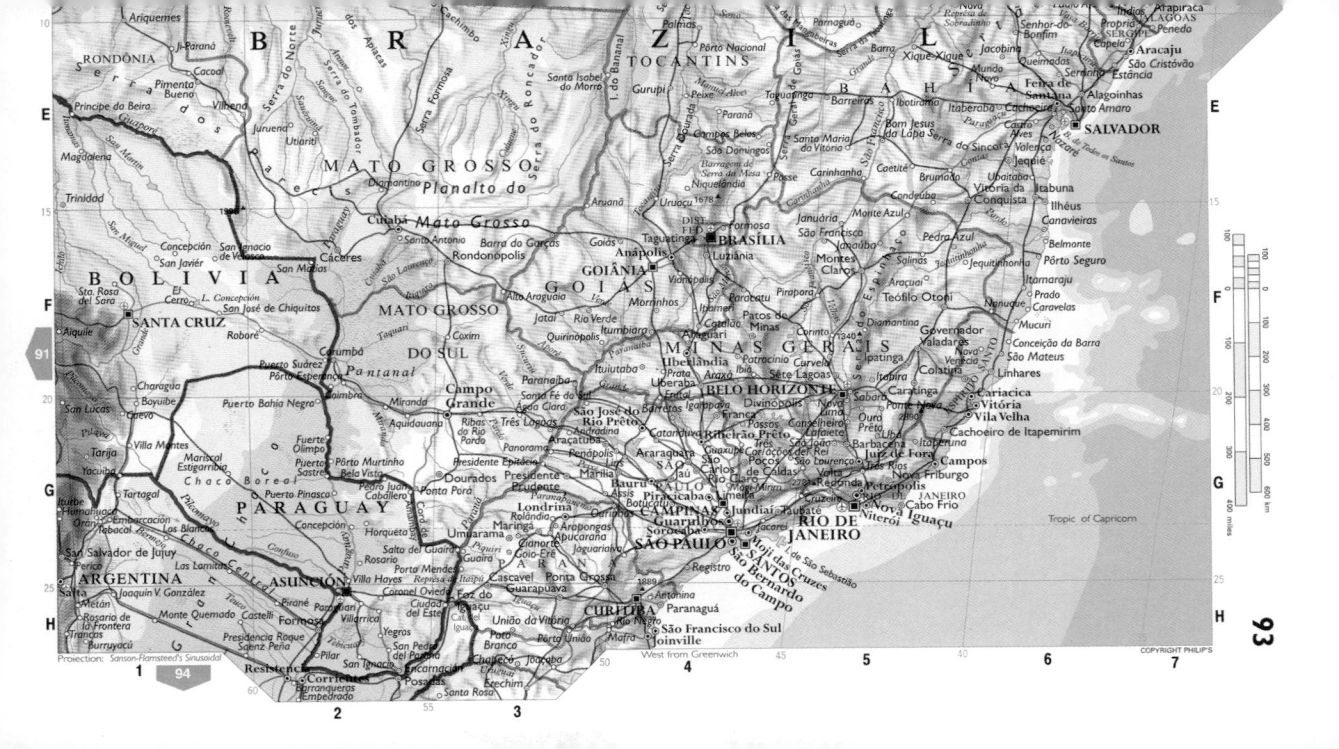
BRAZIL
RONDÔNIA
TOCANTINS
MATO GROSSO
Planalto do Mato Grosso
BOLIVIA
SANTA CRUZ
GOIÁS
GOIÂNIA
BRASÍLIA
MATO GROSSO DO SUL
Pantanal
MINAS GERAIS
BELO HORIZONTE
BAHIA
SALVADOR
Feira de Santana
Aracaju
Maceió
Recife
Campo Grande
Cuiabá
Corumbá
Cáceres
Rio Preto
Ribeirão Preto
Uberlândia
Uberaba
Campos
Vitória
Vila Velha
Cariacica
Cachoeiro de Itapemirim
Juiz de Fora
Petrópolis
RIO DE JANEIRO
Niterói
Nova Iguaçu
Cabo Frio
SÃO PAULO
Santos
Sorocaba
Campinas
Piracicaba
Jundiaí
Guarulhos
Londrina
Maringá
Curitiba
Joinville
São Francisco do Sul
Paranaguá
Ponta Grossa
Cascavel
Foz do Iguaçu
Guarapuava
PARAGUAY
ASUNCIÓN
Ciudad del Este
Pedro Juan Caballero
Concepción
Pilar
Resistencia
Corrientes
Posadas
ARGENTINA
Salta
Jujuy
Tucumán
Santiago del Estero
Formosa
Tropic of Capricorn
West from Greenwich
Projection: Sanson-Flamsteed's Sinusoidal
COPYRIGHT PHILIP'S
93
91
94

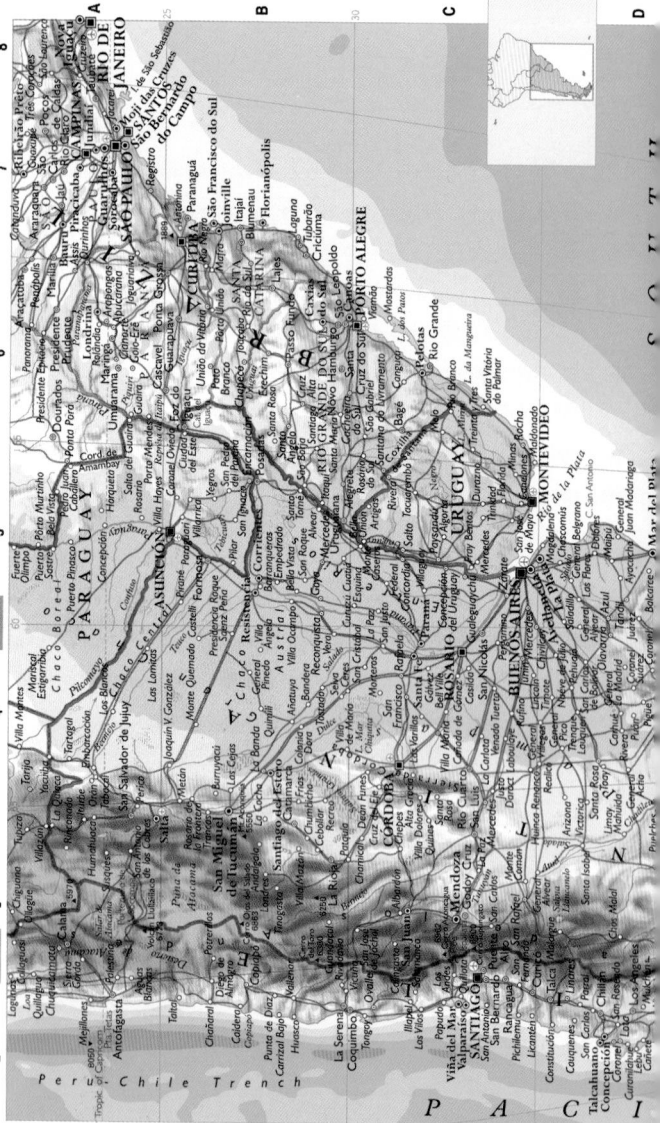
PARAGUAY
URUGUAY
BUENOS AIRES
ROSARIO
CORDOBA
MONTEVIDEO
SÃO PAULO
RIO DE JANEIRO
CURITIBA
PORTO ALEGRE
SANTIAGO
Mendoza
Santiago del Estero
San Miguel de Tucumán
Salta
Asunción
Resistencia
Corrientes
Formosa
Santa Cruz de la Sierra
Antofagasta
Copiapó
La Serena
Valparaíso
Viña del Mar
Concepción
Talcahuano
Temuco
Rio Grande
Mar del Plata
Bahía Blanca
Neuquén
Perú-Chile Trench
Tropic of Capricorn
Mar del Plata
Pacific Ocean
Rio Grande do Sul
Santa Catarina
Paraná
Rio de Janeiro
São Paulo
Chaco Boreal
Chaco Central
Chaco Austral
Pampas
Puna

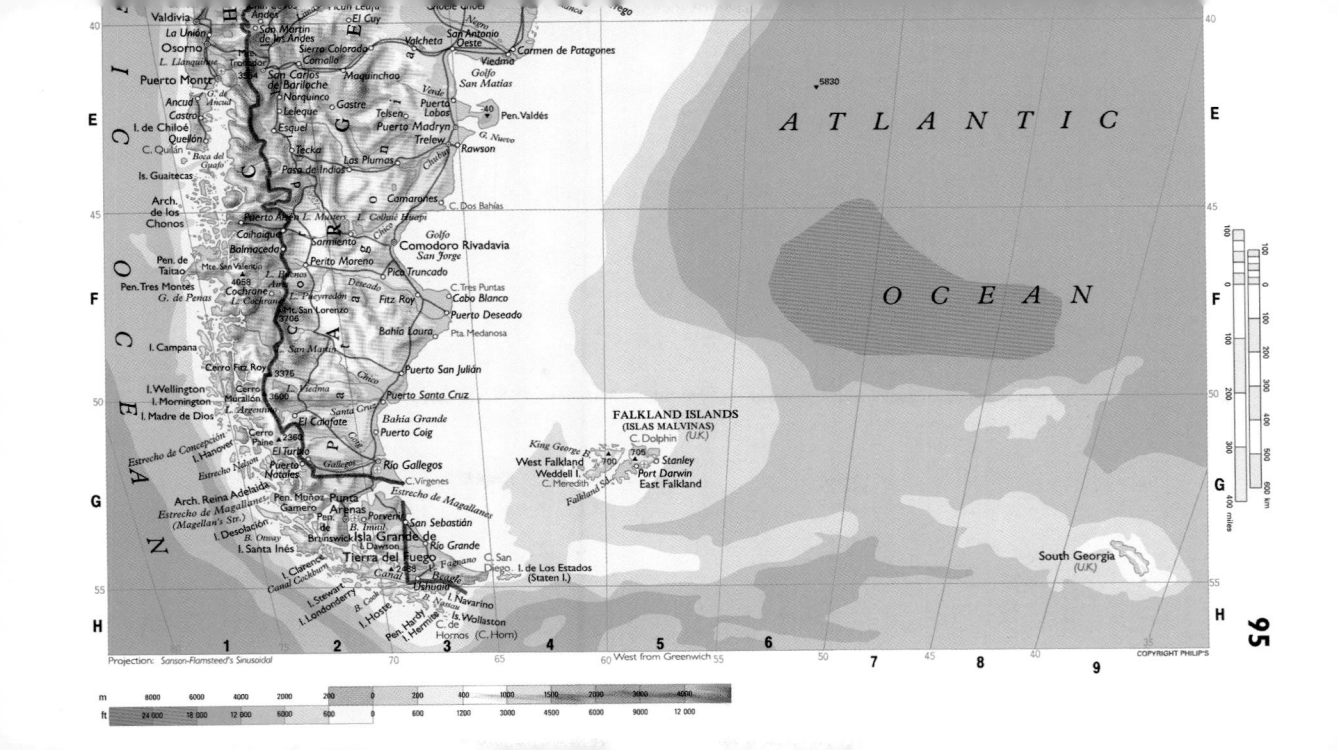
ATLANTIC
OCEAN
PACIFIC
OCEAN
Valdivia
La Unión
Osorno
Puerto Montt
Andes
San Martín de los Andes
El Cuy
Sierra Colorado
Comallo
San Carlos de Bariloche
Maquinchao
Valcheta
San Antonio Oeste
Viedma
Carmen de Patagones
Golfo San Matías
Pen. Valdés
Puerto Madryn
Trelew
Rawson
Puerto Lobos
Telsen
Gastre
Esquel
Lelegue
Norquinco
Tecka
Paso de Indios
Las Plumas
Comodoro Rivadavia
Golfo San Jorge
Sarmiento
Perito Moreno
Pico Truncado
Caleta Olivia
Comarones
C. Dos Bahías
Puerto Aysén
Coihaique
Balmaceda
Cochrane
Fitz Roy
Cerro Fitz Roy
Cerro Murallón
El Calafate
Bahía Grande
Puerto Coig
Río Gallegos
C. Vírgenes
Puerto Santa Cruz
Puerto San Julián
Bahía Laura
Puerto Deseado
Cabo Blanco
C. Tres Puntas
Pta. Medanosa
Estrecho de Magallanes
Punta Arenas
Porvenir
San Sebastián
Río Grande
Isla Grande de Tierra del Fuego
Ushuaia
C. San Diego
I. de los Estados (Staten I.)
I. Navarino
Is. Wollaston
C. de Hornos (C. Horn)
FALKLAND ISLANDS
(ISLAS MALVINAS)
(U.K.)
C. Dolphin
West Falkland
Stanley
Port Darwin
East Falkland
Weddell I.
C. Meredith
South Georgia
(U.K.)
5830
Projection: Sanson-Flamsteed's Sinusoidal
West from Greenwich
COPYRIGHT PHILIP'S
95

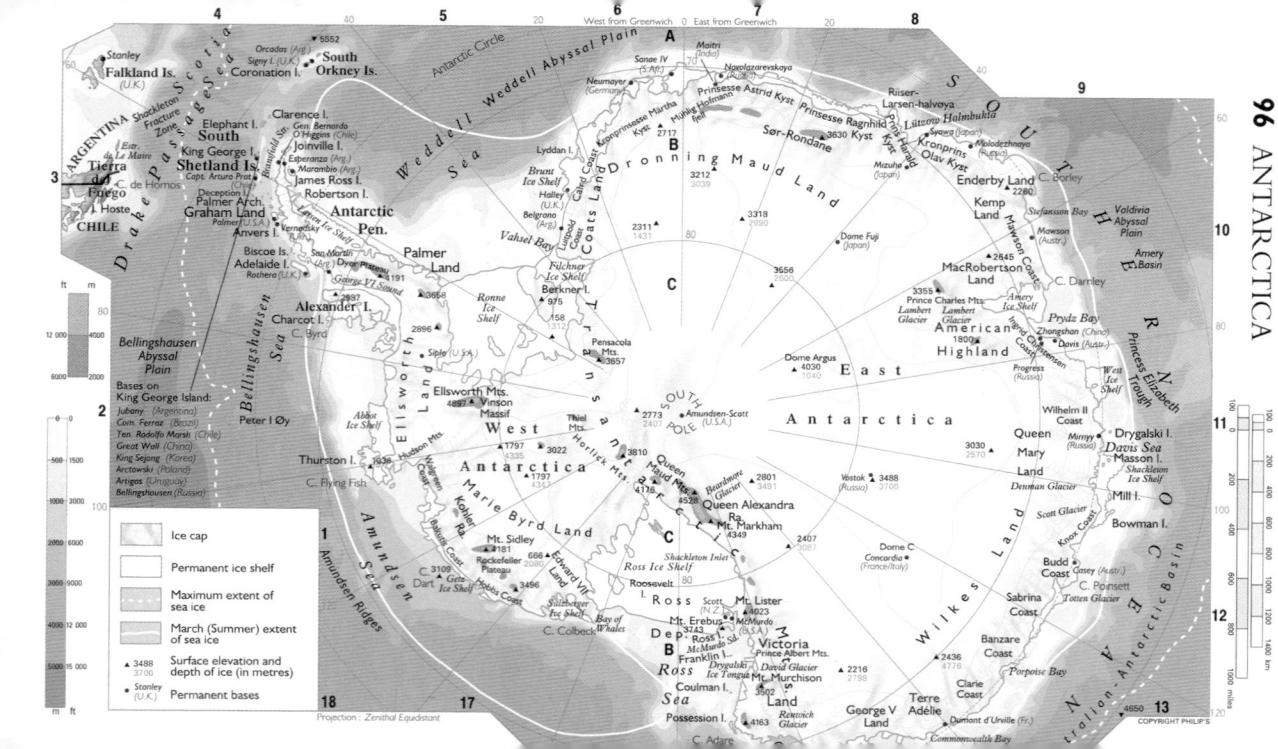
West from Greenwich 0 East from Greenwich
Antarctic Circle
Weddell Abyssal Plain
Weddell Sea
Scotia Sea
Drake Passage
ARGENTINA
Shackleton Fracture Zone
CHILE
Falkland Is. (U.K.)
Stanley
Tierra del Fuego
C. de Hornos
I. Hoste
Orcadas (Arg.)
Signy I. (U.K.)
Coronation I.
South Orkney Is.
Elephant I.
South Shetland Is.
King George I.
Joinville I.
Clarence I.
Gen. Bernardo O'Higgins (Chile)
Esperanza (Arg.)
Marambio (Arg.)
James Ross I.
Robertson I.
Antarctic Pen.
Palmer Arch.
Graham Land
Palmer (U.S.A.)
Anvers I.
Biscoe Is.
Adelaide I.
Rothera (U.K.)
Palmer Land
Alexander I.
Charcot I.
C. Byrd
Bellingshausen Sea
Bellingshausen Abyssal Plain
Peter I Øy
Bases on King George Island:
Jubany (Argentina)
Com. Ferraz (Brazil)
Ten. Rodolfo Marsh (Chile)
Great Wall (China)
King Sejong (Korea)
Arctowski (Poland)
Artigas (Uruguay)
Bellingshausen (Russia)
Ellsworth Land
Ellsworth Mts.
Vinson Massif
Thurston I.
C. Flying Fish
Marie Byrd Land
Amundsen Sea
Amundsen Ridges
Dronning Maud Land
Coats Land
Enderby Land
Kemp Land
MacRobertson Land
Prince Charles Mts.
American Highland
Dome Argus
East Antarctica
Wilhelm II Coast
Queen Mary Land
Drygalski I.
Davis Sea
Masson I.
Shackleton Ice Shelf
Mill I.
Bowman I.
Budd Coast
Sabrina Coast
Banzare Coast
Porpoise Bay
Clarie Coast
Terre Adélie
George V Land
Dumont d'Urville (Fr.)
Commonwealth Bay
Wilkes Land
Victoria Land
Ross Sea
Ross Ice Shelf
Roosevelt I.
Mt. Erebus
Mt. Terror
Franklin I.
Coulman I.
Possession I.
C. Adare
Mt. Markham
Queen Alexandra Rs.
Mt. Sidley
Ross Dependency
Amundsen-Scott (U.S.A.)
SOUTH POLE
Vostok (Russia)
Dome C Concordia (France/Italy)
Dome Fuji (Japan)
Mawson (Austr.)
Davis (Austr.)
Zhongshan (China)
Progress (Russia)
Mirny (Russia)
Casey (Austr.)
Syowa (Japan)
Molodezhnaya (Russia)
Maitri (India)
Novolazarevskaya (Russia)
Sanae IV (S. Afr.)
Neumayer (Germany)
Princesse Astrid Kyst
Princesse Ragnhild Kyst
Sør-Rondane
Riiser-Larsen-halvøya
Prinsesse Martha Kyst
Prinsesse Ingrid Kyst
Kronprins Olav Kyst
Kronprins Harald Kyst
Mizuho (Japan)
Lyddan I.
Halley (U.K.)
Belgrano (Arg.)
Vahsel Bay
Filchner Ice Shelf
Berkner I.
Ronne Ice Shelf
Pensacola Mts.
Thiel Mts.
Horlick Mts.
Queen Maud Mts.
Beardmore Glacier
Shackleton Inlet
Ross Ice Shelf
Scott Glacier
Knox Coast
Wilkes Land
Totten Glacier
Sabrina Coast
Prydz Bay
Amery Ice Shelf
Lambert Glacier
Mawson Coast
Stefansson Bay
Voldivia Abyssal Plain
Amery Basin
Princess Elizabeth Trough
West Ice Shelf
Indian-Antarctic Basin
Projection : Zenithal Equidistant
COPYRIGHT PHILIP'S
Ice cap
Permanent ice shelf
Maximum extent of sea ice
March (Summer) extent of sea ice
Surface elevation and depth of ice (in metres)
Permanent bases
ft m
fm ft
1000 miles
1400 km

Index to Map Pages

The index contains the names of all the principal places and features shown on the world maps. Physical features composed of a proper name (Erie) and a description (Lake) are positioned alphabetically by the proper name. The description is positioned after the proper name and is usually abbreviated:

Erie, L. **76 C5**

Where a description forms part of a settlement or administrative name, however, it is always written in full and put in its true alphabetical position:

Lake Charles **81 D7**

Names beginning St. are alphabetized under Saint, but Sankt, Sant, Santa and San are all spelt in full and are alphabetized accordingly.

The number in bold type which follows each name in the index refers to the number of the map page where that feature or place will be found. This is usually the largest scale at which the place or feature appears.

The letter and figure which are in bold type immediately after the page number give the grid square on the map page, within which the feature is situated.

Rivers are indexed to their mouths or confluences, and carry the symbol ➔ after their names. The following symbols are also used in the index: ■ country, ⧄ overseas territory or dependency, □ first order administrative area, △ national park.

A

A Coruña **18 A1**
A Estrada **18 A1**
A Fonsagrada **18 A2**
Aachen **14 C4**
Aalborg **9 D7**
Aalen **14 D6**
Aarhus = Århus **9 D8**
Aba **53 G7**
Abaco I. **86 A4**
Ābādān **47 E7**
Ābādeh **44 D3**
Abadla **52 B5**
Abaetetuba **92 C4**
Abakan **30 D7**
Abancay **91 F4**
Abarqū **44 D3**
Abashiri **32 A9**
Abashiri-Wan **32 B9**
Ābay = Nīl el Azraq ➔ **55 E5**
Abay **29 E8**
Abaya, L. **57 C7**
Abbay = Nīl el Azraq ➔ **55 E5**
Abbeville **12 A4**
Abbieglassie **63 A4**
Abbot Ice Shelf **96 B2**
ABC Islands = Netherlands Antilles ⧄ **87 D6**
Abd al Kūrī **49 E5**
Abéché **55 F3**
Abel Tasman △ **64 D5**
Abeokuta **53 G6**
Abercorn **63 A5**
Aberdeen *Australia* **63 B5**
Aberdeen *U.K.* **10 C5**
Aberdeen *S. Dak., U.S.A.* **74 C5**
Aberdeen *Wash., U.S.A.* **72 C2**
Aberystwyth **11 E4**
Abidjan **53 G5**
Abilene **80 C4**
Abitibi, L. **71 E6**
Abkhaz Republic = Abkhazia □ **25 E5**
Abkhazia □ **25 E5**
Abminga **62 A1**
Åbo = Turku **9 C10**
Abohar **42 D9**
Abomey **53 G6**
Abong-Mbang **56 D2**
Abou-Deïa **55 F2**
Absaroka Range **73 D9**
Abū 'Alī **47 F7**
Abu Dhabi = Abū Ẓāby **44 E3**
Abu Hamed **55 E5**
Abū Kamāl **46 D5**
Abū Madd, Ra's **47 F4**
Abu Rudeis **47 E3**
Abū Zabad **55 F4**
Abū Ẓāby **44 E3**
Abuja **53 G7**
Abunā **91 E5**
Abunā ➔ **91 E5**
Abut Hd. **65 E4**
Acaponeta **84 C3**
Acapulco **84 D5**
Acarigua **90 B5**
Accra **53 G5**
Aceh □ **38 D1**
Achalpur **43 J10**
Acharnes **23 E4**
Acheloos ➔ **23 E3**
Achill I. **11 E1**
Achinsk **30 D7**
Acireale **21 F5**
Acklins I. **86 B5**
Aconcagua, Cerro **94 C3**
Aconquija, Mt. **94 B3**
Açores, Is. dos **50 C1**
Acraman, L. **62 B2**
Acre = 'Akko **46 D3**
Acre □ **91 E4**
Acre ➔ **91 E5**
Ad Dahnā **47 F7**
Ad Dammām **47 F7**
Ad Dawādimī **47 F6**
Ad Dawḩah **44 E2**
Ad Dīlam **47 G6**
Ad Dīwānīyah **47 E6**
Ada **81 B5**
Adair, C. **70 B6**
Adaja ➔ **18 B3**
Adam **44 F4**
Adamaoua, Massif de l' **55 G1**
Adamawa Highlands = Adamaoua, Massif de l' **55 G1**
Adamello, Mte. **13 C9**
Adaminaby **63 C4**
Adams, Mt. **72 C3**
Adam's Bridge **43 Q11**
Adana **46 C3**
Adapazarı = Sakarya **25 E3**
Adarama **55 E5**
Adare, C. **96 B15**
Adaut **37 F4**
Adavale **63 A3**
Adda ➔ **13 D8**
Addis Ababa = Addis Abeba **49 F2**
Addis Abeba **49 F2**
Adelaide **62 B2**
Adelaide I. **96 A3**
Adelaide Pen. **68 B10**
Adélie, Terre **96 A14**
Adelie Land = Adélie, Terre **96 A14**
Aden = Al 'Adan **49 E4**
Aden, G. of **49 E4**
Adi **37 E4**
Adige ➔ **20 B4**
Adilabad **43 K11**
Adirondack Mts. **77 C8**
Adis Abeba = Addis Abeba **49 F2**
Admiralty I. **68 C6**
Admiralty Is. **64 K9**
Adonara **37 F2**
Adoni **43 M10**
Adour ➔ **12 E3**
Adra **18 D4**
Adrano **21 F5**
Adrar **52 D6**
Adrar des Iforas **52 E6**
Adriatic Sea **20 C5**
Adua **37 E3**
Adzhar Republic = Ajaria □ **25 E5**
Ægean Sea **23 E5**
Aerhtai Shan **34 B4**

Afghanistan ■ 45 C6
'Afif 47 G5
Afuá 92 C3
Afyon 46 C2
Afyonkarahisar = Afyon 46 C2
Agadès = Agadez 53 E7
Agadez 53 E7
Agadir 52 B4
Agapa 30 B6
Agartala 41 F8
Agats 37 F5
Agboville 53 G5
Agde 13 E5
Agen 12 D4
Aghios Efstratios 23 E5
Aghiou Orous, Kolpos 23 D5
Agra 42 F10
Ağri 25 F5
Agri ➔ 21 D6
Ağrı Dağı 25 F5
Ağri Karakose = Ağri 25 F5
Agrigento 21 F4
Agrinio 23 E3
Água Clara 93 G3
Agua Prieta 84 A3
Aguarico ➔ 90 D3
Aguas Blancas 94 A3
Aguascalientes 84 C4
Aguilas 19 D5
Agulhas, C. 58 E4
Agung, Gunung 39 F5
Agusan ➔ 36 C3
Ahaggar 52 D7
Ahar 46 C6
Ahipara B. 64 A5
Ahiri 43 K12
Ahmadabad 43 H8
Ahmadnagar 43 K9
Ahmadpur 42 E7
Ahmedabad = Ahmadabad 43 H8
Ahmednagar = Ahmadnagar 43 K9
Ahvāz 47 E7
Ahvenanmaa = Åland 9 C10
Aḩwar 49 E4
Aigues-Mortes 13 E6
Aihui = Heihe 35 A7
Aija 91 E3
Aikawa 33 D6
Aiken 83 C7
Aimere 37 F2
Ain Banaiyan 44 F2
Aïn Ben Tili 52 C4
Aïn Sefra 52 B5
Aïr 53 E7
Air Force I. 70 C6
Aisne ➔ 13 B5
Aitutaki 65 L14
Aix-en-Provence 13 E6
Aix-la-Chapelle = Aachen 14 C4
Aix-les-Bains 13 D6
Aizawl 41 F9
Aizuwakamatsu 33 E6
Ajaccio 13 F8
Ajanta Ra. 43 J9
Ajari Rep. = Ajaria □ 25 E5
Ajaria □ 25 E5
Ajdābiyā 54 B3
Ajka 16 E3
'Ajmān 44 E3
Ajmer 42 F9
Ajo, C. de 18 A4
Akaroa 65 E5
Akelamo 37 D3
Aketi 56 D4
Akhisar 23 E6
Akimiski I. 71 D5
Akita 32 D7
Akjoujt 53 E3
Akkeshi 32 B9
'Akko 46 D3
Akkol = Aqköl 29 E8
Aklavik 68 B6
Akola 43 J10
Akordat 57 A7
Akpatok I. 70 C7
Akranes 8 C1
Akron 76 D5
Aksai Chin 42 B11
Aksaray 46 C3
Aksarka 28 C7
Akşehir 46 C2
Aksu 34 B3
Aktsyabrski 17 B9
Aktyubinsk = Aqtöbe 29 D6
Akure 53 G7
Akureyri 8 B2
Akyab = Sittwe 41 G9
Al 'Adan 49 E4
Al Aḥsā = Hasa 47 F7
Al Amādīyah 46 C5
Al 'Amārah 47 E6
Al 'Aqabah 47 E3
Al 'Aramah 47 F6
Al Ashkhara 45 F4
Al Badī' 47 G6
Al Baḥrai Mayyit = Dead Sea 47 E3
Al Baṣrah 47 E6
Al Batinah 44 F4
Al Bayḍā 54 B3
Al Faḍīlī 47 F7
Al Fallūjah 46 D5
Al Fāw 47 E7
Al Fujayrah 44 E4
Al Hābah 47 F6
Al Ḥaddār 47 G6
Al Ḥāmad 47 E4
Al Ḥamar 47 G6
Al Ḥamrā' 47 F4
Al Ḥarīq 47 G6
Al Ḥasakah 46 C5
Al Ḥayy 47 D6
Al Ḥillah *Iraq* 47 D6
Al Ḥillah *Si. Arabia* 47 G6
Al Hoceïma 52 A5
Al Ḥudaydah 49 E3
Al Hufūf 47 F7
Al Ḥulwah 47 G6
Al Jāfūrah 47 F7
Al Jaghbūb 54 C3
Al Jahrah 47 E6
Al Jalāmīd 47 E4
Al Jawf *Libya* 54 D3
Al Jawf *Si. Arabia* 47 E4
Al Jazair = Algeria ■ 52 C6
Al Jazirah 46 D5
Al Jubayl 47 F7
Al Jubaylah 47 F6
Al Junaynah 55 F3
Al Khābūra 44 F4
Al Khalīl 47 E3
Al Kharfah 47 G6
Al Kharsānīyah 47 F7
Al Khaṣab 44 E4
Al Kufrah 54 D3
Al Kūt 47 D6
Al Kuwayt 47 E7
Al Lādhiqīyah 46 D3
Al Luḥayyah 49 D3
Al Madīnah 47 F4
Al Maghreb = Morocco ■ 52 B4
Al Majma'ah 47 F6
Al Manāmah 44 E2
Al Marj 54 B3
Al Mawṣil 46 C5
Al Midhnab 47 F6
Al Mish'āb 47 E7
Al Mubarraz 47 F7
Al Muḥarraq 44 E2
Al Mukallā 49 E4
Al Mukhā 49 E3
Al Musayyib 47 D6
Al Muwayliḥ 47 F3
Al Qaḍīmah 47 G4
Al Qā'iyah 47 F5
Al Qāmishlī 46 C5
Al Qaṣīm □ 47 F5
Al Qaṭif 47 F7
Al Qaṭrūn 54 D2
Al Quaisūmah 47 E6
Al Quds = Jerusalem 47 E3
Al Qurayyāt 45 F4
Al Qurnah 47 E6
Al 'Ulā 47 F4
Al 'Uqayr 47 F7
Al 'Uthmānīyah 47 F7
Al 'Uwaynid 47 F6
Al 'Uwayqīlah 47 E5
Al 'Uyūn 47 F5
Al Wakrah 44 E2
Al Yamāmah 47 F6
Al Yaman = Yemen ■ 49 D4
Alabama □ 82 C4
Alabama ➔ 82 D4
Alaçam Dağları 23 E7
Alacant = Alicante 19 C5
Alagoa Grande 92 D6
Alagoas □ 93 D6
Alagoinhas 93 E6
Alajuela 86 D3
Alamosa 79 B10
Åland 9 C10
Alania = North Ossetia □ 25 E5
Alanya 46 C2
Alapayevsk 29 D7
Alappuzha = Alleppey 43 Q10
Alaşehir 23 E7
Alaska □ 69 B4
Alaska, G. of 69 C5
Alaska Peninsula 69 C4
Alaska Range 69 B4
Alataw Shankou 34 B3
Alatyr 24 C6
Alausi 90 D3
Alawoona 62 B3
Alba 13 D8
Albacete 19 C5
Albacutya, L. 62 C3
Albanel, L. 71 D6
Albania ■ 23 D3
Albany *Australia* 60 H2
Albany *Ga., U.S.A.* 83 D5
Albany *N.Y., U.S.A.* 77 C9
Albany *Oreg., U.S.A.* 72 D2
Albany ➔ 71 D5
Albardón 94 C3
Albemarle 83 B7
Alberche ➔ 18 C3
Alberga ➔ 62 A2
Albert, L. *Africa* 57 D6
Albert, L. *Australia* 62 C2
Albert Nile ➔ 57 D6
Albertville 13 D7
Albi 12 E5
Albina 92 A3
Alborán 18 E4
Ålborg = Aalborg 9 D7
Alborz, Reshteh-ye Kūhā-ye 44 B3
Albuquerque 79 C9
Albury 63 C4
Alcalá de Henares 18 B4
Alcalá la Real 18 D4
Álcamo 21 F4
Alcaníz 19 B5
Alcântara 92 C5
Alcántara, Embalse de 18 C2
Alcantarilla 19 D5
Alcaraz, Sierra de 19 C4
Alcaudete 18 D3
Alcázar de San Juan 18 C4
Alchevsk 25 D4
Alcira = Alzira 19 C5
Alcoy 19 C5
Aldabra Is. 51 G8
Aldan ➔ 31 C10
Alderney 11 G5
Aleg 53 E3
Alegrete 94 B5
Aleksandriya = Oleksandriya 17 C8
Aleksandrovskoye 29 C8
Alençon 12 B4
Aleppo = Ḥalab 46 C4
Alert 70 A7
Alès 13 D6
Alessándria 13 D8
Ålesund 8 C7
Aleutian Is. 69 C2
Alexander Arch. 69 C6
Alexander I. 96 A3
Alexandra *Australia* 63 C4
Alexandra *N.Z.* 65 F3

Alexandria = El Iskandarîya **54 B4**
Alexandria *Romania* **22 C5**
Alexandria *La., U.S.A.* **81 D7**
Alexandria *Va., U.S.A.* **77 E7**
Alexandrina, L. **62 C2**
Alexandroupoli **22 D5**
Aleysk **29 D9**
Alga **29 E6**
Algarve **18 D1**
Algeciras **18 D3**
Algemesí **19 C5**
Alger **52 A6**
Algeria ■ **52 C6**
Alghero **21 D2**
Algiers = Alger **52 A6**
Alhucemas = Al Hoceïma **52 A5**
'Alī al Gharbī **47 D6**
'Alī Khēl **42 C6**
Aliağa **23 E6**
Alicante **19 C5**
Alice Springs **60 E5**
Aligarh **42 F11**
Alīgūdarz **46 D7**
Alipur **42 E7**
Alipur Duar **41 D7**
Aliwal North **59 E5**
Aljustrel **18 D1**
Alkmaar **14 B3**
All American Canal **78 D5**
Allahabad **40 E3**
Allegheny ➔ **77 D5**
Allegheny Mts. **77 F5**
Allentown **77 D8**
Alleppey **43 Q10**
Aller ➔ **14 B5**
Allier ➔ **13 C5**
Allora **63 A5**
Alma Ata = Almaty **29 E8**
Almada **18 C1**
Almadén **18 C3**
Almansa **19 C5**
Almanzor, Pico **18 B3**
Almanzora ➔ **19 D5**
Almaty **29 E8**
Almazán **19 B4**
Almeirim **92 C3**
Almelo **14 B4**
Almendralejo **18 C2**
Almería **19 D4**
Almora **42 E11**
Alnwick **10 D6**
Alon **41 F10**
Alor **37 F2**
Alor Setar **38 C2**
Alps **14 E5**
Alsace □ **13 B7**
Alsask **69 C9**
Alsasua **19 A4**
Alta Gracia **94 C4**
Altai = Aerhtai Shan **34 B4**
Altai = Gorno-Altay □ **29 D9**
Altamira **92 C3**
Altamura **21 D6**
Altanbulag **35 A5**
Altay **34 B3**
Altea **19 C5**
Alto Araguaia **93 F3**
Alto Molocue **59 B7**
Alton **75 F9**
Alton Downs **62 A2**
Altoona **77 D6**
Altun Shan **34 C3**
Alusi **37 F4**
Alvear **94 B5**
Alvie **62 C3**
Alwar **42 F10**
Alxa Zuoqi **35 C5**
Alzira **19 C5**
Am Timan **55 F3**
Amādi **55 G5**
Amadjuak **70 C6**
Amadjuak L. **70 C6**
Amagasaki **33 F4**
Amahai **37 E3**
Amakusa-Shotō **33 G2**
Amaliada **23 F3**
Amalner **43 J9**
Amambay, Cordillera de **94 A5**
Amankeldi **29 D7**
Amapá **92 B3**
Amapá □ **92 B3**
Amarante **92 D5**
Amarillo **80 B3**
Amaro, Mte. **20 C5**
Amasra **46 B3**
Amazon = Amazonas ➔ **92 C3**
Amazonas □ **90 D6**
Amazonas ➔ **92 C3**
Ambala **42 D10**
Ambalavao **59 C9**
Ambanja **59 A9**
Ambartsevo **29 D9**
Ambato **90 D3**
Ambatolampy **59 B9**
Ambatondrazaka **59 B9**
Amberg **15 D6**
Ambergris Cay **85 D7**
Amberley **65 E5**
Ambikapur **40 F4**
Ambilobé **59 A9**
Ambo **91 F3**
Amboise **12 C4**
Ambon **37 E3**
Ambositra **59 C9**
Ambovombe **59 D9**
Amboyna Cay **38 C4**
Ambriz **56 F2**
Amby **63 A4**
Amchitka I. **69 C1**
Amderma **28 C7**
Ameca **84 C4**
Ameland **14 B3**
American Highland **96 B10**
American Samoa ☑ **65 L13**
Americus **83 C5**
Amery **69 C10**
Amery Ice Shelf **96 A10**
Ames **75 D8**
Amherst *Burma* **41 J11**
Amherst *Canada* **71 E7**
Amiata, Mte. **20 C3**
Amiens **12 B5**
Amirante Is. **26 K9**
'Ammān **47 E3**
Ammochostos = Famagusta **46 D3**
Amorgos **23 F5**
Amos **71 E6**
Amoy = Xiamen **35 D6**
Ampanihy **59 C8**
Ampenan **39 F5**
Amper ➔ **15 D6**
Amravati **43 J10**
Amreli **43 J7**
Amritsar **42 D9**
Amroha **42 E11**
Amsterdam **14 B3**
Amstetten **15 D8**
Amudarya ➔ **29 E6**
Amund Ringnes I. **70 B4**
Amundsen Gulf **68 A7**
Amundsen Sea **96 B1**
Amuntai **39 E5**
Amur ➔ **31 D12**
Amurang **37 D2**
Amyderya = Amudarya ➔ **29 E6**
An Nafūd **47 E5**
An Najaf **47 D6**
An Nhon **38 B3**
An Nu'ayrīyah **47 F7**
Anabar ➔ **30 B9**
Anaconda **73 C7**
Anadolu **25 F3**
'Ānah **46 D5**
Anaheim **78 D4**
Anakapalle **40 J4**
Anambas, Kepulauan **39 D3**
Anambas Is. = Anambas, Kepulauan **39 D3**
Anamur **46 C3**
Anan **33 G4**
Anantnag **42 C9**
Ananyiv **17 E9**
Anápolis **93 F4**
Anār **44 D3**
Anārak **44 C3**
Anatolia = Anadolu **25 F3**
Añatuya **94 B4**
Anchorage **69 B5**
Ancohuma, Nevado **91 G5**
Ancón **91 F3**
Ancona **20 C4**
Ancud **95 E2**
Ancud, G. de **95 E2**
Andalgalá **94 B3**
Andalucía □ **18 D3**
Andalusia = Andalucía □ **18 D3**
Andalusia **82 D4**
Andaman Is. **27 G11**
Andaman Sea **38 B1**
Andapa **59 A9**
Anderson **76 D3**
Anderson ➔ **68 B7**
Andes, Cord. de los **91 G4**
Andhra Pradesh □ **43 L11**
Andijon **29 E8**
Andikithira = Antikythira **23 G4**
Andizhan = Andijon **29 E8**
Andkhvoy **45 B6**
Andoany **59 A9**
Andorra ■ **19 A6**
Andorra La Vella **12 E4**
Andreanof Is. **69 C2**
Andrewilla **62 A2**
Ándria **20 D6**
Andros **23 F5**
Andros I. **86 B4**
Andújar **18 C3**
Andulo **56 G3**
Aneto, Pico de **19 A6**
Ang'angxi **35 B7**
Angara ➔ **30 D7**
Angarsk **30 D8**
Angaston **62 B2**
Ånge **8 C9**
Angeles **36 A2**
Angellala **63 A4**
Ångermanälven ➔ **8 C9**
Angers **12 C3**
Anglesey **11 E4**
Ango **57 D5**
Angoche **59 B7**
Angola ■ **58 A3**
Angoulême **12 D4**
Angoumois **12 D4**
Angren **29 E8**
Anguilla ☑ **87 C7**
Anhui □ **35 C6**
Anhwei = Anhui □ **35 C6**
Anjou **12 C3**
Ankaboa, Tanjona **59 C8**
Ankang **35 C5**
Ankara **25 F3**
Ankaratra **59 B9**
Ann Arbor **76 C4**
Annaba **52 A7**
Annan **11 D5**
Annapolis **77 E7**
Annecy **13 D7**
Anning **34 D5**
Anniston **82 C5**
Annobón **51 G4**
Annuello **62 B3**
Anqing **35 C6**
Ansbach **14 D6**
Anshan **35 B7**
Anshun **35 D5**
Ansongo **53 E6**
Ansudu **37 E5**
Antabamba **91 F4**
Antakya = Hatay **46 C4**
Antalaha **59 A10**
Antalya **46 C2**
Antalya Körfezi **46 C2**
Antananarivo **59 B9**
Antarctic Pen. **96 A4**
Antarctica **96 C**
Antequera **18 D3**
Anti Atlas **52 C4**
Antibes **13 E7**
Anticosti, Î. d' **71 E7**
Antigonish **71 E7**
Antigua & Barbuda ■ **87 C7**
Antikythira **23 G4**
Antioquia **90 B3**
Antofagasta **94 A2**

Antonina 94 B7
Antrim 11 D3
Antsirabe 59 B9
Antsiranana 59 A9
Antsohihy 59 A9
Antwerp = Antwerpen 14 C3
Antwerpen 14 C3
Anupgarh 42 E8
Anvers = Antwerpen 14 C3
Anvers I. 96 A3
Anxi 34 B4
Anxious B. 62 B1
Anyang 35 C6
Anzhero-Sudzhensk 29 D9
Ánzio 20 D4
Aoga-Shima 33 G6
Aomen = Macau 35 D6
Aomori 32 C7
Aoraki Mount Cook 65 E4
Aosta 13 D7
Aotearoa = New Zealand ■ 64 D7
Aouk, Bahr ➔ 56 C3
Apalachicola ➔ 82 E5
Apaporis ➔ 90 D5
Aparri 36 A2
Apeldoorn 14 B3
Apennines = Appennini 20 B3
Apia 65 L13
Apiacás, Serra dos 91 E7
Aplao 91 G4
Apo, Mt. 36 C3
Apolo 91 F5
Apoteri 90 C7
Appalachian Mts. 77 F5
Appennini 20 B3
Appleton 76 B1
Aprília 20 D4
Apucarana 94 A6
Apure ➔ 90 B5
Apurimac ➔ 91 F4
Aqaba = Al 'Aqabah 47 E3
Aqaba, G. of 47 E3
'Aqabah, Khalīj al = Aqaba, G. of 47 E3
Āqchah 45 B6
Aqköl 29 E8
'Aqrah 46 C5
Aqtöbe 29 D6
Aqtoghay 29 E8
Aquidauana 93 G2
Aquitain, Bassin 12 D3
Ar Rachidiya = Er Rachidia 52 B5
Ar Ramādī 46 D5
Ar Raqqah 46 D4
Ar Rass 47 F5
Ar Rifā'ī 47 E6
Ar Riyāḍ 47 F6
Ar Ruṭbah 46 D5
Ar Ruwayḍah 47 G6
Ara 40 E5
'Arab, Bahr el ➔ 55 G4
Arab, Shatt al ➔ 47 E7
Arabian Desert = Es Sahrâ' Esh Sharqîya 54 C5
Arabian Gulf = Persian Gulf 44 E2
Arabian Sea 26 G8
Araç 46 B3
Aracaju 93 E6
Aracati 92 C6
Araçatuba 93 G3
Aracena 18 D2
Araçuaí 93 F5
Arad 16 E5
Arafura Sea 37 F4
Aragón □ 19 B5
Aragón ➔ 19 A5
Araguacema 92 D4
Araguaia ➔ 92 D4
Araguari 93 F4
Araguari ➔ 92 B4
Arak 52 C6
Arakan Coast 41 H9
Arakan Yoma 41 H10
Araks = Aras, Rüd-e ➔ 46 B7
Aral 29 E7
Aral Sea 29 E6
Aral Tengizi = Aral Sea 29 E6
Aralsk = Aral 29 E7
Aralskoye More = Aral Sea 29 E6
Aran I. 10 D2
Aran Is. 11 E2
Aranda de Duero 18 B4
Aranjuez 18 B4
Arapgir 46 C4
Arapiraca 93 D6
Arapongas 94 A6
Araraquara 93 G4
Ararat 62 C3
Ararat, Mt. = Ağrı Dağı 25 F5
Araripe, Chapada do 92 D6
Aras, Rüd-e ➔ 46 B7
Arauca 90 B4
Arauca ➔ 90 B5
Araxá 93 F4
Araya, Pen. de 90 A6
Árbatax 21 E2
Arbīl 46 C6
Arbroath 10 C5
Arcachon 12 D3
Archangel = Arkhangelsk 28 C5
Arckaringa 62 A1
Arckaringa Cr. ➔ 62 A2
Arcos de la Frontera 18 D3
Arcot 43 N11
Arctic Bay 70 B5
Arctic Red River = Tsiigehtchic 68 B6
Arda ➔ 22 D6
Ardabīl 46 C7
Ardahan 46 B5
Ardenne 14 D3
Ardennes = Ardenne 14 D3
Ardestān 44 C3
Ardlethan 63 B4
Ardmore 80 B5
Ardrossan 62 B2
Arecibo 87 C6
Areia Branca 92 C6
Arendal 9 D7
Arequipa 91 G4
Arévalo 18 B3
Arezzo 20 C3
Arganda 18 B4
Argentan 12 B3
Argentário, Mte. 20 C3
Argentina ■ 94 D3
Argentina Is. 96 A3
Argentino, L. 95 G2
Argeş ➔ 22 B6
Arghandab ➔ 42 D4
Argolikos Kolpos 23 F4
Argos 23 F4
Argostoli 23 E3
Århus 9 D8
Ariadnoye 32 A4
Arica *Chile* 91 G4
Arica *Colombia* 90 D4
Aridh 47 F6
Arinos ➔ 91 F7
Aripuanã 91 E6
Aripuanã ➔ 90 E6
Ariquemes 91 E6
Arizona 94 D3
Arizona □ 79 C7
Arjona 90 A3
Arkalyk = Arqalyk 29 D7
Arkansas □ 81 B7
Arkansas ➔ 81 C8
Arkansas City 80 A5
Arkhangelsk 28 C5
Arklow 11 E3
Arkticheskiy, Mys 30 A7
Arlanzón ➔ 18 A3
Arlbergpass 14 E6
Arles 13 E6
Arlington *Va., U.S.A.* 77 E7
Arlington *Wash., U.S.A.* 72 B2
Arlon 14 D3
Armagh 11 D3
Armavir 25 D5
Armenia 90 C3
Armenia ■ 25 E5
Armidale 63 B5
Arnaud ➔ 70 C6
Arnauti, C. 46 D3
Arnhem 14 C3
Arnhem, C. 60 C6
Arnhem Land 60 C5
Arno ➔ 20 C3
Arno Bay 62 B2
Arnsberg 14 C5
Arqalyk 29 D7
Arrabury 62 A3
Arrah = Ara 40 E5
Arran 10 D4
Arras 13 A5
Arrecife 52 C3
Arrée, Mts. d' 12 B2
Arrowtown 65 F3
Arsenev 32 A3
Arta 23 E3
Artem 32 B3
Arthur ➔ 62 D3
Arthur's Pass △ 65 E4
Arthur's Pass △ 65 E4
Artigas 94 C5
Artois 12 A5
Artsyz 17 E9
Artvin 25 E5
Aru, Kepulauan 37 F4
Aru Is. = Aru, Kepulauan 37 F4
Arua 57 D6
Aruanã 93 E3
Aruba ⊠ 87 D6
Arunachal Pradesh □ 41 C10
Arusha 57 E7
Aruwimi ➔ 56 D4
Arviat 68 B10
Arxan 35 B6
Arys 29 E7
Arzamas 24 B5
As Saffānīyah 47 E7
As Samāwah 47 E6
As Sohar = Ṣuḥār 44 E4
As Sulaymānīyah *Iraq* 46 D6
As Sulaymānīyah *Si. Arabia* 47 F6
As Summān 47 F6
As Sūq 47 G5
As Suwaydā' 46 D4
As Suwayḥ 45 F4
Aṣ Ṣuwayrah 47 D6
Asahigawa 32 B8
Asansol 40 F6
Ascension I. 51 G2
Aschaffenburg 14 D5
Aschersleben 15 C6
Áscoli Piceno 20 C4
Ascope 91 E3
Aseb 49 E3
Asenovgrad 22 C5
Aşgabat = Ashgabat 29 F6
Ash Shāmīyah 47 E6
Ash Shāriqah 44 E3
Ash Shaṭrah 47 E6
Ash Shu'aybah 47 F6
Ash Shu'bah 47 E6
Ashburton 65 E4
Asheville 83 B6
Ashford *Australia* 63 A5
Ashford *U.K.* 11 F7
Ashgabat 29 F6
Ashizuri-Zaki 33 G3
Ashkhabad = Ashgabat 29 F6
Ashmyany 17 A7
Ashqelon 47 E3
Ashtabula 76 D5
Ashuanipi, L. 71 D7
Asia, Kepulauan 37 D4
Asifabad 43 K11
Asinara 20 D2
Asinara, G. dell' 20 D2
Asino 29 D9
Asipovichy 17 B9
'Asīr 48 D3
Asir, Ras 49 E5
Asmara = Asmera 57 A7
Asmera 57 A7
Aspiring, Mt. 65 F3
Assab = Aseb 49 E3

Assam □ 41 D9
Assen 14 B4
Assiniboia 69 D9
Assiniboine ➔ 69 D10
Assis 94 A6
Assisi 20 C4
Astana 29 D8
Asti 13 D8
Astipalea 23 F6
Astorga 18 A2
Astoria 72 C2
Astrakhan 25 D6
Astrakhan-Bazàr 25 F6
Asturias □ 18 A3
Asunción 94 B5
Aswân 54 D5
Aswan Dam = Sadd el Aali 54 D5
Asyût 54 C5
Aṭ Ṭafilah 47 E3
Aṭ Tā'if 48 C3
Atacama, Desierto de 94 A3
Atacama, Salar de 94 A3
Atalaya 91 F4
Atamyrat 29 F7
Atapupu 37 F2
Atâr 52 D3
Atasū 29 E8
Atauro 37 F3
Atbara 55 E5
'Atbara, Nahr ➔ 55 E5
Atbasar 29 D7
Athabasca 69 C8
Athabasca ➔ 68 C8
Athabasca, L. 68 C8
Athens = Athina 23 F4
Athens *Ala., U.S.A.* 82 B4
Athens *Ga., U.S.A.* 83 C6
Athina 23 F4
Athínai = Athina 23 F4
Athlone 11 E3
Athos 23 D5
Athy 11 E3
Ati 55 F2
Atlanta 83 C5
Atlantic City 77 E8
Atlas Mts. = Haut Atlas 52 B4
Atrak = Atrek ➔ 44 B3
Atrek ➔ 44 B3
Atsuta 32 B7
Attapu 38 B3
Attawapiskat 71 D5
Attawapiskat ➔ 71 D5
Attock 42 C8
Attopeu = Attapu 38 B3
Attur 43 P11
Atuel ➔ 94 D3
Atyraŭ 29 E6
Aubagne 13 E6
Aube ➔ 13 B5
Auburn 82 C5
Auburn Ra. 63 A5
Aubusson 12 D5
Auch 12 E4
Auckland 64 B6
Aude ➔ 13 E5
Augathella 63 A4
Augsburg 14 D6
Augusta *Italy* 21 F5
Augusta *Ga., U.S.A.* 83 C7
Augusta *Maine, U.S.A.* 77 B11
Aujuittuq = Grise Fiord 70 B5
Aunis 12 C3
Auponhia 37 E3
Aurangabad *Bihar, India* 40 E5
Aurangabad *Maharashtra, India* 43 K9
Aurich 14 B4
Aurillac 12 D5
Aurora *Colo., U.S.A.* 74 F2
Aurora *Ill., U.S.A.* 76 D1
Austin *Minn., U.S.A.* 75 D8
Austin *Tex., U.S.A.* 80 D5
Austral Is. = Tubuaï, Îs. 65 M16
Austral Seamount Chain 65 M16
Australia ■ 60 E6
Australian Alps 63 C4
Australian Capital Territory □ 63 C4
Austria ■ 15 E8
Autun 13 C6
Auvergne □ 13 D5
Auvergne, Mts. d' 13 D5
Auxerre 13 C5
Avallon 13 C5
Aveiro *Brazil* 92 C2
Aveiro *Portugal* 18 B1
Āvej 46 D7
Avellaneda 94 C5
Avellino 21 D5
Aversa 21 D5
Avesta 9 C9
Avezzano 20 C4
Aviemore 10 C5
Avignon 13 E6
Ávila 18 B3
Avilés 18 A3
Avoca ➔ 62 C3
Avola 21 F5
Avranches 12 B3
Awaji-Shima 33 F4
Awash 49 F3
Awatere ➔ 65 D6
Awbārī 54 C1
Awbārī, Idehan 54 C1
Awjilah 54 C3
Axel Heiberg I. 70 B5
Axim 53 H5
Axios ➔ 23 D4
Ayabaca 90 D3
Ayabe 33 F4
Ayacucho *Argentina* 94 D5
Ayacucho *Peru* 91 F4
Ayaguz = Ayaköz 29 E9
Ayaköz 29 E9
Ayamonte 18 D2
Ayaviri 91 F4
Äybak 45 B7
Aydın 23 F6
Ayers Rock = Uluru 60 F5
Ayeyarwady = Irrawaddy ➔ 41 K10
Aylmer, L. 68 B8
Ayn Dār 47 F7
Ayr 10 D4
Aytos 22 C6
Ayu, Kepulauan 37 D4
Ayvacık 23 E6
Ayvalık 23 E6
Az Ẓahrān 47 F7
Az Zarqā 46 D4
Az Zilfī 47 F6
Az Zubayr 47 E6
Azamgarh 40 D4
Azārbayjan = Azerbaijan ■ 25 E6
Āzarbāyjān-e Gharbī □ 46 C6
Āzarbāyjān-e Sharqī □ 46 C6
Azare 53 F8
Azbine = Aïr 53 E7
Azerbaijan ■ 25 E6
Azogues 90 D3
Azores = Açores, Is. dos 50 C1
Azov 25 D4
Azov, Sea of 25 D4
Azovskoye More = Azov, Sea of 25 D4
Azovy 28 C7
Azuaga 18 C3
Azuero, Pen. de 86 E3
Azul 94 D5

B

Ba Don 38 A3
Ba Ria 38 B3
Baardeere = Bardera 49 G3
Bab el Mandeb 49 E3
Bābā, Koh-i- 42 B5
Baba Burnu 23 E6
Babadag 22 B7
Babadayhan 29 F7
Babaeski 22 D6
Babahoyo 90 D3
Babar 37 F3
Babo 37 E4
Bābol 44 B3
Bābol Sar 44 B3
Babruysk 17 B9
Babuyan Chan. 36 A2
Babylon 47 D6
Bacabal 92 C5
Bacan, Kepulauan 37 E3
Bacarra 36 A2
Bacău 17 E8
Bachelina 29 D7
Back ➔ 68 B9
Bacolod 36 B2
Bad Ischl 15 E7
Bad Kissingen 14 C6
Badagara 43 P9
Badajoz 18 C2
Badalona 19 B7
Badampahar 40 F6
Badanah 47 E5
Badarinath 42 D11
Badas 38 D4
Badas, Kepulauan 39 D3
Baddo ➔ 42 E4
Bade 37 F5
Baden 15 D9
Baden-Baden 14 D5
Baden-Württemberg □ 14 D5
Badgastein 15 E7
Bādghīs □ 42 B3
Badin 43 G6
Badlands 74 D3
Baena 18 D3
Baeza 18 D4
Baffin B. 70 B7
Baffin I. 70 C6
Bafia 53 H8
Bafing ➔ 53 F3
Bafoulabé 53 F3
Bāfq 44 D3
Bāft 44 D4
Bafwasende 57 D5
Bagamoyo 57 F7
Baganga 36 C3
Bagansiapiapi 39 D2
Bagdarin 30 D9
Bagé 94 C6
Baghdād 46 D6
Bagheria 21 E4
Baghlān 42 A6
Baghlān □ 45 C7
Bago = Pegu 41 J11
Baguio 36 A2
Bahamas ■ 86 A4
Baharampur 40 E7
Bahawalpur 42 E7
Bahía = Salvador 93 E6
Bahía □ 93 E5
Bahía Blanca 94 D4
Bahía de Caráquez 90 D2
Bahía Laura 95 F3
Bahía Negra 91 H7
Bahraich 40 D3
Bahrain ■ 44 E2
Baia Mare 17 E6
Baibokoum 55 G2
Baidoa 49 G3
Baie-Comeau 71 E7
Baie Verte 71 E8
Ba'ijī 46 D5
Baikal, L. = Baykal, Oz. 30 D8
Baikonur = Bayqongyr 29 E7
Baile Atha Cliath = Dublin 11 E3
Băileşti 22 B4
Bā'ir 47 E4
Bairiki = Tarawa 64 J12
Bairnsdale 63 C4
Baitadi 40 C3
Baiyin 35 C5
Baja 16 E4
Baja, Pta. 84 B1
Baja California 84 A1
Bajimba, Mt. 63 A5
Bakala 55 G3
Bakchar 29 D9
Bakel 53 F3
Baker, L. 68 B10
Baker, Mt. 72 B3
Baker I. 64 J13
Baker Lake 68 B10

Bakers Dozen Is. **71 D6**
Bakersfield **78 C3**
Bākhtarān = Kermānshāh **46 D6**
Bakı **25 E6**
Bakony **16 E3**
Bakony Forest = Bakony **16 E3**
Bakouma **55 G3**
Baku = Bakı **25 E6**
Bakutis Coast **96 B1**
Baky = Bakı **25 E6**
Balabac I. **38 C5**
Balabac Str. **38 C5**
Balabalangan, Kepulauan **39 E5**
Balaghat Ra. **43 K10**
Balaguer **19 B6**
Balaklava **25 E3**
Balakovo **24 C6**
Balashov **24 C5**
Balasore = Baleshwar **40 G6**
Balaton **16 E3**
Balbina, Reprêsa de **90 D7**
Balchik **22 C7**
Balclutha **65 G3**
Baleares, Is. **19 C7**
Balearic Is. = Baleares, Is. **19 C7**
Baleine = Whale ➔ **70 D7**
Baler **36 A2**
Baleshwar **40 G6**
Bali **39 F5**
Bali □ **39 F5**
Baliem ➔ **37 F5**
Balikeşir **23 E6**
Balikpapan **39 E5**
Balimbing **36 C1**
Balipara **41 D9**
Balkan Mts. = Stara Planina **22 C4**
Balkanabat **29 F6**
Balkh **45 B6**
Balkhash = Balqash **29 E8**
Balkhash, Ozero = Balqash Köli **29 E8**
Balla **41 E8**
Ballarat **62 C3**
Ballater **10 C5**
Ballina *Australia* **63 A5**
Ballina *Ireland* **11 D2**
Ballinasloe **11 E2**
Ballymena **11 D3**
Balmaceda **95 F2**
Balmoral **62 C3**
Balochistan = Baluchistan □ **42 F4**
Balonne ➔ **63 A4**
Balqash **29 E8**
Balqash Köli **29 E8**
Balrampur **40 D4**
Balranald **62 B3**
Balsas ➔ **84 D4**
Balta **17 D9**
Bālṭi **17 E8**
Baltic Sea **9 D9**
Baltimore **77 E7**
Baluchistan □ **42 F4**
Balya **23 E6**
Bam **44 D4**
Bama **55 F1**
Bamako **53 F4**
Bambari **55 G3**
Bamberg **14 D6**
Bamenda **53 G8**
Bāmīān □ **42 B5**
Bampūr **45 E5**
Ban Don = Surat Thani **38 C1**
Ban Kantang **38 C1**
Ban Mê Thuôt = Buon Ma Thuot **38 B3**
Banaba **64 K11**
Banalia **57 D5**
Bananal, I. do **93 E3**
Banaras = Varanasi **40 E4**
Bānās, Ras **54 D6**
Band-e Torkestan **45 C6**
Banda, Kepulauan **37 E3**
Banda Aceh **38 C1**
Banda Banda, Mt. **63 B5**
Banda Elat **37 F4**
Banda Is. = Banda, Kepulauan **37 E3**
Banda Sea **37 F3**
Bandanaira **37 E3**
Bandar = Machilipatnam **40 J3**
Bandar-e Abbās **44 E4**
Bandar-e Anzalī **46 C7**
Bandar-e Bushehr = Būshehr **44 D2**
Bandar-e Chārak **44 E3**
Bandar-e Deylam **47 E7**
Bandar-e Emām Khomeynī **47 E7**
Bandar-e Lengeh **44 E3**
Bandar-e Nakhīlū **44 E3**
Bandar-e Rīg **44 D2**
Bandar-e Torkeman **44 B3**
Bandar Lampung **39 F3**
Bandar Maharani = Muar **39 D2**
Bandar Penggaram = Batu Pahat **39 D2**
Bandar Seri Begawan **38 D5**
Bandar Sri Aman = Sri Aman **39 D4**
Bandera **94 B4**
Bandirma **23 D7**
Bandjarmasin = Banjarmasin **39 E4**
Bandon **11 F2**
Bandundu **56 E3**
Bandung **39 F3**
Banff *Canada* **69 C8**
Banff *U.K.* **10 C5**
Bang Saphan **38 B1**
Bangalore **43 N10**
Bangassou **56 D4**
Banggai, Kepulauan **37 E2**
Banggai Arch. = Banggai, Kepulauan **37 E2**
Banggi, Pulau **38 C5**
Banghāzī **54 B3**
Bangka *Sulawesi, Indonesia* **37 D3**
Bangka *Sumatera, Indonesia* **39 E3**
Bangka, Selat **39 E3**
Bangkinang **39 D2**
Bangko **39 E2**
Bangkok **38 B2**
Bangladesh ■ **41 E7**
Bangong Co **42 B11**
Bangor *Down, U.K.* **11 D4**
Bangor *Gwynedd, U.K.* **11 E4**
Bangor *U.S.A.* **77 B11**
Bangued **36 A2**
Bangui **56 D3**
Bangweulu, L. **57 G6**
Baní **87 C5**
Banī Walīd **54 B1**
Bāniyās **46 D3**
Banja Luka **20 B6**
Banjarmasin **39 E4**
Banjul **53 F2**
Bankipore **40 E5**
Banks I. **68 A7**
Banks Pen. **65 E5**
Banks Str. **62 D4**
Bankura **40 F6**
Bannu **42 C7**
Banswara **43 H9**
Bantry **11 F2**
Banu **42 B6**
Banyak, Kepulauan **39 D1**
Banzare Coast **96 A13**
Baoding **35 C6**
Baoji **35 C5**
Baoshan **34 D4**
Baotou **35 B6**
Bapatla **40 K3**
Ba'qūbah **46 D6**
Bar *Montenegro* **22 C2**
Bar *Ukraine* **17 D8**
Bar-le-Duc **13 B6**
Barabai **39 E5**
Barabinsk **29 D8**
Baracoa **86 B5**
Barahona **87 C5**
Barail Range **41 E9**
Barakaldo **19 A4**
Barakhola **41 E9**
Barakpur **41 F7**
Barakula **63 A5**
Baramula **42 B9**
Baran **43 G10**
Baranavichy **17 B8**
Baranof I. **69 C6**
Barapasi **37 E5**
Barat Daya, Kepulauan **37 F3**
Barbacena **93 G5**
Barbados ■ **87 D8**
Barbastro **19 A6**
Barcellona Pozzo di Gotto **21 E5**
Barcelona *Spain* **19 B7**
Barcelona *Venezuela* **90 A6**
Barcelos **90 D6**
Bardaï **54 D2**
Barddhaman **40 F6**
Bardera **49 G3**
Bardīyah **54 B4**
Bareilly **42 E11**
Barfleur, Pte. de **12 B3**
Barga **34 C3**
Barhi **40 E5**
Bari **20 D6**
Bari Doab **42 D8**
Barīdī, Ra's **47 F4**
Barinas **90 B4**
Baring, C. **68 B8**
Barisal **41 F8**
Barisan, Pegunungan **39 E2**
Barito ➔ **39 E4**
Barkly Tableland **60 D6**
Bārlad ➔ **17 F8**
Barlee, L. **60 F2**
Barletta **20 D6**
Barmedman **63 B4**
Barmer **42 G7**
Barmera **62 B3**
Barnaul **29 D9**
Barnsley **11 E6**
Barnstaple **11 F4**
Baro **53 G7**
Baroda = Vadodara **43 H8**
Barotseland **58 B4**
Barpeta **41 D8**
Barquisimeto **90 A5**
Barra *Brazil* **93 E5**
Barra *U.K.* **10 C3**
Barra do Corda **92 D4**
Barra Falsa, Pta. da **59 C7**
Barraba **63 B5**
Barrackpur = Barakpur **41 F7**
Barraigh = Barra **10 C3**
Barranca *Lima, Peru* **91 F3**
Barranca *Loreto, Peru* **90 D3**
Barrancabermeja **90 B4**
Barrancas **90 B6**
Barrancos **18 C2**
Barranqueras **94 B5**
Barranquilla **90 A4**
Barreiras **93 E5**
Barreirinhas **92 C5**
Barreiro **18 C1**
Barretos **93 G4**
Barrie **71 E6**
Barrier Ra. **62 B3**
Barrington Tops **63 B5**
Barringun **63 A4**
Barrow **69 A4**
Barrow-in-Furness **11 D5**
Barry **11 F5**
Barsi **43 K9**
Barsoi **40 E6**
Barstow **78 C4**
Bartica **90 B7**
Bartin **46 B3**
Bartlesville **81 A6**
Barysaw **17 A9**
Bāsa'idū **44 E3**
Basankusa **56 D3**
Basarabeasca **17 E9**
Basarabia = Bessarabiya **17 E9**
Basel **14 E4**
Bashkir Republic = Bashkortostan □ **29 D6**

Bashkortostan □ 29 D6
Basilan 36 C2
Basilan Str. 36 C2
Basildon 11 F7
Basim = Washim 43 J10
Basingstoke 11 F6
Basle = Basel 14 E4
Basoko 56 D4
Basque Provinces = País Vasco □ 19 A4
Basra = Al Baṣrah 47 E6
Bass Str. 61 H8
Bassano del Grappa 20 B3
Bassas da India 59 C7
Basse-Terre 87 C7
Bassein 41 J10
Basseterre 87 C7
Bastak 44 E3
Bastar 40 H3
Basti 40 D4
Bastia 13 E8
Bastogne 14 C3
Bata 56 D1
Bataan □ 36 B2
Batabanó, G. de 86 B3
Batac 36 A2
Batagai 31 C11
Batamay 31 C10
Batangafo 55 G2
Batangas 36 B2
Batanta 37 E4
Batdambang 38 B2
Batemans B. 63 C5
Batemans Bay 63 C5
Bath 11 F5
Bathurst *Australia* 63 B4
Bathurst *Canada* 71 E7
Bathurst, C. 68 A7
Bathurst Harb. 62 D4
Bathurst I. 70 B3
Bathurst Inlet 68 B9
Batlow 63 C4
Batman 46 C5
Batna 52 A7
Baton Rouge 81 D8
Batouri 56 D2
Battambang = Batdambang 38 B2
Battipáglia 21 D5
Battle Creek 76 C3
Batu 49 F2
Batu, Kepulauan 39 E1
Batu Is. = Batu, Kepulauan 39 E1
Batu Pahat 39 D2
Batuata 37 F2
Batumi 25 E5
Baturaja 39 E2
Baturité 92 C6
Bau 39 D4
Baubau 37 F2
Baucau 37 F3
Bauchi 53 F7
Bauer, C. 62 B1
Baukau = Baucau 37 F3
Bauld, C. 71 D8
Bauru 93 G4
Bautzen 15 C8
Bavaria = Bayern □ 15 D6
Bawdwin 41 F11
Bawean 39 F4
Bawku 53 F5
Bawlake 41 H11
Bay City 76 C4
Bay View 64 C7
Bayamo 86 B4
Bayan Har Shan 34 C4
Bayan Hot = Alxa Zuoqi 35 C5
Bayanaüyl 29 D8
Bayanhongor 35 B5
Bayázeh 44 C3
Baybay 36 B2
Baydhabo = Baidoa 49 G3
Bayern □ 15 D6
Bayeux 12 B3
Bayındır 23 E6
Baykal, Oz. 30 D8
Baykit 30 C7
Bayombong 36 A2
Bayonne 12 E3
Bayovar 91 E2
Bayqongyr 29 E7
Bayram-Ali = Baýramaly 29 F7
Baýramaly 29 F7
Bayramiç 23 E6
Bayreuth 15 D6
Bayrūt 46 D3
Baytown 81 E6
Baza 19 D4
Bazaruto, I. do 59 C7
Beachport 62 C2
Beagle, Canal 95 G3
Beardmore Glacier 96 C14
Béarn 12 E3
Beauce, Plaine de la 12 B4
Beaudesert 63 A5
Beaufort 38 C5
Beaufort Sea 66 B6
Beaufort West 58 E4
Beaumont 81 D6
Beaune 13 C6
Beauvais 12 B5
Beaver ➔ 69 C9
Beawar 42 F9
Bečej 22 B3
Béchar 52 B5
Bedford 11 E6
Beenleigh 63 A5
Be'er Sheva 47 E3
Beersheba = Be'er Sheva 47 E3
Befale 56 D4
Bega 63 C4
Behbehān 47 E7
Behshahr 44 B3
Bei Jiang ➔ 35 D6
Bei'an 35 B7
Beihai 35 D5
Beijing 35 C6
Beilpajah 63 B3
Beinn na Faoghla = Benbecula 10 C3
Beira 59 B6
Beirut = Bayrūt 46 D3
Beitbridge 59 C6
Beja *Portugal* 18 C2
Béja *Tunisia* 54 A1
Bejaïa 52 A7
Béjar 18 B3
Bejestān 44 C4
Békéscsaba 16 E5
Bela *India* 40 E4
Bela *Pakistan* 42 F5
Bela Crkva 22 B3
Bela Vista *Brazil* 94 A5
Bela Vista *Mozam.* 59 D6
Belarus ■ 24 C2
Belau = Palau ■ 36 C4
Belawan 39 D1
Belaya Tserkov = Bila Tserkva 17 D10
Belcher Chan. 70 B4
Belcher Is. 71 D6
Beled Weyne = Belet Uen 49 G4
Belém 92 C4
Belet Uen 49 G4
Belev 24 C4
Belfast 11 D4
Belfort 13 C7
Belgaum 43 M9
Belgium ■ 14 C3
Belgorod 24 C4
Belgorod-Dnestrovskiy = Bilhorod-Dnistrovskyy 25 D3
Belgrade = Beograd 22 B3
Beli Drim ➔ 22 C3
Belinyu 39 E3
Beliton Is. = Belitung 39 E3
Belitung 39 E3
Belize ■ 85 D7
Belize City 85 D7
Belkovskiy, Ostrov 30 B11
Bell Bay 62 D4
Bell Peninsula 70 C5
Bell Ville 94 C4
Bella Unión 94 C5
Bella Vista 94 B5
Bellary 43 M10
Bellata 63 A4
Belle-Île 12 C2
Belle Isle 71 D8
Belle Isle, Str. of 71 D8
Belleville *Canada* 71 E6
Belleville *U.S.A.* 75 F10
Bellin = Kangirsuk 70 D7
Bellingen 63 B5
Bellingham 72 B2
Bellingshausen Sea 96 A2
Bellinzona 13 C8
Belluno 20 A4
Belmonte 93 F6
Belmopan 85 D7
Belo Horizonte 93 F5
Belo-Tsiribihina 59 B8
Beloit 75 D10
Belokorovichi 17 C9
Belomorsk 28 C4
Belonia 41 F8
Belorussia = Belarus ■ 24 C2
Belovo 29 D9
Beloye, Ozero 24 A4
Beloye More 8 B13
Belozersk 24 A4
Beltana 62 B2
Belterra 92 C3
Beltsy = Bălţi 17 E8
Belukha 29 E9
Beluran 38 C5
Belyy, Ostrov 28 B8
Belyy Yar 29 D9
Bembéréke 53 F6
Bemidji 75 B7
Ben Lomond *N.S.W., Australia* 63 B5
Ben Lomond *Tas., Australia* 62 D4
Ben Nevis 10 C4
Bena 53 F7
Bena-Dibele 56 E4
Benalla 63 C4
Benares = Varanasi 40 E4
Benavente 18 A3
Benbecula 10 C3
Benbonyathe Hill 62 B2
Bend 72 D3
Bender Beila 49 F5
Bendery = Tighina 17 E9
Bendigo 63 C3
Benevento 20 D5
Bengal, Bay of 41 J7
Bengalūru = Bangalore 43 N10
Bengbu 35 C6
Benghazi = Banghāzī 54 B3
Bengkalis 39 D2
Bengkulu 39 E2
Bengkulu □ 39 E2
Benguela 58 A2
Beni 57 D5
Beni ➔ 91 F5
Beni Mellal 52 B4
Beni Suef 54 C5
Benidorm 19 C5
Benin ■ 53 G6
Benin, Bight of 53 H6
Benin City 53 G7
Benjamin Constant 90 D4
Benoni 59 D5
Bent 44 E4
Benteng 37 F2
Benton Harbor 76 C2
Benue ➔ 53 G7
Benxi 35 B7
Beo 36 D3
Beograd 22 B3
Beppu 33 G2
Berat 23 D2
Berau, Teluk 37 E4
Berber 55 E5
Berbera 49 E4
Berbérati 56 D3
Berbice ➔ 90 B7
Berdichev = Berdychiv 17 D9
Berdsk 29 D9
Berdyansk 25 D4
Berdychiv 17 D9
Berebere 37 D3
Bereda 49 E5
Berehove 17 D6
Berekum 53 G5

Berestechko **17 C7**
Bereza = Byaroza **17 B7**
Berezhany **17 D7**
Berezina = Byarezina ➔ **17 B10**
Berezniki **28 D6**
Berezovo **28 C7**
Berga **19 A6**
Bergama **23 E6**
Bérgamo **13 D8**
Bergen **8 C7**
Bergerac **12 D4**
Berhala, Selat **39 E2**
Berhampore = Baharampur **40 E7**
Berhampur = Brahmapur **40 H5**
Bering Sea **69 C1**
Bering Strait **69 B3**
Berja **19 D4**
Berkeley **72 H2**
Berkner I. **96 B4**
Berlin **15 B7**
Bermejo ➔ *Formosa, Argentina* **94 B5**
Bermejo ➔ *San Juan, Argentina* **94 C3**
Bermejo, Paso = Uspallata, P. de **94 C3**
Bermuda ⌀ **67 F13**
Bern **14 E4**
Bernburg **15 C6**
Berne = Bern **14 E4**
Bernina, Piz **13 C8**
Beroun **16 D2**
Berri **62 B3**
Berry *Australia* **63 B5**
Berry *France* **12 C5**
Bershad **17 D9**
Bertoua **56 D2**
Berwick-upon-Tweed **10 D6**
Besalampy **59 B8**
Besançon **13 C7**
Besar **39 E5**
Bessarabiya **17 E9**
Bessarabka = Basarabeasca **17 E9**
Bessemer **82 C4**
Betanzos **18 A1**
Bétaré Oya **56 C2**
Bethel **69 B3**
Bethlehem *S. Africa* **59 D5**
Bethlehem *U.S.A.* **77 D8**
Béthune **13 A5**
Betong **39 D4**
Betroka **59 C9**
Bettiah **40 D5**
Betul **43 J10**
Beverley **11 E6**
Beverly Hills **78 C3**
Beyneu **29 E6**
Beypazarı **25 E3**
Beyşehir Gölü **46 C2**
Bezhitsa **24 C3**
Béziers **13 E5**
Bezwada = Vijayawada **40 J3**
Bhachau **43 H7**
Bhadrakh **40 G6**
Bhadravati **43 N9**
Bhagalpur **40 E6**
Bhakra Dam **42 D10**
Bhamo **41 E11**
Bhandara **43 J11**
Bhanrer Ra. **43 H11**
Bharat = India ■ **43 J10**
Bharatpur **42 F10**
Bhatpara **41 F7**
Bhaunagar = Bhavnagar **43 J8**
Bhavnagar **43 J8**
Bhawanipatna **40 H4**
Bhilai = Bhilainagar-Durg **40 G3**
Bhilainagar-Durg **40 G3**
Bhilsa = Vidisha **43 H10**
Bhilwara **43 G9**
Bhima ➔ **43 L10**
Bhind **42 F11**
Bhiwandi **43 K8**
Bhiwani **42 E10**
Bhola **41 F8**
Bhopal **43 H10**
Bhubaneshwar **40 G5**
Bhuj **43 H6**
Bhumiphol Dam = Phumiphon, Khuan **38 A1**
Bhusawal **43 J9**
Bhutan ■ **41 D8**
Biafra, B. of = Bonny, Bight of **56 D1**
Biak **37 E5**
Biała Podlaska **17 B6**
Białogard **16 A2**
Białystok **17 B6**
Biaro **37 D3**
Biarritz **12 E3**
Bibai **32 B7**
Biberach **14 D5**
Bida **53 G7**
Bidar **43 L10**
Biddeford **77 C10**
Bié, Planalto de **58 A3**
Bielefeld **14 B5**
Biella **13 D8**
Bielsk Podlaski **17 B6**
Bielsko-Biała **16 D4**
Bien Hoa **38 B3**
Bienville, L. **71 D6**
Big Horn Mts. = Bighorn Mts. **73 D10**
Big Spring **80 C3**
Big Trout L. **71 D5**
Biğa **23 D6**
Bigadiç **23 E7**
Biggar **69 C9**
Biggenden **63 A5**
Bighorn ➔ **73 C10**
Bighorn Mts. **73 D10**
Bihać **20 B5**
Bihar **40 E5**
Bihar □ **40 E5**
Bihor, Munţii **17 E6**
Bijagós, Arquipélago dos **53 F2**
Bijapur *Chhattisgarh, India* **40 H3**
Bijapur *Karnataka, India* **43 L9**
Bijār **46 D6**
Bijeljina **20 B7**
Bijnor **42 E11**
Bikaner **42 E8**
Bikini Atoll **64 H11**
Bila Tserkva **17 D10**
Bilara **42 F8**
Bilaspur **40 F4**
Bilauk Taungdan **38 B1**
Bilbao **19 A4**
Bilbo = Bilbao **19 A4**
Bilecik **25 E3**
Bilhorod-Dnistrovskyy **25 D3**
Bilir **31 C11**
Billings **73 D9**
Billiton Is. = Belitung **39 E3**
Bilma **55 E1**
Biloxi **81 D9**
Biltine **55 F3**
Bima **37 F1**
Bina-Etawah **43 G11**
Binalbagan **36 B2**
Binalong **63 B4**
Bīnālūd, Kūh-e **44 B4**
Binatang = Bintangau **39 D4**
Binda **63 A4**
Bindle **63 A4**
Bindura **59 B6**
Bingara *N.S.W., Australia* **63 A5**
Bingara *Queens., Australia* **63 A3**
Binghamton **77 C8**
Bingöl **46 C5**
Binh Dinh = An Nhon **38 B3**
Binh Son **38 A3**
Binjai **39 D1**
Binnaway **63 B4**
Binongko **37 F2**
Bintan **39 D2**
Bintangau **39 D4**
Bintulu **39 D4**
Bintuni **37 E4**
Binzert = Bizerte **54 A1**
Bioko **53 H7**
Bir **43 K9**
Bir Atrun **55 E4**
Bīr Mogreīn **52 C3**
Birāk **54 C1**
Birchip **62 C3**
Birecik **46 C4**
Bireuen **38 C1**
Birlik **29 E8**
Birmingham *U.K.* **11 E6**
Birmingham *U.S.A.* **82 C4**
Birmitrapur **40 F5**
Birni Nkonni **53 F7**
Birnin Kebbi **53 F6**
Birr **11 E3**
Birrie ➔ **63 A4**
Birsk **29 D6**
Birur **43 N9**
Bisa **37 E3**
Biscay, B. of **12 D2**
Biscoe Bay **96 B17**
Biscoe Is. **96 A3**
Bishkek **29 E8**
Biskra **52 B7**
Bislig **36 C3**
Bismarck **74 B4**
Bismarck Arch. **64 K9**
Bissagos = Bijagós, Arquipélago dos **53 F2**
Bissau **53 F2**
Bistriţa **17 E7**
Bistriţa ➔ **17 E8**
Bitlis **46 C5**
Bitola **22 D3**
Bitolj = Bitola **22 D3**
Bitterfontein **58 E3**
Bitterroot Range **73 D6**
Biu **55 F1**
Biwa-Ko **33 F5**
Biysk **29 D9**
Bizerte **54 A1**
Bjelovar **20 B6**
Björneborg = Pori **8 C10**
Black Forest = Schwarzwald **14 D5**
Black Hills **74 D3**
Black Sea **25 E3**
Black Volta ➔ **53 G5**
Blackball **65 E4**
Blackburn **11 E5**
Blackpool **11 E5**
Blackwater ➔ **11 E2**
Blagodarnoye = Blagodarnyy **25 D5**
Blagodarnyy **25 D5**
Blagoevgrad **22 C4**
Blagoveshchensk **31 D10**
Blanc, Mont **13 D7**
Blanca, B. **95 D4**
Blanca Peak **79 B10**
Blanche, C. **62 B1**
Blanche, L. **62 A2**
Blanes **19 B7**
Blantyre **59 B6**
Blayney **63 B4**
Blednaya, Gora **28 B7**
Blenheim **65 D5**
Blida **52 A6**
Bligh Sound **65 F2**
Blodgett Iceberg Tongue **96 A13**
Bloemfontein **59 D5**
Bloemhof **59 D5**
Blois **12 C4**
Bloomington *Ill., U.S.A.* **75 E10**
Bloomington *Ind., U.S.A.* **76 E2**
Blue Mts. **72 D4**
Blue Nile = Nīl el Azraq ➔ **55 E5**
Blue Ridge **83 A7**
Bluefields **86 D3**
Bluff **65 G3**
Blumenau **94 B7**
Bo **53 G3**
Bo Hai **35 C6**
Boa Vista **90 C6**
Boatman **63 A4**
Bobadah **63 B4**
Bobbili **40 H4**
Bobo-Dioulasso **53 F5**

Bóbr → 16 B2
Bobraomby, Tanjon' i 59 A9
Bobruysk = Babruysk 17 B9
Boby, Pic 59 C9
Bôca do Acre 91 E5
Boca Raton 83 F7
Bocaranga 55 G2
Bochum 14 C4
Bodaybo 30 D9
Boden 8 B10
Bodensee 13 C8
Bodhan 43 K10
Bodø 8 B8
Bodrog → 16 D5
Bodrum 23 F6
Boende 56 E4
Bogalusa 81 D9
Bogan Gate 63 B4
Boggabilla 63 A5
Boggabri 63 B5
Bogo 36 B2
Bogong, Mt. 63 C4
Bogor 39 F3
Bogotá 90 C4
Bogotol 29 D9
Bogra 41 E7
Bohemian Forest = Böhmerwald 15 D7
Böhmerwald 15 D7
Bohol □ 36 C2
Bohol Sea 36 C2
Boise 72 E5
Boise City 80 A2
Bojador, C. 52 C3
Bojana → 22 D2
Bojnürd 44 B4
Bokhara → 63 A4
Bokoro 55 F2
Bolan Pass 42 E5
Bolbec 12 B4
Bole 34 B3
Bolekhiv 17 D6
Bolesławiec 16 C2
Bolgrad = Bolhrad 17 F9
Bolhrad 17 F9
Bolivia ■ 91 G6
Bollon 63 A4
Bolobo 56 E3
Bologna 20 B3
Bologoye 24 B3
Bolsena, L. di 20 C3
Bolshereche 29 D8
Bolshevik, Ostrov 30 B8
Bolshoy Atlym 28 C7
Bolshoy Begichev, Ostrov 30 B9
Bolshoy Kavkas = Caucasus Mountains 25 E5
Bolshoy Lyakhovskiy, Ostrov 31 B12
Bolton 11 E5
Bolu 25 E3
Bolvadin 46 C2
Bolzano 20 A3
Bom Jesus da Lapa 93 E5
Boma 56 F2
Bombala 63 C4
Bombay = Mumbai 43 K8
Bomboma 56 D3
Bomu → 56 D4
Bon, C. 21 F3
Bonaire 87 D6
Bonang 63 C4
Bonavista 71 E8
Bondo 56 D4
Bondoukou 53 G5
Bone, Teluk 37 E2
Bonerate 37 F2
Bonerate, Kepulauan 37 F2
Bong Son = Hoai Nhon 38 B3
Bongor 55 F2
Bonifacio 13 F8
Bonin Is. = Ogasawara Gunto 27 F16
Bonn 14 C4
Bonney, L. 62 C3
Bonny, Bight of 56 D1
Bonoi 37 E5
Bontang 39 D5
Bonthain 37 F1
Bonthe 53 G3
Bontoc 36 A2
Boolaboolka L. 62 B3
Booligal 63 B3
Boonah 63 A5
Boorindal 63 B4
Boorowa 63 B4
Boosaaso = Bosaso 49 E4
Boothia, Gulf of 70 B5
Boothia Pen. 68 A10
Booué 56 E2
Bor *Serbia* 22 B4
Bôr *Sudan* 55 G5
Borås 9 D8
Borāzjān 44 D2
Borba 90 D7
Borda, C. 62 C2
Bordeaux 12 D3
Borden I. 70 B2
Borden Pen. 70 B5
Bordertown 62 C3
Bordj Fly Ste. Marie 52 C5
Bordj-in-Eker 52 D7
Bordj Omar Driss 52 C7
Borger 80 B3
Borhoyn Tal 35 B6
Borisoglebsk 24 C5
Borisov = Barysaw 17 A9
Borja 90 D3
Borkou 55 E2
Borkum 14 B4
Borley, C. 96 A9
Borneo 39 D4
Bornholm 9 D9
Borongan 36 B3
Borovichi 24 B3
Borşa 17 E7
Borüjerd 46 D7
Boryslav 17 D6
Bosa 21 D2
Bosanska Gradiška 20 B6
Bosaso 49 E4
Boshrüyeh 44 C4
Bosna → 20 B7
Bosna i Hercegovina = Bosnia-Herzegovina ■ 20 B6
Bosnia-Herzegovina ■ 20 B6
Bosnik 37 E5
Bosobolo 56 D3
Bosporus = İstanbul Boğazı 22 D7
Bossangoa 55 G2
Bosso 55 F1
Bosten Hu 34 B3
Boston *U.K.* 11 E6
Boston *U.S.A.* 77 C10
Bothnia, G. of 8 C10
Bothwell 62 D4
Botletle → 58 C4
Botoşani 17 E8
Botswana ■ 58 C4
Botucatu 93 G4
Bouaké 53 G4
Bouar 56 C3
Bouârfa 52 B5
Bouca 55 G2
Bougainville I. 64 K10
Bougie = Bejaïa 52 A7
Bougouni 53 F4
Boulder 74 E2
Boulder Dam = Hoover Dam 78 B5
Boulogne-sur-Mer 12 A4
Bouna 53 G5
Boundiali 53 G4
Bourbonnais 13 C5
Bourem 53 E5
Bourg-en-Bresse 13 C6
Bourg-St-Maurice 13 D7
Bourgas = Burgas 22 C6
Bourges 12 C5
Bourgogne □ 13 C6
Bourke 63 B4
Bournemouth 11 F6
Bowen Mts. 63 C4
Bowman I. 96 A12
Bowmans 62 B2
Bowral 63 B5
Bowraville 63 B5
Boyne → 11 E3
Boyoma, Chutes 57 D5
Boz Dağları 23 E7
Bozburun 23 F7
Bozcaada 23 E6
Bozdoğan 23 F7
Bozeman 73 D8
Bozen = Bolzano 20 A3
Bozoum 55 G2
Bra 13 D7
Brač 20 C6
Bracciano, L. di 20 C4
Bräcke 8 C9
Bradenton 83 F6
Bradford 11 E6
Braga 18 B1
Bragança *Brazil* 92 C4
Bragança *Portugal* 18 B2
Brahestad = Raahe 8 C10
Brahmanbaria 41 F8
Brahmani → 40 G6
Brahmapur 40 H5
Brahmaputra → 41 F7
Braidwood 63 C4
Brăila 17 F8
Branco → 90 D6
Brandenburg = Neubrandenburg 15 B7
Brandenburg 15 B7
Brandenburg □ 15 B7
Brandon 69 D10
Braniewo 16 A4
Bransfield Str. 96 A4
Brantford 76 C5
Brasil = Brazil ■ 93 E4
Brasiléia 91 F5
Brasília 93 F4
Braşov 17 F7
Brassey, Banjaran 38 D5
Bratislava 16 D3
Bratsk 30 D8
Braunau 15 D7
Braunschweig 14 B6
Bravo del Norte, Rio = Grande, Rio → 84 B5
Brawley 78 D5
Bray 11 E3
Bray, Pays de 12 B4
Brazil ■ 93 E4
Brazos → 81 E6
Brazzaville 56 E3
Brčko 20 B7
Breaksea Sd. 65 F2
Bream B. 64 A6
Bream Hd. 64 A6
Brecon 11 F5
Breda 14 C3
Bredasdorp 58 E4
Bregenz 14 E5
Breiðafjörður 8 B1
Brejo 92 C5
Bremen 14 B5
Bremerhaven 14 B5
Bremerton 72 C2
Brennerpass 15 E6
Brescia 13 D9
Breslau = Wrocław 16 C3
Bressanone 20 A3
Brest *Belarus* 17 B6
Brest *France* 12 B1
Brest-Litovsk = Brest 17 B6
Bretagne □ 12 B2
Brett, C. 64 A6
Brewarrina 63 A4
Bria 55 G3
Briançon 13 D7
Bribie I. 63 A5
Bridgeport 77 D9
Bridgetown 87 D8
Bridgewater 71 E7
Bridgewater, C. 62 C3
Bridlington 11 D6
Bridport 62 D4
Brigham City 73 F7
Bright 63 C4
Brighton *Australia* 62 C2
Brighton *U.K.* 11 F6
Brindisi 21 D6
Brisbane 63 A5
Brisbane → 63 A5
Bristol *U.K.* 11 F5
Bristol *U.S.A.* 83 A6
Bristol B. 69 C3
Bristol Channel 11 F4
British Indian Ocean Terr. = Chagos Arch. ⊠ 26 J9

British Isles 11 D4
British Virgin Is. ⊠ 87 C7
Brittany = Bretagne □ 12 B2
Brive-la-Gaillarde 12 D4
Brixen = Bressanone 20 A3
Brlik = Birlik 29 E8
Brno 16 D3
Brock I. 70 B2
Brocken 14 C6
Brodeur Pen. 70 B5
Brodnica 16 B4
Brody 17 C7
Broken Hill 62 B3
Bronte Park 62 D4
Brooks Range 69 B5
Brooloo 63 A5
Broome 60 D3
Broughton Island = Qikiqtarjuaq 70 C7
Brown, Pt. 62 B1
Brownsville 81 G5
Brownwood 80 D4
Bruay-la-Buissière 13 A5
Bruce, Mt. 60 E2
Bruck an der Mur 15 E8
Bruges = Brugge 14 C2
Brugge 14 C2
Brumado 93 E5
Brunei = Bandar Seri Begawan 38 D5
Brunei ■ 38 D4
Brunner, L. 65 E4
Brunswick = Braunschweig 14 B6
Brunswick 83 D7
Brunswick, Pen. de 95 G2
Brussel 14 C3
Brussels = Brussel 14 C3
Bruthen 63 C4
Bruxelles = Brussel 14 C3
Bryan 81 D5
Bryan, Mt. 62 B2
Bryansk 24 C3
Bu Craa 52 C3
Buapinang 37 E2
Buayan 36 C3
Bucak 46 C2
Bucaramanga 90 B4
Buchach 17 D7
Buchanan 53 G3
Bucharest = Bucureşti 22 B6
Buckie 10 C5
Buckleboo 62 B2
Bucureşti 22 B6
Budalin 41 F10
Budapest 16 E4
Budd Coast 96 A12
Bude 11 F4
Budennovsk 25 E5
Budgewoi 63 B5
Budjala 56 D3
Buenaventura 90 C3
Buenos Aires 94 C5
Buenos Aires, L. 95 F2
Buffalo 77 C6
Bug = Buh ➔ 25 D3
Bug ➔ 16 B5
Buga 90 C3
Bugel, Tanjung 39 F4
Bugsuk I. 38 C5
Bugun Shara 35 B5
Buguruslan 29 D6
Buh ➔ 25 D3
Buir Nur 35 B6
Bujumbura 57 E5
Bukavu 57 E5
Bukhara = Bukhoro 29 F7
Bukhoro 29 F7
Bukittinggi 39 E2
Bukoba 57 E6
Bula 37 E4
Bulahdelah 63 B5
Bulan 36 B2
Bulandshahr 42 E10
Bulawayo 59 C5
Buldan 23 E7
Bulgan 35 B5
Bulgaria ■ 22 C5
Bulgroo 63 A3
Bulgunnia 62 B1
Buli, Teluk 37 D3
Buliluyan, C. 38 C5
Bulloo ➔ 63 A3
Bulloo Downs 62 A3
Bulloo L. 62 A3
Bulls 64 D6
Bulsar = Valsad 43 J8
Bulukumba 37 F2
Bulun 30 B10
Bumba 56 D4
Bumhpa Bum 41 D11
Bunbury 60 G2
Buncrana 11 D3
Bundaberg 63 A5
Bundi 43 G9
Bundoran 11 D2
Bungo-Suidō 33 G3
Bunia 57 D6
Bunji 42 B9
Buntok 39 E4
Bunyu 39 D5
Buol 37 D2
Buon Ma Thuot 38 B3
Buorkhaya, Mys 31 B11
Buqayq 47 F7
Bur Acaba 49 G3
Būr Safâga 54 C5
Būr Sa'īd 54 B5
Būr Sūdān 55 E6
Burao 49 F4
Buraydah 47 F5
Buraymī, Al Wāhāt al 44 E3
Burdur 46 C2
Burdwan = Barddhaman 40 F6
Burgas 22 C6
Burgos 18 A4
Burgundy = Bourgogne □ 13 C6
Burhaniye 23 E6
Burhanpur 43 J10
Burias I. 36 B2
Buriram 38 A2
Burkina Faso ■ 53 F5
Burlington *Iowa, U.S.A.* 75 E9
Burlington *N.C., U.S.A.* 83 A8
Burlington *Vt., U.S.A.* 77 B9
Burlyu-Tyube 29 E8
Burma ■ 41 G11
Burnie 62 D4
Burnley 11 E5
Burnside ➔ 68 B9
Burqān 47 E6
Burqin 34 B3
Burra 62 B2
Burren Junction 63 B4
Burrendong Dam 63 B4
Burrinjuck Res. 63 C4
Burruyacú 94 B4
Bursa 23 D7
Buru 37 E3
Burundi ■ 57 E6
Burutu 53 G7
Bury St. Edmunds 11 E7
Busan 35 C7
Büshehr 44 D2
Büshehr □ 44 D2
Bushire = Büshehr 44 D2
Businga 56 D4
Buşra ash Shām 46 D4
Busto Arsizio 13 D8
Busu Djanoa 56 D4
Busuanga I. 36 B1
Buta 57 D4
Butare 57 E5
Butaritari 64 J12
Butembo 57 D5
Butha Qi 35 B7
Buton 37 E2
Butte 73 C7
Butterworth = Gcuwa 59 E5
Butterworth 38 C2
Butuan 36 C3
Butung = Buton 37 E2
Buturlinovka 24 C5
Buur Hakaba = Bur Acaba 49 G3
Buxoro = Bukhoro 29 F7
Buxtehude 14 B5
Buy 24 B5
Buyant-Uhaa 35 B6
Büyük Menderes ➔ 23 F6
Büyükçekmece 22 D7
Buzău 17 F8
Buzău ➔ 17 F8
Buzen 33 G2
Buzi ➔ 59 B6
Buzuluk 29 D6
Byarezina ➔ 17 B10
Byaroza 17 B7
Bydgoszcz 16 B3
Byelorussia = Belarus ■ 24 C2
Bykhaw 17 B10
Bykhov = Bykhaw 17 B10
Bylot I. 70 B6
Byrd, C. 96 A3
Byrock 63 B4
Byron Bay 63 A5
Byrranga, Gory 30 B8
Byrranga Mts. = Byrranga, Gory 30 B8
Bytom 16 C4
Bytów 16 A3

C

Ca Mau 38 C3
Caála 58 A3
Cabanatuan 36 A2
Cabedelo 92 D7
Cabimas 90 A4
Cabinda 56 F2
Cabinda □ 56 F2
Cabinet Mts. 73 C6
Cabo Blanco 95 F3
Cabo Frio 93 G5
Cabo Pantoja 90 D3
Cabo Verde = Cape Verde Is. ■ 50 E1
Cabonga, Réservoir 71 E6
Caboolture 63 A5
Cabora Bassa Dam = Cahora Bassa, Reprêsa de 59 B6
Cabot Str. 71 E8
Cabra 18 D3
Cabrera 19 C7
Cabriel ➔ 19 C5
Čačak 22 C3
Cáceres *Brazil* 91 G7
Cáceres *Spain* 18 C2
Cachimbo, Serra do 93 D2
Cachoeira 93 E6
Cachoeira do Sul 94 C6
Cachoeiro de Itapemirim 93 G5
Cacólo 56 G3
Caconda 58 A3
Cadibarrawirracanna, L. 62 A2
Cadiz *Phil.* 36 B2
Cádiz *Spain* 18 D2
Cádiz, G. de 18 D2
Cadney Park 62 A1
Caen 12 B3
Caetité 93 E5
Cagayan de Oro 36 C2
Cágliari 21 E2
Cágliari, G. di 21 E2
Caguas 87 C6
Cahora Bassa, Reprêsa de 59 B6
Cahors 12 D4
Cahul 17 F9
Caicara 90 B5
Caicó 92 D6
Caird Coast 96 B5
Cairns 61 D8
Cairo = El Qāhira 54 B5
Cairo 81 A9
Cajamarca 91 E3
Cajàzeiras 92 D6
Calabar 53 H7
Calábria □ 21 E6
Calafate 95 G2
Calahorra 19 A5
Calais 12 A4
Calama *Brazil* 91 E6
Calama *Chile* 94 A3
Calamar 90 A4
Calamian Group 36 B1
Calamocha 19 B5
Calang 38 D1
Calapan 36 B2

Călăraşi 22 B6
Calatayud 19 B5
Calauag 36 B2
Calavite, C. 36 B2
Calbayog 36 B2
Calca 91 F4
Calcutta = Kolkata 41 F7
Caldas da Rainha 18 C1
Caldera 94 B2
Caldwell 72 E5
Caledon → 59 E5
Calgary 69 C8
Cali 90 C3
Calicut 43 P9
California □ 78 B3
California, G. de 84 B2
Calingasta 94 C3
Callabonna, L. 62 A3
Callao 91 F3
Caloundra 63 A5
Caltagirone 21 F5
Caltanissetta 21 F5
Calulo 56 G2
Calvi 13 E8
Calviá 19 C7
Calvinia 58 E3
Camabatela 56 F3
Camacupa 58 A3
Camagüey 86 B4
Camaná 91 G4
Camargue 13 E6
Camarones 95 E3
Cambay = Khambhat 43 H8
Cambay, G. of = Khambhat, G. of 43 J8
Cambodia ■ 38 B3
Cambrai 13 A5
Cambrian Mts. 11 E5
Cambridge *N.Z.* 64 B6
Cambridge *U.K.* 11 E7
Cambridge *U.S.A.* 77 C10
Cambridge Bay = Ikaluktutiak 68 B9
Cambundi-Catembo 56 G3
Camden *Ark., U.S.A.* 81 C7
Camden *N.J., U.S.A.* 77 E8
Cameroon ■ 56 C2
Cameroun, Mt. 53 H7
Cametá 92 C4
Caminha 18 B1
Camira Creek 63 A5
Camocim 92 C5
Campana, I. 95 F1
Campánia □ 21 D5
Campbell Town 62 D4
Campbellton 71 E7
Campbelltown 63 B5
Campbeltown 10 D4
Campeche 85 D6
Campeche, Golfo de 85 D6
Camperdown 62 C3
Câmpina 17 F7
Campina Grande 92 D6
Campinas 94 A7
Campo Grande 93 G3
Campo Maior 92 C5
Campobasso 20 D5
Campos 93 G5
Campos Belos 93 E4
Câmpulung 17 F7
Camrose 69 C8
Çan 23 D6
Can Tho 38 B3
Canada ■ 68 C8
Cañada de Gómez 94 C4
Çanakkale 23 D6
Çanakkale Boğazı 23 D6
Cananea 84 A2
Canarias, Is. 52 C2
Canary Is. = Canarias, Is. 52 C2
Canavieiras 93 F6
Canberra 63 C4
Candelo 63 C4
Candia = Iraklio 23 G5
Canea = Chania 23 G5
Canelones 94 C5
Cañete *Chile* 94 D2
Cañete *Peru* 91 F3
Cangas de Narcea 18 A2
Canguaretama 92 D6
Canguçu 94 C6
Caniapiscau → 70 D7
Caniapiscau, L. 71 D7
Canicattì 21 F4
Canigou, Mt. 12 E5
Canipaan 38 C5
Çankırı 25 E3
Cann River 63 C4
Cannanore 43 P9
Cannes 13 E7
Canoas 94 B6
Canora 69 C9
Canowindra 63 B4
Cantabria □ 18 A4
Cantabrian Mts. = Cantábrica, Cordillera 18 A3
Cantábrica, Cordillera 18 A3
Cantal, Plomb du 13 D5
Canterbury 11 F7
Canterbury Bight 65 F4
Canterbury Plains 65 E4
Canton = Guangzhou 35 D6
Canton 76 D5
Canudos 91 E7
Canutama 91 E6
Cap-Haïtien 87 C5
Capanaparo → 90 B5
Cape Barren I. 62 D4
Cape Breton I. 71 E7
Cape Coast 53 G5
Cape Dorset 70 C6
Cape Dyer 70 C7
Cape Girardeau 81 A9
Cape Lisburne = Wevok 69 B3
Cape Town 58 E3
Cape Verde Is. ■ 50 E1
Cape York Peninsula 61 C7
Capela 93 E6
Capim → 92 C4
Capraia 13 E8
Capri 21 D5
Caprivi Strip 58 B4
Captain's Flat 63 C4
Caquetá → 90 D5
Caracal 22 B5
Caracas 90 A5
Caracol 93 D5
Caradoc 62 B3
Carajás, Serra dos 92 D3
Caransebeş 17 F6
Caratasca, L. 86 C3
Caratinga 93 F5
Caraúbas 92 D6
Caravaca de la Cruz 19 C5
Caravelas 93 F6
Caraveli 91 G4
Carballo 18 A1
Carbonara, C. 21 E2
Carbondale 81 A9
Carbonear 71 E8
Carbónia 21 E2
Carcassonne 12 E5
Carcross 68 B6
Cardamon Hills 43 Q10
Cárdenas 86 B3
Cardiff 11 F5
Cardigan B. 11 E4
Cardston 69 D8
Carei 17 E6
Carhué 94 D4
Caria 23 F7
Cariacica 93 G5
Caribbean Sea 86 D5
Cariboo Mts. 69 C7
Carinda 63 B4
Carinhanha 93 E5
Carinthia = Kärnten □ 15 E7
Caripito 90 A6
Carlisle 11 D5
Carlow 11 E3
Carlsbad 80 C1
Carmacks 68 B6
Carmarthen 11 F4
Carmaux 12 D5
Carmen 90 B3
Carmen de Patagones 95 E4
Carmona 18 D3
Carnac 12 C2
Carnarvon *Australia* 60 E1
Carnarvon *S. Africa* 58 E4
Carnegie, L. 60 F3
Carnot 56 D3
Carnot, C. 62 B2
Carolina 92 D4
Caroline I. 65 K15
Caroline Is. 64 J10
Caroni → 90 B6
Caronía = Nébrodi, Monti 21 F5
Caroona 63 B5
Carpathians 16 D5
Carpaţii Meridionali 17 F7
Carpentaria, G. of 60 C6
Carpentras 13 D6
Carpi 20 B3
Carpolac = Morea 62 C3
Carrara 13 D9
Carrauntoohill 11 E2
Carrick-on-Suir 11 E3
Carrieton 62 B2
Carrizal Bajo 94 B2
Carson City 72 G4
Cartagena *Colombia* 90 A3
Cartagena *Spain* 19 D5
Cartago *Colombia* 90 C3
Cartago *Costa Rica* 86 E3
Carterton 65 D6
Carthage 81 A6
Cartwright 70 D8
Caruaru 92 D6
Carúpano 90 A6
Carvoeiro 90 D6
Carvoeiro, C. 18 C1
Casablanca 52 B4
Cascade Ra. 72 C3
Cascais 18 C1
Cascavel 94 A6
Cáscina 20 C3
Caserta 20 D5
Caseyr, Raas = Asir, Ras 49 E5
Casiguran 36 A2
Casilda 94 C4
Casino 63 A5
Casiquiare → 90 C5
Casma 91 E3
Caspe 19 B5
Casper 73 E10
Caspian Sea 29 E6
Castellammare di Stábia 21 D5
Castelló de la Plana 19 C5
Castelo Branco 18 C2
Castelsarrasin 12 D4
Castelvetrano 21 F4
Casterton 62 C3
Castilla-La Mancha □ 18 C4
Castilla y Leon □ 18 A3
Castlebar 11 E2
Castleblaney 11 D3
Castlemaine 63 C3
Castlereagh → 63 B4
Castres 12 E5
Castries 87 D7
Castro 95 E2
Castro Alves 93 E6
Castuera 18 C3
Cat I. 86 B4
Catalão 93 F4
Çatalca 22 D7
Catalonia = Cataluña □ 19 B6
Cataluña □ 19 B6
Catamarca 94 B3
Catanduanes □ 36 B2
Catanduva 93 G4
Catánia 21 F5
Catanzaro 21 E6
Catarman 36 B2
Cateel 36 C3
Catoche, C. 85 C7
Catrimani 90 C6
Catskill Mts. 77 C8
Cauca → 90 B4

Caucaia 92 C6
Caucasus Mountains 25 E5
Caungula 56 F3
Cauquenes 94 D2
Caura ➔ 90 B6
Cauvery ➔ 43 P11
Caux, Pays de 12 B4
Cavan 11 D3
Cavendish 62 C3
Caviana, I. 92 B3
Cavite 36 B2
Cawndilla L. 62 B3
Cawnpore = Kanpur 40 D3
Caxias 92 C5
Caxias do Sul 94 B6
Cayambe 90 C3
Cayenne 92 A3
Cayman Is. ⧄ 86 C3
Cazombo 58 A4
Ceanannus Mor 11 E3
Ceará = Fortaleza 92 C6
Ceará □ 92 D6
Ceará Mirim 92 D6
Cebollar 94 B3
Cebu 36 B2
Cecil Plains 63 A5
Cedar L. 69 C10
Cedar Rapids 75 E9
Cedro 92 D6
Ceduna 62 B1
Ceerigaabo = Erigavo 49 E4
Cefalù 21 E5
Cegléd 16 E4
Celaya 84 C4
Celebes = Sulawesi 37 E2
Celebes Sea 37 D2
Celje 20 A5
Celle 14 B6
Celtic Sea 11 F2
Central, Cordillera 90 C3
Central African Rep. ■ 56 C4
Central Makran Range 42 F4
Cephalonia = Kefalonia 23 E3
Ceram = Seram 37 E3
Ceram Sea = Seram Sea 37 E3
Ceres 94 B4
Cerignola 20 D5
Cerigo = Kythira 23 F4
Çerkeş 46 B3
Çerkezköy 22 D6
Cervera 19 B6
Cesena 20 B4
Ceská Rep. = Czech Rep. ■ 16 D2
České Budějovice 16 D2
Českomoravská Vrchovina 16 D2
Çeşme 23 E6
Cessnock 63 B5
Cetinje 22 C2
Cetraro 21 E5
Ceuta 18 E3
Cévennes 13 D5
Ceylon = Sri Lanka ■ 43 R12
Chachapoyas 91 E3
Chachran 42 E7
Chad ■ 55 E2
Chad, L. = Tchad, L. 55 F1
Chadileuvú ➔ 94 D3
Chadyr-Lunga = Ciadâr-Lunga 17 E9
Chagai Hills = Chāh Gay Hills 42 E3
Chagos Arch. ⧄ 26 J9
Chāh Bahar 45 E5
Chāh Gay Hills 42 E3
Chahār Borjak 42 D3
Chaibasa 40 F5
Chakhānsūr 42 D3
Chakradharpur 40 F5
Chakwal 42 C8
Chala 91 G4
Chalcis = Halkida 23 E4
Chalhuanca 91 F4
Chalisgaon 43 J9
Chalky Inlet 65 G2
Challapata 91 G5
Chalon-sur-Saône 13 C6
Châlons-en-Champagne 13 B6
Chaman 42 D5
Chamba 42 C10
Chambal ➔ 42 F11
Chambéry 13 D6
Chamical 94 C3
Chamonix-Mont Blanc 13 D7
Champagne 13 B6
Champaign 76 D1
Champlain, L. 77 B9
Chañaral 94 B2
Chandigarh 42 D10
Chandler 62 A1
Chandmani 34 B4
Chandpur 41 F8
Chandrapur 43 K11
Ch'ang Chiang = Chang Jiang ➔ 35 C7
Chang Jiang ➔ 35 C7
Changanacheri 43 Q10
Changane ➔ 59 C6
Changchiak'ou = Zhangjiakou 35 B6
Ch'angchou = Changzhou 35 C6
Changchun 35 B7
Changde 35 D6
Changhai = Shanghai 35 C7
Changhua 35 D7
Changsha 35 D6
Changzhi 35 C6
Changzhou 35 C6
Chania 23 G5
Chanion, Kolpos 23 G4
Channapatna 43 N10
Channel Is. 11 G5
Channel-Port aux Basques 71 E8
Chantada 18 A2
Chanthaburi 38 B2
Chantrey Inlet 68 B10
Chanute 81 A6
Chao Phraya ➔ 38 B2
Chaozhou 35 D6
Chapala, L. de 84 C4
Chapayevsk 24 C6
Chapleau 71 E5
Chapra = Chhapra 40 E5
Chara 31 D9
Charagua 91 G6
Charaña 91 G5
Chardara 29 E7
Chardzhou = Türkmenabat 29 F7
Charente ➔ 12 D3
Chari ➔ 55 F1
Chārīkār 42 B6
Chārjew = Türkmenabat 29 F7
Charleroi 14 C3
Charles, C. 77 F8
Charleston *S.C., U.S.A.* 83 C8
Charleston *W. Va., U.S.A.* 76 E5
Charlesville 56 F4
Charleville 63 A4
Charleville-Mézières 13 B6
Charlotte 83 B7
Charlotte Amalie 87 C6
Charlottesville 77 E6
Charlottetown 71 E7
Charlton 62 C3
Charlton I. 71 D6
Charolles 13 C6
Charters Towers 61 E8
Chartres 12 B4
Chascomús 94 D5
Châteaubriant 12 C3
Châteaulin 12 B1
Châteauroux 12 C4
Châtellerault 12 C4
Chatham = Chatham-Kent 71 E5
Chatham = Miramichi 71 E7
Chatham 11 F7
Chatham-Kent 71 E5
Chatrapur 40 H5
Châttagâm = Chittagong 41 F8
Chattahoochee ➔ 82 D5
Chattanooga 82 B5
Chaukan Pass 41 D11
Chaumont 13 B6
Chaves *Brazil* 92 C4
Chaves *Portugal* 18 B2
Cheb 16 C1
Cheboksary 24 B6
Chech, Erg 52 D5
Chechenia □ 25 E6
Checheno-Ingush Republic = Chechenia □ 25 E6
Chechnya = Chechenia □ 25 E6
Cheduba I. 41 H9
Cheepie 63 A4
Chegga 52 C4
Chegutu 59 B6
Chehalis 72 C2
Cheju-do = Jeju-do 35 C7
Chekiang = Zhejiang □ 35 D7
Cheleken = Hazar 29 F6
Chelforó 95 D3
Chelkar = Shalqar 29 E6
Chelkar Tengiz, Solonchak 29 E7
Chełm 17 C6
Chełmno 16 B4
Chelmsford 11 F7
Cheltenham 11 F5
Chelyabinsk 29 D7
Chelyuskin, C. = Chelyuskin, Mys 30 B8
Chelyuskin, Mys 30 B8
Chemba 59 B6
Chemnitz 15 C7
Chenab ➔ 42 D7
Chengchou = Zhengzhou 35 C6
Chengde 35 B6
Chengdu 35 C5
Chengjiang 34 D5
Ch'engtu = Chengdu 35 C5
Chennai 43 N12
Chenzhou 35 D6
Cheo Reo 38 B3
Cheom Ksan 38 B2
Cheongju 35 C7
Chepén 91 E3
Chepes 94 C3
Cher ➔ 12 C4
Cherbourg 12 B3
Cherdyn 28 C6
Cherepanovo 29 D9
Cherepovets 24 B4
Chergui, Chott ech 52 B6
Cherikov = Cherykaw 17 B10
Cherkasy 24 D3
Cherlak 29 D8
Chernaya 30 B6
Chernigov = Chernihiv 24 C3
Chernihiv 24 C3
Chernivtsi 17 D7
Chernobyl = Chornobyl 17 C10
Chernovtsy = Chernivtsi 17 D7
Cherrapunji 41 E8
Cherven 17 B9
Chervonohrad 17 C7
Cherykaw 17 B10
Chesapeake 77 F7
Chesapeake B. 77 E7
Cheshskaya Guba 28 C5
Chester *U.K.* 11 E5
Chester *U.S.A.* 77 E8
Chesterfield 11 E6
Chesterfield, Îs. 64 L10
Chesterfield Inlet 68 B10
Chesterton Ra. 63 A4
Chetumal 85 D7
Cheviot Hills 10 D5
Chew Bahir 55 H6
Cheyenne 74 E2

Cheyenne ➔ 74 C4
Chhapra 40 E5
Chhatarpur 43 G11
Chhindwara 43 H11
Chi ➔ 38 A2
Chiai 35 D7
Chiávari 13 D8
Chiavenna 13 C8
Chiba 33 F7
Chibemba 58 B2
Chibia 58 B2
Chibougamau 71 E6
Chicacole = Srikakulam 40 H4
Chicago 76 D2
Chichagof I. 69 C6
Chichester 11 F6
Ch'ich'ihaerh = Qiqihar 35 B7
Chickasha 80 B5
Chiclana de la Frontera 18 D2
Chiclayo 91 E3
Chico 72 G3
Chico ➔ *Chubut, Argentina* 95 E3
Chico ➔ *Santa Cruz, Argentina* 95 F3
Chicoutimi 71 E6
Chidambaram 43 P11
Chidley, C. 70 C7
Chiemsee 15 E7
Chiese ➔ 13 D9
Chieti 20 C5
Chiguana 91 H5
Chihli, G. of = Bo Hai 35 C6
Chihuahua 84 B3
Chiili = Shïeli 29 E7
Chik Bollapur 43 N10
Chikmagalur 43 N9
Chilapa 84 D5
Chilas 42 B9
Chilaw 43 R11
Childers 63 A5
Chile ■ 94 D2
Chilete 91 E3
Chililabombwe 59 A5
Chilin = Jilin 35 B7
Chilka L. 40 H5
Chillán 94 D2
Chiloé, I. de 95 E2
Chilpancingo 84 D5
Chilung 35 D7
Chilwa, L. 59 B7
Chimbay 29 E6
Chimborazo 90 D3
Chimbote 91 E3
Chimkent = Shymkent 29 E7
Chimoio 59 B6
Chin □ 41 F9
China ■ 35 C5
Chinan = Jinan 35 C6
Chinandega 85 E7
Chincha Alta 91 F3
Chinchilla 63 A5
Chinchou = Jinzhou 35 B7
Chinde 59 B7
Chindwin ➔ 41 G10
Chingola 59 A5
Ch'ingtao = Qingdao 35 C7
Chinguetti 52 D3
Chinhoyi 59 B6
Chiniot 42 D8
Chinnampo = Namp'o 35 C7
Chinon 12 C4
Chióggia 20 B4
Chíos = Hios 23 E6
Chipata 59 A6
Chiquián 91 F3
Chiquinquira 90 B4
Chirchiq 29 E7
Chiredzi 59 C6
Chirmiri 40 F4
Chisapani Garhi 40 D5
Chisasibi 71 D6
Chisimaio 49 H3
Chişinău 17 E9
Chistopol 24 B7
Chita 30 D9
Chitral 42 B7
Chitré 86 E3
Chittagong 41 F8
Chittagong □ 41 E8
Chittaurgarh 43 G9
Chittoor 43 N11
Chitungwiza 59 B6
Chiusi 20 C3
Chivasso 13 D7
Chivilcoy 94 B4
Chkalov = Orenburg 29 D6
Choele Choel 95 D3
Chojnice 16 B3
Cholet 12 C3
Choluteca 85 E7
Choma 59 B5
Chomolungma = Everest, Mt. 40 C6
Chomutov 16 C1
Chon Buri 38 B2
Chone 90 D3
Ch'öngjin 35 B7
Chongqing 35 D5
Chongui 30 F
Chonos, Arch. de los 95 F2
Chop 17 D6
Chora Sfakion 23 G5
Chornobyl 17 C10
Chortkiv 17 D7
Chorzów 16 C4
Chos-Malal 94 D2
Choszczno 16 B2
Chotila 43 H7
Choybalsan 35 B6
Christchurch 65 E5
Christmas I. = Kiritimati 65 J15
Chü = Shü 29 E8
Ch'uanchou = Quanzhou 35 D6
Chubut ➔ 95 E3
Chudskoye, Ozero 24 B2
Chūgoku-Sanchi 33 F3
Chula Vista 78 D4
Chulucanas 90 E2
Chulym ➔ 29 D9
Chumbicha 94 B3
Chumphon 38 B1
Chuna ➔ 30 D7
Chuncheon 35 C7
Chungking = Chongqing 35 D5
Chunya 57 F6
Chuquibamba 91 G4
Chuquicamata 94 A3
Chur 13 C8
Churachandpur 41 E9
Churchill 68 C10
Churchill ➔ *Man., Canada* 68 C10
Churchill ➔ *Nfld. & L., Canada* 71 D7
Churchill, C. 68 C10
Churchill Falls 71 D7
Churchill L. 69 C9
Churu 42 E9
Chushal 42 C11
Chusovoy 28 D6
Chuuk = Truk 64 J10
Chuvash Republic = Chuvashia □ 24 B6
Chuvashia □ 24 B6
Ciadâr-Lunga 17 E9
Cicero 76 D2
Ciechanów 16 B5
Ciego de Ávila 86 B4
Ciénaga 90 A4
Cienfuegos 86 B3
Cieza 19 C5
Cijara, Embalse de 18 C3
Cilician Gates P. 46 C3
Cill Chainnigh = Kilkenny 11 E3
Cimişlia 17 E9
Cimone, Mte. 20 B3
Cinca ➔ 19 B6
Cincar 20 C6
Cincinnati 76 E3
Çine 23 F7
Cinto, Mte. 13 E8
Circle 69 B5
Cirebon 39 F3
Citlaltépetl = Orizaba, Pico de 84 D5
Città del Vaticano = Vatican City ■ 20 D4
Città di Castello 20 C4
Ciudad Bolívar 90 B6
Ciudad de México 84 D5
Ciudad del Carmen 85 D6
Ciudad Delicias = Delicias 84 B3
Ciudad Guayana 90 B6
Ciudad Juárez 84 A3
Ciudad Madero 84 C5
Ciudad Mante 84 C5
Ciudad Obregón 84 B3
Ciudad Real 18 C4
Ciudad Rodrigo 18 B2
Ciudad Victoria 84 C5
Civitanova Marche 20 C4
Civitavécchia 20 C3
Cizre 46 C5
Clare 62 B2
Clarence ➔ *Australia* 63 A5
Clarence ➔ *N.Z.* 65 E5
Clarence, I. 95 G2
Clarence I. 96 A4
Clarie Coast 96 A13
Clarke I. 62 D4
Clarksdale 81 B8
Clarksville 82 A4
Claveria 36 A2
Clear, C. 11 F2
Clearwater 83 F6
Clearwater Mts. 73 C6
Clermont-Ferrand 13 D5
Cleveland *Australia* 63 A5
Cleveland *U.S.A.* 76 D5
Clifden 65 G2
Clifton 63 A5
Clifton Hills 62 A2
Clinton *N.Z.* 65 G3
Clinton *U.S.A.* 75 E9
Clinton Colden L. 68 B9
Clones 11 D3
Clonmel 11 E3
Clovis 80 B2
Cluj-Napoca 17 E6
Clunes 62 C3
Clutha ➔ 65 G3
Clyde 65 F3
Clyde ➔ 10 D4
Clyde, Firth of 10 D4
Clyde River 70 B7
Coari 90 D6
Coast Mts. 68 C7
Coast Ranges 72 F2
Coats I. 70 C5
Coats Land 96 B5
Coatzacoalcos 85 D6
Cobar 63 B4
Cóbh 11 F2
Cobham 62 B3
Cobija 91 F5
Cobram 63 C4
Coburg 15 C6
Cocanada = Kakinada 40 J4
Cochabamba 91 G5
Cochin 43 Q10
Cochin China = Nam-Phan 38 B3
Cochrane 71 E5
Cochrane, L. 95 F2
Cockburn 62 B3
Cockburn, Canal 95 G2
Coco ➔ 86 D3
Cocobeach 56 D1
Cod, C. 77 C10
Codajás 90 D6
Codó 92 C5
Coeur d'Alene 72 C5
Coffeyville 81 A6
Coffin B. 62 B2
Coffin Bay Peninsula 62 B2
Coffs Harbour 63 B5
Cognac 12 D3
Cohuna 63 C3
Coiba, I. de 86 E3
Coig ➔ 95 G3
Coihaique 95 F2
Coimbatore 43 P10
Coimbra *Brazil* 91 G7

Coimbra *Portugal* **18 B1**
Coín **18 D3**
Cojimies **90 C3**
Colac **62 C3**
Colatina **93 F5**
Colbeck, C. **96 B17**
Colbinabbin **63 C3**
Colchester **11 F7**
Colebrook **62 D4**
Coleman **69 D8**
Coleraine *Australia* **62 C3**
Coleraine *U.K.* **11 D3**
Coleridge, L. **65 E4**
Colesberg **59 E5**
Colhué Huapi, L. **95 F3**
Colima **84 D4**
Colinas **92 D5**
Coll **10 C3**
Collaguasi **91 H5**
Collarenebri **63 A4**
Collina, Passo di **20 B3**
Collingwood **64 D5**
Colmar **13 B7**
Colo ➔ **63 B5**
Cologne = Köln **14 C4**
Colomb-Béchar = Béchar **52 B5**
Colombia ■ **90 C4**
Colombo **43 R11**
Colón *Cuba* **86 B3**
Colón *Panama* **85 F9**
Colonia del Sacramento **94 C5**
Colonia Dora **94 B4**
Colonsay **10 C3**
Colorado □ **79 A10**
Colorado ➔ *Argentina* **95 D4**
Colorado ➔ *N. Amer.* **78 E5**
Colorado Plateau **79 B7**
Colorado Springs **74 F2**
Columbia *Mo., U.S.A.* **75 F8**
Columbia *S.C., U.S.A.* **83 B7**
Columbia *Tenn., U.S.A.* **82 B4**
Columbia ➔ **72 C1**
Columbia, C. **70 A7**
Columbia, District of □ **77 E7**
Columbia Basin **72 C4**
Columbretes, Is. **19 C6**
Columbus *Ga., U.S.A.* **82 C5**
Columbus *Miss., U.S.A.* **82 C3**
Columbus *Ohio, U.S.A.* **76 E4**
Colville ➔ **69 A4**
Colville, C. **64 B6**
Colwyn Bay **11 E5**
Comácchio **20 B4**
Comallo **95 E2**
Comilla **41 F8**
Comino, C. **21 D2**
Committee B. **70 C5**
Commonwealth B. **96 A14**
Commoron Cr. ➔ **63 A5**
Communism Pk. = imeni Ismail Samani, Pik **29 F8**
Como **13 D8**
Como, Lago di **13 D8**
Comodoro Rivadavia **95 F3**
Comorin, C. = Kanyakumari **43 Q10**
Comoros ■ **51 H8**
Compiègne **13 B5**
Compton Downs **63 B4**
Comrat **17 E9**
Conakry **53 G3**
Conara **62 D4**
Concarneau **12 C2**
Conceição da Barra **93 F6**
Concepción *Bolivia* **91 G6**
Concepción *Chile* **94 D2**
Concepción *Paraguay* **94 A5**
Concepción, L. **91 G6**
Concepción del Oro **84 C4**
Concepción del Uruguay **94 C5**
Conchos ➔ **84 B3**
Concord *N.C., U.S.A.* **83 B7**
Concord *N.H., U.S.A.* **77 C10**
Concordia *Argentina* **94 C5**
Concórdia *Brazil* **90 D5**
Condamine **63 A5**
Condeúba **93 E5**
Condobolin **63 B4**
Conegliano **20 B4**
Confuso ➔ **94 B5**
Congo (Brazzaville) = Congo ■ **56 E3**
Congo (Kinshasa) = Congo, Dem. Rep. of the ■ **56 E4**
Congo ■ **56 E3**
Congo ➔ **56 F2**
Congo, Dem. Rep. of the ■ **56 E4**
Conjeeveram = Kanchipuram **43 N11**
Conlea **63 B3**
Conn, L. **11 D2**
Connacht □ **11 E2**
Connecticut □ **77 D9**
Connecticut ➔ **77 D9**
Connemara **11 E2**
Conran, C. **63 C4**
Conselheiro Lafaiete **93 G5**
Constance = Konstanz **14 E5**
Constance, L. = Bodensee **13 C8**
Constanţa **22 B7**
Constantine **52 A7**
Constitución **94 D2**
Contai **40 G6**
Contamana **91 E4**
Contas ➔ **93 E6**
Conway, L. **62 A2**
Coober Pedy **62 A1**
Cooch Behar = Koch Bihar **41 D7**
Cook, B. **95 H2**
Cook, Mt. = Aoraki Mount Cook **65 E4**
Cook Inlet **69 C4**
Cook Is. **65 L14**
Cook Strait **65 D6**
Cooktown **61 D8**
Coolabah **63 B4**
Cooladdi **63 A4**
Coolah **63 B4**
Coolamon **63 B4**
Coolangatta **63 A5**
Cooma **63 C4**
Coonabarabran **63 B4**
Coonamble **63 B4**
Coondapoor **43 N9**
Coongie **62 A3**
Coongoola **63 A4**
Cooninnie, L. **62 A2**
Cooper Cr. ➔ *N. Terr., Australia* **60 C5**
Cooper Cr. ➔ *S. Austral., Australia* **62 A2**
Coorong, The **62 C2**
Cooroy **63 A5**
Cootamundra **63 B4**
Cooyar **63 A5**
Copenhagen = København **9 D8**
Copiapó **94 B2**
Copiapó ➔ **94 B2**
Coppermine = Kugluktuk **68 B8**
Coppermine ➔ **68 B8**
Coquimbo **94 C2**
Corabia **22 C5**
Coracora **91 G4**
Coral Harbour **70 C5**
Coral Sea **64 L10**
Corato **21 D6**
Corby **11 E6**
Corcaigh = Cork **11 F2**
Corcubión **18 A1**
Córdoba *Argentina* **94 C4**
Córdoba *Spain* **18 D3**
Córdoba, Sierra de **94 C4**
Cordova **69 B5**
Corfu = Kerkyra **23 E2**
Coria **18 C2**
Corigliano Cálabro **21 E6**
Corinna **62 D4**
Corinth = Korinthos **23 F4**
Corinth, G. of = Korinthiakos Kolpos **23 E4**
Corinto **93 F5**
Cork **11 F2**
Çorlu **22 D6**
Corner Brook **71 E8**
Corneşti **17 E9**
Cornwall **71 E6**
Cornwall I. **70 B4**
Cornwallis I. **70 B4**
Corny Pt. **62 B2**
Coro **90 A5**
Coroatá **92 C5**
Corocoro **91 G5**
Coroico **91 G5**
Coromandel **64 B6**
Corona **62 B3**
Coronation Gulf **68 B8**
Coronation I. **96 A4**
Coronel **94 D2**
Coronel Dorrego **94 D4**
Coronel Suárez **94 D4**
Corowa **63 C4**
Corpus Christi **80 F5**
Corrib, L. **11 E2**
Corrientes **94 B5**
Corrientes ➔ **90 D4**
Corrientes, C. *Colombia* **90 B3**
Corrientes, C. *Mexico* **84 C3**
Corriverton **90 B7**
Corse □ **13 E8**
Corse, C. **13 E8**
Corsica = Corse □ **13 E8**
Corsicana **81 C5**
Corte **13 E8**
Cortés, Mar de = California, G. de **84 B2**
Çorum **25 E3**
Corumbá **91 G7**
Corunna = A Coruña **18 A1**
Corvallis **72 D2**
Cosenza **21 E6**
Costa Blanca **19 C5**
Costa Brava **19 B7**
Costa del Sol **18 D3**
Costa Dorada **19 B6**
Costa Rica ■ **86 E3**
Cotabato **36 C2**
Cotagaita **91 H5**
Côte d'Azur **13 E7**
Côte-d'Ivoire = Ivory Coast ■ **53 G4**
Cotentin **12 B3**
Cotonou **53 G6**
Cotopaxi **90 D3**
Cotswold Hills **11 F5**
Cottbus **15 C8**
Couedic, C. du **62 C2**
Coulman I. **96 B15**
Council Bluffs **75 E7**
Courantyne ➔ **90 B7**
Courtrai = Kortrijk **14 C2**
Coventry **11 E6**
Covilhã **18 B2**
Covington **76 E3**
Cowal, L. **63 B4**
Cowangie **62 C3**
Cowarie **62 A2**
Cowell **62 B2**
Cowra **63 B4**
Coxim **93 F3**
Cox's Bazar **41 G8**
Cozumel, Isla **85 C7**
Craboon **63 B4**
Cracow = Kraków **16 C4**
Cracow **63 A5**
Cradock **59 E5**
Craigavon **11 D3**
Crailsheim **14 D6**
Craiova **22 B4**
Cranbrook *Australia* **62 D4**
Cranbrook *Canada* **69 D8**

Crateús 92 D5
Crato 92 D6
Crawley 11 F6
Crazy Mts. 73 C8
Crema 13 D8
Cremona 13 D9
Cres 20 B5
Crete = Kriti 23 G5
Créteil 12 B5
Creus, C. de 19 A7
Creuse ➔ 12 C4
Crewe 11 E5
Criciúma 94 B7
Crimean Pen. = Krymskyy Pivostriv 25 D3
Crişul Negru ➔ 16 E5
Crna ➔ 22 D3
Crna Gora = Montenegro ■ 22 C2
Crna Gora 22 C3
Crna Reka = Crna ➔ 22 D3
Croatia ■ 20 B6
Crocker, Banjaran 38 C5
Croker, C. 60 C5
Cromer 11 E7
Cromwell 65 F3
Cronulla 63 B5
Crookwell 63 B4
Cross Sound 69 C6
Crotone 21 E6
Crows Nest 63 A5
Crowsnest Pass 69 D8
Cruz Alta 94 B6
Cruz del Eje 94 C4
Cruzeiro do Sul 91 E4
Crystal Brook 62 B2
Csongrád 16 E5
Cuamba 59 A7
Cuando ➔ 58 B4
Cuango = Kwango ➔ 56 E3
Cuanza ➔ 56 F2
Cuba ■ 86 B4
Cubango ➔ 58 B4
Cúcuta 90 B4
Cuddalore 43 P11
Cuddapah 43 M11
Cuenca *Ecuador* 90 D3
Cuenca *Spain* 19 B4
Cuenca, Serranía de 19 C5
Cuernavaca 84 D5
Cuevas del Almanzora 19 D5
Cuevo 91 H6
Cuiabá 93 F2
Cuiabá ➔ 93 F2
Cuito ➔ 58 B4
Culcairn 63 C4
Culgoa ➔ 63 A4
Culiacán 84 C3
Culion 36 B2
Cullarin Ra. 63 B4
Cullera 19 C5
Culuene ➔ 93 E3
Culverden 65 E5
Cumaná 90 A6
Cumberland 77 E6
Cumberland Pen. 70 C7
Cumberland Plateau 76 F3
Cumberland Sd. 70 C7
Cumborah 63 A4
Cumbum 43 M11
Cummins 62 B2
Cumnock 63 B4
Cunene ➔ 58 B2
Cúneo 13 D7
Cunnamulla 63 A4
Cupica, G. de 90 B3
Curaçao 87 D6
Curaray ➔ 90 D4
Curiapo 90 B6
Curicó 94 C2
Curitiba 94 B7
Currabubula 63 B5
Currais Novos 92 D6
Curralinho 92 C4
Currie 62 C3
Curtea de Argeş 17 F7
Curtis Group 62 C4
Curuápanema ➔ 92 C2
Curuçá 92 C4
Curup 39 E2
Cururupu 92 C5
Curuzú Cuatiá 94 B5
Cusco = Cuzco 91 F4
Cuttaburra ➔ 63 A3
Cuttack 40 G5
Cuvier I. 64 B6
Cuxhaven 14 B5
Cuyo 36 B2
Cuzco *Bolivia* 91 H5
Cuzco *Peru* 91 F4
Cwmbran 11 F5
Cyclades 23 F5
Cygnet 62 D4
Cyprus ■ 46 D3
Cyrenaica 54 C3
Czech Rep. ■ 16 D2
Częstochowa 16 C4

D

Da Hinggan Ling 35 B7
Da Lat 38 B3
Da Nang 38 A3
Da Qaidam 34 C4
Daba Shan 35 C5
Dabo = Pasirkuning 39 E2
Dabola 53 F3
Dacca = Dhaka 41 F8
Dacca = Dhaka □ 41 E8
Dachau 15 D6
Dadanawa 90 C7
Dadra & Nagar Haveli □ 43 J8
Dadu 42 F5
Daegu 35 C7
Daejeon 35 C7
Daet 36 B2
Dagana 53 E2
Dagestan □ 25 E6
Daghestan Republic = Dagestan □ 25 E6
Dagö = Hiiumaa 24 B1
Dagupan 36 A2
Dahlak Kebir 49 D3
Dahod 43 H9
Daiō-Misaki 33 F5
Daisetsu-Zan 32 B8
Dakar 53 F2
Dakhla 52 D2
Dakhla, El Wâhât el- 54 C4
Dakhovskaya 25 E5
Đakovica 22 C3
Dalälven ➔ 9 C9
Dalaman ➔ 23 F7
Dalandzadgad 35 B5
Dalap-Uliga-Darrit = Majuro 64 J12
Dālbandīn 42 E4
Dalby 63 A5
Dali 34 D5
Dalian 35 C7
Daliang Shan 34 D5
Dallarnil 63 A5
Dallas 81 C5
Dalmacija 20 C6
Dalmatia = Dalmacija 20 C6
Dalnegorsk 32 A4
Daloa 53 G4
Dalton 82 B5
Dalton Iceberg Tongue 96 A13
Daly Waters 60 D5
Daman 43 J8
Damanhūr 54 B5
Damar 37 F3
Damaraland 58 C3
Damascus = Dimashq 46 D4
Damāvand 44 C3
Damāvand, Qolleh-ye 44 C3
Damba 56 F3
Dâmboviţa ➔ 22 B6
Dāmghān 44 B3
Damiel 18 C4
Damietta = Dumyāt 54 B5
Dammam = Ad Dammām 47 F7
Damoh 43 H11
Dampier 60 E2
Dampier, Selat 37 E4
Danbury 77 D9
Dandeldhura 40 C3
Dandeli 43 M9
Dandenong 63 C4
Dandong 35 B7
Danger Is. = Pukapuka 65 L14
Dangla Shan = Tanggula Shan 34 C4
Danilov 24 B5
Dankhar Gompa 42 C11
Danmark = Denmark ■ 9 D7
Dannemora 9 F11
Dannevirke 64 D7
Danube = Dunărea ➔ 17 F9
Danville 83 A8
Danzig = Gdańsk 16 A4
Dao = Tobias Fornier 36 B2
Dar el Beida = Casablanca 52 B4
Dar es Salaam 57 F7
Dārāb 44 D3
Daraj 54 B1
Darband 42 B8
Darbhanga 40 D5
Dardanelles = Çanakkale Boğazı 23 D6
Dârfûr 55 F3
Dargai 42 B7
Darganata 29 E7
Dargaville 64 A5
Darica 22 D7
Darién, G. del 90 B3
Darjeeling = Darjiling 40 D7
Darjiling 40 D7
Darling ➔ 62 B3
Darling Downs 63 A5
Darling Ra. 60 G2
Darlington 11 D6
Darłowo 16 A3
Darmstadt 14 D5
Darnah 54 B3
Darnley, C. 96 A10
Darnley B. 68 B7
Dart, C. 96 B18
Dartmoor 11 F5
Dartmouth 71 E7
Dartmouth Res. 63 A4
Darvaza 29 E6
Darvel, Teluk = Lahad Datu, Telok 36 D1
Darwha 43 J10
Darwin 60 C5
Daryoi Amu = Amudarya ➔ 29 E6
Dās 44 E3
Dashen, Ras 57 B7
Dashoguz 29 E6
Dasht ➔ 42 G2
Datça 23 F6
Datia 43 G11
Datong 35 B6
Datu, Tanjung 39 D3
Datu Piang 36 C2
Datuk, Tanjong = Datu, Tanjung 39 D3
Daugava ➔ 24 B1
Daugavpils 24 B2
Daulpur 42 F10
Dauphin 69 C9
Dauphiné 13 D6
Davangere 43 M9
Davao 36 C3
Davao G. 36 C3
Dāvar Panāh = Sarāvān 45 E5
Davenport 75 E9
David 86 E3
David Gorodok = Davyd Haradok 17 B8
Davis Sea 96 A11
Davis Str. 6 C14
Davos 13 C8
Davyd Haradok 17 B8
Dawei = Tavoy 38 B1
Dawna Ra. 41 J12
Dawson 68 B6
Dawson, I. 95 G2
Dax 12 E3

Daxian **35 C5**
Daxue Shan **34 C5**
Daylesford **62 C3**
Dayr az Zawr **46 D5**
Dayton **76 E3**
Daytona Beach **83 E7**
De Aar **58 E4**
Dead Sea **47 E3**
Deakin **60 G4**
Deal I. **62 C4**
Deán Funes **94 C4**
Death Valley **78 B4**
Debar **22 D3**
Debre Markos **55 F6**
Debrecen **16 E5**
Decatur *Ala., U.S.A.* **82 B4**
Decatur *Ill., U.S.A.* **75 F10**
Deccan **43 L11**
Děčín **16 C2**
Dedéagach = Alexandroupoli **22 D5**
Dee ➔ **10 C5**
Deepwater **63 A5**
Deer Lake **71 E8**
Deggendorf **15 D7**
Deh Bīd **44 D3**
Dehi Titan **42 C3**
Dehibat **54 B1**
Dehkareqan **46 C6**
Dehra Dun **42 D11**
Dej **17 E6**
Dekese **56 E4**
Delano **78 C3**
Delaware □ **77 E8**
Delegate **63 C4**
Delgado, C. **57 G8**
Delgo **55 D5**
Delhi **42 E10**
Delice ➔ **25 F3**
Delicias **84 B3**
Déline **68 B7**
Delmenhorst **14 B5**
Deloraine **62 D4**
Delungra **63 A5**
Delvinë **23 E3**
Demanda, Sierra de la **18 A4**
Demavend = Damāvand, Qolleh-ye **44 C3**
Dembidolo **55 G5**
Demini ➔ **90 D6**
Demirci **23 E7**
Demirköy **22 D6**
Dempo **39 E2**
Den Bosch = 's-Hertogenbosch **14 C3**
Den Haag = 's-Gravenhage **14 B3**
Den Helder **14 B3**
Denali = McKinley, Mt. **69 B4**
Denau **29 F7**
Dendang **39 E3**
Denia **19 C6**
Denial B. **62 B1**
Deniliquin **63 C3**
Denizli **46 C2**
Denman Glacier **96 A11**
Denmark ■ **9 D7**
Denmark Str. **66 C17**
Denpasar **39 F5**
Denton **80 C5**
D'Entrecasteaux Is. **61 B9**
Denver **74 F2**
Deoghar **40 E6**
Deolali **43 K8**
Deoria **40 D4**
Deosai Mts. **42 B9**
Dera Ghazi Khan **42 D7**
Dera Ismail Khan **42 D7**
Derbent **25 E6**
Derby *Australia* **60 D3**
Derby *U.K.* **11 E6**
Derg, L. **11 E2**
Dergaon **41 D9**
Derry = Londonderry **11 D3**
Des Moines **75 E8**
Des Moines ➔ **75 E9**
Desaguadero ➔ **91 G5**
Dese **49 E2**
Desna ➔ **17 C10**
Desolación, I. **95 G2**
Despeñaperros, Paso **18 C4**
Dessau **15 C7**
Dessye = Dese **49 E2**
D'Estrees B. **62 C2**
Detmold **14 C5**
Detroit **76 C4**
Deutsche Bucht **14 A5**
Deutschland = Germany ■ **14 C6**
Deva **17 F6**
Devakottai **43 Q11**
Deventer **14 B4**
Devon I. **70 B5**
Devonport *Australia* **62 D4**
Devonport *N.Z.* **64 B6**
Dewas **43 H10**
Deyhūk **44 C4**
Deyyer **44 E2**
Dezfūl **47 D7**
Dezhneva, Mys **31 C16**
Dhafra **44 F3**
Dhahira **44 F4**
Dhahran = Aẓ Ẓahrān **47 F7**
Dhaka **41 F8**
Dhaka □ **41 E8**
Dhamtari **40 G3**
Dhanbad **40 F6**
Dhangarhi **40 C3**
Dhankuta **40 D6**
Dhar **43 H9**
Dharmapuri **43 N11**
Dhaulagiri **40 C4**
Dhenkanal **40 G5**
Dhodhekánisos = Dodecanese **23 F6**
Dhrol **43 H7**
Dhubaibah **44 F3**
Dhuburi **41 D7**
Dhule **43 J9**
Dhut ➔ **49 E5**
Diafarabé **53 F5**
Diamantina **93 F5**
Diamantina ➔ **62 A2**
Diamantino **93 E2**
Diamond Harbour **40 F7**
Dibaya-Lubue **56 E3**
Dibbi **49 G3**
Dibrugarh **41 D10**
Didiéni **53 F4**
Diefenbaker, L. **69 C9**
Diego Suarez = Antsiranana **59 A9**
Dieppe **12 B4**
Digby **71 E7**
Dighinala **41 F9**
Digne-les-Bains **13 D7**
Digos **36 C3**
Digul ➔ **37 F5**
Dihang = Brahmaputra ➔ **41 F7**
Dijlah, Nahr ➔ **47 E6**
Dijon **13 C6**
Dikimdya **31 D10**
Dikson **28 B9**
Dikti Oros **23 G5**
Dili **37 F3**
Dilli = Delhi **42 E10**
Dillingham **69 C4**
Dilolo **56 G4**
Dilston **62 D4**
Dimashq **46 D4**
Dimboola **62 C3**
Dîmbovița = Dâmbovița ➔ **22 B6**
Dimitrovgrad *Bulgaria* **22 C5**
Dimitrovgrad *Russia* **24 C6**
Dimitrovo = Pernik **22 C4**
Dinagat **36 B3**
Dinajpur **41 E7**
Dinan **12 B2**
Dinant **14 C3**
Dinar **46 C2**
Dīnār, Küh-e **44 D2**
Dinara Planina **20 B6**
Dinard **12 B2**
Dinaric Alps = Dinara Planina **20 B6**
Dindigul **43 P11**
Dingle **11 E1**
Dingwall **10 C4**
Dinosaur ⌂ **73 F9**
Dipolog **36 C2**
Dir **42 B7**
Dire Dawa **49 F3**
Dirfis Oros **23 E4**
Dirranbandi **63 A4**
Disa **43 G8**
Disappointment, L. **60 E3**
Disaster B. **63 C4**
Discovery B. **62 C3**
Disteghil Sar **42 A9**
District of Columbia □ **77 E7**
Distrito Federal □ **93 F4**
Diu **43 J7**
Divinópolis **93 G5**
Divnoye **25 D5**
Diyarbakır **46 C5**
Diz Chah **44 C3**
Djakarta = Jakarta **39 F3**
Djambala **56 E2**
Djanet **52 D7**
Djawa = Jawa **39 F3**
Djelfa **52 B6**
Djerba, Ī. de **54 B1**
Djerid, Chott **52 B7**
Djibouti **49 E3**
Djibouti ■ **49 E3**
Djolu **56 D4**
Djoum **56 D2**
Djourab, Erg du **55 E2**
Dmitriya Lapteva, Proliv **31 B12**
Dnepr = Dnipro ➔ **25 D3**
Dneprodzerzhinsk = Dniprodzerzhynsk **25 D3**
Dnepropetrovsk = Dnipropetrovsk **25 D4**
Dnestr = Dnister ➔ **17 E10**
Dnieper = Dnipro ➔ **25 D3**
Dniester = Dnister ➔ **17 E10**
Dnipro ➔ **25 D3**
Dniprodzerzhynsk **25 D3**
Dnipropetrovsk **25 D4**
Dnister ➔ **17 E10**
Dnistrovskyy Lyman **17 E10**
Dnyapro = Dnipro ➔ **25 D3**
Doba **55 G2**
Doberai, Jazirah **37 E4**
Dobo **37 F4**
Doboj **20 B7**
Dobrich **22 C6**
Dobruja **22 B7**
Dobrush **17 B10**
Dodecanese **23 F6**
Dodekanisa = Dodecanese **23 F6**
Dodge City **80 A3**
Dodoma **57 F7**
Doha = Ad Dawḥah **44 E2**
Dohazari **41 F9**
Doi **37 D3**
Dois Irmãos, Sa. **93 D5**
Dolak, Pulau **37 F5**
Dolbeau-Mistassini **71 E6**
Dole **13 C6**
Dolomites = Dolomiti **20 A3**
Dolomiti **20 A3**
Dolores **94 D5**
Dolphin, C. **95 G5**
Dolphin and Union Str. **68 B8**
Dombarovskiy **29 D6**
Dominica ■ **87 C7**
Dominican Rep. ■ **87 C5**
Domodóssola **13 C8**
Domville, Mt. **63 A5**
Don ➔ *Russia* **25 D4**
Don ➔ *U.K.* **10 C5**
Don Benito **18 C3**
Donald **62 C3**
Donau = Dunărea ➔ **17 F9**
Donauwörth **14 D6**
Doncaster **11 E6**
Dondo, Teluk **37 D2**

Donegal 11 D2
Donets ➔ 25 D5
Donetsk 25 D4
Donggala 37 E1
Dongola 55 E5
Dongting Hu 35 D6
Donington, C. 62 B2
Donnelly's Crossing 64 A5
Donostia = Donostia-San Sebastián 19 A5
Donostia-San Sebastián 19 A5
Dora Báltea ➔ 13 D8
Dorchester, C. 70 C6
Dordogne ➔ 12 D3
Dordrecht 14 C3
Dori 53 F5
Dornbirn 14 E5
Doro, Kavo 23 E5
Dorohoi 17 E8
Döröö Nuur 34 B4
Dorrigo 63 B5
Dortmund 14 C4
Dos Bahías, C. 95 E3
Dos Hermanas 18 D3
Dosso 53 F6
Dothan 82 D5
Douai 13 A5
Douala 53 H7
Douarnenez 12 B1
Double Island Pt. 63 A5
Doubs ➔ 13 C6
Doubtful Sd. 65 F2
Doubtless B. 64 A5
Douglas *I. of Man* 11 D4
Douglas *U.S.A.* 79 E8
Dourados 94 A6
Douro ➔ 18 B1
Dover *Australia* 62 D4
Dover *U.K.* 11 F7
Dover, Str. of 11 F7
Dovrefjell 8 C7
Dowlat Yār 45 C6
Dowlatābād 44 D4
Drăgășani 22 B5
Dragichyn 17 B7
Dragoman, Prokhod 22 C4
Draguignan 13 E7
Drake 63 A5
Drakensberg 59 E5
Drama 22 D5
Drammen 9 D8
Drau = Drava ➔ 20 B7
Drava ➔ 20 B7
Dresden 15 C7
Dreux 12 B4
Drin ➔ 22 C2
Drina ➔ 20 B7
Drobeta-Turnu Severin 22 B4
Drochia 17 D8
Drogheda 11 E3
Drogichin = Dragichyn 17 B7
Drogobych = Drohobych 17 D6
Drohobych 17 D6
Droichead Atha = Drogheda 11 E3
Dromedary, C. 63 C5
Dronning Maud Land 96 B7
Druk Yul = Bhutan ■ 41 D8
Drumheller 69 C8
Drummond Pt. 62 B2
Drut ➔ 17 B10
Drygalski I. 96 A11
Ḍubā 47 F3
Dubai = Dubayy 44 E3
Dubăsari 17 E9
Dubăsari Vdkhr. 17 E9
Dubawnt ➔ 68 B9
Dubawnt L. 68 B9
Dubayy 44 E3
Dubbo 63 B4
Dublin *Ireland* 11 E3
Dublin *U.S.A.* 83 C6
Dubno 17 C7
Dubossary = Dubăsari 17 E9
Dubossary Vdkhr. = Dubăsari Vdkhr. 17 E9
Dubovka 24 D5
Dubréka 53 G3
Dubrovitsa = Dubrovytsya 17 C8
Dubrovnik 20 C7
Dubrovytsya 17 C8
Dudhi 40 E4
Dudinka 30 C6
Duero = Douro ➔ 18 B1
Dūghī Kalā 42 C3
Dugi Otok 20 B5
Duisburg 14 C4
Dujiangyan 34 C5
Dukhān 44 E2
Duki 42 D6
Dulce ➔ 94 C4
Dulit, Banjaran 39 D4
Duluth 75 B8
Dum Duma 41 D10
Dumaguete 36 C2
Dumai 39 D2
Dumaran 36 B1
Dumfries 11 D5
Dumyāt 54 B5
Dún Dealgan = Dundalk 11 D3
Dún Laoghaire 11 E3
Duna = Dunărea ➔ 17 F9
Dunaj = Dunărea ➔ 17 F9
Dunakeszi 16 E4
Dunărea ➔ 17 F9
Dunaújváros 16 E4
Dunav = Dunărea ➔ 17 F9
Dunback 65 F4
Dunbar 10 D5
Duncan 80 B5
Dundalk 11 D3
Dundee 10 C5
Dundoo 63 A3
Dunedin 65 F4
Dunfermline 10 C5
Dungarvan 11 E3
Dungog 63 B5
Dungu 57 D5
Dunhuang 34 B4
Dunkerque 12 A5
Dunkirk = Dunkerque 12 A5
Dúnleary = Dún Laoghaire 11 E3
Dunolly 62 C3
Dunstan Mts. 65 F3
Durance ➔ 13 E6
Durango *Mexico* 84 C4
Durango *Spain* 19 A4
Durazno 94 C5
Durazzo = Durrës 22 D2
Durban 59 D6
Düren 14 C4
Durg = Bhilainagar-Durg 40 G3
Durgapur 40 F6
Durham *U.K.* 11 D6
Durham *U.S.A.* 83 B8
Durham Downs 63 A4
Durmitor 22 C2
Durrës 22 D2
Dursunbey 23 E7
D'Urville, Tanjung 37 E5
D'Urville I. 65 D5
Dushak 29 F7
Dushanbe 29 F7
Dusky Sd. 65 F2
Düsseldorf 14 C4
Dutch Harbor 69 C3
Duyun 35 D5
Dvina, Severnaya ➔ 28 C5
Dvinsk = Daugavpils 24 B2
Dwarka 43 H6
Dyatlovo = Dzyatlava 17 B7
Dyer, C. 70 C7
Dyer Plateau 96 B3
Dyersburg 81 A9
Dymer 17 C10
Dynevor Downs 63 A3
Dzerzhinsk 24 B5
Dzhambul = Taraz 29 E8
Dzhankoy 25 D3
Dzhardzhan 30 C10
Dzhezkazgan = Zhezqazghan 29 E7
Dzhizak = Jizzakh 29 E7
Działdowo 16 B5
Dzierżoniów 16 C3
Dzungaria = Junggar Pendi 34 B3
Dzungarian Basin = Junggar Pendi 34 B3
Dzungarian Gate = Alataw Shankou 34 B3
Dzüünmod 35 B5
Dzyarzhynsk 17 B8
Dzyatlava 17 B7

E

Earnslaw, Mt. 65 F3
East Bengal 41 E7
East Beskids = Vychodné Beskydy 17 D5
East C. = Dezhneva, Mys 31 C16
East C. 64 B8
East China Sea 35 C7
East Falkland 95 G5
East Kilbride 10 D4
East London 59 E5
East Main = Eastmain 71 D6
East Orange 77 D8
East St. Louis 75 F9
East Sea = Japan, Sea of 32 D4
East Timor ■ 37 F3
East Toorale 63 B4
Eastbourne *N.Z.* 65 D6
Eastbourne *U.K.* 11 F7
Eastern Ghats 43 N11
Eastmain 71 D6
Eastmain ➔ 71 D6
Eau Claire 75 C9
Eau Claire, L. à l' 71 D6
Eberswalde-Finow 15 B7
Ebetsu 32 B7
Ebolowa 56 D2
Ebro ➔ 19 B6
Eceabat 23 D6
Ech Chéliff 52 A6
Echo Bay 68 B8
Echuca 63 C3
Ecija 18 D3
Eclipse Sd. 70 B6
Ecuador ■ 90 D3
Ed Dar el Beida = Casablanca 52 B4
Ed Debba 55 E5
Ed Dueim 55 F5
Eddystone Pt. 62 D4
Édéa 53 H8
Eden 63 C4
Eder ➔ 14 C5
Edessa 23 D4
Édhessa = Edessa 23 D4
Edievale 65 F3
Edinburg 80 F4
Edinburgh 10 D5
Edineţ 17 D8
Edirne 22 D6
Edithburgh 62 C2
Edmonton 69 C8
Edmundston 71 E7
Edremit 23 E6
Edremit Körfezi 23 E6
Edson 69 C8
Edward ➔ 62 C3
Edward, L. 57 E5
Edward VII Land 96 C17
Edwards Plateau 80 D3
Eesti = Estonia ■ 24 B2
Égadi, Isole 21 F4
Eger = Cheb 16 C1
Eger 16 E5
Egio 23 E4
Eglinton I. 70 B2
Egmont, C. 64 C5
Egmont, Mt. = Taranaki, Mt. 64 C6
Egmont △ 64 C6
Eğridir 46 C2
Eğridir Gölü 46 C2
Egypt ■ 54 C5
Eibar 19 A4

Eidsvold 63 A5
Eifel 14 C4
Eigg 10 C3
Eil 49 F4
Eildon, L. 63 C4
Eindhoven 14 C3
Eire = Ireland ■ 11 E3
Eirunepé 91 E5
Eisenach 14 C6
Eisenerz 15 E8
Eivissa 19 C6
Ekaterinburg = Yekaterinburg 29 D7
Eketahuna 64 D6
Ekibastuz 29 D8
El Aaiún 52 C3
El 'Alamein 54 B4
El Asnam = Ech Chéliff 52 A6
El Bayadh 52 B6
El Centro 78 D5
El Cerro 91 G6
El Cuy 95 D3
El Dere 49 G4
El Diviso 90 C3
El Djouf 53 D4
El Dorado *Ark., U.S.A.* 81 C7
El Dorado *Kans., U.S.A.* 80 A5
El Dorado *Venezuela* 90 B6
El Escorial 18 B3
El Faiyûm 54 C5
El Fâsher 55 F4
El Ferrol = Ferrol 18 A1
El Fuerte 84 B3
El Gal 49 E5
El Geneina = Al Junaynah 55 F3
El Gîza 54 C5
El Homeur 52 C6
El Iskandarîya 54 B4
El Jadida 52 B4
El Khârga 54 C5
El Khartûm 55 E5
El Lucero 84 A3
El Maestrazgo 19 B5
El Mahalla el Kubra 54 B5
El Mansûra 54 B5
El Minyâ 54 C5
El Obeid 55 F5
El Odaiya 55 F4
El Oued 52 B7
El Paso 79 E9
El Prat de Llobregat 19 B7
El Puerto de Santa María 18 D2
El Qâhira 54 B5
El Reno 80 B5
El Salvador ■ 85 E7
El Suweis 54 C5
El Tigre 90 B6
El Turbio 95 G2
El Uqsur 54 C5
El Vigía 90 B4
El Wak 57 D8
El Wuz 55 E5
Elat 47 E3
Elâzığ 46 C4
Elba 20 C3
Elbasan 22 D3
Elbe ➔ 14 B5
Elbert, Mt. 79 A9
Elbeuf 12 B4
Elbing = Elbląg 16 A4
Elbląg 16 A4
Elbrus 25 E5
Elburz Mts. = Alborz, Reshteh-ye Kūhhā-ye 44 B3
Elche 19 C5
Elda 19 C5
Elde ➔ 15 B6
Eldoret 57 D7
Elefantes ➔ 59 C6
Elektrostal 24 B4
Elephant I. 96 A4
Eleuthera 86 A4
Elgin *U.K.* 10 C5
Elgin *U.S.A.* 76 C1
Elgon, Mt. 57 D6
Eliase 37 F4
Elista 25 D5
Elizabeth *Australia* 62 B2
Elizabeth *U.S.A.* 77 D8
Elizabeth City 83 A9
Elizabethton 83 A6
Elk 16 B6
Elkhart 76 D3
Elkhovo 22 C6
Elko 72 F6
Ellas = Greece ■ 23 E4
Ellef Ringnes I. 70 B3
Ellery, Mt. 63 C4
Ellesmere, L. 65 G5
Ellesmere I. 70 B6
Ellice Is. = Tuvalu ■ 64 K12
Elliot Lake 71 E5
Elliston 62 B1
Ellore = Eluru 40 J3
Ellsworth Land 96 B2
Ellsworth Mts. 96 B2
Elmore 63 C3
Elmshorn 14 B5
Eltham 64 C6
Eluru 40 J3
Elvas 18 C2
Elx = Elche 19 C5
Ely 11 E7
eMalahleni 59 D5
Emāmrūd 44 B3
Embarcación 94 A4
Embetsu 32 A7
Embi 29 E6
Embi ➔ 29 E6
Embrun 13 D7
Emden 14 B4
Emet 23 E7
Emi Koussi 55 E2
Emine, Nos 22 C6
Emissi, Tarso 54 D2
Emmen 14 B4
Empalme 84 B2
Empangeni 59 D6
Empedrado 94 B5
Empty Quarter = Rub' al Khālī 48 D4
Ems ➔ 14 B4
En Nahud 55 F4
Enare = Inarijärvi 8 B11
Enarotali 37 E5
Encanto, C. 36 A2
Encarnación 94 B5
Encounter B. 62 C2
Ende 37 F2
Enderby Land 96 A9
Enewetak Atoll 64 H11
Enez 23 D6
Engaño, C. 36 A2
Engaru 32 A8
Engels 24 C6
Enggano 39 F2
England □ 11 E6
Englewood 74 F2
English Bazar = Ingraj Bazar 40 E7
English Channel 11 F5
Enid 80 A5
Enna 21 F5
Ennedi 55 E3
Enngonia 63 A4
Ennis 11 E2
Enniskillen 11 D3
Enns ➔ 15 D8
Enschede 14 B4
Ensenada 84 A1
Entebbe 57 D6
Entre Ríos □ 94 C5
Entroncamento 18 C1
Enugu 53 G7
Eólie, Îs. 21 E5
Épernay 13 B5
Ephesus 23 F6
Épinal 13 B7
Equatorial Guinea ■ 56 D1
Er Rachidia 52 B5
Er Rahad 55 F5
Er Rif 52 A5
Erāwadī Myit = Irrawaddy ➔ 41 K10
Erāwadī Myitwanya = Irrawaddy, Mouths of the 41 K10
Erbil = Arbil 46 C6
Ercıyaş Dağı 46 C3
Érd 16 E4
Erdek 23 D6
Erebus, Mt. 96 B15
Erechim 94 B6
Ereğli *Konya, Turkey* 46 C3
Ereğli *Zonguldak, Turkey* 25 E3
Eresma ➔ 18 B3
Erfurt 15 C6
Ergani 46 C4
Érice 21 E4
Erie 77 C5
Erie, L. 76 C5
Erigavo 49 E4
Erimanthos 23 F3
Erimo-misaki 32 C8
Eritrea ■ 49 E2
Erlangen 15 D6
Ermenek 46 C3
Erne, Lower L. 11 D3
Erode 43 P10
Eromanga 63 A3
Erramala Hills 43 M11
Ertis = Irtysh ➔ 28 C7
Erzgebirge 15 C7
Erzincan 25 F4
Erzurum 25 F5
Es Sahrā' Esh Sharqīya 54 C5
Es Sīnā' 54 C5
Esan-Misaki 32 C7
Esashi *Hokkaidō, Japan* 32 A8
Esashi *Hokkaidō, Japan* 32 C7
Esbjerg 9 D7
Esbo = Espoo 9 C10
Esch-sur-Alzette 13 B6
Escuinapa de Hidalgo 84 C3
Esenguly 29 F6
Eşfahān 44 C2
Esh Sham = Dimashq 46 D4
Esil = Ishim ➔ 29 D8
Esker 71 D7
Eskilstuna 9 D9
Eskimo Point = Arviat 68 B10
Eskişehir 25 F3
Esla ➔ 18 B2
Eslāmābād-e Gharb 46 D6
Eşme 23 E7
Esmeraldas 90 C3
España = Spain ■ 18 C4
Esperance 60 G3
Espichel, C. 18 C1
Espinazo, Sierra del = Espinhaço, Serra do 93 F5
Espinhaço, Serra do 93 F5
Espírito Santo □ 93 G5
Espíritu Santo 64 L11
Espoo 9 C10
Esquel 95 E2
Esquina 94 C5
Essaouira 52 B4
Essen 14 C4
Essequibo ➔ 90 B7
Esslingen 14 D5
Estados, I. de Los 95 G4
Estância 93 E6
Estevan 69 D9
Estonia ■ 24 B2
Estrela, Serra da 18 B2
Estremoz 18 C2
Estrondo, Serra do 92 D4
Esztergom 16 E4
Etadunna 62 A2
Étampes 12 B5
Etawah 42 F11
eThekwini = Durban 59 D6
Ethiopia ■ 49 F2
Ethiopian Highlands 49 F2
Etna 21 F5
Etosha Pan 58 B3
Euboea = Evia 23 E5
Eucumbene, L. 63 C4
Eufaula 82 D5
Eugene 72 E2
Eugowra 63 B4

Eulo 63 A4
Euphrates = Furāt, Nahr al ➔ 47 E6
Eureka *Canada* 70 B5
Eureka *U.S.A.* 72 F1
Euroa 63 C4
Europa, Île 59 C8
Europa, Picos de 18 A3
Europa, Pt. 18 D3
Evans Head 63 A5
Evanston 76 C2
Evansville 76 F2
Everard, L. 62 B1
Everest, Mt. 40 C6
Everett 72 C2
Everglades △ 83 G7
Evia 23 E5
Évora 18 C2
Évreux 12 B4
Evros ➔ 22 D6
Évry 12 B5
Évvoia = Evia 23 E5
Ewo 56 E2
Exaltación 91 F5
Exeter 11 F5
Exmoor 11 F5
Exmouth 11 F5
Extremadura □ 18 C2
Eyasi, L. 57 E6
Eyre (North), L. 62 A2
Eyre (South), L. 62 A2
Eyre, L. 60 F6
Eyre Mts. 65 F3
Eyre Pen. 62 B2
Ezine 23 E6

F

F.Y.R.O.M. = Macedonia ■ 22 D3
Fabriano 20 C4
Fada 55 E3
Fada-n-Gourma 53 F6
Faddeyevskiy, Ostrov 31 B12
Faenza 20 B3
Færoe Is. = Føroyar ☑ 6 C4
Făgăras 17 F7
Fagnano, L. 95 G3
Fahraj 45 D4
Fahüd 44 F4
Fair Isle 10 B6
Fairbanks 69 B5
Fairfield *Ala., U.S.A.* 82 C4
Fairfield *Calif., U.S.A.* 72 G2
Fairlie 65 F4
Fairweather, Mt. 69 C6
Faisalabad 42 D8
Faizabad 40 D4
Fakfak 37 E4
Falaise 12 B3
Falam 41 F9
Falconara Marittima 20 C4
Falcone, C. del 20 D2
Faleshty = Fălești 17 E8
Fălești 17 E8
Falkland Is. ☑ 95 G5
Falkland Sd. 95 G5
Fall River 77 D10
Falmouth 11 F4
Fălticeni 17 E8
Falun 9 C9
Famagusta 46 D3
Fano 20 C4
Fao = Al Fāw 47 E7
Faradje 57 D5
Farafangana 59 C9
Farāh 42 C3
Farāh □ 42 C3
Faranah 53 F3
Farasān, Jazā'ir 49 D3
Farasan Is. = Farasān, Jazā'ir 49 D3
Fareham 11 F6
Farewell, C. 64 D5
Farghona 29 E8
Fargo 74 B6
Farīmān 45 C4
Farina 62 B2
Faro *Brazil* 92 C2
Faro *Portugal* 18 D2
Farrāshband 44 D3
Farrukhabad-cum-Fatehgarh 42 F11
Fārs □ 44 D3
Farsala 23 E4
Fartak, Rās 47 E3
Fāryāb □ 45 B6
Fasā 44 D3
Fasano 21 D6
Fastiv 17 C9
Fastov = Fastiv 17 C9
Fatagar, Tanjung 37 E4
Fatehgarh 42 F11
Fatehpur *Raj., India* 42 F9
Fatehpur *Ut. P., India* 40 E3
Favara 21 F4
Favignana 21 F4
Faxaflói 8 C1
Faya-Largeau 55 E2
Fayd 47 F5
Fayetteville *Ark., U.S.A.* 81 A6
Fayetteville *N.C., U.S.A.* 83 B8
Fazilka 42 D9
Fdérik 52 D3
Feather ➔ 72 G3
Featherston 65 D6
Fécamp 12 B4
Fehmarn 15 A6
Feilding 64 D6
Feira de Santana 93 E6
Feldkirch 14 E5
Felipe Carrillo Puerto 85 D7
Felixstowe 11 F7
Fenoarivo Atsinanana 59 B9
Fenyang 35 C6
Feodosiya 25 D4
Ferdows 44 C4
Ferfer 49 F4
Fergana = Farghona 29 E8
Fermo 20 C4
Fermont 71 D7
Fernando de Noronha 92 C7
Fernando Póo = Bioko 53 H7
Ferozepore = Firozpur 42 D9
Ferrara 20 B3
Ferreñafe 91 E3
Ferret, C. 12 D3
Ferrol 18 A1
Fès 52 B5
Feteşti 22 B6
Fetlar 10 A6
Feuilles ➔ 70 D6
Fez = Fès 52 B5
Fezzan 54 C2
Fianarantsoa 59 C9
Fier 23 D2
Figeac 12 D5
Figueira da Foz 18 B1
Figueres 19 A7
Figuig 52 B5
Fiji ■ 64 L12
Filiatra 23 F3
Filyos Cayi ➔ 46 B3
Fíngoè 59 A6
Finike 46 C2
Finisterre, C. = Fisterra, C. 18 A1
Finland ■ 8 C11
Finland, G. of 9 D11
Finlay ➔ 68 C7
Finley 63 C4
Finniss, C. 62 B1
Fiora ➔ 20 C3
Fiordland △ 65 F2
Firat = Furāt, Nahr al ➔ 47 E6
Firenze 20 C3
Firozabad 42 F11
Firozpur 42 D9
Firūzābād 44 D3
Firūzkūh 44 C3
Fish ➔ 58 D3
Fishguard 11 E4
Fisterra, C. 18 A1
Fitz Roy 95 F3
Fiume = Rijeka 20 B5
Fizi 57 E5
Flagstaff 79 C7
Flåm 8 C7
Flaming Gorge Res. 73 F9
Flamingo, Teluk 37 F5
Flanders = Flandre 14 C2
Flandre 14 C2
Flathead L. 73 C7
Flattery, C. 72 B1
Flensburg 14 A5
Flers 12 B3
Flesko, Tanjung 37 D2
Flin Flon 69 C9
Flinders ➔ 61 D7
Flinders I. 62 C4
Flinders Ranges 62 B2
Flint 76 C4
Flint I. 65 L15
Flinton 63 A4
Florence = Firenze 20 C3
Florence *Ala., U.S.A.* 82 B4
Florence *S.C., U.S.A.* 83 B8
Florence, L. 62 A2
Flores 37 F2
Flores Sea 37 F2
Floreşti 17 E9
Floriano 92 D5
Florianópolis 94 B7
Florida 94 C5
Florida □ 83 F6
Florida, Straits of 86 B3
Florina 23 D3
Florø 8 C7
Fluk 37 E3
Flushing = Vlissingen 14 C2
Fly ➔ 61 B7
Flying Fish, C. 96 B1
Foça 23 E6
Focşani 17 F8
Fóggia 20 D5
Föhr 14 A5
Foix 12 E4
Folda 8 B8
Foligno 20 C4
Folkestone 11 F7
Fond du Lac 75 D10
Fondi 20 D4
Fongafale 64 K12
Fonsagrada = A Fonsagrada 18 A2
Fonseca, G. de 85 E7
Fontainebleau 13 B5
Fonte Boa 90 D5
Fontenay-le-Comte 12 C3
Foochow = Fuzhou 35 D6
Forbes 63 B4
Fords Bridge 63 A4
Forestier Pen. 62 D4
Forfar 10 C5
Forlì 20 B4
Formentera 19 C6
Formentor, C. de 19 C7
Former Yugoslav Republic of Macedonia = Macedonia ■ 22 D3
Fórmia 20 D4
Formosa = Taiwan ■ 35 D7
Formosa 94 B5
Formosa, Serra 93 E3
Formosa B. = Ungwana B. 57 E8
Føroyar ☑ 6 C4
Forsayth 61 D7
Forst 15 C8
Fort Albany 71 D5
Fort Collins 74 E2
Fort Dauphin = Taolanaro 59 D9
Fort-de-France 87 D7
Fort Dodge 75 D7
Fort Franklin = Déline 68 B7
Fort George = Chisasibi 71 D6
Fort Good Hope 68 B7
Fort Lauderdale 83 F7
Fort Liard 68 B7
Fort Macleod 69 D8
Fort McPherson 68 B6

Fort Myers **83 F7**
Fort Norman = Tulita **68 B7**
Fort Peck L. **73 C10**
Fort Pierce **83 F7**
Fort Providence **68 B8**
Fort Resolution **68 B8**
Fort Rupert = Waskaganish **71 D6**
Fort Scott **81 A6**
Fort Shevchenko **29 E6**
Fort Simpson **68 B7**
Fort Smith *Canada* **68 B8**
Fort Smith *U.S.A.* **81 B6**
Fort Walton Beach **82 D4**
Fort Wayne **76 D3**
Fort William **10 C4**
Fort Worth **80 C5**
Fort Yukon **69 B5**
Fortaleza **92 C6**
Forür **44 E3**
Foshan **35 D6**
Fossano **13 D7**
Fougères **12 B3**
Foula **10 A5**
Fourni **23 F6**
Fouta Djallon **53 F3**
Foveaux Str. **65 G3**
Foxe Basin **70 C6**
Foxe Chan. **70 C5**
Foxe Pen. **70 C6**
Foxton **64 D6**
Foz do Iguaçu **94 B6**
Franca **93 G4**
Francavilla Fontana **21 D6**
France ■ **13 C5**
Frances **62 C3**
Franceville **56 E2**
Franche-Comté □ **13 C6**
Francistown **59 C5**
Frankfurt *Brandenburg, Germany* **15 B8**
Frankfurt *Hessen, Germany* **14 C5**
Fränkische Alb **15 D6**
Franklin B. **68 B7**
Franklin I. **96 B15**
Franklin Mts. **68 B7**
Franklin Str. **68 A10**
Frankston **63 C4**
Frantsa Iosifa, Zemlya **28 A6**
Franz Josef Land = Frantsa Iosifa, Zemlya **28 A6**
Fraser ➔ **69 D7**
Fraser I. **63 A5**
Fraserburgh **10 C5**
Fray Bentos **94 C5**
Fredericksburg **77 E7**
Fredericton **71 E7**
Frederikshavn **9 D8**
Fredrikstad **9 D8**
Free State □ **59 D5**
Freeport *Bahamas* **86 A4**
Freeport *U.S.A.* **75 D10**
Freetown **53 G3**
Fregenal de la Sierra **18 C2**
Freiburg **14 E4**
Freire **95 D2**
Freising **15 D6**
Freistadt **15 D8**
Fréjus **13 E7**
Fremont **78 B2**
French Guiana ⊠ **92 B3**
French Polynesia ⊠ **65 M16**
Fresco ➔ **92 D3**
Freshfield, C. **96 A14**
Fresnillo **84 C4**
Fresno **78 B3**
Freycinet Pen. **62 D4**
Fria, C. **58 B2**
Frías **94 B3**
Friedrichshafen **14 E5**
Frobisher B. **70 C7**
Frobisher Bay = Iqaluit **70 C7**
Frome ➔ **62 A2**
Frome, L. **62 B2**
Frosinone **20 D4**
Frunze = Bishkek **29 E8**
Frutal **93 F4**
Frýdek-Místek **16 D4**
Fuchou = Fuzhou **35 D6**
Fuchū **33 F3**
Fuengirola **18 D3**
Fuentes de Oñoro **18 B2**
Fuerte ➔ **84 B3**
Fuerte Olimpo **91 H7**
Fuerteventura **52 C3**
Fuhai **34 B3**
Fuji **33 F6**
Fuji-San **33 F6**
Fujian □ **35 D6**
Fujiyama, Mt. = Fuji-San **33 F6**
Fukien = Fujian □ **35 D6**
Fukuchiyama **33 F4**
Fukue-Shima **33 G1**
Fukui **33 E5**
Fukuoka **33 G2**
Fukushima **33 E7**
Fukuyama **33 F3**
Fulda **14 C5**
Fulda ➔ **14 C5**
Funabashi **33 F7**
Funafuti = Fongafale **64 K12**
Funchal **52 B2**
Fundación **90 A4**
Fundão **18 B2**
Fundy, B. of **71 E7**
Funtua **53 F7**
Furāt, Nahr al ➔ **47 E6**
Furneaux Group **62 D4**
Fürstenwalde **15 B8**
Fürth **14 D6**
Furukawa **32 D7**
Fury and Hecla Str. **70 C5**
Fusagasuga **90 C4**
Fushun **35 B7**
Futuna **64 L12**
Fuxin **35 B7**
Fuyuan **35 B8**
Fuzhou **35 D6**
Fyn **9 D8**

G

Gabela **56 G2**
Gabès **54 B1**
Gabès, G. de **54 B1**
Gabon ■ **56 E2**
Gaborone **59 C5**
Gabrovo **22 C5**
Gachsārān **44 D2**
Gadag **43 M9**
Gadarwara **43 H11**
Gadhada **43 J7**
Gadsden **82 B4**
Gadwal **43 L10**
Gafsa **52 B7**
Gagnoa **53 G4**
Gagnon **71 D7**
Gaillimh = Galway **11 E2**
Gainesville *Fla., U.S.A.* **83 E6**
Gainesville *Ga., U.S.A.* **83 B6**
Gainesville *Tex., U.S.A.* **80 C5**
Gairdner, L. **62 B2**
Galashiels **10 D5**
Galați **17 F9**
Galatina **21 D7**
Galcaio **49 F4**
Galdhøpiggen **8 C7**
Galela **37 D3**
Galesburg **75 E9**
Galich **24 B5**
Galicia □ **18 A2**
Galilee, Sea of = Yam Kinneret **46 D3**
Gállego ➔ **19 B5**
Gallegos ➔ **95 G3**
Gallinas, Pta. **90 A4**
Gallipoli = Gelibolu **23 D6**
Gallípoli **21 D6**
Gällivare **8 B10**
Galloway, Mull of **11 D4**
Galveston **81 E6**
Gálvez **94 C4**
Galway **11 E2**
Galway B. **11 E2**
Gambia ■ **53 F2**
Gambia ➔ **53 F2**
Gambier, Îs. **65 M17**
Gambier Is. **62 C2**
Gamboma **56 E3**
Gan Jiang ➔ **35 D6**
Ganāveh **44 D2**
Gāncā **25 E6**
Gand = Gent **14 C2**
Ganda **58 A2**
Gandak ➔ **40 E5**
Gandava **42 E5**
Gander **71 E8**
Gandhi Sagar **43 G9**
Gandía **19 C5**
Ganedidalem = Gani **37 E3**
Ganga ➔ **41 F8**
Ganganagar **42 E8**
Gangaw **41 F10**
Gangdisê Shan **40 B3**
Ganges = Ganga ➔ **41 F8**
Gangneung **35 C7**
Gangtok **41 D7**
Gani **37 E3**
Gansu □ **34 C5**
Ganta **53 G4**
Gantheaume, C. **62 C2**
Gantsevichi = Hantsavichy **17 B8**
Ganyem = Genyem **37 E6**
Ganzhou **35 D6**
Gaoua **53 F5**
Gaoual **53 F3**
Gaoxiong = Kaohsiung **35 D7**
Gap **13 D7**
Gar **34 C2**
Garabogazköl Aylagy **29 E6**
Garagum **29 F6**
Garanhuns **92 D6**
Garda, L. di **20 B3**
Garden City **80 A3**
Gardēz **42 C6**
Gardo **49 F4**
Gargano, Mte. **20 D5**
Garigliano ➔ **20 D4**
Garland **73 F7**
Garm **29 F8**
Garmisch-Partenkirchen **14 E6**
Garmsār **44 C3**
Garoe **49 F4**
Garonne ➔ **12 D3**
Garoowe = Garoe **49 F4**
Garoua **55 G1**
Garrison Res. = Sakakawea, L. **74 B4**
Garry, L. **68 B9**
Garvie Mts. **65 F3**
Garwa = Garoua **55 G1**
Gary **76 D2**
Garzê **34 C5**
Garzón **90 C3**
Gasan Kuli = Esenguly **29 F6**
Gascogne **12 E4**
Gascogne, G. de **12 D2**
Gascony = Gascogne **12 E4**
Gaspé **71 E7**
Gaspé, C. **71 E7**
Gaspé Pen. = Gaspésie, Pén. de la **71 E7**
Gaspésie, Pén. de la **71 E7**
Gasteiz = Vitoria-Gasteiz **19 A4**
Gastonia **83 B7**
Gastre **95 E3**
Gata, C. de **19 D4**
Gata, Sierra de **18 B2**
Gateshead **11 D6**
Gauhati = Guwahati **41 D8**
Gavāter **45 E5**
Gavdos **23 G5**
Gävle **9 C9**
Gawilgarh Hills **43 J10**
Gawler **62 B2**
Gaxun Nur **34 B5**
Gaya *India* **40 E5**
Gaya *Niger* **53 F6**

Gayndah **63 A5**
Gaysin = Haysyn **17 D9**
Gayvoron = Hayvoron **17 D9**
Gaza **47 E3**
Gaza Strip ■ **47 E3**
Gaziantep **46 C4**
Gazimağosa = Famagusta **46 D3**
Gazli **29 E7**
Gcuwa **59 E5**
Gdańsk **16 A4**
Gdańska, Zatoka **16 A4**
Gdov **24 B2**
Gdynia **16 A4**
Gebe **37 D3**
Gebze **22 D7**
Gedaref **55 F6**
Gediz ➔ **23 E6**
Gedser **9 E8**
Geelong **63 C3**
Geesthacht **14 B6**
Geidam **55 F1**
Gejiu **34 D5**
Gela **21 F5**
Gelibolu **23 D6**
Gelsenkirchen **14 C4**
Gemena **56 D3**
Gemerek **46 C4**
Gemlik **23 D7**
General Acha **94 D4**
General Alvear *B. Aires, Argentina* **94 D5**
General Alvear *Mendoza, Argentina* **94 D3**
General Belgrano **94 D5**
General Juan Madariaga **94 D5**
General La Madrid **94 D4**
General MacArthur **36 B3**
General Pico **94 D4**
General Pinedo **94 B4**
General Santos **36 C3**
General Villegas **94 D4**
Geneva = Genève **14 E4**
Geneva, L. = Léman, L. **13 C7**
Genève **14 E4**
Genil ➔ **18 D3**
Gennargentu, Mti. del **21 D2**
Genoa = Génova **13 D8**
Genoa **63 C4**
Génova **13 D8**
Génova, G. di **20 C2**
Gent **14 C2**
Genyem **37 E6**
Georga, Zemlya **28 A5**
George **58 E4**
George ➔ **70 D7**
George, L. *N.S.W., Australia* **63 C4**
George, L. *S. Austral., Australia* **62 C3**
George River = Kangiqsualujjuaq **70 D7**
George Sound **65 F2**
George Town *Cayman Is.* **86 C3**
George Town *Malaysia* **38 C2**
George V Land **96 A14**
George VI Sound **96 B3**
Georgetown = Janjanbureh **53 F3**
Georgetown **90 B7**
Georgia □ **83 C6**
Georgia ■ **25 E5**
Georgian B. **71 E5**
Georgiyevsk **25 E5**
Gera **15 C7**
Geral de Goiás, Serra **93 E4**
Geraldton **60 F1**
Gerede **46 B3**
Gereshk **42 D4**
Germany ■ **14 C6**
Germiston **59 D5**
Gernika-Lumo **19 A4**
Gerona = Girona **19 B7**
Geser **37 E4**
Getafe **18 B4**
Gettysburg **77 E7**
Getxo **19 A4**
Getz Ice Shelf **96 B18**
Ghaghara ➔ **40 E5**
Ghana ■ **53 G5**
Ghanzi **58 C4**
Ghardaïa **52 B6**
Gharyān **54 B1**
Ghat **54 D1**
Ghats, Eastern **43 N11**
Ghats, Western **43 N9**
Ghawdex = Gozo **21 F5**
Ghayl **47 G6**
Ghazal, Bahr el ➔ *Chad* **55 F2**
Ghazâl, Bahr el ➔ *Sudan* **55 G5**
Ghaziabad **42 E10**
Ghazipur **40 E4**
Ghaznī **42 C6**
Ghaznī □ **42 C6**
Ghent = Gent **14 C2**
Gheorghe Gheorghiu-Dej = Onești **17 E8**
Ghowr □ **42 C4**
Ghugus **43 K11**
Ghūrīān **42 B2**
Gia Lai = Plei Ku **38 B3**
Gian **36 C3**
Gianitsa **23 D4**
Giarabub = Al Jaghbūb **54 C3**
Giarre **21 F5**
Gibeon **58 D3**
Gibraltar ⊠ **18 D3**
Gibraltar, Str. of **18 E3**
Gibson Desert **60 E4**
Giebnegáisi = Kebnekaise **8 B9**
Giessen **14 C5**
Gifu **33 F5**
Gíglio **20 C3**
Gijón **18 A3**
Gila ➔ **78 D5**
Gilān □ **46 C7**
Gilbert Is. **64 J12**
Gilgandra **63 B4**
Gilgit **42 B9**
Gilles, L. **62 B2**
Gilmore **63 C4**
Gin Gin **63 A5**
Ginir **49 F3**
Giona, Oros **23 E4**
Giresun **25 E4**
Girga **54 C5**
Giridih **40 E6**
Girne = Kyrenia **46 D3**
Giron = Kiruna **8 B10**
Girona **19 B7**
Gironde ➔ **12 D3**
Girvan **10 D4**
Gisborne **64 C8**
Gisenyi **57 E5**
Gitega **57 E5**
Githio **23 F4**
Giuba ➔ **49 G3**
Giurgiu **22 C5**
Giza = El Gîza **54 C5**
Gizab **42 C4**
Giżycko **16 A5**
Gjirokastër **23 D3**
Gjoa Haven **68 B10**
Glace Bay **71 E8**
Gladstone *Queens., Australia* **61 E9**
Gladstone *S. Austral., Australia* **62 B2**
Glåma = Glomma ➔ **9 C8**
Glasgow **10 D4**
Glazov **28 D6**
Gleiwitz = Gliwice **16 C4**
Glen Canyon ⌓ **79 B7**
Glen Innes **63 A5**
Glendale **78 C3**
Glenelg ➔ **62 C3**
Glenmorgan **63 A4**
Glenorchy **62 D4**
Glenreagh **63 B5**
Glenrothes **10 C5**
Glens Falls **77 C9**
Gliwice **16 C4**
Głogów **16 C3**
Glomma ➔ **9 C8**
Glorieuses, Îs. **59 A9**
Gloucester *Australia* **63 B5**
Gloucester *U.K.* **11 F5**
Glusk **17 B9**
Gmünd **15 D8**
Gmunden **15 E7**
Gniezno **16 B3**
Goa **43 M8**
Goa □ **43 M8**
Goalen Hd. **63 C5**
Goalpara **41 D8**
Goba **49 F2**
Gobabis **58 C3**
Gobi **35 B6**
Godavari ➔ **40 J4**
Godavari Pt. **40 J4**
Godhra **43 H8**
Gods ➔ **69 C10**
Gods L. **69 C10**
Godthåb = Nuuk **66 C14**
Goeie Hoop, Kaap die = Good Hope, C. of **58 E3**
Gogra = Ghaghara ➔ **40 E5**
Goiânia **93 F4**
Goiás **93 F3**
Goiás □ **93 E4**
Goio-Erê **94 A6**
Gojra **42 D8**
Gökçeada **23 D5**
Gökova Körfezi **23 F6**
Gokteik **41 F11**
Gold Coast **63 A5**
Golden B. **64 D5**
Golden Gate **72 H2**
Goldsboro **83 B9**
Goleniów **16 B2**
Golfo Aranci **20 D2**
Golspie **10 C5**
Goma **57 E5**
Gomel = Homyel **17 B10**
Gomera **52 C2**
Gómez Palacio **84 B4**
Gomogomo **37 F4**
Gomoh **40 F6**
Gompa = Ganta **53 G4**
Gonābād **44 C4**
Gonaïves **87 C5**
Gonbad-e Kāvūs **44 B3**
Gonda **40 D3**
Gonder **55 F6**
Gönen **23 D6**
Gonghe **34 C5**
Gongolgon **63 B4**
Good Hope, C. of **58 E3**
Goodooga **63 A4**
Goolgowi **63 B4**
Goombalie **63 A4**
Goondiwindi **63 A5**
Gooray **63 A5**
Gop **43 H6**
Göppingen **14 D5**
Gorakhpur **40 D4**
Goražde **20 C7**
Gordon ➔ **62 D4**
Gore *Australia* **63 A5**
Gore *Ethiopia* **55 G6**
Gore *N.Z.* **65 G3**
Gorgān **44 B3**
Gorgona, I. **90 C3**
Gorizia **20 B4**
Gorkiy = Nizhniy Novgorod **24 B5**
Gorkovskoye Vdkhr. **24 B5**
Görlitz **15 C8**
Gorlovka = Horlivka **25 D4**
Gorna Dzhumayo = Blagoevgrad **22 C4**
Gorna Oryakhovitsa **22 C5**
Gorno-Altay □ **29 D9**
Gorno-Altaysk **29 D9**
Gorno Slinkino = Gornopravdinsk **29 C8**
Gornopravdinsk **29 C8**
Gornyy **32 A3**
Gorodenka = Horodenka **17 D7**
Gorodok = Horodok **17 D6**
Gorokhov = Horokhiv **17 C7**
Gorontalo **37 D2**
Gorzów Wielkopolski **16 B2**
Gosford **63 B5**
Goshogawara **32 C7**

Goslar **14 C6**
Gospič **20 B5**
Göta kanal **9 D9**
Göteborg **9 D8**
Gotha **14 C6**
Gothenburg = Göteborg **9 D8**
Gotland **9 D9**
Gotō-Rettō **33 G1**
Göttingen **14 C5**
Gottwaldov = Zlín **16 D3**
Gouda **14 B3**
Gouin, Rés. **71 E6**
Goulburn **63 B4**
Gouro **55 E2**
Governador Valadares **93 F5**
Goya **94 B5**
Goyder Lagoon **62 A2**
Goyllarisquisga **91 F3**
Goz Beïda **55 F3**
Gozo **21 F5**
Graaff-Reinet **58 E4**
Gračac **20 B5**
Gracias a Dios, C. **86 D3**
Grado **18 A2**
Gradule **63 A4**
Grafton **63 A5**
Graham Bell, Ostrov = Greem-Bell, Ostrov **28 A7**
Graham Land **96 A3**
Grahamstown **59 E5**
Grajaú **92 D4**
Grajaú ➔ **92 C5**
Grampian Highlands = Grampian Mts. **10 C4**
Grampian Mts. **10 C4**
Grampians, The **62 C3**
Gran Canaria **52 C2**
Gran Chaco **94 B4**
Gran Paradiso **13 D7**
Gran Sasso d'Itália **20 C4**
Granada *Nic.* **85 E7**
Granada *Spain* **18 D4**
Granby **71 E6**
Grand Bahama I. **86 A4**
Grand Bassam **53 G5**
Grand Canyon **79 B6**
Grand Cayman **86 C3**
Grand Coulee Dam **72 C4**
Grand Falls **71 E7**
Grand Falls-Windsor **71 E8**
Grand Forks **74 B6**
Grand Island **74 E5**
Grand Rapids *Canada* **69 C10**
Grand Rapids *U.S.A.* **76 C3**
Grand St-Bernard, Col du **13 D7**
Grand Teton **73 E8**
Grande ➔ *Bolivia* **91 G6**
Grande ➔ *Bahia, Brazil* **93 E5**
Grande ➔ *Minas Gerais, Brazil* **93 G3**
Grande, B. **95 G3**
Grande, Rio ➔ **84 B5**
Grande Baleine, R. de la ➔ **71 D6**
Granite City **75 F9**
Granity **65 D4**
Granja **92 C5**
Granollers **19 B7**
Grantham **11 E6**
Granville **12 B3**
Grasse **13 E7**
Grassmere **62 B3**
Graulhet **12 E4**
's-Gravenhage **14 B3**
Gravesend **63 A5**
Graz **15 E8**
Great Abaco I. = Abaco I. **86 A4**
Great Australian Bight **60 G4**
Great Barrier I. **64 B6**
Great Barrier Reef **61 D8**
Great Basin **72 G5**
Great Bear ➔ **68 B7**
Great Bear L. **68 B7**
Great Belt = Store Bælt **9 D8**
Great Divide, The = Great Dividing Ra. **61 E8**
Great Dividing Ra. **61 E8**
Great Falls **73 C8**
Great Inagua I. **86 B5**
Great Indian Desert = Thar Desert **42 F7**
Great Karoo **58 E4**
Great Khingan Mts. = Da Hinggan Ling **35 B7**
Great Lake **62 D4**
Great Ouse ➔ **11 E7**
Great Ruaha ➔ **57 F7**
Great Saint Bernard Pass = Grand St-Bernard, Col du **13 D7**
Great Salt Desert = Kavīr, Dasht-e **44 C3**
Great Salt L. **73 F7**
Great Salt Lake Desert **73 F7**
Great Sandy Desert **60 E3**
Great Sangi = Sangihe, Pulau **37 D3**
Great Slave L. **68 B8**
Great Smoky Mts. △ **83 B6**
Great Victoria Desert **60 F4**
Great Wall **35 C5**
Great Yarmouth **11 E7**
Great Zab = Zāb al Kabīr ➔ **46 C5**
Greater Antilles **86 C5**
Greater Sudbury = Sudbury **71 E5**
Greater Sunda Is. **39 F4**
Gredos, Sierra de **18 B3**
Greece ■ **23 E4**
Greeley **74 E2**
Greely Fd. **70 A5**
Greem-Bell, Ostrov **28 A7**
Green ➔ **79 A8**
Green Bay **76 B2**
Green C. **63 C5**
Greenland ⊠ **66 C9**
Greenock **10 D4**
Greensboro **83 A8**
Greenville *Ala., U.S.A.* **82 D4**
Greenville *Miss., U.S.A.* **81 C8**
Greenville *N.C., U.S.A.* **83 B9**
Greenville *S.C., U.S.A.* **83 B6**
Greenwood *Miss., U.S.A.* **81 C8**
Greenwood *S.C., U.S.A.* **83 B6**
Gregory, L. **62 A2**
Greifswald **15 A7**
Greiz **15 C7**
Gremikha **28 C4**
Grenada ■ **87 D7**
Grenfell **63 B4**
Grenoble **13 D6**
Grey ➔ **65 E4**
Grey Ra. **63 A3**
Greymouth **65 E4**
Greytown **65 D6**
Griffin **83 C5**
Griffith **63 B4**
Grimari **55 G3**
Grimaylov = Hrymayliv **17 D8**
Grimsby **11 E6**
Gris-Nez, C. **12 A4**
Grise Fiord **70 B5**
Grodno = Hrodna **17 B6**
Grodzyanka = Hrodzyanka **17 B9**
Grójec **16 C5**
Groningen **14 B4**
Grootfontein **58 B3**
Grosser Arber **15 D7**
Grosseto **20 C3**
Grossglockner **15 E7**
Groznyy **25 E6**
Grudziądz **16 B4**
Gryazi **24 C4**
Gryazovets **28 D5**
Gua **40 F5**
Guadalajara *Mexico* **84 C4**
Guadalajara *Spain* **18 B4**
Guadalcanal **64 K11**
Guadalete ➔ **18 D2**
Guadalquivir ➔ **18 D2**
Guadalupe = Guadeloupe ⊠ **87 C7**
Guadalupe, Sierra de **18 C3**
Guadarrama, Sierra de **18 B4**
Guadeloupe ⊠ **87 C7**
Guadiana ➔ **18 D2**
Guadix **18 D4**
Guafo, Boca del **95 E2**
Guaíra **94 A6**
Guaitecas, Is. **95 E2**
Guajará-Mirim **91 F5**
Guajira, Pen. de la **90 A4**
Gualeguaychú **94 C5**
Guam ⊠ **64 H9**
Guamúchil **84 B3**
Guanahani = San Salvador I. **86 B5**
Guanajuato **84 C4**
Guandacol **94 B3**
Guane **86 B3**
Guangdong □ **35 D6**
Guangxi Zhuangzu Zizhiqu □ **35 D5**
Guangzhou **35 D6**
Guanipa ➔ **90 B6**
Guantánamo **86 B4**
Guantánamo B. **86 B5**
Guaporé ➔ **91 F5**
Guaqui **91 G5**
Guarapuava **94 B6**
Guarda **18 B2**
Guardafui, C. = Asir, Ras **49 E5**
Guasdualito **90 B4**
Guatemala **85 E6**
Guatemala ■ **85 D6**
Guaviare ➔ **90 C5**
Guaxupé **93 G4**
Guayaquil **90 D3**
Guayaquil, G. de **90 D2**
Guaymas **84 B2**
Guddu Barrage **42 E6**
Gudur **43 M11**
Guecho = Getxo **19 A4**
Guelph **76 C5**
Guéret **12 C4**
Guernica = Gernika-Lumo **19 A4**
Guernsey **11 G5**
Guidónia-Montecélio **20 C4**
Guijá **59 C6**
Guildford **11 F6**
Guilin **35 D6**
Guimarães **18 B1**
Guimaras □ **36 B2**
Guinea ■ **53 F3**
Guinea, Gulf of **51 F3**
Guinea-Bissau ■ **53 F3**
Guingamp **12 B2**
Güiria **90 A6**
Guiuan **36 B3**
Guiyang **35 D5**
Guizhou □ **35 D5**
Gujarat □ **43 H7**
Gujranwala **42 C9**
Gujrat **42 C9**
Gulbarga **43 L10**
Gulf, The = Persian Gulf **44 E2**
Gulgong **63 B4**
Güllük **23 F6**
Gülshat **29 E8**
Gulu **57 D6**
Gümüşhane **46 B4**
Gumzai **37 F4**
Guna **43 G10**
Gunnedah **63 B5**
Gunningbar Cr. ➔ **63 B4**
Gunsan **35 C7**
Guntakal **43 M10**
Guntur **40 J3**
Gunungapi **37 F3**
Gunungsitoli **39 D1**
Gunza **56 G2**

Gupis 42 A8
Gürchän 46 D7
Gurdaspur 42 C9
Gurkha 40 C5
Gurley 63 A4
Gurupá 92 C3
Gurupá, I. Grande de 92 C3
Gurupi ➔ 92 C4
Guryev = Atyraü 29 E6
Gusau 53 F7
Güstrow 15 B7
Gütersloh 14 C5
Guthrie 80 B5
Guwahati 41 D8
Guyana ■ 90 B7
Guyane française = French Guiana ⧄ 92 B3
Guyenne 12 D4
Guyra 63 B5
Güzelyurt = Morphou 46 D3
Gwa 41 J10
Gwabegar 63 B4
Gwādar 42 G3
Gwalior 42 F11
Gwanda 59 C5
Gwangju 35 C7
Gwanju = Gwangju 35 C7
Gweru 59 B5
Gwydir ➔ 63 A4
Gyandzha = Gäncä 25 E6
Gyaring Hu 34 C4
Gydanskiy Poluostrov 28 B8
Gympie 63 A5
Gyöngyös 16 E4
Győr 16 E3
Gyula 16 E5
Gyumri 25 E5
Gyzylarbat = Serdar 29 F6

H

Haarlem 14 B3
Haast ➔ 65 E3
Haboro 32 A7
Hachijō-Jima 33 G6
Hachinohe 32 C7
Hadarba, Ras 54 D6
Ḥadd, Ra's al 45 F4
Hadejia 53 F7
Haden 63 A5
Hadera 46 D3
Hadhramaut = Haḍramawt 49 D4
Haḍramawt 49 D4
Haeju 35 C7
Haerhpin = Harbin 35 B7
Hafar al Bāṭin 47 E6
Hafizabad 42 C8
Haflong 41 E9
Haft Gel 47 E7
Hagen 14 C4
Hagerstown 77 E7
Hagi 33 F2
Hagondange 13 B7
Hague, C. de la 12 B3
Hague, The = 's-Gravenhage 14 B3
Haguenau 13 B7
Haidarābād = Hyderabad 43 L11
Haifa = Ḥefa 46 D3
Haikou 35 D6
Ḥā'il 47 F5
Hailar 35 B6
Hailun 35 B7
Hailuoto 8 B10
Hainan □ 35 E5
Haiphong 35 D5
Haiti ■ 87 C5
Haiya 55 E6
Hajdúböszörmény 16 E5
Haji Ibrahim 46 C6
Hajnówka 17 B6
Hakodate 32 C7
Hala 42 G6
Ḥalab 46 C4
Ḥalabjah 46 D6
Halaib 54 D6
Halberstadt 15 C6
Halcombe 64 D6
Halcon 36 B2
Halden 9 D8
Haldia 40 F7
Haldwani 42 E11
Halfmoon Bay 65 G3
Halifax *Canada* 71 E7
Halifax *U.K.* 11 E6
Halīl ➔ 44 E4
Halkida 23 E4
Hall Beach = Sanirajak 70 C5
Hall Pen. 70 C7
Hallāniyat, Jazā'ir al 49 D6
Halle 15 C6
Hallett 62 B2
Halmahera 37 D3
Halmstad 9 D8
Hälsingborg = Helsingborg 9 D8
Ḥālūl 44 E3
Hamada 33 F3
Hamadān 46 D7
Hamadān □ 46 D7
Ḥamāh 46 D4
Hamamatsu 33 F5
Hamar 8 C8
Hamburg 14 B5
Hämeenlinna 8 C10
Hameln 14 B5
Hamersley Ra. 60 E2
Hamhüng 35 C7
Hami 34 B4
Hamilton *Australia* 62 C3
Hamilton *Canada* 71 E6
Hamilton *N.Z.* 64 B6
Hamilton *U.K.* 10 D4
Hamilton ➔ 62 A2
Hamley Bridge 62 B2
Hamlin = Hameln 14 B5
Hamm 14 C4
Hammerfest 8 A10
Hammond 76 D2
Hampden 65 F4
Hampton 77 F7
Han Pijesak 20 B7
Hanamaki 32 D7
Hanau 14 C5
Hancock 75 C7
Handan 35 C6
Hangayn Nuruu 34 B4
Hangchou = Hangzhou 35 C7
Hangzhou 35 C7
Hangzhou Wan 35 C7
Hania = Chania 23 G5
Ḥanīsh 49 E3
Hankö 9 D10
Hanle 42 C11
Hanmer Springs 65 E5
Hanna 69 C8
Hannibal 75 F9
Hannover 14 B5
Hanoi 35 D5
Hanover = Hannover 14 B5
Hanover, I. 95 G2
Hansi 42 E9
Hanson, L. 62 B2
Hantsavichy 17 B8
Hanzhong 35 C5
Haora 40 F7
Haparanda 8 B10
Happy Valley-Goose Bay 71 D7
Hapur 42 E10
Ḥaql 47 E3
Har 37 F4
Har Hu 34 C4
Har Us Nuur 34 B4
Ḥarad 47 F7
Haraisan Plateau = Hurayṣān 47 G6
Haranomachi 33 E7
Harare 59 B6
Haraz 55 F2
Harbin 35 B7
Hardangerfjorden 8 C7
Hardwar = Haridwar 42 E11
Hardy, Pen. 95 H3
Harer 49 F3
Hargeisa 49 F3
Hari ➔ 39 E2
Haridwar 42 E11
Haringhata ➔ 41 G7
Harīrūd 45 C5
Harīrūd ➔ 42 A2
Harlingen 80 F5
Harlow 11 F7
Harney Basin 72 E4
Härnösand 8 C9
Harricana ➔ 71 D6
Harris 10 C3
Harris, L. 62 B2
Harrisburg 77 D7
Harrison, C. 70 D8
Harrogate 11 D6
Hart, L. 62 B2
Hartford 77 D9
Hartlepool 11 D6
Harvey 76 D2
Harwich 11 F7
Haryana □ 42 E10
Haryn ➔ 17 B8
Harz 14 C6
Hasa 47 F7
Haskovo = Khaskovo 22 D5
Hassi Messaoud 52 B7
Hastings *N.Z.* 64 C7
Hastings *U.K.* 11 F7
Hastings *U.S.A.* 74 E5
Hastings Ra. 63 B5
Hatay 46 C4
Hatfield P.O. 62 B3
Hatgal 34 A5
Hathras 42 F11
Hatia 41 F8
Hattah 62 B3
Hatteras, C. 83 B10
Hattiesburg 81 D9
Hatvan 16 E4
Hau Bon = Cheo Reo 38 B3
Haugesund 9 D7
Hauraki G. 64 B6
Haut Atlas 52 B4
Hautah, Wahāt al 47 G6
Havana = La Habana 86 B3
Havant 11 F6
Havel ➔ 15 B7
Havelock 65 D5
Haverfordwest 11 F4
Havličkův Brod 16 D2
Havre 73 B9
Havre-St.-Pierre 71 D7
Havza 46 B3
Hawai'i ⧄ 78 H12
Hawaiian Is. 78 H12
Hawea, L. 65 F3
Hawera 64 C6
Hawick 10 D5
Hawke B. 64 C7
Hawker 62 B2
Hawkwood 63 A5
Hay 63 B3
Hay River 68 B8
Haya = Tehoru 37 E3
Hayastan = Armenia ■ 25 E5
Hayes ➔ 69 C10
Hayrabolu 22 D6
Haysyn 17 D9
Hayvoron 17 D9
Hazar 29 F6
Hazārān, Küh-e 44 D4
Hazaribag 40 F5
Healesville 63 C4
Hearst 71 E5
Hebei □ 35 C6
Hebel 63 A4
Hebron = Al Khalīl 47 E3
Hebron 70 D7
Hechi 35 D5
Hechuan 35 C5
Heerlen 13 A6
Ḥefa 46 D3
Hefei 35 C6
Hegang 35 B8
Heidelberg 14 D5
Heihe 35 A7
Heilbronn 14 D5
Heilongjiang □ 35 B7
Heilunkiang = Heilongjiang □ 35 B7
Heimaey 8 C1
Heinze Kyun 41 K11

Hejaz = Ḥijāz 47 F4
Hekımhan 46 C4
Hekou 34 D5
Helena *Ark., U.S.A.* 81 B8
Helena *Mont., U.S.A.* 73 C7
Helensville 64 B6
Helgoland 14 A4
Heligoland = Helgoland 14 A4
Heligoland B. = Deutsche Bucht 14 A5
Hellas = Greece ■ 23 E4
Hellespont = Çanakkale Boğazı 23 D6
Hellín 19 C5
Helmand □ 42 D3
Helmand ➔ 42 D2
Helmand, Hamun 45 D5
Helmsdale 10 B5
Helsingborg 9 D8
Helsingfors = Helsinki 9 C11
Helsinki 9 C11
Helwân 54 C5
Hemel Hempstead 11 F6
Henan □ 35 C6
Henares ➔ 18 B4
Henashi-Misaki 32 C6
Henderson 83 A8
Hendon 63 A5
Hengyang 35 D6
Henrietta Maria, C. 71 D5
Hentiyn Nuruu 35 B5
Henty 63 C4
Henzada 41 J10
Heraklion = Iraklio 23 G5
Herät 42 B3
Herät □ 42 B3
Herceg-Novi 22 C2
Hereford 11 E5
Herford 14 B5
Hermidale 63 B4
Hermite, I. 95 H3
Hermon, Mt. = Shaykh, J. ash 46 D3
Hermosillo 84 B2
Hernád ➔ 16 E5
Heroica Nogales = Nogales 84 A2
Herrick 62 D4
's-Hertogenbosch 14 C3
Hesse = Hessen □ 14 C5
Hessen □ 14 C5
Hexham 11 D5
Heywood 62 C3
Hialeah 83 G7
Hibbing 75 B8
Hibbs B. 62 D4
Hickory 83 B7
Hicks, Pt. 63 C4
Hidalgo del Parral 84 B3
Higashiajima-San 33 E7
Higashiōsaka 33 F4
High Point 83 B8
High River 69 C8
High Tatra = Tatry 16 D4
High Wycombe 11 F6
Hiiumaa 24 B1
Ḥijārah, Ṣaḥrā' al 47 E6
Ḥijāz 47 F4
Hijo = Tagum 36 C3
Hikurangi *Gisborne, N.Z.* 64 C7
Hikurangi *Northland, N.Z.* 64 A6
Hildesheim 14 B5
Hillston 63 B4
Hilo 78 J13
Hilversum 14 B3
Himachal Pradesh □ 42 D10
Himalaya 40 C5
Himatnagar 43 H8
Himeji 33 F4
Himi 33 E5
Ḥimṣ 46 D4
Hindmarsh, L. 62 C3
Hindu Bagh 42 D5
Hindu Kush 42 B7
Hindupur 43 N10
Hinganghat 43 J11
Hingoli 43 K10
Hinna = Imi 49 F3
Hinojosa del Duque 18 C3
Hinthada = Henzada 41 J10
Hios 23 E6
Hirakud Dam 40 G4
Hiroo 32 B8
Hirosaki 32 C7
Hiroshima 33 F3
Hisar 42 E9
Hispaniola 87 C5
Hitachi 33 E7
Hjälmaren 9 D9
Hkakabo Razi 41 C11
Hlyboka 17 D7
Ho Chi Minh City = Thanh Pho Ho Chi Minh 38 B3
Hoai Nhon 38 B3
Hoare B. 70 C7
Hobart 62 D4
Hobbs Coast 96 B18
Hodaka-Dake 33 E5
Hodeida = Al Ḥudaydah 49 E3
Hodgson 69 C10
Hódmezővásárhely 16 E5
Hodna, Chott el 52 A6
Hodonín 16 D3
Hoek van Holland 14 B3
Hof 15 C6
Hofsjökull 8 C2
Höfu 33 F2
Hogan Group 62 C4
Hoggar = Ahaggar 52 D7
Hoh Xil Shan 34 C3
Hoher Rhön = Rhön 14 C5
Hohhot 35 B6
Hoi An 38 A3
Hokianga Harbour 64 A5
Hokitika 65 E4
Hokkaidō □ 32 B8
Holbrook 63 C4
Holguín 86 B4
Hollywood 83 G7
Holman 68 A8
Holstebro 9 D7
Holyhead 11 E4
Homalin 41 E10
Hombori 53 E5
Home B. 70 C7
Homer 69 C4
Homs = Ḥimṣ 46 D4
Homyel 17 B10
Hon Chong 38 B2
Honan = Henan □ 35 C6
Honbetsu 32 B8
Honduras ■ 85 E7
Honduras, G. de 85 D7
Hønefoss 9 C8
Honfleur 12 B4
Hong Kong □ 35 D6
Hongjiang 35 D5
Hongshui He ➔ 35 D5
Hongze Hu 35 C6
Honiara 64 K10
Honjō 32 D7
Honolulu 78 H12
Honshū 33 F4
Hood, Mt. 72 D3
Hooghly = Hugli ➔ 40 G7
Hook of Holland = Hoek van Holland 14 B3
Hoorn 14 B3
Hoover Dam 78 B5
Hope, L. 62 A2
Hopedale 70 D7
Hopei = Hebei □ 35 C6
Hopetoun 62 C3
Hopetown 58 D4
Hoquiam 72 C2
Horlick Mts. 96 C1
Horlivka 25 D4
Hormoz 44 E3
Hormoz, Jaz.-ye 44 E4
Hormozgān □ 44 E3
Hormuz, Str. of 44 E4
Horn 15 D8
Horn, Cape = Hornos, C. de 95 H3
Hornavan 8 B9
Hornos, C. de 95 H3
Horodenka 17 D7
Horodok *Khmelnytskyy, Ukraine* 17 D8
Horodok *Lviv, Ukraine* 17 D6
Horokhiv 17 C7
Horqin Youyi Qianqi 35 B7
Horqueta 94 A5
Horsham 62 C3
Horton ➔ 68 B7
Hose, Gunung-Gunung 39 D4
Hoshangabad 43 H10
Hoshiarpur 42 D9
Hospet 43 M10
Hoste, I. 95 H3
Hot Springs 81 B7
Hotan 34 C2
Hotazel 58 D4
Houhora Heads 64 A5
Houlton 77 A12
Houma 81 E8
Houston 81 E6
Hovd □ 34 B4
Hövsgöl Nuur 34 A5
Howard 63 A5
Howe, C. 63 C5
Howitt, L. 62 A2
Howrah = Haora 40 F7
Höxter 14 C5
Hoy 10 B5
Høyanger 8 C7
Hoyerswerda 15 C8
Hpa-an = Pa-an 41 J11
Hpunan Pass 41 D11
Hradec Králové 16 C2
Hrodna 17 B6
Hrodzyanka 17 B9
Hrvatska = Croatia ■ 20 B6
Hrymayliv 17 D8
Hsenwi 41 F11
Hsiamen = Xiamen 35 D6
Hsian = Xi'an 35 C5
Hsinhailien = Lianyungang 35 C6
Hsüchou = Xuzhou 35 C6
Hua Hin 38 B1
Huacho 91 F3
Huai He ➔ 35 C6
Huainan 35 C6
Huallaga ➔ 90 E3
Huambo 58 A3
Huancabamba 91 E3
Huancane 91 G5
Huancavelica 91 F3
Huancayo 91 F3
Huang Hai = Yellow Sea 35 C7
Huang He ➔ 35 C6
Huangliu 35 E5
Huangshan 35 D6
Huangshi 35 C6
Huánuco 91 E3
Huaraz 91 E3
Huarmey 91 F3
Huascarán, Nevado 91 E3
Huasco 94 B2
Huatabampo 84 B3
Hubei □ 35 C6
Hubli 43 M9
Huddersfield 11 E6
Hudiksvall 8 C9
Hudson ➔ 77 D8
Hudson Bay 70 C5
Hudson Mts. 96 B2
Hudson Str. 70 C7
Hue 38 A3
Huelva 18 D2
Huesca 19 A5
Hughenden 61 E7
Hugli ➔ 40 G7
Huila, Nevado del 90 C3
Huinca Renancó 94 C4
Huize 34 D5
Hukawng Valley 41 D11
Hulan 35 B7
Ḥulayfā' 47 F5
Hull = Kingston upon Hull 11 E6
Hull 71 E6
Hulun Nur 35 B6
Humahuaca 94 A3
Humaitá 91 E6
Humber ➔ 11 E6
Humboldt 69 C9

Humboldt ➔ 72 F4
Hume, L. 63 C4
Hün 54 C2
Húnaflói 8 B1
Hunan □ 35 D6
Hunedoara 17 F6
Hungary ■ 16 E4
Hungerford 63 A3
Hũngnam 35 C7
Hunsrück 14 D4
Hunter I. 62 D3
Hunter Ra. 63 B5
Hunterville 64 C6
Huntington 76 E4
Huntington Beach 78 D3
Huntly *N.Z.* 64 B6
Huntly *U.K.* 10 C5
Huntsville *Canada* 71 E6
Huntsville *U.S.A.* 82 B4
Huonville 62 D4
Hupeh = Hubei □ 35 C6
Huraysān 47 G6
Huron, L. 76 B4
Hurunui ➔ 65 E5
Húsavík 8 B2
Huşi 17 E9
Hutchinson 80 A5
Hutton, Mt. 63 A4
Hvar 20 C6
Hwang Ho = Huang He ➔ 35 C6
Hwange 59 B5
Hyargas Nuur 34 B4
Hyderabad *India* 43 L11
Hyderabad *Pakistan* 42 G6
Hydra 23 F4
Hyères 13 E7
Hyères, Îs. d' 13 E7
Hyūga 33 G2

I

I-n-Gall 53 E7
Iaco ➔ 91 E5
Ialomiţa ➔ 22 B6
Iaşi 17 E8
Iba 36 A2
Ibadan 53 G6
Ibagué 90 C3
Ibar ➔ 22 C3
Ibarra 90 C3
Ibiá 93 F4
Ibiapaba, Sa. da 92 C5
Ibiza = Eivissa 19 C6
Ibonma 37 E4
Ibotirama 93 E5
Ibu 37 D3
Ibusuki 33 H2
Ica 91 F3
Iça ➔ 90 D5
Içana 90 C5
Içel 46 C3
Iceland ■ 8 B2
Ich'ang = Yichang 35 C6
Ichchapuram 40 H5
Ichihara 33 F7
Ichilo ➔ 91 G6
Ichinomiya 33 F5
Ichinoseki 32 D7
Idaho □ 73 D7
Idaho Falls 73 E7
Idar-Oberstein 14 D4
Idensalmi = Iisalmi 8 C11
Idfū 54 D5
Īdhra = Hydra 23 F4
Idi 38 C1
Idi, Oros = Psiloritis, Oros 23 G5
Idiofa 56 E3
Idlib 46 D4
Idlip 46 D4
Ierapetra 23 G5
Iesi 20 C4
Ife 53 G6
Iforas, Adrar des 52 E6
Igarapava 93 G4
Igarka 28 C9
Iglésias 21 E2
Igloolik 70 C5
Igluligaarjuk = Chesterfield Inlet 68 B10
Iglulik = Igloolik 70 C5
Iğneada Burnu 22 D7
Igoumenitsa 23 E3
Iguaçu ➔ 94 B6
Iguaçu, Cat. del 94 B6
Iguaçu Falls = Iguaçu, Cat. del 94 B6
Iguala 84 D5
Igualada 19 B6
Iguassu = Iguaçu ➔ 94 B6
Iguatu 92 D6
Iharana 59 A10
Ihosy 59 C9
Iida 33 F5
Iisalmi 8 C11
Ijebu-Ode 53 G6
IJsselmeer 14 B3
Ikaluktutiak 68 B9
Ikaria 23 F6
Ikeda 33 F3
Ikela 56 E4
Iki 33 G1
Ikopa ➔ 59 B9
Ikparjuk = Arctic Bay 70 B5
Ilagan 36 A2
Īlām 46 D6
Iława 16 B4
Ile ➔ 29 E8
Île-de-France □ 12 B5
Ilebo 56 E4
Ilesha 53 G6
Ilhéus 93 E6
Ili = Ile ➔ 29 E8
Iligan 36 C2
Illampu = Ancohuma, Nevado 91 G5
Illana B. 36 C2
Illapel 94 C2
Iller ➔ 14 D5
Illimani, Nevado 91 G5
Ilmen, Ozero 24 B3
Ilo 91 G4
Iloilo 36 B2
Ilorin 53 G6
Ilwaki 37 F3
Imabari 33 F3
Imandra, Ozero 28 C4
Imari 33 G1
Imatra 8 C11
imeni 26 Bakinskikh Komissarov = Neftçala 46 C7
imeni Ismail Samani, Pik 29 F8
Imeri, Serra 90 C5
Imi 49 F3
Ímola 20 B3
Imperatriz 92 D4
Império 13 E8
Imperial Dam 78 D5
Impfondo 56 D3
Imphal 41 E9
Ímroz = Gökçeada 23 D5
Imuruan B. 36 B1
In Salah 52 C6
Ina 33 F5
Inangahua 65 D4
Inanwatan 37 E4
Iñapari 91 F5
Inari 8 B11
Inarijärvi 8 B11
Inca 19 C7
Ince Burun 25 E3
Incheon 35 C7
Incirliova 23 F6
Incomáti ➔ 59 D6
Indalsälven ➔ 8 C9
Indaw 41 E11
Independence *Kans., U.S.A.* 81 A6
Independence *Mo., U.S.A.* 75 F7
India ■ 43 J10
Indian ➔ 83 F7
Indiana □ 76 D3
Indianapolis 76 E2
Indigirka ➔ 31 B12
Indira Gandhi Canal 42 F8
Indonesia ■ 39 E4
Indore 43 H9
Indravati ➔ 40 H3
Indre ➔ 12 C4
Indus ➔ 43 G5
Inebolu 25 E3
Inglewood *Queens., Australia* 63 A5
Inglewood *Vic., Australia* 62 C3
Inglewood *N.Z.* 64 C6
Ingolstadt 15 D6
Ingraj Bazar 40 E7
Ingrid Christensen Coast 96 A10
Ingulec = Inhulec 25 D3
Inhambane 59 C7
Inharrime 59 C7
Inhulec 25 D3
Ining = Yining 29 E9
Inírida ➔ 90 C5
Injune 63 A4
Inland Kaikoura Ra. 65 D5
Inland Sea = Setonaikai 33 F3
Inle L. 41 G11
Inn ➔ 15 D7
Innamincka 62 A3
Inner Hebrides 10 C3
Inner Mongolia = Nei Monggol Zizhiqu □ 35 B6
Innsbruck 15 E6
Inongo 56 E3
Inoucdjouac = Inukjuak 70 D6
Inowrocław 16 B4
Insein 41 J11
International Falls 75 A8
Inukjuak 70 D6
Inútil, B. 95 G2
Inuvik 68 B6
Invercargill 65 G3
Inverell 63 A5
Invergordon 10 C4
Inverness 10 C4
Inverurie 10 C5
Investigator Group 62 B1
Investigator Str. 62 C2
Inya 29 D9
Inza 24 C6
Ioannina 23 E3
Ionian Is. = Ionioi Nisoi 23 E3
Ionian Sea 21 F6
Ionioi Nisoi 23 E3
Ios 23 F5
Iowa □ 75 D8
Iowa City 75 E9
Ipameri 93 F4
Ipatinga 93 F5
Ipiales 90 C3
Ipin = Yibin 35 D5
Ipixuna 91 E4
Ipoh 38 D2
Ippy 55 G3
Ipsala 22 D6
Ipswich *Australia* 63 A5
Ipswich *U.K.* 11 E7
Ipu 92 C5
Iqaluit 70 C7
Iquique 91 H4
Iquitos 90 D4
Iracoubo 92 A3
Iraklio 23 G5
Iráklion = Iraklio 23 G5
Iran ■ 44 C3
Iran, Pegunungan 39 D4
Iran Ra. = Iran, Pegunungan 39 D4
Īrānshahr 45 E5
Irapuato 84 C4
Iraq ■ 46 D5
Ireland ■ 11 E3
Irian Jaya = Papua □ 37 E5
Iringa 57 F7
Iriri ➔ 92 C3
Irish Republic ■ 11 E3
Irish Sea 11 E4
Irkineyeva 30 D7
Irkutsk 30 D8
Irō-Zaki 33 F6
Iron Baron 62 B2
Iron Gate = Portile de Fier 22 B4
Iron Knob 62 B2
Ironwood 75 B9
Irpin 17 C10

Irrara Cr. ➔ 63 A4
Irrawaddy □ 41 J10
Irrawaddy ➔ 41 K10
Irrawaddy, Mouths of the 41 K10
Irtysh ➔ 28 C7
Irún 19 A5
Irunea = Pamplona 19 A5
Irvine 10 D4
Irymple 62 B3
Isabela 36 C2
Ísafjörður 8 B1
Isahaya 33 G2
Isar ➔ 15 D7
Ischia 21 D4
Ise-Wan 33 F5
Isère ➔ 13 D6
Isérnia 20 D5
Isfahan = Eşfahān 44 C2
Ishikari-Gawa ➔ 32 B7
Ishikari-Wan 32 B7
Ishim ➔ 29 D8
Ishinomaki 32 D7
Ishkuman 42 A8
Isil Kul 29 D8
Isiro 57 D5
İskenderun 46 C4
Iskŭr ➔ 22 C5
Islamabad 42 C8
Island = Iceland ■ 8 B2
Island L. 69 C10
Island Lagoon 62 B2
Islands, B. of 64 A6
Islay 10 D3
Isle ➔ 12 D3
Isle of Wight □ 11 F6
Ismail = Izmayil 17 F9
Ismā'īlīya 47 E3
Isparta 46 C2
Íspica 21 F5
Israel ■ 46 E3
Issoire 13 D5
Issyk-Kul, Ozero = Ysyk-Köl 29 E8
İstanbul 22 D7
İstanbul Boğazı 22 D7
Istiea 23 E4
Istra 20 B4
Istres 13 E6
Istria = Istra 20 B4
Itaberaba 93 E5
Itabira 93 F5
Itabuna 93 E6
Itaipú, Reprêsa de 94 B6
Itaituba 92 C2
Itajaí 94 B7
Italy ■ 20 C4
Itapecuru-Mirim 92 C5
Itaperuna 93 G5
Itapicuru ➔ *Bahia, Brazil* 93 E6
Itapicuru ➔ *Maranhão, Brazil* 92 C5
Itapipoca 92 C6
Itaquí 94 B5
Ithaca = Ithaki 23 E3
Ithaki 23 E3
Itō 33 F6
Itonamas ➔ 91 F6
Ituiutaba 93 F4
Itumbiara 93 F4
Iturbe 94 A3
Itzehoe 14 B5
Ivanava 17 B7
Ivanhoe 63 B3
Ivano-Frankivsk 17 D7
Ivanovo = Ivanava 17 B7
Ivanovo 24 B5
Ivatsevichy 17 B7
Ivory Coast ■ 53 G4
Ivrea 13 D7
Ivujivik 70 C6
Iwahig 38 C5
Iwaizumi 32 D7
Iwaki 33 E7
Iwakuni 33 F3
Iwamizawa 32 B7
Iwanai 32 B7
Iwata 33 F5
Iwate-San 32 D7
Iwo 53 G6
Ixiamas 91 F5
Izhevsk 28 D6
Izmayil 17 F9
İzmir 23 E6
İzmit = Kocaeli 25 E2
İznik Gölü 23 D7
Izu-Shotō 33 F7
Izumi-Sano 33 F4
Izumo 33 F3
Izyaslav 17 C8

J

Jabalpur 43 H11
Jablah 46 D4
Jablanica 22 D3
Jablonec nad Nisou 16 C2
Jaboatão 92 D6
Jaca 19 A5
Jacareí 94 A7
Jackson *Australia* 63 A4
Jackson *Mich., U.S.A.* 76 C3
Jackson *Miss., U.S.A.* 81 C8
Jackson *Tenn., U.S.A.* 82 B3
Jackson B. 65 E3
Jacksons 65 E4
Jacksonville *Fla., U.S.A.* 83 D7
Jacksonville *Ill., U.S.A.* 75 F9
Jacksonville *N.C., U.S.A.* 83 B9
Jacmel 87 C5
Jacobabad 42 E6
Jacobina 93 E5
Jacundá ➔ 92 C3
Jade Mt. = Yü Shan 35 D7
Jaén *Peru* 91 E3
Jaén *Spain* 18 D4
Jaffa = Tel Aviv-Yafo 46 D3
Jaffa, C. 62 C2
Jaffna 43 Q12
Jagadhri 42 D10
Jagdalpur 40 H3
Jagodina 22 B3
Jagraon 42 D9
Jagtial 43 K11
Jaguariaíva 94 A7
Jaguaribe ➔ 92 C6
Jahrom 44 D3
Jailolo 37 D3
Jailolo, Selat 37 D3
Jaipur 42 F9
Jakarta 39 F3
Jalālābād 42 B7
Jalapa Enriquez = Xalapa 84 D5
Jalas, Jabal al 47 F4
Jalgaon *Maharashtra, India* 43 J10
Jalgaon *Maharashtra, India* 43 J9
Jalna 43 K9
Jalón ➔ 19 B5
Jalpaiguri 41 D7
Jaluit I. 64 J11
Jamaica ■ 86 C4
Jamalpur *Bangla.* 41 E7
Jamalpur *India* 40 E6
Jamanxim ➔ 92 C2
Jambe 37 E4
Jambi 39 E2
Jambi □ 39 E2
Jambongan, Pulau 38 C5
James ➔ 74 D6
James B. 71 D5
James Ross I. 96 A4
Jamestown *Australia* 62 B2
Jamestown *N. Dak., U.S.A.* 74 B5
Jamestown *N.Y., U.S.A.* 77 C6
Jamkhandi 43 L9
Jammu 42 C9
Jammu & Kashmir □ 42 B10
Jamnagar 43 H7
Jamshedpur 40 F6
Jand 42 C8
Jandaq 44 C3
Jandowae 63 A5
Janesville 75 D10
Janjanbureh 53 F3
Januária 93 F5
Jaora 43 H9
Japan ■ 33 F5
Japan, Sea of 32 D4
Japen = Yapen 37 E5
Japurá ➔ 90 D5
Jaqué 90 B3
Jarama ➔ 18 B4
Jarvis I. 65 K15
Jarwa 40 D4
Jäsk 44 E4
Jasper 82 C4
Jászberény 16 E4
Jataí 93 F3
Játiva = Xátiva 19 C5
Jaú 93 G4
Jauja 91 F3
Jaunpur 40 E4
Java = Jawa 39 F3
Java Sea 39 E3
Jawa 39 F3
Jaya, Puncak 37 E5
Jayanti 41 D7
Jayapura 37 E6
Jayawijaya, Pegunungan 37 E5
Jaynagar 40 D6
Jebel, Bahr el ➔ 55 G5
Jedburgh 10 D5
Jedda = Jiddah 47 G4
Jędrzejów 16 C5
Jefferson City 75 F8
Jega 53 F6
Jeju-do 35 C7
Jelenia Góra 16 C2
Jelgava 24 B1
Jena 15 C6
Jeonju 35 C7
Jeparit 62 C3
Jequié 93 E5
Jequitinhonha 93 F5
Jequitinhonha ➔ 93 F6
Jérémie 86 C5
Jerez de la Frontera 18 D2
Jerez de los Caballeros 18 C2
Jerid, Chott el = Djerid, Chott 52 B7
Jerilderie 63 C4
Jersey 11 G5
Jersey City 77 D8
Jerusalem 47 E3
Jervis B. 63 C5
Jesi = Iesi 20 C4
Jessore 41 F7
Jeypore 40 H4
Jhal Jhao 42 F4
Jhalawar 43 G10
Jhang Maghiana 42 D8
Jhansi 43 G11
Jharsuguda 40 G5
Jhelum 42 C8
Jhelum ➔ 42 D8
Jhunjhunu 42 E9
Jiamusi 35 B8
Ji'an 35 D6
Jiangmen 35 D6
Jiangsu □ 35 C6
Jiangxi □ 35 D6
Jiao Xian = Jiaozhou 35 C7
Jiaozhou 35 C7
Jiaxing 35 C7
Jiayi = Chiai 35 D7
Jibuti = Djibouti ■ 49 E3
Jiddah 47 G4
Jido 41 C10
Jihlava 16 D2
Jihlava ➔ 16 D3
Jijiga 49 F3
Jilin 35 B7
Jilong = Chilung 35 D7
Jima 55 G6
Jiménez 84 B4
Jinan 35 C6
Jindabyne 63 C4
Jindřichův Hradec 16 D2
Jingdezhen 35 D6
Jinggu 34 D5
Jinhua 35 D6
Jining *Nei Monggol Zizhiqu, China* 35 B6

Jining *Shandong, China* **35 C6**
Jinja **57 D6**
Jinnah Barrage **42 C7**
Jinzhou **35 B7**
Jiparaná ➔ **91 E6**
Jipijapa **90 D2**
Jiu ➔ **22 C4**
Jiujiang **35 D6**
Jiuquan **34 C4**
Jixi **35 B8**
Jizzakh **29 E7**
Joaçaba **94 B6**
João Pessoa **92 D7**
Joaquín V. González **94 B4**
Jodhpur **42 F8**
Joensuu **8 C11**
Jogjakarta = Yogyakarta **39 F4**
Johannesburg **59 D5**
Johnson City **83 A6**
Johnston Falls = Mambilima Falls **57 G5**
Johnstown **77 D6**
Johor Bahru **39 D2**
Joinville **94 B7**
Joinville I. **96 A4**
Joliet **76 D1**
Joliette **71 E6**
Jolo **36 C2**
Jome **37 E3**
Jones Sound **70 B5**
Jonesboro **81 B8**
Jönköping **9 D8**
Jonquière **71 E6**
Joplin **81 A6**
Jordan ■ **47 E4**
Jorhat **41 D10**
Jorong **39 E4**
Jos **53 G7**
Jotunheimen **8 C7**
Jowzjān □ **45 B6**
Juan de Fuca, Str of. **72 B1**
Juan Fernández, Arch. de **89 G3**
Juárez **94 D5**
Juàzeiro **93 D5**
Juàzeiro do Norte **92 D6**
Juba = Giuba ➔ **49 G3**
Jubbulpore = Jabalpur **43 H11**
Juby, C. **52 C3**
Júcar = Xúquer ➔ **19 C5**
Juchitán de Zaragoza **85 D5**
Jugoslavia = Serbia ■ **22 B3**
Juiz de Fora **93 G5**
Juli **91 G5**
Juliaca **91 G4**
Jullundur **42 D9**
Jumilla **19 C5**
Jumla **40 C4**
Jumna = Yamuna ➔ **40 E3**
Junagadh **43 J7**
Jundiaí **94 A7**
Juneau **69 C6**
Junee **63 B4**
Junggar Pendi **34 B3**
Junín **94 C4**
Junín de los Andes **95 D2**
Jūniyah **46 D3**
Jur, Nahr el ➔ **55 G4**
Jura = Jura, Mts. du **13 C7**
Jura = Schwäbische Alb **14 D5**
Jura **10 D4**
Jura, Mts. du **13 C7**
Juruá ➔ **90 D5**
Juruena ➔ **91 E7**
Juruti **92 C2**
Justo Daract **94 C3**
Jutland = Jylland **9 D7**
Juventud, I. de la **86 B3**
Jwaneng **58 C4**
Jylland **9 D7**
Jyväskylä **8 C11**

K

K2 **42 B10**
Kaapstad = Cape Town **58 E3**
Kabaena **37 F2**
Kabala **53 G3**
Kabale **57 E6**
Kabalo **57 F5**
Kabanjahe **39 D1**
Kabarai **37 E4**
Kabardino-Balkar Republic = Kabardino-Balkaria □ **25 E5**
Kabardino-Balkaria □ **25 E5**
Kabarega Falls = Murchison Falls **57 D6**
Kabasalan **36 C2**
Kabīr Kūh **47 D6**
Kabompo ➔ **58 A4**
Kabongo **57 F5**
Kabūd Gonbad **44 B4**
Kābul **42 B6**
Kābul □ **42 B6**
Kābul ➔ **42 C8**
Kaburuang **37 D3**
Kabwe **59 A5**
Kachchh, Gulf of **43 H6**
Kachchh, Rann of **43 G6**
Kachin □ **41 D11**
Kachiry **29 D8**
Kaçkar **25 E5**
Kadan Kyun **38 B1**
Kadina **62 B2**
Kadiyevka = Stakhanov **25 D4**
Kadoma **59 B5**
Kâdugli **55 F4**
Kaduna **53 F7**
Kaédi **53 E3**
Kaesŏng **35 C7**
Käf **47 E4**
Kafan = Kapan **25 F6**
Kafanchan **53 G7**
Kafue ➔ **59 B5**
Kaga Bandoro **55 G2**
Kagan **29 F7**
Kağızman **46 B5**
Kagoshima **33 H2**
Kagul = Cahul **17 F9**
Kahayan ➔ **39 E4**
Kahnūj **44 E4**
Kaho'olawe **78 H12**
Kahramanmaraş **46 C4**
Kahurangi △ **65 D5**
Kai, Kepulauan **37 F4**
Kai Besar **37 F4**
Kai Is. = Kai, Kepulauan **37 F4**
Kai Kecil **37 F4**
Kaiapoi **65 E5**
Kaieteur Falls **90 B7**
Kaifeng **35 C6**
Kaikohe **64 A5**
Kaikoura **65 E5**
Kaimana **37 E4**
Kaimanawa Mts. **64 C6**
Kainji Res. **53 F6**
Kaipara Harbour **64 B6**
Kaironi **37 E4**
Kairouan **54 A1**
Kaiserslautern **14 D4**
Kaitaia **64 A5**
Kaitangata **65 G3**
Kajaani **8 C11**
Kajabbi **61 D6**
Kajana = Kajaani **8 C11**
Kajo Kaji **55 H5**
Kakamega **57 D6**
Kakanui Mts. **65 F4**
Kakhovka **25 D3**
Kakhovske Vdskh. **25 D3**
Kakinada **40 J4**
Kalaallit Nunaat = Greenland ⊠ **66 C9**
Kalabagh **42 C7**
Kalabahi **37 F2**
Kalach **24 C5**
Kaladan ➔ **41 G9**
Kalahari **58 C4**
Kalakan **31 D9**
K'alak'unlun Shank'ou = Karakoram Pass **42 B10**
Kalamata **23 F4**
Kalamazoo **76 C3**
Kalan **46 C4**
Kalao **37 F2**
Kalaotoa **37 F2**
Kalat **42 E5**
Kalce **20 B5**
Kale **23 F7**
Kalegauk Kyun **41 K11**
Kalemie **57 F5**
Kalewa **41 F10**
Kalgoorlie-Boulder **60 G3**
Kaliakra, Nos **22 C7**
Kalianda **39 F3**
Kalibo **36 B2**
Kalima **57 E5**
Kalimantan **39 E4**
Kalimantan Barat □ **39 D4**
Kalimantan Selatan □ **39 E5**
Kalimantan Tengah □ **39 E4**
Kalimantan Timur □ **39 D5**
Kálimnos **23 F6**
Kaliningrad **24 C1**
Kalinkavichy **17 B9**
Kalinkovichi = Kalinkavichy **17 B9**
Kalispell **73 B6**
Kalisz **16 C4**
Kallsjön **8 C8**
Kalmar **9 D9**
Kalmyk Republic = Kalmykia □ **25 D6**
Kalmykia □ **25 D6**
Kalocsa **16 E4**
Kaluga **24 C4**
Kalush **17 D7**
Kalutara **43 R11**
Kama ➔ **29 D6**
Kamaishi **32 D7**
Kamarān **49 D3**
Kamchatka, Poluostrov **31 D13**
Kamchatka Pen. = Kamchatka, Poluostrov **31 D13**
Kamchiya ➔ **22 C6**
Kamen **29 D9**
Kamen-Rybolov **32 A3**
Kamenjak, Rt **20 B4**
Kamenka Bugskaya = Kamyanka-Buzka **17 C7**
Kamensk Uralskiy **29 D7**
Kamin-Kashyrskyy **17 C7**
Kamina **57 F5**
Kamloops **69 C7**
Kampala **57 D6**
Kampar ➔ **39 D2**
Kampen **14 B3**
Kampong Chhnang **38 B2**
Kampong Saom **38 B2**
Kampot **38 B2**
Kampuchea = Cambodia ■ **38 B3**
Kampungbaru = Tolitoli **37 D2**
Kamrau, Teluk **37 E4**
Kamui-Misaki **32 B7**
Kamyanets-Podilskyy **17 D8**
Kamyanka-Buzka **17 C7**
Kamyshin **24 C6**
Kanaaupscow **71 D6**
Kanagi **32 C7**
Kananga **56 F4**
Kanash **24 B6**
Kanastraíon, Ákra = Paliouri, Akra **23 E4**
Kanazawa **33 E5**
Kanchanaburi **38 B1**
Kanchenjunga **40 D7**
Kanchipuram **43 N11**
Kandahār **42 D4**
Kandahār □ **42 D4**
Kandalaksha **8 B12**
Kandalu **42 E3**
Kandangan **39 E5**
Kandi **53 F6**
Kandla **43 H7**
Kandos **63 B4**
Kandy **43 R12**
Kangaroo I. **62 C2**
Kangāvar **46 D7**
Kangean, Kepulauan **39 F5**

Kangean Is. = Kangean, Kepulauan **39 F5**
Kangiqliniq = Rankin Inlet **68 B10**
Kangiqsualujjuaq **70 D7**
Kangiqsujuaq **70 C6**
Kangiqtugaapik = Clyde River **70 B7**
Kangirsuk **70 D7**
Kangto **41 D9**
Kaniapiskau = Caniapiscau ➔ **70 D7**
Kaniapiskau, L. = Caniapiscau, L. **71 D7**
Kanin, Poluostrov **28 C5**
Kanin Nos, Mys **28 C5**
Kanin Pen. = Kanin, Poluostrov **28 C5**
Kaniva **62 C3**
Kankakee **76 D2**
Kankan **53 F4**
Kankendy = Xankändi **25 F6**
Kanker **40 G3**
Kannapolis **83 B7**
Kannauj **42 F11**
Kannod **43 H10**
Kano **53 F7**
Kanowit **39 D4**
Kanoya **33 H2**
Kanpetlet **41 G9**
Kanpur **40 D3**
Kansas □ **74 F5**
Kansas City *Kans., U.S.A.* **75 F7**
Kansas City *Mo., U.S.A.* **75 F7**
Kansk **30 D7**
Kansu = Gansu □ **34 C5**
Kanyakumari **43 Q10**
Kanye **59 C5**
Kaohsiung **35 D7**
Kaolack **53 F2**
Kapan **25 F6**
Kapanga **56 F4**
Kapchagai = Qapshaghay **29 E8**
Kapela = Velika Kapela **20 B5**
Kapfenberg **15 E8**
Kapiri Mposhi **59 A5**
Kāpīsā □ **45 C7**
Kapit **39 D4**
Kapiti I. **65 D6**
Kapoeta **55 H5**
Kaposvár **16 E3**
Kaptai L. **41 F9**
Kapuas ➔ **39 E3**
Kapuas Hulu, Pegunungan **39 D4**
Kapuas Hulu Ra. = Kapuas Hulu, Pegunungan **39 D4**
Kapunda **62 B2**
Kapuni **64 C6**
Kaputar, Mt. **63 B5**
Kara **28 C7**
Kara Bogaz Gol, Zaliv = Garabogazköl Aylagy **29 E6**
Kara Kalpak Republic = Qoraqalpoghistan □ **29 E6**
Kara Kum = Garagum **29 F6**
Kara Sea **28 B8**
Karabiğa **23 D6**
Karabük **46 B3**
Karaburun **23 E6**
Karabutak = Qarabutaq **29 E7**
Karacabey **23 D7**
Karacasu **23 F7**
Karachi **43 G5**
Karad **43 L9**
Karaganda = Qaraghandy **29 E8**
Karagayly = Qaraghayly **29 E8**
Karaikal **43 P11**
Karaikkudi **43 P11**
Karakalpakstan = Qoraqalpoghistan □ **29 E6**
Karakas **29 E9**
Karakelong **36 D3**
Karakitang **37 D3**
Karakol **29 E8**
Karakoram Pass **42 B10**
Karakoram Ra. **42 B10**
Karalon **30 D9**
Karaman **46 C3**
Karamay **34 B3**
Karambu **39 E5**
Karamea Bight **65 D4**
Karasburg **58 D3**
Karasino **28 C9**
Karasuk **29 D8**
Karatau, Khrebet = Qarataŭ **29 E7**
Karatsu **33 G2**
Karawanken **20 A5**
Karazhal = Qarazhal **29 E8**
Karbalā' **47 D6**
Karcag **16 E5**
Karditsa **23 E3**
Karelia □ **8 C12**
Karelian Republic = Karelia □ **8 C12**
Kargänrüd **46 C7**
Kargasok **29 D9**
Kargat **29 D9**
Kargil **42 B10**
Kariba, L. **59 B5**
Kariba Dam **59 B5**
Kariba Gorge **59 B5**
Karimata, Kepulauan **39 E3**
Karimata, Selat **39 E3**
Karimata Is. = Karimata, Kepulauan **39 E3**
Karimnagar **43 K11**
Karimunjawa, Kepulauan **39 F4**
Karin **49 E4**
Karkaralinsk = Qarqaraly **29 E8**
Karkinitska Zatoka **25 D3**
Karkinitskiy Zaliv = Karkinitska Zatoka **25 D3**
Karkuk = Kirkük **46 D6**
Karlovac **20 B5**
Karlovo **22 C5**
Karlovy Vary **16 C1**
Karlsbad = Karlovy Vary **16 C1**
Karlskrona **9 D9**
Karlsruhe **14 D5**
Karlstad **9 D8**
Karnal **42 E10**
Karnali ➔ **40 C3**
Karnaphuli Res. = Kaptai L. **41 F9**
Karnataka □ **43 N10**
Kärnten □ **15 E7**
Karonga **57 F6**
Karoonda **62 C2**
Karora **55 E6**
Karpathos **23 G6**
Kars **25 E5**
Karsakpay **29 E7**
Karshi = Qarshi **29 F7**
Karsun **24 C6**
Karufa **37 E4**
Karungu **57 E6**
Karviná **16 D4**
Karwar **43 M9**
Kasai ➔ **56 E3**
Kasama **57 G6**
Kasandra Kolpos **23 D4**
Kasaragod **43 N9**
Kasba L. **68 B9**
Kasempa **59 A5**
Kasenga **57 G5**
Kāshān **44 C2**
Kashgar = Kashi **34 C2**
Kashi **34 C2**
Kashk-e Kohneh **42 B3**
Kāshmar **44 C4**
Kashun Noerh = Gaxun Nur **34 B5**
Kasimov **24 C5**
Kasiruta **37 E3**
Kasongo **57 E5**
Kasongo Lunda **56 F3**
Kasos **23 G6**
Kassalā **55 E6**
Kassel **14 C5**
Kastamonu **25 E3**
Kasur **42 D9**
Katanga □ **57 F4**
Katangi **43 J11**
Katerini **23 D4**
Katha **41 E11**
Kathiawar **43 H7**
Kathmandu = Katmandu **40 D5**
Katihar **40 E6**
Katima Mulilo **58 B4**
Katingan = Mendawai ➔ **39 E4**
Katiola **53 G4**
Katmandu **40 D5**
Katoomba **63 B5**
Katowice **16 C4**
Katsina **53 F7**
Kattegat **9 D8**
Kaua'i **78 G11**
Kaunas **24 C1**
Kavala **22 D5**
Kavalerovo **32 A4**
Kavīr, Dasht-e **44 C3**
Kaw **92 B3**
Kawagoe **33 F6**
Kawaguchi **33 F6**
Kawardha **40 G3**
Kawasaki **33 F6**
Kawasi **37 E3**
Kawawachikamach **71 D7**
Kawerau **64 C7**
Kawhia **64 C6**
Kawhia Harbour **64 C6**
Kawio, Kepulauan **36 D3**
Kawnro **41 F12**
Kawthoolei = Kayin □ **41 H11**
Kawthule = Kayin □ **41 H11**
Kaya **53 F5**
Kayah □ **41 H11**
Kayan ➔ **39 D5**
Kayeli **37 E3**
Kayes **53 F3**
Kayin □ **41 H11**
Kayoa **37 D3**
Kayrunnera **62 B3**
Kayseri **46 C3**
Kazachye **31 B11**
Kazakhstan ■ **29 E7**
Kazan **24 B6**
Kazanlŭk **22 C5**
Kazatin = Kozyatyn **17 D9**
Kāzerūn **44 D2**
Kazym ➔ **28 C7**
Kea **23 F5**
Kebnekaise **8 B9**
Kebri Dehar **49 F3**
Kecskemét **16 E4**
Kediri **39 F4**
Keelung = Chilung **35 D7**
Keetmanshoop **58 D3**
Kefalonia **23 E3**
Kefamenanu **37 F2**
Keffi **53 G7**
Keflavík **8 C1**
Keighley **11 E6**
Keimoes **58 D4**
Keith **62 C3**
Kekri **42 G9**
Kël **30 C10**
Kelang = Klang **39 D2**
Kells = Ceanannus Mor **11 E3**
Kelowna **69 D8**
Kelso **65 F3**
Keluang = Kluang **39 D2**
Kem **28 C4**
Kema **37 D3**
Kemah **46 C4**
Kemerovo **29 D9**
Kemi **8 B10**
Kemi älv = Kemijoki ➔ **8 B10**
Kemi träsk = Kemijärvi **8 B11**
Kemijärvi **8 B11**
Kemijoki ➔ **8 B10**
Kemp Land **96 A9**
Kempsey **63 B5**
Kempten **14 E6**

Kendal 39 F4
Kendall 63 B5
Kendari 37 E2
Kendawangan 39 E4
Kendrapara 40 G6
Kenema 53 G3
Keng Tawng 41 G12
Keng Tung 41 G12
Kenitra 52 B4
Kennedy, Mt. 41 F9
Kennewick 72 C4
Kenogami → 71 D5
Kenosha 76 C2
Kent Group 62 C4
Kent Pen. 68 B9
Kentaü 29 E7
Kentucky □ 76 F3
Kentville 71 E7
Kenya ■ 57 D7
Kenya, Mt. 57 E7
Kepi 37 F5
Kerala □ 43 P10
Kerang 62 C3
Kerch 25 D4
Kericho 57 E7
Kerinci 39 E2
Kerki = Atamyrat 29 F7
Kerkyra 23 E2
Kermadec Is. 64 M13
Kermadec Trench 65 N13
Kermān 44 D4
Kermān □ 44 D4
Kermānshāh 46 D6
Kerrobert 69 C9
Kerulen → 35 B6
Kerzaz 52 C5
Keşan 22 D6
Kesennuma 32 D7
Kestenga 28 C4
Ket → 29 D9
Ketapang 39 E4
Ketchikan 69 C6
Kętrzyn 16 A5
Key West 86 B3
Khabarovo 28 C7
Khabarovsk 31 E11
Khābūr → 46 D5
Khairpur 42 F6
Khakassia □ 30 D6
Khalkhāl 46 C7
Khalkís = Halkida 23 E4
Khalmer Yu 28 C7
Khalturin 24 B6
Khalūf 48 C6
Khambhat 43 H8
Khambhat, G. of 43 J8
Khamir 49 D3
Khānābād 45 B7
Khānaqīn 46 D6
Khandwa 43 J10
Khanewal 42 D7
Khaniá = Chania 23 G5
Khanka, L. 32 A3
Khankendy = Xankändi 25 F6
Khanty-Mansiysk 29 C7
Khapcheranga 30 E9
Kharagpur 40 F6
Kharan Kalat 42 E4
Kharānaq 44 C3
Kharda 43 K9
Kharg = Khārk, Jazīreh-ye 47 E7
Khârga, El Wâhât-el 54 C5
Khargon 43 J9
Khārk, Jazīreh-ye 47 E7
Kharkiv 24 D4
Kharkov = Kharkiv 24 D4
Kharovsk 24 B5
Kharta 22 D7
Khartoum = El Khartûm 55 E5
Khasan 32 B2
Khāsh 42 E2
Khashm el Girba 55 F6
Khaskovo 22 D5
Khatanga 30 B8
Khatanga → 30 B8
Khaybar, Ḥarrat 47 F5
Khed Brahma 43 G8
Khemmarat 38 A3
Khenchela 52 A7
Kherson 25 D3
Kheta → 30 B8
Khilok 30 D9
Khíos = Hios 23 E6
Khiuma = Hiiumaa 24 B1
Khiva 29 E7
Khīyāv 46 C6
Khmelnik 17 D8
Khmelnitskiy = Khmelnytskyy 17 D8
Khmelnytskyy 17 D8
Khmer Rep. = Cambodia ■ 38 B3
Khodoriv 17 D7
Khodzent = Khŭjand 29 E7
Khojak Pass 42 D5
Kholm *Afghan.* 45 B6
Kholm *Russia* 24 B3
Khomeyn 44 C2
Khon Kaen 38 A2
Khorat = Nakhon Ratchasima 38 B2
Khorramābād 46 D7
Khorrāmshahr 47 E7
Khotyn 17 D8
Khouribga 52 B4
Khowst 42 C6
Khoyniki 17 C9
Khu Khan 38 B2
Khudzhand = Khŭjand 29 E7
Khūgiāni 42 D4
Khŭjand 29 E7
Khulna 41 F7
Khulna □ 41 F7
Khūr 44 C4
Khurayş 47 F7
Khush 42 C3
Khushab 42 C8
Khust 17 D6
Khuzdar 42 F5
Khvor 44 C3
Khvormūj 44 D2
Khvoy 46 C6
Khyber Pass 42 B7
Kiama 63 B5
Kiamba 36 C2
Kiangsi = Jiangxi □ 35 D6
Kiangsu = Jiangsu □ 35 C6
Kibombo 57 E5
Kıbrıs = Cyprus ■ 46 D3
Kibwezi 57 E7
Kicking Horse Pass 69 C8
Kidal 53 E6
Kidnappers, C. 64 C7
Kiel 14 A6
Kiel Canal = Nord-Ostsee-Kanal 14 A5
Kielce 16 C5
Kieler Bucht 14 A6
Kiev = Kyyiv 17 C10
Kiffa 53 E3
Kifrī 46 D6
Kigali 57 E6
Kigoma-Ujiji 57 E5
Kihee 62 A3
Kii-Sanchi 33 F5
Kikinda 22 B3
Kikládhes = Cyclades 23 F5
Kikwit 56 E3
Kilcoy 63 A5
Kilimanjaro 57 E7
Kilis 46 C4
Kiliya 17 F9
Kilkenny 11 E3
Kilkis 23 D4
Killarney *Australia* 63 A5
Killarney *Ireland* 11 E2
Killeen 80 D5
Killini 23 F4
Kilmarnock 10 D4
Kilmore 63 C3
Kilosa 57 F7
Kilrush 11 E2
Kilwa Kivinje 57 F7
Kimaam 37 F5
Kimba 62 B2
Kimberley *Australia* 60 D4
Kimberley *S. Africa* 58 D4
Kimmirut 70 C7
Kimry 24 B4
Kinabalu, Gunung 38 C5
Kindia 53 F3
Kindu 57 E5
Kineshma 24 B5
King George B. 95 G4
King George I. 96 A4
King George Is. 71 D5
King I. = Kadan Kyun 38 B1
King I. 62 C3
King William I. 68 B10
Kingait = Cape Dorset 70 C6
Kingaok = Bathurst Inlet 68 B9
Kingaroy 63 A5
Kingoonya 62 B2
Kings Canyon △ 78 B3
King's Lynn 11 E7
Kingscote 62 C2
Kingsport 83 A6
Kingston *Canada* 71 E6
Kingston *Jamaica* 86 C4
Kingston *N.Z.* 65 F3
Kingston South East 62 C2
Kingston upon Hull 11 E6
Kingstown 87 D7
Kingsville 80 F5
Kınık 23 E6
Kinkala 56 E2
Kinleith 64 C6
Kinsale 11 F2
Kinsha = Chang Jiang → 35 C7
Kinshasa 56 E3
Kinston 83 B9
Kiparissia 23 F3
Kiparissiakos Kolpos 23 F3
Kipushi 59 A5
Kirghizia = Kyrgyzstan ■ 29 E8
Kiribati ■ 64 K12
Kırıkkale 25 F3
Kirillov 24 B4
Kirin = Jilin 35 B7
Kirinyaga = Kenya, Mt. 57 E7
Kiritimati 65 J15
Kirkcaldy 10 C5
Kirkcudbright 11 D4
Kirkee 43 K8
Kirkland Lake 71 E5
Kırklareli 22 D6
Kirkük 46 D6
Kirkwall 10 B5
Kirov 28 D5
Kirovabad = Gäncä 25 E6
Kirovograd = Kirovohrad 25 D3
Kirovohrad 25 D3
Kirovsk = Babadayhan 29 F7
Kirovskiy 32 A3
Kirsanov 24 C5
Kırşehir 25 F3
Kirthar Range 42 F5
Kiruna 8 B10
Kiryū 33 E6
Kisangani 57 D5
Kisar 37 F3
Kiselevsk 29 D9
Kishanganj 40 D7
Kishangarh 42 F7
Kishb, Ḥarrat al 47 G5
Kishinev = Chişinău 17 E9
Kishtwar 42 C9
Kisii 57 E6
Kiskőrös 16 E4
Kiskunfélegyháza 16 E4
Kiskunhalas 16 E4
Kislovodsk 25 E5
Kismayu = Chisimaio 49 H3
Kiso-Gawa → 33 F5
Kissidougou 53 G3
Kisumu 57 E6
Kita 53 F4
Kitaibaraki 33 E7
Kitakyūshū 33 G2
Kitale 57 D7
Kitami 32 B8
Kitchener 71 E5

Kitega = Gitega **57 E5**
Kíthira = Kythira **23 F4**
Kíthnos **23 F5**
Kitikmeot □ **68 B9**
Kittakittaooloo, L. **62 A2**
Kitui **57 E7**
Kitwe **59 A5**
Kivertsi **17 C7**
Kivu, L. **57 E5**
Kiyev = Kyyiv **17 C10**
Kiyevskoye Vdkhr. = Kyyivske Vdskh. **17 C10**
Kızıl Irmak ➔ **25 E4**
Kizlyar **25 E6**
Kizyl-Arvat = Serdar **29 F6**
Kladno **16 C2**
Klagenfurt **15 E8**
Klaipėda **24 B1**
Klamath Falls **72 E3**
Klamath Mts. **72 F2**
Klang **39 D2**
Klarälven ➔ **9 C8**
Klatovy **16 D1**
Klerksdorp **59 D5**
Kletsk = Klyetsk **17 B8**
Kłodzko **16 C3**
Klondike **68 B6**
Klouto **53 G6**
Kluane L. **68 B6**
Kluang **39 D2**
Kluczbork **16 C4**
Klyetsk **17 B8**
Knossos **23 G5**
Knox Coast **96 A12**
Knoxville **83 B6**
Koartac = Quaqtaq **70 C7**
Koba **37 F4**
Kobarid **20 A4**
Köbe **33 F4**
København **9 D8**
Koblenz **14 C4**
Kobroor **37 F4**
Kobryn **17 B7**
Kocaeli **25 E2**
Kočani **22 D4**
Koch Bihar **41 D7**
Kochi = Cochin **43 Q10**
Köchi **33 G3**
Kochiu = Gejiu **34 D5**
Kodiak **69 C4**
Kodiak I. **69 C4**
Kofiau **37 E3**
Koforidua **53 G5**
Köfu **33 F6**
Kogan **63 A5**
Kohat **42 C7**
Kohima **41 E10**
Kohkīlūyeh va Būyer Aḥmadi □ **44 D2**
Kohler Ra. **96 B1**
Kokand = Qūqon **29 E8**
Kokas **37 E4**
Kokchetav = Kökshetaü **29 D7**
Koko Kyunzu **41 K9**
Kokomo **76 D2**
Kökshetaü **29 D7**
Koksoak ➔ **70 D7**
Kokstad **59 E5**
Kola **37 F4**
Kola Pen. = Kolskiy Poluostrov **8 B13**
Kolaka **37 E2**
Kolar **43 N11**
Kolar Gold Fields **43 N11**
Kolayat **42 F8**
Kolepom = Dolak, Pulau **37 F5**
Kolguyev, Ostrov **28 C5**
Kolhapur **43 L9**
Kolín **16 C2**
Kolkata **41 F7**
Kollam = Quilon **43 Q10**
Köln **14 C4**
Koło **16 B4**
Kołobrzeg **16 A2**
Kolomna **24 B4**
Kolomyya **17 D7**
Kolonodale **37 E2**
Kolosib **41 E9**
Kolpashevo **29 D9**
Kolpino **24 B3**
Kolskiy Poluostrov **8 B13**
Kolwezi **57 G5**
Kolyma ➔ **31 C13**
Komatsu **33 E5**
Komi □ **28 C6**
Kommunarsk = Alchevsk **25 D4**
Kommunizma, Pik = imeni Ismail Samani, Pik **29 F8**
Komodo **37 F1**
Komoran, Pulau **37 F5**
Komotini **22 D5**
Kompong Cham **38 B3**
Kompong Chhnang = Kampong Chhnang **38 B2**
Kompong Som = Kampong Saom **38 B2**
Komrat = Comrat **17 E9**
Komsomolets, Ostrov **30 A7**
Kon Tum **38 B3**
Konar □ **42 B7**
Konch **42 G11**
Kondoa **57 E7**
Kondoz **45 B7**
Kondoz □ **45 B7**
Köneürgench **29 E6**
Kong **53 G5**
Kong, Koh **38 B2**
Konglu **41 D11**
Kongolo **57 F5**
Konin **16 B4**
Konjic **20 C6**
Konosha **28 C5**
Konotop **24 C3**
Konqi He ➔ **34 B4**
Końskie **16 C5**
Konstanz **14 E5**
Kontagora **53 F7**
Konya **46 C3**
Konya Ovası **46 C3**
Kooloonong **62 B3**
Koonibba **62 B1**
Koorawatha **63 B4**
Kootenay L. **69 D8**
Kopaonik **22 C3**
Koper **20 B4**
Kopi **62 B2**
Koprivnica **20 A6**
Kopychyntsi **17 D7**
Korab **22 D3**
Korçë **23 D3**
Korčula **20 C6**
Kordestan = Kurdistan **46 D5**
Kordestān □ **46 D6**
Kordofān **55 F4**
Korea, North ■ **35 C7**
Korea, South ■ **35 C7**
Korea Bay **35 C7**
Korea Strait **35 C7**
Korets **17 C8**
Korhogo **53 G4**
Korinthiakos Kolpos **23 E4**
Korinthos **23 F4**
Kōriyama **33 E7**
Korneshty = Cornești **17 E9**
Koro **53 G4**
Korogwe **57 F7**
Koror = Melekeok **36 C4**
Körös ➔ **16 E5**
Korosten **17 C9**
Korostyshev **17 C9**
Kortrijk **14 C2**
Kos **23 F6**
Kościan **16 B3**
Kosciuszko, Mt. **63 C4**
Kosha **54 D5**
K'oshih = Kashi **34 C2**
Koshiki-Rettō **33 H1**
Košice **16 D5**
Kosovo ■ **22 C3**
Kosovska Mitrovica **22 C3**
Kōstī **55 F5**
Kostopil **17 C8**
Kostroma **24 B5**
Kostrzyn **16 B2**
Koszalin **16 A3**
Kota **43 G9**
Kota Belud **38 C5**
Kota Bharu **38 C2**
Kota Kinabalu **38 C5**
Kota Kubu Bharu **39 D2**
Kota Tinggi **39 D2**
Kotaagung **39 F2**
Kotabaru **39 E5**
Kotabumi **39 E2**
Kotamobagu **37 D2**
Kotelnich **24 B6**
Kotelnyy, Ostrov **31 B11**
Kotka **9 C11**
Kotlas **28 C5**
Kotor **22 C2**
Kotovsk **17 E9**
Kotri **42 G6**
Kotturu **43 M10**
Kotuy ➔ **30 B8**
Kotzebue **69 B3**
Koudougou **53 F5**
Kouilou ➔ **56 E2**
Koula Moutou **56 E2**
Koulen = Kulen **38 B2**
Koumra **55 G2**
Kounradskiy **29 E8**
Kousseri **55 F1**
Kouvola **8 C11**
Kovel **17 C7**
Kovrov **24 B5**
Koyampattur = Coimbatore **43 P10**
Köyceğiz **23 F7**
Kozan **46 C3**
Kozani **23 D3**
Kozhikode = Calicut **43 P9**
Kozyatyn **17 D9**
Kra, Isthmus of = Kra, Kho Khot **38 B1**
Kra, Kho Khot **38 B1**
Kracheh **38 B3**
Kragujevac **22 B3**
Krajina **20 B6**
Krakatau = Rakata, Pulau **39 F3**
Krakatoa = Rakata, Pulau **39 F3**
Kraków **16 C4**
Kraljevo **22 C3**
Kramatorsk **25 D4**
Kranj **20 A5**
Kraśnik **16 C6**
Krasnoarmeysk **29 D5**
Krasnodar **25 D4**
Krasnoperekopsk **25 D3**
Krasnoselkup **28 C9**
Krasnoturinsk **28 D7**
Krasnoyarsk **30 D7**
Krasnyy Luch **25 D4**
Krasnyy Yar **25 D6**
Kratie = Kracheh **38 B3**
Krau **37 E6**
Krefeld **14 C4**
Kremen **20 B5**
Kremenchuk **24 D3**
Kremenchuksk Vdskh. **24 D3**
Kremenets **17 C7**
Krems **15 D8**
Kribi **56 D1**
Krichev = Krychaw **17 B10**
Krishna ➔ **40 K3**
Krishnanagar **41 F7**
Kristiansand **9 D7**
Kristiansund **8 C7**
Kriti **23 G5**
Krivoy Rog = Kryvyy Rih **25 D3**
Krk **20 B5**
Kronprins Olav Kyst **96 A9**
Kronshtadt **24 B2**
Kroonstad **59 D5**
Kropotkin *Irkutsk, Russia* **30 D9**
Kropotkin *Krasnodar, Russia* **25 D5**
Krotoszyn **16 C3**
Krung Thep = Bangkok **38 B2**
Krupki **17 A9**
Kruševac **22 C3**
Krychaw **17 B10**
Krymskiy Poluostrov = Krymskyy Pivostriv **25 D3**
Krymskyy Pivostriv **25 D3**
Kryvyy Rih **25 D3**

Ksar el Kebir 52 B4
Ksar es Souk = Er Rachidia 52 B5
Kuala Lipis 39 D2
Kuala Lumpur 39 D2
Kuala Sepetang 38 D2
Kuala Terengganu 38 C2
Kualajelai 39 E4
Kualakapuas 39 E4
Kualakurun 39 E4
Kualapembuang 39 E4
Kualasimpang 39 D1
Kuandang 37 D2
Kuangchou = Guangzhou 35 D6
Kuantan 39 D2
Kuba = Quba 25 E6
Kuban ➔ 25 D4
Kuching 39 D4
Kucing = Kuching 39 D4
Kuda 43 H7
Kudat 38 C5
Kudymkar 28 D6
Kueiyang = Guiyang 35 D5
Kufra Oasis = Al Kufrah 54 D3
Kufstein 15 E7
Kugaaruk = Pelly Bay 70 C5
Kugluktuk 68 B8
Küh-e 'Alijūq 44 D2
Küh-e Sorkh 44 C4
Kūhak 42 F3
Kūhhā-ye-Bashākerd 45 E4
Kūhpāyeh 44 C3
Kuito 58 A3
Kuji 32 C7
Kukës 22 C3
Kula 23 E7
Kulasekarappattinam 43 Q11
Kulen 38 B2
Külob 29 F7
Kulsary 29 E6
Kulunda 29 D8
Kulwin 62 C3
Kulyab = Külob 29 F7
Kum Tekei 29 E8
Kuma ➔ 25 E6
Kumagaya 33 E6
Kumai 39 E4
Kumamba, Kepulauan 37 E5
Kumamoto 33 G2
Kumanovo 22 C3
Kumara 65 E4
Kumasi 53 G5
Kumba 53 H7
Kumbakonam 43 P11
Kumbarilla 63 A5
Kumon Bum 41 D11
Kunama 63 C4
Kungala 63 A5
Kungrad = Qūnghirot 29 E6
Kungur 29 D6
Kunlong 41 F12
Kunlun Shan 34 C3
Kunming 34 D5
Kunya-Urgench = Köneürgench 29 E6
Kuopio 8 C11
Kupa ➔ 20 B6
Kuqa 34 B3
Kür ➔ 25 E6
Kura = Kür ➔ 25 E6
Kurdistan 46 D5
Kürdzhali 22 D5
Kure 33 F3
Kurgaldzhinskiy 29 D8
Kurgan 29 D7
Kuria Maria Is. = Hallāniyat, Jazā'ir al 49 D6
Kurigram 41 E7
Kuril Is. = Kurilskiye Ostrova 31 E12
Kurilskiye Ostrova 31 E12
Kurnool 43 L11
Kurow 65 F4
Kurri Kurri 63 B5
Kursk 24 C4
Kuruktag 34 B3
Kuruman 58 D4
Kurume 33 G2
Kus Gölü 23 D6
Kuşadası 23 F6
Kushimoto 33 G4
Kushiro 32 B9
Kushtia 41 F7
Kuskokwim B. 69 C3
Kustanay = Qostanay 29 D7
Kütahya 25 F3
Kutaisi 25 E5
Kutaraja = Banda Aceh 38 C1
Kutch, Gulf of = Kachchh, Gulf of 43 H6
Kutch, Rann of = Kachchh, Rann of 43 G6
Kutno 16 B4
Kutu 56 E3
Kutum 55 F3
Kuujjuaq 70 D7
Kuujjuarapik 71 D6
Kuusamo 8 B11
Kuwait = Al Kuwayt 47 E7
Kuwait ■ 47 E6
Kuybyshev = Samara 24 C7
Kuybyshev 29 D8
Kuybyshevskoye Vdkhr. 24 B6
Kuyumba 30 C7
Kuzey Anadolu Dağları 25 E4
Kuznetsk 24 C6
Kvarner 20 B5
Kvarnerič 20 B5
Kwajalein 64 J11
Kwakoegron 92 A2
KwaMashu 59 D6
Kwando ➔ 58 B4
Kwangchow = Guangzhou 35 D6
Kwango ➔ 56 E3
Kwangsi-Chuang = Guangxi Zhuangzu Zizhiqu □ 35 D5
Kwangtung = Guangdong □ 35 D6
Kwatisore 37 E4
KwaZulu Natal □ 59 D6
Kweichow = Guizhou □ 35 D5
Kwekwe 59 B5
Kwidzyn 16 B4
Kwoka 37 E4
Kyabra Cr. ➔ 63 A3
Kyabram 63 C4
Kyancutta 62 B2
Kyaukpadaung 41 G10
Kyaukpyu 41 H9
Kyaukse 41 G11
Kyneton 63 C3
Kyō-ga-Saki 33 F4
Kyoga, L. 57 D6
Kyogle 63 A5
Kyonpyaw 41 J10
Kyōto 33 F4
Kypros = Cyprus ■ 46 D3
Kyrenia 46 D3
Kyrgyzstan ■ 29 E8
Kyrtylakh 31 C10
Kystatyam 30 C10
Kythira 23 F4
Kyunhla 41 F10
Kyūshū 33 G2
Kyustendil 22 C4
Kyusyur 30 B10
Kyyiv 17 C10
Kyyivske Vdskh. 17 C10
Kyzyl Kum 29 E7
Kyzyl-Kyya 29 E8
Kyzyl-Orda = Qyzylorda 29 E7

L

La Alcarria 19 B4
La Asunción 90 A6
La Banda 94 B4
La Carlota 94 C4
La Ceiba 85 D7
La Cocha 94 B3
La Coruña = A Coruña 18 A1
La Crosse 75 D9
La Estrada = A Estrada 18 A1
La Grande ➔ 71 D6
La Grange 82 C5
La Guaira 90 A5
La Habana 86 B3
La Línea de la Concepción 18 D3
La Mancha 19 C4
La Palma 52 C2
La Palma del Condado 18 D2
La Paragua 90 B6
La Paz *Entre Ríos, Argentina* 94 C5
La Paz *San Luis, Argentina* 94 C3
La Paz *Bolivia* 91 G5
La Paz *Mexico* 84 C2
La Pedrera 90 D5
La Plata 94 D5
La Quiaca 94 A3
La Rioja 94 B3
La Rioja □ 19 A4
La Robla 18 A3
La Roche-sur-Yon 12 C3
La Rochelle 12 C3
La Roda 19 C4
La Romana 87 C6
La Serena 94 B2
La Seu d'Urgell 19 A6
La Seyne-sur-Mer 13 E6
La Spézia 13 D8
La Tortuga 87 D6
La Tuque 71 E6
La Unión 95 E2
La Urbana 90 B5
La Vall d'Uixó 19 C5
La Vega 87 C5
Laas Caanood = Las Anod 49 F4
Labe = Elbe ➔ 14 B5
Labé 53 F3
Laboulaye 94 C4
Labrador 71 D7
Labrador City 71 D7
Labrador Sea 70 D8
Lábrea 91 E6
Labuan 38 C5
Labuan, Pulau 38 C5
Labuha 37 E3
Labuhanbajo 37 F2
Labuk, Telok 38 C5
Labyrinth, L. 62 B2
Labytnangi 28 C7
Lac La Biche 69 C8
Lac la Martre = Wha Ti 68 B8
Lacanau 12 D3
Laccadive Is. = Lakshadweep Is. 26 G9
Lacepede B. 62 C2
Lachlan ➔ 63 B3
Lacombe 69 C8
Ladakh Ra. 42 B10
Lādīz 45 D5
Ladoga, L. = Ladozhskoye Ozero 8 C12
Ladozhskoye Ozero 8 C12
Ladysmith 59 D5
Lae 61 B8
Lafayette 81 D7
Lafia 53 G7
Laghmān □ 45 C7
Laghouat 52 B6
Lagonoy G. 36 B2
Lagos *Nigeria* 53 G6
Lagos *Portugal* 18 D1
Laguna 94 B7
Lagunas 90 E3
Lahad Datu 36 C1
Lahad Datu, Telok 36 D1
Lahat 39 E2
Lahewa 39 D1
Lāhījān 46 C7
Lahn ➔ 14 C4
Lahore 42 D9
Lahti 8 C11
Lahtis = Lahti 8 C11
Laï 55 G2
Laidley 63 A5

Laila = Layla **47 G6**
Lairg **10 B4**
Laizhou **35 C6**
Lajes **94 B6**
Lake Cargelligo **63 B4**
Lake Charles **81 D7**
Lake City **83 D6**
Lake Harbour = Kimmirut **70 C7**
Lake Worth **83 F7**
Lakeland **83 E7**
Lakes Entrance **63 C4**
Lakewood **76 D5**
Lakhnau = Lucknow **40 D3**
Lakonikos Kolpos **23 F4**
Lakor **37 F3**
Lakota **53 G4**
Lakshadweep Is. **26 G9**
Lalaghat **41 E9**
L'Albufera **19 C5**
Lalín **18 A1**
Lalitapur **40 D5**
Lamaing **41 K11**
Lamas **91 E3**
Lambaréné **56 E2**
Lambert Glacier **96 B10**
Lamego **18 B2**
Lameroo **62 C3**
Lamia **23 E4**
Lamon B. **36 B2**
Lampa **91 G4**
Lampedusa **21 G4**
Lampione **21 G4**
Lampung □ **39 F2**
Lamu **57 E8**
Lāna'i **78 H12**
Lanak La **42 B11**
Lanak'o Shank'ou = Lanak La **42 B11**
Lancaster *U.K.* **11 D5**
Lancaster *U.S.A.* **77 D7**
Lancaster Sd. **70 B5**
Lanchow = Lanzhou **35 C5**
Lanciano **20 C5**
Landeck **14 E6**
Landes **12 D3**
Landi Kotal **42 B7**
Land's End **11 F4**
Landshut **15 D7**
La'nga Co **40 B3**
Langjökull **8 C2**
Langkawi, Pulau **38 C1**
Langkon **38 C5**
Langreo **18 A3**
Langres **13 C6**
Langres, Plateau de **13 C6**
Langsa **38 D1**
Languedoc **13 E5**
Lannion **12 B2**
Lansdowne **63 B5**
Lansing **76 C3**
Lanusei **21 E2**
Lanzarote **52 C3**
Lanzhou **35 C5**
Laoag **36 A2**
Laoang **36 B3**
Laohekou **35 C6**
Laon **13 B5**
Laos ■ **38 A3**
Laparan **36 C1**
Lapland = Lappland **8 B10**
Lappland **8 B10**
Lapseki **23 D6**
Laptev Sea **30 B10**
L'Àquila **20 C4**
Lär **44 E3**
Laramie **74 E2**
Larantuka **37 F2**
Larap **36 B2**
Larat **37 F4**
Laredo **80 F4**
Lariang **37 E1**
Larisa **23 E4**
Larnaca **46 D3**
Larne **11 D4**
Larrimah **60 D5**
Larsen Ice Shelf **96 A3**
Larvik **9 D8**
Laryak **29 C8**
Las Anod **49 F4**
Las Cruces **79 D9**
Las Flores **94 D5**
Las Lajas **94 D2**
Las Lomitas **94 A4**
Las Palmas **52 C2**
Las Plumas **95 E3**
Las Varillas **94 C4**
Las Vegas **78 B5**
Lash-e Joveyn **42 D2**
Lashio **41 F11**
Lassen Pk. **72 F3**
Lastoursville **56 E2**
Lastovo **20 C6**
Latacunga **90 D3**
Latakia = Al Lādhiqīyah **46 D3**
Latina **20 D4**
Latium = Lazio □ **20 C4**
Latrobe **62 D4**
Latvia ■ **24 B1**
Lauchhammer **15 C7**
Launceston **62 D4**
Laurel **81 D9**
Lauria **21 D5**
Lausanne **14 E4**
Laut **38 D3**
Laut Kecil, Kepulauan **39 E5**
Laval **12 B3**
Lavrio **23 F5**
Lawas **38 D5**
Lawele **37 F2**
Lawng Pit **41 E11**
Lawrence *N.Z.* **65 F3**
Lawrence *U.S.A.* **75 F7**
Lawton **80 B4**
Layla **47 G6**
Lazio □ **20 C4**
Lazo **32 B3**
Le Creusot **13 C6**
Le Havre **12 B4**
Le Mans **12 C4**
Le Mont-St-Michel **12 B3**
Le Puy-en-Velay **13 D5**
Le Touquet-Paris-Plage **12 A4**
Le Tréport **12 A4**
Le Verdon-sur-Mer **12 D3**
Leamington Spa = Royal Leamington Spa **11 E6**
Leavenworth **75 F7**
Lebak **36 C2**
Lebanon ■ **46 D3**
Lębork **16 A3**
Lebrija **18 D2**
Lebu **94 D2**
Lecce **21 D7**
Lecco **13 D8**
Lech ➔ **14 D6**
Łęczyca **16 B4**
Leeds **11 E6**
Leer **14 B4**
Leeton **63 B4**
Leeuwarden **14 B3**
Leeuwin, C. **60 G2**
Leeward Is. **87 C7**
Lefkada **23 E3**
Leganés **18 B4**
Legazpi **36 B2**
Leghorn = Livorno **20 C3**
Legionowo **16 B5**
Legnago **20 B3**
Legnica **16 C3**
Legume **63 A5**
Leh **42 B10**
Leicester **11 E6**
Leiden **14 B3**
Leie ➔ **14 C2**
Leine ➔ **14 B5**
Leinster □ **11 E3**
Leipzig **15 C7**
Leiria **18 C1**
Leitrim **11 D2**
Leizhou Bandao **35 D6**
Leleque **95 E2**
Léman, L. **13 C7**
Lemhi Ra. **73 D7**
Lena ➔ **30 B10**
Leninogorsk **29 D9**
Leninsk **25 D6**
Leninsk-Kuznetskiy **29 D9**
Lenmalu **37 E4**
Lens **13 A5**
Lentini **21 F5**
Leoben **15 E8**
Leodhas = Lewis **10 B3**
León *Mexico* **84 C4**
León *Nic.* **85 E7**
León *Spain* **18 A3**
León, Montes de **18 A2**
Leongatha **63 C4**
Leova **17 E9**
Lepel = Lyepyel **24 C2**
Lepikha **31 C10**
Lérida = Lleida **19 B6**
Lerwick **10 A6**
Les Cayes **86 C5**
Les Sables-d'Olonne **12 C3**
Lesbos **23 E6**
Leskovac **22 C3**
Lesotho ■ **59 D5**
Lesozavodsk **32 A3**
Lesser Antilles **87 D7**
Lesser Sunda Is. **37 F2**
Lésvos = Lesbos **23 E6**
Leszno **16 C3**
Lethbridge **69 D8**
Leti, Kepulauan **37 F3**
Leti Is. = Leti, Kepulauan **37 F3**
Leticia **90 D4**
Letpadan **41 J10**
Letpan **41 H10**
Letterkenny **11 D3**
Leuser, G. **39 D1**
Leuven **14 C3**
Levanger **8 C8**
Levin **64 D6**
Lévis **71 E6**
Levka Oros **23 G5**
Levkás = Lefkada **23 E3**
Levkôsia = Nicosia **46 D3**
Levskigrad = Karlovo **22 C5**
Lewis **10 B3**
Lewisporte **71 E8**
Lewiston *Idaho, U.S.A.* **72 C5**
Lewiston *Maine, U.S.A.* **77 B10**
Lexington *Ky., U.S.A.* **76 E3**
Lexington *N.C., U.S.A.* **83 B7**
Leyte □ **36 B2**
Lezhë **22 D2**
Lhasa **34 D4**
Lhazê **34 D3**
Lhokkruet **38 D1**
Lhokseumawe **38 C1**
L'Hospitalet de Llobregat **19 B7**
Liancourt Rocks **33 E2**
Lianga **36 C3**
Lianyungang **35 C6**
Liaoning □ **35 B7**
Liaoyuan **35 B7**
Liard ➔ **68 B7**
Libau = Liepāja **24 B1**
Libenge **56 D3**
Liberal **80 A3**
Liberec **16 C2**
Liberia ■ **53 G4**
Lībīya, Sahrā' **54 C4**
Libobo, Tanjung **37 E3**
Libourne **12 D3**
Libreville **56 D1**
Libya ■ **54 C2**
Libyan Desert = Lībīya, Sahrā' **54 C4**
Licantén **94 D2**
Licata **21 F4**
Lichinga **59 A7**
Lida **17 B7**
Liechtenstein ■ **14 E5**
Liège **14 C3**
Liegnitz = Legnica **16 C3**
Lienyünchiangshih = Lianyungang **35 C6**
Lienz **15 E7**
Liepāja **24 B1**
Lietuva = Lithuania ■ **24 B1**
Liffey ➔ **11 E3**
Lifford **11 D3**
Lightning Ridge **63 A4**
Liguria □ **13 D8**

Ligurian Sea **20 C2**
Lijiang **34 D5**
Likasi **57 G5**
Lille **13 A5**
Lillehammer **8 C8**
Lilongwe **59 A6**
Liloy **36 C2**
Lim ➔ **20 C7**
Lima *Indonesia* **37 E3**
Lima *Peru* **91 F3**
Lima *U.S.A.* **76 D3**
Lima ➔ **18 B1**
Limassol **46 D3**
Limay Mahuida **94 D3**
Limbang **38 D5**
Limbe **53 H7**
Limbri **63 B5**
Limburg **14 C5**
Limeira **93 G4**
Limerick **11 E2**
Limfjorden **9 D7**
Limia = Lima ➔ **18 B1**
Limnos **23 E5**
Limoges **12 D4**
Limón **86 E3**
Limousin □ **12 D4**
Limoux **12 E5**
Limpopo ➔ **59 D6**
Limuru **57 E7**
Linares *Chile* **94 D2**
Linares *Mexico* **84 C5**
Linares *Spain* **18 C4**
Lincoln *Argentina* **94 C4**
Lincoln *N.Z.* **65 E5**
Lincoln *U.K.* **11 E6**
Lincoln *U.S.A.* **75 E6**
Linden **90 B7**
Lindesnes **9 D7**
Lindi **57 F7**
Lindos **23 F7**
Lingayen **36 A2**
Lingayen G. **36 A2**
Lingen **14 B4**
Lingga **39 E2**
Lingga, Kepulauan **39 E2**
Lingga Arch. = Lingga, Kepulauan **39 E2**
Linguère **53 E2**
Linhai **35 D7**
Linhares **93 F5**
Linköping **9 D9**
Linosa **21 G4**
Lins **93 G4**
Linville **63 A5**
Linxia **34 C5**
Linz **15 D8**
Lion, G. du **13 E6**
Lions, G. of = Lion, G. du **13 E6**
Lipa **36 B2**
Lípari **21 E5**
Lípari, Is. = Eólie, Ís. **21 E5**
Lipcani **17 D8**
Lipetsk **24 C4**
Lipkany = Lipcani **17 D8**
Lipovets **17 D9**
Lippe ➔ **14 C4**
Liptrap, C. **63 C4**
Lira **57 D6**
Liria = Lliria **19 C5**
Lisala **56 D4**
Lisboa **18 C1**
Lisbon = Lisboa **18 C1**
Lisburn **11 D3**
Lisichansk = Lysychansk **25 D4**
Lisieux **12 B4**
Liski **24 C4**
Lismore **63 A5**
Lister, Mt. **96 B15**
Liston **63 A5**
Listowel **11 E2**
Litani ➔ *Lebanon* **46 D3**
Litani ➔ *S. Amer.* **30 E**
Lithgow **63 B5**
Lithino, Akra **23 G5**
Lithuania ■ **24 B1**
Litoměřice **16 C2**
Little Barrier I. **64 B6**
Little Khingan Mts. = Xiao Hinggan Ling **35 B7**
Little Laut Is. = Laut Kecil, Kepulauan **39 E5**
Little Missouri ➔ **74 B3**
Little River **65 E5**
Little Rock **81 B7**
Little Zab = Zāb aş Şaghīr ➔ **46 D5**
Liukang Tenggaja = Sabalana, Kepulauan **37 F1**
Liuwa Plain **58 A4**
Liuzhou **35 D5**
Livadia **23 E4**
Liverpool *Canada* **71 E7**
Liverpool *U.K.* **11 E5**
Liverpool Plains **63 B5**
Liverpool Ra. **63 B5**
Livingstone **59 B5**
Livny **24 C4**
Livorno **20 C3**
Ljubljana **20 A5**
Llancanelo, Salina **94 D3**
Llanelli **11 F4**
Llanes **18 A3**
Llano Estacado **80 C2**
Llanos **90 C4**
Lleida **19 B6**
Lliria **19 C5**
Llobregat ➔ **19 B7**
Lloret de Mar **19 B7**
Llucmajor **19 C7**
Llullaillaco, Volcán **94 A3**
Loa ➔ **94 A2**
Lobatse **59 D5**
Lobería **94 D5**
Lobito **58 A2**
Locarno **13 C8**
Loch Garman = Wexford **11 E3**
Loches **12 C4**
Lock **62 B2**
Lodhran **42 E7**
Lodi *Italy* **13 D8**
Lodi *U.S.A.* **72 G3**
Lodja **56 E4**
Lodwar **57 D7**
Łódź **16 C4**
Lofoten **8 B9**
Logan **73 F8**
Logan, Mt. **68 B5**
Logone ➔ **55 F2**
Logroño **19 A4**
Lohardaga **40 F5**
Loi-kaw **41 H11**
Loir ➔ **12 C3**
Loire ➔ **12 C2**
Loja *Ecuador* **90 D3**
Loja *Spain* **18 D3**
Loji = Kawasi **37 E3**
Lokitaung **57 D7**
Lokkan tekojärvi **8 B11**
Lokoja **53 G7**
Lom **22 C4**
Lomami ➔ **56 D4**
Lombárdia □ **13 D8**
Lombardy = Lombárdia □ **13 D8**
Lomblen **37 F2**
Lombok **39 F5**
Lomé **53 G6**
Lomela **56 E4**
Lomela ➔ **56 E4**
Lomond, L. **10 C4**
Lompobatang **37 F1**
Łomża **16 B6**
Loncoche **95 D2**
Londa **43 M9**
London *Canada* **71 E5**
London *U.K.* **11 F6**
Londonderry **11 D3**
Londonderry, C. **60 C4**
Londonderry, I. **95 H2**
Londrina **94 A6**
Long Beach **78 D3**
Long I. *Bahamas* **86 B4**
Long I. *U.S.A.* **77 D9**
Long Xuyen **38 B3**
Longford *Australia* **62 D4**
Longford *Ireland* **11 E3**
Longiram **39 E5**
Longnawan **39 D4**
Longreach **61 E7**
Longview *Tex., U.S.A.* **81 C6**
Longview *Wash., U.S.A.* **72 C2**
Lons-le-Saunier **13 C6**
Lop Nor = Lop Nur **34 B4**
Lop Nur **34 B4**
Lopez, C. **56 E1**
Lora ➔ **42 D4**
Lora, Hāmūn-i- **42 E4**
Lora Cr. ➔ **62 A2**
Lora del Río **18 D3**
Lorain **76 D4**
Loralai **42 D6**
Lorca **19 D5**
Lord Howe I. **64 N10**
Lord Howe Rise **64 N11**
Lorestān □ **46 D6**
Loreto **92 D4**
Lorient **12 C2**
Lorne **62 C3**
Lorraine □ **13 B7**
Los Alamos **79 C9**
Los Andes **94 C2**
Los Angeles *Chile* **94 D2**
Los Angeles *U.S.A.* **78 C3**
Los Blancos **94 A4**
Los Hermanos Is. **90 A6**
Los Mochis **84 B3**
Los Roques Is. **90 A5**
Los Testigos, Is. **90 A6**
Los Vilos **94 C2**
Lošinj **20 B5**
Lot ➔ **12 D4**
Lota **94 D2**
Loubomo **56 E2**
Louga **53 E2**
Lougheed I. **70 B3**
Louis Trichardt **59 C5**
Louis XIV, Pte. **71 D6**
Louisiade Arch. **61 C9**
Louisiana □ **81 D8**
Louisville **76 E3**
Loulé **18 D1**
Lourdes **12 E3**
Louth *Australia* **63 B4**
Louth *U.K.* **11 E6**
Louvain = Leuven **14 C3**
Lovech **22 C5**
Lowell **77 C10**
Lower California = Baja California **84 A1**
Lower Hutt **65 D6**
Lower Saxony = Niedersachsen □ **14 B5**
Lower Tunguska = Tunguska, Nizhnyaya ➔ **30 C6**
Lowestoft **11 E7**
Lowgar □ **45 C7**
Łowicz **16 B4**
Loxton **62 B3**
Loyalty Is. = Loyauté, Îs. **64 M11**
Loyang = Luoyang **35 C6**
Loyauté, Îs. **64 M11**
Loyev = Loyew **17 C10**
Loyew **17 C10**
Luachimo **56 F4**
Lualaba ➔ **57 D5**
Luanda **56 F2**
Luangwa ➔ **59 A6**
Luanshya **59 A5**
Luapula ➔ **57 F5**
Luarca **18 A2**
Luau **56 G4**
Lubang Is. **36 B2**
Lubango **58 A2**
Lubbock **80 C3**
Lübeck **15 B6**
Lubero = Luofu **57 E5**
Lubin **16 C3**
Lublin **17 C6**
Lubnān = Lebanon ■ **46 D3**
Lubuk Antu **39 D4**
Lubuklinggau **39 E2**
Lubuksikaping **39 D2**
Lubumbashi **59 A5**
Lubutu **57 E5**
Lucca **20 C3**
Lucena *Phil.* **36 B2**
Lucena *Spain* **18 D3**
Lucerne = Luzern **13 C8**
Luckenwalde **15 B7**
Lucknow **40 D3**
Lüda = Dalian **35 C7**

Lüderitz **58 D3**
Ludhiana **42 D9**
Ludwigsburg **14 D5**
Ludwigshafen **14 D5**
Lufira ➔ **57 F5**
Lufkin **81 D6**
Luga **24 B2**
Lugano **13 C8**
Lugansk = Luhansk **25 D4**
Lugh Ganana **49 G3**
Lugo *Italy* **20 B3**
Lugo *Spain* **18 A2**
Lugoj **17 F5**
Lugovoy = Qulan **29 E8**
Luhansk **25 D4**
Luichow Pen. = Leizhou Bandao **35 D6**
Luimneach = Limerick **11 E2**
Luís Correia **92 C5**
Luitpold Coast **96 B5**
Luiza **56 F4**
Lukanga Swamp **59 A5**
Lukenie ➔ **56 E3**
Łuków **17 C6**
Luleå **8 B10**
Luleälven ➔ **8 B10**
Lüleburgaz **22 D6**
Lulonga ➔ **56 D3**
Lulua ➔ **56 E4**
Lumbala N'guimbo **58 A4**
Lumsden **65 F3**
Lumut, Tanjung **39 E3**
Lund **9 D8**
Lundazi **59 A6**
Lundu **39 D3**
Lüneburg **14 B6**
Lüneburg Heath = Lüneburger Heide **14 B6**
Lüneburger Heide **14 B6**
Lunéville **13 B7**
Lunglei **41 F9**
Luni **42 G8**
Luni ➔ **43 G7**
Luninets = Luninyets **17 B8**
Luninyets **17 B8**
Luofu **57 E5**
Luoyang **35 C6**
Lurgan **11 D3**
Lusaka **59 B5**
Lusambo **56 E4**
Lushnjë **23 D2**
Luta = Dalian **35 C7**
Lutherstadt Wittenberg **15 C7**
Luton **11 F6**
Łutselk'e **68 B8**
Lutsk **17 C7**
Lützow Holmbukta **96 A8**
Luuq = Lugh Ganana **49 G3**
Luwuk **37 E2**
Luxembourg **13 B7**
Luxembourg ■ **14 D4**
Luxor = El Uqsur **54 C5**
Luza **24 A6**
Luzern **13 C8**
Luzhou **35 D5**
Luziânia **93 F4**
Luzon **36 A2**
Lviv **17 D7**
Lvov = Lviv **17 D7**
Lyakhavichy **17 B8**
Lyakhovskiye, Ostrova **31 B12**
Lydenburg **59 D6**
Lydia **23 E7**
Lyell **65 D5**
Lyepyel **24 C2**
Łyna ➔ **16 A5**
Lynchburg **77 F6**
Lynd Ra. **63 A4**
Lyndhurst **62 B2**
Lynn Lake **69 C9**
Lyon **13 D6**
Lyonnais **13 D6**
Lyons = Lyon **13 D6**
Lys = Leie ➔ **14 C2**
Lysychansk **25 D4**
Lyttelton **65 E5**
Lyubertsy **24 B4**
Lyuboml **17 C7**

M

Ma'alah **47 F6**
Ma'ān **47 E3**
Ma'anshan **35 C6**
Ma'arrat an Nu'mān **46 D4**
Maas ➔ **14 C3**
Maastricht **13 A6**
McAllen **80 F4**
Macao = Macau **35 D6**
Macapá **92 B3**
Macau *Brazil* **92 D6**
Macau *China* **35 D6**
M'Clintock Chan. **68 A9**
M'Clure Str. **70 B2**
McComb **81 D8**
MacDonnell Ranges **60 E5**
McDouall Peak **62 A1**
Macdougall L. **68 B10**
Macedonia □ **23 D4**
Macedonia ■ **22 D3**
Maceió **93 D6**
Macerata **20 C4**
Macfarlane, L. **62 B2**
Macgillycuddy's Reeks **11 F2**
McGregor Ra. **62 A3**
Mach **42 E5**
Machado = Jiparaná ➔ **91 E6**
Machakos **57 E7**
Machala **90 D3**
Machilipatnam **40 J3**
Machiques **90 A4**
Machupicchu **91 F4**
Macintyre ➔ **63 A5**
Mackay **61 E8**
Mackay, L. **60 E4**
Mackenzie ➔ **68 B6**
Mackenzie City = Linden **90 B7**
Mackenzie King I. **70 B2**
Mackenzie Mts. **68 B6**
McKinley, Mt. **69 B4**
McKinney **81 C5**
Macksville **63 B5**
Maclean **63 A5**
Maclear **59 E5**
Macleay ➔ **63 B5**
McMurdo Sd. **96 B15**
Mâcon *France* **13 C6**
Macon *U.S.A.* **83 C6**
McPherson Ra. **63 A5**
Macquarie Harbour **62 D4**
MacRobertson Land **96 B10**
Macumba ➔ **62 A2**
Madadeni **59 D6**
Madagascar ■ **59 C9**
Madā'in Sālih **47 F4**
Madama **54 D1**
Madang **61 B8**
Madaripur **41 F8**
Madauk **41 J11**
Madaya **41 F11**
Maddalena **20 D2**
Madeira **52 B2**
Madeira ➔ **90 D7**
Madeleine, Îs. de la **71 E7**
Madha **43 L9**
Madhya Pradesh □ **43 H10**
Madikeri **43 N9**
Madimba **56 E3**
Madingou **56 E2**
Madison **75 D10**
Madiun **39 F4**
Madras = Chennai **43 N12**
Madras = Tamil Nadu □ **43 P10**
Madre, L. **80 F5**
Madre, Sierra **36 A2**
Madre de Dios ➔ **91 F5**
Madre de Dios, I. **95 G1**
Madre Occidental, Sierra **84 B3**
Madrid **18 B4**
Madurai **43 Q11**
Madurantakam **43 N11**
Mae Sot **38 A1**
Maebashi **33 E6**
Maevatanana **59 B9**
Mafeteng **59 D5**
Maffra **63 C4**
Mafia I. **57 F7**
Mafra *Brazil* **94 B7**
Mafra *Portugal* **18 C1**
Magadan **31 D13**
Magallanes, Estrecho de **95 G2**
Magangué **90 B4**
Magdalen Is. = Madeleine, Îs. de la **71 E7**
Magdalena *Argentina* **94 D5**
Magdalena *Bolivia* **91 F6**
Magdalena ➔ **90 A4**
Magdeburg **15 B6**
Magelang **39 F4**
Magellan's Str. = Magallanes, Estrecho de **95 G2**
Maggiore, Lago **13 D8**
Magnetic Pole (North) **70 A2**
Magnetic Pole (South) **96 A13**
Magnitogorsk **29 D6**
Magoša = Famagusta **46 D3**
Maguarinho, C. **92 C4**
Mağusa = Famagusta **46 D3**
Magwe **41 G10**
Magyarország = Hungary ■ **16 E4**
Mahābād **46 C6**
Mahabo **59 C8**
Mahajanga **59 B9**
Mahakam ➔ **39 E5**
Mahalapye **59 C5**
Maḥallāt **44 C2**
Mahanadi ➔ **40 G6**
Maharashtra □ **43 J9**
Mahbubnagar **43 L10**
Mahdia **54 A1**
Mahenge **57 F7**
Maheno **65 F4**
Mahesana **43 H8**
Mahia Pen. **64 C7**
Mahilyow **17 B10**
Mahinerangi, L. **65 F3**
Mahón = Maó **19 C8**
Mai-Ndombe, L. **56 E3**
Maicurú ➔ **92 C3**
Maidstone **11 F7**
Maiduguri **55 F1**
Maijdi **41 F8**
Maikala Ra. **40 G3**
Main ➔ **14 D5**
Maine **12 C3**
Maingkwan **41 D11**
Mainit, L. **36 C3**
Mainland *Orkney, U.K.* **10 B5**
Mainland *Shet., U.K.* **10 A6**
Mainz **14 C5**
Maipú **94 D5**
Maiquetía **90 A5**
Mairabari **41 D9**
Maitland *N.S.W., Australia* **63 B5**
Maitland *S. Austral., Australia* **62 B2**
Maizuru **33 F4**
Majene **37 E1**
Majorca = Mallorca **19 C7**
Majuro **64 J12**
Makale **37 E1**
Makarikari = Makgadikgadi Salt Pans **59 C5**
Makasar = Ujung Pandang **37 F1**
Makasar, Selat **37 E1**
Makasar, Str. of = Makasar, Selat **37 E1**
Makat = Maqat **29 E6**
Makedonija = Macedonia ■ **22 D3**
Makeyevka = Makiyivka **25 D4**
Makgadikgadi Salt Pans **59 C5**
Makhachkala **25 E6**
Makhado = Louis Trichardt **59 C5**

Makhfar al Buşayyah 47 E6
Makian 37 D3
Makĭnsk 29 D8
Makiyivka 25 D4
Makkah 47 G4
Makó 16 E5
Makokou 56 D2
Makrai 43 H10
Makran 45 E5
Makran Coast Range 42 G4
Maksimkin Yar 29 D9
Mākū 46 C6
Makurazaki 33 H2
Makurdi 53 G7
Malabar Coast 43 P9
Malacca, Straits of 38 D1
Maladzyechna 17 A8
Málaga 18 D3
Malagasy Rep. = Madagascar ■ 59 C9
Malakâl 55 G5
Malakand 42 B7
Malang 39 F4
Malanje 56 F3
Mälaren 9 D9
Malargüe 94 D3
Malaryta 17 C7
Malatya 46 C4
Malawi ■ 59 A6
Malawi, L. 59 A6
Malay Pen. 38 C2
Malaybalay 36 C3
Malāyer 46 D7
Malaysia ■ 38 D4
Malazgirt 25 F5
Malbooma 62 B1
Malbork 16 A4
Malden I. 65 K15
Maldives ■ 26 H9
Maldonado 94 C6
Maleas, Akra 23 F4
Malegaon 43 J9
Malema 59 A7
Malha 55 E4
Mali ■ 53 E5
Mali ➔ 41 E11
Maliku 37 E2
Malili 37 E2
Malin Hd. 10 D3
Malindi 57 E8
Malines = Mechelen 14 C3
Malino 37 D2
Malita 36 C3
Malkara 22 D6
Mallacoota Inlet 63 C4
Mallaig 10 C4
Mallawi 54 C5
Mallorca 19 C7
Mallow 11 E2
Malmö 9 D8
Malolos 36 B2
Malpelo, I. de 90 C2
Malta ■ 21 G5
Maltahöhe 58 C3
Maluku 37 E3
Maluku □ 37 E3
Maluku Sea = Molucca Sea 37 E2
Malvan 43 L8
Malvinas, Is. = Falkland Is. ⌀ 95 G5
Malyn 17 C9
Malyy Lyakhovskiy, Ostrov 31 B12
Mamahatun 46 C5
Mamanguape 92 D6
Mamasa 37 E1
Mamberamo ➔ 37 E5
Mambilima Falls 57 G5
Mamburao 36 B2
Mamoré ➔ 91 F5
Mamou 53 F3
Mamuju 37 E1
Man 53 G4
Man, I. of 11 D4
Man Na 41 F11
Manaar, G. of = Mannar, G. of 43 Q11
Manacapuru 90 D6
Manacor 19 C7
Manado 37 D2
Managua 85 E7
Manakara 59 C9
Manama = Al Manāmah 44 E2
Mananjary 59 C9
Manaos = Manaus 90 D7
Manapouri 65 F2
Manapouri, L. 65 F2
Manas 34 B3
Manas ➔ 41 D8
Manasir 44 E2
Manaung 41 H9
Manaus 90 D7
Manchester *U.K.* 11 E5
Manchester *U.S.A.* 77 C10
Mand ➔ 44 D3
Mandal 9 D7
Mandala, Puncak 37 E6
Mandalay 41 F11
Mandale = Mandalay 41 F11
Mandalī 46 D6
Mandar, Teluk 37 E1
Mandaue 36 B2
Mandi 42 D10
Mandimba 59 A7
Mandioli 37 E3
Mandla 40 F3
Mandritsara 59 B9
Mandsaur 43 G9
Mandvi 43 H6
Mandya 43 N10
Manfalūt 54 C5
Manfredónia 20 D5
Mangalia 22 C7
Mangalore 43 N9
Mangaweka 64 C6
Manggar 39 E3
Manggawitu 37 E4
Mangghystaū Tübegi 29 E6
Mangkalihat, Tanjung 37 D1
Mangla Dam 42 C8
Mangnai 34 C4
Mango 53 F6
Mangoche 59 A7
Mangoky ➔ 59 C8
Mangole 37 E3
Mangonui 64 A5
Mangueira, L. da 94 C6
Mangyshlak, Poluostrov = Mangghystaū Tübegi 29 E6
Manica 59 B6
Manicoré 91 E6
Manicouagan ➔ 71 E7
Manicouagan, Rés. 71 D7
Manifah 47 F7
Manihiki 65 L14
Manila 36 B2
Manila B. 36 B2
Manilla 63 B5
Manipur □ 41 E9
Manipur ➔ 41 F10
Manisa 23 E6
Manitoba □ 69 C10
Manitoba, L. 69 C10
Manitoulin I. 71 E5
Manitowoc 76 B2
Manizales 90 B3
Manjhand 42 G6
Manjra ➔ 43 K10
Manmad 43 J9
Manna 39 E2
Mannahill 62 B3
Mannar 43 Q11
Mannar, G. of 43 Q11
Mannar I. 43 Q11
Mannheim 14 D5
Mannum 62 B2
Manokwari 37 E4
Manono 57 F5
Manosque 13 E6
Manresa 19 B6
Mansa 57 G5
Mansel I. 70 C5
Mansfield *Australia* 63 C4
Mansfield *U.K.* 11 E6
Mansfield *U.S.A.* 76 D4
Manta 90 D2
Mantalingajan, Mt. 38 C5
Mantes-la-Jolie 12 B4
Manthani 43 K11
Mántova 20 B3
Mantua = Mántova 20 B3
Manu 91 F4
Manuel Alves ➔ 93 E4
Manui 37 E2
Manukau 64 B6
Manych-Gudilo, Ozero 25 D5
Manzai 42 C7
Manzanares 18 C4
Manzanillo *Cuba* 86 B4
Manzanillo *Mexico* 84 D4
Manzhouli 35 B6
Mao *Chad* 55 F2
Maó *Spain* 19 C8
Maoke, Pegunungan 37 E5
Maoming 35 D6
Mapam Yumco 40 B3
Mapia, Kepulauan 37 D4
Mapuera ➔ 90 D7
Maputo 59 D6
Maqat 29 E6
Maqnā 47 E3
Maquan He = Brahmaputra ➔ 41 F7
Maquela do Zombo 56 F3
Maquinchao 95 E3
Mar Chiquita, L. 94 C4
Mar del Plata 94 D5
Mar Menor 19 D5
Maraã 90 D5
Marabá 92 D4
Maracá, I. de 92 B3
Maracaibo 90 A4
Maracaibo, L. de 90 B4
Maracay 90 A5
Maradi 53 F7
Marāgheh 46 C6
Marāh 47 F6
Marajó, I. de 92 C4
Marand 46 C6
Maranguape 92 C6
Maranhão = São Luís 92 C5
Maranhão □ 92 D4
Maranoa ➔ 63 A4
Marañón ➔ 90 D4
Marão 59 C6
Maraş = Kahramanmaraş 46 C4
Maratua 37 D1
Marbella 18 D3
Marburg 14 C5
Marche 12 C4
Marchena 18 D3
Mardan 42 B8
Mardin 46 C5
Marek = Stanke Dimitrov 22 C4
Margarita, I. de 90 A6
Margaritovo 32 B4
Margate 11 F7
Marghilon 29 E8
Mārgow, Dasht-e 42 D3
Mari El □ 24 B6
Mari Republic = Mari El □ 24 B6
Maria I. 62 D4
Maria van Diemen, C. 64 A5
Mariana Trench 64 H9
Maribor 20 A5
Marie Byrd Land 96 B18
Mariecourt = Kangiqsujuaq 70 C6
Mariental 58 C3
Mariinsk 29 D9
Marília 93 G3
Marín 18 A1
Marinduque 36 B2
Maringá 94 A6
Marion 81 A9
Mariscal Estigarribia 91 H6
Maritime Alps = Maritimes, Alpes 13 D7
Maritimes, Alpes 13 D7
Maritsa = Evros ➔ 22 D6
Mariupol 25 D4
Marīvān 46 D6
Marka = Merca 49 G3
Markham, Mt. 96 C15

Marks **24 C6**
Marla **62 A1**
Marmagao **43 M8**
Marmara **23 D6**
Marmara, Sea of = Marmara Denizi **22 D7**
Marmara Denizi **22 D7**
Marmaris **23 F7**
Marmolada, Mte. **20 A3**
Marne ➔ **12 B5**
Maroantsetra **59 B9**
Marondera **59 B6**
Maroni ➔ **92 A3**
Maroochydore **63 A5**
Maroona **62 C3**
Maroua **55 F1**
Marovoay **59 B9**
Marquesas Is. = Marquises, Îs. **65 K17**
Marquises, Îs. **65 K17**
Marrakech **52 B4**
Marrawah **62 D3**
Marree **62 A2**
Marrowie Cr. ➔ **63 B4**
Marrupa **59 A7**
Marsá Matrûh **54 B4**
Marsabit **57 D7**
Marsala **21 F4**
Marsden **63 B4**
Marseille **13 E6**
Marseilles = Marseille **13 E6**
Marshall **81 C6**
Marshall Is. ■ **64 J12**
Marshalltown **75 D8**
Martaban **41 J11**
Martaban, G. of **41 J11**
Martapura *Kalimantan, Indonesia* **39 E4**
Martapura *Sumatera, Indonesia* **39 E2**
Martigues **13 E6**
Martinborough **65 D6**
Martinique ⊘ **87 D7**
Martinsville **83 A8**
Marton **64 D6**
Martos **18 D4**
Marudi **39 D4**
Maruf **42 D5**
Marugame **33 F3**
Marwar **42 G8**
Mary **29 F7**
Maryborough = Port Laoise **11 E3**
Maryborough *Queens., Australia* **63 A5**
Maryborough *Vic., Australia* **62 C3**
Maryland □ **77 E7**
Marystown **71 E8**
Maryvale **63 A5**
Marzūq **54 C1**
Marzūq, Idehān **54 D1**
Masaka **57 E6**
Masalembo, Kepulauan **39 F4**
Masalima, Kepulauan **39 F5**
Masamba **37 E2**
Masan **35 C7**
Masandam, Ra's **44 E4**
Masasi **57 G7**
Masaya **85 E7**
Masbate **36 B2**
Mascara **52 A6**
Masela **37 F3**
Maseru **59 D5**
Mashābih **47 F4**
Mashhad **44 B4**
Māshkel, Hāmūn-i- **42 E3**
Mashki Chāh **42 E3**
Mashonaland **59 B6**
Masindi **57 D6**
Masjed Soleyman **47 E7**
Mask, L. **11 E2**
Maskin **44 F4**
Masoala, Tanjon' i **59 B10**
Masohi = Amahai **37 E3**
Mason City **75 D8**
Masqat **45 F4**
Massa **13 D9**
Massachusetts □ **77 C9**
Massakory **55 F2**
Massangena **59 C6**
Massena **77 B8**
Massénya **55 F2**
Massif Central **13 D5**
Massinga **59 C7**
Masson I. **96 A11**
Mastanli = Momchilgrad **22 D5**
Masterton **65 D6**
Mastuj **42 A8**
Mastung **42 E5**
Masty **17 B7**
Masuda **33 F2**
Masvingo **59 C6**
Mata-au = Clutha ➔ **65 G3**
Matabeleland **59 B5**
Matad **35 B6**
Matadi **56 F2**
Matagalpa **85 E7**
Matagami **71 E6**
Matagami, L. **71 E6**
Matak **39 D3**
Matam **53 E3**
Matamoros *Coahuila, Mexico* **84 B4**
Matamoros *Tamaulipas, Mexico* **84 B5**
Ma'ṭan as Sarra **54 D3**
Matane **71 E7**
Matanzas **86 B3**
Matapan, C. = Tenaro, Akra **23 F4**
Mataram **39 F5**
Matarani **91 G4**
Mataró **19 B7**
Mataura **65 G3**
Matehuala **84 C4**
Matera **21 D6**
Mathraki **21 E7**
Mathura **42 F10**
Mati **36 C3**
Matiri Ra. **65 D5**
Mato Grosso □ **93 E3**
Mato Grosso, Planalto do **93 F3**
Mato Grosso do Sul □ **93 F3**
Matochkin Shar **28 B6**
Matosinhos **18 B1**
Maṭruḥ **45 F4**
Matsue **33 F3**
Matsumae **32 C7**
Matsumoto **33 E6**
Matsusaka **33 F5**
Matsuyama **33 G3**
Mattagami ➔ **71 D5**
Mattancheri **43 Q10**
Matthews Ridge **90 B6**
Matucana **91 F3**
Matūn = Khowst **42 C6**
Maturín **90 B6**
Mau Ranipur **43 G11**
Maubeuge **13 A5**
Maude **63 B3**
Maudin Sun **41 K10**
Maués **90 D7**
Mauganj **40 E3**
Maui **78 H12**
Maulamyaing = Moulmein **41 J11**
Maumere **37 F2**
Maun **58 B4**
Maungmagan Kyunzu **41 K11**
Mauritania ■ **53 E3**
Mauritius ■ **51 H9**
Mawk Mai **41 G11**
Mawlaik **41 F10**
Mawlamyine = Moulmein **41 J11**
Mawson Coast **96 A10**
Mayaguana **87 B5**
Mayagüez **87 C6**
Maydena **62 D4**
Mayenne ➔ **12 C3**
Maykop **25 E5**
Mayo **68 B6**
Mayo L. **68 B6**
Mayon Volcano **36 B2**
Mayor I. **64 B7**
Mayotte ⊘ **59 A9**
Mayu **37 D3**
Mazabuka **59 B5**
Mazagán = El Jadida **52 B4**
Mazagão **92 C3**
Mazán **90 D4**
Māzandarān □ **44 B3**
Mazār-e Sharīf **45 B6**
Mazara del Vallo **21 F4**
Mazarrón **19 D5**
Mazaruni ➔ **90 B7**
Mazatlán **84 C3**
Māzhān **44 C4**
Mazīnān **44 B4**
Mazoe ➔ **59 B6**
Mazurian Lakes = Mazurski, Pojezierze **16 B5**
Mazurski, Pojezierze **16 B5**
Mazyr **17 C9**
Mbabane **59 D6**
Mbaïki **56 D3**
Mbala **57 F6**
Mbale **57 D6**
Mbalmayo **56 D2**
Mbandaka **56 D3**
Mbanza Congo **56 F2**
Mbanza Ngungu **56 F2**
Mbarara **57 E6**
Mbeya **57 F6**
Mbini = Río Muni □ **56 D2**
Mbour **53 F2**
Mbuji-Mayi **56 F4**
Mdantsane **59 E5**
Mead, L. **78 B5**
Mearim ➔ **92 C5**
Meaux **13 B5**
Mecca = Makkah **47 G4**
Mechelen **14 C3**
Mecheria **52 B5**
Mecklenburg **15 B6**
Mecklenburger Bucht **15 A6**
Medan **39 D1**
Medanosa, Pta. **95 F3**
Médéa **52 A6**
Medellín **90 B3**
Medford **72 E2**
Medgidia **22 B7**
Medicine Bow Mts. **73 F10**
Medicine Hat **69 C8**
Medina = Al Madīnah **47 F4**
Medina del Campo **18 B3**
Medina Sidonia **18 D3**
Medinipur **40 F6**
Mediterranean Sea **50 C5**
Médoc **12 D3**
Medveditsa ➔ **24 D5**
Medvezhyegorsk **28 C4**
Meekatharra **60 F2**
Meerut **42 E10**
Megara **23 F4**
Meghalaya □ **41 E8**
Meighen I. **70 B4**
Meiktila **41 G10**
Meissen **15 C7**
Meizhou **35 D6**
Mejillones **94 A2**
Mekhtar **42 D6**
Meknès **52 B4**
Mekong ➔ **38 C3**
Mekongga **37 E2**
Mekvari = Kür ➔ **25 E6**
Melagiri Hills **43 N10**
Melaka **39 D2**
Melalap **38 C5**
Melanesia **64 K10**
Melbourne *Australia* **63 C3**
Melbourne *U.S.A.* **83 E7**
Melekeok **36 C4**
Mélèzes ➔ **70 D6**
Melfort **69 C9**
Melilla **19 E4**
Melitopol **25 D4**
Melk **15 D8**
Melo **94 C6**
Melolo **37 F2**
Melrose **63 B4**
Melun **13 B5**
Melville **69 C9**
Melville I. *Australia* **60 C5**
Melville I. *Canada* **70 B2**
Melville Pen. **70 C5**
Memboro **37 F1**

Memel = Klaipėda **24 B1**
Memmingen **14 E6**
Mempawah **39 D3**
Memphis *Tenn., U.S.A.* **82 B3**
Memphis *Tex., U.S.A.* **80 B3**
Ménaka **53 E6**
Menan = Chao Phraya ➔ **38 B2**
Mendawai ➔ **39 E4**
Mende **13 D5**
Mendocino, C. **72 F1**
Mendoza **94 C3**
Mene Grande **90 B4**
Menemen **23 E6**
Menggala **39 E3**
Mengzi **34 D5**
Menindee **62 B3**
Menindee L. **62 B3**
Meningie **62 C2**
Menominee **76 B2**
Menongue **58 A3**
Menorca **19 C7**
Mentawai, Kepulauan **39 E1**
Menton **13 E7**
Meppel **14 B4**
Meran = Merano **20 A3**
Merano **20 A3**
Merauke **37 F6**
Merbein **62 B3**
Merca **49 G3**
Merced **78 B2**
Mercedes *B. Aires, Argentina* **94 C5**
Mercedes *Corrientes, Argentina* **94 B5**
Mercedes *San Luis, Argentina* **94 C3**
Mercedes *Uruguay* **94 C5**
Mercer **64 B6**
Mercy, C. **70 C7**
Meredith, C. **95 G4**
Mergui Arch. = Myeik Kyunzu **38 B1**
Mérida *Mexico* **85 C7**
Mérida *Spain* **18 C2**
Mérida *Venezuela* **90 B4**
Meridian **82 C3**
Merirumā **92 B3**
Merriwa **63 B5**
Merseburg **15 C6**
Mersin = İçel **46 C3**
Mersing **39 D2**
Merthyr Tydfil **11 F5**
Mértola **18 D2**
Meru **57 D7**
Mesa **79 D7**
Meshed = Mashhad **44 B4**
Mesologi **23 E3**
Mesopotamia = Al Jazirah **46 D5**
Messina = Musina **59 C6**
Messina **21 E5**
Messina, Str. di **21 E5**
Messini **23 F4**
Messiniakos Kolpos **23 F4**
Mesta ➔ **22 D5**
Meta ➔ **90 B5**
Meta Incognita Pen. **70 C7**
Metairie **81 E8**
Metán **94 B4**
Methven **65 E4**
Metlakatla **69 C6**
Mettur Dam **43 P10**
Metz **13 B7**
Meulaboh **39 D1**
Meureudu **38 C1**
Meuse ➔ **13 A6**
Mexiana, I. **92 C4**
Mexicali **84 A1**
México **84 D5**
Mexico ■ **84 C4**
México, Ciudad de **84 D5**
Mexico, G. of **85 B7**
Meymaneh **42 B4**
Mezen **28 C5**
Mezen ➔ **28 C5**
Mézenc, Mt. **13 D6**
Mezőkövesd **16 E5**
Mezőtúr **16 E5**
Mhow **43 H9**
Miami **83 G7**
Miami Beach **83 G7**
Mīāndowāb **46 C6**
Miandrivazo **59 B9**
Mīāneh **46 C6**
Mianwali **42 C7**
Miass **29 D7**
Michigan □ **76 C3**
Michigan, L. **76 C2**
Michurin **22 C6**
Michurinsk **24 C5**
Micronesia **64 H11**
Micronesia, Federated States of ■ **64 J10**
Middelburg **58 E5**
Middlesbrough **11 D6**
Midi, Canal du ➔ **12 E4**
Midland **80 D3**
Midyat **46 C5**
Midzōr **22 C4**
Międzychód **16 B2**
Międzyrzec Podlaski **17 C6**
Mielec **16 C5**
Mieres **18 A3**
Mikhaylovgrad = Montana **22 C4**
Mikines **23 F4**
Mikonos = Mykonos **23 F5**
Milagro **90 D3**
Milan = Milano **13 D8**
Milang **62 B2**
Milano **13 D8**
Milās **23 F6**
Milazzo **21 E5**
Mildura **62 B3**
Miles **63 A5**
Miletus **23 F6**
Milford Haven **11 F4**
Milford Sd. **65 F2**
Milford Sound **65 F2**
Milḥ, Baḥr al = Razāzah, Buḥayrat ar **47 D5**
Mill I. **96 A12**
Millau **13 D5**
Millennium I. = Caroline I. **65 K15**
Millicent **62 C3**
Millinocket **77 B11**
Millmerran **63 A5**
Milne Inlet **70 B5**
Milos **23 F5**
Milparinka **62 A3**
Milton **65 G3**
Milton Keynes **11 E6**
Milwaukee **76 C2**
Min Jiang ➔ *Fujian, China* **35 D6**
Min Jiang ➔ *Sichuan, China* **35 D5**
Mīnā Su'ud **47 E7**
Mīnā'al Aḥmadī **47 E7**
Mīnāb **44 E4**
Minamata **33 G2**
Minas **94 C5**
Minas Gerais □ **93 F4**
Minbu **41 G10**
Mindanao **36 C2**
Mindanao Sea = Bohol Sea **36 C2**
Mindanao Trench **36 B3**
Minden **14 B5**
Mindiptana **37 F6**
Mindoro **36 B2**
Mindoro Str. **36 B2**
Mingäçevir Su Anbarı **25 E6**
Mingechaurskoye Vdkhr. = Mingäçevir Su Anbarı **25 E6**
Mingin **41 F10**
Mingteke Daban = Mintaka Pass **42 A9**
Minho = Miño ➔ **18 B1**
Minho **18 B1**
Minna **53 G7**
Minneapolis **75 C8**
Minnesota □ **75 B7**
Minnipa **62 B2**
Miño ➔ **18 B1**
Minorca = Menorca **19 C7**
Minot **74 A4**
Minsk **24 C2**
Mińsk Mazowiecki **16 B5**
Mintaka Pass **42 A9**
Minto, L. **70 D6**
Minutang **41 C11**
Mira **20 B4**
Mirabello, Kolpos **23 G5**
Miraj **43 L9**
Miram Shah **42 C7**
Miramichi **71 E7**
Miranda **93 G2**
Miranda de Ebro **19 A4**
Miranda do Douro **18 B2**
Miri **38 D4**
Mirim, L. **94 C6**
Mirpur Khas **42 G6**
Mirzapur **40 E4**
Mirzapur-cum-Vindhyachal = Mirzapur **40 E4**
Mish'āb, Ra's al **47 E7**
Mishan **35 B8**
Miskolc **16 D5**
Misool **37 E4**
Miṣr = Egypt ■ **54 C5**
Miṣrātah **54 B2**
Misriç **46 C5**
Missinaibi ➔ **71 D5**
Mississippi □ **81 C9**
Mississippi ➔ **81 E9**
Mississippi River Delta **81 E9**
Missoula **73 C7**
Missouri □ **75 F8**
Missouri ➔ **75 F9**
Mistassini, L. **71 D6**
Misurata = Miṣrātah **54 B2**
Mitchell *Australia* **63 A4**
Mitchell *U.S.A.* **74 D5**
Mitchell ➔ **61 D7**
Mitilini **23 E6**
Mito **33 E7**
Mitrovica = Kosovska Mitrovica **22 C3**
Mittagong **63 B5**
Mittimatalik = Pond Inlet **70 B6**
Mitú **90 C4**
Mitumba, Mts. **57 F5**
Mitwaba **57 F5**
Miyake-Jima **33 F6**
Miyako **32 D7**
Miyakonojō **33 H2**
Miyazaki **33 H2**
Miyet, Bahr el = Dead Sea **47 E3**
Mizal **47 G6**
Mizdah **54 B1**
Mizoram □ **41 F9**
Mjøsa **8 C8**
Mladá Boleslav **16 C2**
Mlange = Mulanje **59 B7**
Mława **16 B5**
Mljet **20 C6**
Mmabatho **59 D5**
Mo i Rana **8 B8**
Moa **37 F3**
Moalie Park **62 A3**
Mobaye **56 D4**
Mobayi **56 D4**
Mobile **82 D3**
Moçambique = Mozambique ■ **59 B7**
Moçambique **59 B8**
Mochudi **59 C5**
Mocimboa da Praia **57 G8**
Mocoa **90 C3**
Mocuba **59 B7**
Modane **13 D7**
Módena **20 B3**
Modesto **78 B2**
Módica **21 F5**
Modimolle **59 C5**
Moe **63 C4**
Moengo **92 A3**
Mogadishu = Muqdisho **49 G4**
Mogador = Essaouira **52 B4**
Mogami-Gawa ➔ **32 D7**
Mogaung **41 E11**
Mogi das Cruzes **94 A7**
Mogilev = Mahilyow **17 B10**
Mogilev-Podolskiy = Mohyliv-Podilskyy **17 D8**

Mogok 41 F11
Mohács 16 F4
Moḥammadābād 44 B4
Mohyliv-Podilskyy 17 D8
Moisie ➔ 71 D7
Mojave Desert 78 C4
Mokai 64 C6
Mokau 64 C6
Mokokchung 41 D10
Mokopane 59 C5
Mokra Gora 22 C3
Molchanovo 29 D9
Moldavia = Moldova ■ 17 E9
Molde 8 C7
Moldova ■ 17 E9
Moldoveanu, Vf. 17 F7
Molepolole 59 C5
Molfetta 20 D6
Moline 75 E9
Mollendo 91 G4
Molodechno = Maladzyechna 17 A8
Moloka'i 78 H12
Molong 63 B4
Molopo ➔ 58 D4
Molu 37 F4
Molucca Sea 37 E2
Moluccas = Maluku 37 E3
Moma 59 B7
Mombasa 57 E7
Mombetsu 32 A8
Momchilgrad 22 D5
Mompós 90 B4
Mon ➔ 41 G10
Mona, Canal de la = Mona Passage 87 C6
Mona Passage 87 C6
Monaco ■ 13 E7
Monahans 80 D2
Monastir = Bitola 22 D3
Moncayo, Sierra del 19 B5
Mönchengladbach 14 C4
Monchique 18 D1
Monclova 84 B4
Moncton 71 E7
Mondego ➔ 18 B1
Mondeodo 37 E2
Mondovì 13 D7
Monforte de Lemos 18 A2
Mong Hsu 41 G12
Mong Kung 41 G11
Mong Nai 41 G11
Mong Pawk 41 F12
Mong Ton 41 G12
Mong Wa 41 G13
Mong Yai 41 F12
Mongalla 55 G5
Monghyr = Munger 40 E6
Mongibello = Etna 21 F5
Mongo 55 F2
Mongolia ■ 35 B5
Mongu 58 B4
Monkoto 56 E4
Monópoli 21 D6
Monroe *La., U.S.A.* 81 C7
Monroe *N.C., U.S.A.* 83 B7
Monrovia 53 G3
Mons 14 C2
Monse 37 E2
Mont-de-Marsan 12 E3
Mont-Laurier 71 E6
Mont-St-Michel, Le 12 B3
Montalbán 19 B5
Montana 22 C4
Montana □ 73 C9
Montargis 13 C5
Montauban 12 D4
Montbéliard 13 C7
Montceau-les-Mines 13 C6
Monte Alegre 92 C3
Monte Azul 93 F5
Monte-Carlo 13 E7
Monte Caseros 94 C5
Monte Comán 94 C3
Monte Santu, C. di 21 D2
Montecristo 20 C3
Montego Bay 86 C4
Montélimar 13 D6
Montemorelos 84 B5
Montenegro ■ 22 C2
Montepuez 59 A7
Monterey 78 B2
Montería 90 B3
Monterrey 84 B4
Montes Claros 93 F5
Montesilvano 20 C5
Montevideo 94 C5
Montgomery 82 C4
Montilla 18 D3
Montluçon 13 C5
Montmorillon 12 C4
Montoro 18 C3
Montpellier 13 E5
Montréal 71 E6
Montrose *U.K.* 10 C5
Montrose *U.S.A.* 79 A9
Montserrat ⊠ 87 C7
Montsinéry 30 E
Monywa 41 F10
Monza 13 D8
Monze 59 B5
Monze, C. 43 G5
Monzón 19 B6
Moolawatana 62 A2
Moomin Cr. ➔ 63 A4
Moonie 63 A5
Moonie ➔ 63 A4
Moonta 62 B2
Moose Jaw 69 C9
Moosomin 69 C9
Moosonee 71 D5
Mopti 53 F5
Moqor 42 C5
Moquegua 91 G4
Mora 8 C8
Moradabad 42 E11
Morafenobe 59 B8
Moramanga 59 B9
Moratuwa 43 R11
Morava ➔ *Serbia* 22 B3
Morava ➔ *Slovak Rep.* 16 D3
Moravian Hts. = Českomoravská Vrchovina 16 D2
Morawhanna 90 B7
Moray Firth 10 C5
Morden 69 D10
Mordovian Republic = Mordvinia □ 24 C5
Mordvinia □ 24 C5
Morea 62 C3
Moree 63 A4
Morelia 84 D4
Morella 19 B5
Morena, Sierra 18 C3
Moreton I. 63 A5
Morgan City 81 E8
Morioka 32 D7
Morlaix 12 B2
Morne Constant 30 C
Mornington 63 C4
Mornington, I. 95 F1
Moro G. 36 C2
Morocco ■ 52 B4
Morogoro 57 F7
Morombe 59 C8
Morón 86 B4
Mörön ➔ 35 B6
Morón de la Frontera 18 D3
Morondava 59 C8
Morotai 37 D3
Moroto 57 D6
Morphou 46 D3
Morrinhos 93 F4
Morrinsville 64 B6
Morristown 83 A6
Morshansk 24 C5
Morteros 94 C4
Mortlake 62 C3
Morundah 63 B4
Moruya 63 C5
Morvan 13 C6
Morven 63 A4
Morwell 63 C4
Moscos Is. 41 L11
Moscow = Moskva 24 B4
Moscow 72 C5
Mosel ➔ 13 A7
Moselle = Mosel ➔ 13 A7
Mosgiel 65 F4
Moshi 57 E7
Mosjøen 8 B8
Moskva 24 B4
Mosonmagyaróvár 16 E3
Mosquera 90 C3
Moss Vale 63 B5
Mossburn 65 F3
Mosselbaai 58 E4
Mossendjo 56 E2
Mossgiel 63 B3
Mossoró 92 D6
Most 16 C1
Mostaganem 52 A6
Mostar 20 C6
Mostardas 94 C6
Mostiska = Mostyska 17 D6
Mosty = Masty 17 B7
Mostyska 17 D6
Mosul = Al Mawṣil 46 C5
Motihari 40 D5
Motril 18 D4
Motueka 65 D5
Motueka ➔ 65 D5
Moudros 23 E5
Mouila 56 E2
Moulamein 63 C3
Moulins 13 C5
Moulmein 41 J11
Moundou 55 G2
Mount Aspiring △ 65 F3
Mount Barker 62 C2
Mount Cook 65 E4
Mount Eba 62 B2
Mount Gambier 62 C3
Mount Hope *N.S.W., Australia* 63 B4
Mount Hope *S. Austral., Australia* 62 B2
Mount Howitt 62 A3
Mount Isa 61 E6
Mount Lofty Ranges 62 B2
Mount Margaret 63 A3
Mount Maunganui 64 B7
Mount Perry 63 A5
Moura *Brazil* 90 D6
Moura *Portugal* 18 C2
Mourdi, Dépression du 55 E3
Moussoro 55 F2
Moutong 37 D2
Moyale 49 G2
Moyen Atlas 52 B4
Moyo 39 F5
Moyyero ➔ 30 C8
Moyynty 29 E8
Mozambique = Moçambique 59 B8
Mozambique ■ 59 B7
Mozambique Chan. 51 H8
Mozdok 25 E5
Mozyr = Mazyr 17 C9
Mpanda 57 F6
Mpika 59 A6
Mpwapwa 57 F7
Mthatha 59 E5
Mu Us Shamo 35 C5
Muar 39 D2
Muarabungo 39 E2
Muaraenim 39 E2
Muarajuloi 39 E4
Muarakaman 39 E5
Muaratebo 39 E2
Muaratembesi 39 E2
Muaratewe 39 E4
Mubarraz = Al Mubarraz 47 F7
Mubi 55 F1
Muckadilla 63 A4
Mucuri 93 F6
Mudanjiang 35 B7
Mudanya 23 D7
Mudgee 63 B4
Mufulira 59 A5
Mugi 33 G4
Muğla 23 F7
Mugu 40 C4
Muhammad Qol 54 D6
Mühlhausen 14 C6
Mühlig Hofmann fjell 96 B7
Mujnak = Muynak 29 E6
Mukacheve 17 D6
Mukachevo = Mukacheve 17 D6

Mukah 39 D4
Mukden = Shenyang 35 B7
Mukomuko 39 E2
Muktsar 42 D9
Mukur = Moqor 42 C5
Mula 19 C5
Mulanje 59 B7
Mulchén 94 D2
Mulde ➔ 15 C7
Mulgathing 62 B1
Mulhacén 18 D4
Mulhouse 13 C7
Mull 10 C4
Mullengudgery 63 B4
Muller, Pegunungan 39 D4
Mullingar 11 E3
Mullumbimby 63 A5
Multan 42 D7
Mumbai 43 K8
Muna 37 F2
München 15 D6
Munchen-Gladbach = Mönchengladbach 14 C4
Muncie 76 D3
Münden 14 C5
Mundo Novo 93 E5
Mungallala 63 A4
Mungallala Cr. ➔ 63 A4
Mungbere 57 D5
Munger 40 E6
Munich = München 15 D6
Muñoz Gamero, Pen. 95 G2
Münster 14 C4
Munster □ 11 E2
Muntok 39 E3
Muqdisho 49 G4
Murallón, Cerro 95 F2
Murang'a 57 E7
Murashi 24 B6
Muratli 22 D6
Murchison ➔ 60 F1
Murchison, Mt. 96 B15
Murchison Falls 57 D6
Murcia 19 C5
Murcia □ 19 D5
Mureş ➔ 22 A3
Mureşul = Mureş ➔ 22 A3
Murfreesboro 82 B4
Murgap 29 F8
Murghob = Murgap 29 F8
Murgon 63 A5
Müritz 15 B7
Murmansk 8 B12
Murom 24 B5
Muroran 32 B7
Muroto 33 G4
Muroto-Misaki 33 G4
Murray ➔ 62 C2
Murray Bridge 62 C2
Murrumbidgee ➔ 62 B3
Murrumburrah 63 B4
Murrurundi 63 B5
Murtoa 62 C3
Murwara 40 F3
Murwillumbah 63 A5
Mürzzuschlag 15 E8
Muş 46 C5
Mûsa, Gebel 47 E3
Musa Khel 42 D6
Mūsa Qal'eh 42 C4
Musala *Bulgaria* 22 C4
Musala *Indonesia* 39 D1
Muscat = Masqat 45 F4
Muscatine 75 E9
Musgrave Ranges 60 F5
Mushie 56 E3
Musi ➔ 39 E2
Musina 59 C6
Muskogee 81 B6
Musoma 57 E6
Mussoorie 42 D11
Mustafakemalpaşa 23 D7
Mustang 40 C4
Musters, L. 95 F3
Muswellbrook 63 B5
Mût *Egypt* 54 C4
Mut *Turkey* 46 C3
Mutare 59 B6
Muting 37 F6
Mutoray 30 C8
Mutsu 32 C7
Mutsu-Wan 32 C7
Muynak 29 E6
Muzaffarabad 42 B8
Muzaffargarh 42 D7
Muzaffarnagar 42 E10
Muzaffarpur 40 D5
Muzhi 28 C7
Muztag 34 C3
Mvuma 59 B6
Mwanza *Dem. Rep. of the Congo* 57 F5
Mwanza *Tanzania* 57 E6
Mweka 56 E4
Mweru, L. 57 F5
Mwinilunga 58 A4
My Tho 38 B3
Myanaung 41 H10
Myanmar = Burma ■ 41 G11
Myaungmya 41 J10
Mycenæ = Mikines 23 F4
Myeik Kyunzu 38 B1
Myingyan 41 G10
Myitkyina 41 E11
Mykolayiv 25 D3
Mykonos 23 F5
Mymensingh 41 E8
Mýrdalsjökull 8 C2
Mysia 23 E6
Mysore = Karnataka □ 43 N10
Mysore 43 N10
Myszków 16 C4
Mytishchi 24 B4

N

Na Hearadh = Harris 10 C3
Naab ➔ 15 D7
Nababeep 58 D3
Naberezhnyye Chelny 29 D6
Nabeul 54 A1
Nabire 37 E5
Nāblus = Nābulus 46 D3
Nābulus 46 D3
Nacala 59 A8
Nachingwea 57 G7
Nacogdoches 81 D6
Nacozari de García 84 A3
Nadiad 43 H8
Nadūshan 44 C3
Nadvirna 17 D7
Nadvornaya = Nadvirna 17 D7
Nadym 28 C8
Nadym ➔ 28 C8
Nafpaktos 23 E3
Nafplio 23 F4
Nafūd ad Dahy 47 G6
Nafud Desert = An Nafūd 47 E5
Naga 36 B2
Nagaland □ 41 E10
Nagano 33 E6
Nagaoka 33 E6
Nagappattinam 43 P11
Nagar Parkar 43 G7
Nagasaki 33 G1
Nagaur 42 F8
Nagercoil 43 Q10
Nagīneh 44 C4
Nagoya 33 F5
Nagpur 43 J11
Nagykanizsa 16 E3
Nagykőrös 16 E4
Naha 35 D7
Nahāvand 46 D7
Nā'īfah 48 D5
Nain *Canada* 70 D7
Nā'īn *Iran* 44 C3
Nairn 10 C5
Nairobi 57 E7
Najaf = An Najaf 47 D6
Najafābād 44 C2
Najd 47 F5
Najibabad 42 E11
Nakamura 33 G3
Nakashibetsu 32 B9
Nakhichevan = Naxçıvan 25 F6
Nakhichevan Rep. = Naxçıvan □ 25 F6
Nakhodka 32 B3
Nakhon Phanom 38 A2
Nakhon Ratchasima 38 B2
Nakhon Sawan 38 A2
Nakhon Si Thammarat 38 C2
Nakina 71 D5
Nakuru 57 E7
Nal ➔ 42 G4
Nalchik 25 E5
Nalgonda 43 L11
Nallamalai Hills 43 M11
Nam Co 34 C4
Nam-Phan 38 B3
Namak, Daryācheh-ye 44 C3
Namak, Kavir-e 44 C4
Namaland 58 D3
Namangan 29 E8
Namapa 59 A7
Namber 37 E4
Nambour 63 A5
Nambucca Heads 63 B5
Namib Desert 58 C2
Namibe 58 B2
Namibia ■ 58 C3
Namibwoestyn = Namib Desert 58 C2
Namlea 37 E3
Namoi ➔ 63 B4
Nampa 72 E5
Namp'o 35 C7
Nampō-Shotō 33 H7
Nampula 59 B7
Namrole 37 E3
Namse Shankou 40 C4
Namtu 41 F11
Namur 14 C3
Nan-ch'ang = Nanchang 35 D6
Nanaimo 69 D7
Nanango 63 A5
Nanao 33 E5
Nanchang 35 D6
Nanching = Nanjing 35 C6
Nanchong 35 C5
Nancy 13 B7
Nanda Devi 42 D11
Nanded 43 K10
Nandewar Ra. 63 B5
Nandurbar 43 J9
Nandyal 43 M11
Nanga-Eboko 56 D2
Nanga Parbat 42 B9
Nangapinoh 39 E4
Nangarhār □ 42 B7
Nangatayap 39 E4
Nanjing 35 C6
Nanking = Nanjing 35 C6
Nanning 35 D5
Nanping 35 D6
Nansei-Shotō = Ryūkyū-rettō 35 D7
Nansen Sd. 70 A4
Nantes 12 C3
Nantucket I. 77 D10
Nanuque 93 F5
Nanusa, Kepulauan 36 D3
Nanyang 35 C6
Nanyuki 57 D7
Nao, C. de la 19 C6
Napa 72 G2
Napier 64 C7
Naples = Nápoli 21 D5
Naples 83 F7
Napo ➔ 90 D4
Nápoli 21 D5
Nappa Merrie 62 A3
Nara 53 E4
Naracoorte 62 C3
Naradhan 63 B4
Narasapur 40 J3
Narathiwat 38 C2
Narayanganj 41 F8
Narayanpet 43 L10
Narbonne 13 E5
Nardò 21 D7
Narew ➔ 16 B5
Narin 42 A6
Narmada ➔ 43 J8
Narodnaya 28 C6
Narooma 63 C5
Narrabri 63 B4

Narran ➔ 63 A4
Narrandera 63 B4
Narromine 63 B4
Narsimhapur 43 H11
Naruto 33 F4
Narva 24 B2
Narvik 8 B9
Naryan-Mar 28 C6
Naryilco 62 A3
Narym 29 D9
Narymskoye 29 E9
Naryn 29 E8
Naseby 65 F4
Naser, Buheirat en 54 D5
Nashville 82 A4
Nasik 43 K8
Nasirabad 42 F9
Nassarawa 53 G7
Nassau 86 A4
Nassau, B. 95 H3
Nasser, L. = Naser, Buheirat en 54 D5
Natal *Brazil* 92 D6
Natal *Indonesia* 39 D1
Naṭanz 44 C2
Natashquan 71 D7
Natashquan ➔ 71 D7
Natchez 81 D8
Nathalia 63 C4
Nathdwara 43 G8
Natitingou 53 F6
Natkyizin 41 K11
Natron, L. 57 E7
Natuna Besar, Kepulauan 39 D3
Natuna Is. = Natuna Besar, Kepulauan 39 D3
Natuna Selatan, Kepulauan 39 D3
Naturaliste, C. 62 D4
Naujaat = Repulse Bay 70 C5
Naumburg 15 C6
Nauru ■ 64 K11
Naushahra = Nowshera 42 B8
Nauta 90 D4
Nautanwa 40 D4
Navahrudak 17 B7
Navalmoral de la Mata 18 C3
Navarino, I. 95 H3
Navarra □ 19 A5
Nāvodari 22 B7
Navoi = Nawoiy 29 E7
Navojoa 84 B3
Navsari 43 J8
Nawabshah 42 F6
Nawakot 40 D5
Nawalgarh 42 F9
Nawāsīf, Ḥarrat 47 G5
Nawoiy 29 E7
Naxçıvan 25 F6
Naxçıvan □ 25 F6
Naxos 23 F5
Nāy Band 44 E3
Naypyidaw 41 H11
Nayoro 32 A8
Nazas ➔ 84 B4
Nazilli 23 F7
Ndalatando 56 F2
Ndélé 55 G3
Ndjamena 55 F1
Ndola 59 A5
Neagh, Lough 11 D3
Neales ➔ 62 A2
Near Is. 69 C1
Neath 11 F5
Nebine Cr. ➔ 63 A4
Nebitdag = Balkanabat 29 F6
Nebraska □ 74 E5
Nébrodi, Monti 21 F5
Neckar ➔ 14 D5
Necochea 94 D5
Nederland = Netherlands ■ 14 B3
Neemuch = Nimach 43 G9
Neepawa 69 C10
Neftçala 46 C7
Negapatam = Nagappattinam 43 P11
Negele 49 F2
Negombo 43 R11
Negotin 22 B4
Negrais, C. = Maudin Sun 41 K10
Negro ➔ *Argentina* 95 E4
Negro ➔ *Brazil* 90 D6
Negro ➔ *Uruguay* 94 C5
Negros 36 C2
Nei Monggol Zizhiqu □ 35 B6
Neijiang 35 D5
Neiva 90 C3
Nejd = Najd 47 F5
Nellore 43 M11
Nelson *Canada* 69 D8
Nelson *N.Z.* 65 D5
Nelson ➔ 69 C10
Nelson, C. 62 C3
Nelson, Estrecho 95 G2
Nelson Lakes △ 65 D5
Nelspruit 59 D6
Néma 53 E4
Neman = Nemunas ➔ 24 B1
Nemunas ➔ 24 B1
Nemuro 32 B9
Nemuro-Kaikyō 32 B9
Nenagh 11 E2
Nenjiang 35 B7
Nepal ■ 40 D5
Nepalganj 40 C3
Neretva ➔ 20 C6
Ness, L. 10 C4
Nesterov 17 C6
Nesvizh = Nyasvizh 17 B8
Netherlands ■ 14 B3
Netherlands Antilles ⊠ 87 D6
Nettilling L. 70 C6
Neubrandenburg 15 B7
Neumünster 14 A5
Neunkirchen 14 D4
Neuquén 94 D3
Neuruppin 15 B7
Neustrelitz 15 B7
Neva ➔ 24 B3
Nevada □ 72 G5
Nevers 13 C5
Nevertire 63 B4
Nevinnomyssk 25 E5
Nevşehir 46 C3
New Amsterdam 90 B7
New Angledool 63 A4
New Bedford 77 D10
New Bern 83 B9
New Brighton 65 E5
New Britain *Papua N. G.* 64 K10
New Britain *U.S.A.* 77 D9
New Brunswick □ 71 E7
New Caledonia ⊠ 64 M11
New Castile = Castilla-La Mancha □ 18 C4
New Delhi 42 E10
New England Ra. 63 B5
New Forest △ 11 F6
New Glasgow 71 E7
New Hampshire □ 77 C10
New Haven 77 D9
New Hebrides = Vanuatu ■ 64 L11
New Ireland 64 K10
New Jersey □ 77 E9
New Liskeard 71 E6
New London 77 D9
New Mexico □ 79 C9
New Norfolk 62 D4
New Orleans 81 E8
New Plymouth 64 C6
New Providence 86 A4
New Siberian Is. = Novosibirskiye Ostrova 31 B12
New South Wales □ 63 B4
New York 77 D9
New York □ 77 C8
New Zealand ■ 64 D7
Newark 77 D8
Newburgh 77 D8
Newbury 11 F6
Newcastle 63 B5
Newcastle-upon-Tyne 11 D6
Newfoundland & Labrador □ 71 D8
Newman 60 E2
Newport *I. of W., U.K.* 11 F6
Newport *Newport, U.K.* 11 F5
Newport *U.S.A.* 77 D10
Newport News 77 F7
Newquay 11 F4
Newry 11 D3
Newton Boyd 63 A5
Neya 24 B5
Neyrīz 44 D3
Neyshābūr 44 B4
Nezhin = Nizhyn 24 C3
Ngabang 39 D3
Ngabordamlu, Tanjung 37 F4
Nganglong Kangri 40 A3
Ngaoundéré 56 C2
Ngapara 65 F4
Ngoring Hu 34 C4
Nguigmi 55 F1
Nha Trang 38 B3
Nhill 62 C3
Niagara Falls *Canada* 71 E6
Niagara Falls *U.S.A.* 77 C6
Niah 39 D4
Niamey 53 F6
Nias 39 D1
Nicaragua ■ 85 E7
Nicaragua, L. de 85 E7
Nicastro 21 E6
Nice 13 E7
Nichinan 33 H2
Nicobar Is. 27 H11
Nicosia 46 D3
Nicoya, Pen. de 85 F7
Niedersachsen □ 14 B5
Niemen = Nemunas ➔ 24 B1
Nienburg 14 B5
Nieuw Amsterdam 92 A2
Nieuw Nickerie 92 A2
Niğde 46 C3
Niger ■ 53 E7
Niger ➔ 53 G7
Nigeria ■ 53 G7
Nightcaps 65 F3
Nihon = Japan ■ 33 F5
Nii-Jima 33 F6
Niigata 33 E6
Ni'ihau 78 H10
Niitsu 33 E6
Nijmegen 14 C3
Nikiniki 37 F2
Nikolayev = Mykolayiv 25 D3
Nikolayevsk 24 C6
Nikopol 25 D3
Nīkshahr 45 E5
Nikšić 22 C2
Nīl, Nahr en ➔ 54 B5
Nīl el Abyad ➔ 55 E5
Nīl el Azraq ➔ 55 E5
Nile = Nīl, Nahr en ➔ 54 B5
Nimach 43 G9
Nîmes 13 E6
Nimfaíon, Ákra = Pines, Akra 23 D5
Nimmitabel 63 C4
Nīmrūz □ 45 D5
Nīnawá 46 C5
Nindigully 63 A4
Nineveh = Nīnawá 46 C5
Ningbo 35 D7
Ningpo = Ningbo 35 D7
Ningsia Hui A.R. = Ningxia Huizu Zizhiqu □ 35 C5
Ningxia Huizu Zizhiqu □ 35 C5
Niobrara ➔ 74 D5
Nioro du Sahel 53 E4
Niort 12 C3
Nipawin 69 C9
Nipigon, L. 71 E5
Nipissing, L. 71 E6
Nippon = Japan ■ 33 F5
Niquelândia 93 E4
Nirmal 43 K11
Nirmali 40 D6
Niš 22 C3

Niṣāb *Sí. Arabia* **47 E6**
Niṣāb *Yemen* **49 E4**
Nistru = Dnister ➔ **17 E10**
Niṭā' **47 F7**
Niterói **93 G5**
Niue **65 L14**
Niut **39 D4**
Nivernais **13 C5**
Nizamabad **43 K11**
Nizamghat **41 C10**
Nizhnevartovsk **29 C8**
Nizhneyansk **31 B11**
Nizhniy Novgorod **24 B5**
Nizhniy Tagil **29 D6**
Nizhyn **24 C3**
Nkhata Bay **57 G6**
Nkhotakota **59 A6**
Nkongsamba **53 H7**
Nmai ➔ **41 E11**
Noakhali = Maijdi **41 F8**
Nobeoka **33 G2**
Nocera Inferiore **21 D5**
Nockatunga **62 A3**
Nogales *Mexico* **84 A2**
Nogales *U.S.A.* **79 E7**
Nōgata **33 G2**
Noginsk **30 C7**
Noires, Mts. **12 B2**
Noirmoutier, Î. de **12 C2**
Nojima-Zaki **33 F6**
Nok Kundi **42 E3**
Nokhtuysk **30 C9**
Nola **56 D3**
Nome **69 B3**
Nong Khai **38 A2**
Noondoo **63 A4**
Noranda = Rouyn-Noranda **71 E6**
Nord-Ostsee-Kanal **14 A5**
Norderney **14 B4**
Norderstedt **14 B5**
Nordfriesische Inseln **14 A5**
Nordhausen **14 C6**
Nordkapp **8 A11**
Nordrhein-Westfalen □ **14 C4**
Nordvik **30 B9**
Norfolk **77 F7**
Norfolk I. **64 M11**
Norge = Norway ■ **8 C8**
Norilsk **30 C6**
Norley **63 A3**
Norman **80 B5**
Norman Wells **68 B7**
Normandie **12 B4**
Normandy = Normandie **12 B4**
Normanton **61 D7**
Norquinco **95 E2**
Norrköping **9 D9**
Norrland **8 C9**
Norseman **60 G3**
North, C. **71 E7**
North Battleford **69 C9**
North Bay **71 E6**
North Bend **72 E1**
North C. **64 A5**
North Cape = Nordkapp **8 A11**
North Carolina □ **83 B7**
North Channel **11 D4**
North Dakota □ **74 B4**
North East Frontier Agency = Arunachal Pradesh □ **41 C10**
North Frisian Is. = Nordfriesische Inseln **14 A5**
North I. **64 B5**
North Korea ■ **35 C7**
North Lakhimpur **41 D10**
North Magnetic Pole **70 A2**
North Minch **10 B4**
North Ossetia □ **25 E5**
North Pagai, I. = Pagai Utara, Pulau **39 E2**
North Platte **74 E4**
North Platte ➔ **74 E4**
North Rhine Westphalia = Nordrhein-Westfalen □ **14 C4**
North Saskatchewan ➔ **69 C8**
North Sea **10 D8**
North Taranaki Bight **64 C6**
North Thompson ➔ **69 C7**
North Uist **10 C3**
North West C. **60 E1**
North West Frontier □ **42 B8**
North West Highlands **10 C4**
North West River **71 D7**
Northampton **11 E6**
Northern Circars **40 J4**
Northern Ireland □ **11 D3**
Northern Marianas ⊘ **64 H9**
Northern Sporades **23 E4**
Northern Territory □ **60 D5**
Northland □ **64 A5**
Northumberland, C. **62 C3**
Northumberland Str. **71 E7**
Northwest Territories □ **68 B9**
Norton Sd. **69 B3**
Norway ■ **8 C8**
Norway House **69 C10**
Norwegian B. **70 B5**
Norwegian Sea **6 B5**
Norwich **11 E7**
Noshiro **32 C7**
Nosok **28 B9**
Noşratābād **45 D4**
Nossob ➔ **58 D4**
Nosy Barren **59 B8**
Nosy Bé **59 A9**
Nosy Boraha **59 B9**
Nosy Varika **59 C9**
Noteć ➔ **16 B2**
Notre Dame B. **71 E8**
Notre-Dame-de-Koartac = Quaqtaq **70 C7**
Notre-Dame-d'Ivugivic = Ivujivik **70 C6**
Nottaway ➔ **71 D6**
Nottingham **11 E6**
Nottingham I. **70 C6**
Nouâdhibou **52 D2**
Nouâdhibou, Râs **52 D2**
Nouakchott **53 E2**
Nouméa **64 M11**
Nouveau Comptoir = Wemindji **71 D6**
Nouvelle-Calédonie = New Caledonia ⊘ **64 M11**
Nova Casa Nova **93 D5**
Nova Friburgo **93 G5**
Nova Iguaçu **93 G5**
Nova Iorque **92 D5**
Nova Lima **93 F5**
Nova Scotia □ **71 E7**
Nova Venécia **93 F5**
Nova Zagora **22 C5**
Novara **13 D8**
Novaya Ladoga **24 A3**
Novaya Lyalya **29 D7**
Novaya Zemlya **28 B6**
Novgorod **24 B3**
Novgorod-Severskiy = Novhorod-Siverskyy **24 C3**
Novhorod-Siverskyy **24 C3**
Novi Ligure **13 D8**
Novi Pazar **22 C3**
Novi Sad **22 B2**
Novo Mesto **20 B5**
Novo Remanso **93 D5**
Novoaltaysk **29 D9**
Novocherkassk **25 D5**
Novogrudok = Navahrudak **17 B7**
Novohrad-Volynskyy **17 C8**
Novokachalinsk **32 A3**
Novokuybyshevsk **24 C6**
Novokuznetsk **29 D9**
Novomoskovsk **24 C4**
Novorossiysk **25 E4**
Novorybnoye **30 B8**
Novoselytsya **17 D8**
Novoshakhtinsk **25 D4**
Novosibirsk **29 D9**
Novosibirskiye Ostrova **31 B12**
Novotroitsk **29 D6**
Novouzensk **24 C6**
Novovolynsk **17 C7**
Novska **20 B6**
Novyy Port **28 C8**
Nowa Sól **16 C2**
Nowgong **41 D9**
Nowra **63 B5**
Nowshera **42 B8**
Nowy Targ **16 D5**
Nowy Tomyśl **16 B3**
Noyon **13 B5**
Nsanje **59 B7**
Nubian Desert = Nûbîya, Es Sahrâ en **54 D5**
Nûbîya, Es Sahrâ en **54 D5**
Nuboai **37 E5**
Nueltin L. **68 B10**
Nueva Rosita **84 B4**
Nuéve de Julio **94 D4**
Nuevitas **86 B4**
Nuevo, G. **95 E4**
Nuevo Laredo **84 B5**
Nugget Pt. **65 G3**
Nuhaka **64 C7**
Nukey Bluff **62 B2**
Nuku'alofa **65 M13**
Nukus **29 E6**
Nullarbor Plain **60 G4**
Numalla, L. **63 A3**
Numan **55 G1**
Numazu **33 F6**
Numfoor **37 E4**
Numurkah **63 C4**
Nunavut □ **70 C5**
Nuneaton **11 E6**
Nunivak I. **69 B3**
Nunkun **42 C10**
Núoro **21 D2**
Nuremberg = Nürnberg **15 D6**
Nuriootpa **62 B2**
Nürnberg **15 D6**
Nurran, L. = Terewah, L. **63 A4**
Nusa Tenggara Barat □ **39 F5**
Nusa Tenggara Timur □ **37 F2**
Nushki **42 E5**
Nuuk **66 C14**
Nuwakot **40 C4**
Nuweveldberge **58 E4**
Nuyts Arch. **62 B1**
Nyahururu **57 D7**
Nyaingêntanglha Shan **34 C4**
Nyâlâ **55 F3**
Nyasa, L. = Malawi, L. **59 A6**
Nyasvizh **17 B8**
Nyda **28 C8**
Nyíregyháza **17 E5**
Nylstroom = Modimolle **59 C5**
Nymagee **63 B4**
Nyngan **63 B4**
Nyoman = Nemunas ➔ **24 B1**
Nysa **16 C3**
Nysa ➔ **16 B2**
Nyslott = Savonlinna **8 C11**
Nystad = Uusikaupunki **9 C10**
Nyurba **30 C9**
Nzega **57 E6**
Nzérékoré **53 G4**
Nzeto **56 F2**

O

Ō-Shima **33 F6**
Oahe, L. **74 C4**
O'ahu **78 H12**
Oak Ridge **83 A5**
Oakey **63 A5**
Oakland **78 B1**

Oamaru 65 F4
Oates Land 96 A15
Oaxaca 84 D5
Ob ➔ 28 C7
Oba 71 E5
Oban 10 C4
Obbia 49 F4
Oberhausen 14 C4
Oberon 63 B4
Obi, Kepulauan 37 E3
Óbidos 92 C2
Obihiro 32 B8
Obilatu 37 E3
Obo 57 C5
Obozerskaya = Obozerskiy 28 C5
Obozerskiy 28 C5
Obskaya Guba 28 C8
Obuasi 53 G5
Ocala 83 E6
Ocaña 18 C4
Occidental, Cordillera 90 C3
Ocean I. = Banaba 64 K11
Oceanside 78 D4
Ocniţa 17 D8
Öda 33 F3
Odate 32 C7
Odawara 33 F6
Ödemiş 23 E7
Odense 9 D8
Oder ➔ 15 B8
Odesa 25 D3
Odessa = Odesa 25 D3
Odessa 80 D2
Odienné 53 G4
Odintsovo 24 B4
Odra = Oder ➔ 15 B8
Odzi 59 B6
Oeiras 92 D5
Ofanto ➔ 20 D6
Offa 53 G6
Offenbach 14 C5
Offenburg 14 D4
Oga 32 D6
Oga-Hantö 32 D6
Ögaki 33 F5
Ogasawara Gunto 27 F16
Ogbomosho 53 G6
Ogden 73 F7
Ogdensburg 77 B8
Oglio ➔ 20 B3
Ogooué ➔ 56 E1
Ogowe = Ogooué ➔ 56 E1
Ohai 65 F2
Ohakune 64 C6
Ohanet 52 C7
Ohata 32 C7
Ohau, L. 65 F3
Ohio □ 76 D4
Ohio ➔ 76 F1
Ohře ➔ 16 C2
Ohrid 22 D3
Ohridsko Jezero 23 D3
Oise ➔ 12 B5
Ōita 33 G2
Oiticica 92 D5
Ojos del Salado, Cerro 94 B3
Oka ➔ 28 D5
Okaba 37 F5
Okahandja 58 C3
Okanogan ➔ 72 B4
Okara 42 D8
Okavango Delta 58 B4
Okavango Swamp = Okavango Delta 58 B4
Okayama 33 F3
Okazaki 33 F5
Okeechobee, L. 83 F7
Okefenokee Swamp 83 D6
Okhotsk, Sea of 31 D12
Oki-Shotō 33 E3
Okinawa-Jima 35 D7
Oklahoma □ 80 B5
Oklahoma City 80 B5
Okmulgee 81 B6
Oknitsa = Ocniţa 17 D8
Oksibil 37 E6
Oktabrsk = Oktyabrsk 29 E6
Oktyabrsk 29 E6
Oktyabrskiy = Aktsyabrski 17 B9
Oktyabrskoy Revolyutsii, Ostrov 30 B7
Oktyabrskoye 28 C7
Okuru 65 E3
Okushiri-Tō 32 B6
Öland 9 D9
Olary 62 B3
Olavarría 94 D4
Oława 16 C3
Ólbia 20 D2
Old Castile = Castilla y Leon □ 18 A3
Old Crow 68 B6
Oldenburg 14 B5
Oldham 11 E5
Olekma ➔ 31 C10
Olekminsk 31 C10
Oleksandriya 17 C8
Olenek 30 C9
Olenek ➔ 30 B10
Oléron, Î. d' 12 D3
Oleśnica 16 C3
Olevsk 17 C8
Olhão 18 D2
Olifants = Elefantes ➔ 59 C6
Ólimbos, Óros = Olympos Oros 23 D4
Olinda 92 D7
Olivenza 18 C2
Ollagüe 91 H5
Olomouc 16 D3
Olongapo 36 B2
Olot 19 A7
Olsztyn 16 B5
Olt ➔ 22 C5
Olteniţa 22 B6
Olympos Oros 23 D4
Olympia *Greece* 23 F3
Olympia *U.S.A.* 72 C2
Olympic Mts. 72 C2
Olympus, Mt. = Olympos Oros 23 D4
Olympus, Mt. = Uludağ 23 D7
Om ➔ 29 D8
Ōmagari 32 D7
Omagh 11 D3
Omaha 75 E7
Oman ■ 48 C6
Oman, G. of 45 E4
Omaruru 58 C3
Omate 91 G4
Ombai, Selat 37 F2
Omboué 56 E1
Ombrone ➔ 20 C3
Omdurmân 55 E5
Ometepec 84 D5
Omo ➔ 55 G6
Omsk 29 D8
Ōmu 32 A8
Omul, Vf. 17 F7
Omuramba Omatako ➔ 58 B4
Ōmuta 33 G2
Onang 37 E1
Onda 19 C5
Ondangwa 58 B3
Öndörhaan 35 B6
Onega 28 C4
Onega, L. = Onezhskoye Ozero 8 C13
Oneşti 17 E8
Onezhskoye Ozero 8 C13
Ongarue 64 C6
Onilahy ➔ 59 C8
Onitsha 53 G7
Ontario □ 71 E5
Ontario, L. 77 C7
Oodnadatta 62 A2
Oostende 14 C2
Ootacamund = Udagamandalam 43 P10
Opala 56 E4
Opava 16 D3
Opole 16 C3
Oporto = Porto 18 B1
Opotiki 64 C7
Opua 64 A6
Opunake 64 C5
Opunohu, B. d' 30 H
Oradea 17 E5
Öræfajökull 8 C2
Orai 42 G11
Oral = Zhayyq ➔ 29 E6
Oral 24 C7
Oran 52 A5
Orange *Australia* 63 B4
Orange *France* 13 D6
Orange *U.S.A.* 81 D7
Orange ➔ 58 D3
Orange, C. 92 B3
Orange Free State = Free State □ 59 D5
Orangeburg 83 C7
Oranienburg 15 B7
Oranje = Orange ➔ 58 D3
Orapa 59 C5
Oras 36 B3
Orbetello 20 C3
Orbost 63 C4
Orchila, I. 90 A5
Ordos = Mu Us Shamo 35 C5
Ordu 46 B4
Ore Mts. = Erzgebirge 15 C7
Örebro 9 D9
Oregon □ 72 E3
Orekhovo-Zuyevo 24 B4
Orel 24 C4
Ören 23 F6
Orenburg 29 D6
Orense = Ourense 18 A2
Orepuki 65 G2
Orfanos Kolpos 23 D5
Orgaz 18 C4
Orgeyev = Orhei 17 E9
Orhaneli 23 E7
Orhangazi 23 D7
Orhei 17 E9
Orhon Gol ➔ 35 A5
Orient 62 A3
Oriental, Cordillera 90 B4
Orihuela 19 C5
Orinoco ➔ 90 B6
Orissa □ 40 G5
Oristano 21 E2
Oristano, G. di 21 E2
Orizaba 84 D5
Orizaba, Pico de 84 D5
Orkney Is. 10 B5
Orlando 83 E7
Orléanais 12 C5
Orléans 12 C4
Ormara 42 G4
Ormoc 36 B2
Ormond 64 C7
Örnsköldsvik 8 C9
Orocué 90 C4
Orol Dengizi = Aral Sea 29 E6
Oroquieta 36 C2
Orosháza 16 E5
Orroroo 62 B2
Orsha 24 C3
Orsk 29 D6
Orşova 22 B4
Ortaca 23 F7
Ortegal, C. 18 A2
Orthez 12 E3
Ortigueira 18 A2
Ortles 13 C9
Ortón ➔ 91 F5
Orümīyeh 46 C6
Orūmīyeh, Daryācheh-ye 46 C6
Oruro 91 G5
Oruzgān □ 42 C5
Orvieto 20 C4
Oryakhovo 22 C4
Ōsaka 33 F4
Ösel = Saaremaa 24 B1
Osh 29 E8
Oshakati 58 B3
Oshawa 71 E6
Oshkosh 74 E3
Oshmyany = Ashmyany 17 A7
Oshogbo 53 G6
Oshwe 56 E3
Osijek 20 B7
Osipovichi = Asipovichy 17 B9

Osizweni 59 D6
Oskarshamn 9 D9
Oskemen 29 E9
Oslo 9 D8
Oslofjorden 9 D8
Osmanabad 43 K10
Osmaniye 46 C4
Osnabrück 14 B5
Osorno 95 E2
Ossa, Mt. 62 D4
Ossa, Oros 23 E4
Ostend = Oostende 14 C2
Oster 17 C10
Österdalälven 8 C8
Österreich = Austria ■ 15 E8
Östersund 8 C8
Ostfriesische Inseln 14 B4
Ostrava 16 D4
Ostróda 16 B4
Ostroh 17 C8
Ostrołęka 16 B5
Ostrów Mazowiecka 16 B5
Ostrów Wielkopolski 16 C3
Ostrowiec-Świętokrzyski 16 C5
Ostuni 21 D6
Osuna 18 D3
Oswego 77 C7
Otago □ 65 F3
Otago Harbour 65 F4
Otaki 64 D6
Otaru 32 B7
Otaru-Wan = Ishikari-Wan 32 B7
Otavalo 90 C3
Otjiwarongo 58 C3
Otoineppu 32 A8
Otorohanga 64 C6
Otranto 21 D7
Otranto, C. d' 21 D7
Otranto, Str. of 21 D7
Ōtsu 33 F4
Ottawa = Outaouais ➔ 71 E6
Ottawa 71 E6
Ottawa Is. 70 D5
Ottumwa 75 E8
Oturkpo 53 G7
Otway, B. 95 G2
Otway, C. 62 C3
Otwock 16 B5
Ouachita Mts. 81 B6
Ouadda 55 G3
Ouagadougou 53 F5
Ouahran = Oran 52 A5
Ouallene 52 D6
Ouanda Djallé 55 G3
Ouaqui 30 E
Ouargla 52 B7
Ouarzazate 52 B4
Oubangi ➔ 56 E3
Oudtshoorn 58 E4
Ouessant, Î. d' 12 B1
Ouesso 56 D3
Ouest, Pte. de l' 30 A
Ouezzane 52 B4
Oujda 52 B5
Oulu 8 B11
Oulujärvi 8 C11
Oulujoki ➔ 8 B11
Oum Chalouba 55 E3
Oum Hadjer 55 F2
Ounianga Sérir 55 E3
Ourense 18 A2
Ouricuri 92 D5
Ouro Prêto 93 G5
Ouse 62 D4
Outaouais ➔ 71 E6
Outer Hebrides 10 C3
Outjo 58 C3
Ouyen 62 C3
Ovalle 94 C2
Ovamboland 58 B3
Oviedo 18 A3
Ovruch 17 C9
Owaka 65 G3
Owambo = Ovamboland 58 B3
Owase 33 F5
Owbeh 42 B3
Owen Sound 71 E5
Owen Stanley Ra. 61 B8
Owo 53 G7
Owyhee ➔ 72 E5
Oxford *N.Z.* 65 E5
Oxford *U.K.* 11 F6
Oxnard 78 C3
Oxus = Amudarya ➔ 29 E6
Oya 39 D4
Oyama 33 E6
Oyem 56 D2
Oyo 53 G6
Ozamiz 36 C2
Ozark Plateau 81 A8
Özd 16 D5

P

Pa-an 41 J11
Paarl 58 E3
Pab Hills 42 F5
Pabianice 16 C4
Pabna 41 E7
Pacaja ➔ 92 C3
Pacaraima, Sa. 90 C6
Pacasmayo 91 E3
Pachpadra 42 G8
Pachuca 84 C5
Padaido, Kepulauan 37 E5
Padang 39 E2
Padangpanjang 39 E2
Padangsidempuan 39 D1
Paderborn 14 C5
Padloping Island 70 C7
Pádova 20 B3
Padua = Pádova 20 B3
Paducah 76 F1
Paeroa 64 B6
Pag 20 B5
Pagadian 36 C2
Pagai Selatan, Pulau 39 E2
Pagai Utara, Pulau 39 E2
Pagalu = Annobón 51 G4
Pagastikos Kolpos 23 E4
Pagatan 39 E5
Pahiatua 64 D6
Päijänne 8 C11
Painan 39 E2
Paint Hills = Wemindji 71 D6
Painted Desert 79 C7
País Vasco □ 19 A4
Paisley 10 D4
Paita 90 E2
Pajares, Puerto de 18 A3
Pakistan ■ 42 E7
Pakokku 41 G10
Paktīā □ 42 C6
Pakxe 38 A3
Pala 55 G2
Palagruža 20 C6
Palam 43 K10
Palampur 42 C10
Palana 62 C4
Palanan 36 A2
Palanan Pt. 36 A2
Palangkaraya 39 E4
Palani Hills 43 P10
Palanpur 43 G8
Palapye 59 C5
Palau ■ 36 C4
Palawan 38 C5
Palayankottai 43 Q10
Paleleh 37 D2
Palembang 39 E2
Palencia 18 A3
Palermo 21 E4
Palestine 81 D6
Paletwa 41 G9
Palghat 43 P10
Pali 42 G8
Palikir 64 J10
Paliouri, Akra 23 E4
Palitana 43 J7
Palk Bay 43 Q11
Palk Strait 43 Q11
Pallanza = Verbánia 13 D8
Palm Springs 78 D4
Palma, B. de 19 C7
Palma de Mallorca 19 C7
Palmares 92 D6
Palmas, C. 53 H4
Pálmas, G. di 21 E2
Palmeira dos Índios 93 D6
Palmer 69 B5
Palmer Arch. 96 A3
Palmer Land 96 B3
Palmerston 65 F4
Palmerston North 64 D6
Palmi 21 E5
Palmira 90 C3
Palmyra = Tudmur 46 D4
Palopo 37 E2
Palos, C. de 19 D5
Palu *Indonesia* 37 E1
Palu *Turkey* 46 C5
Pamiers 12 E4
Pamir 29 F8
Pamlico Sd. 83 B10
Pampa 80 B3
Pampanua 37 E2
Pampas *Argentina* 94 D4
Pampas *Peru* 91 F4
Pamplona *Colombia* 90 B4
Pamplona *Spain* 19 A5
Panaji 43 M8
Panamá 85 F9
Panama ■ 86 E4
Panamá, G. de 86 E4
Panama Canal 86 E4
Panama City 82 D5
Panão 91 E3
Panay 36 B2
Panay G. 36 B2
Pančevo 22 B3
Pandan 36 B2
Pandharpur 43 L9
Pando, L. = Hope, L. 62 A2
Panevėžys 24 B1
Pang-Long 41 F12
Pang-Yang 41 F12
Pangani 57 F7
Pangfou = Bengbu 35 C6
Pangkajene 37 E1
Pangkalanbrandan 39 D1
Pangkalanbuun 39 E4
Pangkalpinang 39 E3
Pangnirtung 70 C7
Pangutaran Group 36 C2
Panjgur 42 F4
Panjim = Panaji 43 M8
Panjnad Barrage 42 E7
Pannirtuuq = Pangnirtung 70 C7
Panorama 94 A6
Pantar 37 F2
Pante Macassar 37 F2
Pante Makasar = Pante Macassar 37 F2
Pantelleria 21 F3
Paoting = Baoding 35 C6
Paot'ou = Baotou 35 B6
Paoua 55 G2
Pápa 16 E3
Papakura 64 B6
Papantla 84 C5
Papar 38 C5
Paparoa △ 65 E4
Papeete 65 L16
Papua □ 37 E5
Papua New Guinea ■ 64 K9
Papudo 94 C2
Papun 41 H11
Pará = Belém 92 C4
Pará □ 92 C3
Paracatu 93 F4
Paracel Is. 38 A4
Parachilna 62 B2
Paradip 40 G6
Parado 37 F1
Paragua ➔ 90 B6
Paraguaçu ➔ 93 E6
Paraguaná, Pen. de 90 A4
Paraguarí 94 B5
Paraguay ■ 94 A5
Paraguay ➔ 94 B5
Paraíba = João Pessoa 92 D7
Paraíba □ 92 D6
Parakou 53 G6
Paramaribo 92 A2
Paraná *Argentina* 94 C4

Paraná *Brazil* **93 E4**
Paraná □ **94 A6**
Paraná ➔ **94 C5**
Paranaguá **94 B7**
Paranaíba **93 F3**
Paranaíba ➔ **93 G3**
Paranapanema ➔ **94 A6**
Paranas **36 B3**
Parang *Maguindanao, Phil.* **36 C2**
Parang *Sulu, Phil.* **36 C2**
Parângul Mare, Vf. **17 F6**
Paraparaumu **64 D6**
Paratinga **93 E5**
Parattah **62 D4**
Parbhani **43 K10**
Parchim **15 B6**
Pardo ➔ *Bahia, Brazil* **93 F6**
Pardo ➔ *Mato Grosso, Brazil* **93 G3**
Pardubice **16 C2**
Parecis, Serra dos **91 F7**
Parepare **37 E1**
Parga **23 E3**
Pariaguán **90 B6**
Parigi **37 E2**
Parika **90 B7**
Parima, Serra **90 C6**
Parinari **90 D4**
Parintins **92 C2**
Pariparit Kyun **41 K9**
Paris *France* **12 B5**
Paris *U.S.A.* **81 C6**
Park Range **73 G10**
Parkersburg **76 E5**
Parkes **63 B4**
Parla **18 B4**
Parma **13 D9**
Parnaguá **93 E5**
Parnaíba **92 C5**
Parnaíba ➔ **92 C5**
Parnassos **23 E4**
Pärnu **24 B1**
Paroo ➔ **63 B3**
Paros **23 F5**
Parral **94 D2**
Parry Is. **70 B3**
Parry Sound **71 E6**
Partinico **21 E4**
Paru ➔ **92 C3**
Parvān □ **42 B6**
Parvatipuram **40 H4**
Pas, The **69 C9**
Pasadena *Calif., U.S.A.* **78 C3**
Pasadena *Tex., U.S.A.* **81 E6**
Pascagoula **81 D9**
Paşcani **17 E8**
Pasco **72 C4**
Pasco, Cerro de **91 F3**
Pasirkuning **39 E2**
Pašman **20 C5**
Pasni **42 G3**
Paso de Indios **95 E3**
Passau **15 D7**
Passero, C. **21 F5**
Passo Fundo **94 B6**
Passos **93 G4**
Pastaza ➔ **90 D3**
Pasto **90 C3**
Patagonia **95 F3**
Patan = Lalitapur **40 D5**
Patan **43 H8**
Patani **37 D3**
Patchewollock **62 C3**
Patea **64 C6**
Paternò **21 F5**
Paterson **77 D8**
Pathankot **42 C9**
Pathein = Bassein **41 J10**
Patiala **42 D10**
Patkai Bum **41 D10**
Patmos **23 F6**
Patna **40 E5**
Patos, L. dos **94 C6**
Patos de Minas **93 F4**
Patquía **94 C3**
Patra **23 E3**
Patraikos Kolpos **23 E3**
Patras = Patra **23 E3**
Patrocínio **93 F4**
Pattani **38 C2**
Patuakhali **41 F8**
Pau **12 E3**
Pauk **41 G10**
Paulistana **92 D5**
Paulo Afonso **93 D6**
Pavia **13 D8**
Pavlodar **29 D8**
Pavlograd = Pavlohrad **25 D4**
Pavlohrad **25 D4**
Pavlovo **24 B5**
Pavlovsk **24 C5**
Pawtucket **77 D10**
Paxi **23 E3**
Payakumbuh **39 E2**
Payne Bay = Kangirsuk **70 D7**
Payne L. **70 D6**
Paysandú **94 C5**
Paz, B. de la **84 C2**
Pazar **46 B5**
Pazardzhik **22 C5**
Peace ➔ **68 C8**
Peak Hill **63 B4**
Peake Cr. ➔ **62 A2**
Peawanuck **71 D5**
Pebane **59 B7**
Pebas **90 D4**
Peć **22 C3**
Pechenga **28 C4**
Pechenizhyn **17 D7**
Pechora ➔ **28 C6**
Pechorskaya Guba **28 C6**
Pecos ➔ **80 E3**
Pécs **16 E4**
Pedder, L. **62 D4**
Pedirka **62 A2**
Pedra Azul **93 F5**
Pedreiras **92 C5**
Pedro Afonso **93 D4**
Pedro Juan Caballero **94 A5**
Peebinga **62 B3**
Peel ➔ *Australia* **63 B5**
Peel ➔ *Canada* **68 B6**
Peera Peera Poolanna L. **62 A2**
Pegasus Bay **65 E5**
Pegu **41 J11**
Pegu Yoma **41 H10**
Pehuajó **94 D4**
Peine **14 B6**
Peip'ing = Beijing **35 C6**
Peipus, L. = Chudskoye, Ozero **24 B2**
Peixe **93 E4**
Pekalongan **39 F3**
Pekanbaru **39 D2**
Pekin **75 E10**
Peking = Beijing **35 C6**
Pelagie, Is. **21 G4**
Pelaihari **39 E4**
Peleaga, Vf. **17 F6**
Peleng **37 E2**
Pelješac **20 C6**
Pelly ➔ **68 B6**
Pelly Bay **70 C5**
Peloponnese □ **23 F4**
Peloro, C. **21 E5**
Pelorus Sd. **65 D5**
Pelotas **94 C6**
Pelvoux, Massif du **13 D7**
Pematangsiantar **39 D1**
Pemba **59 A8**
Pemba I. **57 F7**
Pembroke *Canada* **71 E6**
Pembroke *U.K.* **11 F4**
Penang = Pinang **38 C2**
Penápolis **94 A6**
Peñarroya-Pueblonuevo **18 C3**
Peñas, C. de **18 A3**
Peñas, G. de **95 F2**
Pench'i = Benxi **35 B7**
Pend Oreille, L. **72 C5**
Pendembu **53 G3**
Pendleton **72 D4**
Penedo **93 E6**
Penguin **62 D4**
Peniche **18 C1**
Penida, Nusa **39 F5**
Peninsular Malaysia □ **39 D2**
Penmarch, Pte. de **12 C1**
Pennines **11 D5**
Pennsylvania □ **77 D7**
Penny Str. **70 B4**
Penola **62 C3**
Penong **60 G5**
Penrhyn **65 K15**
Penrith **63 B5**
Pensacola **82 D4**
Pensacola Mts. **96 C4**
Penshurst **62 C3**
Penticton **69 D8**
Pentland Firth **10 B5**
Penza **24 C6**
Penzance **11 F4**
Peoria **75 E10**
Perabumulih **39 E2**
Perche, Collines du **12 B4**
Perdido, Mte. **19 A6**
Perdu, Mt. = Perdido, Mte. **19 A6**
Pereira **90 C3**
Perekerten **62 B3**
Pereyaslav-Khmelnytskyy **24 C3**
Pergamino **94 C4**
Péribonka ➔ **71 E6**
Perico **94 A3**
Périgueux **12 D4**
Perijá, Sierra de **90 B4**
Perlas, Arch. de las **86 E4**
Perm **29 D6**
Pernambuco = Recife **92 D7**
Pernatty Lagoon **62 B2**
Pernik **22 C4**
Perpendicular Pt. **63 B5**
Perpignan **13 E5**
Persepolis **44 D3**
Pershotravensk **17 C8**
Persia = Iran ■ **44 C3**
Persian Gulf **44 E2**
Perth *Australia* **60 G2**
Perth *U.K.* **10 C5**
Perth Amboy **77 D8**
Peru ■ **90 C3**
Perúgia **20 C4**
Pervomaysk **25 D3**
Pervouralsk **29 D6**
Pésaro **20 C4**
Pescara **20 C5**
Peshawar **42 B7**
Peshkopi **22 D3**
Pesqueira **92 D6**
Petah Tiqwa **46 D3**
Petauke **59 A6**
Peter I. Øy **96 A2**
Peterborough *Australia* **62 B2**
Peterborough *Canada* **71 E6**
Peterborough *U.K.* **11 E6**
Peterhead **10 C6**
Petersburg *Alaska, U.S.A.* **69 C6**
Petersburg *Va., U.S.A.* **77 F7**
Petit Barachois **30 A**
Petitsikapau L. **71 D7**
Petlad **43 H8**
Peto **85 C7**
Petone **65 D6**
Petra Velikogo, Zaliv **32 B3**
Petrich **22 D4**
Petrikov = Pyetrikaw **17 B9**
Petrolândia **93 D6**
Petrolina **93 D5**
Petropavl **29 D7**
Petropavlovsk = Petropavl **29 D7**
Petropavlovsk-Kamchatskiy **31 D13**
Petrópolis **93 G5**
Petroşani **17 F6**
Petrovaradin **22 B2**
Petrovsk **24 C6**
Petrozavodsk **8 C12**
Peureulak **38 D1**
Pforzheim **14 D5**
Phagwara **42 D9**
Phalodi **42 F8**
Phan Rang **38 B3**
Phangan, Ko **38 C2**
Phangnga **38 C1**

Phatthalung **38 C2**
Phetchabun **38 A2**
Philadelphia **77 E8**
Philippine Trench = Mindanao Trench **36 B3**
Philippines ■ **36 B2**
Philippopolis = Plovdiv **22 C5**
Phillip I. **63 C4**
Phillott **63 A4**
Phitsanulok **38 A2**
Phnom Dangrek **38 B2**
Phnom Penh **38 B2**
Phnum Penh = Phnom Penh **38 B2**
Phoenix **79 D6**
Phra Nakhon Si Ayutthaya **38 B2**
Phuket **38 C1**
Phumiphon, Khuan **38 A1**
Piacenza **13 D8**
Pialba **63 A5**
Pian Cr. ➔ **63 B4**
Pianosa **20 C3**
Piatra Neamţ **17 E8**
Piauí □ **92 D5**
Piave ➔ **20 B4**
Pibor Post **55 G5**
Picardie □ **13 B5**
Picardy = Picardie □ **13 B5**
Pichilemu **94 C2**
Pico Truncado **95 F3**
Picton *Australia* **63 B5**
Picton *N.Z.* **65 D6**
Picún Leufú **95 D3**
Piedmont = Piemonte □ **13 D7**
Piedras, R. de las ➔ **91 F5**
Piedras Negras **84 B4**
Pielinen **8 C11**
Piemonte □ **13 D7**
Piet Retief **59 D6**
Pietermaritzburg **59 D6**
Pietersburg = Polokwane **59 C5**
Pietrosul, Vf. *Maramureş, Romania* **17 E7**
Pietrosul, Vf. *Suceava, Romania* **17 E7**
Pigüe **94 D4**
Piła **16 B3**
Pilar **94 B5**
Pilcomayo ➔ **94 B5**
Pilibhit **42 E11**
Pilica ➔ **16 C5**
Pilipinas = Philippines ■ **36 B2**
Pilos **23 F3**
Pimba **62 B2**
Pimenta Bueno **91 F6**
Pimentel **91 E3**
Pinang **38 C2**
Pinar del Río **86 B3**
Pınarhisar **22 D6**
Pińczów **16 C5**
Pindos Oros **23 E3**
Pindus Mts. = Pindos Oros **23 E3**
Pine Bluff **81 B7**
Pine Point **68 B8**
Pinega ➔ **28 C5**
Pinerolo **13 D7**
Pines, Akra **23 D5**
Ping ➔ **38 A2**
Pingdong **35 D7**
Pingliang **35 C5**
Pingxiang **35 D5**
Pinhel **18 B2**
Pini **39 D1**
Pinios ➔ **23 E4**
Pinnaroo **62 C3**
Pinrang **37 E1**
Pinsk **17 B8**
Pintados **91 H5**
Pinyug **24 A6**
Piombino **20 C3**
Pioner, Ostrov **30 B7**
Piopiotaki = Milford Sd. **65 F2**
Piorini, L. **90 D6**
Piotrków Trybunalski **16 C4**
Pīp **45 E5**
Piquiri ➔ **94 A6**
Piracicaba **94 A7**
Piracuruca **92 C5**
Piraeus = Pireas **23 F4**
Piraiévs = Pireas **23 F4**
Pirané **94 B5**
Pirapora **93 F5**
Pireas **23 F4**
Pirgos **23 F3**
Pirin Planina **22 D4**
Pírineos = Pyrénées **12 E4**
Piripiri **92 C5**
Pirmasens **14 D4**
Pirot **22 C4**
Piru **37 E3**
Pisa **20 C3**
Pisagua **91 G4**
Pisciotta **21 D5**
Pisco **91 F3**
Písek **16 D2**
Pishan **34 C2**
Pising **37 F2**
Pistóia **20 C3**
Pisuerga ➔ **18 B3**
Pitarpunga L. **62 B3**
Pitcairn I. **65 M17**
Piteå **8 B10**
Piteşti **22 B5**
Pithapuram **40 J4**
Pittsburg **81 A6**
Pittsburgh **77 D5**
Pittsworth **63 A5**
Piura **90 E2**
Placentia **71 E8**
Placentia B. **71 E8**
Plainview **80 B3**
Plaka, Akra **23 G6**
Plakhino **28 C9**
Plasencia **18 B2**
Plastun **32 A5**
Plata, Río de la ➔ **94 C5**
Plátani ➔ **21 F4**
Platte ➔ **75 F7**
Plauen **15 C7**
Plei Ku **38 B3**
Plenty, B. of **64 B7**
Pleven **22 C5**
Plevlja **22 C2**
Płock **16 B4**
Plöckenstein **15 D7**
Ploieşti **22 B6**
Plovdiv **22 C5**
Plumtree **59 C5**
Plymouth **11 F4**
Plzeň **16 D1**
Po ➔ **20 B4**
Po Hai = Bo Hai **35 C6**
Pobedy, Pik **29 E8**
Pocatello **73 E7**
Poços de Caldas **93 G4**
Podgorica **22 C2**
Podilska Vysochyna **17 D8**
Podolsk **24 B4**
Poh **37 E2**
Pohnpei **64 J10**
Poinsett, C. **96 A12**
Pointe-à-Pitre **87 C7**
Pointe-Noire **56 E2**
Poitiers **12 C4**
Poitou **12 C3**
Pokaran **42 F7**
Pokataroo **63 A4**
Pola = Pula **20 B4**
Polan **45 E5**
Poland ■ **16 B5**
Polatsk **24 B2**
Polesye = Pripet Marshes **17 B9**
Police **16 B2**
Poligiros **23 D4**
Polillo Is. **36 B2**
Pollachi **43 P10**
Polnovat **28 C7**
Polokwane **59 C5**
Polonne **17 C8**
Polonnoye = Polonne **17 C8**
Poltava **24 D3**
Polunochnoye **28 C7**
Polynesia **65 L15**
Polynésie française = French Polynesia ☑ **65 M16**
Pombal **18 C1**
Pomézia **20 D4**
Pomorskie, Pojezierze **16 B3**
Ponape = Pohnpei **64 J10**
Ponca City **80 A5**
Ponce **87 C6**
Pond Inlet **70 B6**
Pondicherry = Puducherry **43 P11**
Ponferrada **18 A2**
Ponnani **43 P9**
Ponnyadaung **41 F10**
Ponta Grossa **94 B6**
Ponta Pora **94 A5**
Pontarlier **13 C7**
Pontchartrain, L. **81 D8**
Ponte Nova **93 G5**
Pontevedra **18 A1**
Pontiac **76 C4**
Pontianak **39 E3**
Pontine Is. = Ponziane, Ísole **21 D4**
Pontine Mts. = Kuzey Anadolu Dağları **25 E4**
Pontivy **12 B2**
Pontoise **12 B5**
Ponziane, Ísole **21 D4**
Poochera **62 B1**
Poole **11 F6**
Poona = Pune **43 K8**
Pooncarie **62 B3**
Poopelloe L. **63 B3**
Poopó, L. de **91 G5**
Popayán **90 C3**
Popigay **30 B9**
Popiltah L. **62 B3**
Popio L. **62 B3**
Poplar Bluff **81 A8**
Popocatépetl, Volcán **84 D5**
Popokabaka **56 F3**
Porbandar **43 J6**
Porcupine ➔ **69 B5**
Pordenone **20 B4**
Pori **8 C10**
Porkala = Porkkala **9 G12**
Porkkala **9 G12**
Porlamar **90 A6**
Poroshiri-Dake **32 B8**
Porpoise B. **96 A13**
Port Alberni **69 D7**
Port Angeles **72 B2**
Port Arthur *Australia* **62 D4**
Port Arthur *U.S.A.* **81 E7**
Port-au-Prince **87 C5**
Port Augusta **62 B2**
Port Augusta West **62 B2**
Port Broughton **62 B2**
Port-Cartier **71 D7**
Port Chalmers **65 F4**
Port Darwin **95 G5**
Port Davey **62 D4**
Port Dickson **39 D2**
Port Elizabeth **59 E5**
Port Fairy **62 C3**
Port-Gentil **56 E1**
Port Harcourt **53 H7**
Port Harrison = Inukjuak **70 D6**
Port Hawkesbury **71 E7**
Port Hedland **60 E2**
Port Hope Simpson **71 D8**
Port Huron **76 C4**
Port Kenny **62 B1**
Port Lairge = Waterford **11 E3**
Port Laoise **11 E3**
Port Lincoln **62 B2**
Port Loko **53 G3**
Port Louis **51 J9**
Port MacDonnell **62 C3**
Port Macquarie **63 B5**
Port Moresby **61 B8**
Port Nelson **69 C10**
Port Nolloth **58 D3**
Port Nouveau-Québec = Kangiqsualujjuaq **70 D7**
Port of Spain **87 D7**
Port Pegasus **65 G2**
Port Phillip B. **63 C3**
Port Pirie **62 B2**
Port Safaga = Bûr Safâga **54 C5**
Port Said = Bûr Sa'īd **54 B5**

Port St. Johns = Umzimvubu **59 E5**
Port Shepstone **59 E6**
Port Stanley = Stanley **95 G5**
Port Sudan = Bûr Sûdân **55 E6**
Port Talbot **11 F5**
Port-Vendres **13 E5**
Port Vila **64 L11**
Port Wakefield **62 B2**
Porta Orientalis **22 B4**
Portadown **11 D3**
Portage la Prairie **69 D10**
Portalegre **18 C2**
Portbou **19 A7**
Portile de Fier **22 B4**
Portimão **18 D1**
Portland *N.S.W., Australia* **63 B4**
Portland *Vic., Australia* **62 C3**
Portland *Maine, U.S.A.* **77 C10**
Portland *Oreg., U.S.A.* **72 D2**
Portland B. **62 C3**
Porto **18 B1**
Pôrto Alegre **94 C6**
Pôrto de Móz **92 C3**
Porto Empédocle **21 F4**
Pôrto Esperança **91 G7**
Pôrto Franco **92 D4**
Pôrto Mendes **94 A6**
Pôrto Murtinho **91 H7**
Pôrto Nacional **93 E4**
Porto-Novo **53 G6**
Porto Santo, I. de **52 B2**
Pôrto Seguro **93 F6**
Porto Tórres **20 D2**
Pôrto União **94 B6**
Pôrto Válter **91 E4**
Porto-Vecchio **13 F8**
Pôrto Velho **91 E6**
Portoferráio **20 C3**
Portoscuso **21 E2**
Portoviejo **90 D2**
Portree **10 C3**
Portsmouth *U.K.* **11 F6**
Portsmouth *U.S.A.* **77 F7**
Porttipahdan tekojärvi **8 B11**
Portugal ■ **18 C1**
Porvenir **95 G2**
Posadas **94 B5**
Poso **37 E2**
Posse **93 E4**
Possession I. **96 B15**
Poste-de-la-Baleine = Kuujjuarapik **71 D6**
Postmasburg **58 D4**
Postojna **20 B5**
Potchefstroom **59 D5**
Potenza **21 D5**
Poteriteri, L. **65 G2**
Potgietersrus = Mokopane **59 C5**
Poti **25 E5**
Potomac ➔ **77 E7**
Potosí **91 G5**
Pototan **36 B2**
Potrerillos **94 B3**
Potsdam **15 B7**
Poughkeepsie **77 D9**
Považská Bystrica **16 D4**
Poverty B. **64 C8**
Póvoa de Varzim **18 B1**
Povungnituk = Puvirnituq **70 C6**
Powder ➔ **74 B2**
Powell, L. **79 B7**
Poyang Hu **35 D6**
Požarevac **22 B3**
Poznań **16 B3**
Pozo Almonte **91 H5**
Pozoblanco **18 C3**
Pozzuoli **21 D5**
Prachuap Khiri Khan **38 B1**
Prado **93 F6**
Prague = Praha **16 C2**
Praha **16 C2**
Prainha *Amazonas, Brazil* **91 E6**
Prainha *Pará, Brazil* **92 C3**
Prairies **69 C9**
Prapat **39 D1**
Prata **93 F4**
Prato **20 C3**
Pravia **18 A2**
Praya **39 F5**
Preobrazheniye **32 B3**
Preparis North Channel **41 K9**
Preparis South Channel **41 K9**
Přerov **16 D3**
Preservation Inlet **65 G2**
Presidencia Roque Saenz Peña **94 B4**
Presidente Epitácio **93 G3**
Presidente Prudente **93 G3**
Prespa, L. = Prespansko Jezero **23 D3**
Prespansko Jezero **23 D3**
Presque Isle **77 A11**
Preston **11 E5**
Pretoria **59 D5**
Preveza **23 E3**
Příbram **16 D2**
Prichard **82 D3**
Prieska **58 D4**
Prilep **22 D3**
Priluki = Pryluky **24 C3**
Prime Seal I. **62 D4**
Prince Albert **69 C9**
Prince Albert Mts. **96 B15**
Prince Albert Pen. **68 A8**
Prince Albert Sd. **68 A8**
Prince Alfred, C. **70 B1**
Prince Charles I. **70 C6**
Prince Charles Mts. **96 B10**
Prince Edward I. □ **71 E7**
Prince of Wales I. **68 A10**
Prince Patrick I. **70 B2**
Principe da Beira **91 F6**
Prins Harald Kyst **96 B8**
Prinsesse Astrid Kyst **96 B7**
Prinsesse Ragnhild Kyst **96 B8**
Pripet = Prypyat ➔ **17 C10**
Pripet Marshes **17 B9**
Pripyat Marshes = Pripet Marshes **17 B9**
Pripyats = Prypyat ➔ **17 C10**
Priština **22 C3**
Privas **13 D6**
Privolzhskaya Vozvyshennost **24 C6**
Prizren **22 C3**
Proddatur **43 M11**
Progreso **85 C7**
Prokopyevsk **29 D9**
Prokuplje **22 C3**
Prome **41 H10**
Propriá **93 E6**
Prosna ➔ **16 B3**
Prostějov **16 D3**
Proston **63 A5**
Provence **13 E6**
Providence **77 D10**
Providencia, I. de **86 D3**
Provins **13 B5**
Provo **73 F8**
Pruszków **16 B5**
Prut ➔ **17 F9**
Pruzhany **17 B7**
Prydz B. **96 A10**
Pryluky **24 C3**
Prypyat ➔ **17 C10**
Przhevalsk = Karakol **29 E8**
Psara **23 E5**
Psiloritis, Oros **23 G5**
Pskov **24 B2**
Ptich = Ptsich ➔ **17 B9**
Ptsich ➔ **17 B9**
Puán **94 D4**
Pucallpa **91 E4**
Puducherry **43 P11**
Pudukkottai **43 P11**
Puebla **84 D5**
Pueblo **74 F2**
Puelches **94 D3**
Puente Alto **94 C2**
Puente-Genil **18 D3**
Puerto Aisén **95 F2**
Puerto Ayacucho **90 B5**
Puerto Barrios **85 D7**
Puerto Bermúdez **91 F4**
Puerto Bolívar **90 D3**
Puerto Cabello **90 A5**
Puerto Cabezas **86 D3**
Puerto Carreño **90 B5**
Puerto Chicama **91 E3**
Puerto Coig **95 G3**
Puerto Cortés **85 D7**
Puerto Cumarebo **90 A5**
Puerto Deseado **95 F3**
Puerto Heath **91 F5**
Puerto La Cruz **90 A6**
Puerto Leguízamo **90 D4**
Puerto Lobos **95 E3**
Puerto Madryn **95 E3**
Puerto Maldonado **91 F5**
Puerto Montt **95 E2**
Puerto Natales **95 G2**
Puerto Páez **90 B5**
Puerto Pinasco **94 A5**
Puerto Plata **87 C5**
Puerto Princesa **36 C1**
Puerto Rico ☑ **87 C6**
Puerto Sastre **91 H7**
Puerto Suárez **91 G7**
Puerto Wilches **90 B4**
Puertollano **18 C3**
Pueyrredón, L. **95 F2**
Pugachev **24 C6**
Puget Sound **72 C2**
Puigcerdà **19 A6**
Pukaki, L. **65 F4**
Pukapuka **65 L14**
Pukekohe **64 B6**
Pula **20 B4**
Pulandian **35 C7**
Puławy **16 C5**
Pullman **72 C5**
Pulog, Mt. **36 A2**
Pułtusk **16 B5**
Puná, I. **90 D2**
Punakaiki **65 E4**
Punakha Dzong **41 D7**
Punata **91 G5**
Punch **42 C9**
Pune **43 K8**
Punjab □ *India* **42 D9**
Punjab □ *Pakistan* **42 D8**
Puno **91 G4**
Punta Alta **94 D4**
Punta Arenas **95 G2**
Punta de Díaz **94 B2**
Puntabie **62 B1**
Puntarenas **86 E3**
Punto Fijo **90 A4**
Puquio **91 F4**
Pur ➔ **28 C8**
Puracé, Vol. **90 C3**
Puralia = Puruliya **40 F6**
Puri **40 H5**
Purnia **40 E6**
Purukcahu **39 E4**
Puruliya **40 F6**
Purus ➔ **90 D6**
Pusan = Busan **35 C7**
Pushkino **24 C6**
Putao **41 D11**
Putaruru **64 C6**
Puthein Myit ➔ **41 K10**
Putignano **21 D6**
Puting, Tanjung **39 E4**
Putorana, Gory **30 C7**
Puttalam **43 Q11**
Puttgarden **15 A6**
Putumayo ➔ **90 D5**
Putussibau **39 D4**
Puvirnituq **70 C6**
Puy-de-Dôme **13 D5**
Pwllheli **11 E4**
Pyapon **41 J10**
Pyasina ➔ **30 B6**
Pyatigorsk **25 E5**
Pyè = Prome **41 H10**
Pyetrikaw **17 B9**
Pyinmana **41 H11**
P'yŏngyang **35 C7**
Pyrénées **12 E4**
Pyu **41 H11**

Q

Qā'emshahr **44 B3**
Qahremānshahr = Kermānshāh **46 D6**
Qaidam Pendi **34 C4**
Qal'at al Akhḍar **47 E4**
Qalât-i-Ghilzai **45 C6**
Qal'eh Shaharak **42 B4**
Qamani'tuaq = Baker Lake **68 B10**
Qamruddin Karez **42 D6**
Qandahār = Kandahār **42 D4**
Qandahār = Kandahār □ **42 D4**
Qapshaghay **29 E8**
Qarabutaq **29 E7**
Qarachuk **46 C5**
Qaraghandy **29 E8**
Qaraghayly **29 E8**
Qarataū *Kazakhstan* **29 E7**
Qarataū *Zhambyl, Kazakhstan* **29 E8**
Qarazhal **29 E8**
Qardho = Gardo **49 F4**
Qarqan **34 C3**
Qarqan He ➔ **34 C3**
Qarqaraly **29 E8**
Qarshi **29 F7**
Qaşr-e Qand **45 E5**
Qasr Farâfra **54 C4**
Qatar ■ **44 E2**
Qattâra, Munkhafed el **54 C4**
Qattâra Depression = Qattâra, Munkhafed el **54 C4**
Qausiuittuq = Resolute **70 B4**
Qāyen **44 C4**
Qazaqstan = Kazakhstan ■ **29 E7**
Qazvīn **46 C7**
Qena **54 C5**
Qeshm **44 E4**
Qikiqtarjuaq **70 C7**
Qila Saifullāh **42 D6**
Qilian Shan **34 C4**
Qingdao **35 C7**
Qinghai □ **34 C4**
Qinghai Hu **34 C5**
Qinhuangdao **35 C6**
Qinzhou **35 D5**
Qiqihar **35 B7**
Qitai **34 B3**
Qom **44 C2**
Qomolangma Feng = Everest, Mt. **40 C6**
Qomsheh **44 C2**
Qondūz = Kondoz **45 B7**
Qondūz = Kondoz □ **45 B7**
Qoqon = Qŭqon **29 E8**
Qoraqalpoghistan □ **29 E6**
Qostanay **29 D7**
Quambatook **62 C3**
Quambone **63 B4**
Quan Long = Ca Mau **38 C3**
Quang Ngai **38 A3**
Quanzhou **35 D6**
Quaqtaq **70 C7**
Quartu Sant'Élena **21 E2**
Quba **25 E6**
Qŭchān **44 B4**
Queanbeyan **63 C4**
Québec **71 E6**
Québec □ **71 E6**
Queen Alexandra Ra. **96 C15**
Queen Charlotte Is. **68 C6**
Queen Charlotte Sd. **69 C7**
Queen Elizabeth Is. **66 B9**
Queen Mary Land **96 B11**
Queen Maud G. **68 B9**
Queen Maud Land = Dronning Maud Land **96 B7**
Queen Maud Mts. **96 C16**
Queenscliff **63 C3**
Queensland □ **61 E7**
Queenstown *Australia* **62 D4**
Queenstown *N.Z.* **65 F3**
Queenstown *S. Africa* **59 E5**
Queimadas **93 E6**
Quelimane **59 B7**
Quelpart = Jeju-do **35 C7**
Querétaro **84 C4**
Quetta **42 D5**
Quezon City **36 B2**
Qui Nhon **38 B3**
Quibaxe **56 F2**
Quibdo **90 B3**
Quiberon **12 C2**
Quilán, C. **95 E2**
Quillabamba **91 F4**
Quillagua **91 H5**
Quillota **94 C2**
Quilon **43 Q10**
Quilpie **63 A3**
Quimilí **94 B4**
Quimper **12 B1**
Quimperlé **12 C2**
Quincy **75 F9**
Quines **94 C3**
Quintanar de la Orden **18 C4**
Quinyambie **62 B3**
Quipungo **58 A2**
Quirindi **63 B5**
Quissanga **59 A8**
Quito **90 D3**
Quixadá **92 C6**
Qulan **29 E8**
Qŭnghirot **29 E6**
Quondong **62 B3**
Quorn **62 B2**
Qŭqon **29 E8**
Quseir **54 C5**
Quzhou **35 D6**
Qyzylorda **29 E7**

R

Raahe **8 C10**
Raba **37 F1**
Rába ➔ **16 E3**
Rabat *Malta* **21 G5**
Rabat *Morocco* **52 B4**
Rabaul **64 K10**
Rābigh **47 G4**
Rândița **17 E9**
Race, C. **71 E8**
Rach Gia **38 B3**
Racine **76 C2**
Rădăuți **17 E7**
Radekhiv **17 C7**
Radekhov = Radekhiv **17 C7**
Radom **16 C5**
Radomsko **16 C4**
Radomyshl **17 C9**
Radstock, C. **62 B1**
Rae **68 B8**
Rae Bareli **40 D3**
Rae Isthmus **70 C5**
Raetihi **64 C6**
Rafaela **94 C4**
Rafḥā **47 E5**
Rafsanjān **44 D4**
Ragachow **17 B10**
Ragama **43 R11**
Raglan **64 B6**
Ragusa **21 F5**
Raha **37 E2**
Rahaeng = Tak **38 A1**
Rahimyar Khan **42 E7**
Raichur **43 L10**
Raigarh **40 G4**
Railton **62 D4**
Rainier, Mt. **72 C3**
Raipur **40 G3**
Ra'is **47 G4**
Raj Nandgaon **40 G3**
Raja, Ujung **39 D1**
Raja Ampat, Kepulauan **37 E3**
Rajahmundry **40 J3**
Rajang ➔ **39 D4**
Rajapalaiyam **43 Q10**
Rajasthan □ **42 F8**
Rajasthan Canal = Indira Gandhi Canal **42 F8**
Rajgarh **43 G10**
Rajkot **43 H7**
Rajpipla **43 J8**
Rajshahi **41 E7**
Rakaia **65 E5**
Rakaia ➔ **65 E5**
Rakan, Ra's **44 E2**
Rakaposhi **42 A9**
Rakata, Pulau **39 F3**
Rakhiv **17 D7**
Rakitnoye **32 A4**
Rakiura △ **65 G2**
Raleigh **83 B8**
Ramanathapuram **43 Q11**
Rame Hd. **63 C4**
Ramechhap **40 D6**
Ramelau **37 F3**
Ramgarh *Jharkhand, India* **40 F5**
Ramgarh *Raj., India* **42 F7**
Ramnad = Ramanathapuram **43 Q11**
Râmnicu Sărat **17 F8**
Râmnicu Vâlcea **17 F7**
Rampur **42 E11**
Rampur Hat **40 E6**
Ramree I. **41 H9**
Ramtek **43 J11**
Ranaghat **41 F7**
Ranau **38 C5**
Rancagua **94 C2**
Ranchi **40 F5**
Randers **9 D8**
Rangaunu B. **64 A5**
Rangia **41 D8**
Rangiora **65 E5**
Rangitaiki ➔ **64 B7**
Rangitata ➔ **65 E4**
Rangitoto ke te tonga = D'Urville I. **65 D5**
Rangon ➔ **41 J11**
Rangoon **41 J11**
Rangpur **41 E7**
Ranibennur **43 M9**
Raniganj **40 F6**
Raniwara **43 G8**
Rankin Inlet **68 B10**
Rankins Springs **63 B4**
Ranohira **59 C9**
Ranong **38 C1**
Ransiki **37 E4**
Rantauprapat **39 D1**
Rantemario **37 E1**
Rapa **65 M16**
Rapallo **13 D8**
Räpch **45 E4**
Raper, C. **70 C7**
Rapid City **74 C3**
Rarotonga **65 M14**
Ra's al Khaymah **44 E4**
Ra's Lānūf **54 B2**
Rasht **46 C7**
Rat Islands **69 C1**
Ratangarh **42 E9**
Rathenow **15 B7**
Ratlam **43 H9**
Ratnagiri **43 L8**
Raukumara Ra. **64 C7**
Rauma **8 C10**
Raumo = Rauma **8 C10**
Raurkela **40 F5**
Rausu-Dake **32 A9**
Rava-Ruska **17 C6**
Rava Russkaya = Rava-Ruska **17 C6**
Rāvar **44 D4**
Ravenna **20 B4**
Ravensburg **14 E5**
Ravi ➔ **42 D7**
Rawalpindi **42 C8**
Rawene **64 A5**
Rawlins **73 F10**
Rawson **95 E3**
Ray, C. **71 E8**
Rayadurg **43 M10**
Rayagada **40 H4**
Raz, Pte. du **12 B1**
Razāzah, Buḥayrat ar **47 D5**
Razazah, L. = Razāzah, Buḥayrat ar **47 D5**
Razdel'naya = Rozdilna **17 E10**

Razgrad 22 C6
Razim, Lacul 22 B7
Ré, Î. de 12 C3
Reading *U.K.* 11 F6
Reading *U.S.A.* 77 D8
Realicó 94 D4
Rebi 37 F4
Rebiana 54 D3
Rebun-Tō 32 A7
Rechytsa 17 B10
Recife 92 D7
Reconquista 94 B5
Recreo 94 B3
Red ➔ 81 D8
Red Cliffs 62 B3
Red Deer 69 C8
Red River of the North ➔ 74 A6
Red Sea 48 C2
Red Tower Pass = Turnu Roşu, P. 17 F7
Redcar 11 D6
Redcliffe 63 A5
Redding 72 F2
Redditch 11 E6
Redon 12 C2
Redondela 18 A1
Redwood City 78 B1
Ree, L. 11 E3
Reefton 65 E4
Regensburg 15 D7
Reggâne = Zaouiet Reggâne 52 C6
Réggio di Calábria 21 E5
Réggio nell'Emília 20 B3
Reghin 17 E7
Regina 69 C9
Rehoboth 58 C3
Rehovot 46 E3
Reichenbach 15 C7
Reidsville 83 A8
Reigate 11 F6
Reims 13 B6
Reina Adelaida, Arch. 95 G2
Reindeer L. 69 C9
Reinga, C. 64 A5
Reinosa 18 A3
Remarkable, Mt. 62 B2
Remeshk 45 E4
Rendsburg 14 A5
Rengat 39 E2
Reni 17 F9
Renmark 62 B3
Rennes 12 B3
Reno 72 G4
Reno ➔ 20 B4
Rentería 19 A5
Republican ➔ 74 F6
Repulse Bay 70 C5
Requena *Peru* 90 E4
Requena *Spain* 19 C5
Reşadiye = Datça 23 F6
Resht = Rasht 46 C7
Resistencia 94 B5
Reşiţa 17 F5
Resolute 70 B4
Resolution I. *Canada* 70 C7
Resolution I. *N.Z.* 65 F2
Rethimno 23 G5
Réunion ⧄ 51 J9
Reus 19 B6
Reutlingen 14 D5
Reval = Tallinn 24 B1
Revelstoke 69 C8
Revillagigedo, Is. de 84 D2
Rewa 40 E3
Rewari 42 E10
Rey Bouba 55 G1
Rey Malabo 53 H7
Reykjavík 8 C1
Reynosa 84 B5
Rhein ➔ 14 C4
Rhein-Main-Donau-Kanal 15 D6
Rheine 14 B4
Rheinland-Pfalz □ 14 C4
Rhin = Rhein ➔ 14 C4
Rhine = Rhein ➔ 14 C4
Rhineland-Palatinate = Rheinland-Pfalz □ 14 C4
Rhode Island □ 77 D10
Rhodes 23 F7
Rhodope Mts. = Rhodopi Planina 22 D5
Rhodopi Planina 22 D5
Rhön 14 C5
Rhondda 11 F5
Rhône ➔ 13 E6
Rhum 10 C3
Riachão 92 D4
Riasi 42 C9
Riau □ 39 E2
Riau, Kepulauan 39 D2
Riau Arch. = Riau, Kepulauan 39 D2
Ribadeo 18 A2
Ribeirão Prêto 93 G4
Riberalta 91 F5
Riccarton 65 E5
Richards Bay 59 D6
Richland 72 C4
Richmond *N.Z.* 65 D5
Richmond *Calif., U.S.A.* 72 H2
Richmond *Va., U.S.A.* 77 F7
Richmond Ra. 63 A5
Ridder = Leninogorsk 29 D9
Ried 15 D7
Riesa 15 C7
Rieti 20 C4
Rif = Er Rif 52 A5
Rīga 24 B1
Riga, G. of 24 B1
Rīgas Jūras Līcis = Riga, G. of 24 B1
Rīgestān 42 D4
Rigolet 70 D8
Riiser-Larsen-halvøya 96 A8
Rijeka 20 B5
Rimah, Wadi ar ➔ 47 F5
Rimini 20 B4
Rimouski 71 E7
Rinca 37 F1
Rinconada 94 A3
Rinjani 39 F5
Rio Branco *Brazil* 91 E5
Rio Branco *Uruguay* 94 C6
Río Cuarto 94 C4
Rio de Janeiro 93 G5
Rio de Janeiro □ 93 G5
Rio do Sul 94 B7
Río Gallegos 95 G3
Río Grande *Argentina* 95 G3
Rio Grande *Brazil* 94 C6
Rio Grande ➔ 84 B5
Río Grande de Santiago ➔ 84 C3
Rio Grande do Norte □ 92 D6
Rio Grande do Sul □ 94 B6
Rio Largo 93 D6
Río Mulatos 91 G5
Río Muni □ 56 D2
Rio Negro 94 B7
Rio Verde 93 F3
Ríobamba 90 D3
Ríohacha 90 A4
Ríosucio *Caldas, Colombia* 90 B3
Ríosucio *Choco, Colombia* 90 B3
Rishiri-Tō 32 A7
Riva del Garda 20 B3
Rivadavia 94 B2
Rivera 94 C5
Riverside 78 D4
Riverton *Australia* 62 B2
Riverton *N.Z.* 65 G2
Riviera di Levante 13 D8
Riviera di Ponente 13 D8
Rivière-du-Loup 71 E7
Rivne 17 C8
Rívoli 13 D7
Rivoli B. 62 C3
Riyadh = Ar Riyāḍ 47 F6
Rize 25 E5
Rizzuto, C. 21 E6
Roanne 13 C6
Roanoke 77 F6
Robbins I. 62 D4
Robertson I. 96 A4
Robertstown 62 B2
Roberval 71 E6
Robinvale 62 B3
Roboré 91 G7
Robson, Mt. 69 C8
Roca, C. da 18 C1
Rocas, I. 92 C7
Rocha 94 C6
Rochefort 12 D3
Rochester *Minn., U.S.A.* 75 C8
Rochester *N.Y., U.S.A.* 77 C7
Rock, The 63 C4
Rock Hill 83 B7
Rock Island 75 E9
Rock Springs 73 F9
Rockefeller Plateau 96 C18
Rockford 75 D10
Rockhampton 61 E9
Rocky Mount 83 B9
Rocky Mts. 68 C7
Rod 42 E3
Rodez 13 D5
Ródhos = Rhodes 23 F7
Rodney, C. 64 B6
Roes Welcome Sd. 70 C5
Rogachev = Ragachow 17 B10
Rogagua, L. 91 F5
Rogatyn 17 D7
Rogoaguado, L. 91 F5
Rohri 42 F6
Rohtak 42 E10
Roi Et 38 A2
Rojo, C. 84 C5
Rokan ➔ 39 D2
Rolândia 94 A6
Roma *Australia* 63 A4
Roma *Italy* 20 D4
Romaine ➔ 71 D7
Roman 17 E8
Romang 37 F3
Romania ■ 22 B5
Romans-sur-Isère 13 D6
Romblon 36 B2
Rome = Roma 20 D4
Rome 82 B5
Romorantin-Lanthenay 12 C4
Roncador, Serra do 93 E3
Ronda 18 D3
Rondônia □ 91 F6
Rondonópolis 93 F3
Ronge, L. la 69 C9
Roniu, Mt. 30 H
Ronne Ice Shelf 96 B3
Roorkee 42 E10
Roosevelt ➔ 91 E6
Roosevelt I. 96 B16
Roquetas de Mar 19 D4
Roraima □ 90 C6
Roraima, Mt. 90 B6
Rosa, Monte 13 D7
Rosario *Argentina* 94 C4
Rosário *Brazil* 92 C5
Rosario *Mexico* 84 C3
Rosario *Paraguay* 94 A5
Rosario de la Frontera 94 B3
Rosário do Sul 94 C6
Roscommon 11 E2
Roseau *Dominica* 87 C7
Roseau *U.S.A.* 75 A7
Rosebery 62 D4
Roseburg 72 E2
Rosenheim 15 E7
Roses, G. de 19 A7
Rosetown 69 C9
Roseville 72 G3
Rosewood 63 A5
Rosignano Marittimo 20 C3
Rosignol 90 B7
Roşiori de Vede 22 B5
Roslavl 24 C3
Roslyn 63 B4
Ross *Australia* 62 D4
Ross *N.Z.* 65 E4

Ross I. 96 B15
Ross Ice Shelf 96 C16
Ross Sea 96 B15
Rossano 21 E6
Rossiya = Russia ■ 26 C10
Rosslare 11 E3
Rosso 53 E2
Rossosh 24 C4
Rostock 15 A7
Rostov *Don, Russia* 25 D4
Rostov *Yaroslavl, Russia* 24 B4
Roswell 80 C1
Rotherham 11 E6
Roto 63 B4
Rotondo, Mte. 13 E8
Rotoroa, L. 65 D5
Rotorua 64 C7
Rotorua, L. 64 C7
Rotterdam 14 C3
Rottweil 14 D5
Rotuma 64 L12
Roubaix 13 A5
Rouen 12 B4
Round Mt. 63 B5
Rousse = Ruse 22 C5
Roussillon 13 E5
Rouyn-Noranda 71 E6
Rovaniemi 8 B11
Rovereto 20 B3
Rovigo 20 B3
Rovinj 20 B4
Rovno = Rivne 17 C8
Rovuma = Ruvuma ➔ 57 G8
Rowena 63 A4
Roxas 36 B2
Roxburgh 65 F3
Royal Leamington Spa 11 E6
Royan 12 D3
Rozdilna 17 E10
Rozhyshche 17 C7
Rtishchevo 24 C5
Ruahine Ra. 64 C7
Ruapehu 64 C6
Ruapuke I. 65 G3
Rub' al Khālī 48 D4
Rubio 90 B4
Rubtsovsk 29 D9
Rudall 62 B2
Rudolfa, Ostrov 28 A6
Rufiji ➔ 57 F7
Rufino 94 C4
Rugby 11 E6
Rügen 15 A7
Ruhr ➔ 14 C4
Rukwa, L. 57 F6
Rum = Rhum 10 C3
Rumāḩ 47 F6
Rumania = Romania ■ 22 B5
Rumbêk 55 G4
Rumia 16 A4
Rumoi 32 B7
Runanga 65 E4
Runaway, C. 64 B7
Rundu 58 B3
Ruoqiang 34 C3
Rupa 41 D9
Rupat 39 D2
Rupert ➔ 71 D6
Rupert House = Waskaganish 71 D6
Rurrenabaque 91 F5
Ruschuk = Ruse 22 C5
Ruse 22 C5
Russas 92 C6
Russellkonda 40 H5
Russia ■ 26 C10
Russkaya Polyana 29 D8
Rustavi 25 E6
Rustenburg 59 D5
Ruteng 37 F2
Ruvuma ➔ 57 G8
Ruwenzori 57 D5
Rwanda ■ 57 E6
Ryazan 24 C4
Ryazhsk 24 C5
Rybache = Rybachye 29 E9
Rybachye 29 E9
Rybinsk 24 B4
Rybinskoye Vdkhr. 24 B4
Rybnitsa = Râbnița 17 E9
Rylstone 63 B4
Ryōtsu 32 D6
Rypin 16 B4
Ryukyu Is. = Ryūkyū-rettō 35 D7
Ryūkyū-rettō 35 D7
Rzeszów 16 C5
Rzhev 24 B3

S

Sa Dec 38 B3
Sa'ādatābād 44 D3
Saale ➔ 15 C6
Saalfeld 15 C6
Saar ➔ 13 B7
Saarbrücken 14 D4
Saaremaa 24 B1
Šabac 22 B2
Sabadell 19 B7
Sabah □ 38 C5
Ṣabāḩ, Wadi ➔ 47 G7
Sabalān, Kūhhā-ye 46 C6
Sabalana, Kepulauan 37 F1
Sábanalarga 90 A4
Sabang 38 C1
Sabará 93 F5
Saberania 37 E5
Sabhā 54 C1
Sabinas 84 B4
Sabinas Hidalgo 84 B4
Sablayan 36 B2
Sable, C. *Canada* 71 E7
Sable, C. *U.S.A.* 86 A3
Sable I. 71 E8
Sabrina Coast 96 A12
Sabulubbek 39 E1
Sabzevār 44 B4
Sabzvārān 44 D4
Săcele 17 F7
Sachsen □ 15 C7
Sachsen-Anhalt □ 15 C7
Sacramento 72 G3
Sacramento ➔ 72 G3
Sacramento Mts. 79 D10
Sadd el Aali 54 D5
Sado 32 E6
Sadon 41 E11
Safi 52 B4
Safid Kūh 42 B3
Saga 33 G2
Sagar 43 M9
Sagarmatha = Everest, Mt. 40 C6
Sagil 34 A4
Saginaw 76 C4
Saglouc = Salluit 70 C6
Sagua la Grande 86 B3
Sagunt 19 C5
Sagunto = Sagunt 19 C5
Sahagún 18 A3
Sahand, Kūh-e 46 C6
Sahara 52 D6
Saharan Atlas = Saharien, Atlas 52 B6
Saharanpur 42 E10
Saharien, Atlas 52 B6
Sahiwal 42 D8
Sahrawi = Western Sahara ■ 52 D3
Sa'id Bundās 55 G3
Sa'īdābād = Sirjān 44 D3
Sa'īdīyeh 46 C7
Saidpur 41 E7
Saidu Sharif 42 B8
Saigon = Thanh Pho Ho Chi Minh 38 B3
Saikhoa Ghat 41 D10
Saiki 33 G2
Sailolof 37 E4
Saimaa 8 C11
Saimen = Saimaa 8 C11
St. Andrews 10 C5
St. Anthony 71 D8
St. Arnaud 62 C3
St-Augustin 71 D8
St. Augustine 83 E7
St. Austell 11 F4
St. Boniface 69 D10
St-Brieuc 12 B2
St. Catharines 77 C6
St-Chamond 13 D6
St. Christopher-Nevis = St. Kitts & Nevis ■ 87 C7
St. Cloud 75 C7
St. Croix 87 C7
St-Denis 12 B5
St-Dizier 13 B6
St. Elias, Mt. 68 B5
St-Étienne 13 D6
St-Flour 13 D5
St. Gallen = Sankt Gallen 13 C8
St-Gaudens 12 E4
St. George 63 A4
St-Georges 92 B3
St. George's 87 D7
St. George's Channel 11 F3
St. Georges Hd. 63 C5
St. Gotthard P. = San Gottardo, P. del 13 C8
St. Helena 51 H3
St. Helena B. 58 E3
St. Helens 62 D4
St. Helier 11 G5
St-Hyacinthe 71 E6
St-Jean, L. 71 E6
St. John 71 E7
St. John's *Antigua & B.* 87 C7
St. John's *Canada* 71 E8
St. Johns ➔ 83 D7
St. Joseph 75 F7
St. Joseph, L. 71 D4
St. Kilda 10 C2
St. Kitts & Nevis ■ 87 C7
St-Laurent 92 A3
St. Lawrence ➔ 71 E7
St. Lawrence, Gulf of 71 E7
St. Lawrence I. 69 B2
St-Lô 12 B3
St. Louis *Senegal* 53 E2
St. Louis *U.S.A.* 75 F9
St. Lucia ■ 87 D7
St-Malo 12 B2
St-Marc 87 C5
St. Mary Pk. 62 B2
St. Marys 62 D4
St-Mathieu, Pte. 12 B1
St-Nazaire 12 C2
St-Omer 12 A5
St. Paul 75 C8
St. Peter Port 11 G5
St. Petersburg = Sankt-Peterburg 24 B3
St. Petersburg 83 F6
St-Pierre-et-Miquelon ☑ 71 E8
St-Quentin 13 B5
St-Tropez 13 E7
St. Vincent, G. 62 C2
St. Vincent & the Grenadines ■ 87 D7
Ste-Marie, Ile = Nosy Boraha 59 B9
Saintes 12 D3
Saintonge 12 D3
Saipan 64 H9
Sairang 41 F9
Sajama 91 G5
Sajószentpéter 16 D5
Sakākah 47 E5
Sakakawea, L. 74 B4
Sakartvelo = Georgia ■ 25 E5
Sakarya 25 E3
Sakata 32 D6
Sakhalin 31 D12
Sakon Nakhon 38 A2
Sala 9 D9
Sala Consilina 21 D5
Saladillo 94 D5
Salado ➔ *B. Aires, Argentina* 94 D5
Salado ➔ *La Pampa, Argentina* 94 D3
Salado ➔ *Santa Fe, Argentina* 94 C4
Salaga 53 G5
Salālah 49 D5
Salamanca *Chile* 94 C2

Salamanca *Spain* **18 B3**
Salamina **23 F4**
Salar de Atacama **94 A3**
Salar de Uyuni **91 H5**
Salaverry **91 E3**
Salawati **37 E4**
Salayar **37 F2**
Saldanha **58 E3**
Sale *Australia* **63 C4**
Salé *Morocco* **52 B4**
Salekhard **28 C7**
Salem *India* **43 P11**
Salem *U.S.A.* **72 D2**
Salerno **21 D5**
Salgótarján **16 D4**
Salihli **23 E7**
Salihorsk **17 B8**
Salima **59 A6**
Salina *Italy* **21 E5**
Salina *U.S.A.* **74 F6**
Salina Cruz **85 D5**
Salinas *Brazil* **93 F5**
Salinas *Ecuador* **90 D2**
Salinas *U.S.A.* **78 B2**
Salinas Grandes **94 C3**
Salinópolis **92 C4**
Salisbury *Australia* **62 B2**
Salisbury *U.K.* **11 F6**
Salisbury *U.S.A.* **83 B7**
Salisbury I. **70 C6**
Salliq = Coral Harbour **70 C5**
Salluit **70 C6**
Salmäs **46 C6**
Salmon ➔ **72 D5**
Salmon River Mts. **73 D6**
Salon-de-Provence **13 E6**
Salonica = Thessaloniki **23 D4**
Salonta **16 E5**
Salsk **25 D5**
Salso ➔ **21 F4**
Salt Creek **62 C2**
Salt L. **62 B3**
Salt Lake City **73 F8**
Salta **94 A3**
Saltillo **84 B4**
Salto **94 C5**
Salto ➔ **20 C4**
Salton Sea **78 D5**
Salûm **54 B4**
Salur **40 H4**
Salvador **93 E6**
Salvador, El ■ **85 E7**
Salwa **44 E2**
Salween ➔ **41 J11**
Salyan **25 F6**
Salzach ➔ **15 D7**
Salzburg **15 E7**
Salzgitter **14 B6**
Salzwedel **15 B6**
Sama **28 C7**
Sama de Langreo = Langreo **18 A3**
Samales Group **36 C2**
Samangân □ **45 B7**
Samani **32 B8**
Samar **36 B3**
Samara **24 C7**
Samarinda **39 E5**
Samarkand = Samarqand **29 F7**
Samarqand **29 F7**
Sāmarrā' **46 D5**
Sambalpur **40 G5**
Sambar, Tanjung **39 E4**
Sambas **39 D3**
Sambhal **42 E11**
Sambhar **42 F9**
Sambiase **21 E6**
Sambir **17 D6**
Samoa ■ **65 L13**
Samokov **22 C4**
Samos **23 F6**
Samothráki = Mathraki **21 E7**
Samothraki **23 D5**
Sampit **39 E4**
Sampit, Teluk **39 E4**
Samra **47 F5**
Samsun **25 E4**
Samui, Ko **38 C2**
Samut Prakan **38 B2**
Samut Songkhram **38 B2**
San **53 F5**
San Agustin, C. **36 C3**
San Andrés, I. de **86 D3**
San Andrés Tuxtla **85 D5**
San Angelo **80 D3**
San Antonio *Chile* **94 C2**
San Antonio *U.S.A.* **80 E4**
San Antonio, C. **94 D5**
San Antonio Oeste **95 E4**
San Benedetto del Tronto **20 C4**
San Bernardino **78 C4**
San Bernardino Str. **36 B2**
San Bernardo **94 C2**
San Bernardo, I. de **90 B3**
San Borja **91 F5**
San Buenaventura = Ventura **78 C3**
San Carlos *Argentina* **94 C3**
San Carlos *Chile* **94 D2**
San Carlos *Phil.* **36 B2**
San Carlos *Amazonas, Venezuela* **90 C5**
San Carlos *Cojedes, Venezuela* **90 B5**
San Carlos de Bariloche **95 E2**
San Carlos del Zulia **90 B4**
San Cristóbal *Argentina* **94 C4**
San Cristóbal *Venezuela* **90 B4**
San Cristóbal de las Casas **85 D6**
San Diego **78 D4**
San Diego, C. **95 G3**
San Felipe *Chile* **94 C2**
San Felipe *Venezuela* **90 A5**
San Fernando *Chile* **94 C2**
San Fernando *La Union, Phil.* **36 A2**
San Fernando *Pampanga, Phil.* **36 A2**
San Fernando *Spain* **18 D2**
San Fernando *Trin. & Tob.* **87 D7**
San Fernando *U.S.A.* **78 C3**
San Fernando de Apure **90 B5**
San Fernando de Atabapo **90 C5**
San Francisco *Argentina* **94 C4**
San Francisco *U.S.A.* **78 B1**
San Francisco de Macorís **87 C5**
San Gottardo, P. del **13 C8**
San Ignacio *Bolivia* **91 G6**
San Ignacio *Paraguay* **94 B5**
San Ildefonso, C. **36 A2**
San Javier **91 G6**
San Joaquin ➔ **78 A2**
San Jorge, G. **95 F3**
San José *Costa Rica* **86 E3**
San Jose *Mind. Occ., Phil.* **36 B2**
San Jose *Nueva Ecija, Phil.* **36 A2**
San Jose *U.S.A.* **78 B2**
San José de Chiquitos **91 G6**
San José de Jáchal **94 C3**
San José de Mayo **94 C5**
San José del Guaviare **90 C4**
San Juan *Argentina* **94 C3**
San Juan *Phil.* **36 C3**
San Juan *Puerto Rico* **87 C6**
San Juan ➔ **86 D3**
San Juan de los Morros **90 B5**
San Juan Mts. **79 B9**
San Justo **94 C4**
San Leandro **78 B1**
San Lorenzo **90 C3**
San Lorenzo, Mte. **95 F2**
San Lucas **91 H5**
San Lucas, C. **84 C2**
San Luis **94 C3**
San Luis Obispo **78 C2**
San Luis Potosí **84 C4**
San Marino **20 C4**
San Marino ■ **20 C4**
San Martín, L. **95 F2**
San Matías **91 G7**
San Matías, G. **95 E4**
San Miguel **85 E7**
San Miguel ➔ **91 F6**
San Miguel de Tucumán **94 B3**
San Narciso **36 A2**
San Nicolás de los Arroyas **94 C4**
San Pedro **53 H4**
San Pedro de las Colonias **84 B4**
San Pedro de Macorís **87 C6**
San Pedro del Paraná **94 B5**
San Pedro Sula **85 D7**
San Pietro **21 E2**
San Rafael *Argentina* **94 C3**
San Rafael *U.S.A.* **72 H2**
San Remo **13 E7**
San Roque *Argentina* **94 B5**
San Roque *Spain* **18 D3**
San Rosendo **94 D2**
San Salvador **85 E7**
San Salvador de Jujuy **94 A4**
San Salvador I. **86 B5**
San Sebastián = Donostia-San Sebastián **19 A5**
San Sebastián **95 G3**
San Severo **20 D5**
San Valentin, Mte. **95 F2**
San Vicente de la Barquera **18 A3**
Sana' **49 D3**
Sana ➔ **20 B6**
Sanaga ➔ **56 D1**
Sanana **37 E3**
Sanandaj **46 D6**
Sancti Spíritus **86 B4**
Sancy, Puy de **13 D5**
Sandakan **38 C5**
Sandanski **22 D4**
Sanday **10 B5**
Sandgate **63 A5**
Sandía **91 F5**
Sandıklı **46 C2**
Sandoa **56 F4**
Sandomierz **16 C5**
Sandoway = Thandwe **41 H10**
Sandusky **76 D4**
Sandwip Chan. **41 F8**
Sandy C. **62 D3**
Sandy L. **69 C10**
Sanford *Fla., U.S.A.* **83 E7**
Sanford *N.C., U.S.A.* **83 B8**
Sanford, Mt. **69 B5**
Sanga ➔ **56 E3**
Sangamner **43 K9**
Sangar **31 C10**
Sangeang **37 F1**
Sangerhausen **15 C6**
Sanggau **39 D4**
Sangihe, Pulau **37 D3**
Sangkapura **39 F4**
Sangli **43 L9**
Sangmélima **56 D2**
Sangre de Cristo Mts. **80 A1**
Sanikiluaq **71 D6**
Sanirajak **70 C5**
Sanjo **33 E6**
Sankt Gallen **13 C8**
Sankt Moritz **13 C8**
Sankt-Peterburg **24 B3**
Sankt Pölten **15 D8**
Sankuru ➔ **56 E4**
Sanliurfa **46 C4**
Sanlúcar de Barrameda **18 D2**

Sanmenxia 35 C6
Sannicandro Gargánico 20 D5
Sant Antoni de Portmany 19 C6
Sant Feliu de Guíxols 19 B7
Sant Jordi, G. de 19 B6
Santa Ana *Bolivia* 91 F5
Santa Ana *El Salv.* 85 E7
Santa Ana *U.S.A.* 78 D4
Sant' Antioco 21 E2
Santa Barbara 78 C3
Santa Catalina I. 78 D3
Santa Catarina □ 94 B7
Santa Clara 86 B4
Santa Clotilde 90 D4
Santa Coloma de Gramenet 19 B7
Santa Cruz *Argentina* 95 G3
Santa Cruz *Bolivia* 91 G6
Santa Cruz *Phil.* 36 B2
Santa Cruz *U.S.A.* 78 B1
Santa Cruz ➔ 95 G3
Santa Cruz de Tenerife 52 C2
Santa Cruz do Sul 94 B6
Santa Cruz Is. 64 L11
Santa Eugenia, Pta. 84 B1
Santa Fé *Argentina* 94 C4
Santa Fe *U.S.A.* 79 C10
Santa Filomena 93 D4
Santa Inés, I. 95 G2
Santa Isabel 94 D3
Santa Isabel do Morro 93 E3
Santa Lucia Range 78 C2
Santa Maria *Brazil* 94 B6
Santa Maria *U.S.A.* 78 C2
Santa María ➔ 84 A3
Santa Maria da Vitória 93 E5
Santa Maria di Léuca, C. 21 E7
Santa Marta 90 A4
Santa Marta, Sierra Nevada de 90 A4
Santa Maura = Lefkada 23 E3
Santa Rosa *La Pampa, Argentina* 94 D4
Santa Rosa *San Luis, Argentina* 94 C3
Santa Rosa *Brazil* 94 B6
Santa Rosa *U.S.A.* 72 G2
Santa Vitória do Palmar 94 C6
Santai 35 C5
Santana, Coxilha de 94 C5
Santana do Livramento 94 C5
Santander 18 A4
Santarém *Brazil* 92 C3
Santarém *Portugal* 18 C1
Santiago = Río Grande de Santiago ➔ 84 C3
Santiago *Brazil* 94 B6
Santiago *Chile* 94 C2
Santiago ➔ 90 D3
Santiago de Compostela 18 A1
Santiago de Cuba 86 C4
Santiago de los Caballeros 87 C5
Santiago del Estero 94 B4
Santo Amaro 93 E6
Santo Ângelo 94 B6
Santo Antônio do Leverger 93 F2
Santo Domingo 87 C6
Santo Tomás 91 F4
Santo Tomé 94 B5
Santo Tomé de Guayana = Ciudad Guayana 90 B6
Santoña 18 A4
Santorini 23 F5
Santos 94 A7
São Bernardo do Campo 93 G4
São Borja 94 B5
São Carlos 94 A7
São Cristóvão 93 E6
São Domingos 93 E4
São Francisco 93 F5
São Francisco ➔ 93 E6
São Francisco do Sul 94 B7
São Gabriel 94 C6
São João da Madeira 18 B1
São João del Rei 93 G5
São João do Araguaia 92 D4
São João do Piauí 92 D5
São José do Rio Prêto 93 G4
São Leopoldo 94 B6
São Lourenço 93 G4
São Lourenço ➔ 93 F2
São Luís 92 C5
São Marcos ➔ 93 F4
São Marcos, B. de 92 C5
São Mateus 93 F6
São Paulo 94 A7
São Paulo □ 94 A7
São Roque, C. de 92 D6
São Sebastião, I. de 94 A7
São Tomé & Príncipe ■ 51 F4
São Vicente, C. de 18 D1
Saône ➔ 13 D6
Saonek 37 E4
Saparua 37 E3
Sapele 53 G7
Saposoa 91 E3
Sapporo 32 B7
Sapulpa 81 B5
Saqqez 46 C6
Sar-e Pol 45 B6
Sar-e Pol □ 45 B6
Sar Planina 22 C3
Saräb 46 C6
Saragossa = Zaragoza 19 B5
Saraguro 90 D3
Sarajevo 20 C7
Saran, Gunung 39 E4
Sarangani B. 36 C3
Sarangani Is. 36 C3
Sarangarh 40 G4
Saransk 24 C6
Sarapul 29 D6
Sarasota 83 F6
Saratov 24 C6
Sarāvān 45 E5
Saravane 38 A3
Sarawak □ 39 D4
Saray 22 D6
Sarayköy 23 F7
Sarbāz 45 E5
Sarbīsheh 45 C4
Sarda ➔ 40 D3
Sardarshahr 42 E9
Sardegna □ 21 D2
Sardinia = Sardegna □ 21 D2
Sardis 23 E7
Sargodha 42 C8
Sarh 55 G2
Sārī 44 B3
Sangöl 23 E7
Sarikamiş 46 B5
Sarikei 39 D4
Sark 11 G5
Şarköy 23 D6
Sarlat-la-Canéda 12 D4
Sarmi 37 E5
Sarmiento 95 F3
Sarnia 71 E5
Sarny 24 C2
Sarolangun 39 E2
Saronikos Kolpos 23 F4
Sarre = Saar ➔ 13 B7
Sarreguemines 13 B7
Sarthe ➔ 12 C3
Sartynya 28 C7
Sarvestān 44 D3
Sary-Tash 29 F8
Saryshaghan 29 E8
Sasaram 40 E5
Sasebo 33 G1
Saser 42 B10
Saskatchewan □ 69 C9
Saskatchewan ➔ 69 C9
Saskatoon 69 C9
Saskylakh 30 B9
Sasovo 24 C5
Sassandra 53 H4
Sassandra ➔ 53 H4
Sássari 21 D2
Sassnitz 15 A7
Sassuolo 20 B3
Sasyk, Ozero 17 F9
Sata-Misaki 33 H2
Satadougou 53 F3
Satara 43 L8
Satmala Hills 43 J9
Satna 40 E3
Sátoraljaújhely 16 D5
Satpura Ra. 43 J10
Satu Mare 17 E6
Satui 39 E5
Saturnina ➔ 91 F7
Sauðarkrókur 8 B2
Saudi Arabia ■ 47 F6
Sauerland 14 C4
Sault Ste. Marie *Canada* 71 E5
Sault Ste. Marie *U.S.A.* 76 A3
Saumlaki 37 F4
Saumur 12 C3
Saunders, C. 65 F4
Saurimo 56 F4
Sava ➔ 22 B3
Savage I. = Niue 65 L14
Savalou 53 G6
Savannah 83 C7
Savannah ➔ 83 C7
Savannakhet 38 A2
Save ➔ 59 C6
Säveh 46 D7
Savelugu 53 G5
Savoie □ 13 D7
Savona 13 D8
Savonlinna 8 C11
Savoy = Savoie □ 13 D7
Sawahlunto 39 E2
Sawai 37 E3
Sawai Madhopur 42 F10
Sawatch Range 79 A9
Sawu 37 F2
Sawu Sea 37 F2
Saxony = Sachsen □ 15 C7
Saxony, Lower = Niedersachsen □ 14 B5
Sayán 91 F3
Sayan, Zapadnyy 30 D7
Saydā 46 D3
Sayghān 45 C6
Sayḩūt 49 D5
Saylac = Zeila 49 E3
Saynshand = Buyant-Uhaa 35 B6
Sazanit 23 D2
Sázava ➔ 16 D2
Sazin 42 B8
Scandicci 20 C3
Scandinavia 8 C8
Scarborough 11 D6
Scebeli, Wabi ➔ 49 G3
Schaffhausen 13 C8
Schefferville = Kawawachikamach 71 D7
Schelde ➔ 14 C3
Schenectady 77 C9
Schiermonnikoog 14 B4
Schio 20 B3
Schleswig 14 A5
Schleswig-Holstein □ 14 A5
Schouten I. 62 D4
Schouten Is. = Supiori 37 E5
Schwäbische Alb 14 D5
Schwaner, Pegunungan 39 E4
Schwarzwald 14 D5
Schwedt 15 B8
Schweinfurt 14 C6
Schweiz = Switzerland ■ 13 C8
Schwenningen = Villingen-Schwenningen 14 D5
Schwerin 15 B6
Schwyz 13 C8

Sciacca 21 F4
Scilla 21 E5
Scilly, Isles of 11 G3
Scone 63 B5
Scotland □ 10 C4
Scott Glacier 96 A12
Scott Inlet 70 B6
Scottsbluff 74 E3
Scottsdale 62 D4
Scranton 77 D8
Scunthorpe 11 E6
Scutari = Shkodër 22 C2
Seaspray 63 C4
Seattle 72 C2
Sebastopol = Sevastopol 25 E3
Sebha = Sabhā 54 C1
Şebinkarahisar 46 B4
Sebta = Ceuta 18 E3
Sebuku 39 E5
Sebuku, Teluk 39 D5
Secretary I. 65 F2
Secunderabad 43 L11
Sedalia 75 F8
Sedan 13 B6
Seddon 65 D6
Seddonville 65 D5
Sédhiou 53 F2
Sedova, Pik 28 B6
Seferihisar 23 E6
Segamat 39 D2
Segesta 21 F4
Seget 37 E4
Ségou 53 F4
Segovia = Coco ➔ 86 D3
Segovia 18 B3
Segre ➔ 19 B6
Séguéla 53 G4
Segura ➔ 19 C5
Sehore 43 H10
Seinäjoki ➔ 8 C10
Seine ➔ 12 B4
Seistan = Sīstān 45 D5
Seistan, Daryācheh-ye = Sīstān, Daryācheh-ye 45 D5
Sekayu 39 E2
Sekondi-Takoradi 53 H5
Selaru 37 F4
Selçuk 23 F6
Sele ➔ 21 D5
Selebi-Pikwe 59 C5
Selenga = Selenge Mörön ➔ 35 A5
Selenge Mörön ➔ 35 A5
Seletan, Tanjung 39 E4
Sélibabi 53 E3
Selīma, El Wāhāt el 54 D4
Selkirk 69 C10
Selkirk Mts. 69 C8
Selma 83 B8
Selpele 37 E4
Selu 37 F4
Selva 94 B4
Selvas 91 E5
Seman ➔ 23 D2
Semarang 39 F4
Semey 29 D9
Semiozernoye 29 D7
Semipalatinsk = Semey 29 D9
Semirara Is. 36 B2
Semitau 39 D4
Semiyarka 29 D8
Semiyarskoye = Semiyarka 29 D8
Semmering P. 15 E8
Semnān 44 C3
Semnān □ 44 C3
Semporna 36 D1
Semuda 39 E4
Sena Madureira 91 E5
Senador Pompeu 92 D6
Senanga 58 B4
Sendai *Kagoshima, Japan* 33 H2
Sendai *Miyagi, Japan* 32 D7
Sendai-Wan 32 D7
Senegal ■ 53 F3
Sénégal ➔ 53 E2
Senge Khambab = Indus ➔ 43 G5
Senhor-do-Bonfim 93 E5
Senigállia 20 C4
Senj 20 B5
Senja 8 B9
Senlis 13 B5
Senmonorom 38 B3
Sens 13 B5
Senta 22 B3
Sentani 37 E6
Seo de Urgel = La Seu d'Urgell 19 A6
Seoul 35 C7
Sept-Îles 71 D7
Sequoia △ 78 B3
Seram 37 E3
Seram Laut 37 E4
Seram Sea 37 E3
Serasan 39 D3
Serbia ■ 22 B3
Serdar 29 F6
Serdobsk 24 C5
Seremban 39 D2
Sereth = Siret ➔ 17 F9
Sergipe □ 93 E6
Sergiyev Posad 24 B4
Seria 38 D4
Serian 39 D4
Seribu, Kepulauan 39 F3
Serifos 23 F5
Sermata 37 F3
Serov 28 D7
Serowe 59 C5
Serpukhov 24 C4
Serres 22 D4
Serrinha 93 E6
Serua 37 F4
Serui 37 E5
Sesepe 37 E3
Setana 32 B6
Sète 13 E5
Sete Lagôas 93 F5
Sétif 52 A7
Setonaikai 33 F3
Settat 52 B4
Setúbal 18 C1
Setúbal, B. de 18 C1
Sevan, Ozero = Sevana Lich 25 E6
Sevana Lich 25 E6
Sevastopol 25 E3
Severn ➔ *Canada* 71 D5
Severn ➔ *U.K.* 11 F5
Severnaya Zemlya 30 B7
Severnyye Uvaly 24 B6
Severo-Yeniseyskiy 30 C7
Severodvinsk 28 C4
Sevilla 18 D2
Seville = Sevilla 18 D2
Sevlievo 22 C5
Seward 69 B5
Seward Peninsula 69 B3
Sewer 37 F4
Seychelles ■ 26 J7
Seyðisfjörður 8 B3
Seymour 63 C4
Sfântu Gheorghe 17 F7
Sfax 54 B1
Shaanxi □ 35 C5
Shaba = Katanga □ 57 F4
Shaballe = Scebeli, Wabi ➔ 49 G3
Shache 34 C2
Shackleton Ice Shelf 96 A11
Shackleton Inlet 96 C15
Shadrinsk 29 D7
Shāhābād 44 B4
Shahdād 44 D4
Shahdād, Namakzār-e 44 D4
Shahdadkot 42 F5
Shahgarh 42 F6
Shahjahanpur 42 F11
Shahr-e Kord 44 C2
Shahrig 42 D5
Shajapur 43 H10
Shakhty 25 D5
Shakhunya 24 B6
Shaki 53 G6
Shalqar 29 E6
Shām, Bādiyat ash 47 D4
Shām, J. ash 44 F4
Shamīl 44 E4
Shammar, Jabal 47 F5
Shamo = Gobi 35 B6
Shamo, L. 55 G6
Shan □ 41 G12
Shandong □ 35 C6
Shangani ➔ 59 B5
Shanghai 35 C7
Shangqiu 35 C6
Shangrao 35 D6
Shangshui 35 C6
Shannon 64 D6
Shannon ➔ 11 E2
Shansi = Shanxi □ 35 C6
Shantou 35 D6
Shantung = Shandong □ 35 C6
Shanxi □ 35 C6
Shaoguan 35 D6
Shaoxing 35 C7
Shaoyang 35 D6
Shaqra' *Si. Arabia* 47 F6
Shaqrā' *Yemen* 49 E4
Shari 32 B9
Sharjah = Ash Shāriqah 44 E3
Sharon 76 D5
Sharya 24 B6
Shashi 35 C6
Shasta, Mt. 72 F2
Shatt al Arab 47 E7
Shawan 34 B3
Shawinigan 71 E6
Shaykh, J. ash 46 D3
Shchūchīnsk 29 D8
Shebele = Scebeli, Wabi ➔ 49 G3
Sheboygan 76 C2
Sheffield 11 E6
Shekhupura 42 D8
Shelby 83 B7
Shelbyville 82 B4
Shellharbour 63 B5
Shenandoah ➔ 77 E7
Shendam 53 G7
Shendī 55 E5
Shensi = Shaanxi □ 35 C5
Shenyang 35 B7
Sheopur Kalan 42 G10
Shepetivka 17 C8
Shepetovka = Shepetivka 17 C8
Shepparton 63 C4
Sherbro I. 53 G3
Sherbrooke 71 E6
Sheridan 73 D10
Sherman 81 C5
Shetland Is. 10 A6
Shibām 49 D4
Shibata 33 E6
Shibecha 32 B9
Shibetsu 32 A8
Shīeli 29 E7
Shihchiachuangi = Shijiazhuang 35 C6
Shijiazhuang 35 C6
Shikarpur 42 F6
Shikoku □ 33 G3
Shikotsu-Ko 32 B7
Shilabo 49 F3
Shiliguri 40 D7
Shillong 41 E8
Shimla 42 D10
Shimoga 43 N9
Shimonoseki 33 G2
Shīndand 42 C3
Shingū 33 G4
Shinyanga 57 E6
Shio-no-Misaki 33 G4
Shipchenski Prokhod 22 C5
Shipki La 42 D11
Shiquan He = Indus ➔ 43 G5
Shīr Kūh 44 D3
Shiragami-Misaki 32 C7
Shīrāz 44 D3
Shire ➔ 59 B7
Shiriya-Zaki 32 C7
Shīrvān 44 B4
Shirwa, L. = Chilwa, L. 59 B7
Shivpuri 43 G10
Shizuoka 33 F6
Shklov = Shklow 17 A10
Shklow 17 A10

Shkodër 22 C2
Shkumbini ➔ 23 D2
Shmidta, Ostrov 30 A7
Sholapur = Solapur 43 L9
Shoshone Mts. 72 G5
Shqipëria = Albania ■ 23 D3
Shreveport 81 C7
Shrewsbury 11 E5
Shrirampur 40 F7
Shū 29 E8
Shuangyashan 35 B8
Shule 34 C2
Shumagin Is. 69 C4
Shumen 22 C6
Shür ➔ 44 D3
Shurugwi 59 B6
Shüsf 45 D5
Shüshtar 47 D7
Shwebo 41 F10
Shwegu 41 E11
Shweli ➔ 41 F11
Shymkent 29 E7
Shyok 42 B11
Shyok ➔ 42 B9
Si Kiang = Xi Jiang ➔ 35 D6
Si-ngan = Xi'an 35 C5
Siah 47 G6
Siahan Range 42 F4
Siaksriindrapura 39 D2
Sialkot 42 C9
Siam = Thailand ■ 38 A2
Sian = Xi'an 35 C5
Siantan 39 D3
Siargao I. 36 C3
Siasi 36 C2
Siau 37 D3
Šiauliai 24 B1
Šibenik 20 C5
Siberia 30 C8
Siberut 39 E1
Sibi 42 E5
Sibil = Oksibil 37 E6
Sibirtsevo 32 A3
Sibiti 56 E2
Sibiu 17 F7
Sibolga 39 D1
Sibsagar 41 D10
Sibu 39 D4
Sibuco 36 C2
Sibuguey B. 36 C2
Sibut 55 G2
Sibutu 36 D1
Sibutu Passage 36 D1
Sibuyan I. 36 B2
Sibuyan Sea 36 B2
Sichuan □ 34 C5
Sicilia 21 F5
Sicily = Sicilia 21 F5
Sicuani 91 F4
Siddipet 43 K11
Sidi-bel-Abbès 52 A5
Sidi Ifni 52 C3
Sidley, Mt. 96 B18
Sidon = Saydā 46 D3
Sidra, G. of = Surt, Khalīj 54 B2
Siedlce 17 B6
Sieg ➔ 14 C4
Siegen 14 C5
Siem Reap = Siemreab 38 B2
Siemreab 38 B2
Siena 20 C3
Sieradz 16 C4
Sierra Colorada 95 E3
Sierra Gorda 94 A3
Sierra Leone ■ 53 G3
Sierra Madre Occidental 84 B3
Sierra Nevada *Spain* 18 D4
Sierra Nevada *U.S.A.* 72 G3
Sifnos 23 F5
Sighetu-Marmaţiei 17 E6
Sigli 38 C1
Siglufjörður 8 B2
Sigsig 90 D3
Sigüenza 19 B4
Siguiri 53 F4
Sikar 42 F9
Sikasso 53 F4
Sikhote Alin, Khrebet 32 A5
Sikhote Alin Ra. = Sikhote Alin, Khrebet 32 A5
Sikinos 23 F5
Sikkim □ 40 D7
Sil ➔ 18 A2
Silchar 41 E9
Silesia = Śląsk 16 C3
Silgarhi Doti 40 C3
Silghat 41 D9
Silifke 46 C3
Siliguri = Shiliguri 40 D7
Siling Co 34 C3
Silistra 22 B6
Silivri 22 D7
Sillajhuay, Cordillera 91 G5
Simanggang = Sri Aman 39 D4
Simav 23 E7
Simbirsk 24 C6
Simeria 17 F6
Simeulue 39 D1
Simferopol 25 E3
Simi 23 F6
Simikot 40 C3
Simla = Shimla 42 D10
Simpson Desert 60 F6
Simpson Pen. 70 C5
Sinabang 39 D1
Sinadogo 49 F4
Sinai = Es Sīnā' 54 C5
Sinai, Mt. = Mūsa, Gebel 47 E3
Sinaloa de Leyva 84 B3
Sincelejo 90 B3
Sincorá, Serra do 93 E5
Sind = Sindh □ 42 F6
Sind Sagar Doab 42 D7
Sindangan 36 C2
Sindh □ 42 F6
Sines 18 D1
Sines, C. de 18 D1
Singa 55 F5
Singapore ■ 39 D2
Singaraja 39 F5
Singida 57 E6
Singkaling Hkamti 41 E10
Singkang 37 E2
Singkawang 39 D3
Singleton 63 B5
Singora = Songkhla 38 C2
Sinjai 37 F2
Sinjär 46 C5
Sinkat 55 E6
Sinkiang = Xinjiang Uygur Zizhiqu □ 34 B3
Sinni ➔ 21 D6
Sinop 25 E4
Sintang 39 D4
Sintra 18 C1
Siocon 36 C2
Siófok 16 E4
Sioux City 75 D6
Sioux Falls 74 D6
Sioux Lookout 69 C10
Siping 35 B7
Sipura 39 E1
Siquijor 36 C2
Siracusa 21 F5
Sirajganj 41 E7
Siret ➔ 17 F9
Sīrjān 44 D3
Sirohi 43 G8
Sironj 43 G10
Síros = Syros 23 F5
Sirsa 42 E9
Sisak 20 B6
Sisaket 38 A2
Sisophon 38 B2
Sīstān 45 D5
Sīstān, Daryācheh-ye 45 D5
Sistān va Balūchestān □ 45 E5
Sitapur 40 D3
Sitges 19 B6
Sitia 23 G6
Sitka 69 C6
Sittang Myit ➔ 41 J11
Sittoung = Sittang Myit ➔ 41 J11
Sittwe 41 G9
Siuri 40 F6
Sivas 25 F4
Siverek 46 C4
Sivrihisar 25 F3
Siwa 54 C4
Siwalik Range 40 D4
Siwan 40 D5
Sjælland 9 D8
Sjumen = Shumen 22 C6
Skadarsko Jezero 22 C2
Skagen 9 D8
Skagerrak 9 D7
Skagway 69 C6
Skala-Podilska 17 D8
Skala Podolskaya = Skala-Podilska 17 D8
Skalat 17 D7
Skardu 42 B9
Skarżysko-Kamienna 16 C5
Skeena ➔ 68 C6
Skegness 11 E7
Skeldon = Corriverton 90 B7
Skeleton Coast 58 C2
Skellefteå 8 C10
Skellefteälven ➔ 8 C10
Skiathos 23 E4
Skien 9 D7
Skierniewice 16 C5
Skikda 52 A7
Skiros 23 E5
Skole 17 D6
Skopelos 23 E4
Skopje 22 C3
Skvyra 17 D9
Skye 10 C3
Skyros = Skiros 23 E5
Śląsk 16 C3
Slatina 22 B5
Slave ➔ 68 B8
Slavgorod 29 D8
Slavonski Brod 20 B7
Slavuta 17 C8
Slavyanka 32 B2
Slavyansk = Slovyansk 25 D4
Slawharad 17 B10
Sleaford B. 62 B2
Sleeper Is. 70 D5
Sligeach = Sligo 11 D2
Sligo 11 D2
Sliven 22 C6
Slobodskoy 24 B7
Slobozia 22 B6
Slonim 17 B7
Slough 11 F6
Slovak Rep. ■ 16 D4
Slovakia = Slovak Rep. ■ 16 D4
Slovakian Ore Mts. = Slovenské Rudohorie 16 D4
Slovenia ■ 20 B5
Slovenija = Slovenia ■ 20 B5
Slovenska = Slovak Rep. ■ 16 D4
Slovenské Rudohorie 16 D4
Slovyansk 25 D4
Sluch ➔ 17 C8
Słupsk 16 A3
Slutsk 17 B8
Smallwood Res. 71 D7
Smara 52 B4
Smarhon 17 A8
Smederevo 22 B3
Smithton 62 D4
Smithtown 63 B5
Smoky Bay 62 B1
Smolensk 24 C3
Smolikas, Oros 23 D3
Smolyan 22 D5
Smorgon = Smarhon 17 A8
Smyrna = İzmir 23 E6
Snake ➔ 72 C4
Snake I. 63 C4
Snake River Plain 73 E7
Sneek 14 B3
Sněžka 16 C2

Snøhetta 8 C7
Snowdon 11 E4
Snowdrift = Łutselk'e 68 B8
Snowtown 62 B2
Snowy ➔ 63 C4
Snowy Mts. 63 C4
Snyatyn 17 D7
Snyder 80 C3
Sobat, Nahr ➔ 55 G5
Sobral 92 C5
Soc Trang 38 C3
Soch'e = Shache 34 C2
Sochi 25 E4
Société, Îs. de la 65 L15
Society Is. = Société, Îs. de la 65 L15
Socompa, Portezuelo de 94 A3
Socotra 49 E5
Söderhamn 8 C9
Sodiri 55 F4
Sofia = Sofiya 22 C4
Sofia ➔ 59 B9
Sofiya 22 C4
Sogamoso 90 B4
Sognefjorden 8 C7
Sohåg 54 C5
Soissons 13 B5
Sokal 17 C7
Söke 23 F6
Sokhumi 25 E5
Sokodé 53 G6
Sokol 24 B5
Sokółka 17 B6
Sokołów Podlaski 17 B6
Sokoto 53 F7
Solander I. 65 G2
Solano 36 A2
Solapur 43 L9
Soledad 90 B6
Soligalich 24 B5
Soligorsk = Salihorsk 17 B8
Solikamsk 28 D6
Solimões = Amazonas ➔ 92 C3
Solingen 14 C4
Sóller 19 C7
Sologne 12 C4
Solok 39 E2
Solomon Is. ■ 64 K10
Solomon Sea 61 B9
Solon 35 B7
Solor 37 F2
Šolta 20 C6
Soltänäbäd 44 B4
Solunska Glava 22 D3
Solwezi 59 A5
Söma *Japan* 32 E7
Soma *Turkey* 23 E6
Somali Rep. ■ 49 F4
Somalia = Somali Rep. ■ 49 F4
Somaliland □ 49 E4
Sombor 22 B2
Sombrerete 84 C4
Somerset I. 68 A10
Someş ➔ 17 E6
Sommariva 63 A4
Somme ➔ 12 A4
Somosierra, Puerto de 18 B4
Somport, Puerto de 12 E3
Sóndrio 13 C8
Sonepur 40 G4
Song Cau 38 B3
Songea 57 G7
Songhua Jiang ➔ 35 B8
Songkhla 38 C2
Songo 59 B6
Songpan 34 C5
Sonipat 42 E10
Sonmiani 42 G5
Sono ➔ 93 D4
Sonora ➔ 84 B2
Sonsonate 85 E7
Soochow = Suzhou 35 C7
Soomaaliya = Somali Rep. ■ 49 F4
Sopi 37 D3
Sopot 16 A4
Sopron 16 E3
Sør-Rondane 96 B8
Sorel-Tracy 71 E6
Sórgono 21 D2
Soria 19 B4
Sorkh, Kuh-e 44 C4
Soroca 17 D9
Sorocaba 94 A7
Soroki = Soroca 17 D9
Sorong 37 E4
Soroti 57 D6
Sørøya 8 A10
Sorrento 63 C3
Sorsogon 36 B2
Sosnowiec 16 C4
Souanké 56 D2
Soudas, Ormos 23 G5
Sŏul = Seoul 35 C7
Sources, Mt. aux 59 D5
Soure 92 C4
Souris ➔ 69 D10
Sousa 92 D6
Sousse 54 A1
South Africa ■ 58 E4
South Australia □ 62 B2
South Bend 76 D2
South Carolina □ 83 C7
South China Sea 38 C4
South Dakota □ 74 C4
South East C. 62 D4
South Horr 57 D7
South I. 65 E3
South Invercargill 65 G3
South Korea ■ 35 C7
South Magnetic Pole 96 A13
South Nahanni ➔ 68 B7
South Natuna Is. = Natuna Selatan, Kepulauan 39 D3
South Orkney Is. 96 A4
South Pagai, I. = Pagai Selatan, Pulau 39 E2
South Platte ➔ 74 E4
South Pole 96 C
South Ronaldsay 10 B5
South Saskatchewan ➔ 69 C9
South Shetland Is. 96 A4
South Shields 11 D6
South Taranaki Bight 64 C6
South Uist 10 C3
South West C. *Australia* 62 D4
South West C. *N.Z.* 65 G2
Southampton 11 F6
Southampton I. 70 C5
Southbridge 65 E5
Southend-on-Sea 11 F7
Southern Alps 65 E4
Southern Indian L. 69 C10
Southern Ocean 96 A9
Southern Uplands 10 D5
Southland □ 65 F3
Southport 63 A5
Sovetsk *Kaliningrad, Russia* 24 B1
Sovetsk *Kirov, Russia* 24 B6
Soweto 59 D5
Sozh ➔ 17 C10
Spain ■ 18 C4
Spalding 62 B2
Spanish Town 86 C4
Sparta = Sparti 23 F4
Spartanburg 83 B7
Sparti 23 F4
Spartivento, C. *Calabria, Italy* 21 F6
Spartivento, C. *Sard., Italy* 21 E2
Spassk Dalniy 32 A3
Spatha, Akra 23 G4
Spence Bay = Taloyoak 68 B10
Spencer, C. 62 C2
Spencer G. 62 B2
Spenser Mts. 65 E5
Spey ➔ 10 C5
Speyer 14 D5
Split 20 C6
Spokane 72 C5
Spoleto 20 C4
Sporyy Navolok, Mys 28 B7
Spratly Is. 38 C4
Spree ➔ 15 B7
Springfield *N.Z.* 65 E4
Springfield *Ill., U.S.A.* 75 F10
Springfield *Mass., U.S.A.* 77 C9
Springfield *Mo., U.S.A.* 81 A7
Springfield *Ohio, U.S.A.* 76 E4
Springfield *Oreg., U.S.A.* 72 D2
Springhurst 63 C4
Springs 59 D5
Srbija = Serbia ■ 22 B3
Sre Ambel 38 B2
Sre Umbell = Sre Ambel 38 B2
Srebrenica 20 B7
Sredinny Ra. = Sredinnyy Khrebet 31 D14
Sredinnyy Khrebet 31 D14
Srednevilyuysk 31 C10
Śrem 16 B3
Sremska Mitrovica 22 B2
Sri Aman 39 D4
Sri Lanka ■ 43 R12
Srikakulam 40 H4
Srinagar 42 B9
Stade 14 B5
Stafford 11 E5
Stakhanov 25 D4
Stalowa Wola 17 C6
Stamford 77 D9
Stanke Dimitrov 22 C4
Stanley *Australia* 62 D4
Stanley *Falk. Is.* 95 G5
Stanovoy Khrebet 31 D10
Stanovoy Ra. = Stanovoy Khrebet 31 D10
Stanthorpe 63 A5
Stara Planina 22 C4
Stara Zagora 22 C5
Starachowice 16 C5
Staraya Russa 24 B3
Starbuck I. 65 K15
Stargard Szczeciński 16 B2
Staritsa 24 B3
Starogard Gdański 16 B4
Starokonstantinov = Starokonstyantyniv 17 D8
Starokonstyantyniv 17 D8
Staryy Chartoriysk 17 C7
Staryy Oskol 24 C4
State College 77 D7
Staten, I. = Estados, I. de Los 95 G4
Statesville 83 B7
Stavanger 9 D7
Staveley 65 E4
Stavropol 25 D5
Stawell 62 C3
Stefanie L. = Chew Bahir 55 H6
Stefansson Bay 96 A9
Steiermark □ 15 E8
Steinkjer 8 C8
Stendal 15 B6
Steornabhaigh = Stornoway 10 B3
Stepanakert = Xankändi 25 F6
Stephens Creek 62 B3
Stephenville 71 E8
Stepnyak 29 D8
Sterlitamak 29 D6
Stettin = Szczecin 16 B2
Stettiner Haff 15 B8
Stettler 69 C8
Steubenville 76 D5
Stevenage 11 F6
Stevenson ➔ 62 A2
Stewart ➔ 68 B6
Stewart, I. 95 G2
Stewart I. 65 G2
Steyr 15 D8
Stillwater *N.Z.* 65 E4
Stillwater *U.S.A.* 80 A5
Štip 22 D4

Stirling 10 C5
Stockerau 15 D9
Stockholm 9 D9
Stockport 11 E5
Stockton 78 B2
Stockton-on-Tees 11 D6
Stoeng Treng 38 B3
Stoke-on-Trent 11 E5
Stokes Pt. 62 D3
Stolac 20 C6
Stolbovoy, Ostrov 30 B11
Stolbtsy = Stowbtsy 17 B8
Stolin 17 C8
Stonehaven 10 C5
Stony Tunguska = Tunguska, Podkamennaya ➔ 30 C7
Stora Lulevatten 8 B9
Storavan 8 B9
Store Bælt 9 D8
Store Creek 63 B4
Storm B. 62 D4
Stormberge 59 E5
Stornoway 10 B3
Storozhinets = Storozhynets 17 D7
Storozhynets 17 D7
Storsjön 8 C8
Storuman 8 B9
Stowbtsy 17 B8
Strahan 62 D4
Stralsund 15 A7
Stranraer 11 D4
Strasbourg 13 B7
Stratford *Canada* 76 C5
Stratford *N.Z.* 64 C6
Strathalbyn 62 C2
Straubing 15 D7
Streaky B. 62 B1
Streaky Bay 62 B1
Strelka 30 D7
Strezhevoy 29 C8
Strimonas ➔ 23 D4
Strómboli 21 E5
Stronsay 10 B5
Stroud Road 63 B5
Strumica 22 D4
Stryy 17 D6
Strzelecki Cr. ➔ 62 A2
Stuart Ra. 62 A1
Stung Treng = Stoeng Treng 38 B3
Stuttgart 14 D5
Styria = Steiermark □ 15 E8
Suakin 55 E6
Subansiri ➔ 41 D9
Subi 39 D3
Subotica 16 E4
Suceava 17 E8
Suchou = Suzhou 35 C7
Süchow = Xuzhou 35 C6
Sucre 91 G5
Sudair 47 F6
Sudan ■ 55 E4
Sudbury 71 E5
Südd 55 G4
Sudeten Mts. = Sudety 16 C3
Sudety 16 C3
Sudirman, Pegunungan 37 E5
Sueca 19 C5
Suez = El Suweis 54 C5
Suez, G. of = Suweis, Khalīg el 54 C5
Sugluk = Salluit 70 C6
Şuhār 44 E4
Sühbaatar 35 A5
Suhl 14 C6
Suihua 35 B7
Suisse = Switzerland ■ 13 C8
Sukadana 39 E3
Sukagawa 33 E7
Sukaraja 39 E4
Sukhona ➔ 28 C5
Sukhumi = Sokhumi 25 E5
Sukkur 42 F6
Sukkur Barrage 42 F6
Sukumo 33 G3
Sula, Kepulauan 37 E3
Sulaiman Range 42 D6
Sulawesi 37 E2
Sulawesi Sea = Celebes Sea 37 D2
Sulawesi Tengah □ 37 E2
Sulawesi Tenggara □ 37 E2
Sulima 53 G3
Sulina 17 F9
Sullana 90 D2
Sultanpur 40 D4
Sulu Arch. 36 C2
Sulu Sea 36 C2
Suluq 54 B3
Sulzberger Ice Shelf 96 B17
Sumalata 37 D2
Sumatera 39 D2
Sumatra = Sumatera 39 D2
Sumba 37 F1
Sumba, Selat 37 F1
Sumbawa 39 F5
Sumbawa Besar 39 F5
Sumbe 56 G2
Šumen = Shumen 22 C6
Sumgait = Sumqayıt 25 E6
Summerside 71 E7
Šumperk 16 D3
Sumqayıt 25 E6
Sumter 83 C7
Sumy 24 C3
Sunbury 63 C3
Sunda, Selat 39 F3
Sunda Str. = Sunda, Selat 39 F3
Sundarbans 41 G7
Sundargarh 40 F5
Sunderland 11 D6
Sundsvall 8 C9
Sungaigerong 39 E2
Sungailiat 39 E3
Sungaipakning 39 D2
Sungaipenuh 39 E2
Sungari = Songhua Jiang ➔ 35 B8
Sunghua Chiang = Songhua Jiang ➔ 35 B8
Sungurlu 46 B3
Sunnyvale 78 B1
Suntar 30 C9
Suomi = Finland ■ 8 C11
Supaul 40 D6
Superior 75 B8
Superior, L. 71 E5
Suphan Dağı 46 C5
Supiori 37 E5
Suquṭra = Socotra 49 E5
Sūr *Lebanon* 46 D3
Ṣūr *Oman* 45 F4
Sura ➔ 24 B6
Surabaja = Surabaya 39 F4
Surabaya 39 F4
Surakarta 39 F4
Surat *Australia* 63 A4
Surat *India* 43 J8
Surat Thani 38 C1
Suratgarh 42 E8
Surgut 29 C8
Suriapet 43 L11
Surigao 36 C3
Surinam = Suriname ■ 92 B2
Suriname ■ 92 B2
Suriname ➔ 92 A2
Surt 54 B2
Surt, Khalīj 54 B2
Surtsey 8 C1
Suruga-Wan 33 F6
Süsangerd 47 E7
Susanville 72 F3
Susquehanna ➔ 77 E7
Susques 94 A3
Susunu 37 E4
Susurluk 23 E7
Sutherland 58 E4
Sutherland Falls 65 F2
Sutlej ➔ 42 E7
Suttsu 32 B7
Suva 64 L12
Suva Planina 22 C4
Suvorov Is. = Suwarrow Is. 65 L14
Suwałki 17 A6
Suwarrow Is. 65 L14
Suweis, Khalīg el 54 C5
Suzdal 24 B5
Suzhou 35 C7
Suzu 33 E5
Suzu-Misaki 33 E5
Svealand □ 9 D9
Sverdrup Chan. 70 B4
Sverdrup Is. 70 B4
Sverige = Sweden ■ 9 D9
Svetlogorsk = Svyetlahorsk 17 B9
Svishtov 22 C5
Svislach 17 B7
Svizzera = Switzerland ■ 13 C8
Svyetlahorsk 17 B9
Swabian Alps = Schwäbische Alb 14 D5
Swakopmund 58 C2
Swan Hill 62 C3
Swansea 11 F5
Swatow = Shantou 35 D6
Swaziland ■ 59 D6
Sweden ■ 9 D9
Sweetwater 80 C3
Swellendam 58 E4
Świdnica 16 C3
Świdnik 17 C6
Świebodzin 16 B2
Świecie 16 B4
Swift Current 69 C9
Swindon 11 F6
Swinemünde = Świnoujście 16 B2
Świnoujście 16 B2
Switzerland ■ 13 C8
Sydney *Australia* 63 B5
Sydney *Canada* 71 E7
Sydra, G. of = Surt, Khalīj 54 B2
Syktyvkar 28 C6
Sylhet 41 E8
Sylt 14 A5
Sym 29 C9
Syracuse 77 C7
Syrdarya ➔ 29 E7
Syria ■ 46 D4
Syrian Desert = Shām, Bādiyat ash 47 D4
Syros 23 F5
Syzran 24 C6
Szczecin 16 B2
Szczecinek 16 B3
Szczeciński, Zalew = Stettiner Haff 15 B8
Szczytno 16 B5
Szechwan = Sichuan □ 34 C5
Szeged 16 E5
Székesfehérvár 16 E4
Szekszárd 16 E4
Szentes 16 E5
Szolnok 16 E5
Szombathely 16 E3

T

Tabacal 94 A4
Tabaco 36 B2
Ṭābah 47 F5
Ṭabas *Khorāsān, Iran* 45 C5
Ṭabas *Yazd, Iran* 44 C4
Tabatinga, Serra da 93 E5
Tablas 36 B2
Table B. 58 E3
Table Mt. 58 E3
Tábor 16 D2
Tabora 57 F6
Tabou 53 H4
Tabrīz 46 C6
Tabük 47 E4
Tacheng 34 B3
Tacloban 36 B2
Tacna 91 G4
Tacoma 72 C2
Tacuarembó 94 C5
Tademaït, Plateau du 52 C6

Tadjoura **49 E3**
Tadmor **65 D5**
Tadzhikistan = Tajikistan ■ **29 F8**
Taegu = Daegu **35 C7**
Taejŏn = Daejeon **35 C7**
Tafalla **19 A5**
Tafelbaai = Table B. **58 E3**
Tafermaar **37 F4**
Taft **36 B3**
Taftan **42 E2**
Taftān, Kūh-e **45 D5**
Taga Dzong **41 D7**
Taganrog **25 D4**
Tagbilaran **36 C2**
Tagliamento ➔ **20 B4**
Taguatinga **93 E5**
Tagum **36 C3**
Tagus = Tejo ➔ **18 C1**
Tahakopa **65 G3**
Tahan, Gunung **38 D2**
Tahat **52 D7**
Tāherī **44 E3**
Tahiti **65 L16**
Tahoe, L. **72 G3**
Tahoua **53 F7**
Tahta **54 C5**
Tahulandang **37 D3**
Tahuna **37 D3**
Taibei = T'aipei **35 D7**
T'aichung **35 D7**
Taidong **35 D7**
Taieri ➔ **65 G4**
Taihape **64 C6**
Tailem Bend **62 C2**
Taimyr Peninsula = Taymyr, Poluostrov **30 B7**
Tain **10 C4**
T'ainan **35 D7**
T'aipei **35 D7**
Taiping **38 D2**
Taitao, Pen. de **95 F1**
Taiwan ■ **35 D7**
Taiyuan **35 C6**
Taizhong = T'aichung **35 D7**
Ta'izz **49 E3**
Tajikistan ■ **29 F8**
Tajima **33 E6**
Tajo = Tejo ➔ **18 C1**
Tak **38 A1**
Takada **33 E6**
Takaka **65 D5**
Takamatsu **33 F4**
Takaoka **33 E5**
Takapuna **64 B6**
Takasaki **33 E6**
Takayama **33 E5**
Takefu **33 F5**
Takengon **38 D1**
Takeshima = Liancourt Rocks **33 E2**
Tākestān **46 D7**
Takev **38 B2**
Takhār □ **45 B7**
Takikawa **32 B7**
Takla Makan **34 C3**
Taklamakan Shamo = Takla Makan **34 C3**
Talara **90 D2**
Talas **29 E8**
Talaud, Kepulauan **36 D3**
Talaud Is. = Talaud, Kepulauan **36 D3**
Talavera de la Reina **18 C3**
Talayan **36 C2**
Talbragar ➔ **63 B4**
Talca **94 D2**
Talcahuano **94 D2**
Talcher **40 G5**
Taldy Kurgan = Taldyqorghan **29 E8**
Taldyqorghan **29 E8**
Tālesh, Kūhhā-ye **46 C7**
Tali Post **55 G5**
Talibon **36 B2**
Taliwang **39 F5**
Tall 'Afar **46 C5**
Talladega **82 C4**
Tallahassee **83 D5**
Tallangatta **63 C4**
Tallinn **24 B1**
Taloyoak **68 B10**
Taltal **94 B2**
Talwood **63 A4**
Talyawalka Cr. ➔ **62 B3**
Tamale **53 G5**
Tamanrasset **52 D7**
Tamarang **63 B5**
Tamatave = Toamasina **59 B9**
Tambacounda **53 F3**
Tambelan, Kepulauan **39 D3**
Tambo de Mora **91 F3**
Tambora **39 F5**
Tambov **24 C5**
Tāmega ➔ **18 B1**
Tamenglong **41 E9**
Tamgak, Mts. **53 E7**
Tamil Nadu □ **43 P10**
Tammerfors = Tampere **8 C10**
Tamo Abu, Banjaran **39 D5**
Tampa **83 F6**
Tampere **8 C10**
Tampico **84 C5**
Tamsagbulag **35 B6**
Tamu **41 E10**
Tamworth **63 B5**
Tana ➔ *Kenya* **57 E8**
Tana ➔ *Norway* **8 A11**
Tana, L. **55 F6**
Tanabe **33 G4**
Tanahbala **39 E1**
Tanahgrogot **39 E5**
Tanahjampea **37 F2**
Tanahmasa **39 E1**
Tanahmerah **37 F6**
Tanakura **33 E7**
Tanami Desert **60 D5**
Tanana ➔ **69 B4**
Tananarive = Antananarivo **59 B9**
Tánaro ➔ **13 D8**
Tandag **36 C3**
Tandil **94 D5**
Tando Adam **42 G6**
Tandou L. **62 B3**
Taneatua **64 C7**
Tanen Tong Dan = Dawna Ra. **41 J12**
Tanezrouft **52 D6**
Tanga **57 F7**
Tanganyika, L. **57 F5**
Tanger **52 A4**
Tanggula Shan **34 C4**
Tanghla Range = Tanggula Shan **34 C4**
Tangier = Tanger **52 A4**
Tangshan **35 C6**
Tanimbar, Kepulauan **37 F4**
Tanimbar Is. = Tanimbar, Kepulauan **37 F4**
Taninthari = Tenasserim **38 B1**
Tanjay **36 C2**
Tanjore = Thanjavur **43 P11**
Tanjung **39 E5**
Tanjungbalai **39 D1**
Tanjungbatu **39 D5**
Tanjungkarang Telukbetung = Bandar Lampung **39 F3**
Tanjungpandan **39 E3**
Tanjungpinang **39 D2**
Tanjungredeb **39 D5**
Tanjungselor **39 D5**
Tanout **53 F7**
Tanta **54 B5**
Tantung = Dandong **35 B7**
Tanunda **62 B2**
Tanzania ■ **57 F6**
Taolanaro **59 D9**
Taoudenni **52 D5**
Tapa Shan = Daba Shan **35 C5**
Tapajós ➔ **92 C3**
Tapaktuan **39 D1**
Tapanui **65 F3**
Tapauá ➔ **91 E6**
Tapeta **53 G4**
Tapirapecó, Serra **90 C6**
Tapti ➔ **43 J8**
Tapuae-o-Uenuku **65 D5**
Tapul Group **36 C2**
Taquari ➔ **91 G7**
Tara *Australia* **63 A5**
Tara *Russia* **29 D8**
Tara ➔ *Montenegro* **22 C2**
Tara ➔ *Russia* **29 D8**
Tarābulus *Lebanon* **46 D3**
Tarābulus *Libya* **54 B1**
Tarakan **39 D5**
Taranaki □ **64 C6**
Taranaki, Mt. **64 C6**
Tarancón **19 B4**
Taranga Hill **43 H8**
Táranto **21 D6**
Táranto, G. di **21 D6**
Tarapacá **90 D5**
Tararua Ra. **64 D6**
Tarashcha **17 D10**
Tarauacá **91 E4**
Tarauacá ➔ **91 E5**
Tarawa **64 J12**
Tarawera **64 C7**
Tarawera, L. **64 C7**
Taraz **29 E8**
Tarazona **19 B5**
Tarbagatay, Khrebet **29 E9**
Tarbela Dam **42 B8**
Tarbes **12 E4**
Tarcoola **62 B1**
Tarcoon **63 B4**
Taree **63 B5**
Tarfaya **52 C3**
Târgovişte **22 B5**
Târgu Jiu **17 F6**
Târgu Mureş **17 E7**
Tarifa **18 D3**
Tarija **94 A4**
Tariku ➔ **37 E5**
Tarim Basin = Tarim Pendi **34 C3**
Tarim He ➔ **34 C3**
Tarim Pendi **34 C3**
Taritatu ➔ **37 E5**
Tarkhankut, Mys **25 D3**
Tarko Sale **28 C8**
Tarkwa **53 G5**
Tarlac **36 A2**
Tarma **91 F3**
Tarn ➔ **12 D4**
Tarnobrzeg **16 C5**
Tarnów **16 C5**
Tarnowskie Góry **16 C4**
Taroom **63 A4**
Taroudannt **52 B4**
Tarragona **19 B6**
Tarrasa = Terrassa **19 B7**
Tarsus **46 C3**
Tartagal **94 A4**
Tartu **24 B2**
Ṭarṭūs **46 D3**
Tarutung **39 D1**
Tash-Kömür **29 E8**
Tash-Kumyr = Tash-Kömür **29 E8**
Tashauz = Dashoguz **29 E6**
Tashi Chho Dzong = Thimphu **41 D7**
Tashkent = Toshkent **29 E7**
Tashtagol **29 D9**
Tasman B. **65 D5**
Tasman Mts. **65 D5**
Tasman Pen. **62 D4**
Tasmania □ **62 D4**
Tatabánya **16 E4**
Tatar Republic = Tatarstan □ **29 D6**
Tatarbunary **17 F9**
Tatarsk **29 D8**
Tatarstan □ **29 D6**
Tateyama **33 F6**
Tathra **63 C4**
Tatnam, C. **71 D4**
Tatra = Tatry **16 D4**
Tatry **16 D4**
Tatta **43 G5**
Tat'ung = Datong **35 B6**

Tatvan **46 C5**
Taubaté **94 A7**
Tauern **15 E7**
Taumarunui **64 C6**
Taumaturgo **91 E4**
Taungdwingyi **41 G10**
Taunggyi **41 G11**
Taungup **41 H10**
Taungup Taunggya **41 H9**
Taunton **11 F5**
Taunus **14 C5**
Taupo **64 C7**
Taupo, L. **64 C6**
Tauranga **64 B7**
Tauranga Harb. **64 B7**
Taurianova **21 E6**
Taurus Mts. = Toros Dağları **46 C3**
Tavastehus = Hämeenlinna **8 C10**
Tavda **29 D7**
Tavda ➔ **29 D7**
Tavira **18 D2**
Tavoy **38 B1**
Tawau **38 D5**
Tawi-Tawi **36 C2**
Tay ➔ **10 C5**
Tayabamba **91 E3**
Taygetos Oros **23 F4**
Taylakova **29 D8**
Taylakovy = Taylakova **29 D8**
Taymā **47 F4**
Taymyr, Oz. **30 B8**
Taymyr, Poluostrov **30 B7**
Taytay **36 B1**
Taz ➔ **28 C8**
Taza **52 B5**
Tazovskiy **28 C8**
Tbilisi **25 E5**
Tchad = Chad ■ **55 E2**
Tchad, L. **55 F1**
Tch'eng-tou = Chengdu **35 C5**
Tchibanga **56 E2**
Tch'ong-k'ing = Chongqing **35 D5**
Tczew **16 A4**
Te Anau, L. **65 F2**
Te Aroha **64 B6**
Te Awamutu **64 C6**
Te Ika a Maui = North I. **64 B5**
Te Kuiti **64 C6**
Te Puke **64 B7**
Te Waewae B. **65 G2**
Te Wai Pounamu = South I. **65 E3**
Tebakang **39 D4**
Tébessa **52 A7**
Tebicuary ➔ **94 B5**
Tebingtinggi **39 D1**
Tecuci **22 B6**
Tedzhen = Tejen **29 F7**
Tefé **90 D6**
Tegal **39 F3**
Tegucigalpa **85 E7**
Tehachapi **78 C3**
Teheran = Tehrān **44 C2**
Tehoru **37 E3**
Tehrān **44 C2**
Tehuantepec **85 D5**
Tehuantepec, G. de **85 D5**
Tehuantepec, Istmo de **85 D6**
Tejen **29 F7**
Tejo ➔ **18 C1**
Tekapo, L. **65 E4**
Tekeli **29 E8**
Tekirdağ **22 D6**
Tekkali **40 H5**
Tel Aviv-Yafo **46 D3**
Tela **85 D7**
Telanaipura = Jambi **39 E2**
Telavi **25 E6**
Telekhany = Tsyelyakhany **17 B7**
Teles Pires ➔ **91 E7**
Telford **11 E5**
Tellicherry **43 P9**
Telsen **95 E3**
Teluk Anson = Teluk Intan **39 D2**
Teluk Betung = Bandar Lampung **39 F3**
Teluk Intan **39 D2**
Telukbutun **39 D3**
Telukdalem **39 D1**
Tema **53 G5**
Temerloh **39 D2**
Temir **29 E6**
Temirtau *Kazakhstan* **29 D8**
Temirtau *Russia* **29 D9**
Temma **62 D3**
Tempe **79 D7**
Temple **80 D5**
Temuco **94 D2**
Temuka **65 F4**
Tenali **40 J3**
Tenaro, Akra **23 F4**
Tenasserim **38 B1**
Tenda, Colle di **13 D7**
Tendaho **49 E3**
Tenerife **52 C2**
Tengah, Kepulauan **39 F5**
Tengchong **34 D4**
Tenggarong **39 E5**
Tengiz Köli **29 D7**
Tenkasi **43 Q10**
Tennessee □ **82 B4**
Tennessee ➔ **76 F1**
Tenom **38 C5**
Tenterfield **63 A5**
Teófilo Otoni **93 F5**
Tepa **37 F3**
Tepic **84 C4**
Teplice **16 C1**
Ter ➔ **19 A7**
Téramo **20 C4**
Terang **62 C3**
Terebovlya **17 D7**
Terek ➔ **25 E6**
Teresina **92 D5**
Terewah, L. **63 A4**
Teridgerie Cr. ➔ **63 B4**
Termez = Termiz **29 F7**
Término Imerese **21 F4**
Termiz **29 F7**
Térmoli **20 C5**
Ternate **37 D3**
Terney **32 A5**
Terni **20 C4**
Ternopil **17 D7**
Ternopol = Ternopil **17 D7**
Terowie *N.S.W., Australia* **63 B4**
Terowie *S. Austral., Australia* **62 B2**
Terracina **20 D4**
Terralba **21 E2**
Terrassa **19 B7**
Terre Haute **76 E2**
Terschelling **14 B3**
Teruel **19 B5**
Teryaweynya L. **62 B3**
Teshio **32 A7**
Teshio-Gawa ➔ **32 A7**
Tesiyn Gol ➔ **34 A4**
Teslin **68 B6**
Tessalit **52 D6**
Tetas, Pta. **94 A2**
Tete **59 B6**
Teterev ➔ **17 C10**
Teteven **22 C5**
Tetiyev **17 D9**
Tétouan **52 A4**
Tetovo **22 C3**
Teuco ➔ **94 B4**
Teun **37 F3**
Teutoburger Wald **14 B5**
Tevere ➔ **20 D4**
Tewantin **63 A5**
Texarkana **81 C6**
Texas **63 A5**
Texas □ **80 D4**
Texas City **81 E6**
Texel **14 B3**
Teyvareh **45 C6**
Tezpur **41 D9**
Thabana Ntlenyana **59 D5**
Thabazimbi **59 C5**
Thailand ■ **38 A2**
Thailand, G. of **38 B2**
Thakhek **38 A2**
Thal **42 C7**
Thala La = Hkakabo Razi **41 C11**
Thallon **63 A4**
Thames **64 B6**
Thames ➔ **11 F7**
Thandwe **41 H10**
Thane **43 K8**
Thanh Pho Ho Chi Minh **38 B3**
Thanjavur **43 P11**
Thar Desert **42 F7**
Tharad **43 G7**
Thargomindah **63 A3**
Tharrawaddy **41 J10**
Thasos **23 D5**
Thaton **41 J11**
Thaungdut **41 E10**
Thayetmyo **41 H10**
Thazi **41 G11**
The Gulf = Persian Gulf **44 E2**
The Hague = 's-Gravenhage **14 B3**
The Pas **69 C9**
The Wash **11 E7**
Thebes = Thiva **23 E4**
Theebine **63 A5**
Thermopylae **23 E4**
Thessaloniki **23 D4**
Thessaloniki, Gulf of = Thessaloniki Kolpos **23 D4**
Thessaloniki Kolpos **23 D4**
Thetford **11 E7**
Thetford Mines **71 E6**
Thevenard **62 B1**
Thiel Mts. **96 C2**
Thiers **13 D5**
Thiès **53 F2**
Thika **57 E7**
Thimphu **41 D7**
Thionville **13 B7**
Thira = Santorini **23 F5**
Thiruvananthapuram = Trivandrum **43 Q10**
Thistle I. **62 C2**
Thiva **23 E4**
Þjórsá ➔ **8 C1**
Thohoyandou **59 C6**
Thomas, L. **62 A2**
Thomasville *Ga., U.S.A.* **83 D6**
Thomasville *N.C., U.S.A.* **83 B7**
Thompson **69 C10**
Thrace **22 D6**
Three Hummock I. **62 D3**
Three Points, C. **53 H5**
Thunder Bay **71 E5**
Thung Song **38 C1**
Thunkar **41 D8**
Thüringer Wald **14 C6**
Thurles **11 E3**
Thurloo Downs **63 A3**
Thurso **10 B5**
Thurston I. **96 B2**
Thylungra **63 A3**
Tia **63 B5**
Tian Shan **34 B3**
Tianjin **35 C6**
Tianshui **35 C5**
Tiaret **52 A6**
Tiber = Tevere ➔ **20 D4**
Tiberias, L. = Yam Kinneret **46 D3**
Tibesti **54 D2**
Tibet = Xizang Zizhiqu □ **34 C3**
Tibooburra **62 A3**
Tiburón, I. **84 B2**
Ticino ➔ **13 D8**
Tiddim **41 F9**
Tidjikja **53 E3**
Tidore **37 D3**
Tien Shan = Tian Shan **34 B3**
Tien-tsin = Tianjin **35 C6**
T'ienching = Tianjin **35 C6**
Tientsin = Tianjin **35 C6**
Tierra de Campos **18 A3**
Tierra del Fuego, I. Gr. de **95 G3**
Tiétar ➔ **18 C2**

Tieyon 62 A1
Tifu 37 E3
Tighina 17 E9
Tigre ➔ 90 D4
Tigris = Dijlah, Nahr ➔ 47 E6
Tigyaing 41 F11
Tijuana 84 A1
Tikamgarh 43 G11
Tikhoretsk 25 D5
Tikiraqjuaq = Whale Cove 68 B10
Tikrīt 46 D5
Tiksi 30 B10
Tilamuta 37 D2
Tilburg 14 C3
Tilos 23 F6
Tilpa 63 B3
Timaru 65 F4
Timbuktu = Tombouctou 53 E5
Timimoun 52 C6
Timiris, Râs 53 E2
Timişoara 16 F5
Timmins 71 E5
Timok ➔ 22 B4
Timor 37 F2
Timor Leste = East Timor ■ 37 F3
Tinaca Pt. 36 C3
Tindouf 52 C4
Tingo Maria 91 E3
Tinian 64 H9
Tinjoub 52 C4
Tinnevelly = Tirunelveli 43 Q10
Tinogasta 94 B3
Tinos 23 F5
Tintinara 62 C3
Tioman, Pulau 39 D2
Tipongpani 41 D10
Tipperary 11 E2
Tirān 44 C2
Tiranë 22 D2
Tiraspol 17 E9
Tire 23 E6
Tirebolu 25 E4
Tiree 10 C3
Tîrgovişte = Târgovişte 22 B5
Tîrgu Jiu = Târgu Jiu 17 F6
Tîrgu Mureş = Târgu Mureş 17 E7
Tirich Mir 42 A7
Tiritiri o te Moana = Southern Alps 65 E4
Tirnavos 23 E4
Tirodi 43 J11
Tirol □ 14 E6
Tirso ➔ 21 E2
Tiruchchirappalli 43 P11
Tirunelveli 43 Q10
Tirupati 43 N11
Tiruppur 43 P10
Tiruvannamalai 43 N11
Tisa ➔ 22 B3
Tisdale 69 C9
Tisza = Tisa ➔ 22 B3
Tit-Ary 30 B10
Titicaca, L. 91 G5
Titule 57 D5
Tivaouane 53 F2
Tívoli 20 D4
Tiwī 45 F4
Tizi-Ouzou 52 A6
Tjirebon = Cirebon 39 F3
Tlaxiaco 84 D5
Tlemcen 52 B5
Toamasina 59 B9
Toay 94 D4
Toba Kakar 42 D6
Tobago 87 D7
Tobelo 37 D3
Tobermory 10 C3
Tobias Fornier 36 B2
Toboali 39 E3
Tobol ➔ 29 D7
Toboli 37 E2
Tobolsk 29 D7
Tobruk = Tubruq 54 B3
Tobyl = Tobol ➔ 29 D7
Tocantinópolis 92 D4
Tocantins □ 93 E4
Tocantins ➔ 92 C4
Tocumwal 63 C4
Tocuyo ➔ 90 A5
Todeli 37 E2
Todos os Santos, B. de 93 E6
Togian, Kepulauan 37 E2
Togliatti 24 C6
Togo ■ 53 G6
Toili 37 E2
Toinya 55 G4
Tojikiston = Tajikistan ■ 29 F8
Tojo 37 E2
Tokala 37 E2
Tōkamachi 33 E6
Tokanui 65 G3
Tokarahi 65 F4
Tokat 46 B4
Tokdo = Liancourt Rocks 33 E2
Tokelau Is. 65 K13
Tokmak 29 E8
Tokushima 33 F4
Tokuyama 33 F2
Tōkyō 33 F6
Tolaga Bay 64 C8
Tolbukhin = Dobrich 22 C6
Toledo *Spain* 18 C3
Toledo *U.S.A.* 76 D4
Toledo, Montes de 18 C3
Toliara 59 C8
Tolima 90 C3
Tolitoli 37 D2
Tolo, Teluk 37 E2
Toluca 84 D5
Tomakomai 32 B7
Tomar 18 C1
Tomaszów Mazowiecki 16 C4
Tombouctou 53 E5
Tombua 58 B2
Tomelloso 18 C4
Tomini 37 D2
Tomini, Teluk 37 E2
Tomorit 23 D3
Tomsk 29 D9
Tonantins 90 D5
Tondano 37 D2
Tonekābon 44 B2
Tonga ■ 65 L13
Tonga Trench 65 L13
Tongareva = Penrhyn 65 K15
Tongariro △ 64 C6
Tongchuan 35 C5
Tonghua 35 B7
Tongjiang 35 B8
Tongking, G. of = Tonkin, G. of 35 D5
Tongoy 94 C2
Tongsa Dzong 41 D8
Tongue ➔ 74 B2
Tonk 42 F9
Tonkin, G. of 35 D5
Tonle Sap 38 B2
Tonnégrande 30 E
Toompine 63 A3
Toora 63 C4
Toowoomba 63 A5
Topeka 75 F7
Topki 29 D9
Topolobampo 84 B3
Torata 91 G4
Torbalı 23 E6
Torbat-e Heydārīyeh 44 C4
Torbat-e Jām 45 C5
Torbay □ 11 F5
Tordesillas 18 B3
Torgau 15 C7
Torino 13 D7
Torit 55 H5
Tormes ➔ 18 B2
Torneå = Tornio 8 E12
Torneälven ➔ 8 B10
Torneträsk 8 B9
Tornio 8 E12
Tornionjoki = Torneälven ➔ 8 B10
Tornquist 94 D4
Toro, Cerro del 94 B3
Toronto 71 E6
Toropets 24 B3
Tororo 57 D6
Toros Dağları 46 C3
Torre de Moncorvo 18 B2
Torre del Greco 21 D5
Torrejón de Ardoz 18 B4
Torrelavega 18 A3
Torremolinos 18 D3
Torrens, L. 62 B2
Torrent 19 C5
Torreón 84 B4
Torres Vedras 18 C1
Torrevieja 19 D5
Tortosa 19 B6
Tortosa, C. 19 B6
Toruď 44 C3
Toruń 16 B4
Tosa-Wan 33 G3
Toscana □ 20 C3
Toshkent 29 E7
Tostado 94 B4
Tosya 46 B3
Totma 24 A5
Totten Glacier 96 A12
Tottenham 63 B4
Tottori 33 F4
Toubkal, Djebel 52 B4
Tougan 53 F5
Tougguort 52 B7
Toul 13 B6
Toulon 13 E6
Toulouse 12 E4
Toummo 54 D1
Toungoo 41 H11
Touraine 12 C4
Tourcoing 13 A5
Touriñán, C. 18 A1
Tournai 14 C2
Tournon-sur-Rhône 13 D6
Tours 12 C4
Towada 32 C7
Towada-Ko 32 C7
Towamba 63 C4
Towang 41 D8
Townsville 61 D8
Toya-Ko 32 B7
Toyama 33 E5
Toyama-Wan 33 E5
Toyohashi 33 F5
Toyooka 33 F4
Toyota 33 F5
Tozeur 52 B7
Tozkhurmato 46 D6
Trá Lí = Tralee 11 E2
Trabzon 25 E4
Trafalgar, C. 18 D2
Trail 69 D8
Tralee 11 E2
Trancas 94 B3
Trang 38 C1
Trangan 37 F4
Trangie 63 B4
Trani 20 D6
Transantarctic Mts. 96 C3
Transilvania 17 F7
Transilvanian Alps = Carpaţii Meridionali 17 F7
Transylvania = Transilvania 17 F7
Trápani 21 E4
Traralgon 63 C4
Trasimeno, L. 20 C4
Traun 15 D8
Travemünde 15 B6
Travers, Mt. 65 E5
Travnik 20 B6
Trébbia ➔ 13 D8
Třebíč 16 D2
Trebinje 20 C7
Treinta y Tres 94 C6
Trelew 95 E3
Tremp 19 A6
Trenque Lauquen 94 D4
Trent ➔ 11 E6
Trento 20 A3
Trenton 77 D8
Tres Arroyos 94 D4
Três Lagoas 93 G3
Tres Montes, C. 95 F1
Tres Puntas, C. 95 F3
Três Rios 93 G5

Treviso 20 B4
Triabunna 62 D4
Trichinopoly = Tiruchchirappalli 43 P11
Trichur 43 P10
Trida 63 B4
Trier 14 D4
Trieste 20 B4
Triglav 20 A4
Trikala 23 E3
Trikora, Puncak 37 E5
Trinidad *Bolivia* 91 F6
Trinidad *Cuba* 86 B3
Trinidad *Uruguay* 94 C5
Trinidad *U.S.A.* 80 A1
Trinidad & Tobago ■ 87 D7
Trinity ➔ 81 E6
Trinity B. 71 E8
Trinity Range 72 F4
Trinkitat 55 E6
Tripoli = Tarābulus *Lebanon* 46 D3
Tripoli = Tarābulus *Libya* 54 B1
Tripoli 23 F4
Tripura □ 41 F8
Trivandrum 43 Q10
Troglav 20 C6
Trois-Rivières 71 E6
Troitsko Pechorsk 28 C6
Trollhättan 9 D8
Tromsø 8 B9
Tronador, Mte. 95 E2
Trondheim 8 C8
Trondheimsfjorden 8 C8
Trout L. 68 B7
Trouville-sur-Mer 12 B4
Troy *Turkey* 23 E6
Troy *Ala., U.S.A.* 82 D5
Troy *N.Y., U.S.A.* 77 C9
Troyes 13 B6
Trucial States = United Arab Emirates ■ 44 F3
Trudovoye 32 B3
Trujillo *Honduras* 85 D7
Trujillo *Peru* 91 E3
Trujillo *Spain* 18 C3
Trujillo *Venezuela* 90 B4
Truk 64 J10
Trundle 63 B4
Truro *Canada* 71 E7
Truro *U.K.* 11 F4
Truskavets 17 D6
Trutnov 16 C2
Tsaratanana 59 B9
Tsetserleg 34 B5
Tshabong 58 D4
Tshane 58 C4
Tshela 56 E2
Tshikapa 56 F4
Tshwane = Pretoria 59 D5
Tsiigehtchic 68 B6
Tsimlyansk Res. = Tsimlyanskoye Vdkhr. 25 D5
Tsimlyanskoye Vdkhr. 25 D5
Tsinan = Jinan 35 C6
Tsinghai = Qinghai □ 34 C4
Tsingtao = Qingdao 35 C7
Tsirigo = Kythira 23 F4
Tskhinvali 25 E5
Tsna ➔ 24 C5
Tsuchiura 33 E7
Tsugaru-Kaikyō 32 C7
Tsumeb 58 B3
Tsuruga 33 F5
Tsuruoka 32 D6
Tsushima 33 F1
Tsuyama 33 F4
Tsyelyakhany 17 B7
Tual 37 F4
Tuamotu, Îs. 65 L16
Tuamotu Arch. = Tuamotu, Îs. 65 L16
Tuamotu Ridge 65 M17
Tuao 36 A2
Tuapse 25 E4
Tuatapere 65 G2
Tubarão 94 B7
Tübingen 14 D5
Tubruq 54 B3
Tubuai, Îs. 65 M16
Tucacas 90 A5
Tucson 79 D7
Tucumcari 80 B2
Tucupita 90 B6
Tucuruí 92 C4
Tucuruí, Reprêsa de 92 C4
Tudela 19 A5
Tudmur 46 D4
Tuen 63 A4
Tuguegarao 36 A2
Tui 18 A1
Tukangbesi, Kepulauan 37 F2
Tuktoyaktuk 68 B6
Tukuyu 57 F6
Tula 24 C4
Tülak 45 C5
Tulare 78 B3
Tulcán 90 C3
Tulcea 17 F9
Tulchyn 17 D9
Tulita 68 B7
Tullamore *Australia* 63 B4
Tullamore *Ireland* 11 E3
Tulle 12 D4
Tullibigeal 63 B4
Tulsa 81 A6
Tulua 90 C3
Tum 37 E4
Tumaco 90 C3
Tumatumari 90 B7
Tumba, L. 56 E3
Tumbarumba 63 C4
Tumbes 90 D2
Tumby Bay 62 B2
Tumeremo 90 B6
Tumkur 43 N10
Tump 42 F3
Tumpat 38 C2
Tumu 53 F5
Tumucumaque, Serra 92 B3
Tumut 63 C4
Tuncurry 63 B5
Tundzha ➔ 22 D6
Tungabhadra ➔ 43 M11
Tunguska, Nizhnyaya ➔ 30 C6
Tunguska, Podkamennaya ➔ 30 C7
Tunis 50 A1
Tunisia ■ 50 B1
Tunja 90 B4
Tunuyán ➔ 94 C3
Tupelo 82 B3
Tupinambaranas 90 D7
Tupiza 94 A3
Tupungato, Cerro 94 C3
Túquerres 90 C3
Tura 30 C8
Turabah 47 E5
Türān 44 C4
Ţurayf 47 E4
Turek 16 B4
Turfan = Turpan 34 B3
Turfan Basin = Turpan Pendi 34 B3
Turfan Depression = Turpan Pendi 34 B3
Türgovishte 22 C6
Turgutlu 23 E6
Turhal 46 B4
Turia ➔ 19 C5
Turiaçu 92 C4
Turiaçu ➔ 92 C4
Turin = Torino 13 D7
Turkana, L. 57 D7
Turkestan = Türkistan 29 E7
Turkey ■ 25 F4
Türkistan 29 E7
Türkmenabat 29 F7
Türkmenbashi 29 E6
Turkmenistan ■ 29 F6
Turks & Caicos Is. ⊠ 87 B5
Turku 9 C10
Turnagain, C. 64 D7
Turneffe Is. 85 D7
Turnhout 14 C3
Türnovo = Veliko Türnovo 22 C5
Turnu Măgurele 22 C5
Turnu Roşu, P. 17 F7
Turpan 34 B3
Turpan Pendi 34 B3
Turukhansk 30 C6
Tuscaloosa 82 C4
Tuscany = Toscana □ 20 C3
Tuticorin 43 Q11
Tutóia 92 C5
Tutong 38 D4
Tutrakan 22 B6
Tuttlingen 14 E5
Tutuala 37 F3
Tutuila 65 L13
Tutume 59 C5
Tuvalu ■ 64 K12
Tuxpan 84 C5
Tuxtla Gutiérrez 85 D6
Tuy = Tui 18 A1
Tuz Gölü 46 C3
Ţūz Khurmātū = Tozkhurmato 46 D6
Tuzla 20 B7
Tver 24 B4
Tweed Heads 63 A5
Twin Falls 73 E6
Twofold B. 63 C4
Tyachiv 17 D6
Tychy 16 C4
Tyler 81 C6
Tyre = Sür 46 D3
Tyrol = Tirol □ 14 E6
Tyrrell ➔ 62 C3
Tyrrell, L. 62 C3
Tyrrhenian Sea 21 E4
Tyumen 29 D7
Tzaneen 59 C6
Tzukong = Zigong 35 D5

U

U.S.A. = United States of America ■ 67 F10
Uato-Udo 37 F3
Uatumã ➔ 90 D7
Uaupés 90 D5
Uaupés ➔ 90 C5
Ubá 93 G5
Ubaitaba 93 E6
Ubangi = Oubangi ➔ 56 E3
Ubauro 42 E6
Ube 33 G2
Úbeda 18 C4
Uberaba 93 F4
Uberlândia 93 F4
Ubon Ratchathani 38 A2
Ubort ➔ 17 B9
Ubundu 57 E5
Ucayali ➔ 90 D4
Uchiura-Wan 32 B7
Udagamandalam 43 P10
Udaipur 43 G8
Udaipur Garhi 40 D6
Udgir 43 K10
Udhampur 42 C9
Údine 20 A4
Udmurtia □ 28 D6
Udon Thani 38 A2
Udupi 43 N9
Uele ➔ 57 D4
Uelzen 14 B6
Ufa 29 D6
Ugab ➔ 58 C2
Ugalla ➔ 57 F6
Uganda ■ 57 D6
Ugljan 20 B5
Ugolyak 30 C10
Uibhist a Deas = South Uist 10 C3
Uibhist a Tuath = North Uist 10 C3
Uíge 56 F2
Uinta Mts. 73 F8
Uitenhage 59 E5
Ujjain 43 H9
Ujung Pandang 37 F1
Ukhrul 41 E10
Ukhta 28 C6
Ukraine ■ 25 D3
Ulaanbaatar 35 B5
Ulaangom 34 A4

Ulaanjirem **35 B5**
Ulan Bator = Ulaanbaatar **35 B5**
Ulan Ude **30 D8**
Ulcinj **22 D2**
Ule älv = Oulujoki ➔ **8 B11**
Ule träsk = Oulujärvi **8 C11**
Uleåborg = Oulu **8 B11**
Ulhasnagar **43 K8**
Uliastay **34 B4**
Ulladulla **63 C5**
Ullapool **10 C4**
Ulleungdo **33 E2**
Ulm **14 D5**
Ulmarra **63 A5**
Ulster □ **11 D3**
Ulubat Gölü **23 D7**
Uludağ **23 D7**
Ulungur He ➔ **34 B3**
Uluru **60 F5**
Ulutau **29 E7**
Ulverstone **62 D4**
Ulyanovsk = Simbirsk **24 C6**
Ulyasutay = Uliastay **34 B4**
Umala **91 G5**
'Umān = Oman ■ **48 C6**
Uman **17 D10**
Umaria **40 F3**
Umarkot **43 G6**
Umbrella Mts. **65 F3**
Umeå **8 C10**
Umeälven ➔ **8 C10**
Umera **37 E3**
Umlazi **59 E6**
Umm al Qaywayn **44 E3**
Umm Durman = Omdurmān **55 E5**
Umm Lajj **47 F4**
Umm Ruwaba **55 F5**
Umnak I. **69 C3**
Umniati ➔ **59 B5**
Umtata = Mthatha **59 E5**
Umuarama **93 G3**
Umzimvubu **59 E5**
Una ➔ **20 B6**
Unalaska **69 C3**
Uncía **91 G5**
Underbool **62 C3**
Ungarie **63 B4**
Ungarra **62 B2**
Ungava, Pén. d' **70 C6**
Ungava B. **70 D7**
Ungeny = Ungheni **17 E8**
Ungheni **17 E8**
Ungwana B. **57 E8**
União da Vitória **94 B6**
Unimak I. **69 C3**
United Arab Emirates ■ **44 F3**
United Kingdom ■ **11 D5**
United States of America ■ **67 F10**
Unnao **40 D3**
Unst **10 A6**
Ünye **46 B4**
Upata **90 B6**
Upemba, L. **57 F5**
Upington **58 D4**
Upper Hutt **65 D6**
Upper Volta = Burkina Faso ■ **53 F5**
Uppsala **9 D9**
Uqsuqtuuq = Gjoa Haven **68 B10**
Ur **47 E6**
Ural = Zhayyq ➔ **29 E6**
Ural **63 B4**
Ural Mts. = Uralskie Gory **28 D6**
Uralla **63 B5**
Uralsk = Oral **24 C7**
Uralskie Gory **28 D6**
Uranquinty **63 C4**
Uray **29 C7**
Urbana **76 D1**
Urbino **20 C4**
Urbión, Picos de **19 A4**
Urcos **91 F4**
Urda **25 D6**
Urewera △ **64 C7**
Urfa = Sanliurfa **46 C4**
Urganch **29 E7**
Urgench = Urganch **29 E7**
Uribia **90 A4**
Urla **23 E6**
Urmia = Orümīyeh **46 C6**
Uroševac **22 C3**
Urubamba ➔ **91 F4**
Uruçara **90 D7**
Uruçuí **92 D5**
Uruguai ➔ **94 B6**
Uruguaiana **94 B5**
Uruguay ■ **94 C5**
Uruguay ➔ **94 C5**
Urumchi = Ürümqi **29 E9**
Ürümqi **29 E9**
Ürzhar **29 E9**
Usakos **58 C3**
Usedom **15 B8**
Ushant = Ouessant, Î. d' **12 B1**
Ushibuka **33 G2**
Üshtöbe **29 E8**
Ushuaia **95 G3**
Usman **24 C4**
Uspallata, P. de **94 C3**
Uspenskiy **29 E8**
Ussuriysk **32 B2**
Ust-Ishim **29 D8**
Ust-Kamenogorsk = Öskemen **29 E9**
Ust-Karenga **31 D9**
Ust-Kuyga **31 B11**
Ust Muya **30 D9**
Ust-Olenek **30 B10**
Ust-Port **28 C9**
Ust-Tsilma **28 C6**
Ust-Urt = Ustyurt Plateau **29 E6**
Ústí nad Labem **16 C2**
Ústica **21 E4**
Ustinov = Izhevsk **28 D6**
Ustye **30 D7**
Ustyurt Plateau **29 E6**
Usu **34 B3**
Usumacinta ➔ **85 D6**
Usumbura = Bujumbura **57 E5**
Uta **37 E5**
Utah □ **73 G8**
Utiariti **91 F7**
Utica **77 C8**
Utrecht **14 B3**
Utrera **18 D3**
Utsunomiya **33 E6**
Uttar Pradesh □ **42 F11**
Uttaradit **38 A2**
Uusikaupunki **9 C10**
Uvat **29 D7**
Uvinza **57 F6**
Uvira **57 E5**
Uvs Nuur **34 A4**
'Uwairidh, Ḥarrat al **47 F4**
Uwajima **33 G3**
Uyuni **91 H5**
Uzbekistan ■ **29 E7**
Uzerche **12 D4**
Uzh ➔ **17 C10**
Uzhgorod = Uzhhorod **17 D6**
Uzhhorod **17 D6**
Užice **22 C2**
Uzunköprü **22 D6**

V

Vaal ➔ **58 D4**
Vaasa **8 C10**
Vác **16 E4**
Vach = Vakh ➔ **29 C8**
Vadodara **43 H8**
Vadsø **8 D13**
Vaduz **13 C8**
Vahsel B. **96 B5**
Váhtjer = Gällivare **8 B10**
Vaigach **28 B6**
Vakh ➔ **29 C8**
Val-d'Or **71 E6**
Valahia **22 B5**
Valandovo **22 D4**
Valcheta **95 E3**
Valdai Hills = Valdayskaya Vozvyshennost **24 B3**
Valdayskaya Vozvyshennost **24 B3**
Valdepeñas **18 C4**
Valdés, Pen. de **94 C3**
Valdez **69 B5**
Valdivia **95 D2**
Valdosta **83 D6**
Valença **93 E6**
Valença do Piauí **92 D5**
Valence **13 D6**
Valencia *Spain* **19 C5**
Valencia *Venezuela* **90 A5**
Valencia □ **19 C5**
Valencia, G. de **19 C6**
Valencia de Alcántara **18 C2**
Valencia I. **11 F1**
Valenciennes **13 A5**
Valentim, Sa. do **92 D5**
Valera **90 B4**
Valjevo **22 B2**
Vall de Uxó = La Vall d'Uixó **19 C5**
Valladolid *Mexico* **85 C7**
Valladolid *Spain* **18 B3**
Valle de la Pascua **90 B5**
Valledupar **90 A4**
Vallejo **72 G2**
Vallenar **94 B2**
Valletta **21 G5**
Valls **19 B6**
Valognes **12 B3**
Valona = Vlorë **23 D2**
Valozhyn **17 A8**
Valparaíso **94 C2**
Vals, Tanjung **37 F5**
Valsad **43 J8**
Valverde del Camino **18 D2**
Van **46 C5**
Van, L. = Van Gölü **46 C5**
Van Gölü **46 C5**
Van Rees, Pegunungan **37 E5**
Vanadzor **25 E5**
Vancouver *Canada* **69 D7**
Vancouver *U.S.A.* **72 D2**
Vancouver I. **69 D7**
Vänern **9 D8**
Vangaindrano **59 C9**
Vännäs **8 C9**
Vannes **12 C2**
Vanrhynsdorp **58 E3**
Vantaa ➔ **9 C11**
Vanua Levu **64 L12**
Vanuatu ■ **64 L11**
Vapnyarka **17 D9**
Varanasi **40 E4**
Varangerfjorden **8 A11**
Varaždin **20 A6**
Varberg **9 D8**
Vardak □ **45 C7**
Vardar = Axios ➔ **23 D4**
Varese **13 D8**
Varna **22 C6**
Varzaneh **44 C3**
Vasa = Vaasa **8 C10**
Vasa Barris ➔ **93 E6**
Vascongadas = País Vasco □ **19 A4**
Vasht = Khāsh **42 E2**
Vasilevichi **17 B9**
Vasilkov = Vasylkiv **17 C10**
Västerås **9 D9**
Västerdalälven ➔ **8 C8**
Västervik **9 D9**
Vasto **20 C5**
Vasylkiv **17 C10**
Vatican City ■ **20 D4**
Vatnajökull **8 C2**
Vatra-Dornei **17 E7**
Vättern **9 D8**
Vaupés = Uaupés ➔ **90 C5**
Vawkavysk **17 B7**
Vaygach, Ostrov **28 C6**
Vedea ➔ **22 C5**
Vega **8 B8**
Vegreville **69 C8**
Vejer de la Frontera **18 D3**
Velebit Planina **20 B5**
Veles **22 D3**
Vélez-Málaga **18 D3**
Vélez Rubio **19 D4**
Velhas ➔ **93 F5**
Velika Kapela **20 B5**

Velikaya ➔ 24 B2
Veliki Ustyug 24 A6
Velikiye Luki 24 B3
Veliko Türnovo 22 C5
Velikonda Range 43 M11
Velletri 20 D4
Vellore 43 N11
Venado Tuerto 94 C4
Vendée □ 12 C3
Vendôme 12 C4
Venézia 20 B4
Venézia, G. di 20 B4
Venezuela ■ 90 B5
Venezuela, G. de 90 A4
Vengurla 43 M8
Venice = Venézia 20 B4
Venkatapuram 40 H3
Ventoténe 21 D4
Ventoux, Mt. 13 D6
Ventspils 24 B1
Ventuarí ➔ 90 C5
Ventura 78 C3
Venus B. 63 C4
Vera *Argentina* 94 B4
Vera *Spain* 19 D5
Veracruz 84 D5
Veraval 43 J7
Verbánia 13 D8
Vercelli 13 D8
Verde ➔ 95 E3
Verden 14 B5
Verdun 13 B6
Vereeniging 59 D5
Verga, C. 53 F3
Veria 23 D4
Verín 18 B2
Verkhnevilyuysk 30 C10
Verkhniy Baskunchak 25 D6
Verkhoyansk 31 C11
Verkhoyansk Ra. = Verkhoyanskiy Khrebet 31 C10
Verkhoyanskiy Khrebet 31 C10
Vermont □ 77 C9
Vernon *Canada* 69 C8
Vernon *U.S.A.* 80 B4
Véroia = Veria 23 D4
Verona 20 B3
Versailles 12 B5
Vert, C. 53 F2
Verviers 14 C3
Veselovskoye Vdkhr. 25 D5
Vesoul 13 C7
Vesterålen 8 B9
Vestfjorden 8 B8
Vesuvio 21 D5
Vesuvius, Mt. = Vesuvio 21 D5
Veszprém 16 E3
Vettore, Mte. 20 C4
Vezhen 22 C5
Viacha 91 G5
Viamão 94 C6
Viana 92 C5
Viana do Alentejo 18 C2
Viana do Castelo 18 B1
Viangchan = Vientiane 38 A2
Vianópolis 93 F4
Viaréggio 20 C3
Vibo Valéntia 21 E6
Vic 19 B7
Vicenza 20 B3
Vich = Vic 19 B7
Vichy 13 C5
Vicksburg 81 C8
Victor 43 J7
Victor Harbor 62 C2
Victoria *Canada* 69 D7
Victoria *Chile* 94 D2
Victoria □ 62 C3
Victoria, L. *Africa* 57 E6
Victoria, L. *Australia* 62 B3
Victoria, Mt. 41 G9
Victoria de Durango = Durango 84 C4
Victoria Falls 59 B5
Victoria I. 68 A8
Victoria Ld. 96 B14
Victorica 94 D3
Vicuña 94 C2
Vidin 22 C4
Vidisha 43 H10
Viedma 95 E4
Viedma, L. 95 F2
Vienna = Wien 15 D9
Vienne 13 D6
Vienne ➔ 12 C4
Vientiane 38 A2
Vierzon 12 C5
Vietnam ■ 38 A3
Vieux-Fort, Pte. du 30 C
Vigan 36 A2
Vigévano 13 D8
Vigia 92 C4
Vigo 18 A1
Vijayawada 40 J3
Vijosë ➔ 23 D2
Vikeke = Viqueque 37 F3
Vikna 8 C8
Vila do Bispo 18 D1
Vila Franca de Xira 18 C1
Vila Nova de Gaia 18 B1
Vila Real 18 B2
Vila-real de los Infantes 19 C5
Vila Real de Santo António 18 D2
Vila Velha 93 G5
Vilagarcía de Arousa 18 A1
Vilaine ➔ 12 C2
Vilanculos 59 C7
Vilanova i la Geltrú 19 B6
Vileyka 17 A8
Vilhelmina 8 C9
Vilhena 91 F6
Vilkitskogo, Proliv 30 B8
Vilkovo = Vylkove 17 F9
Villa Ángela 94 B4
Villa Bella 91 F5
Villa de María 94 B4
Villa Dolores 94 C3
Villa Hayes 94 B5
Villa María 94 C4
Villa Mazán 94 B3
Villa Montes 94 A4
Villa Ocampo 94 B5
Villacarrillo 18 C4
Villach 15 E7
Villaguay 94 C5
Villahermosa 85 D6
Villajoyosa 19 C5
Villalba 18 A2
Villanueva de la Serena 18 C3
Villanueva y Geltrú = Vilanova i la Geltrú 19 B6
Villarreal = Vila-real de los Infantes 19 C5
Villarrica *Chile* 95 D2
Villarrica *Paraguay* 94 B5
Villarrobledo 19 C4
Villavicencio 90 C4
Villaviciosa 18 A3
Villazón 94 A3
Villena 19 C5
Villeneuve-d'Ascq 13 A5
Villeneuve-sur-Lot 12 D4
Villingen-Schwenningen 14 D5
Vilnius 24 C2
Vilyuy ➔ 31 C10
Vilyuysk 31 C10
Viña del Mar 94 C2
Vinarós 19 B6
Vindhya Ra. 43 H10
Vineland 77 E8
Vinkovci 20 B7
Vinnitsa = Vinnytsya 17 D9
Vinnytsya 17 D9
Viqueque 37 F3
Virac 36 B2
Viramgam 43 H8
Virden 69 D9
Vire 12 B3
Vírgenes, C. 95 G3
Virgin Is. (British) ☑ 87 C7
Virginia 59 D5
Virginia □ 77 F6
Virginia Beach 77 F8
Virovitica 20 B6
Virudunagar 43 Q10
Vis 20 C6
Visalia 78 B3
Visayan Sea 36 B2
Visby 9 D9
Viscount Melville Sd. 70 B3
Višegrad 20 C7
Viseu *Brazil* 92 C4
Viseu *Portugal* 18 B2
Vishakhapatnam 40 J4
Viso, Mte. 13 D7
Vistula = Wisła ➔ 16 A4
Vitebsk = Vitsyebsk 24 B3
Viterbo 20 C4
Viti Levu 64 L12
Vitigudino 18 B2
Vitória 93 G5
Vitória da Conquista 93 E5
Vitoria-Gasteiz 19 A4
Vitsyebsk 24 B3
Vittória 21 F5
Vittório Véneto 20 B4
Viveiro 18 A2
Vize 22 D6
Vizianagaram 40 H4
Vladikavkaz 25 E5
Vladimir 24 B5
Vladimir Volynskiy = Volodymyr-Volynskyy 17 C7
Vladivostok 32 B2
Vlissingen 14 C2
Vlorë 23 D2
Vltava ➔ 16 C2
Vogelkop = Doberai, Jazirah 37 E4
Vogelsberg 14 C5
Voghera 13 D8
Vohimarina = Iharana 59 A10
Vohimena, Tanjon' i 59 D9
Voi 57 E7
Voiron 13 D6
Vojvodina □ 22 B2
Volga ➔ 25 D6
Volga Hts. = Privolzhskaya Vozvyshennost 24 C6
Volgodonsk 25 D5
Volgograd 25 D5
Volgogradskoye Vdkhr. 24 C6
Volkhov ➔ 24 A3
Volkovysk = Vawkavysk 17 B7
Volochanka 30 B7
Volodymyr-Volynskyy 17 C7
Vologda 24 B4
Volos 23 E4
Volovets 17 D6
Volozhin = Valozhyn 17 A8
Volsk 24 C6
Volta, L. 53 G6
Volta Redonda 93 G5
Volterra 20 C3
Volturno ➔ 20 D4
Volzhskiy 25 D5
Vorkuta 28 C7
Voronezh 24 C4
Vosges 13 B7
Vostok I. 65 L15
Vouga ➔ 18 B1
Voznesensk 25 D3
Vrangelya, Ostrov 31 B15
Vranje 22 C3
Vratsa 22 C4
Vrbas ➔ 20 B6
Vršac 22 B3
Vryburg 58 D4
Vryheid 59 D6
Vukovar 20 B7
Vulcan 17 F6
Vulcanești 17 F9
Vulcano 21 E5
Vulkaneshty = Vulcanești 17 F9
Vung Tau 38 B3
Vyatka = Kirov 28 D5
Vyatskiye Polyany 24 B7
Vyazma 24 B3
Vyborg 28 C3
Vychegda ➔ 28 C5
Vychodné Beskydy 17 D5
Vylkove 17 F9
Vynohradiv 17 D6
Vyshniy Volochek 24 B3
Vyškov 16 D3

W

Waal ➔ 14 C3
Wabash ➔ 76 F1
Waco 80 D5
Wad Hamid 55 E5
Wad Medanī 55 F5
Waddington, Mt. 69 C7
Waddy Pt. 63 A5
Wadi Halfa 54 D5
Wafrah 47 E6
Wager B. 70 C5
Wager Bay 70 C4
Wagga Wagga 63 C4
Waghete 37 E5
Wah 42 C8
Wahai 37 E3
Waiau ➔ 65 E5
Waibeem 37 E4
Waigeo 37 E4
Waihi 64 B6
Waihou ➔ 64 B6
Waikabubak 37 F1
Waikaremoana, L. 64 C7
Waikari 65 E5
Waikato ➔ 64 B6
Waikerie 62 B2
Waikokopu 64 C7
Waikouaiti 65 F4
Waimakariri ➔ 65 E5
Waimate 65 F4
Wainganga ➔ 43 K11
Waingapu 37 F2
Waiouru 64 C6
Waipara 65 E5
Waipawa 64 C7
Waipiro 64 C8
Waipoua Forest 64 A5
Waipu 64 A6
Waipukurau 64 D7
Wairakei 64 C7
Wairarapa, L. 65 D6
Wairoa 64 C7
Waitaki ➔ 65 F4
Waitangi 64 A6
Waitara 64 C6
Waitomo Caves 64 C6
Waiuku 64 B6
Wajima 33 E5
Wajir 57 D8
Wakasa-Wan 33 F4
Wakatipu, L. 65 F3
Wakayama 33 F4
Wakefield 65 D5
Wakkanai 32 A7
Wakool 63 C3
Wakool ➔ 62 C3
Wakre 37 E4
Wałbrzych 16 C3
Walcha 63 B5
Wałcz 16 B3
Wales □ 11 E4
Walgett 63 A4
Walgreen Coast 96 B1
Walla Walla 72 C4
Wallachia = Valahia 22 B5
Wallal 63 A4
Wallaroo 62 B2
Wallis & Futuna, Is. 64 L13
Wallowa Mts. 72 D5
Wallumbilla 63 A4
Walvis Bay 58 C2
Walvisbaai = Walvis Bay 58 C2
Wamba 57 D5
Wamena 37 E5
Wamulan 37 E3
Wana 42 C6
Wanaaring 63 A3
Wanaka 65 F3
Wanaka, L. 65 F3
Wandoan 63 A4
Wangal 37 F4
Wanganella 63 C3
Wanganui 64 C6
Wangaratta 63 C4
Wangary 62 B2
Wangerooge 14 B4
Wangiwangi 37 F2
Warangal 43 L11
Waratah 62 D4
Waratah B. 63 C4
Warburton 63 C4
Warburton ➔ 62 A2
Ward 65 D6
Ward ➔ 63 A4
Wardha 43 J11
Wardha ➔ 43 K11
Warialda 63 A5
Wariap 37 E4
Warkopi 37 E4
Warner Mts. 72 F3
Warracknabeal 62 C3
Warragul 63 C4
Warrego ➔ 63 B4
Warren *Australia* 63 B4
Warren *U.S.A.* 76 C4
Warrenville 63 A4
Warri 53 G7
Warrina 62 A2
Warrington *U.K.* 11 E5
Warrington *U.S.A.* 82 D4
Warrnambool 62 C3
Warsa 37 E5
Warsaw = Warszawa 16 B5
Warszawa 16 B5
Warta ➔ 16 B2
Warthe = Warta ➔ 16 B2
Waru 37 E4
Warwick 63 A5
Wasatch Ra. 73 F8
Wash, The 11 E7
Washim 43 J10
Washington 77 E7
Washington □ 72 C3
Washington, Mt. 77 B10
Wasian 37 E4
Wasior 37 E4
Waskaganish 71 D6
Wasserkuppe 14 C5
Watampone 37 E2
Waterbury 77 D9
Waterford 11 E3
Waterloo 75 D8
Watertown 77 C8
Waterville 77 B11
Watford 11 F6
Watling I. = San Salvador I. 86 B5
Watrous 69 C9
Watsa 57 D5
Watson Lake 68 B7
Watsonville 78 B2
Wattiwarriganna Cr. ➔ 62 A2
Watuata = Batuata 37 F2
Watubela, Kepulauan 37 E4
Watubela Is. = Watubela, Kepulauan 37 E4
Wau = Wāw 55 G4
Wauchope 63 B5
Waukegan 76 C2
Waukesha 76 C1
Wausau 75 C10
Wauwatosa 76 C2
Waverley 64 C6
Wāw 55 G4
Wāw al Kabīr 54 C2
Waxahachie 81 C5
Wayabula 37 D3
Wayatinah 62 D4
Waycross 83 D6
Wazirabad 42 C9
We 38 C1
Weda 37 D3
Weda, Teluk 37 D3
Weddell I. 95 G4
Weddell Sea 96 A4
Wedderburn 62 C3
Wee Waa 63 B4
Weemelah 63 A4
Weiden 15 D7
Weifang 35 C6
Weimar 15 C6
Weipa 61 C7
Weir ➔ 63 A4
Wejherowo 16 A4
Welbourn Hill 62 A1
Welkom 59 D5
Wellesley Is. 60 D6
Wellington *Australia* 63 B4
Wellington *N.Z.* 65 D6
Wellington, I. 95 F1
Wellington, L. 63 C4
Wellington Chan. 70 B4
Wels 15 D8
Welshpool 11 E5
Wemindji 71 D6
Wenatchee 72 C3
Wenchi 53 G5
Wenchow = Wenzhou 35 D7
Wendesi 37 E4
Wensu 34 B3
Wentworth 62 B3
Wenut 37 E4
Wenzhou 35 D7
Weri 37 E4
Werra ➔ 14 C5
Werrimull 62 B3
Werris Creek 63 B5
Wersar 37 E4
Weser ➔ 14 B5
Wesiri 37 F3
West Bank ■ 46 D3
West Bengal □ 40 F7
West Beskids = Západné Beskydy 16 D4
West Falkland 95 G4
West Fjord = Vestfjorden 8 B8
West Ice Shelf 96 A11
West Palm Beach 83 F7
West Pt. 62 C2
West Virginia □ 76 E5
West Wyalong 63 B4
Westall, Pt. 62 B1
Westbury 62 D4
Westerland 14 A5
Western Australia □ 60 F3
Western Dvina = Daugava ➔ 24 B1
Western Ghats 43 N9
Western Sahara ■ 52 D3
Western Samoa = Samoa ■ 65 L13
Western Sierra Madre = Madre Occidental, Sierra 84 B3
Westerwald 14 C4
Westland △ 65 E4
Westland Bight 65 E4
Weston-super-Mare 11 F5
Westport *Ireland* 11 E2
Westport *N.Z.* 65 D4
Westray 10 B5
Wetar 37 F3
Wetaskiwin 69 C8
Wetzlar 14 C5
Wevok 69 B3
Wexford 11 E3
Weyburn 69 D9
Weymouth 11 F5
Wha Ti 68 B8
Whakaari = White I. 64 B7
Whakatane 64 B7
Whale ➔ 70 D7
Whale Cove 68 B10
Whales, B. of 96 B16
Whangamata 64 B6
Whangamomona 64 C6
Whanganui △ 64 C6
Whangarei 64 A6
Whangarei Harb. 64 A6
Wheeling 76 D5
White ➔ *Ark., U.S.A.* 81 C8
White ➔ *Ind., U.S.A.* 76 E2
White Cliffs 62 B3
White I. 64 B7
White Nile = Nīl el Abyad ➔ 55 E5
White Russia = Belarus ■ 24 C2
White Sea = Beloye More 8 B13
Whitecliffs 65 E4
Whitehaven 11 D5
Whitehorse 68 B6
Whitemark 62 D4
Whitianga 64 B6
Whitney, Mt. 78 B3
Whittlesea 63 C4
Wholdaia L. 68 B9
Whyalla 62 B2
Whyjonta 62 A3
Wichita 80 A5
Wichita Falls 80 C4
Wick 10 B5
Wickham, C. 62 C3
Wicklow Mts. 11 E3

Wieluń 16 C4
Wien 15 D9
Wiener Neustadt 15 E9
Wiesbaden 14 C5
Wight, I. of 11 F6
Wilcannia 62 B3
Wildspitze 14 E6
Wilhelm, Mt. 61 B8
Wilhelm II Coast 96 A11
Wilhelmshaven 14 B5
Wilkes-Barre 77 D8
Willandra Creek → 63 B4
Willemstad 87 D6
William Creek 62 A2
Williams Lake 69 C7
Williamsburg 77 F7
Williamsport 77 D7
Williamstown 63 C3
Williston 74 A3
Willunga 62 C2
Wilmington *Australia* 62 B2
Wilmington *Del., U.S.A.* 77 E8
Wilmington *N.C., U.S.A.* 83 B9
Wilpena Cr. → 62 B2
Wilson 83 B9
Wilson → 62 A3
Wilsons Promontory 63 C4
Wimmera → 62 C3
Winchester 11 F6
Wind River Range 73 E9
Windau = Ventspils 24 B1
Windhoek 58 C3
Windsor *Australia* 63 B5
Windsor *Canada* 71 E5
Wingen 63 B5
Wingham 63 B5
Winisk → 71 D5
Winnipeg 69 D10
Winnipeg, L. 69 C10
Winnipegosis L. 69 C9
Winona 75 C9
Winston-Salem 83 A7
Winterthur 13 C8
Winton *Australia* 61 E7
Winton *N.Z.* 65 G3
Wirrulla 62 B1
Wisconsin □ 75 C10
Wisła → 16 A4
Wismar 15 B6
Witbank = eMalahleni 59 D5
Wittenberge 15 B6
Wkra → 16 B5
Włocławek 16 B4
Włodawa 17 C6
Wokam 37 F4
Wolfsberg 15 E8
Wolfsburg 15 B6
Wolin 16 B2
Wollaston, Is. 95 H3
Wollaston Pen. 68 B8
Wollongong 63 B5
Wolverhampton 11 E5
Wondai 63 A5
Wongalarroo L. 63 B3
Wönsan 35 C7
Wonthaggi 63 C4
Woocalla 62 B2
Woodburn 63 A5
Woodenbong 63 A5
Woodend 63 C3
Woodland 72 G3
Woodroffe, Mt. 60 F5
Woods, L. of the 69 D10
Woodstock 71 E7
Woodville 64 D6
Woolamai, C. 63 C4
Woolgoolga 63 B5
Woombye 63 A5
Woomera 62 B2
Worcester *S. Africa* 58 E3
Worcester *U.K.* 11 E5
Worcester *U.S.A.* 77 C10
Workington 11 D5
Worms 14 D5
Worthing 11 F6
Wosi 37 E3
Wou-han = Wuhan 35 C6
Wousi = Wuxi 35 C7
Wowoni 37 E2
Wrangel I. = Vrangelya, Ostrov 31 B15
Wrangell 69 C6
Wrangell Mts. 69 B5
Wrath, C. 10 B4
Wrexham 11 E5
Wright = Paranas 36 B3
Wrigley 68 B7
Wrocław 16 C3
Września 16 B3
Wu Jiang → 35 D5
Wuhan 35 C6
Wuhsi = Wuxi 35 C7
Wuhu 35 C6
Wukari 53 G7
Wuliaru 37 F4
Wulumuchi = Ürümqi 29 E9
Wuntho 41 F10
Wuppertal 14 C4
Würzburg 14 D5
Wutongqiao 34 D5
Wuwei 34 C5
Wuxi 35 C7
Wuyi Shan 35 D6
Wuzhong 35 C5
Wuzhou 35 D6
Wyandotte 76 C4
Wyandra 63 A4
Wyangala, L. 63 B4
Wyara, L. 63 A3
Wycheproof 62 C3
Wynbring 62 B1
Wyndham *Australia* 60 D4
Wyndham *N.Z.* 65 G3
Wynnum 63 A5
Wynyard 62 D4
Wyoming □ 73 E10
Wyong 63 B5

X

Xaafuun 49 E5
Xaafuun, Ras 49 E5
Xai-Xai 59 D6
Xainza 34 C3
Xalapa 84 D5
Xangongo 58 B3
Xankändi 25 F6
Xanthi 22 D5
Xapuri 91 F5
Xátiva 19 C5
Xi Jiang → 35 D6
Xiaguan 34 D5
Xiamen 35 D6
Xi'an 35 C5
Xiang Jiang → 35 D6
Xiangfan 35 C6
Xianggang = Hong Kong □ 35 D6
Xiangquan He = Sutlej → 42 E7
Xiangtan 35 D6
Xiao Hinggan Ling 35 B7
Xichang 34 D5
Xigazê 34 D3
Xing'an 35 D6
Xingu → 92 C3
Xining 34 C5
Xinjiang Uygur Zizhiqu □ 34 B3
Xinjin = Pulandian 35 C7
Xinxiang 35 C6
Xinyang 35 C6
Xinzhu 35 D7
Xique-Xique 93 E5
Xisha Qundao = Paracel Is. 38 A4
Xixabangma Feng 40 C5
Xixón = Gijón 18 A3
Xizang Zizhiqu □ 34 C3
Xuanhua 35 B6
Xúquer → 19 C5
Xuzhou 35 C6

Y

Ya'an 34 D5
Yaapeet 62 C3
Yablonovyy Khrebet 30 D9
Yablonovyy Ra. = Yablonovyy Khrebet 30 D9
Yacuiba 94 A4
Yadgir 43 L10
Yahuma 56 D4
Yakima 72 C3
Yakovlevka 32 A3
Yakumo 32 B7
Yakutat 69 C6
Yakutsk 31 C10
Yala 38 C2
Yalinga 55 G3
Yalong Jiang → 34 D5
Yalova 22 D7
Yalta 25 E3
Yalutorovsk 29 D7
Yam Ha Melaḥ = Dead Sea 47 E3
Yam Kinneret 46 D3
Yamagata 32 D7
Yamaguchi 33 F2
Yamal, Poluostrov 28 B8
Yamal Pen. = Yamal, Poluostrov 28 B8
Yamantau, Gora 29 D6
Yamba *N.S.W., Australia* 63 A5
Yamba *S. Austral., Australia* 62 B3
Yambiō 55 H4
Yambol 22 C6
Yamdena 37 F4
Yamethin 41 G11
Yamma Yamma, L. 62 A3
Yamoussoukro 53 G4
Yampil 17 D9
Yampol = Yampil 17 D9
Yamuna → 40 E3
Yamzho Yumco 34 D4
Yana → 31 B11
Yanac 62 C3
Yanbu 'al Baḥr 47 F4
Yancannia 62 B3
Yanco Cr. → 63 C4
Yandoon 41 J10
Yangambi 56 D4
Yangch'ü = Taiyuan 35 C6
Yangjiang 35 D6
Yangon = Rangoon 41 J11
Yangquan 35 C6
Yangtse = Chang Jiang → 35 C7
Yangtze Kiang = Chang Jiang → 35 C7
Yanji 35 B7
Yanna 63 A4
Yanqi 34 B3
Yantabulla 63 A4
Yantai 35 C7
Yanykurgan = Zhangaqūrghan 29 E7
Yaoundé 56 D2
Yapen 37 E5
Yapen, Selat 37 E5
Yaqui → 84 B2
Yar-Sale 28 C8
Yaraka 61 E7
Yaransk 24 B6
Yardea P.O. 62 B2
Yaremcha 17 D7
Yarensk 28 C5
Yari → 90 D4
Yarkand = Shache 34 C2
Yarkhun → 42 A8
Yarlung Ziangbo Jiang = Brahmaputra → 41 F7
Yarmouth 71 E7
Yaroslavl 24 B4
Yarram 63 C4
Yarraman 63 A5
Yarranvale 63 A4
Yarras 63 B5
Yartsevo 30 C7
Yaselda 17 B8
Yasinya 17 D7
Yass 63 B4
Yatağan 23 F7
Yathkyed L. 68 B10
Yatsushiro 33 G2
Yavari → 90 D4
Yavatmal 43 J11
Yavoriv 17 D6
Yavorov = Yavoriv 17 D6
Yawatahama 33 G3
Yazd 44 D3
Yazd □ 44 C3

Yazdān **45 C5**
Yazoo ➔ **81 C8**
Yebyu **41 K12**
Yecla **19 C5**
Yedintsy = Edineţ **17 D8**
Yeelanna **62 B2**
Yegros **94 B5**
Yei **55 H5**
Yekaterinburg **29 D7**
Yelarbon **63 A5**
Yelets **24 C4**
Yelizavetgrad = Kirovohrad **25 D3**
Yell **10 A6**
Yellow = Huang He ➔ **35 C6**
Yellow Sea **35 C7**
Yellowhead Pass **69 C8**
Yellowknife **68 B8**
Yellowstone ➔ **74 B3**
Yellowstone △ **73 D9**
Yelsk **17 C9**
Yemen ■ **49 D4**
Yenangyaung **41 G10**
Yenbo = Yanbu 'al Baḥr **47 F4**
Yenda **63 B4**
Yenice **23 E6**
Yenisey ➔ **28 B9**
Yeniseysk **30 D7**
Yeniseyskiy Zaliv **28 B9**
Yenyuka **31 D10**
Yeola **43 J9**
Yeovil **11 F5**
Yerbent **29 F6**
Yerevan **25 E5**
Yermak **29 D8**
Yershov **24 C6**
Yerushalayim = Jerusalem **47 E3**
Yessey **30 C8**
Yeu, Î. d' **12 C2**
Yevpatoriya **25 D3**
Yeysk **25 D4**
Yezd = Yazd **44 D3**
Yibin **35 D5**
Yichang **35 C6**
Yichun **35 B7**
Yilan **35 D7**
Yıldız Dağları **22 D6**
Yinchuan **35 C5**
Yingkou **35 B7**
Yining **29 E9**
Yinmabin **41 F10**
Yishan **35 D5**
Yiyang **35 D6**
Yog Pt. **36 B2**
Yogyakarta **39 F4**
Yokadouma **56 D2**
Yokkaichi **33 F5**
Yokohama **33 F6**
Yokosuka **33 F6**
Yola **55 G1**
Yonago **33 F3**
Yonibana **53 G3**
Yonkers **77 D9**
Yonne ➔ **13 B5**
York *U.K.* **11 E6**
York *U.S.A.* **77 E7**
York, C. **61 C7**
Yorke Pen. **62 B2**
Yorkton **69 C9**
Yos Sudarso, Pulau = Dolak, Pulau **37 F5**
Yosemite △ **78 B3**
Yoshkar Ola **24 B6**
Youghal **11 F3**
Young **63 B4**
Younghusband, L. **62 B2**
Younghusband Pen. **62 C2**
Youngstown **76 D5**
Yozgat **25 F3**
Ysyk-Köl **29 E8**
Yu Jiang ➔ **35 D6**
Yü Shan **35 D7**
Yuan Jiang ➔ **35 D6**
Yuba City **72 G3**
Yübetsu **32 A8**
Yucatán □ **85 C7**
Yucatán, Canal de **85 C7**
Yucatán, Península de **85 D7**
Yucatan Channel = Yucatán, Canal de **85 C7**
Yuci **35 C6**
Yugoslavia = Serbia ■ **22 B3**
Yukon ➔ **69 B3**
Yukon Territory □ **68 B6**
Yukta **30 C8**
Yuma **78 D5**
Yumen **34 C4**
Yungas **91 G5**
Yunnan □ **34 D5**
Yunta **62 B2**
Yurga **29 D9**
Yuribei **28 B8**
Yurimaguas **91 E3**
Yuryung Kaya **30 B9**
Yushu **34 C4**
Yuzhno-Sakhalinsk **31 E12**
Yvetot **12 B4**

Z

Zāb al Kabīr ➔ **46 C5**
Zāb aş Şaghīr ➔ **46 D5**
Zābol □ **45 D6**
Zābolī **45 E5**
Zabrze **16 C4**
Zacatecas **84 C4**
Zadar **20 B5**
Zadetkyi Kyun **38 C1**
Zafra **18 C2**
Żagań **16 C2**
Zagazig **54 B5**
Zagreb **20 B6**
Zāgros, Kūhhā-ye **44 C2**
Zagros Mts. = Zāgros, Kūhhā-ye **44 C2**
Zāhedān **45 D5**
Zahlah **46 D3**
Zaïre = Congo ➔ **56 F2**
Zaječar **22 C4**
Zakhodnaya Dzvina = Daugava ➔ **24 B1**
Zākhū **46 C5**
Zakinthos = Zakynthos **23 F3**
Zakynthos **23 F3**
Zalaegerszeg **16 E3**
Zalāu **17 E6**
Zaleshchiki = Zalishchyky **17 D7**
Zalew Wiślany **16 A4**
Zalingei **55 F3**
Zalishchyky **17 D7**
Zambeze ➔ **59 B7**
Zambezi = Zambeze ➔ **59 B7**
Zambezi **58 A4**
Zambia ■ **59 B5**
Zamboanga **36 C2**
Zamora *Mexico* **84 D4**
Zamora *Spain* **18 B3**
Zamość **17 C6**
Zanesville **76 E4**
Zanjān **46 C7**
Zanjān □ **46 C7**
Zante = Zakynthos **23 F3**
Zanzibar **57 F7**
Zaouiet El-Kala = Bordj Omar Driss **52 C7**
Zaouiet Reggâne **52 C6**
Zap Suyu = Zāb al Kabīr ➔ **46 C5**
Zapadnaya Dvina = Daugava ➔ **24 B1**
Západné Beskydy **16 D4**
Zaporizhzhya **25 D4**
Zaporozhye = Zaporizhzhya **25 D4**
Zara **46 C4**
Zaragoza **19 B5**
Zarand **44 D4**
Zaranj **42 D2**
Zaria **53 F7**
Zaruma **90 D3**
Žary **16 C2**
Zarzis **54 B1**
Zaskar Mts. **42 C10**
Zavāreh **44 C3**
Zawiercie **16 C4**
Zāwiyat al Bayḍā = Al Bayḍā **54 B3**
Zāyandeh ➔ **44 C3**
Zaysan **29 E9**
Zaysan Köli **29 E9**
Zbarazh **17 D7**
Zdolbuniv **17 C8**
Zduńska Wola **16 C4**
Zeebrugge **14 C2**
Zeehan **62 D4**
Zeila **49 E3**
Zeitz **15 C7**
Zelenograd **24 B4**
Zemun **22 B3**
Zenica **20 B6**
Žepče **20 B7**
Zêzere ➔ **18 C1**
Zgorzelec **16 C2**
Zhabinka **17 B7**
Zhailma **29 D7**
Zhambyl = Taraz **29 E8**
Zhangaqazaly **29 E7**
Zhangaqūrghan **29 E7**
Zhanghua **35 D7**
Zhangjiakou **35 B6**
Zhangye **34 C5**
Zhangzhou **35 D6**
Zhanjiang **35 D6**
Zhanyi **34 D5**
Zhaotong **34 D5**
Zharkent **29 E8**
Zhashkiv **17 D10**
Zhayyq ➔ **29 E6**
Zhdanov = Mariupol **25 D4**
Zhejiang □ **35 D7**
Zhengzhou **35 C6**
Zhezqazghan **29 E7**
Zhigansk **30 C10**
Zhilinda **30 B9**
Zhitomir = Zhytomyr **17 C9**
Zhlobin **17 B10**
Zhmerinka = Zhmerynka **17 D9**
Zhmerynka **17 D9**
Zhob **42 D6**
Zhodino = Zhodzina **17 A9**
Zhodzina **17 A9**
Zhongdian **34 D4**
Zhumadian **35 C6**
Zhytomyr **17 C9**
Zibo **35 C6**
Zielona Góra **16 C2**
Zigey **55 F2**
Zigong **35 D5**
Ziguinchor **53 F2**
Zile **46 B3**
Zillah **54 C2**
Zimbabwe ■ **59 B5**
Zimnicea **22 C5**
Zinder **53 F7**
Zion △ **79 B6**
Zirreh, Gowd-e **42 E3**
Zlatograd **22 D5**
Zlatoust **29 D6**
Zlín **16 D3**
Zmeinogorsk **29 D9**
Znojmo **16 D3**
Zolochev = Zolochiv **17 D7**
Zolochiv **17 D7**
Zomba **59 B7**
Zongo **56 D3**
Zonguldak **25 E3**
Zorritos **90 D2**
Zouar **54 D2**
Zouérate = Zouîrât **52 D3**
Zouîrât **52 D3**
Zrenjanin **22 B3**
Ẓufār **48 D5**
Zug **13 C8**
Zugspitze **14 E6**
Zumbo **59 B6**
Zunyi **35 D5**
Zürich **13 C8**
Zuwārah **54 B1**
Zvishavane **59 C6**
Zwelitsha **59 E5**
Zwettl **15 D8**
Zwickau **15 C7**
Zwolle **14 B4**
Żyrardów **16 B5**

Alaska (U.S.A.)
Arctic Circle
GREENLAND (Den.)
CANADA
North America
UNITED STATES
Chicago
Detroit
Toronto
Boston
New York
Philadelphia
Washington D.C.
San Francisco
Los Angeles
Dallas
Houston
Atlanta
Miami
BAHAMAS
CUBA
Bermuda (U.K.)
NORTH ATLANTIC OCEAN
Azores (Port.)
Canary Is. (Spain)
WESTERN SAHARA
MAURITANIA
MOROCCO
PORTUGAL
Tropic of Cancer
Hawaiian Is. (U.S.A.)
MEXICO
Mexico
BELIZE
GUATEMALA
HONDURAS
EL SALVADOR
NICARAGUA
COSTA RICA
PANAMA
JAMAICA
HAITI
DOM. REP.
Puerto Rico (U.S.A.)
ST. KITTS & NEVIS
ANTIGUA & BARBUDA
DOMINICA
ST. LUCIA
BARBADOS
ST. VINCENT
TRINIDAD & TOBAGO
VENEZUELA
GUYANA
SURINAM
FRENCH GUIANA
Bogota
COLOMBIA
ECUADOR
Galapagos Is. (Ecuador)
CAPE VERDE IS.
SENEGAL
GAMBIA
GUINEA BISSAU
GUINEA
SIERRA LEONE
LIBERIA
PACIFIC OCEAN
Kiritimati
Equator
Marquesas Islands (France)
FRENCH POLYNESIA
Society Islands (France)
Tahiti (France)
Tuamotu Archipelago (France)
Cook Islands (N.Z.)
Tropic of Capricorn
Tubuai Islands (France)
Pitcairn Island (U.K.)
Easter Island (Chile)
South America
PERU
Lima
BRAZIL
BOLIVIA
PARAGUAY
Sao Paulo
Rio de Janeiro
CHILE
Santiago
ARGENTINA
URUGUAY
Buenos Aires
SOUTH ATLANTIC OCEAN
Ascension (U.K.)
St. Helena (U.K.)
Tristan da Cunha
Chatham Islands (N.Z.)
Falkland Is. (U.K.)
South Georgia (U.K.)
Projection: *Hammer Equal Area*
Antarctic Circle
West from Green
Anta